Nationalism and Ethnicity in a Hindu Kingdom

Studies in Anthropology and History

Studies in Anthropology and History is a series which develops new theoretical perspectives, and combines comparative and ethnographic studies with historical research.

Edited by James G. Carrier, University of Durham, UK. Associate editors: Nicholas Thomas, The Australian National University, Canberra and Emiko Ohnuki-Tierney, University of Wisconsin, USA.

This book is part of a series. The publisher will accept continuation orders which may be cancelled at any time and which provide for automatic billing and shipping of each title in the series upon publication. Please write for details.

David N. Gellner, Joanna Pfaff-Czarnecka, and John Whelpton

Nationalism and Ethnicity in a Hindu Kingdom

The Politics of Culture in Contemporary Nepal

harwood academic publishers

Australia ♦ Canada ♦ China ♦ France ♦ Germany ♦ India ♦ Japan
Luxembourg ♦ Malaysia ♦ The Netherlands ♦ Russia ♦ Singapore
Switzerland ♦ Thailand ♦ United Kingdom

Amsteldijk 166
1st Floor
1079 LH Amsterdam
The Netherlands

British Library Cataloguing in Publication Data
Nationalism and ethnicity in a Hindu Kingdom : the politics
    of culture in contemporary Nepal. — (Studies in
    anthropology and history ; v. 20)
    1. Ethnicity — Nepal   2. Ethnicity — Nepal — Religious aspects
    3. Nepal — Ethnic relations   4. Nepal — Politics and
    government — 1990–
    I. Gellner, David N.   II. Pfaff-Czarnecka, Joanna
    III. Whelpton, John
    305.8′91495

    ISBN 90-5702-089-0 (Hardcover)

Front Cover
Joanna Pfaff-Czarnecka

In memory of Richard Burghart (1944–1994)

"Do not leave your ancient religion. Don't forsake the salt of the King ..."

Prithvi Narayan Shah
Dibya Upadesh (Stiller 1968:44)

"... a subject of the king of Gorkha at the turn of the nineteenth century was entitled to change his political affiliation as freely as a citizen of the Kingdom of Nepal in the mid-twentieth century can change his employment ... [By contrast] a country [*deś*] was a territorial affiliation that the native did not ordinarily give up; when he did, such emigration was likened to an act of renunciation (*deś tyāg*) ...

"At the turn of the nineteenth century each of [Nepal's ethnic] groups was thought of as a country, and in [the Legal Code of] 1854 as a species [*jāt*]; now [in 1984] they are all registered in the census as language groups."

Richard Burghart
'The Formation of the Concept of Nation-State in Nepal'

Contents

List of Figures

xiii

List of Tables

Preface

This book had its origins in a one-day conference and an associated eight-week seminar series on culture, politics, and identity in the Himalayan region, held in the autumn of 1992 at the Institute for Social and Cultural Anthropology (ISCA), University of Oxford. The papers by Whelpton, Burkert, McDonaugh, and Gaenszle were commissioned afterwards in order to fill obvious gaps in a collection which we had decided would focus on Nepal. Prayag Raj Sharma and Harka Gurung were invited to provide Nepalese and on-the-spot perspectives as part of the concluding section of the book.

We thank ISCA for its support. We would also like to thank Charles Ramble for his help and diplomacy in Kathmandu, as well as for advice on all things Tibetan. Anil Sakya lent a hand with diacritics in a mammoth session preparing the final manuscript. Except where authors have explicitly stated that they follow for the system of Turner (1980), it has been attempted, as far as possible, to adopt the spellings of the Royal Nepal Academy's *Nepālī Bṛhat Śabdakoś* (1983). We are grateful to Harka Gurung for supplying the computerized maps (Figures 1 and 48) and to Marcus Banks and his Mac for help in reading them.

The matters dealt with in this book are inevitably controversial and extremely serious for Nepalis themselves. It should be borne in mind that to describe events and movements does not in any sense indicate approval or support for any specific political position. As foreign academics our job is simply to provide a record and analysis. It is for the Nepali people themselves to determine their own political destiny.

The editors

Contributors

N.J. Allen is university lecturer in the anthropology of South Asia at the University of Oxford. After a background in classics and then in medicine, he started studying social anthropology at Oxford in 1965. Twenty months' fieldwork in Nepal led to a series of publications, many of them situating data from the Thulung Rai within the framework of Himalayan comparativism. Over the last fifteen years his research has extended into general kinship theory and Indo-European comparativism (conceived of as casting light on Hinduism). After teaching at Durham, he has been in Oxford since 1976 as a fellow of Wolfson College and university lecturer.

Claire Burkert is the advisor to the Janakpur Women's Development Centre, which she founded in 1989. She currently divides her time between Nepal and Vietnam, where she works helping women of ethnic minorities to produce handicrafts.

Ben Campbell first encountered the Tamangs of Rasuwa on a trek in 1980, after graduating in social anthropology at Cambridge. He did fieldwork between 1989 and 1991, and completed his PhD at the School of Development Studies, University of East Anglia, funded by the ESRC. He has been a lecturer in the Department of Social Anthropology of the University of Edinburgh, and is currently a fellow of the International Centre for Contemporary Cultural Research of Manchester University.

Martin Gaenszle is affiliated with the South Asia Institute, Heidelberg University, where he teaches at the Department of Ethnology. From 1987 to 1993 he was the resident representative of the South Asia Institute in Kathmandu. Since 1984 he has been engaged in research on the Mewahang Rai, a result of which was his book *Verwandtschaft und Mythologie bei den Mewahang Rai: Eine ethnographische Studie zum Problem der 'ethnischen Identität'* (1991) and various articles. He is currently working on a book about the ritual traditions of this group.

David N. Gellner is lecturer in social anthropology in the Department of Human Sciences, Brunel University, London. His main fieldwork,

xix

part of a DPhil for Oxford University, was carried out from 1982 to 1984 and he has returned to Nepal on six occasions since then. He is the author of *Monk, Householder, and Tantric Priest: Newar Buddhism and its Hierarchy of Ritual* (1992) and co-editor, with Declan Quigley, of *Contested Hierarchies: A Collaborative Ethnography of Caste among the Newars of the Kathmandu Valley, Nepal* (1995).

Harka Gurung, son of a Gurkha subedar who fought at Gallipoli and in the 1919 Waziristan campaign, received his early education in India. He was a geography demonstrator at Edinburgh University, where he obtained his doctorate, and then a research fellow at the School of Oriental and African Studies, London, and a lecturer in Tribhuvan University, Kathmandu. In 1968 he was appointed a member of Nepal's National Planning Commission and in 1972 became Vice-Chairman. He served as Minister of State for Education and for Industry and Commerce (1972–7) and subsequently for Tourism, Public Works, and Transport (1977–8), and he chaired the committee which produced the 1983 report on internal and international migration for the National Commission on Population. He has extensive experience as a consultant and project director and is currently director of the Asian and Pacific Development Centre, an intergovernmental research organization based in Kuala Lumpur. His many publications include *Vignettes of Nepal* (1980), *Nepal: Dimensions of Development* (1984), *Nature and Culture: Random Reflections* (1989), *Regional Patterns of Migration in Nepal* (1989), and (with Jan Salter) *Faces of Nepal* (1996).

Michael Hutt is senior lecturer in Nepali at the School of Oriental and African Studies, London University. He is the author of *Nepali: A National Language and its Literature* (1988) and *Himalayan Voices: An Introduction to Modern Nepali Literature* (1991), and the editor of *Nepal in the Nineties* (1994) and *Nepal: A Guide to the Art and Architecture of the Kathmandu Valley* (1994). He made research trips to Bhutan in 1992 and to Darjeeling in 1981 and 1995, and is a regular visitor to Nepal.

Christian McDonaugh is senior lecturer in social anthropology at Oxford Brookes University. His main research has been with Tharu communities in Dang, with whom he has carried out fieldwork at regular intervals since 1979. He has published several papers on various aspects of Dang Tharu society. He also works occasionally as a social development consultant, mostly in Nepal and India.

Alan Macfarlane is professor of anthropological science at the University of Cambridge and a fellow of King's College. His books include *Witchcraft in Tudor and Stuart England* (1970), *Resources and Population: A Study of the Gurungs of Nepal* (1976), *The Origins of English Individualism* (1978), and *The Culture of Capitalism* (1987). With Sarah Harrison he translated and edited *The Gurungs* by Bernard Pignède (1993). He is currently working on a comparison of England, Japan, and Nepal.

Axel Michaels is professor of classical Indology at the South Asia Institute of Heidelberg University, having previously been professor of religious studies at Berne University. He obtained his PhD in Indology from Hamburg University. He was assistant professor at Kiel University from 1981 to 1992, director of the Nepal Research Centre, Kathmandu, from 1981 to 1983, and Spalding visiting fellow at Wolfson College, Oxford, in 1986. He is the author of *Beweisverfahren in der vedischen Sakral-Geometrie* (1978), *A Comprehensive Śulvasūtra Word Index* (1983), *Ritual und Gesellschaft in Indien* (1986), *The Making of a Statue: Lost-Wax Casting in Nepal* (1988, with N. Gutschow), *Der indische Tanz* (1988, with F. Baldissera), *Benares* (1993, with N. Gutschow), and *Die Reisen der Götter: Der nepalische Paśupatinātha-Tempel und sein rituelles Umfeld* (1994).

Joanna Pfaff-Czarnecka is lecturer in social anthropology at Zürich University. She is a specialist on Hindu societies and has carried out extensive research on ethnicity in the South Asian context, including fieldwork in Nepal of more than three years in total. She is the author of *Macht und rituelle Reinheit: Hinduistisches Kastenwesen und ethnische Beziehungen im Entwicklungsprozess Nepals* (1989).

Charles Ramble is a British social anthropologist, currently employed as a research fellow at the Central Asian Seminar of Bonn University. He has worked in various parts of Nepal and Tibet, specializing in aspects of the Bon religion and local political systems. He is now engaged in research in Mustang District, Nepal, in association with the Nepal-German Project on High Mountain Archaeology, a multi-disciplinary study funded by the German Research Council.

Andrew Russell is lecturer in the Department of Anthropology, University of Durham, and is currently director of the Health and Human Sciences degree at University College, Stockton. His DPhil in social anthropology, 'The Yakha: Culture, Environment and

Development in East Nepal', was supervised by Drs N.J. Allen and Vernon Reynolds at the University of Oxford. He also has a Masters degree in Biomedical Anthropology from the University of Pennsylvania. He is currently undertaking medical anthropological research in the field of primary health care in the north of England, as well as continuing his research interests in the environment, development, and cross-cultural education in Nepal and elsewhere.

Prayag Raj Sharma is professor of ancient history at the Centre for Nepalese and Asian Studies (CNAS), Tribhuvan University. He received his MA from Allahabad University and his PhD from Pune University. He is the author of *A Preliminary Study of the Art and Architecture of the Karnali Basin* and many articles on state and society in Nepal. He has been associated with CNAS from its inception and was the founding Dean of its predecessor, INAS, from 1972 to 1978, as well as the founding editor of *Contributions to Nepalese Studies*.

John Whelpton studied classics at the University of Oxford and then lectured in English at Shri Thakur Ram (Birganj) and Amrit Science (Kathmandu) campuses of Tribhuvan University from 1972 to 1974. He worked in the Ministry of Defence in London between 1975 and 1981 and was then associated with the School of Oriental and African Studies as a postgraduate student, editor of *South Asia Research*, and occasional teacher of Nepali. Since 1987 he has been teaching English in Hong Kong whilst making regular visits to Kathmandu and continuing work on Nepalese history and politics. His main publications are *Jang Bahadur in Europe: The First Nepalese Mission to the West* (1983), *Nepal* (World Bibliographical Series, vol. 38) (1990), and *Kings, Soldiers and Priests: Nepalese Politics and the Rise of Jang Bahadur Rana, 1830–57* (1991).

INTRODUCTION

Ethnicity and Nationalism in the World's Only Hindu State

David N. Gellner

A CHANGING HINDU POLITY

This book focuses on nationalism, ethnicity, resistance, and change in Nepal, the world's only Hindu state. As an officially Hindu kingdom, Nepal's political culture and recent history have been very different from its officially secular neighbour, the Republic of India, with which it otherwise shares so much. Just what it means to live in a Hindu polity varies a great deal depending on who you are. Nepal itself has also changed considerably over the last 200 years, and these changes are examined in detail throughout this book, from both top-down and bottom-up perspectives.

The modern state of Nepal was created in the second half of the eighteenth century and was very largely the work of one man, Prithvi Narayan Shah (1723–75), ancestor of the present monarch, King Birendra. For this, Prithvi Narayan is nowadays styled 'the Great' by Nepali nationalists. Prithvi Narayan began life as the king of the little statelet of Gorkha, about 50 miles west of Kathmandu. The key to his success was the conquest of the Kathmandu Valley which took him twenty-six years of sieges, blockades, and assaults to achieve. Thereafter he and his successors conquered an enormous length of the Himalayan foothills, as far as Sikkim in the east and Kangra in the west.

The ethnic backbone of the new state was formed by the Parbatiya or 'hill people'; both they and their language were, and occasionally still are, known as Gorkhali. They have a simple caste system consisting of Brahmans (Bahuns) and Kshatriyas (Chetris) at the top and three or four Untouchable artisan castes at the bottom. In addition there is a small royal caste, called Thakuri. The Chetris used to be known as Khas and the language was therefore known as Khas Kura ('the speech of the Khas'); today the word 'Khas' is generally considered somewhat insulting in central Nepal but versions of it continue to be used in other Nepalese languages. The Gorkhali, Parbatiya, or Khas Kura language is now known as Nepali.

The present boundaries of the kingdom were fixed, more or less as they are today, by the 1816 Treaty of Sagauli after a two-year war with the British East India Company. Although the eastern and western ends of the kingdom were truncated and contacts with other countries curtailed, the British allowed the Gorkhalis (as the dominant Nepalis were then called) to keep a substantial strip of Gangetic plain, known as the Tarai. This contained both thick forest (a valuable defence against invasion, as the Gorkhalis saw it) and fertile agricultural land (the support base for the Gorkhali elite). The Gorkhalis had successfully prevented the Company from absorbing them into their expanding empire; the Company had earned itself a reliable ally on its northern flank. The loyalty of the Gorkhalis to the British in the 1857 Indian Mutiny/Uprising was rewarded with the return of previously annexed land in the western Tarai.

The Gorkhali kingdom was strung out along the Himalayas and included very diverse geographical and cultural regions. To the north of the foothills or middle hills which were its backbone, there were high peaks and valleys with a thin population of Tibetan culture. To the south were the Tarai plains populated both by tribals (principally Tharus) and by caste people, such as the Maithils, whose culture and language were found equally on the other side of the border with India.

The modern history of Nepal can be divided into the early Shah period (1769–1846), the Rana period (1846–1951), a period of transition from 1951 to 1962, the Panchayat period (1962–1990) when Nepal 'enjoyed' a system known as Partyless Panchayat Democracy, and most recently the period of multiparty democracy introduced by the People's Movement (*jan āndolan*) or revolution of 1990. The Rana period was inaugurated by Jang Bahadur Kunwar's seizure of power in 1846: he subsequently raised his family to Thakuri status and took the title Rana. He ensured that his family became thoroughly intermarried with the Shah kings who were reduced to the status of symbolic and powerless figureheads, and he made the Prime Ministership hereditary within his own family.

The political and cultural aspects of Rana rule, especially the Ranas' use of Hindu ritual and the codification of castes and ethnic groups in the Muluki Ain (Legal Code) of 1854, are analysed in many of the contributions below. Here we need only note that it was only about 1909 that the Ranas began to define the country they ruled as a nation-state called Nepal. Before that, as admirably described by Burghart (1984), 'Nepal' referred only to the Kathmandu Valley, and what we now think of as Nepal consisted of various 'countries' (*deśa*) all subject to the house of Gorkha. As part of the construction of the new national identity the dominant language, having been known as Gorkhali or colloquially as Khas Kura, was renamed 'Nepali' in about 1933. The official government newspaper has retained its old name, *Gorkhapatra*, to this day.

The Ranas deliberately kept the country isolated, forbidding entry to Westerners as far as they could. They could not prevent Nepalis from studying in India, however, and the influence of Indian nationalism could not in the end be resisted. With the fall of the Ranas in 1950–51, the country was opened up. Social change was slow at first, but has occurred with increasing rapidity since the 1960s. In and around the capital and other cities the outward signs are obvious in the explosion of new buildings, Hong Kong goods, and satellite dishes. But even in the rural hinterland dramatic shifts in familial relations, economic practices, and ethnic self-perceptions have occurred, as discussed in many of the contributions below (cf. Fricke, 1994: 205–9). At the same time it has been widely recognized that the aspirations of the vast mass of the people have not been met: education and basic health care may have become more widely available, but there has been little economic growth, much ecological degradation, a decline in the average diet, and continued population growth and emigration – all this in spite of one of the highest per capita levels of foreign aid in the world (Seddon, 1987).

For the last forty years it has been a cliché of Nepalese politics and tourist brochures that the many different castes, religions, languages, and 'races' of Nepal live together in tolerant harmony, without the violent conflict which has blighted the other countries of South Asia. The harmony may have been exaggerated – Bhattachan (1995: 125) condemns it as a "blatantly manufactured myth" of the Panchayat period – but it is equally true that ethnic violence has so far been avoided. Understanding how this has been achieved, and how it can be perpetuated, are questions which rightly concern Nepalis and all those who study Nepal.

The majority of the contributors to this volume are social anthropologists, others are historians: all have spent many years studying aspects of Nepali culture. All of them have been led to reflect on the changing nature of cultural identity in Nepal as a whole and for different groups of Nepalis, in the light of the 1990 People's Movement.

As in much of the rest of the world, so too in Nepal, the years 1989 and 1990 marked a watershed: the new Constitution of 1990 changed the previous definition of Nepal as "an independent, indivisible and sovereign monarchical Hindu Kingdom" to "a multi-ethnic, multilingual, democratic, independent, indivisible, sovereign, Hindu and Constitutional Monarchical Kingdom."[1] With that, at least on paper, ethnic affiliations were given a degree of official recognition they certainly did not have in the institutions or ideology of the preceding Panchayat regime. In a further step towards pluralism, on August 14th, 1994, Radio Nepal began broadcasting the news in eight minority languages for the first time: they were Rai (Bantawa), Gurung, Magar, Limbu, Bhojpuri, Awadhi, Tharu, and Tamang. Maithili had already been used from January 1993 and Newari from 1990.[2] This unprecedented public use of these eight new languages indicated a dramatic shift in official policy.

SOME PRELIMINARY DEFINITIONS

In discussions of ethnicity and nationalism, two positions are conventionally distinguished, the primordialist, on the one hand,

and the instrumentalist or modernist, on the other. According to the primordialist position, ethnic (and potentially national) identity has always been an aspect of social identity. Ethnic and national units are therefore assumed to have persisted over long periods of time and to have generated deep emotional attachments in an unproblematic manner. Consequently the primordialist view is also often characterized as essentialist. This view is held by ordinary people in the modern world, and is enthusiastically and usually uncritically endorsed by nationalist historians. However, few social scientists today, even those who seek to establish a continuity between the premodern forms of identity and modern states (e.g. Smith, 1986), accept that they themselves are primordialists.[3]

Opponents of primordialism are known by the two different labels already mentioned, namely instrumentalism and modernism. In fact these two terms are used in different contexts and have different implications. In discussions of ethnicity it is instrumentalism that is opposed to primordialism, the idea being that the point of emphasizing ethnic distinctiveness is to gain some political or economic advantage. In discussions of nationalism, on the other hand, it is *modernism* that is opposed to primordialism: the claim being made here is that nationalism is essentially a modern phenomenon, not predating the eighteenth century.

Instrumentalism raises the issue of motivation; or at least asserts that considerations of political and economic advantage offer the best grounding for explaining the success or failure of different ethnic movements. Modernism makes a much more straightforward historical claim about origins. No extreme instrumentalist position will be defended here: it is unlikely that ethnic activists are motivated solely by the pursuit of economic or political advantage either for themselves or for the group (they often view themselves as devoted to the selfless pursuit of larger goals, to the detriment of their own, and their household's, economic advantage; at the same time, as Whelpton points out below, they often have a crude instrumentalist view of their *opponents'* motivations). And yet, the competition of different elites, which sometimes takes ethnic forms, does usually have political and/or economic consequences. Indeed political and economic benefits are specifically targetted when there are campaigns for job quotas or autonomous regions (see chapters 1 and 13 below). For present purposes, the more modest (though still far from uncontroversial) modernist claim is upheld, that both nationalism and ethnicity – but not ethnic identity, which is ancient, as explained below – are relatively new phenomena on the world scene, and even more recent arrivals in Nepal. Just how they have emerged in the Nepalese context, and how they have been constrained by and built upon the past, is explored in the contributions to this book.[4]

Before proceeding to examine the problems with the primordialist position, it is worth trying to clarify the relationship of ethnicity and nationalism. Where a group is large enough to dominate a given political unit, or may reasonably aspire to form its own, we have a nation. Where we are dealing with a minority, it is invariably labelled an ethnic group or community. The term 'ethnicity' is generally confined to scholarly discourse and is parasitic on the expression 'ethnic group'. "Ethnicity", as Chapman *et al.* note (1989: 15), is "what it is you have if you are an 'ethnic group'."

Many scholars follow wider usage in considering ethnic groups to be, by definition, minorities (as in the English expressions, 'ethnic dress', 'ethnic food'). Other social scientists apply the term to all distinctive groups, even majorities (e.g. Han Chinese) (contrast chapters 1 and 13 below). By this latter criterion the dominant Parbatiyas (Parbates) of Nepal – that is, the Bahun (Brahman), Thakuri, and Chetri castes and their associated low-status artisan castes – are also an ethnic group or category, though it is certain that they do not usually think of themselves as such. However, with the publication of the 1991 census, Parbatiyas have discovered themselves to be a minority in the country as a whole – 40% of the population, about 30% if one omits the low castes. Since they are increasingly under attack from other groups, it is likely that they (or at least the high castes among them) will come to see themselves as an ethnic group. Scholars have recently begun to talk about incipient Bahun and Chetri ethnicity (Bhattachan, 1995: 135). The assertion of Bahun identity (an appeal to Bahun voters), attacked by others as 'Brahmanism' (*bāhunbād*), was surely behind both the Congress government's decision in 1993 to make Sanskrit compulsory in secondary schools and the Communist government's decision to introduce newscasts in Sanskrit in 1995.

There is an important distinction in the Nepalese context between the Parbatiyas and the Pahari (Pahāḍī), although both terms literally mean 'hill people'.[5] The term Pahari refers to *all* the people of the hills, both the Parbatiyas and other ethnic groups. As Sharma points out in chapter 14 (p.485), minority hill ethnic groups object to *Parbatiya* domination [and, especially today, Brahman domination], whereas the people of the Tarai object to *Pahari* domination. What this illustrates is that ethnic feelings develop in very specific contexts of opposition and competition. The ethnic Nepali refugees from Bhutan, united as they are by a common subordination in Bhutan, find the emerging politicized divisions in Nepal to be quite alien to them (Hutt and Sharkey, 1995: 34). Conversely, as Hutt describes below (p.109), Nepali intellectuals in Kathmandu find the hostility of Gorkhaland activists in Darjeeling to the poet Bhanubhakta to be quite incredible.

In South Asia there is a much older term than 'ethnic group', namely 'community' (*sampradāya*), with its derogatory counterpart 'communalism' (*sampradāyiktā*). This refers, in a negative way, to movements on behalf of a specific community. Such communities can be defined in terms of caste, language, or religion, but paradigmatically the latter. Colonial observers and historians thought in terms of primordial identities, projecting back into history contemporary Hindu-Muslim and Hindu-Sikh conflicts. As Gyanendra Pandey argues,

> The concept stands for the puerile and the primitive – all that colonialism, in its own reckoning, was not. The paradox is that the nationalists have done more than anyone to propagate its use ... Like 'tribalism' in Africa, communalism in the colonialist perception served to designate a pathological condition (Pandey, 1990: 6, 9–10).

As far as Indian nationalists' own self-perceptions were concerned, the crucial period, according to Pandey, was the 1920s. Before that time India

> was visualized as a composite body, consisting of several
> communities, each with its own history and culture and
> own special contribution to make to the common
> nationality . . . Sometime around the 1920s this vision was
> substantially altered, and India came to be seen very much
> more as a collection of individuals, of Indian 'citizens'
> (Pandey, 1990: 210).

Thus 'communalism' passed into the general political discourse of
South Asia as the term for any minority sentiment or movement
detrimental to the construction of the nation.

In Nepal too, both before and after 1990, the dominant
political discourse marks the English word 'nationalism' as entirely
positive, and the terms 'tribe' and 'communalism' as negative.
Foreigners who take an interest in minorities or 'tribes' are often
suspected of encouraging backward-looking allegiances.[6] By contrast, it would be unthinkable for any political party to be *against*
'nationalism'. 'Nationalism' (*rāṣṭriyatā*), 'democracy' (*prajātantra*),
and 'development' (*bikās*) are the three holy mantras of Nepalese
politics. Politicians always claim to be building them, and always
accuse their opponents of undermining them.

ETHNICITY, NATIONALISM, AND THE PROBLEMS WITH PRIMORDIALISM

Regardless of these differences of terminology, we need to be
clear that there is in fact only a difference in relative scale between
ethnicity and nationalism. As Cohen has pointed out (1974: xi), the
identities 'Indian' and 'Chinese' are national in India and China
respectively, but ethnic when Indians or Chinese migrate to other
countries. In many languages there is in fact no obvious
terminological distinction between ethnicity and nationalism. Thus,
any theoretical approach which pretends that ethnicity and
nationalism are unrelated is unlikely to be fruitful.

Having said that, it also needs to be noted that the difference of scale has important consequences. Successful nationalisms acquire an institutional backing which allows them to be imposed on, or at least to impinge upon, large numbers of people. Ethnic movements, on the other hand, may be wholly cultural in intent, without any aspiration to national status, as the Newar example clearly shows (chapter 4 below). This implies a completely different relationship to the state: ethnic movements may only seek recognition, and perhaps financial support, from the state, whereas national movements seek their own state, or at least their own administrative unit within the state.[7] Most nationalisms build on the ethnic identity of the majority while rejecting or containing minority identities; but some nationalist ideologies, particularly in classic 'pluralist' societies such as Switzerland, Kenya, Trinidad, or Mauritius, attempt – with greater or lesser success – to build a sense of national identity on the basis of the equal treatment of all constituent ethnic identities (Eriksen, 1993: 116–18).

What, then, is the problem with the popular primordialist viewpoint? We should begin by noting that there is an interesting contrast in the Western 'common sense' view of nationalism and ethnicity respectively. Whilst national identity is nowadays usually thought of as natural and universal, ethnicity, though seen as equally primordial, is very often considered unnecessary and backward in modern society. ('Our' obvious and justified national identity is contrasted with 'their' irrational and instinctive ethnicity.) Scholars also once assumed, as journalistic and popular accounts usually still do, that ethnicity is a throwback or survival, an unfortunate atavism perpetuated in the nooks and crannies of otherwise modernized or modernizing states.

Contrary to the popular assumption, close study in context after context has led sociologists and anthropologists to conclude that the importance of ethnicity generally *grows* as modernization and globalization proceed, and that ethnicity as understood and experienced today is, to a very large extent, a modern phenomenon. It must therefore be explained as a response to contemporary pressures, and not as a leftover of some previous type of society or period of history. In an influential early account, Abner Cohen described how Hausa from northern Nigeria who had settled among the Yoruba of southern Nigeria gained considerable advantages from their intensified sense of ethnic identity as Muslims belonging to the Tijanniya brotherhood. Cohen concluded:

> Ethnicity is thus basically a political and not a cultural phenomenon, and it operates with contemporary political contexts and is not an archaic survival arrangement carried over into the present by a conservative people (Cohen, 1969: 190).

This is not to say that modern ethnicity emerges, or can be created, *ex nihilo*. Another Nigerian specialist, J. D. Y. Peel, has taken Cohen to task for his 'presentism', i.e. his denial of any significance to the historical antecedents of present-day Hausa ethnicity, and for his privileging of the political over the cultural. Peel suggests that in the Yoruba case "the further we go back, the more . . . ethnicity was a cultural project before it was political" (Peel, 1989: 201). Whether ethnicity is primarily cultural or primarily political, the important point is that it has to be created. It is not an essential and universal aspect of the human condition. The problem with primordialism, in short, is that the identities it postulates are unproblematic.[8]

THE STATE, ETHNIC CATEGORIES, AND ETHNIC GROUPS

Another Africanist, Aidan Southall, has eloquently and passionately argued that many of the ethnic units which now exist only came into existence as a response to the nation-state or to the colonial state which in many cases preceded it (Southall, 1970). What existed before were usually multiple, overlapping, flexible identities; only in exceptional cases did these approximate to the one-and-only-one tribe per person model. Sweeping all this away, the modern state has been determined to classify its population into sets of exclusive units, often taking diverse labels out of their original context and applying them to a new and homoeneous set of categories. These classifications are recorded in censuses, maps, and museums, as Anderson notes (1991: chapter 10).

The modernist view asserts, as we have seen, that ethnicity and nationalism are distinctively modern phenomena. Depending on one's preferred emphasis, they have arisen in, and are essentially linked to, the age of 'print capitalism' (Anderson, 1991), the rise of industrial or would-be industrial states with their 'requirement' of cultural homogeneity (E. Gellner, 1983), or competition between elites for control of or access to the resources of the state (Brass, 1991; Breuilly, 1993).

A third position, in addition to the primordialist and the modernist, has recently been posited by J. D. Rogers (1994). He calls it the "Post-orientalist", and it is in effect a distinctive form of modernism. This is a good label for those writers who have claimed that the state's classification project and the identities which resulted from it were the creation of colonialism. However, as Rogers points out, "A shift toward rigid categorization . . . was not uniquely colonial . . . [A] parallel process was taking place in Britain itself and in other countries not under colonial rule" (Rogers, 1994: 20). Nepal, in fact, would be a good example of the latter. In the Nepalese case, the self-consciously Hindu Rana regime (1846–1951) designated the social units it recognized as *jāt*, essentially 'caste', though the term could apply equally well to units that outside observers would view as tribes or ethnic groups (see chapters 1, 3, 9, and 13 below). (In fact the term *jāt*, derived from the Sanskrit root *jan* meaning 'birth' or 'origin', is so broad it means 'type' or 'kind'; Burghart (1984) rendered it 'species'.)

Modernists do not deny that ethnic *categories*, collections of people sharing a common language and/or culture, existed and often persisted in the premodern era.[9] Nor do they deny that in many situations ethnic categories and cultural allegiances had some political significance. But they do deny that, with one or two exceptions, before the eighteenth century national and ethnic identity were ever seen as the single overriding factor determining a person's political rights and duties. Breuilly (1993: 3–4) cites the case of Dante, who by precept and example established the Italian language, and urged other poets and writers to use it, defend it, and develop it. At the same time Dante wrote in favour of a universal Christian monarch. It never occurred to him that his cultural preference for Italian and the Italian nation could or should have political implications.

If one wants a definition of what makes an ethnic category, A.D. Smith's list of six characteristics or "dimensions" is a useful starting point (1986: 22–31):

– a collective name
– a common myth of descent
– a shared history
– a distinctive shared culture
– an association with a specific territory
– a sense of solidarity.

What are here being called ethnic categories were in the past named 'races', 'peoples', 'nations', or 'tribes'. All these terms have been abandoned as too misleading or too pejorative.[10] For present purposes, four important reservations to Smith's list of six characteristics need to be kept in mind:

1. There can be very great variation in the depth or intensity of Smith's six 'dimensions' of ethnic identity (some ethnic categories possess little sense of solidarity or shared history).
2. The list should be taken as polythetic: that is, all six are important and frequently found bases of ethnic identity; but in specific cases one or other criterion may be lacking; no one criterion is present in every case (the Newars, for example, lack a myth of common origin: see chapter 4 below).[11] Furthermore, Smith's list omits the criterion which is central to many ethnic activists' efforts at mobilization in Nepal, as well as in much of South Asia and elsewhere, namely *a distinctive language.*
3. In premodern situations boundaries between ethnic categories could be fluid and context-dependent. People might pass from one category to another and back, or combine different 'ethnic' identities according to context; and one should not assume this

was in any way anomalous. Some groups manage to continue such strategies well into the modern period. The Yakha of east Nepal (see chapter 10) are a good example of this.

4.   Consequently, differences *within* ethnic categories may be greater than those *between* them. As Toffin remarks of Nepal, "classifications of the Tibeto-Burman hill tribes into Tamang, Gurung, Magar, Rai, Thakali, etc., correspond only very imperfectly to reality and can only be accepted as working hypotheses. In fact, none of these groups forms a homogeneous ethnic group, either culturally or linguistically" (Toffin, 1981: 39; cf. Levine, 1987).

Smith himself distinguishes what he calls *ethnie* which always possess all six characteristics from *ethnic categories* which lack a sense of solidarity. He cites the Ukrainians in the past as an example of the latter. The first two qualifications I have made to Smith's criteria effectively dispose of this distinction. Instead we need only to distinguish ethnic categories – which are often overlapping, context-dependent, formed on a variety of bases, and characteristic of the premodern world – from ethnic groups and nations which emerge from and are forged out of some ('successful') ethnic categories in a dialectical or symbiotic relation to the modern state, colonial or other.

Anthropologists have been much influenced by Frederik Barth's seminal article (1969) which was an important early attack on static views of ethnic groups and cultures. His view was that ethnic groups define themselves by the boundaries they erect against each other; several contributors take issue with this below. While Barth is clearly not a primordialist, since he emphasizes that there may well be no continuity to the "cultural stuff" enclosed by the boundary, he is at the same time not a modernist, since he assumes that ethnic groups have existed at all times and in all places.

Caste societies provide an interesting angle on theories of ethnicity. In the first place, they immediately show up one often-noted problem with Barth's theory: it is much too broad in its application. In South Asia, to define ethnic groups in terms of boundary maintenance creates as many ethnic groups as there are castes, or even sub-castes, since each caste will have a separate myth of origin and a vivid sense of its own difference from other castes. And despite the fact that castes may sometimes behave like ethnic groups, and in some cases increasingly begin to resemble ethnic groups, we surely do not wish to be committed to saying, depending on which theory of caste we may favour, that within a given population there are twenty-five ethnic groups ranked in a hierarchy of purity and impurity, or ranked according to the dignity of their position in the king's sacrificial organization.[12]

I would prefer to say that when a given population shares a common language, a common culture, and a common attachment to a given territory, or at least a historical link to these shared features, it thereby constitutes an ethnic group. And this is so *even though* it is made up of different castes who believe that they have different origins. In line with qualifications made to Smith's definition above, an ethnic group does not need to share a myth of common origin.

Whichever stance one adopts – primordialist, modernist, or some synthesis of the two – the great majority of observers seem to agree that ethnicity has become *more* of a practical problem, i.e. more of a problem for governments and elites, under modern conditions.[13] Furthermore, the fact that it has become a problem derives from its essentially political nature. As Paul Brass, one of the foremost students of Indian communalism and politics, puts it,

> whether or not the culture of the group is ancient or is newly-fashioned, the study of ethnicity and nationality is in large part the study of politically induced cultural change. More precisely, it is the study of the process by which elites and counterelites within ethnic groups select aspects of the group's culture, attach new value and meaning to them, and use them as symbols to mobilize the group, to defend its interests, and to compete with other groups. In this process, those elites have an advantage whose leaders can operate most skillfully in relation both to the deeply-felt primordial attachments of group members and the shifting relationships of politics (Brass, 1991: 75).

Mines (1975) claims to have identified a case in which an intensification of ethnic identity has occurred propelled entirely by internal group dynamics, without political competition with other groups being an issue, namely among urban Muslims in Tamil Nadu. Yet even here, one can argue that these internal dynamics are themselves fed by the wider context of urban, middle-class South Asia, where competition between Muslims and Hindus in the political sphere certainly is important.

RESISTANCE AND THE ANTHROPOLOGICAL 'VIEW FROM BELOW'

With the diffusion of democratic and human rights ideals, resistance to authority, that other fashionable anthropological topic, has, like ethnicity, become more of a problem. Everywhere old patterns of deference are discarded; everywhere equal rights are claimed (even if the point for many is to participate in global consumerism rather than in political processes). Yet within anthropology the distribution of interest in resistance is much more uneven. While ethnicity is discussed by social scientists everywhere from Kraków, to Kandy, to Kathmandu, interest in resistance, as a topic independent of ethnicity, is much more patchy. In north American academe it is all the rage, encouraged by the policy and the ideals of multiculturalism. Evidence of resistance is unearthed even in the most unpromising contexts (routine rituals of obeisance, for example).

In this volume the focus is rather on resistance as more conventionally defined, and as viewed by (at least some) Nepalis themselves. Alan Macfarlane, in chapter 5, describes a striking occurrence. In March 1992 Gurung activists held a conference in Pokhara and passed three resolutions: that Gurung history had been distorted by Brahmans, that there were no superior or inferior Gurung clans, and that the original Gurung priests were the Pa-chyu and Khlibri. These statements represent a clear rejection of Hindu and Brahman dominance and a clear rejection of the

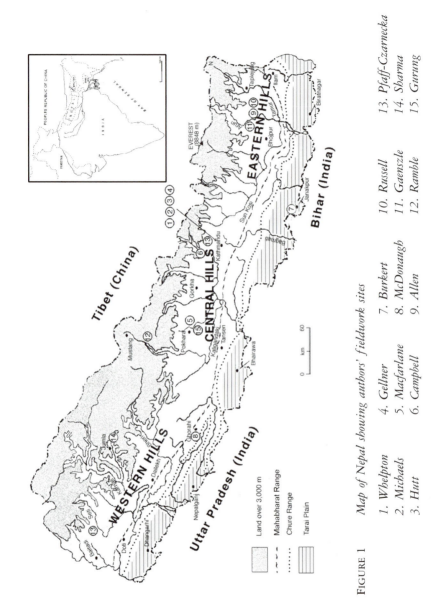

FIGURE 1   Map of Nepal showing authors' fieldwork sites

1. Whelpton
2. Michaels
3. Hutt
4. Gellner
5. Macfarlane
6. Campbell
7. Burkert
8. McDonaugh
9. Allen
10. Russell
11. Gaenszle
12. Ramble
13. Pfaff-Czarnecka
14. Sharma
15. Gurung

Gurungs' own recent past. The Rais of east Nepal, on the other hand, are far more internally divided. Rather than making such overtly political statements they have confined their activity to the invention of a new annual dance tradition which expresses their "unity in diversity" (see chapter 11, p.367, below) and to publishing (in Nepali) magazines written by Rais for Rais. On a more mundane level, Campbell (chapter 6) describes how Tamangs continue to resist the attempts of the state to impose its standards on them, with respect to distilling alcohol and killing female buffaloes.

Most of the contributors to the present volume share a concern to give sufficient weight to the 'view from below'. This entails an examination of ordinary modes of being, and not necessarily giving full credence to the most vocal and most active proponents of ethnic identity. Burkert's discussion of Maithil identity (chapter 7), for example, shows how the preservation of much that is thought of as distinctively Maithil is preserved by *women*; but women's concerns and perspectives are crucially distorted or ignored by the self-appointed spokes*men* of Maithil culture.[14]

We do not have any *a priori* commitment to reading *every* aspect of ethnic groups' life as resistance. In fact, the most impressive fact of the social history of Nepal in recent years, at least in the hill areas, is the active *adoption and adaptation* of high-caste and Parbatiya cultural forms, in varying degrees. Related to this, there has been the increasing adoption of the Nepali language by the minorities of Nepal, and increasing influence of Nepali on other Nepalese languages. As Pfaff-Czarnecka (1991: 256) has noted (cf. chapter 13 below), "the spread of Hinduism in wide parts of Nepalese territory (especially in the hill area) was not the result of the central government's endeavors ... [T]he local elites had to learn the rulers' language and at least display Hindu symbols in order to prove loyal and be treated on an equal footing with emerging Hindu elites."

In this connection the paper by N. J. Allen (chapter 9), originally written at the beginning of the 1970s, is a very useful corrective to the enthusiasms generated by the events of 1990. It reminds us that the normal state of most Nepalese people is one of barely conscious, piecemeal, but profound and on-going

Hinduization. By a familiar kind of irony, even those ethnic activists who seek to defend their languages and cultures can only come together and do so through Nepali, as in the conference on language problems held in 1993 by the Nepal Janajati Mahasangh (Nepal Federation of Nationalities or NEFEN).[15] NEFEN had been founded in 1990 as a federation of seven different organizations: four represented Newars, Tamangs, Magars, and Gurungs; the other three were Kiranti bodies, one representing Limbus, two Rais. By 1995 it had been reorganized so that there could only be one representative body per ethnic group (one of the Rai institutions became an 'associate member'); there are 21 such groups, the new ones being the Chantel, Danuwar, Dhimal, Dura, Jirel, Meche, Chepang, Hyolmo [people of Helambu], the Kushwar Majhi, Thami, Tharu, Rajbanshi, Sunuwar, Thakali, and Yhambu [Sherpa].

In the face of the erosion of many local languages and cultures in Nepal, one important fact needs stressing. For many ordinary Nepalis today their local language and traditions have no particular value, and are, they often feel, a disadvantage in the highly competitive scramble for employment and survival. Local languages are often divided by dialect (the Rais are an extreme, but not untypical case: see chapters 10 and 12). Consequently it often happens that two members of the same ethnic group prefer to speak Nepali to each other, either to increase comprehensibility or to avoid the status implications of specific dialects. Ethnic activists therefore face an uphill task in standardizing and generating attachment to the languages they campaign for; and it has frequently been observed that such activists themselves speak Nepali to their children.[16]

Ethnic activists in Nepal have grown in sophistication. Together with other interested parties, in March 1994 NEFEN formed a committee in response to the UN resolution of December 1993 calling for a decade of Indigenous Peoples. The definition offered by them of indigenous peoples in Nepal is worth quoting in full:

"The Indigenous People" refer to those communities –

    1. which possess their own distinct and original lingual and cultural traditions and whose religious faith is based

on ancient animism (worshipper of ancestors, land, season, nature), or who do not claim "The Hinduism" enforced by the state, as their traditional and original religion.

2. those existing descendants of the peoples whose ancestors had established themselves as the first settlers or principal inhabitants in any part of the land falling within the territory of modern state (Nepal), or and who inhabitate [sic] the present territory of Nepal at the time when persons of different culture or ethnic origin arrived there and who have their own history (written or oral) and historical continuity.

3. which have been displaced from their own land for the last 4 centuries, particularly during the expansion and establishment of modern Hindu nation State and have been deprived of their traditional rights to own the natural resources (Kipat {communal land}, cultivable land, water, minerals, trading points etc.).

4. who have been subjugated in the State's political power set-up (decision-making process), whose ancient culture, language and religion are non-dominant and social values neglected and humiliated;

5. whose society is traditionally erected on the principle of egalitarianism – rather than the hierarchy of the Indo-Aryan caste system and gender equality (or rather women enjoying more advantageous positions) – rather than social, economic and religious subordination of woman, but whose social norms and values have been slighted by the state;

6. which formally or informally, admit or claim to be "the indigenous peoples of Nepal" on the basis of the aforementioned characteristics.
(Indigenous, 1994: 2–3; punctuation etc. as original.)

The conference went on to make many familiar demands, e.g. for the state to provide mother-tongue primary education, for the removal of Sanskrit from the school curriculum, for the right to defend oneself in court in one's own language, for a secular state, and for an ethnographic museum of Nepal's indigenous peoples. The leaders of NEFEN are willing to consider the possibility of the

Chetris being accepted as members if – reversing at least the last 150 years of their social history – they define themselves as Khas, organize themselves, and reject their Hinduization. Dor Bahadur Bista (1995: 46) has likewise put the Khas, at least those of far west Nepal, in the *janajāti* category. By contrast, NEFEN has turned down an approach by the leaders of Dalit organizations (representing Parbatiya Untouchables) on the grounds that their cultural identity is ineluctably Hindu. They would, for the same reason, reject Tarai-dwellers other than the Tharu and similar groups. In effect, then, NEFEN is an anti-Hindu and, more specifically, an anti-Brahman organization.

It is particularly striking how this set of definitions put forward by NEFEN and others reworks a crude contrast between supposedly hierarchical Hindus (the Parbatiyas) and egalitarian 'tribes' that has been the stock in trade of foreign observers of Nepal for a long time. It is immediately obvious that the Newars, with their practice of both Hinduism and Buddhism, and their complex internal caste hierarchy, do not fit anywhere in this framework.[17] But even for other groups, the opposition is by no means as clear cut as this list would present it, as many of the chapters below indicate. There is a bitter irony in the fact, as pointed out by Denis Vidal in the 1992 conference from which this book grew, that just when a scholarly and anthropological consensus is emerging that a Hindu-tribe dichotomy was hopelessly flawed as a tool for understanding Nepalese society, Nepalese intellectuals themselves should begin to take it up with a vengeance. Of course, the politically charged construction of ethnic identities by local intellectuals is a global phenomenon, as are anthropological qualms at the essentialist views of culture and cultures so propagated.[18]

Alan Macfarlane writes (p.204, below) that anthropologists are now "actively engaged in the process of the creation and reinter-pretation of ethnic identity ... [in] a co-operative venture with the people themselves." He implies that this is entirely right and proper. This is a controversial claim both in the Western and in the Nepalese context. I would say rather that anthropologists, with their tradition of studying the everyday lives of ordinary people, have a particular duty to document the *lack of fit* between what activists say and the feelings and perceptions of those on whose behalf the activists claim to speak. In Eriksen's words:

> Movements of ethnic revitalisation are much more spectacular than the quiet daily movement towards mutual accommodation in complex societies, and they are perhaps more attractive as objects of study. This does not, however, necessarily mean that such movements are more representative than moves towards the end of ethnicity in particular societies. After all, seen through the perspective of *la longue durée*, the eventual disappearance of ethnic groups is no less certain than their appearance (Eriksen, 1993: 160).

Not only do anthropologists have a duty to pay attention to the values and worldviews of ordinary people: they have an obvious advantage in doing so. Social historians equally wish to capture the 'view from below', but they have to be very creative in their use of sources and still face gaps in what can be known. Anthropologists, on the other hand, actually spend their time with the people they are studying.

THE ORGANIZATION OF 'ETHNIC' CATEGORIES IN PREMODERN NEPAL

The founder of the modern state of Nepal, Prithvi Narayan Shah, called his new kingdom, in a much-quoted phrase, a garden of the four *varna*s and thirty-six *jāt*s. *Varṇa* refers to the four scripturally sanctioned status groups of Hinduism: the Brahmans (priests), Kshatriyas (rulers or warriors), Vaishyas (traders or herdsmen), and Shudras (servants). One possible translation of *varṇa* is therefore 'estates' in the sense of the three status groups of Medieval Europe, the clergy, nobility, and peasantry. *Jāt*, as mentioned above, means caste.

Conventionally this phrase of Prithvi Narayan's is taken as endorsing a policy of ethnic harmony and coexistence. The words attributed to Rishikeshab Raj Regmi in a recent interview are a good example:

> After king Prithvi Narayan unified Nepal, he let the traditions and customs of all groups to continue. That policy proved to be excellent as every group today enjoys its practices and traditions. And that is the main reason why they are diversely unified.
>
> But the much talked-about goal of king Prithvi Narayan Shah – to make Nepal a common garden of four castes and thirty-six tribes [sic] – was not practised by his successors. The Rana regime exploited most of the castes before the introduction of democracy in the country. But, the late king Mahendra and king Birendra have contributed to the country by following the footsteps of their forefather king Prithvi Narayan Shah (Regmi, 1996: 20).

However, examining the actual context of what Prithvi Narayan was saying, we see – if I have understood this difficult passage correctly – that his main concern was to keep Indians out, so that (in line with his mercantilist assumptions) wealth would not go out of the country. To this end he wanted to *prevent* his kingdom from becoming a garden of 'every sort of people': only then would it remain a true (*asal*) Hindustan of the four *varṇa*s and thirty-six *jāt*s.[19] The 'Father of the Nation' was therefore very far from being a multiculturalist celebrating cultural diversity for its own sake as he is so often depicted. Nor was he really a nationalist in the modern sense, as his indifference to the question of language shows.

We need to remember that, politically, the history of South Asia has been marked by interethnic cooperation rather than ethnic conflict (cf. Brass, 1994: 151). The dominant traditional model for such cooperation, in areas with Hindu rulers, was that of the caste system. Jang Bahadur Rana attempted to systematize this in his celebrated law code, the Muluki Ain of 1854 (Höfer, 1979).

Anderson (1991) has plausibly argued that, in the past, large-scale imagined communities (as opposed to the practical local-level communities in which people actually lived) were of two sorts: the dynastic and the religious. Nepal experienced both of these: the ancestors of the Nepalese citizens of today were both subjects of the King of Gorkha and, to a greater or lesser extent, Hindus (only Muslims were exempted from this inclusivist definition). Interestingly, however, when Anderson writes of the "great sacral cultures" of the past, he specifically includes Islam, Christianity, Buddhism, and even Confucianism, but does not mention Hinduism.

Hinduism is indeed a problem for the conceptual apparatus of Western social science.[20] It is not just that, in the various ideals it propagates, hierarchical imagined communities receive relatively greater weight than egalitarian ones. Nor is it that Hinduism requires hierarchically arranged sub-communities which we have come to call castes: the traditional forms of Christianity, Buddhism, and Islam legitimated hierarchy too. The real problem with Hinduism is the great *diversity* of imagined communities – different sorts of caste, sect, tribe, and others – it contains within it, all coexisting and competing. These different visions are held together by the Hindu king (see chapters 2, 13; cf. Quigley, 1993). And this is one reason why Nepal, the last Hindu polity, has so much to teach those interested in Hinduism.

In practice, under Hinduism, Anderson's two forms of premodern imagined community fuse: the dynasty is semi-divine; the king is the centre of the country, even if he rules over several countries.[21] The crucial point is that before the age of nationalism "the fundamental conceptions about social groups were centripetal and hierarchical, rather than boundary-oriented and horizontal" (Anderson, 1991: 22). Though not composed with Hinduism in mind, this characterizes the traditional Hindu polity very well.[22]

Still today the sheer diversity of identities which Nepalis can bring into play needs to be stressed. The lack of a sense of nationality – whether as a Nepali, on the one hand, or as a Tamang, Gurung etc., on the other – is the despair of both nation-builders and ethnic activists respectively. They can perhaps take heart from each others' lack of success! By a familiar paradox, it is primarily when Nepalis emigrate or seek work outside Nepal that their identity as Nepalis or Gorkhalis becomes supremely important (see chapter 3 below).[23] At the same time, as chapters 5, 6, and 10 all show, migration also serves to generate ethnic identities.

Within Nepal broad trends of 'modernizing' change were – at least till recently – a long way behind India. In India a process has been identified that has been variously called the 'substantialization' (Dumont, 1980: 227) or 'ethnicization' (Barnett, 1976) of caste. With modernization, small differences between sub-castes disappear, intercaste interdependence declines, and castes themselves become solid 'blocs' somewhat akin to ethnic groups, as already noted above in discussing Barth. One aspect of this process is the development of caste associations, caste-based student hostels, and other similar institutions (Khare, 1970). However, it is by no means certain that Nepal will follow exactly the same path as India. As many of the chapters below show and Harka Gurung documents (chapter 15), the demographic balance between Parbatiya groups who cannot think of themselves as anything but Hindu, and others who can plausibly, if occasionally with some difficulty, reject that label, is very different from India: in Nepal the 'non-Hindus' are very numerous, even, as they often claim, actually a majority.

CONCLUSION: THREATS TO NATIONAL UNITY?

In a recent overview, Dahal (1995) points out that many of the 'ethnic minorities' are in fact much better off than the national average, and that Bahun over-representation in the 1991 Parliament was not as extraordinary as often claimed: compared to their population size Bahuns were 194.5% over-represented, Limbus were 162.5% over-represented, Gurungs were 41.6% over-represented, Newars were 33.8% over-represented, and Thakalis were 2142% over-represented. Although "ethnic awareness has become an ubiquitous aspect of political life in Nepal after democracy", he argues that "ethnic problems show the characteristics of a non-peasant, urban phenomena [sic]. In other words, ethnic politics has no base at the grass-roots level and pose no immediate danger to political stability and national integration" (Dahal, 1995: 166–7). Dahal does urge, however, that "multi-culturalism or the plurality of Nepalese culture must be accepted as officially [sic] in every field of life" (*ibid.*: 168). He also thinks that it was a serious mistake on the part of the government to make Sanskrit compulsory in secondary schools.

In contrast to Dahal's essentially optimistic assessment, Bhattachan and Pyakhurel (n.d.) give a much more sombre picture and list a number of "hotspots" which could give rise to severe and destabilizing conflict: these include Mustang (where there is supposed to be support for the Free Tibet movement), the Tarai, the position of the "Janajatis", the position of the Dalits (Untouchables), the Bhutanese refugees, and the backwardness and neglect felt by the people of far west Nepal who sympathize with the recent movement for a separate state of Uttarakhand in the Himalayan part of India's Uttar Pradesh.

Can we say which of these various potential ethnic identities, forged out of the manifold heterogeneous forms of association found in older caste-dominated societies, will become more than merely mobilizers of votes, and actually constitute a serious threat to political unity? The work of Paul Brass (1974, 1994) suggests that in India at least they pose a threat when the focus of the identity is primarily religious, as with Muslims and Sikhs, rather than merely linguistic or cultural.[24] Other cases around the world – N. Ireland, Sri Lanka, former Yugoslavia, and Cyprus – point in the same direction.

These considerations suggest, then, that Nepal has less to fear: Buddhism is the only possible contender in the middle hills (despite NEFEN's invocation of 'animism' quoted above, there is no chance of a politically significant movement being generated by any attempt at animist fundamentalism). However, in strong contrast to Myanmar (Burma), Thailand, or Sri Lanka, Buddhism in the Nepalese context does not generate a marked boundary: too many Gurungs and too many Newars are committed to Hinduism. Other Tibeto-Burman-speaking groups are even further from identifying with Buddhism. While the allegiance of Tamangs and 'Bhotiyas' to Buddhism is much clearer, they are internally divided by other powerful factors (see chapters 6 and 12). Furthermore, the stigma attached to 'Bhotiyas', described by Ramble and Campbell, is likely to prevent any deep-seated alliance with the Newar Buddhists of the Kathmandu Valley, except on specifically Buddhist or religious issues. This is not to adopt a primordialist position; but it is to say that ethnic activists do not make history just as they please. They must work with what they inherit and religion does not reinforce other divisions in the Nepalese context.

The main fear of Nepali intellectuals and politicians is that the Tarai might wish to secede (e.g. Sharma, 1992: 9). The Tarai's proximity to and open access to India, combined with the size and power of India itself, do indeed make that a substantial danger. In the Tarai, where there were Hindu-Muslim riots in 1995, religion is clearly important, but it cannot be used to unite the Tarai against the hills. Yet, both beyond and within South Asia, there are examples of severe separatist or ethnic problems where religion is not a factor (e.g. Belgium, regionalisms in Spain and Italy, and, nearer to Nepal, in Pakistan). A recent analysis suggests that internal divisions within the Tarai are perhaps insuperably great for unity *vis-à-vis* the rest of Nepal to be achieved (Dahal, 1992), and the same is suggested by Burkert's and McDonaugh's chapters below (chapters 7 and 8). It is hard to imagine how the Tharus, represented in the hill-dominated NEFEN and now claiming descent from the Buddha, could throw in their lot with the caste Hindus of the Tarai, in spite of their older traditions claiming Rajput/Kshatriya origin in India.

Thus, although Nepal certainly faces very great economic and ecological problems, the worst fears of some commentators about the politicization of culture may well prove to be unfounded. With the more pluralist model of national culture that has already emerged, it is to be hoped that, despite increasing demands for a place at the national table, few ethnic activists, and fewer still of their potential followers, will wish to depart from it altogether.

NOTES

I am grateful to N. J. Allen, M. Banks, H. Gurung, M. Hutt, J. Pfaff-Czarnecka, D. P. Martinez, A. Michaels, D. Quigley, A. Russell, and J. Whelpton for helpful comments and suggestions on earlier drafts of this introduction. They are in no way to be held responsible for the views expressed.

[1] *The Constitution of Nepal* (fourth edition, 1981), p.2, and *The Constitution of the Kingdom of Nepal 2047 (1990)* (1992), p. 3, respectively (Kathmandu: Law Books Management Board). The 1962 version of the Constitution had used the word 'state' *(rājya)* but this was changed to 'kingdom' *(adhirājya)* by the Third Amendment in 1980. It may not have been obvious to the Constitution's compilers in 1962 that the Nepali (and Hindi) word *rājya* could apply equally to a republic. On the events of 1990 and after, see Bonk (1990), Hacchethu (1990), Gaenszle (1991b), Gaenszle and Burghart (1991), Gaige and Scholz (1991), Hutt (1991b), Raeper and Hoftun (1992), Baral (1993), Hutt ed. (1994b), Kondos (1994), and Brown (1996). On Nepalese politics since 1991, see Whelpton (1995) and Kumar (1995).

[2] Previously, from 1959 to 1964, the news had been broadcast in Hindi and Newari in addition to the national media's principal language, Nepali. Hindi and Newari were immediately reinstated in 1990. As a result of the changes of 1994 only Nepali and Newari are in use throughout the whole country; Hindi was dropped. The country was divided into four zones and news in the various languages is only broadcast in the appropriate zone. I was told in Lamjung in January 1996 that the news in Gurung broadcast from Pokhara is difficult to understand "because it is in Kaski dialect". All programming other than these news broadcasts continues to be in Nepali. On language policy and Radio Nepal, see further Sonntag (1995). As Sonntag points out, the Tamangs are a language group in search of ethnic identity, whereas the Tharus are an ethnic group in search of a language

[3] Smith is keen to dissociate himself both from the primordialist position (contemporary nations have always existed) and from the perennialist one (there have always been nations).

[4] For discussion of points in this and the preceding paragraph, I am indebted to John Whelpton and Marcus Banks. Banks (1995) and Eriksen (1993) are recommended as general guides to anthropological approaches to ethnicity and nationalism.

[5] For the sake of consistency and readability, we, the editors, have taken a local distinction and made it sharper than it probably is in much local usage.

[6] For example, see Dahal's (1979) attack on the term 'tribe'.

[7] In practice, of course, there are likely to be cases which fall between these ideal types.

[8] For a much more detailed attack on primordialism, which examines the works of the scholars who first appealed to 'primordial sentiments' to explain ethnicity, Shils and Geertz (1967), see Eller and Coughlan (1993).

[9] In line with the usage of several other writers, the term 'ethnic category' (as opposed to 'ethnic group' or 'ethnic community') is used to leave open the question of the extent to which, and the manner in which, members of the category conceive of themselves as constituting a group. Thus 'ethnic categories' and 'ethnic groups' are, in this terminology, different forms of 'ethnic identity'.

[10] On this, and on the origins of the term 'ethnicity', see the useful survey by Chapman, McDonald, and Tonkin (1989).

[11] The term and the idea of polythetic classes were introduced to anthropological discussion by Needham (1975), borrowing from Wittgenstein. Since then very many of the analytic concepts of anthropology – marriage, kinship, and religion, for example – have been argued to be polythetic.

[12] Barth himself does seem happy to embrace some such conclusion: "From this perspective, the Indian caste system would appear to be a special case of a stratified polyethnic system" (Barth, 1969: 27).

[13] This has been argued at length by Smith (1981). As for different approaches by the contributors to this book, one could contrast Gaenszle, who is more favourable to primordialism, in chapter 11, with Campbell's relatively materialist and instrumentalist framework, in chapter 6.

[14] For a discussion of how stereotypes about women have determined the way Newars as a group have been viewed, see Gellner (1991).

[15] It listed 17 such problems, e.g. "the problem of national recognition", "the consequences of the 'one nation, one language' doctrine", and "the lack of national consciousness on the part of nationalities (*janajāti*)". Most of the solutions canvassed involved financial support from the government (Tamang *et al.*, 1993). The term *janajāti*, used for ethnic minorities (but not including the Hindu castes of the Tarai), came into general educated usage only after 1990. On the Nepal Janajati Mahasangh, see further Fisher (1993) and chapters 14 and 15 below.

[16] Newar activists set up a private Newari-language primary school in 1991; many parents seem to have been attracted by the English tuition on offer (for some details, see Shrestha and van den Hoek, 1995). I would be surprised if many of the activists' own children were enrolled.

[17] See Gellner (1986, 1991), Gellner and Quigley (1995).

18 Sahlins (1993) has ironized the anthropologists' position and defended the idea that there are distinguishable and different cultures against a corrosive postmodernism. He points out that when European intellectuals hybridized their cultural heritage in the sixteenth century, this was taken to be a great achievement and called The Renaissance; who are we, then, to point to the supposed inauthenticity of indigenous intellectuals remaking their cultural inheritance in the rapidly changing circumstances of the modern world ? However, what Sahlins seems to omit is any consideration of the political implications of doing so.

19 This was incorrectly transposed as the four *jāts* and thirty-six *varṇa*s in the original (Stiller, 1968: 44; Pradhan, 1991: 155). Pradhan (*ibid.*) and Gaenszle (p.372 n.21 below) also point out that this quotation has usually been taken out of context. See also Sharma's discussion on pp. 478–9.

20 See Sontheimer and Kulke (1991) for some interesting discussions of this. For the conceptual problems faced by modern Hindu nationalists in India, see, i.a., Pandey (1993).

21 For discussion of this in the Kathmandu Valley, see Burghart (1984), Levy (1990), Toffin (1993), and Gellner (1993). Cf. p.476 below.

22 For a detailed attempt to apply Anderson's framework to Nepal, see Clarke (1996).

23 Pfaff-Czarnecka (1993b) has described how Bajhangis from far west Nepal, many among them Brahmans, make use of their identity as 'Gorkhas' to maintain a monopoly of positions as nightwatchman in the south Indian city of Bangalore.

24 For an important recent synthesis, which analyses the growth and development of Muslim and Hindu communalism in South Asia with a focus on the symbolic and emic aspects not treated by Brass, see van der Veer (1994).

PART ONE

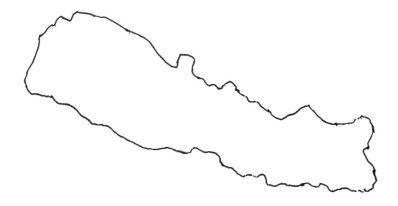

Dominant and Diaspora Identities

In studies of Nepal it is conventional to observe that, strung out as Nepal is along the Himalayas, it lies at the interface between two great civilizations, India to the south and Tibet and China to the north. Prithvi Narayan Shah, the founder of the modern state of Nepal in the eighteenth century, famously compared his country to a "gourd between two rocks" (Stiller, 1968: 42). His kingdom was both geographically and culturally very diverse, covering everything from the high Himalayas to the Gangetic plains, with many people speaking numerous different languages.

In so far as Prithvi Narayan's state had a unifying 'ethnic' basis it was the people known as Parbatiyas who provided it. They may be enumerated as the Bahun (Brahman), Thakuri (royal), and Chetri (Kshatriya) castes at the top of the social scale, and several Untouchable artisan castes at the bottom: Damai (Tailors), Kami (Blacksmiths), and Sarki (Cobblers) are the main ones. It is their language, Nepali, which has become the national language of Nepal and the lingua franca of the Himalayas from Nepal eastwards.

35

Probably originating to the west of what is now Nepal, the Parbatiyas have been gradually migrating eastwards for many centuries. Some Nepalese ethnic groups were closely associated with them from at least the sixteenth century: especially the Magars, and to a lesser extent, the Gurungs. In the nineteenth century these different groups were absorbed into an all-Nepal polity and society. Political and economic interdependence developed between the Parbatiyas and other groups. Usually (though not in every case) the Parbatiyas had the upper hand in these relationships. What sort of national identity developed on this basis, which groups accepted it, and how far they accepted it, are questions analysed in Chapter 1.

The cultural concomitant of this 'unification', as Nepali nationalists call it, was a gradual process of Hinduization: the festivals, the values, and many of the social practices of the Parbatiyas have been adopted along with the Nepali language by other hill Nepalis. Just how far this Hinduization went, how it is to be interpreted, and whether and how it can or should be reversed, are all questions discussed in Parts 2, 4, and 6 below. It is often forgotten that the Parbatiyas themselves have also undergone considerable change in a similar direction. However, since they are assumed to have always been Hindus, this is usually called 'Sanskritization' (that is, adoption of the standards of Sanskritic or Brahmanical Hinduism), rather than 'Hinduization'.

In the eighteenth and nineteenth centuries the newly forged Nepali state relied on Hinduism as its main religious legitimation. In this context the cow was a key symbol, as described in Chapter 2. That it remains a key symbol, and that the interpretation of the official designation of Nepal as a Hindu state remains highly contested, became clear in 1995. Controversy erupted after the Minister of Health in the Communist government, Padma Ratna Tuladhar, made a speech at a meeting on human rights in which he is alleged to have said that Muslims and Tamangs, whose traditional custom it is to eat beef, were being denied religious freedom by the ban on cow slaughter. Initially Congress opponents of the Communist government attacked him for encouraging cow slaughter. Then various Hindu organizations joined the fray, denouncing the Minister, and some called for general strikes. Ethnic activists declared that they would fight a strike in Kathmandu with force. Until a compromise was engineered, and the strike there called off, there were fears of severe ethnic violence.

Many parts of the Nepalese hills have long been 'deficit areas': people have had to emigrate for work and in search of new agricultural land. Many of those moving eastwards have been from 'tribal' groups. Outside of Nepal the distinction between the Parbatiyas and other ex-tribal Nepalis, though not disappearing entirely, does lose its salience: to a much greater extent than inside Nepal, all become equally Nepali. As such, they have a strong sense of cultural solidarity and a strong attachment to the Nepali or Gorkhali language. But the search for an appropriate identity in India and Bhutan is problematic. Since they are identified by others as Nepali and are wrongly accused by other Indians of harbouring designs of creating a 'greater Nepal', some are militantly opposed to being known as Nepalis rather than, as they prefer, as Gorkhas. This is described in Chapter 3.

CHAPTER ONE

Political Identity in Nepal: State, Nation, and Community

John Whelpton

INTRODUCTION

In a recent survey article (Onta, 1993), historians of Nepal were taken to task for ignoring the emphasis on 'history from below' now prominent in work on other parts of South Asia and continuing instead to concentrate almost exclusively on the Nepali state and on elite activities and attitudes. That warning reminded me of two conversations with individual Nepalis. In 1972, shortly after my first arrival in the country, when I was walking only a few miles from Kathmandu I asked a villager where he was going and received the same reply that initially puzzles many foreigners: *Nepāl jāne* ("I'm going to Nepal"). For this man, 'Nepal' retained its old meaning of the Kathmandu Valley, not the country of which he was a citizen. Eighteen years later, in the aftermath of the Movement for the Restoration of Democracy, I was discussing the current situation with a Nepali scholar, whose background was very traditional and who, I think, spoke spontaneously without any influence from Marxist theories of 'petit-bourgeois nationalism'. "It's only we, the middle class, who are really concerned about Nepal," he said. "The poor are just interested in getting enough to eat and the very rich people around the palace are only worried about getting more money and storing it in India." Being Nepali, then, means different things to different Nepalis and we need to be constantly aware of the gap that may exist between official aspirations and the actual feelings of a population divided along ethnic, caste, and class lines.

39

That does not, however, mean that we are wrong to take the Nepali state and groups occupying the most central position within it as the starting point in any discussion of Nepali identity. The consolidation of many older nation-states has involved the diffusion to a wider community of sentiments originally confined to a much smaller circle. We need to examine the undoubtedly strong feelings of 'Nepaliness' which are so evident amongst educated members of the dominant Parbatiya castes (Thakuris, Chetris, and Brahmans) and then look at how far they have spread, or are spreading, to other groups in the population.

THE ROOTS OF A NATIONAL IDENTITY

It is common to regard 'Nepali nationalism' as simply a borrowing in this century, via the Indian nationalist movement, of a nineteenth-century European ideology. This is perhaps true if we are talking about the fully articulated and self-conscious nationalism which the school system and mass media promulgate today, but not if we are looking for the origins of the sense of political identity which is the key characteristic of groups we recognize as 'nations'. Ernest Gellner (1983) is certainly right in discerning a connection between industrialization's need for an homogeneous workforce and the acceptance of the integrated nation-state as a political ideal, but industrialization deepened and accelerated an existing trend rather than producing an entirely new phenomenon. Cultural amalgamation and the growth of a sense of identity between hitherto disparate elements was moulding nation-states in Europe long before the industrial revolution, and in Nepal a somewhat similar, though more limited, process was underway before the importation of Western political ideas could play any significant role.

The 'unification' of Nepal by King Prithvi Narayan Shah of Gorkha and his successors in the late eighteenth and early nineteenth century was in the first place a straightforward military conquest: there was certainly no demand for unity of the kind expressed by many Germans and Italians before German and Italian unification was achieved.[1] Nevertheless there were certain common factors distinguishing the Hindu population from Kumaon eastwards through the Himalayan foothills from Hindus elsewhere in South Asia. There was a shared sense of being Paharis[2] (hillmen) as opposed to plainsdwellers, a continuum of dialects classified as the Pahari division of Indo-Aryan, and a discernible Pahari culture, marked by features such as a less rigorous regulation of caste and sexual relations and the importance of spirit possession in religious life (Berreman, 1972).

This degree of commonality is even greater if we exclude Kumaon and Garhwal and consider the Karnali and Gandaki basins, which before Prithvi Narayan's conquests were divided between some forty-eight independent principalities including Gorkha itself. Here the dominant ethnic group, the Parbatiyas or Indo-Nepalis, were set apart by the peculiarity of their caste structure, anchored around the Chetri (i.e. Kshatriya) caste. Before the mid-nineteenth century the Chetris were known as Khas, and they were in fact a continuation of the people of that name who had lived in the Himalayas since ancient times. Above them in the Parbatiya hierarchy were the Thakuris, who claimed descent from Indian Rajput refugees, and the Brahmans, who were also supposedly of Indian origin. Many of the Thakuris were in fact certainly of Khas extraction themselves, whilst the Brahmans were bound together with the Khas-Chetris because the children of a Brahman father and Khas mother were admitted to Khas-Chetri status. Khas ranks were also swelled by the offspring of unions between a Khas or Brahman male and women from Tibeto-Burman-speaking ethnic groups such as the Magars or Gurungs. This pattern contrasted with the area west of the Mahakali, now forming part of the Indian state of Uttar Pradesh, where there was a much stricter separation between Khas and (real or supposed) immigrants from India and where there were very few non-Hindu 'tribals' remaining.[3]

These pre-existing cultural links were reinforced once the area had been brought within the Gorkha state – we need to say 'Gorkha' because the term 'Nepal' was not officially adopted for the entire kingdom until the 1930s. A key factor right from the start was the use of Hinduism as a source of legitimation. Prithvi Narayan himself described his kingdom as an *asal* (real) *hindustān*[4] thus at once asserting membership of an over-arching Hindu community but also claiming a special status within it as a territory not polluted by Muslim or Christian rule. This was a recurrent theme throughout the Rana period (1846–1951) and, as the debate on the issue of Hindu versus secular state during the drafting of the 1990 Constitution showed, it is still very much alive. There is a clear parallel here with medieval Europe, where claims of a special role within Christendom for a dynasty and the territory it controlled were important in the formation of national identities in France, Spain, and elsewhere (Armstrong, 1982).

The imposition of a precisely delineated border by the 1816 Treaty of Sagauli, which concluded the two-year war with the East India Company, strengthened the ascription of a religious significance to the entire Gorkha domain. As Richard Burghart (1984) has argued, the rulers could now see the whole kingdom as one *deśa* (country) – a word previously reserved either for the region under the protection of the king's tutelary deity (i.e. the Kathmandu Valley and a section of the surrounding hills), or the traditional homeland of one ethnic group (e.g. Magrat, Khasan etc.).[5] A culmination of this process was the promulgation of a single caste hierarchy for the entire territory in the Muluki Ain (national Legal Code) of 1854 (Höfer, 1979).

Alongside the religious factor, Mahesh Regmi has drawn attention to the emergence from Prithvi Narayan's time of the concept of loyalty to the state or *dhuṅgo* (lit. 'stone') as distinct from the purely personal bond between king and follower in the pre-unification statelets (Regmi, 1978b; Gaenszle, 1992: 44). In 1806 Rana Bahadur Shah, who had abdicated the throne in favour of his infant son but regained power as minister, told his half-brother Sher Bahadur that he forgave him for plotting against his own person but that he still had to answer to the nobles (*bhāradār*s) for his crimes against the *dhuṅgo*.[6] Allied with this notion was the general recognition that the *bhāradār*s as a body had the right to over-ride the wishes of an individual king in the interests of the dynasty and kingdom. This point was impressed on Colonel Kirkpatrick during his 1793 visit to Kathmandu, and seen in practice at critical points during the nineteenth century (Kirkpatrick, 1811: 24; Whelpton, 1991: 19–20 and 116–20).

Whilst we can thus certainly speak of at least a Gorkhali 'proto-nation' at this time, did the non-Parbatiya groups, or indeed the Parbatiya untouchables such as the Sarkis, identify with it to any extent or regard it purely as the engine of domination by the Parbatiya twice-born castes? There was certainly no identification with the state amongst the peoples of the Tarai, who were not even Paharis. There was also very little amongst the Kiranti peoples of eastern Nepal, who, although in some cases nominally subjects of Rajput rulers based in the Tarai, had enjoyed virtual independence until the Gorkha conquest: significantly, many of them rebelled against their new masters at the time of the Chinese invasion in 1792 (Pradhan, 1991: 136–7). The Newars of the Kathmandu Valley made no move against their Parbatiya overlords, and Newar traders spreading beyond the Valley found opportunities for profit in the newly unified state, but the Newar population as a whole, excluded as it was from political power and from military service, certainly did not think of themselves as Gorkhalis.

In contrast, some at least of the Magars and Gurungs may have felt a sense of belonging to the Gorkha state in Prithvi's time, because both of these groups had long been accustomed to Parbatiya rule and because they provided a significant proportion of the Gorkha army. Until some years into the nineteenth century, the political elite surrounding the Gorkha monarchy included Magars and Gurungs who were acknowledged at such. The link between the Magars and the Shah dynasty was particularly strong: prominent Magars could be granted the right to wear the sacred thread as Chetris in the same way as the Khas (Kirkpatrick, 1811: 123) and Francis Hamilton reported after his 1801–1803 visit that many Magar soldiers had forgotten their own language and spoke only Parbatiya (i.e. Nepali) and that 'many people' in Kathmandu expected the Magars to become simply another Parbatiya caste (Hamilton, 1986: 26).[7] Cultural integration between Gurung and Parbatiya was less complete, but Gurungs generally accepted the Brahmanical account which placed their origins in South Asia rather than Tibet and early in the nineteenth century agreed to give up eating beef (Ragsdale, 1989: 41).[8]

Once the period of Gorkha expansion ended, prospects for 'promotion' through the caste system naturally lessened and by the 1830s British observers believed that there were no Magars or Gurungs amongst army officers.[9] Nevertheless, memories of their role in the establishment of the state were still alive: Nathu and Prahlad

Gurung, two officers who played a prominent role in the conquest of Kumaon and Garhwal, are well remembered amongst the Gurungs to this day.[10] Magars, Gurungs and (after 1847) Rais and Limbus also continued to serve in the army in large numbers and were recruited into the Gurkha regiments of the British Indian Army. Service with either army helped to produce a 'Gorkha identity': soldiers were exposed to military tradition and to a Nepali language and Hinduizing environment, whilst in both the British forces and in those of their own country they were required to swear an oath of allegiance to the King of Nepal and to the Rana Maharaja (Ragsdale, 1989: 49–50, 53). Mary Des Chene (1991) is thus not entirely correct to argue that this identity was purely a colonial construction without impact on the feelings of individual soldiers,[11] but the Gorkha, Magar, Rai, or Limbu soldier's sense of being a 'Gorkhali' was weak when compared to the sense of belonging to their own community, a community which might or might not correspond with one of the ethnic or caste categories recognized by the Nepali state. This mentality was largely the result of social conditions within Nepal but also reinforced by the partial or complete segregation of different ethnic groups within the armies.

MODERN NEPALI NATIONALISM

Although the intensity of identification with the Gorkha state thus varied significantly from group to group, it was sufficiently strong amongst the more privileged groups to ensure that when a minority drawn from these strata was exposed in the twentieth century to Western political ideas, nationalism as an explicitly formulated doctrine married easily with attachments already formed. Thus both before and after the overthrow of the Rana regime in 1950–51, Nepali nationalism was an important factor in the struggle for political power with all sides appealing to nationalist feelings as a means of mobilizing support.

For their part, the Ranas naturally responded to radical nationalist ideas spreading from India by seeking to promote a patriotism centred on themselves as the group controlling the state. This was part of Maharaja Chandra Shamsher Rana's motivation in pressing for formal recognition by Britain of Nepal's total independence, which was granted in 1923; the British had previously hedged on the issue, as, for example, in the Foreign Secretary's 1888 assertion that Nepal was 'in a state of quasi-subordination to us' (Rose, 1971: 145). The official adoption in the 1930s of the name 'Nepal' for the whole kingdom and of 'Nepali' for its principal language, replacing 'Gorkha' and 'Gorkhali' respectively, is presented by Burghart (1984: 118–119) as a falling into line with British usage,[12] but its motivation may rather have been the encouragement of a wider sense of identification with the state, especially amongst the Newar inhabitants of the Kathmandu Valley, who filled many positions in the bureaucracy but could not regard themselves as 'Gorkhali'. The Rana administration's action served a recognizably nationalist objective: underlining a linkage between the seat of government, the whole territory under their control, and the dominant language. The Ranas also appealed to national feeling when reporting dissident activity, branding the Praja Parishad conspirators of 1940 as "traitors to their country" (*deśdrohī*) rather than simply as disloyal to the king and Maharaja.[13]

Nationalism was also a central element in the propaganda of the Ranas' opponents, drawn from the Parbatiya upper castes and from the Newars of the Kathmandu Valley, and for them, too, 'Nepal' rather than 'Gorkha' was becoming the more appropriate term for the nation. The Ranas' policy of close collaboration with the British left them open to attack on nationalist grounds, but the nationalism of many radical Nepalis, particularly among the Nepali community in India, was tempered by their commitment to the wider struggle against British rule in South Asia. This regional dimension was underlined by the fact that the Nepali Congress's 1950–51 uprising against the Ranas was launched from Indian soil, depended on Indian support for its success, and had to be terminated because of Indian pressure to reach a compromise agreement rather than continue fighting for an immediate and total transfer of state power.

The result of this was that in the post-1951 struggles for power, the Nepali Congress, whilst accepted by many as the vehicle of national liberation, was also itself open to attack on nationalist grounds. The Rana revivalist forces, which were an important factor in the political equation until 1960,[14] used this weapon, as did the monarchy and other political parties. Particularly vulnerable was the Congress leader, B. P. Koirala, whose family were hill Brahmans but had migrated to Biratnagar in the Tarai. Koirala himself had been born in Banaras and returned there at the age of three when his father fell foul of Chandra Shamsher and went into exile. Whilst strongly aware of his own Nepali identity, B. P. in his early days did not see 'Nepali' and 'Indian' as mutually exclusive categories. At the inaugural session of the Nepal Rastriya Congress he had declared that because of racial, religious, and economic links "Nepal and India are not two countries" and that "the political difference you find is basically the game of selfish diplomats and politicians" (Uprety, 1992: 94). Once engaged in practical politics inside Nepal, Koirala and his party nevertheless proved able to play a more stridently nationalist tune if required. In 1954, when B. P.'s brother and political rival, M. P. Koirala, headed the government, B. P. and the Congress party attacked it for surrendering control of Nepali territory to India under the Kosi River Project Agreement (Shaha, 1990: vol.2, 305–309). In his last years, after returning from exile in India in 1976, Koirala sought a reconciliation between the monarchy and liberal democratic forces, arguing that otherwise national independence would be in danger.

The 'revolution' had commenced in October 1950 with King Tribhuvan's dramatic flight to the Indian embassy and this Indian connection enabled the Rana regime to attempt an appeal to nationalist sentiment against him. Once the Ranas were dislodged, however, the monarchy was in a strong position to portray itself as the embodiment of national identity, particularly after the accession of Mahendra, who was less beholden to India than his father had been. In addition to the religious awe surrounding Hindu kingship and to his prestige as the direct descendant of the founder of the nation, the occupant of the throne was helped by the royal family's century of political emasculation: it was the Ranas, not the Shah kings, who bore the responsibility for collaboration with British colonialism. The monarchy was in fact able both to claim credit for ending Rana autocracy and also to count on the loyalty of individual members of the Rana family who retained high positions in national life, in particular in the army: a century of inter-marriage between Ranas and Shahs meant that, in a sense, 1950–51 simply saw an exchange of junior and senior roles between two wings of the same family.[15] Using this base, Mahendra presented his 'Panchayat democracy' under 'the active leadership of the king' as an indigenous alternative to Western (and Indian) parliamentarianism. He also made full use of Congress's Indian links, alleging when he ousted Koirala in 1960 that Congress was compromising national independence. Throughout Mahendra's reign and the early years of Birendra's, the official media continued to refer to Congress and other dissidents operating in exile in India as 'anti-national elements' – similar phraseology to that which the Ranas had employed in the 1930s and 1940s.

Also competing for the nationalist mantle were the various factions of the Communist Party of Nepal. Their Marxism drew heavily on Mao Tse Tung's emphasis on oppressed nations as well as oppressed classes, and, since the foreign capital which had most significance for the Nepali economy was Indian capital, it was and is easy for them to appeal to traditional Pahari prejudice against Madheshis whilst not appearing to compromise their internationalist principles. This resulted in a degree of convergence of interest between the Left and the monarchy, and in the 1960s in particular there were tales of Communist activists collecting financial handouts from both the Chinese Embassy and the royal palace! The anti-India theme continues today as exemplified by the ferocious campaign by the Communist groups inside and outside of parliament against the 1991–94 Congress government for sanctioning the Indian construction of a dam on Nepali territory at Tanakpur.[16]

If the opposition between hill and plains has historically provided a negative definition for Nepali national identity, one important positive factor is the simple fact of being included within a single political unit for two hundred years; although merely being under the same set of rulers has little immediate effect on individuals' sense of identity, it becomes more significant in the long term. In Max Weber's words: "It is primarily the political community, no matter how artificially organized, that inspires the belief in common ethnicity" (Weber, 1968: vol.1, p. 389). The modern nation-state is able to accelerate this process through mass education and in

FIGURE 2   *A Communist group invokes the Indian bogey in this banner from the 1991 election campaign: dhoti-clad Indian Prime Minister Chandrashekhar cracks the whip over the Congress troika (left to right: K. P. Bhattarai, G. P. Koirala, and Ganesh Man Singh), instructing them in Hindi: "Dance, and say, 'The rivers and waterways are common'." Bhattarai's use in Delhi of the phrase "common rivers" had been seen by the opposition as conceding to India partial control of the tributaries of the Ganges flowing through Nepal (Jhilko, April–September 1991)*

particular by teaching history in a way which encourages citizens to think of the state's past achievements as their own. As education was expanded rapidly from the very low level of 1951, and especially with the introduction of a standardized national system in the 1960s, children were taught to see themselves as members of a national community in a stronger way than previously.[17]

NATION AND ETHNIC COMMUNITY

The Nepali identity which the education system sought to inculcate continued a pattern established long before 1951, being based on the culture of the dominant Parbatiyas rather than of other groups within the population. In 1955, a landmark report on education planning conceded the need to use minority languages for oral communication with students just starting primary school but advocated a switch to exclusive use of Nepali as soon as possible so that "other languages will gradually disappear and greater national strength and unity will result" (Nepal National Education Planning Commission, 1955: 96–97). An emphasis on the Nepali (Parbatiya or Gorkhali) language is as old as the founding of the state (even older, in that Parbatiya was already in use as a lingua franca before the Gorkha conquests), though the formal declaration of Nepali as the official language was only made under Maharaja Chandra Shamsher (1901–1929).[18] The case is similar with Hinduism, which both linked the country with pan-South-Asian values and also separated it from an India which was initially under non-Hindu rule and then, following independence in 1947, avowedly secular. Nepal was only formally proclaimed a Hindu kingdom in Mahendra's 1962 constitution, but this merely gave modern expression to a long-standing reality, as witnessed by Prithvi Narayan's *asal hindustān* formulation or by Maharaja Chandra Shamsher's 1913 description of the country as 'an ancient Hindu kingdom' when he rejected a proposal from the new Chinese resident in Lhasa for a union between Nepal and the Chinese republic (Husain, 1970: 280).

The new legal code promulgated by King Mahendra in 1962 removed statutory backing for the caste hierarchy, but the reliance by the regime on the traditional aspects of Nepalese political culture meant that languages other than Nepali and values other than those of the *tāgādhārī* Parbatiyas continued to be disregarded. Official propaganda did not always state this preference explicitly, but the underlying ethos was that expressed by Yogi Naraharinath, almost the only ideologue to openly mourn the 1990 downfall of the Panchayat system: "there should be a single language (*bhāṣā*) and writing system ... one style of dress (*bhes*), one aim and one leader."[19]

The opponents of Rana and then Shah autocracy were obviously not committed to such a narrow view of Nepalese identity. The leaders of Congress and other political parties were nevertheless drawn mostly from the Parbatiya elite groups, spoke Nepali as their mother tongue rather than a minority language, and were strongly affected by Hindu caste values even if they had adopted an avowedly egalitarian ideology. Modernism and tradition were strangely combined in the pamphlets put out by the Raktapat (bloodshed) Committee, a dissident group active in Kathmandu during the Second World War. These echoed the language of Russian anarchism and boasted of contacts with the Soviet and Japanese governments, yet indicted Maharaja Juddha Shamsher Rana from a clearly Brahmanical standpoint:

> You will not be blessed with peace and tranquillity in this Hindu Raj as long as . . . administration . . . is in the hand of this ignoble outcaste with whom, according to the laws of our Shastras we should not even drink and dine . . . one who captures the budding, beautiful, innocent Brahman damsels to be his concubines.[20]

Congress and Leftist ranks were to include members of lower castes, and in 1950–51 the insurgents relied heavily on the minorities in the eastern hills, but the highest ranks were normally still in the hands of Brahmans, Thakuri-Chetris, or high-caste Newars.

Since 1951, under both multi-party and Panchayat systems, the Brahmans, Thakuri-Chetris, and Newars, who between them account for about a third of Nepal's total population, have normally held 60% of the seats in parliament or Rastriya Panchayat.[21] The only difference has been that Brahmans, the bulk of the intelligentsia, were boosted by the multi-party system and the Thakuri-Chetris, the traditionally dominant caste on whom both Ranas and Shahs had chiefly relied, benefitted under the Panchayat system. The preponderance is even more marked in the bureaucracy: in 1989, section officers were 55% Brahman, 27% Newar, and 11% Chetri, whilst at the highest rank (secretary), where appointment was determined by political considerations as well as access to education, Brahmans and Chetris each accounted for 31% and Newars for 25%. The three groups together also occupied 81% of the teaching posts at Tribhuvan University in 1990 (Poudyal, 1992: 140–1).

The overwhelming predominance of a Parbatiya-Newar elite in Nepalese society attracted attention and comment even during the Panchayat years, and a number of organizations were set up to campaign for the interests of particular minorities as far as was possible within the political constraints of the day. In the heady atmosphere following the spring 1990 triumph of the Movement for the Restoration of Democracy, the number of such bodies rapidly increased: an umbrella organization set up in July 1990, the Nepal Janajati Mahasangh (Nepal Nationalities Federation), brought together some twenty of them.[22] Minority demands were put forward with a new intensity. The fervency with which some among the educated took up the ethnic cause was greater than that amongst the mass of the population: surveys in the aftermath of the 1991 election showed little importance attached to the issue amongst parliamentarians and party members and virtually none amongst the mass of voters (Borre *et al.*, 1994: 112). Nevertheless, almost every Nepali is keenly aware of his or her membership of a particular caste or ethnic group and the degree of political salience of such identities may obviously increase with changes in circumstances. The present ferment amongst an activist minority is therefore worth some attention.

The discussion so far has given a general view of the diversity of Nepali society. Table 1 provides a more detailed picture, including figures for the relative size of the main groups. A question on caste/ethnic affiliation has regularly been included in census questionnaires but because of the potential sensitivity of the subject, the Nepali government did not publish the results until the census of 1991.[23] The resulting statistics still need to be used with some caution, but they are more reliable than earlier published estimates based on a mixture of limited surveys and guesswork.

More fundamental than arguments over precise figures is a conceptual problem which concerns especially those groupings normally regarded as ethnic and which is addressed by most of the contributors to this volume. The point is that we cannot regard all such groups as 'natural' units in contrast to an 'artificial' Nepali nation. They differ greatly in the intensity of group identification amongst their members and many of them are intricately subdivided. The Newars, the most economically and culturally advanced of the hill minorities, are regarded as a single *jāti* by other Nepalis and treated as such in the census statistics, but they possess an intricate caste structure of their own and these castes were allocated different positions within the overall hierarchy for Nepali society prescribed in the 1854 Muluki Ain. It is only the higher Newar castes (i.e. those shown in the table as entitled to full Hindu or Buddhist tantric initiation) which can be regarded as forming part of the Nepalese elite with Parbatiya Brahmans and Chetris. The divisions are such that it is a matter of controversy whether there was any strong sense of 'Newarness' amongst the Newar population until faced with the prospect of conquest by Gorkha. Two recent studies of Newar ethnicity differ over the prospects of success for those promoting Newar ethnic assertiveness but agree that at present it is still locality and the circle of families accepted as of equal caste status which matters for most Newars.[24]

Whilst other hill minorities possess a less complex and more egalitarian social structure and are commonly referred to as 'tribes', the Nepalese anthropologist Dilli Ram Dahal has argued that none of these groups is a tribe by any of the standard definitions because they lack such basic tribal characteristics as a common territory or over-arching political institutions (Dahal, 1979). The question is a difficult one to adjudicate with so many 'standard definitions' of 'tribe' to choose between, but Dahal does have a point, and one which is also supported by the absence in colloquial Nepali usage of a distinction between 'caste' and 'ethnic group': whilst Nepalis exposed to Western anthropological thinking consistently use the Sanskrit loan-word *jāti* for 'tribes' and its vernacular derivative *jāt* for castes, most of their countrymen either have only *jāt* in their vocabulary or regard the two words as interchangeable.[25] This usage reflects not just a lack of intellectual sophistication but an understanding of an important reality: the ethnic labels commonly employed often conceal internal differences and mask similarities between groups. These labels have often been assigned by outsiders, in particular by the state, to fit within a hierarchically conceived scheme of classification. In other cases, individuals or communities have themselves adopted a name to find an advantageous slot in that structure. The Rai, for example, are a collection of peoples speaking mutually unintelligible languages – hence the Nepali proverb *jati rāī, uti kurā* ("As many dialects as there are Rais"). Their collective eponym is derived from the title given to their chieftains by Nepali speakers.

The elasticity of group boundaries is well illustrated by the Gurung, Tamang, and Thakali (a very small but economically

TABLE 1.1   CASTES AND ETHNIC GROUPS

(1) Parbatiyas (40.3%)

Twice-born:	BRAHMAN	12.9%
	THAKURI	1.6%
	CHETRI (formerly KHAS)	16.1%
Renouncers:	Dashnami Sanyasi and Kanphata Yogi	1.0%
Untouchables:	Kami (iron-workers)	5.2%
	Damai (tailors)	2.0%
	Sarki (cobblers)	1.5%

(2) NEWARS[a] (5.6%)

Entitled to full initiation:

BRAHMAN	0.1%	BAJRACHARYA/ SHAKYA	0.5%
SHRESTHA	1.0%	Uray	0.3%

Other pure castes:

MAHARJAN (JYAPU)	2.3%
'Ekthariya' etc.	0.5−0.7%

Impure castes:

Khadgi (Kasai), Dyahla (Pore) etc.	0.3%

(3) Other hill or mountain ethnic groups ('tribes') (20.1%)

MAGAR	7.2%	Chepang	0.2%
TAMANG	5.5%	Sunuwar	0.2%
RAI	2.8%	Bhotiya	0.1%
GURUNG	2.4%	THAKALI	0.1%
LIMBU	1.6%	Thami	0.1%
SHERPA	0.6%		

(4) Madheshis (32%)

(a) Castes (16.1%)

Twice-born: BRAHMAN		0.9%
RAJPUT		0.3%
Kayastha	(Kshatriya)	0.3%
Rajbhat[b]		0.2%
Baniya (Vaishya)		0.6%

Table 1.1 (Continued):

Other pure castes:	YADAV/Ahir (herdsmen)	4.1%
	Khushawaha[c] (vegetable-growers)	1.1%
	Kurmi (cultivators)	0.9%
	Mallah (fishermen)	0.6%
	Kewat (fishermen)	0.5%
	Kumhar (potters)	0.4%
	Halwai (confectioners)	0.2%
Impure, but Touchable:	Kalawar (brewers/merchants)	0.9%
	Dhobi (washermen)	0.5%
	Teli (oil-pressers)	1.4%
	Kanu (oil-pressers)	0.4%
Untouchable:	Chamar (leather-workers)	1.1%
	Dushadh (basket-makers)	0.5%
	Khatawe (labourers)	0.4%
	Musahar	0.8%

(b) Ethnic groups (9%):

Inner Tarai:	Kumal	0.4%
	Majhi	0.3%
	Danuwar	0.3%
	Darai	0.1%
Tarai Proper:	THARU	6.5%
	Dhanuk	0.7%
	Rajbanshi	0.4%
	Gangai	0.1%
	Dhimal	0.1%

(c) Muslims	(3.5%)
(d) Marwaris[d]	(0.2%)
(e) Sikhs	(0.1%)

Source: Percentages of the total population (18.5 million) are normally taken from the 1991 census data (Central Bureau of Statistics 1993: vol. 2, Part VII, Table 25) and layout is partly based on that of Harka Gurung (Salter and Gurung 1996: Table 1). The table excludes the 4.7% of the population either falling in the census category of 'Others' (the bulk of these being people of Tarai origin) or belonging to groups accounting for less than 0.1% of the population. Due to roundings, totals do not tally exactly. The census distinguishes between groups of mountain, hill, or Tarai origin, but the hill and mountain category are amalgamated here. The ranking of castes in the Tarai is frequently in dispute and is presented here largely on the basis of Gaborieau (1978). The largest and/or best-known groups have been capitalized.

[a] The census treats the Newars as a single group. Figures for the main sub-divisions are calculated from the estimates of the relative size of the different sub-divisions in Gaborieau (1978: 198–206).

[b] Also known as Rajbhar or Bhat. Though classified as a Tarai group in the census, the are also found in the hills. Both in the Tarai and in the western hills they still function as genealogists and match-makers for the other twice-born castes, though Bhat elsewhere in the hills are more usually the offspring of irregular unions between Brahmans and Chetri or Sanyasi (Gaborieau, 1978: 180 and 217–8).

[c] Formerly known as 'Koiris'. Their new name indicates supposed descent from Ram's second son, Kusha, and thus a claim to Kshatriya status, but this has not yet been accepted by other groups (Madhusudhan Thakur, personal communication).

[d] Harka Gurung (personal communication) now treats Marwaris as a category outside the Tarai caste hierarchy both because many are Jains and because the are seen as outsiders by the Tarai population generally. Many do, however, claim to be Hindus and there is also a case for placing them like, the Baniya, in the Vaishya category.

important trading community from the upper Kali Gandaki Valley), who speak closely related languages and whose common forerunners appear to have been a single ethnic group in southern Tibet about a thousand years ago (Höfer, 1981: 7). The present-day Tamang, second largest of the hill minorities, were previously known as 'Murmi' or not differentiated from the lowly-regarded Bhotiyas (groups of Tibetan cultural affinity). It was only in 1932 that they received formal recognition as a group and permission to use the surname 'Tamang' (a Tibetan honorific term meaning 'cavalryman') (Tamang, 1992: 25; Gaborieau, 1978: 132).[26] The related terms 'Tamhang' and 'Tamu' are still used as a name for themselves by the Thakalis and the Gurungs respectively and those Tamang who live west of the Kathmandu Valley generally feel as closely related to the Gurung as to the eastern Tamang. Since the cultural and linguistic differences are slight and Gurungs are a higher-status group, many Tamangs have chosen to 'pass' as Gurung, particularly to enlist in the Nepali and foreign armies where recruitment was traditionally restricted to specific groups (Campbell, pp. 224–5 below). The Tamang/Bhotiya ethnic boundary is similarly porous: some decades ago Tibetan speakers in the north-western district of Humla were ordered by the government to call themselves Tamangs to strengthen Nepal's hand in a border dispute with Tibet (Levine, 1987: 79–80).[27] Campbell also shows how members of Ghale clans in Rasuwa district are regarded as non-Tamang at village level, but nevertheless speak the local Tamang dialect, intermarry with 'true' Tamangs, and are classified in the census as Tamangs.

Similarly to the boundaries between groups, the degree of internal cohesion can shift over time, a possibility on which the hopes of the ethnic activists obviously depend. Whether or not as a result of consciousness-raising efforts by the Nepal Tamang Ghedung (Nepal Tamang Council), marriages between eastern and western Tamangs are considered more acceptable than before. Similarly, amongst the Gurungs the importance of the division between the allegedly higher-status (and more Sanskritized) Char Jat ('Four Castes') and the Sorah Jat ('Sixteen Castes'), which was identified as the source of considerable conflict by Messerschmidt in the 1970s, has virtually disappeared in the villages where Pignède and Messerschmidt worked (Messerschmidt, 1976; Pignède, 1993: 465).[28]

Like the data on ethnic affiliation, the census statistics on mother-tongues (Table 1.2) have to be used with caution. Given the Nepalese situation of many languages in contact and one official language having by far the greatest number of speakers and the greatest prestige, a child may be hearing two or more languages in the home right from the start. What, for example, is the mother-tongue of a Newar child whose parents speak to him in Nepali to prepare him for Nepali-medium education but continue to speak to each other in Newari in his presence? There is also the problem presented by a dialect continuum, where the speech of all members of a given locality is generally mutually comprehensible and any classification into separate languages may seem arbitrary. This is essentially the situation in the Tarai (Rastriya Bhasha Niti Sujhav Ayog, 1994: 8), resulting in particularly frequent disputes about the status and number of speakers of particular languages. The 1952–54 census report, for example, using a very restrictive definition of Maithili, put the number of speakers at under 0.4 million whereas V. Kansakar (1989) and Harka Gurung (1989a: 99, Map 6) arrive at totals of almost a million and 1.5 million respectively by adding in local dialects over differing sections of the eastern Tarai (see note to Table 1.2). Finally, the Panchayat era's stress on the dominant Parbatiya culture may have caused individuals responding to a census question (or the government employee writing down the data) to record 'Nepali' when in fact they made equal or greater use of a minority language in their daily lives. This would explain why the total percentage of Nepali speakers appears to rise steadily for many years and then dips suddenly in 1991, whilst the main hill minority tongues seemed to have recovered some of their lost ground.

ETHNIC POLITICS

Despite all these uncertainties, certain political consequences can be deduced at once from the census data. The first of these is the strength of the Parbatiya upper castes' position among the groups native to the hills. Brahmans, Thakuris, and Chetris make up 45.5% of the population of hill origin (i.e. excluding Madheshis), and although they are thus technically a minority, the remaining 54.5% is divided into a plethora of small groups, with the largest, the Magars (10.8%), long in close association with the Parbatiyas and now 70% Nepali-speaking. Furthermore the non-Parbatiya groups are widely dispersed geographically: the second largest, the Tamangs, do form the largest ethnic bloc in a belt of seven districts surrounding the Kathmandu Valley, but are only an absolute majority in the northern border district of Rasuwa (Harka Gurung, 1994: 8–14). Finally there is the fact that all the hill ethnic groups, even if retaining their original language in the home, accept Nepali as the hill lingua franca and also share an identity as Paharis rather than Madheshis.

In the Tarai, too, there is great diversity, with no group holding the predominant position which the Parbatiyas have in the hills. There are tensions between the recent settlers from the hills (now between 35 and 40% of the Tarai population), the indigenous 'tribal' groups and the caste-Hindus of plains origin.[29] The last-mentioned grouping

TABLE 1.2   MOTHER–TONGUE SPEAKERS OF MAIN
             LANGUAGES (PERCENTAGE OF TOTAL
             POPULATION)

Language	1952/4	1961	1971	1981	1991
Nepali	48.7	50.1	52.5	58.4	50.3
Tarai (Indo-Aryan):					
Maithili	11.2	12.0	11.5	11.1	11.8
Bhojpuri	0.2	6.1	7.0	7.6	7.5
Awadhi	N.A.	4.8	2.7	1.6	2.0
Tharu[a]	4.4	4.3	4.3	3.6	5.4
Hill (Tibeto-Burman):					
Tamang	6.0	5.6	4.8	3.5	4.9
Newari	4.7	4.0	3.9	3.0	3.7
Magar	3.3	2.7	2.5	1.4	2.3
Rai/Kirati	2.9	2.5	2.0	1.5	2.4
Gurung	2.0	1.7	1.5	1.2	1.2
Limbu	1.8	1.5	1.5	0.9	1.4

Source: 1952–1981 census statistics from table in Kansakar (1989: 43–44; 1991
figures calculated from Table 1.5 in Central Bureau of Statistics 1994: 18–19).
For his 1952 Maithili figure, Kansakar has combined the census report's
categories of 'Maithili' and 'Rural languages – Central East Tarai'. For the same
year, Gurung (Salter and Gurung 1996: Table 8) gives 1952 percentages of 18
for Maithili (including 'rural languages' of the Central–East, Eastern, and Far
East Tarai), 3.3 for Bhojpuri (including 'rural languages' for Central–West
Tarai, and 0.8 for Awadhi ('rural languages' for Far West Tarai).[b] Subsequent
census reports abandoned these 'hold-all regional linguistic categories. The
particular complexities behind the acceptance or rejection of the 'Maithili' label
are discussed by Burkert (this volume).

[a] Although 'Tharu' is shown in the census as Nepal's fourth largest language
and is now one of the languages in which Radio Nepal broadcasts news, the
speech of the Tharu 'tribe' has been so heavily influenced by that of the
surrounding caste societies that some analysts (e.g. Jha, 1993: 28) argue that
it is not a distinct language but is simply a label for Awadhi, Bhojpuri, or
Maithili as spoken by ethnic Tharus. Even more than with other groups in
Nepal, Tharus' own overwhelming (83.2%) acceptance of this label is evidence
for the strength of subjective group-identification rather than for purely
linguistic difference.

Table 1.2 (continued)

[b] Details of the basis for his own and Kansakar's figures were supplied by Harka Gurung in a personal communication.

TABLE 1.3   LANGUAGE SHIFT IN SELECTED MINORITY GROUPS (1991)

| Magar | 67.9% | Newar | 33.7% | Limbu | 14.5% |
| Gurung | 49.3% | Rai | 16.4% | Tamang | 11.2% |

Source: Figures are for the proportion of each group *not* reporting the group's own language as their mother tongue and are calculated from the data in Central Bureau of Statistics (1994: Tables 1.5 and 1.6).[a] The shift will normally have been to Nepali.

[a] Minority language retention rates for these and 17 other ethnic groups are shown in the full census report (Central Bureau of Statistics, 1993: vol.2, Part VI, Table 22). See also Harka Gurung, this volume.

dominates in a belt of nine districts in the east-central Tarai and a regional party, Sadbhavana, secured six seats from this area in 1991. Although the party's representation fell to three seats in 1994, there is still potential for the creation of a Tarai identity based on the use of Hindi (the lingua franca of the region),[30] and also on a shared sense of grievance against hill domination. In view of these marked differences between hills and plain, the minority issue in the hills will be considered first before returning to the Tarai situation.

Although Nepal's 1990 Constitution prohibits the Election Commission from recognizing ethnic or regional parties, the principle apparently followed has been to deny registration only to parties whose name or constitution makes their ethnic or regional objectives too explicit. Thus, in 1991, of the parties appealing specifically to the hill minorities, the Mongol National Organization and the Nepal Rastriya Janajati ('National Ethnic Communities') Party were refused recognition and the Limbuwan Liberation Front announced a boycott of the elections in protest against the restrictions, but the Nepal Rastriya Janamukti Party, campaigning basically for ethnic quotas within the political and administrative system, was allowed to participate. None of these groups have a large following, and the largest share of the vote gained by the Rastriya Janamukti Party in any constituency has so far only been 14%.[31] The share of the Nepal-wide vote obtained by the party's 82 candidates in 1994 was 1.05%, more than double the 0.47% secured with 50 candidates in 1991 but still well short of the 3% needed for recognition as a national party. Even if the 3% barrier were to be removed, the demographic situation together with the first-past-the-post electoral system would make it unlikely that parties with an appeal only to minorities could gain a significant number of parliamentary seats.

In this situation, the natural method for putting forward hill ethnic demands is a combination of lobbying by non-party pressure groups and mobilization of ethnic votes through parties which also appeal to the Parbatiyas. Both the main political parties, the Communist Party of Nepal (Unified Marxist-Leninist) and the Nepali Congress, are led mainly by Parbatiya Brahmans, but the Communists have made the stronger effort to appeal to the minorities and have gathered more of their vote. This parallels the situation in many other multi-party democracies: in the UK and in the USA it is the Labour Party and the Democrats, rather than their right-wing rivals, who can generally rely on the votes of disadvantaged ethnic groups. The pattern is likely to persist in Nepal, though the complexities of politics at the local level may result in Congress also developing links with ethnic activism; there were reports in 1993 of a Congress party official being linked with the distribution of a pamphlet calling for Brahmans and Chetris to "go back to Banaras".[32]

Another possible channel for ethnic discontent would be the more radical left-wing groups. The United People's Front, a Maoist group, which held nine seats in the 1991–94 parliament, has voiced vocal support for ethnic demands, and in summer 1992 endorsed the idea of self-determination for every ethnic minority (Lama, 1992). The UPF subsequently split and the section which contested the 1994 election won no seats, but the present parliament contains two 'independents' backed by another Maoist faction, the Communist Party of Nepal (Masal). The Masal, which had called for a boycott of the 1991 election, is close ideologically to the Peruvian Shining Path guerilla movement and it has been suggested that insurgency based partly on ethnic discontent is a strong possibility for Nepal if the parliamentary system fails to deliver real economic improvement (Nickson, 1992).[33] At least amongst some Limbus in east Nepal there was an ethnic aspect to the insurgency against the Rana regime in 1950–51. Clashes between supporters of the non-parliamentary, Baburam Bhattarai faction of the UPF and those of other parties in Rolpa district, which prompted a large police operation in late 1995, have been ascribed to the frustration of disadvantaged Magar youths (Hughes, 1995). Magar activists of this group were also believed to be behind 'Maoist' raids which began causing casualties in several districts in early 1996. Additionally, Masal also draws its strength from an area where the Magars are the main minority group. It should, however, be remembered that the Magars as a whole are the group which has adapted the most thoroughly to Parbatiya culture.

Hill ethnic demands, so far advanced overwhelmingly through constitutional channels, fall into three main categories: institutional, cultural, and economic. Many activists call for recognition of the 'separate national identity' and 'right to self-determination' of all Nepal's ethnic groups, the formula endorsed by the United People's Front. This could in theory lead to federalism, and Khagendra Jang Gurung, leader of the Nepal Rastriya Janajati Party, advocates the division of the country into a dozen ethnic regions (Raeper and Hoftun, 1992: 170). Given the present distribution of the population it would be impossible to create even approximately homogeneous ethnic states without resorting to 'ethnic cleansing' on a massive scale, and the impracticability of this approach is recognized by most *janajāti* spokesmen (Fisher, 1993: 12). More feasible would be some kind of cantonal arrangement, and one Tamang activist has proposed reorganization of local government to allow a decentralization of power to ethnic community level; at present the 'Village Development Committees' (formerly Village Panchayats) do not correspond to physical villages and include settlements of many different communities. For the centre, the proposal is to turn the Upper House (Rastriya Sabha), which is at present largely elected by the members of the lower house (Pratinidhi Sabha), into a 'House of Nationalities', with representation for all ethnic groups in proportion to their numbers.[34] The idea of guaranteed representation for minorities in the Rastriya Sabha has been accepted in election manifestos of both the United People's Front and the Unified Marxist-Leninists (UML) (Tamang, 1991a: 30; NCP(UML), 1994: 30), whilst the Rastriya Janamukti Party advocates proportional representation at all levels below the very top in both the administration and political parties.[35] Since there is UML support, a formula for Upper House representation remains a possibility but anything more radical would run up against the twin hurdles of acceptability to mainstream political parties and deciding just how many of the myriad 'ethnic' divisions in Nepal are to be regarded as politically relevant.

Two cultural issues, both with possible ramifications in the power structure, have also been keenly debated: religion and language. Religious controversy in the wake of the 1990 democracy movement focused on whether the new Constitution should retain the 1962 description of the country as a Hindu kingdom. Secularism for its own sake is not attractive to any outside a small intellectual elite, but it serves as a symbol of opposition to the high-caste Hindus and their dominant position in the social structure. That dominant position formerly had a greater degree of legitimacy in the eyes of less privileged groups because some at least did believe in the spiritual powers of the Brahmans, the main legitimators of the system. With their sacred aura now greatly reduced, the perception of injustice has naturally increased. The problem is complicated by an argument over just how Hindu the kingdom really is. The upper castes amongst the Parbatiyas and in the Tarai, one section of the Newar upper castes, and those most strongly assimilated to these groups are undoubtedly Hindu, whilst other Newar upper castes are undoubtedly Buddhist. The remainder of the population include elements from both 'Great Traditions' and 'tribal' elements in their religious practice.[36] By reckoning as Hindu all who do not categorically reject that identity, the traditionalists can claim an overwhelming Hindu majority, whilst Buddhist activists can deny it by counting as Hindus only wearers of the sacred thread: the statistics produced by both sides are equally suspect.[37] Any attempt to settle the argument by arguing that Buddhism is really a branch of Hinduism is of course resented by fervent Buddhists as domination by inclusion.

Although the conservatives carried the day in the Constitution drafting committee, the issue remains a live one. The debate was given a new twist with the publication in 1991 of Dor Bahadur Bista's *Fatalism and Development*, which laid the blame for many of Nepal's ills on the hierarchical and fatalistic values of 'Brahmanism', which he contrasted with the egalitarian and work-orientated ethic of the hill minorities. Bista's thesis has come under attack from those who wish to link Nepal's poverty with the country's position in the world economic system rather than mental attitudes and also from aggrieved Brahmans (the two categories sometimes coincide!) accusing him of trying to divert attention from his own close association with the former Panchayat regime.[38] Less notice was taken of his attempt to decouple one aspect of the official view of Nepalese history, veneration for Prithvi Narayan Shah, from dependence on Brahmanical Hinduism. Bista (1991: 45) presents Prithvi Narayan as an egalitarian who regarded Brahmans, Khas, and Magars simply as different ethnic groups with none of them superior or inferior to the others. Such an interpretation distorts the eighteenth century realities: caste hierarchy was already well entrenched in pre-unification Gorkha, even if the system was not yet as rigid as it was to become later. Bista is, however, right in sensing Nepal's need now for a common understanding of Nepali history freed from the notion of caste superiority.

On the language issue, the Constitution declared Nepali 'the language of the nation' (*rāṣṭrabhāṣā*) and 'official language' but made concessions to pluralism by declaring that all languages spoken as mother tongues in Nepal were 'national languages' (*rāṣṭriyabhāṣā*)[39] and that any community had the right to operate primary schools in their own language. This fell well short of activist demands for complete equality between languages and for the government itself to provide mother-tongue education.[40] During the 1991 election campaign the United People's Front again went furthest towards meeting activist demands, promising the use of mother-tongue at all levels in the education system and in the courts and administration (United People's Front, 1991). In 1993, the Congress government appointed an advisory commission on the minority languages, with members largely drawn from the minorities themselves, and this recommended establishing a council to oversee language development and introducing mother-tongue teaching in primary schools where all students are from one minority group and a bilingual system where students speak Nepali and one other language. The 1994 election manifestos of the three main parties all included a commitment in general terms to the promotion of mother-tongue education (Nepali Congress, 1994: 37; NCP(UML), 1994: 24; Rastriya Prajatantra Party, 1994: 23) and some preparatory work on textbook production is underway. In addition, the Sadbhavana party, which backs increased use of hill minority languages as well as of Hindi and the Tarai regional languages is now (March 1996) a partner in a coalition government. Nevertheless few observers expect more than token action on the Report.

As the commission itself acknowledged, the practical difficulties in accepting any demand for 'linguistic equality' in Nepal are considerable. Among the hill minority languages, Newari has a well-developed literary tradition and a more-or-less standardized written form, whilst Limbu is already in use as a medium of education in Sikkim, but there is much more work to be done with most of the others. Providing primary education in, for example, Tamang would require selecting one dialect for development as a written standard and then a lengthy effort in textbook production. Then, because even in their principal area Tamangs are often interspersed with members of other ethnic groups and non-Tamang-speaking parents would be unlikely to accept the bilingual option the Commission advocates in such cases, there would be the additional problem of providing the extra teachers and classrooms to allow a choice between Tamang or Nepali-medium education. Tamang and all the other languages of Nepal do in theory have the potential to be developed as a 'language of school and office', but should the Nepali state be required to devote scarce educational resources to realizing that potential for every one of them?

It is certainly doubtful whether the mass of speakers of the hill minority languages even want this. Wherever languages are in contact, people have generally been willing to use another language outside the home if they are given the opportunity to learn it and if speaking the other language would clearly be to their economic advantage. The process results in widespread bilingualism and then in possible loss of the original language. In the British Isles, though the decline of Scots Gaelic was certainly accelerated by the expulsion of whole communities from the Highlands during the eighteenth and nineteenth-century clearances and that of Irish by famine in the 1840s, the switch to English normally resulted more from the Celtic population's wish for greater economic opportunities than from any compulsion by the government (Durkacz, 1983).[41] The increasing use of Nepali in the hills can be similarly explained and it is particularly noteworthy that Nepali has managed to establish itself as the lingua franca of the Himalayas even east of the Nepal border where it lacks the advantage of state backing.[42]

In the last third of the nineteenth century in Europe, campaigns for the use of hitherto undeveloped vernaculars as languages of culture and administration became a more important aspect of nationalist movements. This trend formed part of the growing stress on the right to self-determination of even the smallest potential nations which laid the foundation for the emergence of so many new nation-states in the 1919 peace settlement. The same trend can be seen at work all over the 'Third World' and now in post-Cold-War Europe, often with violent consequences. In his analysis of the nineteenth century development, a leading British Marxist historian, Eric Hobsbawm unkindly characterizes the vernacularist movements as in part "a vested interest of the lesser examination-passing classes" (Hobsbawm, 1990: 118): the very ablest or wealthiest of a minority group have a chance of competing with the dominant community on that community's own terms whilst the poorest can readily pick up enough of the dominant language to operate in the manual labour market, but the educated middle strata feel the need to turn their own language into an economic asset. Such 'instrumentalist' interpretations of linguistic nationalism are much favoured amongst students of South Asia also, with Paul Brass's work on north India (Brass, 1974) perhaps the best known example.[43] The implication of cynical manipulation which sometimes forms an undercurrent of this school of explanation is often unfair and it is wrong to ignore factors such as a minority's need for a sense of self-respect. All the same, elites and would-be elites seeking a smaller pool in which to be bigger fish certainly are an important factor in the situation.

It is where job opportunities are directly at stake that there is probably the greatest resonance between the activist demands and the current aspirations of most of the hill minority population. The key issue is that of increasing the proportion of minority members in public-sector employment. Following the long-standing Indian example, ethnic pressure groups demand a quota system ('reservations' in the standard South Asian terminology) to redress the present imbalance in favour of the higher castes. On this question there is a very clear left/right divide between the mainstream parties, with the UML and other communist groups endorsing the proposal and Congress firmly opposed. The introduction of reservations at a time of increasing economic pressure on all sections of the population is indeed likely to be highly divisive, as in India. The hill Brahmans, the group who would feel most threatened by such a system, would acquire more of the characteristics of an assertive ethnic minority themselves (Sharma, 1992: 8). Such group assertiveness has not been necessary in the past as they were secure first in the privileged position granted them when the caste system was legally enforced and afterwards because of their higher level of education. Friction between other groups would also increase with argument over the relative degree of disadvantage of different minorities and on the definition of minority boundaries.

The perceived unfairness of any kind of ethnic/caste quota system is not purely a matter of the privileged defending their privileges. Caste in India or Nepal (like race in the USA) is only an approximate indicator of economic status. Brahmans are on average a lot wealthier than Tamangs but there are many exceptions, and, as McDonaugh (this volume) shows for the Tharus of Dang, the relative economic position of different ethnic groups can change over time. In any case, it is, of course, the better-off individuals within the minorities who would be best-placed to take advantage of opportunities reserved for the group to which they belong. Restriction of job opportunities for Chetris or Newars as groups would raise even greater problems of equity. Especially in far western Nepal, where the non-Parbatiya proportion of the population is very small, there are many

Chetris amongst the 'have-nots'. Within the Kathmandu Valley, upper-caste Newars count amongst the elite, but very few members of the Jyapu cultivator caste and certainly not Newar Untouchables. Rather than allowing the best-placed individuals within each group to turn caste and ethnicity into political and economic resources for intra-elite competition, and in so doing harden presently flexible inter-ethnic boundaries, 'affirmative action' would be better focused directly on backward regions and on individuals with income or landholding below a prescribed limit.[44] Despite these dangers, however, it is likely that the electoral convenience of caste or community-based appeals, together with the present 'ethnicity wave', will produce irresistible pressure for the introduction of reservations in some form or another. The prospect in the hills is thus for increased ethnic/caste tensions, but there is hope for keeping these within manageable limits, and, given the demographic situation, little prospect of real pressure for autonomous areas.

In the Tarai, which contains around 50% of Nepal's population and generates about two-thirds of its wealth, the diversity of the population means that many of the points made concerning the hill situation also apply. There are, however, two crucial differences. The first is the common culture linking many Tarai communities with the other side of the Indian border and the concomitant movement of people and goods, which is not under control and is probably in fact uncontrollable without disproportionate effort by the Nepalese authorities. A direct consequence of this is the use of Hindi as a link language between the different Tarai communities. The second factor is a tradition of regionally-based political organization, starting with Vedanand Jha's Tarai Congress and the campaign to retain Hindi as a medium of education in the 1950s and now represented by the Sadbhavana Party. In 1991 Sadbhavana won six seats in Parliament, all from Lumbini or Sagarmatha zones and all except one won because the majority of the voters were split between different nationally-based parties.[45] It was reduced to only three seats in the 1994 general election. The party's appeal appears to be limited both because the mainstream parties have tried to respond to Tarai concerns and also probably because of distrust by other communities of Sadbhavana's Rajput leadership. However, the party's inclusion in the coalition government formed in September 1995 may strengthen it and so long as the feeling persists amongst the Indian-origin Tarai-dwellers that they are disadvantaged *as Madheshis*, they pose a serious challenge to the present unitary Nepali state. Any attempted implementation of their demand for a federal constitution would probably lead to serious conflict between Madheshis and settlers from the hills.

The demand for Hindi to become a second official language is a major part of the Sadbhavana platform, and, although the issue is not yet a pressing one for Madheshi voters, it might become so. Many hill Nepalis believe such a demand could be diffused by allowing instead a limited role for the principal spoken languages of the Tarai (Maithili, Bhojpuri, Awadhi, and Tharu) with Nepali then accepted as the link language between communities. Whilst it is true that standard Hindi is spoken as a mother-tongue by very few in the Tarai, 81% of Madheshi households included in a 1992 sample survey reported that they used Hindi as their link language to other communities (Jha, 1993: 32), and the Maithili, Bhojpuri, and Awadhi speakers on the other side of the open border have long been used to employing Hindi in this way and as their main language of literacy. Furthermore, the perception of Maithili as linked to Brahman dominance could incline lower-caste speakers more towards Hindi, just as it helped thwart the campaign for a Maithil state in India in the 1950s (Burkert, chapter 7, pp. 256–7, 259–60; Brass, 1974). If, in addition, the people of the Tarai perceive Nepali as something imposed on them rather than as a door to wider economic opportunities, the demand for mother tongue and Hindi rather than mother tongue plus Nepali can only continue to grow.

The linguistic solution for the Tarai might be retention of Nepali as the language of written record, but encouragement of all Tarai languages, including Hindi, as spoken languages and as vehicles for literature. Hindi, Nepali, and Maithili are closely-related languages written in the same script and all drawing on Sanskrit for their higher-level vocabulary.[46] All urban Nepalis can at least understand spoken Hindi if only because of exposure to the Hindi cinema, and literacy in any of the three languages opens the door to literacy in the others.

Both in language and in other matters, 'non-Indianness' cannot be a unifying force in the Tarai as it has long been in the hills. Total integration into a relatively homogeneous, Nepali-speaking Parbatiya culture may be a long-term possibility for hill minorities but not for those of the Tarai. This does not mean that the Nepali government will become totally unable to take an independent line from the Indian government, but the presentation of any clash as one between rival cultures can only increase alienation in the Tarai. I was made keenly aware of this in 1974 when demonstrators protesting against the integration of Sikkim into the Indian Union roamed the streets of Kathmandu shouting *Dhotīwālā murdābād!* ("Death to the dhoti-wearers". For Paharis, the dhoti is quintessentially Indian (see illustration, p.48) but a Maithil Indian friend staying with me at the time pertinently remarked that very many Nepali citizens also wear the garment.

Acceptance that citizens of Nepal do not have to make an all-or-nothing choice between a Nepali or Indian cultural identity is a precondition for resolving the Tarai problem. A similar spirit would help in Darjeeling where the Nepali-speaking community has the problem of minority status within West Bengal, and in Bhutan where the Drukpa highlanders view the ethnic Nepalese in the south of their country much as many Pahari Nepalis view people of Indian origin in the Tarai (see Hutt, p.136 below). The Madheshis' situation in the Nepali state is much more secure than that of the Lhotshampas in Bhutan, but the potential for conflict is still there unless both the hill elites and the Tarai people show sufficient political maturity.

CONCLUSION

An Englishman surveying the issue of national identity and ethnicity in Nepal has to bear in mind Anthony Smith's words of rebuke:

> It is fashionable for Western observers, securely ensconced in
> their own national identities forged in blood and toil several

centuries ago, to pour scorn on the rhetorical excess and misguided scholarship of nationalist intellectuals in nineteenth-century Europe or twentieth century Africa and Asia. Those whose identities are rarely questioned and who have never known exile or subjugation of land and culture, have little need to trace their 'roots' . . . Yet theirs is only an implicit and unarticulated form of what elsewhere must be shouted from the roof-tops: 'We belong, we have a unique identity, we know it by our ancestry and history' (Smith, 1986: 2).

The particular national or ethnic identities which people assume are not primordial, but brought into being through a historical process in which deliberate design may or may not play a part. However, the longing for group identity, which Smith draws attention to, is a universal reality since it meets two great human needs: a sense of solidarity with other human beings and a sense of power. It is this second aspect which explains why rivalry with other groups is so often a key element in the formation of identity and why a vital role is played by successful armed struggle, or at least the collective memory of such struggle. Power does not, of course, have to accrue directly to each member: in assuming a particular identity, individuals are often motivated by their material interests but once a strong sense of identity has been established individual group members derive vicarious satisfaction from successes of the group as a whole, and their membership is not just an instrument for the attainment of personal goals. In a similar way, group boundaries may originally have had some economic rationale, but the maintenance of the identity's emotional salience for its members normally depends on common, 'cultural' characteristics functioning as the Barthian 'border guards'.

Language often seems to play this differentiating role, and aspects of nineteenth-century European experience still lead many to see this as the most important criterion, but religion has historically been at least as important, and, taking only Europe itself as an example, it is ethnicity based directly on religious affiliation which has fuelled civil strife in former Yugoslavia and in Northern Ireland. A sense of community generated by religion can provide the basis for a distinct ethnic or national identity, and, if religious faith diminishes,

FIGURE 3   *Geopolitical realities tying Nepal to India persist whoever comes to power. In this cartoon, which appeared after the formation of the UML government in 1994, Prime Minister Adhikari tells the Kathmandu crowd: ". . . We too will sign treaties, accords, and agreements, but there will be a fundamental change . . . Congress signed with their right hands but we will do it with our left . . ."* (Saptahik Bimarsha, 16/12/1994)

the explicit ideology of nationalism can offer the sense of continuity through history which religion formerly provided.[47] The fuel may change, but the same flame remains.

Hinduism has played the role of midwife to Nepali nationalism, but its efficacy is limited by the central role caste plays within it. Buddhism, Christianity, and Islam can be combined with highly inegalitarian social arrangements, and have indeed frequently been used to legitimize such arrangements, but they none the less assert the equal membership of all believers and demonstrate this both through their ritual structure and through the lack of any restriction on intermarriage within the religious community; the Muluki Ain is quite correct in regarding Muslims as a single caste, regardless of their ethnicity, and Newar critics of the traditional Vajrayana Buddhism of the Kathmandu Valley are correct in seeing its acceptance of caste divisions within the Buddhist community as contradicting a fundamental Buddhist principle.[48] Hinduism works as an integrative factor for the whole of a Hindu society only for so long as the lower castes accept the legitimacy of their own position. Even in the past that acceptance was never total, and it certainly does not exist today.

How, then, to broaden the sense of 'Nepaliness' described in the first part of this essay so that it embraces the whole population of Nepal? It has to be admitted straight away that, given the geographic and demographic situation, it is never going to be possible to inculcate as strong and unique a sense of being Nepali as the sense of being Japanese is in Japan. A greater degree of integration than at present is nonetheless possible, and an obvious route would be generally increasing prosperity, with perceived possibilities of upwards social mobility for all regions and groups. But if sharing in future economic success is vital, more Nepalis should also be able to feel that the past achievements of their own region or ethnic group is a valued part of a common Nepali past.

One way of achieving this would be by broadening the 'official' culture promulgated through the school system; as Saubhagya Shaha (1993: 9) has put it, "the national pantheon must ... include personalities and events, historic as well as mythical, from all communities." The historical links between the Mithila region of the

Tarai and the Newar kingdoms of the Kathmandu Valley could be emphasized and translations of Maithili, Newari, and Kiranti literature made an important part of the national school syllabus. The role of the Magars and Gurungs in the creation of the Nepali state could be properly recognized and the original fluidity of the boundary between the hill 'tribes' and the Parbatiyas, which is well known to scholars, made part of the average Nepali's consciousness. Reassessment could start at the centre of the state's symbolic structure with the tradition of the Shah dynasty's Rajput origins. We know that the genealogy linking them with the Ranas of Mewar is almost certainly spurious,[49] and that some of Prithvi Narayan's contemporaries regarded him as a Magar. The best guess must be that he was of mixed ancestry, and that the family claimed a purely plains origin for political purposes. Today, the political requirements are very different and it is surely time for the House of Gorkha to reclaim its Magar heritage.

NOTES

This essay derives from a paper (Whelpton,1993b) presented to the 34th. ICANAS (University of Hong Kong, August 1993), to be published in a forthcoming issue of *Modern Asian Studies*. I am grateful to Conference participants for comments on the original version, to Harka Gurung for extensive help with census data and other suggestions, and also to Dhruba Hari Adhikari, David Gellner, Pratyoush Onta, Joanna Pfaff-Czarnecka, and Madhushan for corrections and comments, and to Abhi Subedi and Nirmal Tuladhar for help in collecting materials.

[1] For an elaboration of the contrast, see Kumar Pradhan (1991: 154).

[2] As the reference is to the foothills generally, the original Hindi form *pahāṛī* is retained here. In Nepali the word becomes *pahāṛe* and *pahāṛiyā* (a loan from Bengali) is also used. Cf. p.9 above.

[3] Hitchcock (1979) suggests that the more integrated Parbatiya structure in the Nepal Himalaya, with a stronger position for the Khas, is partly due to the legacy of the Khas-dominated 'Malla Empire' which united a large area of western Nepal and south-western Tibet in the thirteenth and fourteenth centuries.

[4] In his 'political testament', the *Dibya Upadesh*, published in Pokhrel (1986/87: 159).

5   Burghart devises different terms for these two meanings by using the original Sanskrit term (with the final 'a' pronounced) for the first and the vernacular form (with silent final 'a') for the latter, but the two words are indistinguishable in Nepali orthography and will not have been regarded as distinct terms by native speakers of the language.

6   Undated *arjī* of Bal Narsingh Kunwar to King Rajendra, published in Nepali (1963/64: 141–7).

7   Hamilton's assertion that Prithvi Narayan was himself a Magar was made on the authority of a Brahman connected with a rival hill principality who may have wanted to belittle the Gorkha king's claim to Rajput status, but he may well have had some Magar blood. On the Magar adaptation to Parbatiya culture, see now Lecomte-Tilouine (1993). She stresses the active role of the Magar elites themselves (cf. Pfaff-Czarnecka, this volume), but also reports (pp. 31–32) a claim by one old informant in Gulmi that the pre-'unification' kings of the area forbade the use of the Magar language.

8   The abandonment of beef eating is documented by royal decrees from 1805 onwards. These have been published in the Regmi Research Series and are cited in Ragsdale (1989), and in Michaels (chapter 2). The current attempt of some members of the Gurung community to reverse this whole Hinduization process in favour of a return to 'authentic' Gurung traditions is discussed in Macfarlane, chapter 5.

9   Hodgson Papers (India Office Library), vol.6, ff. 175–6.

10 Pignède, (1993: 18 & 425). The second page reference is to a supplementary note by Pignède's reasearch assistant, C.B. Ghotane. The Gurung role in Nepal's unification is described in detail by Jagman Gurung (1985).

11 Aside from the direct experience of military service, the foreign stereotype of the bold Gurkha has itself been internalized to some extent by the groups concerned, as argued for the Magars by Lecomte-Tilouine (1993: 48).

12 'Nepali' seems already to have been the preferred term in 1930 when the Gorkha Bhasha Prakashini Samiti (Gorkha Language Publication Committee) was restyled the Nepali Bhasha Prakashini Samiti (Hutt, 1988: 34).

13 See for example, the speech to *bhāradār*s by Maharaja Juddha Shamsher published in Gautam (1989/90: 405–6).

14 The Gorkha Parishad, led by the grandson of the brother of the last Rana Maharaja, was the largest party in the 1959 parliament after the ruling Nepali Congress. The choice of 'Gorkha' rather than 'Nepali' symbolized

an appeal to the traditionally dominant Thakuri-Chetris and to hill groups such as the Gurungs, in opposition to the 'non-martial' Brahmans and Newars in leading positions in the Congress.

[15] Although the Ranas in general were content to become part of the circle around the king, there were exceptions. Bharat Shamsher, who led the 'Rana revivalist' Gorkha Parishad in the 1959 election, gave his support to Congress demands for a return to parliamentary democracy after the 1960 royal takeover.

[16] For details of the various Communist factions and their ideological differences, see POLSAN (1992) and Whelpton (1993a, 1995).

[17] For a succinct analysis, see Shah (1993: 8).

[18] No contemporary record has been discovered but Malla (1979: 135) dates this to 1920, and Clark (1969: 252) implies it was some time before the change of officially favoured name from Gorkhali to Nepali. As early as 1905, Chandra had ordered that only documents in Nepali should be admissible in court cases (Malla, 1989: 457). For evidence of state promotion of the Parbatiya language before 'unification' see note 7, above.

[19] Yogi Naraharinath, interview in *Saptahik Bimarsha*, 12 July 1991. The Panchayat slogan *Ek bhāṣā, ek bhes, ek deś* ('One language, one dress, one country') was derived from the poet Balkrishna Sama's earlier formulation: *Hāmro rājā, hāmro deś; hāmro bhāṣā, hāmro bhes* ('Our King, our country; our language, our dress') (Shah, 1993: 8).

[20] Pamphlet circulated on 7 September 1940, translated in Uprety (1992:189). Juddha's habit of virtual abducting any young girl who caught his fancy on the streets of Kathmandu is confirmed in British Residency Records (Shaha, 1990: vol.2, 127–128). Cf. chapter 15 note 12, below.

[21] Because caste affiliation is not always formally recorded and some common surnames are used by more than one caste, figures cannot be completely precise. Harka Gurung's figures yield 62.4%, 65.4%, 57.1%, and 61.9% respectively for 1959 (multi-party direct election), 1978 (non-party, indirect election), 1981 (non-party, direct election – nominated members excluded), and 1991 (multi-party, direct) respectively (H. Gurung, 1992: 20).

[22] See Fisher (1993:12), p.20 above, and chapter 12 note 26, below.

[23] I am grateful to Harka Gurung for pointing this out and providing an advance copy of his tabulations of the census data now published in Salter and Gurung (1996).

[24] David Gellner (1986) emphasizes the emergence of a sense of Newar identity amongst educated Newar youth, whilst Quigley (1987) sees no

room for this intermediate level between the traditional, smaller-scale loyalty and identity as a Nepali citizen. In this volume, Gellner continues to argue for a definite group-consciousness amongst at least some Newars but notes the limited nature of its political expression.

25 Reflecting colloquial usage (cf. Allen, ch.9), the Muluki Ain uses *jāt* for both meanings, and Burghart (1984) preserves the ambiguity in English by using the translation 'species'. The standard dictionary of modern Nepali (Royal Nepal Academy, 1983) employs each of the terms *jāt* and *jāti* in its definition of the other. However, Harka Gurung (personal communication) believes that *jāti* may carry connotations of inferiority because the 'i' ending in Nepali can imply being 'small, weak or feminine'.

26 Harka Gurung (chapter 15, this volume) prefers to interpret 'Tamang' as 'highlander' (*ta*, 'up', plus *mang*, 'people'). Holmberg (1989) has an extended discussion which also stresses the role of the Gorkha/Nepali state in cutting off the Tamang of his research area (north-west of Trisuli) from some of their earlier ties to the north.

27 An alternative local version, heard by Harka Gurung in 1966, is that the Tibetan speakers themselves successfully petitioned to be allowed to use the name 'Tamang' after they had helped the Nepal government in the 1856 war with Tibet.

28 In summer 1994, however, a Char Jat Gurung friend told me it was again showing signs of increasing again, with Gurung cultural revivalists branding the more Hinduized ways of the Char Jat as less 'authentic'. He put much of the blame for this on foreign or foreign-inspired studies such as that by Macfarlane in this volume. Macfarlane shows that the revivalists are themselves divided between advocates of Lamaism and of the Pa-chyu tradition and Harka Gurung (personal communication) sees the religious debate itself as overtaking considerations of group status.

29 Dilli Ram Dahal (1992) gives a succinct summary of the demographical situation in the Tarai.

30 The 1991 Census puts the number speaking Hindi as a first language at only 170, 997, viz. about 3% of the total Madheshi population (Central Bureau of Statistics, 1994: 19). A sample survey by Hari Bansh Jha (1993: 30), however, found a proportion of 20%. For the role of Hindi in the Tarai, see the discussion in Jha and also Gaige (1975).

31 This was obtained by the party's leader, Gore Bahadur Khapangi, in Sunsari-l in 1994.

32 *Saptahik Bimarsha*, 23 April 1993.

33 For a critical analysis of enthusiasm for the Shining Path among Nepali communists see also Mikesell (1993).

[34] Tamang (1991 b). In his 1992 article, Tamang instead advocates equal representation in the upper house for all communities, irrespective of numbers.

[35] Statements by party leader Gore Bahadur Khapangi, reported in *Nepali Awaj*, 15 June 1990, and in Raeper & Hoftun (1992: 170).

[36] This kind of syncretism is particularly marked in Nepal but also common in other agrarian societies. A recent survey of Chinese religions notes that "at the most self-consciously literate levels distinctions between traditions can be made, but in ordinary practice they can be difficult to discern" (Overmyer *et al.*, 1995: 315).

[37] The 1991 census reports 86.2% of the population as Hindu. Pashuram Tamang (1991 c) claims that 77% are non-Hindu.

[38] See, for example, Surya Subedi (1992).

[39] Earlier, unofficial translations of the constitution had it the other way about: 'national language' for *rāṣṭrabhāṣā* (Nepali) and 'languages of the nation' for *rāṣṭriyabhāṣā* (Ellingson, 1991:68).

[40] Demands for complete equality between languages were advanced in the period following the 1980 referendum, principally by Leftist groups taking their cue from an early article by Lenin questioning the need for an imposed official language (Malla, 1989: 462–3).

[41] In nineteenth-century Ireland, the nationalists campaigning for home rule were initially unperturbed by the replacement of the Irish language by English. The best known of their early leaders, Daniel O'Connor, though a native speaker of Irish, is said only to have given two speeches in that language – when he feared police spies were listening (McCrum *et al.*, 1986: 182–3). Russell (chapter 10) describes a similar pragmatic attitude among Nepal's Yakha.

[42] Parental wishes aside, advocates of mother-tongue education rely heavily on the UNESCO (1953) argument that children's cognitive and emotional development is adversely affected if their initial education is not in their home language. More recent research suggests that it is the social context rather than the second language itself which causes the problem (So, 1987: 255): children need to feel that they themselves and their home language are respected by the wider society but not necessarily to be taught in that language. Children *will*, however, be at a disadvantage in their early education if their teachers cannot at least understand their mother tongue when the children speak to them in it.

[43] See the useful discussion in Yapp (1979). Ethnic activists have themselves been quick to provide an 'instrumentalist' expalanation of the recent

attempt by Brahman legislators from both major parties to boost the place of Sanskrit within the education system!

[44] There has been a limited recognition of this in India itself: the Central government and many state governments have since 1963 added an economic criterion to that of caste membership when reservations are granted. Narasinha Rao's government has partly defused the controversy over the Mandal Commission recommendations by adding the most economically disadvantaged amongst the 'forward castes' to the beneficiaries of the proposed extension to the reservations system (Hardgrave and Kochanek, 1993: 189, 194).

[45] See Whelpton (1993a, 1995) for Sadbhavana's 1991 manifesto and intra-party disputes. A brief account of the party's background is given in Raeper and Hoftun (1992: 173–5).

[46] Raj (1992) makes this point strongly and even implies that the Nepali speakers in the hills should regard the speakers of other Indo-Aryan languages in southern Nepal as linguistic allies against the advocates of the Tibetan-Burman hill minority languages.

[47] This second factor is a key point in the explanation of nationalism offered by Anthony Smith (1971).

[48] David Gellner, who has tried hard both in his 1992 monograph and elsewhere to rebut the reformists' charge, has pointed out to me that compromise with the caste system has been a feature of Buddhism right from the beginning and that groups such as the Lingayats and the Arya Samaj have rejected Brahman supremacy whilst still being regarded as Hindu. However, Buddhist compromises with casteism have always been vulnerable to attack as 'non-Buddhist' since they are not legitimized by Buddhist sacred texts, whereas the notion that certain groups are inherently superior to others is stressed in many Hindu scriptures and is thus much harder to stigmatize as 'non-Hindu'.

[49] See Baral (1964: chapter 3). The even less plausible claim by Jang Bahadur's family is discussed in Whelpton (1987: 161–4).

CHAPTER TWO

The King and the Cow: On a Crucial Symbol of Hinduization in Nepal

Axel Michaels

INTRODUCTION

'The last Hindu kingdom of the world', Nepal likes to declare herself: for long she saw herself as a stronghold against the West which had already overcome the other Indian kingdoms. On the basis of the old law books, the king was regarded as the protector of Hindu *dharma.* Both king and state saw themselves as the defenders of sacred values against a world in which not even the cow is holy any more.

But what are the sacred values of Hinduism? And what does Hinduism mean in Nepal? To avoid the numerous problems in defining a religion which until recently did not understand itself as just one religion (cf. Stietencron, 1989), it may be helpful to look for the acceptance of signs and symbols rather than concepts, ideas, or fundamentals. Visible symbols always played a crucial role in the process of Hinduization. I agree with A. W. Macdonald and Anne Vergati Stahl that "Nepal was hinduised by displaying and inform-ing, by looking and listening, rather than by the dissemination and reception of written messages" (Macdonald and Stahl, 1979: 6; cf. Höfer, 1986: 44).

One would expect the cow to figure prominently in this regard. However, even at the regularly held World Hindu Con-ferences the representatives of various castes, sects, and religious communities have not been able to find common symbols of Hinduism. To be sure, the cow has been mentioned quite often, but at the Second World Hindu Conference, held in Allahabad (February, 1979), this animal was not included among the six do's for Hindus. Instead one finds in this "six-point Acharsanhita (code of conduct) for all Hindus" (*Organizer* 11/12/1979: 16) the following points: (1) worship of the sun and a kind of physical exercise (*sūryapraṇāma*), (2) reading of the *Bhagavad Gītā*, (3) daily prayer (*prārthana*), (4) the freedom to keep in one's home a portrait or statue (*mūrti*) of any favourite deity, (5) the freedom to use the holy syllable and symbol *oṃ*, (6) the right to plant the basil (Tulsī) plant, sacred to Vishnu, on one's premises.

In Nepal, interestingly, the cow did get included among the national symbols, alongside the crown, sceptre, flag, royal standard, royal crest, the coat-of-arms, the rhododendron plant, the Himalayan pheasant, and vermilion, so beautifully depicted on the usual posters of these emblems as a dark red blob. And at another Conference of the Vishwa Hindu Parishad (VHP, World Hindu Federation) held in Kathmandu (25–28 March, 1988), the former Prime Minister and at that time president of the VHP, Nagendra Prasad Rijal, declared, that "all are Hindus who regard the syllable *oṃ* as holy, who accept the holiness of the cow, who pay reverence to the teachers of *dharma* [i.e. Brahmans?], who follow the path of truth and holiness, who believe in the immortality of the soul, who trust in an all-mighty God and who seek liberation" (quoted by Krämer, 1991: 84, my translation).

In Hindu South Asia the protection of the cow was often connected with Hinduization. "Hinduism is alive as long as there are Hindus who protect cows," wrote Mahatma Gandhi in a famous article.[1] However, it seems to have been the Shah kings, who have ruled over Nepal since 1768 and later the Ranas, who provided hereditary prime ministers for more than a century (1846–1951), who both practically identified the state ideology with a ban on cow slaughter. In the Legal Code of 1854, the (Muluki) Ain, to which I will return below, it is said: "In the Kaliyuga this kingdom is the only kingdom in the world where cows, women, and Brahmans may not be killed."[2] Although the order is somewhat strange, cows mentioned first, then women,[3] and Brahmans only at the end, all three are guarantors of purity, and in an text on politics from the nineteenth century, the *Śukranīti*, the killing of all three of them by enemies is reason enough for immediate war, since it is a *mahāpātaka*, a great sin, which cannot be expiated.[4]

The cow in Nepal played a very special role in the process of defining both Nepal's Hindu identity and the limits of centralized power. What I want to show in the following is based on a twofold hypothesis:

(1) The cow has been used as a means of promoting national integration and sovereignty over various ethnic groups and remote areas. Control of territory is not only given through coercion enforced by the military.[5] It has to do not only with directly coercive means of defining and controlling such units, but also with ritual and religious or political symbols. The cow seems to me to be just one of these religious symbols which had an integrative impact on Nepal's political and cultural identity.

(2) However, the cow is different from the other national emblems mentioned above, since its protection is linked with legal steps against cow slaughter or consuming beef which was quite commonly practised in several areas of Nepal. Enforcing strictly the general ban on cow slaughter could (and, in fact did) endanger Nepal's political cohesion.

This dilemma between the integrative and disintegrative functions of the cow had to be faced by the king. All royal authority was derived from the *dharma* ideal of which the holiness of the cow is a part. But the *dharma* ideal was sometimes in conflict with local customs (*deśadharma*) (cf. Wezler, 1985). This relation between two concepts of law is a critical one in a country as diverse as Nepal. Both *dharma*s were regarded as unchangeable and valid since time immemorial, imposed either by gods, seers, or ancestors. Both were tolerated by the king. "The king, however did not tolerate the customary law of a country that defiled the realm over which he ruled ... The tribal peoples in the eastern Himalayas did, however, observe certain practices that defiled the realm, most notably (in the eyes of the Gorkhali) the slaughter of cattle and the consumption of the flesh of dead cattle" (Burghart, 1984: 110).

In the following, I will focus on the origin and development of legal steps against cow slaughter in eighteenth and nineteenth century Nepal. I will confine myself more or less to legal material found in Nepali sources, royal orders (*lālmohor*) or letters, and the Muluki Ain. I will not deal with the wider question of the alleged rationality of the cow's sacred status, that is to say, I will not join the long debate on Marvin Harris's theory that the taboo on killing cows was a cultural norm based on sound ecological reasons.[6]

THE SIGNIFICANCE OF THE COW FOR THE KING

From the very beginning the Shah dynasty left no room for doubt about their worship and protection of the cow. The very name of their ancestral seat, namely Gorkha or, in Sanskrit, *gorakṣa*, means literally 'cow protector' and, in a secondary meaning, 'protector of the earth' which is believed to be as nourishing as the cow.[7] The name Gorkha was certainly adopted because of the Shahs' connection with Gorakhnath and the Kanphata Yogis (see *infra* and Unbescheid, 1980), but the literal meaning of the name fitted in very well with their concepts of authority and purity.

For the king it was important to preserve the purity of his realm since any defilement would endanger his authority. The notion of purity is thus linked with the concept of power. "The purity of the realm was endangered not only by social disorder but also by the king's rulership. The intimate relationship between the king, his subjects, and the realm is borne out in the claim of the Newar and Hill Brahmans that the Hindus living in Mughal territory had been defiled by virtue of their being governed by Muslim rulers" (Burghart, 1984: 104). Newar travellers who left the country had to undergo elaborate purification rituals with the five products of the cow (*pañcagavya*) after their return, as had already been noted in 1722 by Father Ippolito Desideri (1932: 316).

Rama Shah (reigned 1606–36) issued a royal order to preserve pasture for cattle.[8] He stated that the protection of cows was the king's duty, otherwise he would incur guilt (*pratyavaya*) and

Brahmans would have difficulties in getting food (*brāhmaṇalāi khāna kana duḥkha huncha*). Royal cattle farms were established in the Tarai, the Kathmandu Valley, and the hills,[9] and in letters to responsible officers from the years 1791–94, Rana Bahadur Shah showed himself concerned about the welfare of these cows, especially about the insufficient supply of salt for the animals. This king had donated many plots of land in order to install so-called *gośālā*, "cow-sheds" or "-homes",[10] or to feed the cows and bulls from the Pashupati temple with maize and salt.[11] On parts of these plots later the Tribhuvan Airport was built which was initially known as Gauchar ('cow pasture') Airport. It's a place, where nowadays – oh terrible Kali Yuga! – more and more beef-eaters land.

In the dynastic mythology of the Shah kings too, cows play a prominent role. This is especially shown in a modern Sanskrit poem, the *Gorakṣa-Śāha-Vaṃśa*, by Hariprasada Sharma (1965/66).[12] According to this eulogistic work Dravya Shah could only become king of Gorkha in 1559 because of the following mythical event: once as a child he was keeping watch over the cows, when Gorakhnath, the founder of the Kanphata sect (or Shiva in the form of a yogin), who lived only on milk, appeared. The little Dravya offered milk to Gorakhnath which so pleased him that he foretold the prince's conquest of Gorkha, Nepal, and other countries. But Dravya said that he didn't feel worth such a boon (*varadāna*) since he had not done any *tapas*, or gained any other religious merit, and had not even taken care of his forefathers. Gorakhnath, however, replied that his cow service (*goseva*) alone was enough to gain such a reward because in the body of every cow resides Lakshmi. In this way he had acquired *śrī*, luck and dignity, so that not even the cow-eaters (*gobhakṣa*), such as the British who attacked Nepal from 1814 to 1816, could harm the Shahs, the cow protectors (*gorakṣa*).[13] Moreover, according to a famous myth from the *Gopālarājavaṃśāvalī* and modern Nepali chronicles, it was a cow which discovered the national holy site and seat of the tutelary deity of Pashupatinath.[14]

The Ranas, too, showed themselves often as pious rulers. Even more than the Shah kings they were forced to display religious symbols in order to please the Brahmans and to legitimate their

FIGURE 4   *Bir Shamsher Jang Bahadur Rana worshipping the wishfulfilling cow, Kamadhenu (courtesy of the Musée d' Ethnographie, Geneva). The painting, dated 1889 (V. S. 1946), measures 1.5 by 2.5 metres. It depicts 40 Hindu divinities (Brahma and Sarasvati, Vishnu and Lakshmi, Shiva, Ganesha, Karttikeya, Hanuman, etc.) with the Prime Minister as main worshipper and an ascetic in the background. The text of the painting is in corrupt Sanskrit and contains invocations to Ganesha, Kamadhenu, and other deities*

rulership. Again the cow was an ideal symbol for such a purpose. Thus, in a huge painting dated Vikram Samvat 1946 (1889 AD) Prime Minister Bir Shamsher Jang Bahadur Rana (who ruled 1885–1901 AD) is depicted as venerating the wish-fulfilling cow Kāmadhenu (Figure 4).[15] In this unique painting, which significantly takes up almost directly the mythological story about Dravya Shah, Bir Shamsher is shown remarkably smaller than Kāmadhenu as if he wants to demonstrate his subordination to the religious power of the cow.

To be sure, this royal protection of cows is nothing unusual. Apparently it did not create any problem in the Kathmandu Valley, where the Newars and Indo-Nepalese Parbatiyas are dominant, when a general ban on cow slaughter was proclaimed at the turn of the nineteenth century.[16]

LEGAL STEPS AGAINST COW SLAUGHTER

How would the central government react towards those minorities and ethnic groups who had not adopted specific Hindu elements and sometimes eat beef? The question thus is how can a king (or prime minister) live with a law he cannot enforce? After all, it is no secret that in the hilly regions even today cows are slaughtered by pushing them down a steep slope (cf. Ortner, 1978: 17). It is also known that the Buddhist religion of the Sherpa forbids them to kill cows. "Nevertheless they appreciate the meat. For that reason every year they ask butchers from Tibet to slaughter some yaks for them" (Hagen, 1960: 76; my translation) – which is actually also against the Buddhist rule that one should not eat the meat of animals killed for one's own consumption.[17]

There is a revealing Nepali saying: *sārkīle moṭo gāī mar bhandaimā marcha ra!?* "Does a fat cow die just because the [beef-eating] leatherworker tells it to?" This proverb does not only point to the gap between desire and reality, but also indicates that the tanner is not just longing for the cow's hides and skins. Michael Oppitz (forthcoming) relates an interesting story which makes the conflict between the Kathmandu Valley and the hill regions even more delicate. The northern Magar say that they used to kill cows especially at times when they had trouble with the government in Kathmandu: they attacked, as it were, a symbol of the state rather than the state itself.

Once again, how did the government react when such cases were reported? As I already mentioned, cow slaughter is a major sin and not just a minor affair. Would the king or prime minister be tolerant and risk rebellion among his Brahman counsellors or would he take strict measurements against such people and risk uprising or a change of loyalty in remote areas? Moreover, what about the yak? Was it considered a cow? And how were those groups treated who did not kill the cow but consumed beef?

The ban on cow slaughter was probably first enforced in the whole kingdom by order of Rana Bahadur Shah[18] in April/May 1805[19] – a year after his return from Banaras. He ordered his district officers in the lands (*ambal*) west of Kanka river (i.e. Darjeeling) and east of Garhwal:

> *ājadekhi govadh nagarnu. garyāko jiya* [*jiu*] *dhanamā parlā bhani sunāidinu. abauprānta govadh garyāko ambālīle jibai māridinu.* From today killing of cows is prohibited. Inform (everybody) that, if somebody does (cow slaughter), capital punishment will take place and his property will be confiscated. From now on the killer of a cow should be killed by the *ambālī* (district officer) (§[*savāl*] 22).

The infliction capital punishment for killing a cow is mentioned even earlier, in a letter of a Capuchin missionary dated May 1740 (D. R. Regmi, 1966: 538). The ban on cow slaughter (RRS XI. 8: 126–8) had probably also to do with Rana Bahadur Shah's anti-British feelings which he developed in Banaras he wanted to show himself as a good and uncorrupted Hindu.

Thus, already at the beginning of the nineteenth century in Nepal there existed a clear 'national' ban on cow slaughter which in India still does not exist. To be sure, in Article 48 of India's

Constitution from 1949 one finds some regulations on this matter, but they are rather vague. The fathers of this Constitution, in contradistinction to today's leaders of several Indian parties, knew how dangerous it was for India to touch religious affairs and to offend the Muslim population. Only in a later amendment of this article did India prohibit the transport and sale of beef and the killing of unproductive cattle (Simoons, 1973; Baird, 1991). Today only seven of India's 31 states impose an almost absolute ban on cow slaughter, while in the other states cows may be slaughtered under certain circumstances, in three states even unconditionally (Lensch, 1985: 40–44).

From 1805 onwards the officials in Nepal were even entitled to kill the wrongdoer by an extremely cruel method. When in 1806 in Kathmandu the rumour spread that the local administration had not punished a Damai (a low-caste Tailor) from west Nepal although he was supposed to have killed a cow, the government ordered new legal proceedings against the person suspected of killing a cow, this time along with an ordeal during which – no wonder – the poor victim confessed. Again the case was reported to Kathmandu and the officials from west Nepal asked for a final decision. The 'Royal Order to Bichari Hiranda Tiwari' dated March 1806 was indeed rigorous because it gave the order: "Cut off flesh from his back, and put salt and condensed citrus juice on the wounds. Make him eat the flesh himself and kill him" (RRS XII. 11: 169).

Similarly severe was the punishment for killing oxen. In 1810, reports were received that people from Salyan had killed an ox. The royal order issued to the chief administrator of the district said: "Persons who commit the heinous crime of slaughtering oxen in Hindu land shall be flayed alive, impaled, or hang(ed) upside down until they are dead. Their property shall be confiscated and members of their family enslaved" (RRS XII. 11: 170). Later in the Muluki Ain of 1854 capital punishment was reduced to imprisonment for life, and a recent amendment (1990, § IV.7.11.) of the Muluki Ain stipulates twelve years' imprisonment.

Despite these deterrent measures local officials apparently did not always enforce the law or orders with the prescribed harshness. Yaks and cross-breeds between yak and cow were anyway not really considered as holy cows. At the beginning of the nineteenth century the killing of such animals was not punished. In the order of Rana Bahadur Shah of April/May 1805, quoted above, the killing of female yaks is explicitly (caurībāhik govadh garyā ...) exempted from capital punishment. In Solu Khumbu it was even permitted to kill yaks, as can be seen from an 'Order regarding the ban on cow slaughter in Solukhumbu', dated September 1805 (RRS I.1: 15). There was at least no capital punishment for such cases (RRS XI.8: 127).

Later, however, some killers of yaks were penalized, even in the most remote areas of Nepal, but only when the central government was informed. This happened in 1853 to two Tibetan families in the very north-west of the kingdom, in Humla. Apparently both families had fallen badly sick and left their village without any food. For some reason (perhaps an epidemic) they could not go to other villages either. Desperate as they were and almost starving to death, they killed four yak calves and consumed them. In fear of punishment they then escaped to China. When Prime Minister Jang Bahadur Rana was informed of this he ordered in a letter dated May 1853 that these families could return to Nepal if they would pay two rupees penalty (RRS IV.11: 215). Among the different editions of the Ain we find only in 1871, which is the first printed version, a paragraph stipulating that a killer of yak had to be punished with the fine of 40 rupees. This was certainly less severe than life imprisonment for killing a cow.

The Shahs and Ranas had good reasons to turn a blind eye to such cases, as well as to the killing of cows. For, on the one hand, they needed certain cow products for their arsenal, while on the other hand they realized that taxes were a much better and more profitable measure than a law which was difficult to enforce in the remote regions. Hides and skins were used for making scabbards of weapons and for the transport of salpeter (RRS XI.2: 21–22; RRS XII.8: 115). That is why certain ethnic groups or castes such as the Limbu, Tibetan, Sherpa, Hayu, Lepcha, and Sarki were regularly asked to supply the hides and skins of buffaloes, elephants, tigers, or deer, but also of cattle as is shown in a royal order regarding the regulations on taking the flesh of dead cattle issued by Girvana Yuddha Shah dated 1805 (RRS III.2: 31–2). These groups could, however, also be exempted from this obligation by paying a certain sum of money. One should note that the fine was received by the palace, not by its Brahmanic advisors (*dharmādhikārī*). The same is true for Gurungs and Lamas east of the Trisuli river but only if they were willing to join the army, to honour Brahmans, and not to eat beef any more (RRS XI.2: 22). Apparently both the worshipping of Brahmans and the abandonment of eating beef made them into good, i.e. virtuous and courageous, warriors. As it seems, it was (and still is) no easy task to connect the usefulness of cows with their holiness.

However, more relevant than the usefulness of carcasses were the taxes for such groups who consumed the meat of cattle that died naturally. This meat is known as *sino* or *sinu*. Girvana Yuddha Shah permitted certain castes to eat *sinu* if they would supply hides and skins, otherwise they had to pay fines (RRS III.2: 31–2). In Solu Khumbu, which is mostly inhabited by Sherpas, one was, up to the beginning of the nineteenth century, even allowed to eat the meat of slaughtered cattle providing an annual fee, the so-called *cokho-daṇḍa*, was paid to the local authorities. When the central government in Kathmandu heard about this custom, it banned cow slaughter in this region too. It was however reported by officials sent to Solu Khumbu that almost everybody would have to be punished if they enforced the law. On the basis of this report it was decided that only those culprits should be sentenced to death whose cases occurred prior to February 1804; all other culprits should be enslaved.[20]

In other regions there were similar arrangements. In a royal order (*lālmohor*) dated July 1810 it is, for instance, mentioned that in Pyuthan (west Nepal) more than 3000 *sinu*-eating people had regularly to pay taxes. However, they protested against these high taxes and offered to supply skins and to pay an annual fee instead. This was granted in the end because the authorities in Kathmandu had realized that they could not outlaw a long-continued custom such as *sinu*-eating (RRC 39: 312–3). Thus the superiority of the king was recognized by accepting the dictum of the holiness of the cow, but what was more important for the people of Pyuthan was that they could continue to eat *sinu*. Law and customary law are different affairs.

COW PROTECTION IN THE MULUKI AIN

All these various orders, letters, and laws were put together in the Ain, the famous code of Jang Bahadur Rana from 1853/54. The name of this law-book, deriving from Persian *āī'n*, itself reveals some of its sources. Only from 1952 onwards do we find the addition, *mulukī*, 'royal, national (lit. of the kingdom)'. The other sources are, indirectly, Dharmaśāstra and, to an astonishing degree, common law (cf. § I. 1: *nīti*, *lok-ko anubhāv*).

The relevance of the Ain – a book more quoted than understood – is shown by the fact that it was among the first printed books of Nepal, presumably on a printing press which was imported from England by Jang Bahadur Rana (Fezas, 1990). Jang Bahadur Rana, during his trip to London and Paris (1850–1851) came to endow printed books and especially the codification of law with an almost magical sense as the expression of Western superiority (cf. Whelpton, 1983: 123). His political aim was mainly to establish a common caste hierarchy and a homogeneous legislation, not an easy task in the heterogeneous kingdom of Nepal. He certainly also wanted by this first national law to control remote areas and ethnic groups. The Ain was promulgated on the 6th of January 1854, and was often amended. The ban on cow slaughter is in the 66th chapter of the printed edition, which A. Höfer (1979) has summarized in his study of the Muluki Ain. It has 14 paragraphs; the manuscripts of this chapter in the earlier Ains vary between 10 and 15 paragraphs.[21]

What is the main content of this chapter? In the Ain itself there is a sharp and remarkable contrast between the intentional and the negligent killing of a cow: life sentence for intentional killing versus just one rupee for negligent killing! This is remarkable for two reasons. Firstly, because much less important offences are punished more heavily; and secondly, because it is always very difficult to differentiate between the subjective and objective facts of the case, or between intention of the culprit and the death of the cow, as in the frequent cases when somebody pushes a cow down a hill in order to make its death appear as an accident. Such cases are not really included in the Ain, except perhaps in paragraph 6 which states that it is not permitted for *sinu*-eating people to buy the meat of cows killed accidentally. Does that mean that if it is one's own cow that dies, one may eat it?

Originally, i.e. in the older manuscripts, the legal ban on cow slaughter in the Ain had only 10 paragraphs. The additionally incorporated paragraphs deal mainly with exceptions from the general rule of rigorous prosecution for killing or hurting cows: cases including veterinary treatments (paragraph 8), accidents (paragraph 13), or unsoundness of mind are not punished. The Ain thus differentiates between criminal and public aspects with respect to the order of the kingdom and the culprit's subjective state of mind in that a purification ritual of repentance (*prāyaścitta, patiyā*) is prescribed for the killer even if he was not to be prosecuted. This differentiation exemplifies the well-known ambivalent attitude towards the cow: it is an holy animal, no doubt, but it is also a working animal. The law tries to do justice to both aspects: a man who beats or hurts a cow while working with it can hardly be punished (paragraphs 3, 6, and 11), but he who injures a cow with a weapon will be enslaved (paragraph 2).

The injunction of the Ain is therefore mainly to protect the life and holiness of the cow for the sake of the king's Hindu orthodoxy and for the sake of a common state ideology (as insisted upon by the rulers), but not for the sake of the animal itself. This has nothing to do with the protection of animals, or with *ahiṃsā* (non-violence) or vegetarianism. Hindu kings as members of the Kshatriya *varṇa* are in any case not obliged to respect *ahiṃsā* and have always been devoted hunters. Nepal is no exception to this rule. Yet, there are tendencies in the Ain which in a way point to *ahiṃsā*: on certain holy days such as Ekādaśī (sacred to Vishnu), Krishna's birthday, and Shivaratri, hunting and, interestingly, also the carrying out of capital punishment are prohibited (paragraph 10).[22] Moreover, twenty years after the first Ain the yak was also made into a holy cow (paragraph 15), although with certain limitations as regards sentencing: this animal lacks, so to say, a proper birth: in a way, it is a fallen Brahman. However, animal sacrifices do not fall under these *ahiṃsā* tendencies which can surely be explained by the old Dharmaśāstra rule that animal sacrifices are not to be considered as killing.[23]

CONCLUSION

The cow as a symbol, as insignia, and also as instrument for national unity through Hinduization – these are the main points in the legal bans on cow slaughter in Nepal. All in all, it has little to do with 'civil' rights or avoidance of juridical uncertainty, and much to do with symbolic protection of the cow. Why only symbolic? In my opinion one misses many aspects which are very important to the farmer and that means to those people who actually have to do with cattle: one misses for instance the differentiation between cow and oxen or between milch cow and draught animals. Could male or draught animals, female buffaloes, or old and sick cows be slaughtered? The Ain gives no direct answer to these questions. One thus notes a striking uncertainty of the law, which is even more surprising when one considers that such inconsistencies or deficiencies were not diminished in later amendments. Apparently there was no need for their removal: they did not hinder the achievement of the law's real objective.

But how then do we have to understand the ban on yak slaughter which was included in the Ain after a comparatively short period? After all, this special case concerned only a minority in the remote regions in the high mountains which lived in sensitive borderlands. The reason for the yak ban was, it seems, that the Bhotiya people of the border areas needed to be brought within the moral kingdom of Nepal, at least symbolically, and thereby marked as subjects of Gorkha, not of Tibet. Only in the twentieth century was the boundary with Tibet "understood to demarcate a fixed and exclusive interest of the state upon a territory and upon the people who lived there" (Burghart, 1984: 115). It must thus be concluded that the ban on cow and yak slaughter served an integrative rather than a practical objective.

A similar function of the cow as a symbol of social and political integration is found in the Hindu reactions towards Muslims and British in India, where it led to violent debates and even fights (Parel, 1969). Except for this latter aspect, the use of the cow as a religious symbol of political unity in nineteenth century Nepal is analogous. But what is still not fully realised in India today,

namely a nationwide ban on cow slaughter, could be promulgated and to a certain extent enforced in Nepal comparatively
early – due to its centralized power. That is how Nepal could show
herself more Catholic than the Pope, more Hindu than India:

> Throughout the eighteenth century Nepal was thought by
> the Nepālese to be a Hindu realm uncontaminated by
> Muslim rule. Prithvi Narayan thought that the Kingdom of
> Gorkha could become a 'true Hindustan' (*asal hindustan*: see
> Stiller, 1968: 43–44). Fifty years later, however, nearly all
> the South Asian subcontinent had been subjugated by the
> cow-eating Firangi [European] and, given the presence, as
> always, of the pig-eating Bhotiya of the Tibetan plateau
> ruled by the barbarous Celestial Emperor at Peking, the
> Gorkha government could assert that Gorkha was the only
> remaining Hindustan on the subcontinent and that its
> political isolation was necessary in order to safeguard its
> purity (Burghart, 1984: 115–6).

The idea of Nepal as more pure than India was often
accepted by Indians (though the contrary was also sometimes
asserted basically because Nepalese Brahmans are not vegetarians).
When Maharaja Juddha Shamsher visited Calcutta and other places
in north India in early 1939, he was praised by newspapers all over
India for being the representative of a country which was regarded
as "Symbol of Hinduism". Such is the subtitle of an article by Indra
Prakash, published in the *Hindu Outlook*, New Delhi (2/8/1939), and
two days later in the *Marhatta*, Poona (4/8/1939). Indra Prakash
eulogizes Nepal with the following words:

> We feel that we cannot be accused guilty of exaggeration if
> we say 'Nepal is Hinduism and Hinduism is Nepal'. If one
> feels the necessity to discover religion of Aryan Rishis in its
> pristine glory, in its original and pure form untouched and
> undefiled by semitic cults, we would point to Nepal.
> Maharaja Sir Joodha Samsher Jang Bahadur Rana is a
> powerful, popular and gracious Ruler with the true spirit of
> 'Hindutva' invigorating his nerves and so long as he and his
> followers live in Nepal, Nepal can never become a land of

Christians, nor can it become a Pakistan. The Maharaja like a pious Hindu, is a great cow-worshipper. He himself attends the cow exhibition, which is held every year in Nepal. Handsome prizes are awarded to the persons who exhibit the best cow or a bull.

The rulers of Nepal not only appreciated such a view of their kingdom, they also propagated it strongly. But if you look at the details of their legal measures against cow slaughter, there is a remarkable gap between claim and reality. And it is also rather ironic that only a few years after the promulgation of the Ain, Gurkha regiments joined the British army to beat down the Great Mutiny of 1857 since this was caused by the rumour that the ammunition for the newly introduced Enfield rifles, which had to be cracked with one's teeth before loading, was greased with cow or pig tallow.

Another striking example of the gap between claim and practice comes from the Nepalese coronation rituals so thoroughly described and analysed by Michael Witzel (1987). According to the traditional ritual handbooks the king should mount a throne, the *bhadrāsana*, covered with the skins of various animals symbolising strength, agility, courage, etc. "Most prominent are those of a tiger (viz. a lion, a cat), of a bull (viz., a hyena), and that of an antilope ... In the medieval *Rājyābhiṣeka* [royal consecration (hand-books)], the following are mentioned: bull, cat, hyena (*tarakṣu*), lion, tiger; they are covered with a white cloth" (Witzel, 1987: 455). The king acquires strength by sitting on the remainder of a dead bull. This raises the topic of the generation of life (or strength) through death or killing which I do not wish to discuss here. However, one wonders how the hide of the bull could be procured, if the animals had to be sacrificed. Witzel does not mention this point, but by chance I came across a clipping from the *Times of India* referring to the coronation of King Mahendra:

> Few know that the sacred skin of an ox on which the throne of King Mahendra of Nepal was mounted for the dazzling coronation ceremonies was personally flown to Kathmandu

by Pakistan's Foreign Minister, Mr. Hamidul Huq Chaudhury. The Nepalese Government had no trouble at all in
getting the skins of cat, tiger, leopard and lion. But the skin
of the ox was difficult to procure. A skin of chestnut hue,
enjoined by 200-year old tradition was wanted. Pakistan
alone could furnish it. Mr Chaudhury packed the semi-cured
hide of an ox of the famous Sindhi breed together with the
horns in a specially constructed crate. It was flown over with
presents from the Pakistan Government, including a sword
(*Times of India* 6/5/1956, quoted from Lal, 1967: 19).

A symbol by which Nepalese kingship propagated Hinduism in
order to enforce power and integrate a diverse country thus turns
out to come from a Muslim country.

The Ain and the royal orders mirror this rather ambiguous
attitude towards the protection of the cow. In other words, everybody
could live with the prohibitions of the Ain quite well. The Brahmans
had the cow legally protected, the rulers legitimated their power
religiously and did not endanger it by too strict measures, which they
could anyway not really enforce in the remote regions, and the
heterogeneous population of Nepal were able to find enough
loopholes to continue customs such as the eating of *sinu*.

The early ban on cow slaughter in Nepal has nothing or little
to do with morality, with sublimation, or with guilt. However, the
ban on cow slaughter in nineteenth-century Nepal indicates a
situation not too far away from what has been described by Norbert
Elias for medieval Europe: the more the state consolidates and the
more its power is enforced at the periphery, the more abstract and
subtle its law becomes. The present amendment of the Muluki Ain
deals the ban on cow slaughter under the broad and rather sober
section 'On quadrupeds' (*Caupāyāko*)!

Given this latest development, it is to be feared that the time
is not too far away when in Nepal and India a cow will be just a
cow, an animal valued merely for its utility in the production of
milk and dung, meat and hide. Progress in combination with
rationality has been dominated too much by the cow eaters so that
even the Indian cow can hardly defend itself any more against the
rules of the market. But where money alone rules over men and

animals and not men over or with men and animals, nothing but money itself will remain holy, and in the long run there will perhaps be nothing edible left, either for cows or for men.

NOTES

Different versions of this paper have been read during a seminar on 'Sovereignty in the Himalayan Region' at the South Asia Institute (Heidelberg, June 1991), a seminar on 'Politics, Identity, and Cultural Change in the Himalayan Region' (University of Oxford, Institute of Social and Cultural Anthropology, November 1992), and at the Himalayan Forum (University of London, SOAS, November 1992). I would like to thank the participants for their comments and critical remarks. I am especially grateful to David Gellner, Mahes Raj Pant, Joanna Pfaff-Czarnecka, S. A. Srinivasan, and John Whelpton for their valuable comments on early drafts of this paper. A German version along with a critical edition and translation of the chapter on cow slaughter in the Muluki Ain of 1854 will published in a volume on *ahiṃsā*, edited by A. Wezler (see Michaels, forthcoming). This paper was revised when I came to know about Richard Burghart's untimely death. Many points as regards to the process of Hinduization and nation-building in Nepal were much better and earlier made by him in his famous article on the concept of nation-state in Nepal. He also first pointed out the significance of the cow for this process (Burghart, 1984: 110 and 116).

[1] *Young India*, 11/8/1920 (*Collected Works*, vol. 18, p. 133).

[2] *himduhrāja gohatyā strīhatyā nahunyā brahmahatyā nahunyā .... kalimā himduko rāja yehī muluk mātrai cha*: Muluki Ain of 1854 (ed. V. S. 2020), 1.1, p. 8; cf. Burghart (1984: 116, referring to the Muluki Ain of 1866).

[3] For the protection of women through the abolition of widow burning, see Michaels (1992; 1993).

[4] *na kālaniyamas tatra gostrī vipravināśane* (IV.7. 453).

[5] See Burghart (1984) for a discussion of the three indigenous concepts of territory as (tenurial) possesions (*muluk*), realm (*deśa*), and country or nation (also *deśa*).

[6] See Michaels (forthcoming: fn. 1) for a discussion of this point.

[7] We find a parallel in the etymology of Khotan from Skt. *go-stana* which refers to the legendary founder of Khotan who got breast-(*stana*) fed by the earth (or cow?) (see Mayer, 1990).

8   Riccardi (1977: 50), Naraharinath (1965/66: 686 bottom).

9   RRS (VI.7: 126–7). RRS = Regmi Research Series: a list of the documents which I have used is given at the end of this chapter.

10 See the detailed study by Lodrick (1981). Many of the Indian Gośālās are today homes for old and sick cows, which are donated and maintained by religious institutions. The largest institution of this kind in Nepal is at the Pashupati Temple. Called Śrī Paśupati Gośālā, it is maintained by Indian Marwaris and has likewise the function to protect and care for cows. On average each of the milk-yielding cows gives approx. 260 kg milk p.a. which is almost half of what Indian cows in similar Gośālās produce (approx. 530 kg) (cf. Lodrick, 1981: Table 2.16). This is surprising when one considers that many of the cows in the Kathmandu valley are cross-breeds between the Indian Zebu and imported Holstein-Frisians.

11 Vajracarya and Srestha (1980/81: inscr. no. 239), M. C. Regmi (1976: 52, fn. 29).

12 Cf. Petersen (1985) and Kölver (1986: 23–25).

13 See also *Dibya Upadesh* where an astrologer foretells Prithvi Narayan Shah's future: "You, O Prince, have held at all times great respect for cows, Brahmans, guests, holy men, the gods, and goddesses ... You will one day be king of Nepal" (Stiller, 1989: 39).

14 *Gopālarājavaṃśāvalī* fol. 17a–b; *Bhāṣāvaṃśāvalī* I, 2–3; Wright (1877: 107); Hasrat (1970: 33); see also Eichinger Ferro-Luzzi (1987: 5), and Michaels (1994: 60–65).

15 For a detailed description of this painting see Eracle (n.d.). Unfortunately the inscriptions on the painting do not mention any historical circumstances by which one could learn about the motives of Bir Shamsher.

16 This may be connected to the ban on using the cow for ploughing in the Kathmandu Valley (on which, see Webster, 1981).

17 Cf. Alsdorf (1962: 8). The widespread practice of killing animals at Buddhist shrines in the Kathmandu Valley (Gellner, 1992: 88–94) even led to an exchange of notes between the Tibetan regent sTag-brag Rin-po-che (1941–50) and Prime Minister Juddha Shumsher Rana: see Cüppers (forthcoming) for an edition and translation of these documents.

18 Rana Bahadur Shah abdicated on 23rd of March 1799 in favour of his son Girvana Yuddha Shah who was then only eighteen months old. He returned to Nepal early in 1804 and gained full power to rule in his son's name as regent until he was assassinated by his younger half-brother Sher Bahadur in April 1806.

[19] See Pant (1969/70: 242). The date of the document is [*vikram*] *saṃvat 1863 sāl miti vaiśākh vadi 3 roj 1* (1806 AD) verified by Dines Raj Pant to V.S. *1862 caitra 26* (*ibid*.: 244, fn.).

[20] See RRS XI.9: 129–130; cf. RRS I.1: 15–16 and RRS XII.11: 169.

[21] See Fezas (1990) for a comprehensive list of the various manuscripts and printed editions.

[22] Already in Ashoka's rock edicts certain days are excluded for killing animals: see Alsdorf (1962: 51). According to the *Arthaśāstra* (XII. 5. 12f.), it was a royal tradition to prohibit animal slaughter on certain days; see also Scharfe (1968: 168–9).

[23] *Mānavadharmaśāstra* 5.39cd: *yajño 'sya bhūtyai sarvasya tasmād yajñe vadho 'vadhaḥ*; cf. Alsdorf (1962: 18ff.).

LEGAL REFERENCES

1. Documents from Regmi Research Series (RRS) and Regmi Research Collection (RRC)

N. B. The handwritten copies of the original documents used by M. C. Regmi and his collaborators (= Regmi Research Collection) have been microfilmed by the Nepal-German Manuscript Preservation Project; for an index of these documents see NGMPP Reel. No. E 2392.

RRS I.1 (1969): 15; RRC 6: 441: 'Order regarding ban on cow slaughter in Solukhumbu', AĀśvina badi 3, V. S. 1862 (September 1805).

RRS III.2 (1971): 31–32; RRC 6: 180: 'Regulations on taking the flesh of dead cattle, 1805', Order (*lālmohar*) of Girvana Yuddha Shah dated V. S. 1862 (1805).

RRS IV.11 (1972): 215; RRC 33: 193–194: 'Punishment for Eating Yak-Meat', letter of Jang Bahadur Rana and others dated Jyeṣṭha śudi 9, V. S. 1910 (May 1853).

RRS VI.7 (1974): 126–127; RRC 5: 79–81 and 756–757: 'Royal Cattle Farms, 1791'.

RRS XI.2 (1979): 21–22; RRC 38: 696–697: 'The Hides and Skins Levy'.

RRS XI.8 (1979): 126; RRC 40: 165–168: 'Ban on Cow Slaughter, 1809'.

RRS XI.8 (1979): 127; RRC 40: 165–168: 'Regulations in the Name of Sheoraj, Kashiram, and Rishi Padhya for the Tamakosi-Tista Region', Pauṣa badi 9, V. S. 1866 (December 1809).

RRC 39: 312–313: 'Royal order to the *sino*-eating communities of Pyuthan', Śrāvaṇa śudi 7, V. S. 1867 (July 1810).

RRS XI.9 (1979): 129–130; RRC 6: 663–665: 'Ban on cow slaughter in Solukhumbu', Mārga badi 9, V. S. 1862 (November 1805).

RRS XII.8 (1980): 115; RRC 43: 6–7 and 44: 389–390: 'The Hides and Skins Levy', AĀṣādha badi 4, V. S. 1874 (1817) and Kārttika śudi 14, V. S. 1888 (1831).

RRS XII.11 (1980): 169; RRC 6: 748: 'Royal Order to Bichari Hirananda Tiwari', Caitra badi 30, V. S. 1862 (March 1806).

RRS XII.11 (1980): 170; RRC 39: 318: 'Royal Order Regarding Punishment for Cow Slaughter in Salyan', Bhadra badi 3, V. S. 1867 (August 1810).

2. Versions of the (Muluki) Ain:

(a) Manuscript dated V. S. 1910 (1853), National Archives, Kathmandu;

(b) *Śrī 5 Surendra Bikram Śāhadevakā Śāsanakālamā Baneko Mulukī Ain.* Kathmandu: Śrī 5-ko Sarkāra [H.M.G.], Kānūna tathā Nyāya Mantrālaya [Ministry of Law and Justice], V. S. 2020 (1963);

(c) *Mulukī Ain*, 4 Pts. and Addenda, Kathmandu: Manorañjan Press, V. S. 1927 (1870);

(d) Ain V. S. 1945 (1888) and V. S. 1961 (1905): ed. Śrī 5-ko Sarkāra, Kānūna tathā Nyāya Mantrālaya [Ministry of Law and Justice], Kathmandu.

(e) *Mulukī Ain* (9th amendment) ed. Śrī 5-ko Sarkāra (H.M.G.), Kathmandu V. S. 2047 (1990).

CHAPTER THREE

Being Nepali without Nepal: Reflections on a South Asian Diaspora

Michael Hutt

INTRODUCTION

The question of identity forms one of the key topics of South Asian history and culture. Debate often centres on issues of nationalism ("the desire of a nation to have a state of its own") and nationism ("the desire of a state to have a nation of its own")[1] and a variety of bases have been posited for contemporary political identity, among them religion, language, locality, caste, and ethnicity. Similar questions have also been pursued with regard to the development of the nation-state of Nepal – a phenomenon that accords more closely with Yapp's definition of nationism. One thinks immediately of the important and much-quoted article by Richard Burghart (1984). John Whelpton also examines the issue in considerable detail in an unpublished paper (1993b), and in his contribution to this volume. This discussion will attempt no more than to begin to establish a factual basis, primarily through a review of the relevant literature, and in some areas to identify a serious lack of reliable information. This lack of data has in recent years allowed distorted versions of history, or at least divergent readings of the past, to be used as justifications for controversial measures in the region concerned. The discussion is therefore pertinent to the concerns not only of scholars and students, but also to those of governments, rulers, and refugees.

Since the latter half of the nineteenth century, Nepalis have constituted a visible and increasingly vocal element of the population in Himalayan and sub-Himalayan districts in the northeast of the Indian subcontinent. Here I shall discuss the definition of 'Nepalis' as a quasi-ethnic group, and the historical reasons for their presence in northeast India and southern Bhutan. I shall also attempt to explain the sense of insecurity that has pervaded this community for much of the present century, and to examine some of the ways in which it has attempted to carve a more secure niche for itself outside Nepal. The discussion is topical in view of recent events in Bhutan, where the ethnic cohesiveness of the Nepalis has come to be viewed as a threat to the prevailing political order. Nevertheless, the nature and history of Nepali ethnicity in the so-called 'Nepali diaspora' was not analysed with any real vigour until the publication of studies by Kumar Pradhan (1982) and Tanka Subba (1992).

Many stories and poems portraying emigration and exile, and several novels, have been written in Nepali during the twentieth century. In fact Līlabahādur Kshetrī's *Basāī* (Settlement), a novel published in 1957 that describes the exploitation, dispossession, and emigration of a peasant family in eastern Nepal, is a set text for many Nepalese school students.[2] Elsewhere too, the phenomenon of emigration is portrayed with a fair degree of pathos, as the final lines of a short story from the 1960s illustrate:

> "You have the right to my house, but you've no right to destroy our honour. I hereby give up my house and my land. You just take it over, we're leaving." Pudke relinquished ownership of the house and land of his forefathers, picked up his son and led Ujeli away. Ujeli clung to her husband. "Where are we going?" she asked. Pudke walked on a little further, then he took his son by the hand. "To Assam", he said, "We'll keep cows" (Malla, 1968/9: 21).[3]

Can the term 'diaspora' be used to denote the permanent presence of a Nepali-speaking community outside the borders of present-day Nepal? 'Emigration and settlement' might describe the historical process that led to their presence more precisely, since the emigrants were not driven out of their homeland, except perhaps by economic conditions, and they do not yearn to return. On the other hand, it can be argued that the present political boundary of Nepal – especially in the east – does not demarcate exactly the region whose population is numerically dominated by the originally disparate ethno-linguistic groups who are now categorized as 'Nepalis'. Nor is it at all clear that the whole of the Nepali 'diaspora' community is descended from emigrants from Nepal: in Sikkim, for instance, there were probably villages inhabited by Limbus and Magars (peoples now often classified as 'Nepali'), as well as the autochthonous Lepchas, during the seventeenth century.[4] So, despite its original Jewish associations, the term 'diaspora' is used here in the sense of "a dispersion or spreading, as of people originally belonging to one nation or having a common culture" (Collins, 1979: 409), although in this diaspora, as in many others, much of the 'common culture' was constructed after the migrations, not prior to them.[5]

THE SIZE OF THE NEPALI DIASPORA COMMUNITY

The size of the Nepali community in India can only be assessed with reference to census data on "language mainly spoken in the household" and "population by place of birth". Useful data on the number of persons resident for more than six months abroad are also available from the Census of Nepal. In Bhutan, where such data are not available, the size of the Nepali-speaking population cannot be assessed with any degree of confidence. All Indian census figures probably lead to under-estimates of the 'ethnic Nepali' minority. A proportion of those who might be categorized as 'Nepali' by non-Nepalis, and who do use Nepali in their everyday discourse, still consider other 'Nepalese' languages to be the language of their household, while the majority of 'Nepalis', 'Gorkhas', and 'Lhotshampas' who are long-term residents of India and Bhutan are not Nepal-born.

The Indian Census of 1981 presents language data in two sections. The first enumerates speakers of the 15 languages of the 8th Schedule of the Indian Constitution, which in 1981 excluded

Nepali (Nepali became one of the languages of the Schedule in 1992: see below). The second enumerates speakers of certain other languages, including Gorkhali/Nepali, Limbu, and Sherpa, but no other language that is also spoken in Nepal. The 1971 Census of India recorded a total of 1,419,835 speakers of Gorkhali/Nepali and the 1981 Census recorded a total of 1,252,444. The fall in this figure between 1971 and 1981 is attributable, at least in part, to the absence of statistics from Assam in the 1981 census. In 1981, twelve states and union territories in India recorded more than 10,000 speakers of Gorkhali/Nepali: see Table 3.1 (the number of "Nepal-born" persons is also noted for each state in 1971).

A comparison of the number of Gorkhali/Nepali speakers in each state with the number of Nepal-born persons is instructive. When the former far exceeds the latter (as it does in West Bengal and Assam), the situation described is evidently that of a Nepali-speaking community composed in the main of persons separated from the original emigrants from Nepal by at least one generation. When the situation is reversed (as it is in Uttar Pradesh and Bihar), it is reasonable to conclude that this is the result of more recent emigration from Nepal by people who do not claim Gorkhali/Nepali as their mother-tongue.

The second category of census data that is of relevance here enumerates long-term emigrés from Nepal (in the Nepal Census) and Nepal-born persons resident in India (in the Indian Census). It is probable that these categories overlap those enumerated under language headings; i.e. a person could be recorded twice, once as a Gorkhali/Nepali speaker, and once as a Nepal-born person, though it is impossible to estimate the degree of overlap. This data has been analysed by Harka Gurung (1989: 15–29) and Table 3.2 summarizes his findings.

It is beyond the scope of this discussion to establish a figure for the size of the Nepali community normally resident in India. However, it is perhaps of use to summarize the available data, as in Table 3.3, and suggest some maximal and minimal figures. If based solely on language statistics, even if one adds in the approximately 350,000 speakers of Gorkhali/Nepali recorded in Assam in 1971 and the 30,927 speakers of Limbu and Sherpa recorded in India in

TABLE 3.1   INDIAN STATES AND UNION TERRITORIES
RECORDING MORE THAN 10,000 SPEAKERS OF
GORKHALI/NEPALI IN CENSUS OF INDIA, 1981[a]

	G/N spkrs.	Total popn.	Nepal-born persons (1971)
Assam (1971)	353,700[b]	14,957,542	107,216[c]
Bihar	20,197	69,638,725	122,528
Himachal Pradesh	40,526	4,257,575	79,718
Madhya Pradesh	11,904	52,000,069	
Maharashtra	23,428	62,230,282	18,422
Manipur	37,046	1,409,239	
Meghalaya	61,259	1,326,748	
Nagaland	24,918	747,071	
Sikkim	192,891	308,262	
Uttar Pradesh	29,570	110,549,826	83,459
West Bengal	711,584	54,207,652	100,365
Darjeeling distt.	540,444	1,007,848	
Jalpaiguri distt.	135,860	2,201,794	
Arunachal Pradesh	45,508	597,862	
Delhi	10,947	6,174,632	9,670

Other Nepalese languages

	Limbu	Sherpa[d]
India	18,320	12,607
Sikkim	17,922	10,726

[a] In only eight states and union territories do speakers of languages other than those included in the 8th Schedule constitute a majority: of these eight, six are in the northeast (including Mizoram, which recorded 5,983 speakers of Gorkhali/Nepali in 1981). The other two are the union territories of Dadra and Nagar Haveli, and Goa, Daman, and Diu.

[b] No census operation was carried out in Assam in 1981, due to the "disturbed situation" there.

[c] In 1971, 'Assam' denoted Assam, Meghalaya, and Arunachal Pradesh.

[d] Speakers of Sherpa outside Nepal might not normally identify themselves as 'Nepalis', but may be identified as such by non-Nepalis.

TABLE 3.2   EMIGRATION FROM NEPAL AND NEPAL-BORN
PERSONS IN INDIA

	1 (NC)[a] Persons abroad for 6 months or more	2 (NC) % of (1) residing in India	3 (IC) Nepal-born persons in India	4 (IC) Nepalese nationals in India
1941	81,817			
1951			278,972	82,071
1952[b]	198,120	79.4		
1961	328,470	92.0	498,836	133,524
1971			486,000	
1981	402,977	93.1	501,292	

[a] IC: Census of India; NC: Census of Nepal.
[b] Data from the 1952-4 Census of Nepal.

1981, and postulates a further absolute maximum of 50,000
speakers of other Nepalese languages (Rai, Magar, Gurung,
Tamang, etc.) in India, the total figure of 'Nepalis' in India, if
Nepalis are defined as 'speakers of languages spoken primarily in
Nepal', cannot be stretched much beyond a total of one and three
quarter millions. According to the 1981 Census of India, a total of
501,292 people enumerated in the Census were born in Nepal.
Gurung attributes the fact that this exceeds the number of people
recorded by the Nepal Census as being absent abroad for more than
six months to "under-reporting" and "whole family emigration".
One assumes that many emigrants from Nepal simply lose touch
and, since their neighbours will not know whether they are living
or dead, they are not recorded in the census. Whether this figure
should be added to the above statistics on mother-tongue to provide
an estimate of the size of the Nepali community in India is unclear:
it may be that 'Nepal-born' people form some part of the "Gorkhali/
Nepali" speaking community, or it may be that they are a separate
and distinct category. If the latter is the case, the census data
seem to suggest that the Nepali community in India consists of

TABLE 3.3   SUMMARY OF STATISTICS ON THE SIZE OF
THE NEPALI–SPEAKING COMMUNITY IN INDIA

1. Gorkhali/Nepali speakers in India excluding
   Assam (1981 Census)   1,252,444
2. Gorkhali/Nepali speakers Assam (1971 Census)   350,000[a]
3. Nepal-born persons resident in India (1981)   501,292
4. Speakers of Limbu and Sherpa in India (1981)   30,927
5. Speakers of other 'Nepalese' language in India   50,000[b]
6. Persons absent abroad from Nepal for more than
   6 months (1981)   402,977

[a] It has been suggested that the number of Nepalis in Assam grew from
350,000 to 500,000 during the 1970s, though this has not been substantiated (see Murty, 1983: 40). Interestingly, Murty reports that the
Assamese parties that were agitating for the expulsion of immigrants
"viewed the presence of Nepalese settlers in Assam as not an important
part of the overall issue of [the] presence of foreigners in Assam"
(*ibid.*: 40). Chaudhuri (1982: 44) asserts that a total of 8,500,000
immigrants had settled permanently in Assam by 1971, constituting 57%
of the total population.

[b] This figure is an educated guess.

approximately 2.25 million people. If the former, the total figure is
rather smaller.

The size of the Indian Nepali community is claimed to be
much larger than this by various parties for a variety of reasons.
Those who have demanded the inclusion of Nepali in the 8th
Schedule of the Indian Constitution have regularly quoted a figure
of 5 or 6 million (see, for instance All-India Nepali Bhasha Samiti,
1979). The government of Bhutan, on the other hand, cites a figure
of 10 million for the Nepali community in India, seeking to
emphasize the threat of mass immigration:[6]

> There are, however, many millions of people of Nepali
> origin living in Nepal, Sikkim, Kalimpong, Darjeeling and
> the surrounding areas who are not only jealous of us, the
> Bhutanese, enjoying so much happiness and prosperity, but
> would like to migrate in millions so as to steal our peace,
> happiness and prosperity from us and our children (RGB,
> 1992: 29–30).

Although government census figures rarely reflect demographic situations exactly, and are vulnerable to manipulation for a variety of ends, it remains unlikely that the true size of the Nepali population in India could be treble that suggested by the above maximal reading of the census figures, as claimed by language campaigners, or nearly five times greater, as claimed by the Bhutan government.

The size of the Nepali population of southern Bhutan (called *Lhotshampa*, 'people of the southern border', in official Bhutanese media) is even more difficult to assess. Officially, the total population of Bhutan is now 600,000: some refugee organizations claim that Nepalis are about 50%,[7] but the highest estimate given by the Bhutan government, in 1979, was 33%. This was before the official figure for the total population was reduced from 1.375 million (in 1988) to 600,000 (in 1991). The truth is probably somewhere in between, although the 'demographic equation' altered between 1990 and 1993, as many Lhotshampas left Bhutan as refugees: in September 1995 the UNHCR-administered camps in southeast Nepal accommodated 88,880 (UNHCR, 1995). If they are all from Bhutan (and their origins are hotly disputed), they represent nearly 14% of the official total population, if the 1991 figure is to be taken as accurate.

NAMES AND TERMS

The language currently recognized by the Sahitya Akademi (Literature Academy) of India, the Indian Constitution, and the West Bengal Official Languages Act is "Nepali", but the 1988 Notification on Citizenship, negotiated with the Gorkhaland National Liberation Front (GNLF) in Darjeeling, refers only to "Gorkhas". The GNLF leader Subhas Ghising has argued that Nepali is a foreign language, and was deeply unhappy with its inclusion in the 8th Schedule (for which, see below). Much of the controversy surrounding the status of Indian Nepalis is concerned with nomenclature: "for the Nepalis of India the search for an appropriate term that indicates Indian nationality or which does not confuse them with the 'Nepalese' has long been a genuine concern" (Subba, 1992:

68). Until about 1980, the terms 'Gorkha', 'Gorkhali', and 'Nepali' were used more or less interchangeably in India, but there has since been a contraction of meaning and each has been invested with political connotations. The Bhutan government's application in 1958 of the Dzongkha term 'Lhotshampa' to the Nepali-speaking southern Bhutanese was clearly intended to be integrative, but outside the official media they are still more usually referred to as 'Nepalis' or 'Nepali Bhutanese'. Since its foundation, the GNLF has been violently opposed to the use of 'Nepali', whereas writers and intellectuals object strongly to the imposition of the name 'Gorkha' or 'Gorkhali' onto the literary language they share with contemporaries in Nepal. Synthetic terms such as *bhārpālī* (a contraction of *bhāratīya* (Indian) + *nepālī*) have failed to take root. In 1991, GNLF activists desecrated statues of Bhānubhaktā Āchārya (1814–68) in Darjeeling and Kalimpong. Bhānubhakta was the author of the first major work of modern Nepali literature, but the GNLF claimed that the statues honoured a foreign poet. In Kathmandu, Nepali intellectuals view such controversies with disbelief, but in India they amount to more than mere pedantry.

THE HISTORICAL BACKGROUND

Historically, migration from Nepal, as from anywhere else, can be explained in terms of both push and pull factors. During the late eighteenth, nineteenth, and early twentieth centuries, the movement was mainly eastward, and resulted in permanent settlement outside the kingdom's modern borders. The eastward drift of a culture based on the Nepali language, on the dominance of Brahmans, and of agricultural practices based on the use of the plough and, latterly, the cultivation of maize, has been a longterm process. The conquest and unification of Nepal by the Shah kings of Gorkha during the latter half of the eighteenth century represented a continuation of this process, which had begun about 800 years earlier with the establishment of a kingdom in the Karnali basin by a line of Khasa kings who probably spoke an archaic form of Nepali. The Khasa allegedly intermarried with Rajput

FIGURE 5   *The bust of Bhanubhakta Acharya in Darjeeling's Chowrasta, desecrated by GNLF activists in 1991 as a "foreign poet" (Michael Hutt)*

immigrants, and with local people, to form an ever-expanding Chetri caste, and their descendants spread from west to east, subjugating the local tribes and displacing their Tibeto-Burman languages, and imposing a more uniform Parbatiya culture. Eastward migration from eastern Nepal probably began on a comparatively small scale as a response to the Gorkhali conquest of districts inhabited mainly by Kiranti (Rai and Limbu) populations. The Gorkhalis conquered the Darjeeling hills and a portion of western Sikkim in 1780, and held on to these territories until 1816. Parbatiya cultivators were encouraged to migrate to the less densely-populated eastern districts, and they began to encroach on the indigenous people's ancestral lands. The Rais and Limbus responded by emigrating in ever-increasing numbers: by 1834 the government of Gorkha found it necessary to declare a ten-year moratorium on the repayment of loans because of the peasants' growing penury, brought on by the conversion of taxes to a cash medium (English, 1983: 258). Pradhan has estimated that between 12 and 15% of the total Kiranti population 'emigrated' from eastern Nepal to Darjeeling between 1840 and 1860 (Pradhan, 1991: 192).[8] Pradhan also refers to Imansingh Chemjong's history of Vijaypur, published in Nepali in 1974/75, in which Chemjong claims, citing a Limbu manuscript, that the Gorkhalis' punishment of local chiefs caused 32,000 Limbus to emigrate in three groups. One group is said to have gone to Assam, one to Sikkim, and one to Bhutan (*ibid.*: 137).

More recently, Nepalis have travelled in large numbers to north Indian cities to seek work, but this is a different phenomenon, and has not yet produced large, culturally cohesive communities like those in the older eastern diaspora (see CNAS, 1987; Dixit, 1988). It has become something of a commonplace in media and government circles in Kathmandu to assert that "sixty lakhs" of Nepalis (i.e. six million) are working in India. As has been shown above, the census data currently available do not support this assertion, and one can only assume that it refers in part to Nepalis employed in India on a short term or temporary basis. In a seminar in London, Joanna Pfaff-Czarnecka gave one example of this. She described how Nepalese nationals from the far-western district of Bajhang provided virtually all the nightwatchmen for the south Indian city of Bangalore. Most would work in Bangalore for a period of two or three years, after which their place would be taken by another Bajhangi.[9] Dr. Pfaff estimated that approximately 16,000 Bajhangi men are employed in Bangalore at any given time.

During the nineteenth and early twentieth centuries, permanent emigration from Nepal was also encouraged by two major pull factors. The first resulted from the so-called 'granting' of Darjeeling to the British by the Maharaja of Sikkim in 1835.[10] Nineteen years earlier, following the Anglo-Nepalese wars, all of the territory captured by the Gorkhalis east of the Mechi river (now Nepal's eastern border) had been handed over to the British. In 1817 the British then returned the tracts of Sikkimese land, plus the Darjeeling hills, to Sikkim.[11] In the early years of British rule, the tiny settlement of Darjeeling became a sanatorium and place of refuge for ailing British civil servants fleeing the heat of the plains. Very soon, however, the teaplanters moved in. Tea was first planted commercially in 1852, and by 1891, 177 gardens had been established, covering a total of 45,000 acres. The production of tea is labour-intensive, but the Darjeeling hills contained few potential labourers. By 1876 the tea industry employed 19,000 workers, of whom over 90% came from the hills of eastern Nepal. However, the Darjeeling tea industry declined throughout the twentieth century and by the mid-1980s less than a third of the gardens were still in production. The establishment of a Nepali community based on the tea industry in Darjeeling therefore appears to have taken place between 1852 and the end of the nineteenth century (Subba, 1992: 27–50).[12] Pradhan argues that there were already large numbers of Nepalis in the district prior to this. He reproduces the texts of two letters written in Nepali in 1815 and 1826 which support the idea of much coming and going between eastern Nepal and Darjeeling (1982: 13–14), and points out that the word used by British officials to denote porters and labourers was not 'coolie' but the Nepali *bhariyā* ("bhurriah" in British records). The body of men formed to build and maintain roads in the Darjeeling district in 1839 was, according to Pradhan, "composed almost entirely of Nepalis" (1982: 20–21).

The second major pull factor was the recruitment of Gurkha soldiers into the British Indian army. This began during, or shortly after, the Anglo-Nepalese wars of 1814–16, when over 4,500 Nepalis enlisted, attracted by the fact that the British paid in cash, not in kind. The Sikhs also recruited Nepalis into their army from a very early stage: a third cousin of Jang Bahadur Rana, for instance, died fighting for the Sikhs in Afghanistan in 1824, and by 1830 the army of Ranjit Singh included a special Gurkha corps (see Whelpton, 1987; Mojumdar, 1973: 63 fn. 110; Pant, 1965/6). This fact is reflected in the Nepali word for a soldier who serves in a foreign army: the term *lāhure* is derived from Lahore, the Sikhs' main recruiting centre. Because the British were not allowed to recruit inside Nepal, they encouraged Nepalis to settle outside its borders. The Ranas turned a blind eye to recruiting inside Nepal by local agents and in 1887 Gorakhpur in India became the formal headquarters of Gurkha recruitment, recruiting mainly Magars and Gurungs from central Nepal. By 1902 a recruitment centre was also in operation at Ghoom near Darjeeling, attracting mainly Rais and Limbus. By 1908, approximately 55,000 men had been enlisted (Subba, 1992: 58). Admittedly, such men left Nepal to enlist, not to emigrate permanently. However, there was a marked tendency for them to settle in India after leaving military service: it has been noted that only about one third of the 11,000 Gurkhas discharged from the British Indian Army after the First World War chose to return to Nepal (Blaikie, Cameron, and Seddon, 1980: 37).

THE DEVELOPMENT OF A NEPALI-GORKHALI ETHNIC IDENTITY IN INDIA

The terms 'Nepali' and 'Nepalese' were first used by the British, but during the 1920s there was a gradual move away from the use of 'Gorkha' and 'Gorkhali' towards 'Nepali' among Nepali-speaking intellectuals too. The Nepālī Sāhitya Sammelan (Nepali Literature Association), founded in Darjeeling in 1924, was the first institution to use the name. The Nepal government's publishing and censorship body was established in 1913 as the *Gorkhā Bhāshā*

Prakāshinī Samiti (Gorkha Language Publication Committee), but in 1930 the word 'Gorkhā' was replaced with 'Nepālī'. The emergence of a cohesive ethnic identity among Nepalis in India dates back no further than this time, and can again be attributed to both positive and negative factors. In isolation, the positive factors would probably account for a passive communal identification, but the negative factors have made this identification assertive.

INTERNAL FACTORS: ETHNICITY, LANGUAGE, AND CULTURE

It is significant that the majority of the Nepali emigrants who founded the diaspora communities were of Tibeto-Burman extraction. Even today, around 84% of the Nepali population of Darjeeling consists of Rais, Limbus, Tamangs, Magars, Gurungs, Sunwars, and Newars. Alongside this 'Nepali' community there live groups who have at times made common cause with them: Lepchas, Bhotiyas, and Tibetans,[13] and plainspeople such as Bengalis, Marwaris, and Biharis who for obvious cultural and linguistic reasons do not identify with them much, if at all. Until 1951, the Darjeeling district census enumerated the members of each *jāt* (caste or ethnic group). Between 1901 and 1951, the number of persons belonging to the various Nepalese *jāt*s doubled in number, but the relative proportions of each *jāt* changed very little. According to figures reproduced by Pradhan, roughly one in seven was a Rai, one in nine was a Tamang, while Brahmans numbered only 11,000 in a total Nepalese population of 445,000 in 1951. Those who might be assumed to have Nepali as their mother-tongue (Brahmans, Chetris, Kamis, Sarkis, and Damais) constituted a minority of around 20% (Pradhan, 1982: 36). A striking feature of the diaspora is the rapidity with which mother-tongues appear from the censuses to fall into disuse in favour of Nepali, often within a single generation. Although Nepali was the ancestral language of only some 20% of the Nepalese population of Darjeeling, the 1961 Census of West Bengal (1967: 238–55) recorded that 59% claimed Nepali as mother-tongue. Here it is important to see censuses not only as exercises that produce data, but also as opportunities for particular groups and communities to assert or emphasize particular strands of their identity. The radical change in these language figures may well reflect not only a change in language use, but also a change in the respondents' *declaration* of their language use. And this change in self-representation must be, at least in part, a response to the internal and external factors outlined in this chapter.

Most Bhotiyas and Tibetans in Sikkim and the Darjeeling district have not abandoned their mother-tongue, although they have for the most part acquired Nepali as an additional language. According to Chie Nakane, "even those Nepalis who have lived in a Lepcha-Bhotia community [in Sikkim] for many years do not, as a rule, speak the Bhotia language... Lepchas and Bhotias seem much more successful in learning Nepali, and those who are accustomed to go to the Gangtok bazaar, or who have contact with government officials, are fluent in Nepali; most Bhotia peasants who have contacts with Nepalis in their own village speak at least broken Nepali" (Nakane, 1966: 261–2). She states that this is partly because "Bhotia" is a "complicated tonal language not easily learnt by the average Nepali peasant" (*ibid*.: 261) and then goes on to mention that "Nepali is a kind of lingua franca used widely throughout the Himalayan area" (*ibid*.: 262). In my view, the second factor is far more important in determining the direction of language shift than the first, which is in any case based on a subjective assessment of the inherent difficulty of the "Bhotia" language and on the supposition that "Nepali peasants" are less able to acquire a new language than Bhotiyas.

The Nepali spoken in West Bengal, Assam, and Bhutan differs from that of central and western Nepal in several important respects. In the spoken language, feminine and plural agreement of adjectives and verbs is largely ignored, and there are differences in pronunciation and intonation. In both the spoken and written versions of the so-called Darjeeling dialect, nouns commonly used in Kathmandu (*jhyāl*, 'window'; *pasal*, 'shop'; *syāu*, 'apple') are largely unknown, and different vocabulary is used, shared with Hindi or, in some cases, drawn from English (*khirkī, dokān, āiphal*). Much the same is true of the spoken Nepali of eastern Nepal, though here the difference is less significant because eastern Nepal does not have a Nepali literary tradition of its own, whereas Darjeeling certainly does. It is not difficult for a Kathmandu Nepali to identify an easterner or a Darjeeling Nepali from his or her accent and perceived grammatical laxity.

The Nepali language is the basis of Nepali ethnic identity outside Nepal: it is the primary basis for self-identification with the diaspora community. This is why so much of the argument about the status of Nepalis in India, and to a lesser extent in Bhutan, has focused on the status of their language. It may also represent a small part of the Bhutanese government's rationale for removing Nepali from the Bhutanese school curriculum at the beginning of the school year in 1990.[14] Ethnically, culturally, and linguistically, the various emigrant groups had comparatively little in common with one another at first. Although various insignia – the *khukri* knife, the Nepalese *ṭopī* (cap) – are adopted as other means of self-identification, and although the Bajhangis in Bangalore play up to the stereotypical image that Indians hold of Gorkhas, because it is to their advantage to do so, Nepali has no single term that adequately conveys the manifold connotations of the English word 'race'. *Jāti* is commonly used in the same contexts – *mānav jāti*, 'the human race', *nepālī jāti*, 'the Nepali race' – but its basic meaning is 'species' or 'type', as distinct from *jāt*, used to mean 'caste' which, in a Nepalese context, is frequently the same as 'ethnic group' – Gurung, Rai, Brahman, etc. However, the terms *jāt* and *jāti* are used almost interchangeably in common Nepali parlance and the standard dictionary (the *Nepālī Bṛhat Shabdakosh*), as Whelpton points out, employs each term in its definition of the other (above, p.76 note 25). Munshi and Chakrabarti's questions on ethnicity and race in Darjeeling in 1974, (Munshi and Chakrabarti, 1979) discussed in more detail below, drew responses in which the respondents identified themselves as members of what one might term a *jāti* (Nepali, or Indian Nepali), a *jāt* (Rai, Gurung, Brahman, etc.), or a *thar* (clan or kinship group, the name of which may also indicate which *jāt* its holder belongs to – though some *jāt*s do have *thar* names in common).

Lengthy discussions on the use of the term 'Nepali' took place during the founding of the Nepālī Sāhitya Sammelan in

Darjeeling in 1924. Hariprasad Pradhan, the chairman of the inaugural meeting, argued:

> We should call this organization the Nepālī Sāhitya Sammelan because the word 'Nepali' has a broad meaning. It refers to all the races (*jāti*) of Nepal – Magar, Gurung, Kirati, Newar, Limbu, and so on – and indicates that these and all the other races here are parts of a great Nepali nation (*rāṣṭra*) ... Nepali nowadays is like a lingua franca in the Himalayan region (*pradeś*). Although the people living in this region speak different tongues (*bolī*), there is no one who does not understand Nepali ... And no one race can claim that this language (*bhāṣā*) belongs to it alone (Pradhan, 1982: 37–9; my translation).

A distinction is made here between *bolī* (spoken tongues, i.e. minor languages or dialects) and *bhāṣā* (languages), and the inference is that the various 'races' of Nepal are to be subsumed into a single greater entity, here termed a 'nation' (*rāṭra*). At the same meeting, Paras Mani Pradhan offered much the same justification for the use of the word 'Nepali', but used slightly different terminology. It is as if the old *jāti* categories – Rai, Limbu etc. – were in the process of being downgraded to the status of *jāt*s, and subsumed within a single new construct: that of the Nepali-speakers constituting a single *jāti*:

> Now, blood (*ragat*), dress, and religion (*dharma*) are completely rejected as bases of racehood (*jātiyatā*). One finds a variety of bloods, costumes, and religions. The Darjeeling Nepalis have become a *jāti* that is bound together by the thread (*sūtra*) of common experience, shared sentiments, and a single language (Pradhan, 1982: 44; my translation).

Up until the twilight years of the Rana regime in Nepal, much of the modernization and development of Nepali and its literature took place in India, where educational facilities were more generally available and Rana censorship largely ineffective. The

earliest Nepali newspaper was the *Gorkhā Bhārat Jīvan*, published in
Banaras during the late 1880s, and this was followed in India by
Gorkhe Khabar Kāgat (Darjeeling, 1901), *Sundarī* (Banaras, 1906),
Mādhavī (Banaras, 1908), *Gorkhālī* (Banaras, 1915), *Chandrikā*
(Kurseong, 1917), and the Gorkha League journals *Gorkhā Saṃsār*
(Dehra Dun, 1926) and *Taruṇa Gorkhā* (Dehra Dun, 1928)
(Devkoṭā, 1967). In 1938 the Nepali Sahitya Sammelan published
Kathā-Kusum, the first anthology of Nepali short stories. A Nepali
intellectual and journalistic tradition therefore existed in India rather
earlier than it did in Nepal itself and, while most of Kathmandu's
literati were Brahmans, Chetris, or Newars, four of the five Nepali
writers honoured by the Indian Sahitya Akademi prior to 1982 were
Rais (Pradhan, 1982: 36).

The majority of the nineteenth-century emigrants came from
hill minorities which had only a thin veneer of Hinduism. The
Muluki Ain, which codified Hindu caste laws and incorporated
traditionally non-Hindu minorities into the caste hierarchy in
Nepal, was promulgated in 1854, just as the tea gardens were being
established. The emigrants continued to attach less importance to
considerations of purity and ritual status than those they left behind,
and there were therefore fewer barriers between them. The Muluki
Ain was derived from a variety of sources, but the most important
were: the *Arthashastra* of Kautilya; the codification of caste laws
supposedly promulgated by Sthiti Malla, the ruler of the Kathmandu
Valley kingdom (r. 1382–95); and actual practice (Höfer, 1979: 41).
However, 'actual practice' with regard to caste differentiation varied
considerably from place to place, and it is entirely logical to assume
that, since Sanskritization was a process that moved (broadly) from
west to east through what is now Nepal, the situation among the
'tribals' of the east diverged most radically from the uniform
orthodoxy that the compilers of the Legal Code sought to impose.[15]
In the more remote corners of the diaspora, there are still vestiges
of old cultural practices. In southern Bhutan, polygyny appears to
be practised to a far greater extent than it is in Nepal – whether this
represents the survival of an old practice or a response to a new
situation (such as, perhaps, a change in the vital ratio of land to
labour) is not clear.

EXTERNAL FACTORS: HARDSHIP AND DISCRIMINATION

Negative factors explain the assertiveness of the Nepali minority more thoroughly than the positive factors outlined above, although both have been essential ingredients in the emergence of a cohesive ethnic identity. The deep-seated sense of insecurity felt by Indian and Bhutanese Nepalis is not well understood, but is an important factor in the political and ethnic turmoil of the regions they inhabit.

Economic Hardship

dāju sardār bainī kullī tupīsamma rin
"Elder brother's a head porter, younger sister's a coolie; debt right over our heads." (Hajirman Rai, 1900, quoted in Pradhan, 1982: 30).

As emigré workers, the Nepalis of north-east India have suffered a high degree of exploitation. In the main industries of the Darjeeling district (tea, timber, and tourism), Nepalis constitute the vast majority of the workforce, but are almost wholly absent from the ownership or management of any concern. Such positions are invariably occupied by plainspeople.[16] The West Bengal state government produced a cascade of statistics during the 1980s to prove that "per capita expenditure by the State government on Darjeeling is double that of other districts and the per capita income of Darjeeling is the fourth highest" (Jyoti Basu, Chief Minister of West Bengal, quoted in Timsina, 1992: 53), but the under-representation of Nepalis in the upper echelons of the local administration seemed to go unaddressed. As Subba notes, "if [an ethnic group] feels that it is neglected, no statistical figures can erase that feeling" (Subba, 1992: 43). This sense of deprivation has been accentuated in Darjeeling in recent years by the contrast with Sikkim. Whereas the Gorkhaland movement brought all economic activity bar agriculture to a halt in the Darjeeling hills between 1986 and 1988, the economy of Sikkim has boomed.[17]

In Bhutan and Sikkim, many Nepali immigrants very rapidly became more prosperous than their 'hosts' by clearing forests, establishing fields, and planting crops. In Bhutan, the Nepali immigrants turned what had until the end of the nineteenth century been an unproductive hinterland into the kingdom's main food producing area. The authors of the unpublished 'History of Sikkim', quoted by Nakane, describe the arrival of these immigrants in language which suggests that they were considered a threat:

> Since the year 1871 ... there was an influx of Gorkhalis from the neighbouring state of Nepal ... They settled down for good, and began digging, hoeing, smashing and overturning rocks, felling down [sic] trees, and turning the courses of streams at such a rate that all jungles were turned into fields, in a very short time (Nakane, 1966: 251).

Nakane attempts to explain the fact that "within a couple of decades after ... the first Nepali immigrant settled down in the Lepcha-Bhotia community, ... many [Nepalis] have become wealthier than the former inhabitants" (Nakane, 1966: 256). She argues that the principal factor has been "closely related to the religious differences between the Buddhists and Hindus" and examines the economic implications of these differences. The main thrust of her argument is that some Lepchas and "Bhotias" engage in "priestly activities" and are thus economically unproductive; that Nepali children and women engage in labour alongside Nepali men; and that Lepchas and "Bhotias" have a higher pattern of consumption because they expend a great deal more than the Nepalis do on religious activities. Nakane's work is of immense value, since it is one of only a few instances where such research has been permitted in Sikkim. However, when dealing with the relative economic status of the Nepalis on the one hand and the "Bhotias" and Lepchas on the other, the article lacks a broader perspective. Trevor Ling's criticism of this aspect of Nakane's analysis as a "monofactoral explanation" is therefore not without validity. Ling argues that the relations between the two communities were

> not only those of Buddhist and Hindu, but also those of *settled inhabitant* and *recent immigrant* ... The *poverty* of the vast majority of Nepal's peasants is the basic datum from

which consideration of the activities of those of them who succeeded in entering and settling in Sikkim has to begin. Given this, it is not difficult to understand that such immigrants would be prepared to work intensively for even a reasonable reward and, being accustomed in Nepal to the lowest possible standards of expenditure on dress and food, they would find no great hardship in being satisfied with a somewhat more restricted consumption than their Bhotia-Lepcha neighbours during at least their early years in Sikkim. The contrast that Chie Nakane draws, therefore, is between the settled inhabitants of the Sikkimese state and impoverished refugees from Gurkhali rule (Ling, 1985: 125; emphasis in the original).

Indian Attitudes to Gurkha Soldiers

In strong contrast to the whole-heartedly positive British attitude to the Gurkha soldier, the Indian attitude has often been ambivalent – particularly during the period of British rule. At independence, the Indian government was anxious to retain its Gorkha regiments, which are now far larger than their British counterparts. This may have been prompted partly by a desire to maintain a strong Hindu element in an army with a large contingent of Muslims and Sikhs, whose loyalty at the time of partition did not go unquestioned. Anti-Gorkha sentiments in India arose from the use of Gorkha soldiers to put down the sepoy rebellion in 1857, in the Jalianwala Bagh massacre, against 'Quit India' demonstrators in 1942 and afterward, and on many other occasions to suppress the Indian Nationalist movement. By the 1920s, some Gorkhas might have been second-generation Indian Nepalis, despite the British prejudice against recruits who had not grown up in the hills.[18] Nonetheless, in letters sent by the Political and Foreign Department to all district commissioners on July 21 1923 and October 1 1926, it was stipulated that the "*raiyats* [subjects] of Nepal" should not be employed except in the armed forces (Subba, 1992: 60). Subba claims that after Gorkhas were deployed to put down communal riots in Calcutta in February 1946, many Indian Nepalis suffered severe harrassment, particularly in Bengal. The government even decided to ban the wearing of the *khukri* – still a potent symbol of ethnic identy – but found the order unenforcable (Subba, 1992: 61; Pradhan, 1982: 28).[19] Indian Nepalis formed a number of organizations to protect their interests – notably the Gorkha Samiti in 1906 and the All-India Gorkha League in 1943 – and publications such as *Gorkhā Saṃsār*, founded in Dehra Dun in 1926, vocalized their concerns.

CITIZENSHIP AND NATIONALITY

Whether they are of Nepalese birth, or Gorkhas born in India, all ethnic Nepalis in India are liable to be assumed to be foreign nationals or immigrants. This attitude persists today, and sinister political motives are often imputed to leaders of the Indian and Bhutanese Nepali communities. Subba quotes from a Bengali writer's analysis of an increase from 19% to 59% in the Nepali population of Darjeeling, as recorded in the censuses of 1951 and 1961. This statistical blip can actually be explained by a change in the census questionnaire (the 1941 figure had been 67%), but Snehamoy Chaklader put it down to "[the Nepalis'] urge for the formation of a bigger group with a view to preserving their separate identity and gaining some benefits in a foreign country" (Subba, 1992: 5). Similar rhetoric appeared regularly during the early 1990s in Bhutanese denunciations of *ngolop*s (anti-nationals; literally, 'rebels') in the southern districts of Bhutan, where a predominantly Nepali-speaking population was encouraged to settle by a government-authorized commissioner at the beginning of the present century (Sinha, 1991: 36–40). It is impossible to venture anything more than a subjective opinion on the proportion of the southern Bhutanese population that consists of illegal post-1958 immigrants (the government of Bhutan claimed in 1988 to have detected 100,000), but the bulk of the southern Bhutanese Nepali community appears to be the product of primary migration from Nepal.[20] British reports are the only sources of information on early Nepali migration to Bhutan: there are references to a "considerable community" along the length of southern Bhutan in the 1890s,[21] to "about 15,000, of whom 14,000 were Nepalese" in Sipchoo and Tsangbe in 1904;[22] to "60,000" in south-west Bhutan in 1932;[23] and in 1938 to a "very practical problem" of whether "the local races are destined to be overwhelmed by the Nepalese".[24] With such a large Nepali population in the south at such an early stage, an annual population growth rate of 3% could conceivably have produced a Nepali community in Bhutan of around 200,000 without any need for immigration, legal or otherwise. The date when the migration commenced may also be somewhat earlier than is usually supposed: Christopher Strawn has reproduced the text of a handwritten deed of settlement with which the pönlop (referred to as "Bhar Raja Rinphu Raja") of Paro granted land in southern Bhutan (Chamarchi) to Sardar Dalchan Gurung and his son Gajarman Gurung in Bhadra V. S. 1944 (August/September 1887) (Strawn, 1993: 292–3).

The likelihood is that the Nepali diaspora in northeast India and Bhutan is the product of primary migration from eastern Nepal that reached its peak at the turn of the century and then subsided, rather than of the emigration from Nepal that has undoubtedly continued, but in a different manner and to different destinations, since 1950. This view is supported by a small piece of relevant research conducted in three tea estates near Darjeeling in 1974, during which 411 randomly-selected hillpeople were interviewed. To the question "what is your *jāti?*", 276 answered "Nepali", 64 answered "Bhāratīya Nepali", and 55 gave Nepalese caste or tribal names. Most were aware that their families had migrated to the district from eastern Nepal, but 67% dated this migration (*basāī sārne*) back two generations, and 32% dated it back three generations. 85% of those interviewed had been born in the Darjeeling district, 48% had never travelled outside the district, and only 13% had ever visited Nepal (Munshi and Chakrabarti, 1979: 701–9). Furthermore, whereas one sixth of the Nepalese population of Darjeeling in 1931 was born in Nepal, by 1951 the number had dropped to only 749 in a total of 445,260 (Pradhan, 1982: 33).

The status of Nepalis in India, and of Indians in Nepal, is governed by article 7 of the Indo-Nepal Treaty of Peace and Friendship, concluded on July 31 1950. The Article states, "the

Governments of India and Nepal agree to grant, on a reciprocal basis, to the nationals of one country in the territories of the other, the same privileges in the matter of residence, ownership of property, participation in trade and commerce, movement and other privileges of a similar nature" (Timsïna, 1992: 79). This article is resented by many Indian Nepalis, and its abrogation was one of the central demands of the Gorkhaland movement. Texts of the article were burned in mass demonstrations throughout the Darjeeling district on 27 July 1986. Indeed, the Indo-Nepal Treaty is one of the principal causes of the Indian Nepalis' sense of insecurity. Ethnic Nepalis all enjoy the same status in India, whether they are Indian nationals or citizens of Nepal. Those who are Indian nationals cannot easily prove their citizenship when the Treaty makes no distinction between them and Nepalese nationals. The reciprocal nature of the Treaty is also problematic: if the government of Nepal takes steps to limit the rights of Indians in Nepal, as it tried to do in 1989, Indian Nepalis feel vulnerable. Although they may have been Indian citizens for generations, their status in India is still dependent upon Nepalese government policies, in which they have no say whatsoever.

In northeastern states such as Meghalaya and Mizoram, the need for a Restricted Area Permit caused Indian Nepalis great problems, perhaps because most were assumed to be Nepalese unless they could prove otherwise. In the course of *bhūmiputra* ('sons of the soil') movements, between 13,000 and 17,000 were expelled from Meghalaya in 1980–86,[25] 8,000 from Mizoram in 1967, 2,000 from Manipur in 1980, and thousands fled from Assam after 1979. Nepalis were also expelled in sizable numbers from Burma during the 1960s.[26] Legal arguments are advanced to justify the various expulsions of Nepalis from north-east India and Bhutan, but in practice they have often occurred on a purely ethnic basis. The Bhutanese government claims that those being expelled from the south of the kingdom are illegal residents according to citizenship laws promulgated in 1958, 1977, and 1985, and that they have been identified as such by a census operation which began in 1988. The exiled Lhotshampas complain that this last act has been implemented retroactively, expelling many who had been granted full citizenship between 1958 and 1985.[27] Refugee statements suggest that in practice many were driven from their homes without any reference to their status or non-status as citizens, because they were suspected of having supported or participated in anti-government demonstrations in September and October 1990.[28]

The simple fact of the matter is that a Newar or a Limbu born in Darjeeling, Bhutan, or Assam will always be considered 'Nepali', even if he or she adopts the label 'Gorkha' or 'Lhotshampa', just as a Bihari or a Marwari who has no home other than Kathmandu will always be considered 'Indian'. Throughout this century, Indian Nepalis have struggled to forge an identity for themselves that distinguishes them from the Nepalese of Nepal, so that they might emerge as a distinct ethnic group within India for, as Ronen has remarked in a more general Third World context, "ethnic identity [during the 1960s] had become an organizational form, a weapon, a tool, and/or a means for the attainment of goals" (Thompson and Ronen, 1986: 6).

THE STATUS OF THE NEPALI LANGUAGE

The long-standing campaign for the inclusion of Nepali in the 8th Schedule of the Indian Constitution came to fruition on 20 August 1992. It had many antecedents: first there came a modest demand for the approval of Nepali as the medium of instruction in Darjeeling schools, achieved at primary level in 1927. Next, the demand was for the adoption of Nepali as an official language in Darjeeling. In 1958, the West Bengal Official Languages Bill opted for Bengali as sole language: this led to widespread protests in the hills and, after an inquiry, Nepali was included as an additional language for the three hill subdivisions, though implementation was delayed until 1971.

The first explicit demand for the inclusion of Nepali in the 8th Schedule was made in 1956. The precise status of the languages included in the Schedule, and the criteria for their selection, are still somewhat unclear. The Schedule originally listed 14 languages,[29] to which Sindhi was added in 1967, and is appended to articles 344(1) and 351 of Part XVII of the Indian Constitution, headed "Official Language". The languages of the 8th Schedule have been described in various ways at different times. According to Article 351, they are "languages of India" and "sources of enrichment" for the national language, Hindi. According to Article 344 (1), they can be used, on the president's recommendation, in High Courts and the Supreme Court. They have been described as "national languages", "regional languages", and "languages that need to be developed". Most significantly, perhaps, a resolution was adopted in 1967 which called for the coordinated development of all 8th Schedule languages, and prescribed that they be allowed as alternative media for All-India and higher central service examinations (Munshi and Chakrabarti, 1979: 704). The criteria governing the inclusion of a language in the 8th Schedule do not appear to include the number of its speakers: according to the 1971 Census of India, there were 1,372,000 speakers of Sindhi (which received constitutional recognition in 1967), but 1,419,000 speakers of Nepali.

A delegation of the Akhil Bharatiya Nepali Bhasha Samiti (All-India Nepali Language Committee) met the Indian Prime Minister, Moraji Desai, in September 1977, asking for the inclusion of Nepali on the grounds that it represented "the long-cherished aspiration of over five million Indians with Nepali as their mother-tongue" who suffered from a "sense of insecurity" because of its exclusion from the Schedule. The delegation's communication argued that the inclusion of Nepali would bring about "the development of a linguistic minority" and "emotional integration", and pointed out that the same demand had been supported by 74 MPs in 1971, and now had the backing of the state governments of West Bengal and Sikkim. However, Desai was opposed to any move to extend the 8th Schedule: referring to Nepali as a "foreign language", he argued that its inclusion would set a precedent for scores of tribal languages (Munshi and Chakrabarti, 1979: 705). The campaign for Nepali subsequently became more strident, but its success in 1992 was probably attributable to the election of a more pro-Indian government in Kathmandu, and to Indian hopes that the inclusion of Nepali would prompt a reciprocal move with respect to Hindi on the part of the Nepalese government, as was being demanded by the Tarai-based Nepal Sadbhavana Party. According recognition to 'Nepali' rather than to 'Gorkhali' also deepened the rift that already existed between the troublesome GNLF leader, Subhas Ghising, who had been pushing for the recognition of 'Gorkhali', and the chief minister of Sikkim, Nar Bahadur Bhandari, who had argued the case of 'Nepali'. Such a rift is in the interests of the central government (Datta-Ray, 1992).[30]

THE SEARCH FOR A HOME WITHIN INDIA

We came here looking for a place where we could see the Himalaya clearly. Now we don't want to go anywhere else. All of us should have a house where we can open the window each morning and look at the Himalaya ... Wherever we go we will take this land with us, wrapped up in little bundles (Indra Bahadur Rai in Hutt, 1991a: 263).

The ethno-political movement of the Indian Nepalis dates back more than 80 years, but it remained largely non-violent until 1986. At first it involved a loose alliance of ethnic groups – 'hillpeople' (Nepalis, Bhotiyas, and Lepchas) united by a common lingua franca and a shared sense of economic and political disadvantage. However, as the movement progressed, it came to be dominated by Nepalis who called themselves 'Gorkhas', and the other factions were marginalized.

The first demand for a "separate administrative set-up" for Darjeeling was put before the government in 1907, and similar demands were made again in 1919 and 1929, inspired by the Home Rule movement. Economic considerations precluded any concessions on the part of the government. In ca. 1917 the Gorkha-dominated Hillmen's Association was formed and the common cause of the various hill communities came under increasing strain. The association's sole Bhotiya member, Laden La, opposed the introduction of Nepali as the medium of primary school instruction in 1927, and in 1934 the Association's demand for an "independent

FIGURE 6   *Indra Bahadur Rai, a leading Nepali writer in Darjeeling*
(Michael Hutt)

administrative unit" made reference only to the "problems of the Gurkha population". In an attempt to bring the hill communities together again, Laden La called a mass meeting in Darjeeling in 1934, which created the Hill People's Union. The Union began the publication of a celebrated Nepali monthly entitled *Nebulā* (i.e.

Ne-B[h]u-L ā: Nepali, Bhutia, Lāpche) in February 1935 (Adhikari, 1975: 145).[31] In the early 1980s, the Gorkhaland National Liberation Front (GNLF) attempted to revive the spirit of *Nebulā* with slogans such as *lāpche, bhutiyā nepālī, hāmī sabai gorkhālī* ("Lepcha, Bhutia, Nepali – we are all Gorkhali"), but by then the Gorkhas' dominance was too well-established, and the Lepchas and Bhotiyas too disenchanted (Subba, 1992: 66).

The All-India Gorkha League (AIGL) was founded in Dehra Dun in 1923, and replaced the Hillmen's Association in Darjeeling in 1943. Its mouthpiece was the monthly *Gorkhā*, and in 1949 it launched the most concerted campaign so far for a separate province, tabling several options all called *Uttarakhand*. These options ranged from separate status for Darjeeling alone to separate status for a region that included Darjeeling, Sikkim, and a portion of the Dooars and Siliguri lowlands. The Uttarakhand movement struck a chord in the public imagination, and was widely discussed and supported throughout the hills. But the anti-Rana uprising in Nepal distracted the attention of its proponents and by 1955, when the West Bengal Congress Committee addressed the issue, the regional scene had changed irrevocably and the movement's leaders had faded away.

Communism was established as a political force in Darjeeling during the 1940s: at first the Communist Party of India (CPI) collaborated with the AIGL, but later delinked from it and began to campaign among the exploited workers on the tea estates. The utopian and impracticable demand for a 'greater Nepal' or 'Gorkhasthan' comprising Nepal, southern Sikkim, and Darjeeling was first raised by the CPI in 1947. The spectre of 'greater Nepal' still inspires fear in Bhutan, and has also been raised by the GNLF leader Subhas Ghising, a staunch anti-communist, who claimed in 1993 that a campaign for a 'greater Nepal' was being coordinated by the Communist opposition in Kathmandu and the CPI(M) in West Bengal. The claim was flatly denied by the Nepalese Communist leader Man Mohan Adhikari (Chaudhuri, 1991; Dixit, 1993).[32]

The demand for separate statehood for Darjeeling and the Dooars area of Jalpaiguri was pressed more systematically after the establishment of the Pranta Parishad and the GNLF in 1980 and the Swatantra Manch in 1985. Between May 1986 and December 1988, the Gorkhaland movement involved extreme violence and the total disruption of everyday life in the hill districts of West Bengal. Violence took place between the nationalists ('Gorkhas') of the GNLF and the communists ('Nepalis') of the CPI(M); between the GNLF and the security forces (especially the Central Reserve Police Force); and between rival factions within the GNLF itself. Total casualty figures are difficult to establish, but it is generally believed that about 200 people died during the two and half years of violence, of whom 50–60 were police personnel.

The GNLF's central demands were made in a meeting between Subhas Ghising and Rajiv Gandhi on July 22 1987. They were: the abrogation of article 7 of the Indo-Nepal Treaty; the creation of a separate state of Gorkhaland within the framework of the Indian Constitution; the establishment of an "Indian Gorkha" regiment and the cessation of recruitment of Indian Nepalis into the 'agreement regiments';[33] and the inclusion of the 'Gorkhali' language in the 8th Schedule (Timsina, 1992: 97–98). Settlement of these demands was delayed and complicated by the strained relations which existed between the Left Front government of West Bengal and the central Congress (I) government in Delhi. Both used the Gorkhaland agitation as a stick with which to beat the other on numerous occasions. Tripartite talks were held in Delhi in January 1987, but final agreement was not reached until July 1988. On August 22 1988 an accord on the creation of a Darjeeling Gorkha Hill Council was signed in Calcutta, and a "notification on citizenship issues" was signed in Delhi the following day. The GNLF had agreed to drop its demand for a separate state "in the overall national interest", and had settled for a 42-member Council, consisting of 28 elected members and 14 state government nominees, to administer the hill sub-divisions of Darjeeling, Kalimpong, and Kurseong, and a section of Siliguri subdivision. In polling on December 13 1988, the GNLF won 26 of the electable seats, and on January 7 1989 the State announced its nominees, 13 of whom were CPI(M) members.

The "notification on citizenship" was not an abrogation of the 1950 Treaty, but underlined the rights of "certain classes of persons commonly known as Gorkhas" to citizenship by virtue of

(a) domicile in India as of 26 January 1950 (the date of the commencement of the Constitution), (b) ordinary residence for a minimum of five years before that date, (c) birth in India, and (d) birth of either parent in India (Subba, 1992: 269–270). The Hill Council and the citizenship notification were the Gorkhaland movement's two principal achievements, and both represented compromises. Their attainment demolished much of Darjeeling's economy, and disillusioned many of the movement's supporters. The violence of the movement itself may also have played a major part in convincing the Bhutanese government that its Nepali population was a political liablility.

THE NEPALIZATION OF SIKKIM

It has today become a commonplace to assert that Sikkim's loss of sovereignty and merger with India were direct consequences of the emergence of a Nepali-speaking majority in the former kingdom. It therefore becomes axiomatic that Bhutan has lessons to learn from the experience of Sikkim. But although many parallels undoubtedly exist between the two demographic and political situations, there are also important differences. First, it is abundantly clear that Sikkim's Nepali majority is not of recent origin. Sinha (1975: 10) presents census data showing that Nepalis formed just over 50% of the total population of 30,458 in 1891, and 75–80% of the total population of 109, 808 in 1931. Of the three main ethnic groups (Nepali, Bhutia, Lepcha), the Bhutias formed the smallest element. After an Indian intervention in 1949, the interests of the two minority groups were safeguarded by labyrinthine electoral conventions designed to maintain "parity" between the Nepalis on the one hand and the Bhutias and Lepchas on the other. In elections to the Sikkim Assembly in 1953, the candidate securing the highest number of votes from the ethnic group he represented had also to secure at least 15% of the votes of one other community. If he failed in this, a runner-up from his own community who *had* secured 15% of the votes of another ethnic group could be elected. The Assembly comprised six Nepali seats and six Bhutia-Lepcha seats, and the electoral process for each half of the House was different (Rao, 1978: 17). That these arrangements were unpopular among the Nepali leaders is unsurprising. But other factors that have little to do with ethnicity also help to explain the apparent paradox of 14 April 1975, when the people of Sikkim voted by a huge majority to merge their state with India.

Here, the personalities of the principal players in the drama seem to have been crucial. Rustomji's account focuses upon the author's long friendship with the last Chogyal, Palden Thondup Namgyal: the two men had known one another since their schooldays, and Rustomji acted for the Government of India as the Dewan in Gangtok from 1954–9. Nonetheless, Rustomji levels the occasional criticism. He observes that "[the then Crown Prince's] nostalgia for the traditional values of the Sikkim of his fathers gave rise to an apprehension amongst the Nepalese that they were not only not wanted in Sikkim but that they would be denied full citizen rights" (Rustomji, 1987: 42). Later, he argues, "even amongst the Nepalese [in 1973] the desideratum was not, perhaps, merger so much as the clipping of the ruler's wings, and their vote was, in effect, a vote for a more democratic form of government as against an absolute monarchy" (*ibid.*: 150). B. S. Das, the Indian government's Chief Executive in Sikkim from April 1973 to September 1974, mentions the Chogyal more caustically, but his account is more important for the light it sheds on the Indian government's view of the situation. In Delhi, he was advised, "[d]o not allow the Chogyal to get on top again. We will never get a second chance like this" (Das, 1983: 2–3). In general, Das treats the Bhutia elite's nationalist aspirations with almost open contempt, and one assumes that this reflects the attitude of the Government of India at the time.

Discontent with the political situation in Sikkim does not appear to have been confined to the Nepali community. Das records that he was approached by a group of Lepcha leaders in May 1973; the Lepchas informed him that they supported the idea of a merger with India because "having suffered under Bhutia rule for centuries" they would become "second class citizens" in a Nepali-dominated Sikkim (Das, 1983: 28–9). It is also significant that the Sikkim

Congress, which won all but one of the 32 seats in the Sikkim Assembly in April 1974, was dominated by Kazi Lhendup Dorji, a Bhutia Lepcha with a Belgian wife, not by a Nepali.

Sikkim today is a Nepali-dominated state of India. Several historical questions remain unanswered. For instance, would Sikkim now be the world's smallest independent, sovereign state if there had been no Nepali immigration? The most one can say is that this is doubtful; none the less, the notion has gained general acceptance, and, along with the legacy of the Gorkhaland movement, exercises a powerful influence on government policies in Bhutan.

BHUTAN AND THE NEPALI DIASPORA

Bhutan's Nepali-speaking population remained politically quiescent until Indian independence sent shock-waves through the neighbouring states. It is significant that the late 1940s and early 1950s saw the creation of Nepali-led reformist or revolutionary groups in Nepal, Sikkim, and Bhutan. In 1952, the Bhutan State Congress was formed across the Indian border in Assam. The Congress membership was entirely Nepali: its programme was aimed initially at improving the lot of peasant farmers in the south, but later it called for a broader democratization of the Bhutanese government. On March 22 1954 Bhutan witnessed what was probably its first ever public political demonstration, but the 100 or so marchers were promptly expelled from the country by the militia. The Bhutan State Congress had no support whatsoever in the north, where modern political concepts remained unknown, and probably very little support in the south either, where a largely uneducated peasantry had no wish to endanger its right to continue to till highly productive lands.[34] Moreover, the Congress adopted the flag of the Indian National Congress, with a *vajra* replacing the Indian spinning-wheel (Sinha, 1991: 180). Within Bhutan, it can hardly have been forgotten that the Shabdrung, the reincarnate monk-ruler whose position in the affairs of state was eclipsed when the first Druk Gyalpo was crowned in 1907, had sent his brother to meet Mahatma Gandhi in India in 1931 to seek support for the restoration of his temporal powers (Sinha, 1991: 150–2). As a result, the Shabdrung was confined to his monastery and died there in suspicious circumstances six months later. The Nepali activists' alliance with the Indian National Congress, a party that was perceived to have marked anti-monarchical tendencies, at a time when Bhutan's first concern was to remain distinct from India, made their demands anathema. The party submitted a petition to Jawarharlal Nehru when he visited Bhutan in 1958, and continued to issue statements from Siliguri in West Bengal, but became inactive in 1969 when its leaders were granted an amnesty and permitted to return to Bhutan.

The abortive State Congress campaign may have been taken as a warning, nevertheless, for the Bhutanese government's attitude to southern Bhutan changed noticeably thereafter. During the reign of King Jigme Dorji Wangchuk (1952–72), the administrative system was reformed substantially. A partially-elected Tshogdu (National Assembly) was established in 1953, Bhutan's first Five-Year Plan was inaugurated in 1961, and great efforts were made to encourage the Nepali-speaking southerners to identify with the nation. The most important event in this process was the passing of legislation in 1958 which granted citizenship and land tenure to the entire southern population, and decreed that the Bhutanese Nepalis should thereafter be referred to as 'Lhotshampas'. A significant feature of the 1958 Citizenship Act was the extent to which local officials were empowered to grant citizenship certificates: Bhutanese nationality could be granted by "an official appointed by His Majesty" to people over the age of majority who owned agricultural land and had lived in Bhutan for over ten years, and to the wives of Bhutanese nationals. Some clarificatory amendments were made to the Act in 1977, but its basic principles remained in force until 1985.

Lhotshampas were also guaranteed some measure of political representation: in 1990 the 158-seat National Assembly had 16 Lhotshampa members, the ten-member Royal Advisory Council as constituted in 1977 must have one Lhotshampa representative, and the six judges of the High Court, established in 1975, must include a Lhotshampa (Sinha, 1991: 190, 191, 197, 202). The Lhotshampa population could study Nepali and Sanskrit in southern schools, despite the official policy of promoting Dzongkha as the national language, and intermarriage between northerners and southerners was for several years encouraged by financial inducements.[35] The government's policy of educating its southern population and absorbing Lhotshampas into the administration met with considerable success: by 1992, 1188 Bhutanese held qualifications ranging from Bachelor's degrees to doctorates; 450 of these were southern Bhutanese (RGB, 1992: 59). By 1990, 39% of all Bhutanese civil servants were Lhotshampas (*Kuensel* 2/11/91).

It is probably too early to state with any finality why it was that relations between the Nepali-speaking southern population and the Bhutanese government soured during the late 1980s, though it is clearly apparent that the trend towards integrative policies outlined above was suddenly reversed. The government's oft-repeated explanation is that this was due to the detection, during a census operation that began in 1988, of massive numbers of illegal immigrants. It should be borne in mind that the census did not appear to have as its objective an enumeration of the inhabitants of Bhutan in the way that censuses of India and Nepal do, but aimed simply to "identify Bhutanese nationals", and therefore also non-nationals, and apparently only in southern Bhutan. The new criteria for citizenship enshrined in the 1985 Citizenship Act of Bhutan represented a major revision of the 1958 legislation – but according to many refugees this would not have presented a problem for the vast majority of southern Bhutanese, who could prove their residence in Bhutan during or before the alleged 'cut-off' year of 1958. The source of the political problem in southern Bhutan, and the resulting refugee crisis, seems to have been the manner in which the code of dress and etiquette known as Driglam Namzhag was introduced in the South, and the Lhotshampas' reaction to it. This led to a hardening of government attitudes as dissident organizations began to grow in centres such as Sherubtse College (the Students' Union of Bhutan) and the National Institute of Education in Samchi (People's Forum for Human Rights), and with the formation in June 1990 of the Bhutan People's Party across the border in India. After these organizations launched very large public demonstrations all across southern Bhutan in September and

October 1990, submitting 13 wide-ranging demands for civil rights, cultural safeguards, and political reforms, the Bhutanese government reacted strongly against all dissidents, whom it could now characterize as 'anti-nationals' or *ngolop*s in terms of its own laws on treason. The flow of refugees began in late 1990 and reached a peak in May 1991 with 11,000 new arrivals in camps in southeast Nepal (Hutt, 1993).

Clearly, the existence of the refugee camps, and also of influential and articulate critics in Kathmandu, threatens the system of government that has developed in Bhutan since its political unification in 1616. Whether or not the presence of a large, culturally unintegrated population of Nepali-speakers in southern Bhutan represented an equal threat is perhaps a moot point. It is unlikely that the government of Bhutan foresaw what would result from its attempt to effect the "internal cohesion and external distinction" (Haugen, 1966) of its culture, but it is clear from the record of the 68th session of the National Assembly debate in 1989 that its "one nation, one people" policies were directed principally at the Nepali population:

> [The Deputy Home Minister] explained that this subject assumed particular significance since some of our ways and practices were identical to the customs and traditions prevailing in other countries and *some of our people tend to identify more closely with the people of other countries.* In a large country, such diversity would have added colour and character to its national heritage without affecting national security. However, in a small country like ours it would adversely affect the growth of social harmony and unity among the people. The Government has, for these reasons, promulgated a policy to promote Driglam Namzha, National Dress and Language among our people. He emphasized that the successful implementation of this policy is vital for the promotion of our national identity. The Deputy Minister said that His Majesty's KASHO clearly states that the dress or the customs of the people living in the north need not necessarily comprise the basis for promoting our national identity. What is imperative he

FIGURE 7   *Woman and child, Khudanabari Bhutanese refugee camp, Jhapa,*
                southeast Nepal, February 1995 (Michael Hutt)

said, was that a small country such as Bhutan should have
a distinct national identity that would always stand as a
proud and common symbol of strength to promote and
safeguard the wellbeing of the people and sovereignty of the
nation (RGB, 1989: res. no. 3; emphasis added).

FIGURE 8   *A 59-year-old former member of Bhutan's National Assembly who now lives in Sanishchare Bhutanese refugee camp in the Morang district of southeast Nepal. He wears the Bhutanese national dress that became compulsory throughout Bhutan in 1989 (Michael Hutt)*

Herein lies the notion that a country as small as Bhutan cannot afford cultural diversity within its borders. But radical integrative measures such as those adopted in Bhutan are rarely based on purely cultural considerations: the political and economic implications of the southerners' cross-border idendfication must also be significant here. The people who "tend to identify more closely with the people of other countries" can be no other than the Nepali Bhutanese. Many of the "people of other countries" are of course Nepalis in the diaspora communities, whose political activities in India and Sikkim are matters of concern to the Bhutanese. The fact that the Bhutanese bureaucracy contained a growing number of Lhotshampa officials and that the South produced most of Bhutan's cashcrops and hydro-electric power must also have increased the government's sense of vulnerability.

CONCLUSION

It is significant that rifts in the diaspora community have until very recently tended to occur along political lines, and between the various segments of the diaspora, although the growth of ethnic movements and political parties in Nepal since 1990 has been mirrored to some extent in the diaspora, and particularly in Sikkim. With the establishment of the Gorkha Hill Council and the Nepali domination, both numerical and political, of Sikkim, the Nepali diaspora communities have become more secure inside India. The future status of Nepali-speakers in Bhutan will depend in large part upon the outcome of negotiations over the return of refugees between the governments of Bhutan and Nepal. The unity of the Nepali/Gorkha diaspora community remains compromised although its members are often objects of suspicion throughout the northeastern reaches of the subcontinent. Dixit points out that "[U]ntil the Lhotshampas emerged as refugees, there seem to have been very few political links between them and the Nepalis of Nepal. If there is any place where there is a feeling for being 'Nepali' today, however, it is in the refugee camps of Jhapa" (Dixit, 1993: 17). He also suggests that "a serious move towards Greater Nepal would have to have its origins in the targeting and humiliation of Nepali-speakers from all over, on an extreme scale, *for being Nepali-speakers*" (*ibid.*: 19), but notes that the expulsions and evictions of Nepalis from various Indian states in the past did not provoke any kind of pan-Nepali response. Indeed, the strongest protests against India's absorption of Sikkim emanated from public demonstrations on the streets of Kathmandu (Das, 1983: 59; Rustomji, 1987: 110–11). The final question raised by 'being Nepali without Nepal' is the responsibility that should be assumed by Nepal itself. Curiously, although they may never have resided in Nepal themselves, it is usually to that country that Nepali-speaking refugees come to seek sanctuary, whether they have come from Meghalaya, Manipur, or Bhutan, and Nepal has usually accepted them. Ultimately, being Nepali without Nepal has often proved impossible, and the diaspora's bond with the motherland, however tenuous it may be, is often renewed in times of crisis.

NOTES

This Chapter has grown from a paper on the Nepali diaspora that was first presented to a workshop on the 'Concept of Race in South Asia' at the School of Oriental and African Studies, London, in 1992, and shortly afterwards at the Institute of Social and Cultural Anthropology in Oxford. The paper in its present form was also presented to a seminar at the CNRS, Aix-en-Provence, in July 1994. My thanks to Lionel Caplan, David Gellner, Pratyoush Onta, Joanna Pfaff-Czarnecka, Françoise Pommaret, Keith Sprigg, Tanka Subba, and John Whelpton for advice, suggestions, and comments on earlier drafts.

[1] Both definitions are suggested by Malcolm Yapp in his introductory essay to Taylor and Yapp (1979: 5).

[2] Other novels that deal with similar themes are Lainsingh Baāngdel's *Muluk Bāhira* ('Outside the Country', 1948), Rudrarāj Pānde's *Prāyashcit* ('The Penance', 1938) and Kshetrī's later *Brahmaputrakā Cheuchāu* ('On the Banks of the Brahmaputra') for which Kshetrī received an award from the Sahitya Akademi in 1987. Kshetrī reviews and discusses these novels in an article in *Samkālīn Sāhitya* 9 (Māgh-Chait 2049), pp. 34–45, Kathmandu 1993.

[3] My translation of this story is published in *Himal*, May – June 1993, pp. 14–15.

4 Pradhan (1982: 6 and 1991: 69) mentions the unpublished "History of Sikkim", compiled "by the lamas of Pemiongchi" and salvaged and translated by members of the royal family of Sikkim in 1908. In this, Pradhan claims, it is stated that the Tibetans had to subdue Lepcha and Magar villages in order to establish control over Sikkim in the seventeenth century. He also repeats Joseph Hooker's claim (*Himalayan Journals*, 1848) that the Magars were indigenous to Sikkim, but had been displaced by the Lepchas (1982: 5). The 'History' is also referred to by Chie Nakane (1966), whose article is discussed below.

5 My thanks to Keith Sprigg for his help in thinking through the connotations of this term, and my apologies for differing with him in my conclusion.

6 The figure of 10 million was mentioned to me in interviews with His Majesty King Jigme Singye Wangchuck, the Home Minister Lyonpo Dago Tshering, and the Foreign Minister Lyonpo Dawa Tsering during a visit to Thimphu in September 1992. It is also cited in Shaw (1994) and Rose (1993).

7 A figure of 52% is given in Pradhan (1992: 1) while a figure of 64% is cited by Chaudhuri (1991). The likelihood of Chaudhuri's figure being accurate is put in serious doubt by the fact that he believes the total population of Bhutan to be "2.46 million"!

8 I use the word 'emigrated' cautiously here. It should be borne in mind that for many such people the distance involved would have been only a few score miles, at a time when nations were less clearly conceptualized and national boundaries less clearly demarcated than they are today.

9 Joanna Pfaff-Czarnecka, 'Lotteries as social order: Nepalese peasants as night watchmen in Bangalore, South India', Himalayan Forum seminar, SOAS, London, November 9, 1992. See also Pfaff-Czarnecka (1993b).

10 The first Bhutia ruler of Sikkim was called the *Chös-rgyal* (lit., 'king of religion') but this title appears to have fallen into disuse during the British colonial period. The ruler of Sikkim was more commonly known as the 'Maharaja' until March 1965, when Palden Thondup Namgyal (who had succeeded his father two years earlier) was crowned *Chös-rgyal* and the queen became the *Gyalmo* (Rao, 1978: 22–3).

11 Sikkim's gift of Darjeeling to the British was probably extracted rather than bestowed (see Pinn, 1986: 119–129).

12 However, Pradhan (1982: 20) states that the first commercial tea estate, the Alubari Kaman, opened in 1856.

13 The Bhotiyas (also called Bhutia or, in Sikkim, Lhori) of Darjeeling and Sikkim are people of Tibetan stock who have inhabited the district for generations, and are distinct from the 'Tibetans' (*bod-pa, khams-pa*), most of whom settled there after the Chinese invasion of Tibet in the 1950s. Nakane (1966: 215 fn. 5) suggests that the Bhutia immigration into Sikkim began during the sixteenth century.

14 The Bhutan government's case rests on three arguments: (1) because English has been the medium of education in Bhutan since 1961, the need for schoolchildren to study a third language in the south put them at a disadvantage; (2) Nepali is only one of many languages spoken in Bhutan and is, moreover, the national language of a foreign country; (3) new curricular materials could not be produced in Nepali in line with the New Approach to Primary Education programme, for reasons of cost (Thinley, 1994).

15 In this regard, see Macdonald (1975). Lionel Caplan has examined relations between the Limbus of Ilam district and the Brahmans who have settled there since its incorporation into the Nepalese state (Caplan, 1970).

16 A table reproduced by Timsina (1992: 55) demonstrates that hillpeople comprise 25% of the clerical staff and lower cadre officers in the Darjeeling forest department administration, but 85% of the menials, e.g. orderlies, drivers, watchmen, etc.

17 The number of tourists visiting Darjeeling per annum declined from 115,000 in 1985 to 5,000 in 1988 and the number of unemployed youths was estimated in 1986 to be 65,000 (Subba, 1992: 65). See also Shakya (1991).

18 Des Chene (1991: 174–5) is probably right to assume that the vast majority of British Gurkha soldiers had their homes in Nepal, not in India, during the 1930s, and that this explained their reluctance to join with "ex-Gurkhas who urged them to join the Indian nationalist cause [who] came from families settled for several generations in India". This situation changed when the demand for soldiers expanded after 1939; and in any case 'martial Gurkhas' were probably as available in the Darjeeling hills by 1930 as they were in Nepal proper.

19 The Arms Act of 1878 permitted the use of the *khukri* for ritual, domestic, and military purposes.

20 In interviews with eight Nepali-speaking farmers in Damphu, in the southern Bhutanese district of Chirang, on 16/9/92, I established that all were second or third-generation Bhutanese residents; only one had visited Nepal, on a pilgrimage to the temple of Pashupati. Of the

fifteen elderly Bhutanese refugees I interviewed in Beldangi and Sanishchare refugee camps in Jhapa, Nepal, in February 1995, eleven knew that their grandfathers had emigrated from Nepal.

[21] John Claude White in ca. 1893; quoted in Sinha (1991: 29).

[22] Charles Bell, in 1904; quoted in Sinha (1991: 38).

[23] Capt. C. J. Morris, in 1932; quoted in Sinha (1991: 39).

[24] Basil Gould, Political Officer in Sikkim, in 1938; quoted in Sinha (1991: 171–2).

[25] Newspaper reports in Nepal in 1990 claimed that about 60,000 Nepalis had been forced out of Meghalaya since 1987 (*Gorkhapatra* 16–17 July 1990, quoted in *Nepal Press Digest* 34.30, 23/7/90).

[26] Pratyoush Onta maintains that a number of Nepalis were recruited by the British for the Burma Police, and that others arrived there as a part of the general north-easterly drift of population through Assam (personal comunication, April 1994).

[27] A strange feature of the continuing war of words between exiled southern Bhutanese dissidents and the Bhutan government is the way in which both sides regularly reproduce the texts of the Bhutanese citizenship acts of 1958, 1977, and 1985 to buttress their own arguments. The Harvard lawyer David Thronson (1993: 8) has remarked, "The laws of Bhutan and its neighbors do not form a seamless web and the combination creates vast potential for statelessness. For one simple example, Nepali citizenship by descent comes through the father, as was the case in Bhutan's laws until 1985. Now that Bhutan requires both parents to be Bhutanese, the children of Bhutanese fathers and Nepali mothers are apparently citizens of neither state."

[28] Testimonies by refugees have been published in S. K. Pradhan (1992); SAARC Jurists (1992); AHURA BHUTAN (1993); Amnesty International (1992, 1994), and elsewhere.

[29] These were: Assamese, Bengali, Gujarati, Hindi, Kannada, Kashmiri, Malayalam, Marathi, Oriya, Punjabi, Sanskrit, Tamil, Telugu, and Urdu.

[30] The bill on the recognition of Nepali apparently includes a rider clause which allows the use of the name 'Gorkha bhasa' in the Darjeeling Gorkha Hill Council area. See Josse (1992: 11).

[31] 'Lepcha' is a English corruption of the Nepali term *lāpche*. *Nebulā* became *Parivartan* ('Change') after its first twelve issues. Both *Nebulā* and *Parivartan* published essays arguing for social unity and communal uplift.

[32] Dixit examines the 'likely conspirators' for Greater Nepal – the Nepali state, the Sikkimese state, and the Lhotshampas of Bhutan—and

concludes that "[W]hile a large portion of the population is able to appreciate the cultural attributes of Nepaliness, the feeling does not go deep enough to emerge as a movement for Greater Nepal anytime soon."

33 The 'agreement regiments' are those covered by the 1947 tripartite agreement on British and Indian recruitment from Nepal.

34 There are brief accounts of the Bhutan State Congress agitation in Sinha (1991: 179–81) and Rose (1977: 109–15). See also D. B. Gurung (1960).

35 The incentive, termed *soelray*, amounted to Nu. 5,000 when introduced, and was increased to Nu. 10,000 by the 68th session of the National Assembly (Tshogdu) in 1989. However, it was abolished by the 69th session in the following year (*Kuensel* 29/3/90,2/11/91).

PART TWO

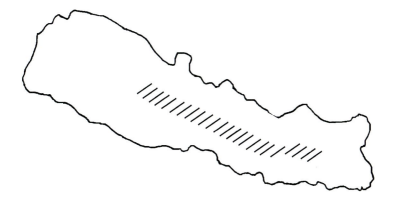

PART TWO

Central Nepal

The geographical heart of Nepal is formed by the stretch of middle hills, high above the Gangetic plains (the Tarai) but below the Himalayan peaks. In the middle of these hills is one valley which is larger and more fertile than the rest because it used to be a lake. This valley high in the mountains has, like Mexico, given its name – Nepal – to the whole country; nowadays it is known, after the capital city, as the Kathmandu Valley. The Newar people of the Kathmandu Valley are a small minority in the country as a whole but are still the largest group in the capital itself. However, as described in chapter 4, they are divided in numerous ways, not least by the fact that they have a caste system more complex and fissiparious than that of the dominant Parbatiyas. The Newars are the only group in Nepal with a truly urban tradition and it is no coincidence that the famous temples and artwork of Nepal were produced by Newar artisans. Most Newars, and

147

certainly high-caste Newars, have an association with Sanskritic culture as old and as profound as the Parbatiyas.

Only in the far west of Nepal do people speaking Sanskrit-derived (Indo-European) language – i.e. Parbatiyas – abut directly onto Buddhist peoples speaking dialects of Tibetan. Everywhere else in the middle hills there is a third category in between these two: a series of what used to be called 'hill tribes' who speak Tibeto-Burman tongues (although many now speak only Nepali). From west to east the largest and most prominent of these ethnic groups are the Magar, the Thakali, the Gurung, the Tamang, the Rai, and the Limbu. The Newars also speak a Tibeto-Burman language, though in their case it has been profoundly influenced by long contact with Sanskrit and other Indo-European languages. All these non-Parbatiya groups were classified as *matwāli*, alcohol-drinkers, in the Legal Code of 1854 (alcohol being, in theory, forbidden to the high-caste Parbatiya wearers of the sacred thread, though there are, notoriously, *matwāli* Khas Chetris in far west Nepal). But the label 'alcohol-drinker' was a hardly a designation that could be used in self-reference as a way of asserting common identity. Since 1990, however, it seems that members of the ethnic groups have begun to use the English loan word 'Mongolian' as a catch-all term for all the Tibeto-Burman-speaking peoples of Nepal, and the Parbatiyas likewise use the term of them. Among intellectuals this word usually appears in the form 'Mongol' or 'Mongoloid', but most now prefer the Sanskritic neologism *janajāti*, variously translated 'nationality', 'ethnic group', or 'indigenous people'. This – *janajāti* – is used for almost the same purpose, though here other groups now speaking Indo-European languages, e.g. the Tharu, are also included.

The Gurungs live to the west and north-west of the Kathmandu Valley. Many Gurung men have served in the British and Indian Gurkha regiments. Once famous as shepherds, they now dominate the second city of the Nepalese middle hills, Pokhara. Pokhara used to be a small Newar bazaar, a staging post on trade routes to India, Tibet, and west Nepal. Now a thriving city, it is also the site of major rethinking of Gurung identity, as documented in chapter 5. An original orientation to Tibet was replaced under Parbatiya influence by chronicles that made them Rajput refugees from India, just like leading Parbatiyas themselves. Now activists seek to reverse what they see as pernicious Hindu influence.

Around the Kathmandu Valley, in a kind of ring like a doughnut, but with greater and more homogeneous concentrations to the north, live the Tamang people. Barred from recruitment to the Gurkhas, the Tamangs formed a reserve army of labour power for the elite in Kathmandu. The Tamangs are among the poorest and least 'developed' people of Nepal. Both the Gurungs and the Tamangs patronize Tibetan lamas, but the Tamangs as a whole are much more firmly within the field of Tibetan Lamaism, more so than any of the other Tibeto-Burman-speaking groups. Tamang intellectuals tend to live in Kathmandu.

CHAPTER FOUR

Caste, Communalism, and Communism: Newars and The Nepalese State

David N. Gellner

INTRODUCTION

The Newars see themselves as the rightful inhabitants of the Kathmandu Valley, the centre of Nepal, and they are the largest single ethnic group within it. In Africa they would be called a 'host tribe' since they form a majority in the capital but are a small minority in the country as a whole. Their position in the capital and their long tradition of literacy mean that they are often viewed by others as part of the Establishment. They have a strong sense of cultural identity which has frequently been envied by the self-appointed leaders of other ethnic minorities in Nepal. And yet it is an interesting and remarkable fact that long after Gurung, Limbu, and Magar activists sought to organize politically no Newar, however marginal, ever seemed interested in attempting to form a communal or ethnic political party. By 1995 and early 1996 the possibility of doing so had become part of activist discourse. Why should this have taken so long to come about?

One immediate answer to this question is that the new Nepali Constitution of 1990 outlaws parties formed "on the basis of religion, community, caste, tribe or region" (Constitution: 95). But this has not prevented such parties from being organized. In 1991 the Election Commission refused to register the Mongol National Organization and the Nepal Rastriya Janajati Party on the grounds that they were communal parties, while the Limbuwan Liberation Front boycotted the elections (see chapter 1 above). A related point is that such parties have little chance of electoral success on their own. Ethnic activists have a much greater chance of having an impact if they work through the established parties, which are, in effect, coalitions. Once again, however, this has not prevented such parties being formed by the would-be representatives of other ethnic groups. A preliminary answer might then be that Newars, unlike other ethnic groups, are too divided by caste for it even to be thinkable that they should unite as Newars. Internal caste divisions are certainly a very important consideration, but, as I shall attempt to show, such an answer is too simple.

In order to forestall misunderstandings which frequently arise in dealing with such a contentious topic, two caveats may be helpful. First, for those, especially Nepalis, who disapprove of foreign scholars giving encouragement to communal movements, I would like to stress that I consider this lack to be a mark of political maturity, not a failing; I do not advocate, and would not support, such a party. But just as sociologists and historians of science have to explain truth and scientific advance as much as the persistence of falsehood, so the anthropologist interested in political processes has an equal duty to explain desirable as undesirable developments, even if that may seem to be a harder task.

My second caveat is directed at theory-conscious anthropologists who are suspicious of all questions of the form, "Why do people X lack trait Y?" as inevitably imposing inappropriate Western concepts in an alien context. Against this doubt, it should be stressed that Nepalis themselves are fully capable of comprehending the question with which I began and in a different form they also pose the same question. It was one of the justifications for the system of Partyless Panchayat Democracy, as it called itself, that it prevented the emergence of communal parties; and Nepalese cultural nationalist intellectuals frequently argue that unless their demands are met, there is the danger that communal parties may become a problem.

A less ambitious aim of the paper is to examine what, if any, role Newar ethnic feelings played in the revolution of 1990; and to explain both the attraction of communism for many Newars, and its partial setback in local elections of 1992. Communism achieved considerable success in Nepal at the very time when it was in full retreat in the ex-Soviet bloc. 'How can communism do well here when it is being rejected all over the world?' argued its opponents in 1991. But in fact it did win widespread support, support which remained firm and led to the Communists winning all ten seats in the Kathmandu Valley in the Parliamentary elections of November 1994. This makes an examination of the local meaning of communism all the more essential.

Behind my main question lies another, which there is no space to address properly here. Today's strong cultural identity may not involve organizing a political party, but it certainly has many consequences for other sorts of activity, many of them with political implications. How far back can we take this cultural identity? More precisely, is it valid to trace it back beyond 1769 when the three Malla kingdoms of the Kathmandu Valley were conquered by Prithvi Narayan Shah of Gorkha and the Newars became a subject people? I have suggested elsewhere (Gellner, 1986) that there is, and has been, in addition to the assertive form of Newar cultural nationalism, a more diffuse kind of Newar identity; but it has to be admitted that, in so far as it did exist in the Malla period, the diffuse form of Newar identity had very few consequences for action, unlike today.

This way of posing the question, raises the more general issue of whether the phenomenon of ethnicity, or communalism as it is known in South Asia, is an entirely modern phenomenon, or whether, as some argue, it is in fact a universal aspect of the human condition. With respect to the Newar case, Quigley has made a strong statement of the modernist or anti-primordialist position. In a criticism of my earlier paper (Gellner, 1986) he asserts that a sense of Newar ethnicity only arose with the threat of Gorkhali conquest, in the seventeenth century:

> To speak of ethnic identity before this period is to conflate ethnicity (a specific historical condition) with identity (a generalized sociological condition). One might say that until this time the people of the Valley did not think of themselves as 'the people of the Valley' at all. If they pondered on their identity, which seems unlikely, it would have been as members of caste or kin groups or, at the

outside, as members of a kingdom to which they owed allegiance or at least tribute. The pre-Gorkhali history of the Kathmandu Valley is one of political fragmentation where the idea of ethnic identity is irrelevant (Quigley, 1987: 168).

Whatever one thinks on the question of whether there was anything like a sense of Newar ethnicity before 1650, it cannot be doubted that ethnic identity is highly relevant today. K. P. Malla, a prominent Newar intellectual, writes:

> With his social and cultural fabric of life slowly being destroyed, the average middle-class Newar of Kathmandu today feels like a displaced Nawab of Lucknow after the Loot. He feels like an alien in his own home pushed too hard [sic] against the wall by ever-stiffer social and economic competition with some 20,000 in-migrants every year. The headlong rush is not only robbing Newars of their jobs, open space, and unpolluted civic life, but also destroying their culture and treating them as a dwindling specimen of aborigines deserving to be confined to the slum areas of Asan and the vegetable markets of Kathmandu (Malla, 1992: 24).

FIVE HISTORICAL TURNING POINTS: 1392, 1769, 1846, 1951, 1990

The 1991 census, which published ethnic or caste affiliation for the first time, revealed that there are today just over a million Newars, or 5.6% of Nepal's total population of 18 million (Gurung, 1992). This can be compared to nearly 3 million Chetris and 2.3 million Bahuns or Brahmans, the two top castes of the dominant Parbatiya ethnic group.

About half of the Newars today live outside their ancestral homeland, the Kathmandu Valley, most of these having emigrated since 1769 to take advantage of commercial, artisanal, or farming opportunities along trade routes within the newly established Gorkhali state. These Newars have assimilated, some almost

entirely, others very considerably, to the dominant Parbatiya culture and language of the middle hills. Thus the new Newar
cultural nationalism, focused specifically on the Newari language,
has little appeal for them. This paper focuses on those Newars who
remained in the Newar heartland, the Kathmandu Valley and
nearby settlements.

Within or near the Kathmandu Valley there are, in addition
to the three cities of Kathmandu, Lalitpur, and Bhaktapur, 39
towns or villages which are predominantly Newar (Müller-Böker,
1988). Today these are interspersed with Parbatiya villages, and
most Newars are bilingual in Newari and Nepali.

In tracing the origin of the modern sense of Newar identity,
five periods need to be distinguished: the later Malla period;
the period of the Shah dynasty after 1769; the Rana dictatorship (1846–1951); the modern period of the Panchayat system
(1951–90); and most recently, the period of multi-party democracy
inaugurated by the 'people's movement' (*jan āndolan*) of 1990. It is
only well into the first of these periods that we have any evidence
of the term 'Newar' being used, and it is fairly clear that it referred
to the dominant (power-holding, Kshatriya) caste, which today
would be known as Shrestha (Gellner, 1986: 140). The term seems
to have derived from the name of the language which was spoken
by the people of the Kathmandu Valley, then known simply as
'Nepal': *newā-bhāy*, or, honorifically, *nepāl-bhāṣā*, i.e. 'the language
of Nepal'. The speakers of *newa-bhāy* were, logically enough, known
as 'Newa'; but this applied principally to the dominant landholders,
and only by extension to their peasants, artisans, servants, and ritual
specialists. In exactly the same way among the Parbatiyas, Khas
Kura, the old name of Nepali, means 'the language of the Khas':
the Khas are the Kshatriya (Chetri) caste among the Parbatiyas.
However, the language is, in fact, equally the language of the
Bahuns (Brahmans) and of the Parbatiya Untouchable artisan castes.

Whereas the name 'Newar' is relatively new, the Newars'
language, Newari, is undoubtedly old. Analysis of the place names in
the Sanskrit inscriptions of the Licchavi period (5–9th centuries)
shows that something like Newari was spoken as the vernacular of
the Kathmandu Valley 1500 years ago (Malla, 1981; 1983). In

analysing the modern period, however, it is unnecessary and would be overambitious to go back that far. The crucial period for the emergence of what counts as traditional Newar culture today was the fourteenth and fifteenth centuries, that is to say, the beginning of the later Malla period. If we wish to be more precise, we may choose as an emblematic date 1392, when Sthiti Malla, or Jaya Sthiti Malla as he is often known, made himself king in Bhaktapur. For the Newars of the nineteenth century he became a kind of mythological founding father, the instigator and legitimator of their traditional customs.[1]

In the fourteenth and for most of the fifteenth century the Valley had not yet been divided into three kingdoms based on its three main cities, Kathmandu, Lalitpur (Patan), and Bhaktapur, but was ruled as one kingdom from Bhaktapur. The Indian plains had come under Muslim rule and the great Buddhist centres of north India, such as Nalanda, were destroyed. Despite continuing influence on Nepali Hinduism and on the court culture from Mithila, the local culture began to be defined more in its own terms. This was the period when the local *Purana*s (religious histories), both Buddhist and Hindu, emerged to prominence and became substantial charters for local religious traditions.[2]

The next major turning point was, as already indicated, the conquest of the Valley by Prithvi Narayan Shah. The nationalist history of today styles him 'the Great': he is the Father of the Nation, and his conquests are referred to as the 'unification' of Nepal. He was undoubtedly a remarkable man. His conquest of the Valley took him twenty-six years of continuous struggle against all the odds.

The establishment of Prithvi Narayan's new state gave a considerable boost to the historic movement eastwards through the Himalayas of the Parbatiya people (see chapter 3 above). It would be quite wrong, however, to see the wars of the eighteenth century in terms of an ethnic struggle. There were Newar artisans and traders settled in Gorkha from the seventeenth century, who owed allegiance to the Shah kings. The Newars of the Valley fought continuously among themselves, and the king of Bhaktapur remained allied with Prithvi Narayan till the very end. The Newar kings themselves made extensive use of Parbatiya and Magar mercenaries, who were quite happy to fight against Parbatiya opponents, until Jaya Prakash, king of Kathmandu, made the mistake of assassinating his Parbatiya general, Kashi Ram Thapa, and seven companions, for being defeated by Prithvi Narayan (Stiller, 1973: 111–12). Only on one occasion during Prithvi Narayan's campaign against the Valley did Newars from other kingdoms come to the aid of fellow Newars: when Prithvi Narayan made his first attack on Kirtipur in 1757 (*ibid*.: 120–1).[3]

All the evidence suggests that the vast majority of Newars reconciled themselves without difficulty to the new rulers. There was considerable emigration from the Valley as Newars settled, often at the invitation of the new rulers, along the trade routes of the new kingdom; they quickly became the traders, shopkeepers, and goldsmiths for most Nepalis.[4] At the same time, it eventually became possible for many Kathmandu and some Lalitpur Newars to win positions in the palaces of the new rulers, as servants (various castes) or bureaucrats (usually Shresthas).

It is the Rana period which serves as the immediate backdrop to modern Nepal. This was inaugurated in 1846 when Jang Bahadur Rana seized power by the simple expedient of bringing loyal soldiers and arms along when the Queen summoned the ruling nobility to the fort next to the Palace and then murdering all the leading contenders for power.[5] Once Jang Bahadur was secure, he left control in his brothers' hands, and went on a one-year trip to Britain and France in 1850 (Whelpton, 1983). In 1854 he promulgated a Legal Code (Muluki Ain) which attempted to weld all the ethnic groups and tribes of the country into a single caste hierarchy. The Newars, who had their own, highly complex, internal hierarchy proved a particularly thorny classificatory problem for the Brahmans who drew the code up (Höfer, 1979: 135–40). In general Newar castes found themselves ranked well below their Parbatiya equivalents. None the less, Newars had a relatively privileged position in the central Valley; unlike many ethnic groups of the hills, Newars were not considered 'enslavable'.

Changes in India in the 1920s, in particular the growth of the independence movement, meant that the Rana rulers felt the need to bolster their rule by appealing to nationalist sentiments: the territory they ruled was now named Nepal, following a usage the British had first adopted a century earlier which extended the name of the Kathmandu Valley to the whole area subject to the Shah king (Burghart, 1984). The language they used was renamed Nepali, instead of Gorkhali, which drew vociferous but ineffective protests from the first Newar cultural nationalist and Buddhist modernist, Dharmaditya Dharmacharyya (Gellner, 1986). In other words, for the first time the territory of the Shah kings began to be conceived as a nation-state. At the same time the Ranas petitioned for, and were granted, an embassy in London, unlike the Indian princely states, a point of considerable importance to Nepali nationalists today, faced as they are by Indian regional ambitions.

The radically new situation in India after 1947 meant that the Ranas could no longer resist change, though earlier attempts had been punished severely. Three of the four martyrs who were executed in January 1941 for campaigning for democracy were Newars (the movement's leader, Tanka Prasad Acharya, was saved by being a Brahman which made him exempt from the death penalty). In November 1950, when King Tribhuvan, who had been kept under virtual house arrest by the Ranas for most of his life, fled to the Indian embassy, opposition to the Ranas grew, the Congress Party began an armed insurrection over the border and in several parts of the hills, and there were massive demonstrations in the capital in which government firing led to two deaths. After powerful Indian intervention, the old regime collapsed. On India's insistence Nepal trod a 'middle path' of compromise between complete revolution and the status quo, so that in the first post-Rana government, five Ranas, including the Prime Minister, continued in office (Joshi and Rose, 1966: 73–85).

Prayag Raj Sharma has written of the period which followed 1951 that

> Nepal made an attempt to break away from its past ... It started immediately with experiments in the new values of political democracy, economic development, egalitarian ideals, and social justice ... [A] single event, happening with the force of an *éclat*, brought new ideas of wholly

Western invention flooding into Nepal ... Neither the
rulers, nor the people were mentally prepared to face up to
the new challenge (Sharma, 1989a: 9).

After considerable manoevring, a general election was finally
held in which the Congress Party won a clear majority of seats. A
Congress Party government was formed under B. P. Koirala. One
year later King Mahendra put the Congress leadership in jail and
declared a new form of government: the system of Partyless
Panchayat Democracy.

This type of guided democracy was supposed to be more
suited to Nepal, and one of the justifications frequently invoked for
it was that it prevented the growth of sectional or communal
interests, which would be encouraged, it was claimed, by a system
of multi-party democracy. Riots and protests in 1979 led King
Birendra, Mahendra's son, to declare a referendum on the issue in
1980. The Partyless system won 55–45%, though not without
considerable bribery, so it is said, orchestrated from the Palace
(Shaha, 1982: chapter 5). None the less, Birendra introduced some
reforms, most importantly direct elections to the National
Assembly. When these took place various known opponents of the
system managed to get elected. In this form the system lasted until
the revolution of 1990.

A SKETCH OF NEWAR SOCIOLOGY

The Newars, as the indigenous inhabitants of the
Kathmandu Valley, have played an important role in all these
events. But since caste is a crucial factor in political attitude we
need first to know something about caste among the Newars. In
the traditional Newar caste hierarchy there were basically six types
of caste (see Table 4.1): (1) priests, (2) nobles and merchants, (3)
agriculturalists, (4) various ritual and artisan specialist castes, (5)
water-unacceptable Butchers and death specialists, (6) Untouchable Sweepers (Gellner and Quigley, 1995: chapter 1). The top
two categories or blocs sub-divide into Buddhist and Hindu

TABLE 4.1   MAIN NEWAR CASTE BLOCS, WITH MOST
COMMON SURNAMES

(1) Priests   (1a) Rajopadhyaya Brahman – Hindu
                                 (1b) Bajracharya and Shakya – Buddhist

(2) Nobles, Merchants,   (2a) Shrestha – mostly Hindu
    Civil Servants   (2b) Tuladhar (Uray) – Buddhist

(3) Agriculturalists (Maharjan)

(4) Various artisan/ritual specialist castes

(5) Butcher-Milkseller caste (Khadgi; Np. Kasai)

(6) Sweepers (Dyahla; Np. Pode)

sections, which need to be sharply distinguished. For the rest of
the society, the distinction is of lesser importance. It is possible to
assign castes or caste sub-groups to the Buddhist or Hindu
category on the basis of which kind of domestic priest they employ
(with the exception of the Sweepers who have to find priests within
their own caste). However, most individuals from these strata,
while aware that the two religions may be treated as separate and
distinct, themselves adopt either a syncretic or an ecumenical
attitude to them.

The Newar Brahmans are, of all the high castes, the group
with the weakest identification as Newars; indeed, like the lowest
caste, they often talk of 'Newars' and do not include themselves in
the category. On the other hand, other Newars do include them as
Newars. The Rajopadhyaya Brahmans were among the first to start
speaking Nepali systematically to their children; and they are
probably still the only caste where *all* children are spoken to in
Nepali (since about the mid-1970s). They still resent the fact that
in the Legal Code of 1854 they were placed below the Parbatiya
Kshatriya castes. Today they are doing their best to be accepted as
similar to Parbatiya Brahmans, and many have adopted Parbatiya
Brahman surnames.

The Buddhist priestly caste is made up of two sub-sections,
the Bajracharyas, who constitute a third of the caste, and the

Shakyas, who make up the other two thirds. It is the Bajracharyas who really deserve the title Buddhist Brahmans, which Sylvain Lévi bestowed on them, as they alone may be domestic priests for other Newars. They are many times more numerous than the Brahmans. They and the Shakyas mostly earn their living by various artisan and craft specialities, though there are also many traders and shop-keepers, as well as some professionals and civil servants, among them. They consider themselves fully Newar, and have no doubts about that identity, or about their Buddhism. On both fronts they feel somewhat embattled.

The Tuladhar caste, based in Kathmandu shares the attitudes and the artisan traditions of the Bajracharyas and Shakyas. They are important, since they have many rich merchants and influential men among their number.

The Shrestha caste is pivotal for Newar identity. It comprises the one-time Kshatriya groups of the Malla kingdoms, plus a very large number of other, upwardly mobile or would-be upwardly mobile groups, many of whom have adopted the Shrestha label and identity rather recently. Shresthas are found wherever there are Newars, and in many settlements they are the largest caste. They are divided into two main sub-castes and numerous grades of status. Shresthas have a tradition of serving as government bureaucrats; they are also shopkeepers, traders, and businessmen of all kinds. Many Newars will tell you, including Shresthas themselves, that, of all Newar castes, they are the most 'spoiled'. Among the Shresthas there are many of Newari's most distinguished poets; but virtually all of them write equally in Nepali and sometimes even in Hindi. Many of the most eloquent spokesmen for Newar cultural nationalism are Shresthas; often these very spokesmen speak high-class Nepali to their own children. The Shresthas serve as the reference group of aspiration for most Newars.

The Maharjan agriculturalists are the largest single Newar caste, and form a considerable majority in the city of Bhaktapur. There are Maharjan sub-castes, but in general they are not divided by the numerous subtle grades of status characteristic of the amorphous Shrestha conglomerate. Maharjans have provided the backbone of support for communism, as will be discussed presently.

The artisan caste bloc includes the Barbers (Napit), Dyers (Ranjitkar), Oil-Pressers (Manandhar), Blacksmiths (Nakarmi), Painters (Chitrakar), and several others. It is at this level also that the geographically peripheral Newar groups, the Pahi (Dwi) and Putuwar, tend to be slotted in. All these castes are very small and dispersed. Today they tend, when educated and urbanized, to aspire to Shrestha status.

The Khadgi caste is the largest of the very low castes. Their own version of their myth of origin has it that they are descended from a younger son of King Harisimhadeva, who was chosen to sacrifice the first buffalo to the royal tutelary goddess, Taleju, because he was found defecating with his back to the sun as it came up (or facing it according to another version). Today a considerable number of those who live in the main Kathmandu-Lalitpur conurbation have prospered, either by selling meat or by driving and owning taxis. The younger Khadgi men fiercely resent unequal treatment at the hands of higher castes and consider themselves as Newar as the next man. There is an interesting contrast here between Khadgis and Maharjans. Maharjan young men seem to be particularly hostile to Shrestha pretensions, perhaps because the castes of bloc 4, formerly their inferiors, often now claim Shrestha status. Khadgi young men, by contrast, feel greatest anger against the Shakyas and Bajracharyas, for preaching Buddhism, supposedly an egalitarian doctrine, while continuing to exclude them, the Khadgi, on the grounds of caste.

In contrast to the Khadgi, the Sweepers still form a kind of sub-culture apart. They too are far less impoverished than they were, most benefiting from regular employment in government offices and municipal rubbish collection. But they do not refer to themselves as Newars. They are most certainly not treated as equal and they have not yet attempted to force the issue, by demanding access to high-caste water spouts, for instance.

Ulrike Müller-Böker has surveyed 39 Newar towns and villages of the Kathmandu Valley outside the three big cities. In 20 Shresthas are the largest caste, and in 18 Maharjans (the other one, Kagatigaon, is inhabited by Balami). In every case, what I have called blocs 2 and 3 together make up more than 70% of the inhabitants (Müller-Böker, 1988: 27–8).

NEWAR CULTURAL NATIONALISM

Newars of the Valley today look back at the three Malla
kingdoms of Kathmandu, Lalitpur, and Bhaktapur, and talk
nostalgically of the 'Newar' kings who never ate their rice without
first going to their roof-top balcony and checking that smoke was
coming from the cooking stoves of every kitchen in their kingdom.
In fact, of course, the Malla kings were by no means always
beneficent towards their subjects. Moreover, for the most part they
did not define themselves as Newars (they wrote more plays in
Maithili than in Newari). They justified their position in terms of
descent from the Mithila king, Harisimhadeva. They, like all the
high-status castes of the time, and many of the lower specialist ones,
defined their status by means of *non-local* affiliations. Ultimately they
claimed to be descended from the god Rama; and it is no coincidence
that they filled their palace squares with temples to Vishnu of whom
Rama is one of the two most important incarnations.

As noted above, the term 'Newar' was used at that time to
refer to the noble and predominantly Hindu caste which today is
known as Shrestha. The first occurrences of the word date from the
second half of the seventeenth century (Gellner, 1986: 140). Right
up to the nineteenth century the term 'Newar' was used primarily
for Shresthas. Since then the denotation of the word has expanded
in its dominant usage to include all those who speak Newari and
belong to the Newar caste system, plus all those descended from
those who used to speak it and used to so belong. But even today
the lowest castes such as some Khadgi and most of the Untouchable
Sweeper caste do not consider themselves Newars. Nor, as we have
seen, do the Newars' Brahmans identify themselves as Newars. In
fact, the old usage, whereby only high-caste Shresthas and those
very similar to them are referred to as Newars, survives in the
outlying town of Panauti (Barré *et al.*, 1981: 25 n. 5).

Over the last century or more it is the Shresthas who have
led the way in assimilating to the culture and the language of the
dominant Parbatiyas, and this has resulted in what I have named
the Shrestha paradox (Gellner, 1986). Although considered by
non-Newars and by themselves to be the paradigmatic Newars, a

claim which we have seen to have considerable historical precedent, other, *non*-Shrestha Newars, especially those with strong Buddhist leanings, regard the Shresthas as the most corrupt and least Newar of Newars. It is surely likely that there are parallels in other parts of South Asia, where members of the dominant local caste are the most prone to adopt cosmopolitan ways, and are therefore seen as simultaneously the most typical and the least authentic representatives of the local culture.

Be that as it may, Shresthas were prominent in the movement I have called Newar cultural nationalism. I call it 'cultural' because it has, for the most part quite deliberately, avoided anything which could be construed as political action, in order to forestall government harassment. It has concentrated mostly on literary activities: producing poetry, plays, newspapers, linguistic analyses (including grammars and dictionaries of Newari), and articles on Newar culture and history. But alongside this there have also been demands for primary schooling to be made available in the mother tongue, for Newari broadcasts on the radio to be resumed as existed before 1965, for the Nepal Era to be recognized as the official Nepali era in place of the 'foreign' Vikram Era identified as Indian, and for Newar poets to appear on Nepali postage stamps.

Only a minority of Newars actually participate in these cultural activities. Writing in 1985, K. P. Malla stated that

> Until recently [the Newari language movement] was *never an organised movement* ... [It was a] disorganised, periodic and irregular articulation of vague resentment and idealistic aspirations ... Politically and culturally, it will begin to matter only when the movement has a firm leadership, a clear programme, some tangible demands and an organised cadre of workers. None exists at the moment.[6]

This was certainly the case then, but much has changed in the intervening decade. As will be discussed below, organizations aspiring to precisely those ends have arisen – too many of them. K. P. Malla commented to me in January 1996 that the problem now is too much organization, not too little.

In the Panchayat period the Newars' literary activities were symptomatic of a wider, quite strong sense of cultural identity. A large part of this modern awareness of being Newar is made up of a feeling of difference from, and resentment at, the dominant Parbatiyas, a feeling which seems to be shared by all Newars, despite all the other factors of caste, religion, dialect, and locality which serve to keep them apart. Non-Newars who live in Kathmandu frequently complain of how communal the Newars are. By this they mean exclusive; a common complaint is that Newars insist on speaking Newari to each other even in the presence of those who do not speak it. Why is it, then, that in spite of a strong cultural identity, the Newars have been slower than other large Nepalese minorities to develop a communalist or nationalist political movement? Why is it that opposition to the state is expressed entirely through the Congress Party and, more particularly, the various Communist Parties?

THE EVENTS OF 1990

During the later 1980s the Kathmandu-Lalitpur conurbation went through a period of intense population growth, in-migration, and economic expansion. Corruption in high places, which many believed went to the very top, became more blatant. The gap between the government rhetoric of democracy and development, and the reality of economic stagnation, ecological degradation, and political opportunism became ever wider (close associates of one of the King's brothers were arrested by Interpol for international heroin smuggling, for example). Now there was a substantial modern–educated middle class in the capital, as well as a peasant-cum-working class youth which had grown up long after the hierarchical and deferential days of the Ranas. I was taken aback on a visit in 1989 to hear a Shakya man tell a young boy in my presence that the King and Queen, and he pointed to their ubiquitous portraits in a most undeferential way, were "camels".

In March 1989 the Trade and Transit Treaty with India ran out without being renegotiated. India closed thirteen of the fifteen border checkposts and imposed what Nepal considered to be a blockade of the country, in retaliation for Nepal having bought small arms from China. India expected Nepal to make immediate concessions, as had happened in similar negotiating positions in the past. Instead the Nepalese government held out, and initially had the support of opposition parties. The capital experienced considerable economic hardship with soaring prices of kerosene and rice. During the so-called blockade the opposition could not campaign against the Panchayat regime. Once the new government of V. P. Singh had come into power in Delhi, although the economic squeeze continued, the opposition felt freer to take advantage of people's pent up frustrations. The movement against the Panchayat system then took off.

The story of the revolution of 1990 has been told elsewhere.[7] There were many factors in its success: the decision of seven out of ten major Communist factions to form the United Left Front (ULF) and to campaign with the Congress Party; the continued opposition of student political bodies; the support of major Indian political parties for change in Nepal;[8] the dire economic situation. But none of these would have succeeded if the people of Bhaktapur and Lalitpur (Patan) had not been willing to revolt and die in front of the soldiers' bullets. The army is recruited almost entirely from the Nepalese hills. If ordered to do so, they would have been willing to go on facing up to demonstrations from the people of the Valley. But the leaders of the Panchayat regime, and in particular the King, were not willing to stomach large numbers of deaths.

The consistently most vociferous opposition to the Panchayat regime, and the staunchest Communists, among the Newars came from the city of Bhaktapur and the town of Kirtipur. The inhabitants of both settlements feel especially disadvantaged. Kirtipur is built on a steep hill just two miles south-west of Kathmandu. In the eighteenth century it twice put up very severe resistence to Prithvi Narayan Shah's armies, and only at the third attempt, after a six-month siege and numerous privations, did they persuade the Kirtipurians to surrender. In return, all the men of Kirtipur had their noses cut off. This event is still vividly remembered by the people of Kirtipur. More recently, in the 1960s, a large amount of Kirtipur's rice land was taken by the government, with token compensation, to create the spacious grounds of the new Tribhuvan university. This too is vividly and angrily remembered.

Bhaktapur, on the other hand, is about eight miles away from Kathmandu. This is far enough that it has not seen the boom in commercial opportunities that have emerged in the Kathmandu – Lalitpur conurbation. The people of Bhaktapur feel that there has been deliberate government neglect. The political leadership of the city is unequivocally in the hands of Narayan Man Bijukche, known as Comrade Rohit. He has his own Communist party, the Nepal Workers' and Peasants' Party. He seems to have the total support of the city's agriculturalists, who form the majority of its population. Many of the Shresthas, the bloc 2 caste, have migrated to Kathmandu over the last century so that peasants, who form the natural constituency of the Communists, are a much larger proportion of the population in Bhaktapur than in either Lalitpur or Kathmandu. Bhaktapur was notorious for its opposition to the government and for its communism throughout the 1980s. All elections, both local and national, were won by Comrade Rohit's candidates, though officially they stood only for themselves. In 1988 Rohit was put in prison after the former MP for Bhaktapur was lynched by an angry crowd which believed that he had misappropriated government relief for earthquake damage.

It is not surprising, then, that the day after the first clashes between police and demonstrators in Kathmandu (February 18th, 1990), there were violent protests in Bhaktapur. At least four people died when police fired dum dum bullets. It was the use of these bullets, banned elsewhere since the First World War, that led to strikes by doctors and nurses at Kathmandu's Bir Hospital. There followed six weeks of violent and non-violent protests in many parts of the country. It was not until the end of March that the Newars of Lalitpur became as active as those of Bhaktapur. There is a story, which has entered the mythology of the events of 1990, that the people of Bhaktapur sent a sari and set of woman's bangles to Lalitpur, with a message that they should either put them on or send them back. The implication was that if they sent them back they would have to rise up against the government. In one version

I heard, the sari was hung on a tree at the shrine of Bal Kumari on the western outskirts of Lalitpur. Several people told me that the story was just made up by politicians to get people going. True or not, it reflects well the simultaneous competition and solidarity between the two Newar cities.

The first violent clashes in Lalitpur occurred on March 30th 1990 and focused on the Panchayat building in the centre of the city. There were two or three deaths and numerous injuries when the police opened fire in Sundhara (Lunhiti). The next day the police came to Lunkhusi and Tyaga, both strongly Maharjan localities in the peasant-dominated eastern end of Lalitpur, assuming, it is said, that in arresting peasants they would be arresting communists.[9] The police also vented their frustration at being the targets of bricks and stones by trashing the insides of several houses. As their young men were led away, the Maharjan women and girls came out to protest: they were teargassed and charged with lathis (staves). This caused great anger, and that night people engineered a blackout, as had happened several times already in Kathmandu. Under cover of darkness barricades were set up and trenches dug at the entrances to the city. About 100 policemen were blockaded in the police station in the royal palace at the city centre; in recalling these events locals stressed that they had not been harmed and that they had sent food in to them. (They escaped two nights later.) The city itself became a no-go area for police and the army and was declared a 'liberated zone' (mukta kṣetra). Young men patrolled the entrances to the city all night on the look out for agents provocateurs known as Mandale, after the Panchayat-sponsored student organization, the Nepal Rastriya Swatantra Vidyarthi Mandal. On the 4th of April Ganesh Man Singh, leader of the Congress Party and of the anti-government agitation, issued a statement from his hospital bed in which he praised the people of Kirtipur and Lalitpur, and compared Lalitpur to Timisoara in Rumania (Dhakal, 1992: 104).

On April 6th the King tried to save the Panchayat system by appointing a new Prime Minister and a new cabinet. Demonstrators in Kathmandu marched to Lalitpur to bring the people from there. This led to the decisive confrontation. The demonstration returned to Kathmandu. After a public meeting at

Ratna Park, the demonstrators, chanting slogans against the King, decided to head towards the royal palace.[10] A common slogan was *bire cor deś choḍ* or 'Thief Birendra quit the country!', a reference to the millions he and his family were widely believed to have stashed away in Switzerland. Outside the royal palace the soldiers opened fire. Some initial reports put the number of dead at 200; the report of the Mallick Commission put the number of dead at just 2; the true figure may have been between 25 and 50. This seems to have proved too much for the king: two days later, after a 24-hour curfew, he summoned the leaders of Congress and the ULF and gave in to their demand for a multi-party system.

There was still a long way to go, and there had to be several more vociferous demonstrations of public anger, and a period of lawless violence blamed on 'Mandales' before the King was finally convinced that he had no choice but to support the interim government; but the battle was essentially won. Observers of the political scene in Kathmandu were struck by many similarities with the 1950s. Many of the same political actors were involved and it was evident that they were trying to avoid the mistakes of the 1950s. After the elections of 1991 the Congress Prime Minister was the younger brother of B. P. Koirala who had been the only previous Congress Prime Minister in 1958–9.

In reality, however, it is the differences with the 1950s which are more significant.[11] For a start, the role of India was much less important in 1990, however much the Panchayat leaders tried to blame everything on foreign interference. Secondly, there had been, in the interim, massive population growth in Kathmandu, and the creation of a modern, professional middle class. The willingness of academics, students, doctors, lawyers, school teachers and school children to strike and protest against government action during late February and March of 1990 was vital to the perpetuation of the movement. "The professional middle class was a totally new feature of Nepali society and formed the backbone of the pro-Democracy movement in 1990."[12] Furthermore, massive amounts of foreign aid, foreign travel, and improved communications, including both Star TV beamed in from Hong Kong and Indian TV, meant that no one in the Valley remained isolated from foreign influences.

Finally, another new and crucial factor, which this account has sought to stress, was the willingness of men *and* women from the Newar agriculturalist castes to appear on the streets and face the dum dum bullets. Congress activists admit that they were surprised by the degree of popular response to their call to action; they never expected the movement to be so successful. It was, I think, the prominence of agriculturalists in the demonstrations which led some locals to tell me in 1991 that the Communists had done the work, but the Congress Party was now reaping the benefit.

One should note also that it is among the agriculturalist castes that women habitually work outside the home and are used to wielding sickles. Whereas high-caste Newar women need a definite and permissible reason to leave the home, Maharjan women will even join in inter-locality fights between groups of Maharjans. The female participation is noted by Dhakal in his history of the people's movement:

> Among Lalitpur's armed demonstrations, those of the women are of historical significance. Every day after the morning meal the women tied their babies on their hips or backs, took up their sickles, mattocks, rakes, hoes, sticks etc., and demonstrated all day against the oppression of the Panchayat system ... Thus on April 6th (Cait 24th), without the slightest trace of fear, more than 100,000 men and women of Lalitpur crossed the Bagmati river to Kathmandu ...[13]

When the dust had died down, the number of deaths from police and army firing that it was possible to verify was found to be 41, including one British tourist. These were declared official martyrs (Dhakal, 1992: 208). Putting aside the tourist, 17 died outside the Valley and 23 within. Of the 23 deaths in the Valley, 4 were in Kirtipur, 5 in Bhaktapur, 4 in Lalitpur, and 10 in Kathmandu. All but 3 of these were Newars: in terms of the caste blocs mentioned above, 5 were Shakyas or Bajracharyas (bloc 1), two were Uray and one a Shrestha (bloc 2), 9 were agriculturalists (bloc 3), one was a Nakarmi (bloc 4), and two were Khadgi (bloc 5). The Parbatiya stereotype of the Newars, dating from 1769 or before, portrays them as vainglorious, feast-addicted, and cowardly, while the Newars view Parbatiyas as rustic and uncouth (Nepali, 1965: 18–19). A Gurung friend observed to me in 1991 that no one would ever be able to accuse Newars of cowardice again.

THE ELECTIONS OF 1991 AND 1992

Six weeks before the elections of 1991 it was fairly clear that the Communists would do well in Lalitpur. What was not anticipated was that they would take eight out of ten seats in the Kathmandu Valley: six went to the UML, the main Communist grouping which had been part of the interim government with the Congress Party, one to the Maoist United People's Front, and one in Bhaktapur to Comrade Rohit, standing for his own party, the NWPP. In the country as a whole Congress just succeeded in winning an overall majority, gaining 54% of the seats with 38% of the vote, whereas the UML won 34% of the seats with 28% of the votes. It was considered especially humiliating that the Congress should lose four out of five seats in the capital city. Furthermore, the Prime Minister, K. P. Bhattarai, and both the wife and son of Ganesh Man Singh, all three standing in Kathmandu for the Congress Party, were beaten.[14]

In the following months a discourse grew up, both among Newars and others, which painted all Newars as Communists, even though the election results clearly showed that Congress had considerable support too. Commentators tried to argue that there was a natural affinity between Newar culture and communism because of the institution of *guthi*s, cooperative organizations traditional to Newar culture. The fact that *guthi*s are mostly exclusivist mono-caste organizations, concerned with maintaining their members' caste purity, was ignored.

Local elections took place a year later in 1992. It was expected that the Communists would again sweep the board in the Kathmandu Valley. In the country as a whole Congress won 50% of the seats in the villages, and 56% in the municipalities, while the

FIGURE 9   *Election banners on the Chyasing Deval and royal palace in*
Mangal Bazaar, the centre of Lalitpur, April–May 1991
(Christine Stingelin Schmid)

FIGURE 10   *Election flags, posters, and graffiti in Sundhara/Lunhiti, Lalitpur, April–May 1991 (Christine Stingelin Schmid)*

UML gained 26% in the villages and 20% in the municipalities. Within the Valley, much to people's surprise, the posts of both Mayor and Vice-Mayor of Kathmandu and Lalitpur were won by the Congress Party, and in both cities Congress won an absolute majority on the city council (19 out of 35 in Kathmandu, 12 out of 22 in Lalitpur). By contrast, the hold of the NWPP on Bhaktapur was secure, and in Kirtipur three constituences were won by Communists, one by the Congress Party. Suddenly no one was saying that all Newars are Communists; many declared that the Communists were finished.

In fact, both 1991 and 1992, the vote was in some cases very close, with less than a thousand votes between the candidates. None the less, there was definitely a turning away from the Communists in Kathmandu and Lalitpur. What lay behind this? Many people were fed up with the continual demonstrations and violence sponsored by Communists since 1991, and with the numerous divisions among them. Second, the Congress Party was much cannier and more organized than in 1991. (It also had the advantage of incumbency and as able to make some use, it is said, of government resources.) In Nag Baha, Lalitpur, a well-known Congress stronghold, I was told that this time they had "imitated the Communists" and gone door to door asking for people's vote. In 1991 Congress had certainly erred by imposing non-local candidates and by assuming they did not have to work hard to win. Nepalis expect to be asked for their vote. Third, many well-off and/or well-connected Newars had come to regret the outcome of the 1991 elections. Communist victories in Kathmandu had left them without any clear avenue or access to the Congress government, since all the representatives for urban areas were in opposition. Ministers with power all came from and had power bases outside the Valley. Prominent Newar families had no alternative but to turn to Ganesh Man Singh, the 80-year-old 'Supreme Leader' of the Congress Party. The pressure he was put under explains some of the friction between him and the other two (non-Newar) leaders of the Congress Party, K. P. Bhattarai, and, more particularly, the new Prime Minister after Bhattarai lost his seat, G. P. Koirala. In short, many Newars in Kathmandu and Lalitpur, as indeed many people throughout the country, understood that if they wanted access to government, and to the resources the government controlled, they had better have Congress representing them. A fourth factor, emphasized by Communist sympathizers, was the relatively greater importance of ties of kinship, caste, and personal obligation in local elections: in 1992 the Communists had no previous organization in many wards and their candidates, unlike those of the Congress Party, were young and unknown.

The results of the local elections greatly strengthened the Congress Party, and in particular shored up the personal position of the Prime Minister, both of which, with continuing economic woes, had begun to look decidedly shaky. The local elections were, in short, evidence of considerable routinization. For most people the great hopes and expectations raised in 1990 had now been dashed or seen to be unrealistic. A common view was that the rules had been changed but the players had remained the same (sic). In fact many thought things had got worse: inflation was more rapid, corruption was far more widespread and open, and the government seemed to have no direction.

THE MEANING OF NEWAR COMMUNISM

Two months before the elections of 1991 I was in the locality of Chyasa, Lalitpur; many houses had communist flags flying from the windows. Talking with a group of young Byanjankars, who said that the area was solid behind the UML, I asked if it wasn't true that the Communists deny the existence of gods. Their leather-jacketed spokesman replied vehemently:

> No! it is Congress that says that. They say you should marry your mother and steal to make a living; they sell off the country to India; and they oppress other people. Communists want to preserve old customs, help other people, and uplift the country. Communists paint election slogans out of their own pocket and do it openly in the daytime. Congress slogans only get written because people have to come and write them at night. Who is it that comes out at night? Thieves, that's who.

This respect for traditional culture and religion is found also among Communist leaders. Siddhi Lal Singh, the UML candidate who won handsomely in Lalitpur-2, the constituency containing most of the old city, told me that Lalitpur had four needs: adequate drainage, preservation of its temples and culture, jobs, and adult education. Tulsi Lal Amatya, a veteran Communist leader from Lalitpur, sees communism as the essence of true Hinduism, and Comrade Rohit in Bhaktapur told Martin Hoftun:

> The aim of religion has always been to reform society ... Every time a new injustice became rampant in society, a new religion would appear. In this way socialism came to Europe in the form of a religion when economic exploitation of the workers had reached its most extreme, just as Buddhism came to India in the age of slavery to give the oppressed liberation (Raeper and Hoftun, 1992: 92–3).

Communists, therefore, both by personal conviction and out of respect to their supporters, do not attack conventional religion. More positively, communism stands for equality, for helping the poor, and for the rights of the tiller.[15] The Communists argue that after a lifetime tilling the land, a tenant ought to have a right to own it. This is part of the great appeal of communism to the agriculturalist castes. What the Communists have never advocated is any kind of collective ownership, which would be anathema to their peasant supporters. Nor have they ever proposed positive discrimination on behalf of Untouchables, in spite of the example of India. This is no doubt for the same reason. By the same token, with the exception of certain activists and other committed individuals, most members of the higher Newar castes, including most landowners, support the Congress Party.

Recently various Communist parties, including the UML, have come out in favour of some kind of ethnic quotas, as a kind of vote-catching exercise (see p.66 above). But these are very double-edged policies which would be very difficult to implement, because of the problems inherent in defining who is eligible for the benefit.

Newar Communists have played an important role, however, in articulating Newar ethnic feelings. Both Siddhi Lal Singh and Comrade Rohit took the oath, when being sworn in to the National

Assembly, in Newari. Other Communists gave speeches in reply to the royal address to the House in July 1991 in Limbu and Tamang, and the leader of the Nepal Sadbhavana Party did so in Hindi (NPD 35, 28: 272). Padma Ratna Tuladhar, a non-aligned communist who was elected first under the Panchayat system but because of his impeccable record of opposition and total incorruptibility was accepted as part of the UML, has always stressed in his speeches that he did not want the votes of those who gave them to him because he is a Newar. But there can be little doubt that, standing for a central Kathmandu constituency, being a Newar has been a big advantage for him. He has lent his name and support to Newar *cultural* nationalist organizations, and advocates mother-tongue schooling at primary level as a preventative measure against the emergence of communalism (Raeper and Hoftun, 1992: 165–6). He too took his oath in the National Assembly in Newari.

ANTIBRAHMANISM, RELIGION, AND NEWAR ETHNICITY AFTER 1990

It is said that some demonstrators in 1990 chanted the slogan *hāmro pālā pheri āyo* or 'Our time has come again'. No party claims this slogan, and I have not been able to verify that it was in fact chanted.[16] But if it was, there is a double irony. In the first place, the slogan, stating that our, i.e. the Newars', time had returned, was chanted in Nepali, the language of politics, not in Newari. Secondly, after the elections of 1991, the number of Parbatiya Brahmans in positions of power increased appreciably: Bahuns, who make up 13% of the population, were 12.5% of the National Assembly in 1981 and 37.4% in 1991. It is not the Newars' time that has come, but the Brahmans'. The big losers were in fact the Chetris, whose representation in the Assembly declined from 36.6% in 1981 to 17.7% in 1991.[17] Newar representation remained virtually unchanged at 8% (H. Gurung, 1992: 20). More importantly, perhaps, the leadership of all the important parties was in the hands of Bahuns.

supposed to be a universalist doctrine, and in its modern forms local Buddhism does indeed recruit from non-Newars if they wish to become monks or nuns. Furthermore, since all the other bases of ethnic identity (territory, language, culture) link Newar Buddhists to others who do not define themselves as Buddhist, this implicit quasi-ethnic identity remains just that: implicit. But for young Shakyas and Bajracharyas their strong awareness of being Newar is run together with their attachment to Buddhism: they feel disadvantaged on both counts.

At the moment differences of caste, locality, religion, and dialect seem to override any wider sense of being Newar on all except literary and cultural occasions. But history is open, and it remains conceivable that for some Newars at least this might change. Apparently it was quite fashionable in Kathmandu in 1993 to wear lapel badges saying *ji newā kha* (I'm a Newar). In May 1993 an organization calling itself Newa Guthi was established by a younger generation of activists. According to the English-language version of its publicity leaflet, its "objective" is as follows:

> To take necessary steps in a systematic manner for
> – Strengthening Nepal Nation by uplifting nationhood of Newas
> – Encouraging and motivating in utilizing Nepalbhasa, the only mother-tongue of Newas with diversity in culture, race and religion
> – Showing all Newas are united as one
> – Reviving the glory and dignity of Newa culture and Nepalbhasa
> – Strengthening democracy by taking necessary steps for obtaining lawful right for Nepalbhasa and Newa nationhood.

Unlike the Nepal Bhasha Manka Khalah, an older umbrella organization bringing together a large number of Newar cultural groups, the Newa Guthi is not a member of the Nepal Federation of Nationalities (NEFEN), which itself has links to the UML. The Newa Guthi was therefore seen to be right-wing and the Manka Khalah left-wing. In an attempt to overcome these splits a nation-wide organization called Newa De Dabu (The Newar National Forum) was set up in September 1995.

It is impossible to say for sure whether the sentiments promoted by such groups will have a political effect or not. The multiplication of different, and presumably competing, organizations suggests that the 'traditional' fissipariousness of Newar social organization continues to be carried over into the political and cultural spheres.

CONCLUSION

The answer I offer to my original question, why no Newar has attempted to organize a communal party, comes in three parts:

1. The potential pool of political leaders is in large part going to be from the Shrestha caste, and here the Shrestha paradox comes into play: although seen as the archetypal Newars, they are simultaneously the most integrated, the most economically successful, and the most internationally minded. Of other potential leaders, the Brahmans are very few and do not identify themselves as Newars. The Bajracharyas and Shakyas have no tradition of political leadership and their strong Buddhist identity has led them to develop a quasi-ethnic identity of their own, as noted above.

2. Further down the social hierarchy, there is no tradition of peasant protest in the Kathmandu Valley, unlike in some parts of India (Dhanagare, 1983) or, arguably, in the eastern hills of Nepal. However there are traditions of Maharjan culture which, together with increased prosperity, greater education, greater self-confidence, and considerable exposure to communist and egalitarian ideologies, contributed to the uprising of 1990. Maharjans are proud of the fact that members of the same locality always help each other and that they have numerous forms of mutual work groups. At the same time different localities vie with each other for prestige, through music, rituals, feasts, and occasionally fighting. In some Newar settlements such competition between different parts of the city is formalized with ritual fighting on specific festivals

(Slusser, 1982: 91, 103; Levy, 1990: 168–74). The Maharjan peasants of the Valley did not traditionally profit from trade or government service under the Ranas. But they have also had no reason to prefer Newar to Parbatiya landlords. Consequently it is Communist leaders who have had the most appeal for them. Even when Communist leaders use cultural nationalist rhetoric, and in spite of the fact that demonstrations have often pitched Newar agriculturalists against non-Newar police and army units, the driving force of their protest is social, not ethnic.

3. There has in fact been a tradition of subordination among the Newars since 1769. It was rather a successful tradition, as shown by figures for Newar representation in government jobs given by Whelpton (above, p.50) . Many Newars would still call it a tradition of loyalty to king and country. Only a few rare individuals have challenged this subordination/loyalty. Until 1990 cultural nationalists almost always preferred to make their demands in as non-political a way as possible, in the hope that the authorities would see them as unthreatening.

In short, a strong sense of Newar identity does not motivate political action directly. This is partly because 'Newar identity' means very different things to different people. But a crucial factor is that the protestors of 1990 had no sense that the (relative) poverty, the exclusions, and the injustices that they suffered from were directed against them *as Newars*.

NOTES

For comments on earlier versions of this paper I am grateful to Chris Fuller, Martin Gaenszle, Declan Quigley, Joanna Pfaff-Czarnecka, Anil Sakya, Gregory Sharkey, John Whelpton, and the members of seminars in San Francisco, Oxford, London (L.S.E.), and Belfast. Nirmal Man Tuladhar deserves special thanks for keeping me in touch. I alone am responsible for any errors of balance or fact. The paper was initially conceived in 1992. Although it was possible to make revisions in the light of a two-week visit to Kathmandu in January 1996, its structure and argument reflect the conditions of the period immediately after 1990.

1   See Slusser (1982: 59), Gellner (1992: 63, 86–7), Gellner and Quigley (1995, chapter 1).

2   See Gellner (1991: 21), Brinkhaus (1993).

3   Kumar Pradhan (1991: 96) writes of "burgeoning [Newar] national consciousness" at this time; but he admits immediately that "it is difficult to gauge how strong the Newar national spirit was."

4   See Lewis and Sakya (1988) on some Newar settlements in east Nepal.

5   Just who was responsible, and to what extent this notorious Kot massacre was premeditated, remain controversial matters. See Whelpton (1991).

6   K. P. Malla, personal communication (comments on an early draft of Gellner, 1986; original emphasis), 9/10/85.

7   See Bonk (1990), Raeper and Hoftun (1992), Dhakal (1992), and other references given in the Introduction, n.1.

8   This included, surprisingly, the Hindu 'fundamentalist' BJP, which has always given particular support to Nepal's Hindu monarchy (Raeper and Hoftun, 1992: 125–6 cf. Hacchethu, 1990: 196–7, and Brown, 1996: 136–7).

9   According to Raeper and Hoftun's informants (1992: 110) the movement in Lalitpur began in Chyasa, but this too is an agriculturalist locality on the eastern side of the city.

10 See Bonk (1990: 31–3).

11 "The 1951 revolution was rightly called a Palace Revolution. What happened in 1990 was a popular uprising – at least in the Kathmandu valley" (Raeper and Hoftun, 1992: 115).

12 Raeper and Hoftun (1992: 79). Cf. Hacchethu (1990: 190–2), Gaenszle (1991a: 241ff.).

13 Dhakal (1992: 125). The figure of 100,000 is being used extremely loosely here: the total number at the demonstration in Kathmandu may have been over 100,000 (Gaenszle, 1991a: 243).

14 In February 1994, in a by-election following the death in 1993 of Madan Bhandari in a motor accident which leftists believed occurred in suspicious circumstances, K. P. Bhattarai was again defeated by Bhandari's widow.

15 For an analysis of the the attempts elsewhere in South Asia to put the slogan 'Land to the Tiller' into practice, see Herring (1983).

16 Too much significance should not be read into a single slogan. Nirmal Man Tuladhar reports hearing Newar youths chanting. "We want *demokrāsi*, we want *dwāyā kwāsi* (bull's testicles)!" (personal communication). Even this, however, while it may have seemed like a

meaningless play on words to many bystanders, could also be read as an assertion of republicanism (the bull being the vehicle of the god Pashupati, the national deity, and therefore a symbol of the king).

[17] This decline puts a rather different light on the controversy surrounding Dor Bahadur Bista's denunciation of Brahmanism and praise of the poor and Nepal's ethnic groups in his *Fatalism and Development* (1991), although the book was in fact composed before the events of 1990. Bista comes from a Chetri family with a history of opposition to the Sanskritizing and Vedicizing tendences of influential Brahman families; he has written frequently since 1990 on the evils of Brahmanism.

[18] Singh's "stand is directed not against nepotism and favouritism but for their extension" (*Deshantar*). "The episode has only harmed Ganesh Man's image. He may now have his way in some appointments of ambassadors, ministers, etc., but does this justify his threat to retire?" (*Nepali Patra*). "If G. P. Koirala is drowned in Brahmanism, Ganesh Man Singh is drowned in Newarism" (*Nepal Bhumi*) (NPD 35, 38: 371–2).

[19] See Gellner (1995). Barnett analyses the ethnicization of caste blocs in Tamil Nadu and notes that "In Madras city, urban untouchables are *excluded* from ethnicization ... the concept of a separate 'untouchable race' is emerging among upper-class city dwellers" (Barnett, 1976: 159; original emphasis).

CHAPTER FIVE

Identity and Change Among the Gurungs (Tamu-mai) of Central Nepal

Alan Macfarlane

INTRODUCTION

On the 13th of March 1992 I received a fax from Pokhara, which included the following:

> You may be interested to know that the following resolutions were unanimously agreed upon at the nation-wide Gurung conference held this week in Pokhara:
>
> 1. Gurung history was written and distorted by Brahmans.
> 2. There are no inferior and superior clan groups in Gurung society.
> 3. The traditional Gurung priests are the Pa-chyu and the Khlibri; lamas are a more recent addition.

In this paper I would like to give a little of the background to these interesting resolutions. In the process I would like to explore how the discussions of identity among the Gurungs have further broken down the gap between the observer and the observed, the anthropologist and the people s/he 'studies'.

SOME PRESSURES UPON THE GURUNGS

The Gurungs are a Tibeto-Burman speaking group who mainly live in the Annapurna region of central Nepal. There are also many Gurungs now living in eastern Nepal and in the cities and

185

plains of Nepal and India. In all, there must be about 200,000 Gurung speakers in the world and another 50,000 or so who call themselves Gurung but do not speak the language. My own work among them started in 1968 and since then I have returned some seven times, in particular to work in the village of Thak, north of Pokhara.

Over a period of twenty-five years I have watched the increasing pressures, material and cultural, which have built up on the Gurungs. Many of these changes are similar to those which are occurring among all the mountain peoples of Nepal and neighbouring regions.

There are, first of all, the demographic pressures. Though the Gurung population is growing less slowly than the Nepalese population as a whole, which is doubling every twenty-five years or so, it is still growing relatively fast, perhaps doubling in twice that time. This is linked to the well-known ecological deterioration in the hills. Forests have been cut back, hillsides eroded. For a number of different reasons there appears to have been somewhere near a 50% decline in crop production over the last twenty-five years in the village of Thak, north of Pokhara, where my fieldwork has been concentrated. This is a result of a number of factors: a shortage of manure, over-cropping, heavy rains leaching the steep terraces, deteriorating standards of field use.

Meanwhile, the effects of the opening of the roads from the south and the development of Pokhara has been to push down the relative value of village land. While prices of land in the Pokhara plain have rocketed, in the villages the land prices have not even kept pace with inflation.

The decline in local productivity is matched by a decline in external sources of income. The major traditional source of income for migrant labourers, the army, and particularly the British army, is now a very minor source of employment in most villages. There are perceived to be very few chances of employment in the small civil service and professional sector in Nepal, which is thought to be dominated by Parbatiyas and Newars. The availability of work in India has also declined and many villagers have told us that wages, if work can be found, are lower in real terms than they were even ten years ago.

Equally serious, but more difficult to quantify, are cultural pressures. Over the twenty-five years since I first visited the Gurungs, the spread of Nepali-medium teaching, the effects of the radio, the growing dominance of the towns, have all eroded the language and culture. The cultural pressures which coincide with the forceful introduction of consumer capitalism, ostentatious tourism, foreign aid projects, television and radio, are apparent in a variety of ways that can only be alluded to here. There is a loss of confidence in the value of Gurung traditions and culture: a revolution of rising expectations, a growing frustration and disillusionment, especially among the young.

Part of this cultural stress comes in the form of religious pressure. There is a growing threat from and dominance by the two competing literate world religions, Hinduism and Buddhism, which threaten the old unwritten shamanic religion of the Gurungs. Likewise, the long tradition of *de facto* political autonomy of the villages is threatened by rapid political centralization and mobilization with the movement from royal absolutism to a form of government modelled on western democracy.

These pressures can most easily be summarized by tabulating the answers to the simple question, 'What does it mean to be a Gurung?' for 1968 and 1992. If we answer this in terms of certain sub-questions, the answer might read as shown in Table 5.1

SOME PRACTICAL REACTIONS TO THE PRESSURES

In this brief account I would like to look at some of the reactions to these pressures. The practical reactions have attracted more attention and I will merely list them, since it is the questions of symbolic reactions and discussions of identity which is the theme of this piece.

Within the village, probably the main change has been in the organization of labour, basically from co-operative farming to share-cropping, which was practically unknown in 1968 in Thak. The

FIGURE 12   *The audience of Gurung priests* (pa-chyu *and* khlibri) *listening to the inaugural meeting of the Pye-ta Lhu-ta, an organization for the study and preservation of Gurung myth and ritual* (Sarah Harrison)

TABLE 5.1 WHAT DOES IT MEAN TO BE GURUNG?

	1968	1992
Where do you live?	a Gurung village	a Nepali town
What do you do?	agriculture or army	various paid jobs
What do you wear?	Gurung clothes	Nepali clothes
What language?	Gurung (Nepali)	Nepali (Gurung)
What politically?	Gurung	Nepali
What hobbies?	dancing and singing	radio, sport
What leisure group?	age groups, *rodi*[a]	friends
What work group?	*gola, nogora*[b]	wages, share-crops

Notes:

[a]   *rodi* is the communal Gurung dormitory, which is based on age groupings.

[b]   *gola* and *nogora* are communal work groups, usually based on friendship and neighbourhood.

FIGURE 13   *Pa-chyu Yarjung Kromche addressing the inaugural meeting of the*
             Pye-ta Lhu-ta in May 1992 (Sarah Harrison)

question of dwindling resources has continued to be dealt with by extensive out-migration and over the twenty-five years I have witnessed three major patterns.

The first, roughly up to the early 1970s was for migration to the army, and retirement in the village. Then from the mid-1970s there was a wave of migration to Indian cities (Bombay, Delhi, etc.), the Middle East, and retirement or movement down to Pokhara. In the last two years or so, young men have begun to search for work in South-East and East Asia: Malaysia, Singapore, Japan, Korea. They are also likely to have left the village for good.

SOME CULTURAL REACTIONS
TO THE PRESSURES

When I returned to Nepal after a long gap of seventeen years in 1986 and talked to my friends, it became clear that there was a new interest in Gurung history and culture. The rapid development of interest in Gurung identity was also increasingly evident in the activities of Gurung cultural groups in both Pokhara and Kathmandu (Tamu Di, Pye Lhu Sangha), which hold large conferences and publish work on Gurung history and traditions.

Further evidence of this increased interest has been the discussion as to how the Gurungs should name themselves. For the last hundred years or more the Gurungs have taken the semi-Hinduized and external names. Now the most active insist on calling themselves 'Tamu' which is their own term for themselves, rather than 'Gurung', which is how they are known by outsiders. Furthermore, they are keen to drop the Hinduized endings: 'Singh', 'Bahadur', 'Maya', etc. Thus a person who might three years ago have called himself Debi Bahadur Gurung will now perhaps call himself Debi Kromje Tamu, though 'Debi', of course, still retains its Sanskritic overtones. 'Kromje' is an important assertion of his clan name, not to be concealed in the new more equal world which the Gurungs hope to achieve.

As an illustration of the re-assessments which this discussion is causing, I would like to discuss briefly some aspects of the process of translating and re-issuing the classic work on the Gurungs by Bernard Pignède. In 1958 a young Frenchman, Bernard Pignède, spent some seven months among the Gurungs, five months of which were in the village of Mohoriya at the western end of Gurung territory. He worked with his assistant Chandra Bahadur Ghotane to undertake the first extended study of these people.[1] Pignède returned to Paris where he drafted out most of the book, but died tragically at the age of twenty-nine in 1961. His colleagues, and particularly Professor Louis Dumont, brought the book to press and it was published in France in 1966. The book has become something of a classic, but was unavailable to many scholars and in particular those in Nepal, because it was written in French. Since it contains so much valuable material, we decided to translate the work, and add detailed footnotes and appendices to bring it up to date.[2]

I had earlier attempted a very small exercise in collaborative representation when I co-authored a small volume with Indra Bahadur Gurung, *Guide to the Gurungs* (1990). This was a title with a deliberate double meaning, for while it was on the surface a short and simple overview intended for trekkers, aid workers, and others, I realized that it would also be used by present and future Gurungs as some kind of 'Guide' or statement of Gurung culture and customs. This small experience, however, did not really prepare me for the complexities of publishing a translation of Bernard Pignède's work.

What we did not fully realize when we started this work was as follows. The growing discussions of identity meant that a number of leading Gurungs, including Pignède's own interpreter C. B. Ghotane, wanted to scrutinize the text and, if necessary, modify the interpretation. This kind of collaborative work, which necessitated writing and re-writing sections of the work, and working closely between Pokhara, Kathmandu, and Cambridge, only really became possible as a result of some simple technological developments. In particular, the flexibility of new computers and desk-top publishing and the availability of fax machines, made it possible to attempt a new, multi-level work.[3]

Firstly, it was important to keep the integrity of Pignède's own text, and the annotations of his original editors. Then a layer of commentary was added by his current translators and editors, Alan Macfarlane and Sarah Harrison, on the basis of their numerous visits to the Gurung area of Nepal, including three visits to Mohoriya. Thirdly, it was obvious that Pignède's original field assistant, C. B. Ghotane, who carefully checked the translation, had much to add. Now that the text was in English he could point to areas where Pignède, who worked under enormous pressure, had misunderstood the situation. Fourthly, two Gurungs particularly interested in the history and traditions of their people, Indra Bahadur and Bhovar Tamu, using their own oral traditions and the written *vaṃśāvalī* or histories, added their own comments. Finally, the secret history of the Gurungs as preserved in the *pye* or oral texts (myths) of the Pa-chyu were scanned by Yarjung Kromche, a leading Pa-chyu, and Pignède's very important work on the work of the priests was checked against Yarjung's own experience.

The integrity and identity of each interpretation has been maintained, for they often conflict. The conflicts between them are, in many ways, the most interesting indication of the current debates.

In essence, it would appear that while Pignède leaned towards an Indianist interpretation of the Gurungs, the recent comments suggest a much more Tibeto-Burman slant to the material. We may illustrate this in relation to some of the key areas of disagreement, which are also among the major discussion points now among the Gurungs.

MARRIAGE, CLAN, AND 'JAT'

One area of disagreement comes in the interpretation of the marriage system of the Gurungs. This has not been of burning concern among the Gurungs themselves, perhaps because most Gurungs were not aware of the way in which Bernard Pignède's writing had been interpreted to suggest links with the asymmetrical marriage systems of India. Yet once the work is translated and widely available in Nepal, it becomes important to point out that Pignède appears to have been mistaken on this point. As summarized in a note to our joint translation, the situation is in fact as follows.

Pignède describes the system as if it is an asymmetrical one, with a marked preference for marriage with a mother's brother's daughter (matrilateral cross-cousin marriage). This would link it to the large group of societies in north India, Assam, and elsewhere, which have this preferential marriage pattern. As I argued some years ago (Macfarlane, 1979: 19), "there is considerable evidence, however, that both in theory and in practice the system is more symmetrical than he suggests with marriages occurring with father's sister's children just as often and with a mixture of symmetry and asymmetry in the kinship terminology." Informants were adamant that both type of marriage were equally desired. The Glovers (Glover, Glover, and Gurung, 1977: 303) also report that "cross cousin marriages are preferred and, in Ghachok area at least, there is no expressed preference as to whether the mate is chosen through the maternal or the paternal link."

When we asked about this in Mohoriya in 1990, people said that both types of marriage were equally desirable and, they thought, equally frequent. Furthermore, the kinship terminology seems to be consistent with this equal preference. There is a strong distinction made between the terms for parallel cousins, who are addressed and referred to in terms used for brothers and sisters, and cross-cousins, who are referred to with special terms. These terms are the same for matrilateral and patrilateral cross-cousins: *nohlo* (male) and *nohlo-syo* (female). It would be interesting to know how Pignède reached his conclusion, but, as we shall see, it fits well with his interpretation of the deeper level of Gurung social structure, and in particular the nature and relationship between the two *'jāts'* or sets of lineages in Gurung society.

Pignède's description of the clan system of the Gurungs is one of the best known and most influential parts of his work. The main section of his account was published in English before his book (Pignède, 1962). The analysis is based on the supposed dichotomies implicit in the four-fold structure of the Char Jat (literally, 'four *jāt*' in Nepali) and, less so, the structure of the Sorah Jat ('sixteen *jāt*'). An elegant argument is based on the opposition of two priestly clans (Lama and Lamechane) and two chiefly clans (Ghale and Ghotane). Pignède was, however, aware that a later rigid classification was probably imposed on a more flexible earlier system. For instance, he noted that in the Central and Eastern region, marriage rules do not conform to the system he elaborated, and that the presence of the Pai clan suggests that "there are in fact, more than four clans". This inconsistency has been confirmed by others; Messerschmidt, for example, found that in his area "there is no evidence of this duality [within the Char Jat] in contemporary marriage practice" (1976: 54).

During the years since Pignède wrote there has been much discussion about these matters. On frequent re-visits, I began to be told of secret documents, *vaṃśāvalī*, which had been hidden even from other Gurungs, which revealed a very different picture from that in Pignède. The revelation of this new material is undoubtedly directly linked with the growing openness of the discussion about who the Gurungs are. Although the matter will require considerably more work, our first impressions, as summarized in an appendix to the Pignède translation, are as follows.

We may look firstly at what Pignède calls the Char Jat to see how far they are, in fact, a four-fold group. We have examined some evidence from several of the older histories of the Gurungs, the *vaṃśāvalī*, and these never refer to the Char Jat at all. The word *jāt*, of Indian origin, is not used, but *gi* (Gurung for group or people) preceded by the Gurung word for three, *song*. Thus certain *vaṃśāvalī* tell of the *song-gi* or *minha song-gi (song-gi* people). These three groups are specified as the *lama, lema,* and *kona/kone*. They may intermarry. The *klye* (Ghale) are treated as an entirely separate group, which is itself divided into three intermarrying groups, *samri klye, relde klye,* and *kh-hyaldi klye.* In these early histories it is suggested that for a long time the "three peoples" were separate, only joining up with the other groups and the Ghale fairly recently. These early histories thus confirm that Pignède was right to be unsure about the four-fold nature of the classification.

When we discussed these matters with one of the so-called Char Jat, he said that in fact Char Jat nothing to do with the Gurungs specifically. It actually referred to the four Hindu *varṇa*, namely Brahman, Kshatriya, Vaishya, and Shudra, which he said later multiplied into thirty-six *jāt*s. This would seem to be an acknowledgement that an external, Hindu, four-fold caste division was later imposed on or absorbed into the Gurung system. C. B. Ghotane agreed that the word *jāt* is inappropriate and that the various groupings are really *thar* or clans, but he included the Ghale in this group, thus confirming Pignède's use of *plih-gi* as an alternative term for Char Jat. He also disputed the existence of a Lama clan.

Turning to the Sorah Jat, Pignède himself noted that he had also been given the name *ku-gi* ('nine-people'), and told that there were not sixteen but only nine clans. He stated that "no Gurung was able to give me a list of the sixteen Solahjat clans" (Pignède, 1993: 175). The list given in one of the legends Pignède quotes is "fanciful enough" (*ibid.*) and corresponds hardly at all to any other lists.

Again it looks as if the "sixteen people" may have been something rather different. In the *vaṃśāvalī* that we have seen, the identifiable groups in the Sorah Jat include Daria, Danuwar, Bramu, Murmi, Hanjhi, Kumal, Hayu, Chepang, Khapang, Pahari, Neware Kumal, Panchhari, Kusalya, Palahari, Musahari, and Hurkya

(Pignède, 1993: 464); there are sixteen named groups in all. They have nothing directly to do with the Gurungs.

In contrast to these, the early history in the *vaṃśāvalī* and the ritual songs (*peda luda*) of the Pa-chyu speak of the *ku-gi* or *kwo-gi*, sometimes later translated into Nepali as *nau-jāt*. The lists of these original nine groups in different *vaṃśāvalī* match well, as follows (Pignède's spellings in brackets): *krommchhain* [*kromcae*], *yobachhain*, *nhansin*, *phijon*, *chormi* [*tohrcae*], *rhilla*, *yoja*, *p-hhachyu* [*paice*], *kepchhain* [*kupcae*]. The list given to Pignède overlaps with this for four of the names, with Pignède's informant giving *mahpcae*, *kercae*, *klihbri*, *lehne*, and *thimce* for the other five (Pignède, 1993: 178).

It is particularly interesting that on the basis of comparing various lists, Pignède gives a list of twenty-seven clans. It might be suggested that the three-fold structure of the nine clans is one version of several systems which are based on multiples of the number three. In the older histories we have looked at, the *ku-gi* are often referred to as the "twelve-twenty-seven" peoples. Twelve is obviously three times four and twenty-seven, a curious number for a group, makes sense as three to the power of three, a perfect number for a three-fold system. It would appear that in place of the rather binary oppositions of Pignède's interpretation, with its Indianist moiety structure, the principles may be of a different, three-fold, structure. Only further research on the early histories and Pa-chyu's mythical stories will illuminate this.

GURUNG RELIGION

Of equal, if not greater, importance to many Gurungs now is to decide what their 'true' religion is and how it is to be performed. This is the subject of very considerable discussion in the various conferences and meetings of Gurungs, where the relative merits and antiquity of Lamaism, Hinduism, and the Pa-chyu and Khlibri priests are debated. A general consensus has emerged, which is reflected in the mythical history partly elaborated at the end of this article, which states that, as in the resolution quoted above, the

Pa-chyus are the most ancient and authentic priests, the Khlibris were the next, and the lamas are more recent.

The situation is complicated, however, by an internal dispute among the Gurungs about the central Gurung ritual, the *pwe lava* or three-day memorial to the dead. This can be seen as one part of that tension between Buddhist and tribal religion which is addressed at length by Mumford (1989). One view is that the present funeral ritual, which involves animal sacrifice, should be simplified and purified. It is too expensive, time-consuming and, possibly, somewhat 'backward'. Some traditional Gurung priests, especially in the Lamjung area have agreed to give up animal sacrifice in the *pwe*.

Other Gurungs take a completely contrary view. They believe that it is essential that some form of real sacrifice at death be continued – a blood sacrifice – as a gift to gods and ancestors. As one leading authority put it to me, "If you do not give blood you do not have a relationship. We need blood and wine." He insisted that there must be some form of destruction of life, even if the object sacrificed has to be diminished down to an egg. He is not prepared to compromise with the lama and Khlibris who would do without blood sacrifice. He argued that this is the Gurungs' real heritage: a blood sacrifice. If it is lost, he argues, the Gurungs will lose all their special identity.

Linked to questions of what kind of funeral the traditional priest should do is the question of what kind of shaman he is. Further revelations on this subject, which are not unrelated to the emergence of secret knowledge as discussions of identity grow, are worth briefly mentioning in the terms described in a note to the Pignède volume. Pignède states that there are no trances or possessions or ecstasy in the Pa-chyu's work (Pignède, 1966: 293; 1993: 308). I thought the same on the basis of working with the Thak Pa-chyu, who never mentioned possession, and did not appear to become possessed. If this were universally true, it would distinguish Gurung Pa-chyus from the classic ecstatic shamanism of inner Asia. It was therefore with considerable surprise that, when attending the *mose tiba* ritual in 1990, at the point when the evil spirit brought down the departed soul and confronted the Pa-chyus,

FIGURE 14   *Yarjung Kromche and Maila Kromche, two shamans* (pa-chyu),
during part of the funeral ritual (pwe) *of Yarjung's father in
November 1994. The central rice image* (khechu) *is the shape
upon which the new ritual centre depicted in Figure 15 is based
(Sarah Harrison)*

FIGURE 15   *The Khoimbo, or Gurung ritual centre in Pokhara, which opened in 1995 (Sarah Harrison)*

we saw them go into what appeared to be a frenzy, beating their drums wildly and shaking back and forth.

Afterwards we asked Yarjung Kromche what had happened and he said *"deota kaba"*. Now the word *kaba*, pronounced slightly differently, can have the meanings of 'to come' (the God has come), or 'to seize hold of'. We confirmed with the Pa-chyu informant that he was using the word in the second sense. He was quite explicit that he was possessed, using the same word, *tarava* (to shake), which is used to describe the very obvious possession in the Ghatu and Sorati dances. He said that he saw the god in his possession and wished that he could draw what he had seen. He was very surprised to hear that a Pa-chyu who works just north of Thak said that he was never possessed.

On asking whether such possession occurred in any other rituals, we were told that it occurs in the *pwelu*, which is a special ritual done in a Pa-chyu's own house to his personal god. We witnessed such a rite in the house of a man who, although not a practising Pa-chyu, was of a Pa-chyu lineage and hence kept the *pwelu* shrine in his house. On this occasion, rather than the Pa-chyu becoming possessed, the person in whose house the rite was performed became possessed, convulsively shaking for three or four minutes. This was clearly possession. We were told that only a few persons have this gift (and it is considered to be a gift). The signs of the ability to become possessed start at about the age of ten or a little younger.

It might be suggested that this possession is a relatively new feature, perhaps copied from the *dhāmī* tradition spreading from India. Indeed, Pignède describes a Pa-chyu going to study the science of the *dhāmī* (1993: 314–15). Yet this was denied by our Pa-chyu informant. He said that his father since becoming a Pa-chyu had always gone into a state of possession and shaken (*tarava*). Our informant had himself done so since he had learnt the Pa-chyu skills in his late teens. This alters our picture of the Pa-chyu, taking him much closer to the shamanic priests of Mongolia and central Asia from where the Gurungs are said to originate. Further similarities to central Asian shamanism are described by Mumford (1989).[4]

THE HISTORY OF THE GURUNGS

All these debates concerning identity become encapsulated into the debate about the history of the Gurungs. In order to know who the Gurungs are, the Gurungs want to find out where they came from and when. Thus the largely oral history of the Gurungs becomes a major debating area for the question of Gurung identity. This has had the fortunate side-effect of again producing much fascinating and hitherto secret material. This is still very confused, but a few of the broad outlines, which are elaborated in greater detail in the notes and appendices to the Pignède translation, may be noted here. At the heart of the debate is the question related to the discussion of the *jāt*s above. Namely, are the Gurungs made up of one people or two? Also relevant, of course, is the question of their overlap with other groups such as the Tamangs and Magars who speak very similar languages and have many social customs in common. Finally, there is the question of the overlay of Gurung culture by Brahmans from the south.

Our summary of these conflicting views in 1989 was briefly as follows:

> The course of the long migration over forested mountain ridges is only remembered in myths and legends. Some suggest that the main route was down to Burma and then westward through Assam and eastern Nepal to their present settlements, where they have been for over seven hundred years. Other legends tell how the Gurungs were wandering shepherds who came down through the high pasture of Tibet, through the kingdom of Mustang to settle the southern slopes of the Annapurna range. Yet other traditions suggest a dual origin, with the 'four jat' as they are known coming from the south, from northern India, and the 'sixteen jat' coming down from the north (Macfarlane and Gurung, 1990: 1–2).

Two other interpretations may now be added. One is by C. B. Ghotane, who writes in a note to the Pignède translation:

> The origins of the Gurungs, Magars, Tamang, Tharus, Sunwar and Danawar of central Nepal seem to be connected with the ancestors of the Kirats, an ancient Indian tribal group, who occupied the northern area of the Indo-Gangetic plain and the foothills of whole Himalayan range which extends from the Kashmir valley to Assam, Nagaland and Manipur. The earliest civilisation of ancient Kathmandu was founded by Kirats. They lived in the foothills and the large inner valleys of Nepal. They appear to have fled to the green mountain tops for safety after the overthrow of the Kirat ruler in the first century A. D. They were pushed further north with the invasion of Indo-Aryans, who infiltrated Nepal in great numbers during the period of the Muslim attacks on India from the fifteenth century (Pignède, 1993: 424).

A very different and fascinating account of the history of the Gurungs has been provided by two Gurungs working in collaboration with Judith Pettigrew and ourselves. Yarjung Kromche, a Pa-chyu, was able to draw on the myths and legends of the priests, written in a mixture of 'Chon-kwyi' (a very archaic form of Gurung, hardly understood today) and 'Tamu-kwyi' (the Gurung language of today). Bhovar Tamu had worked on the ancient histories of the Gurungs, the *vaṃśāvalī*. The account which they have pieced together is reproduced in full as an appendix to the new translation of Pignède (1993: 479–93). In essence the story is as follows (I have reordered some of the material).

The Gurungs originated in Mongolia and western China about eight or nine thousand years ago. They wandered down through China, reaching the Yarlu valley of the Lhoka region of eastern Tibet in about one thousand B. C. They brought with them their traditional priests.

> Here they were known as Tamu (Tubo) by 1,000 B. C. and during the course of time developed Bonism, the pre-Buddhist religion, with its priest, the *Nam-bo* or *Pa-chyu* . . . Bonism, the pre-Buddhist religion of Tibet, was a very advanced form of animism. It is still preserved, almost solely, by the Tamu priests in the form of the *Pye-Ta Lhu-Ta* . . .
>
> According to Tibetan mythology, Bonism is categorised as:
>
> 1. Nam-bo (Dol or Black Bon) whose priest is the *Pa-chyu* which is the oldest.
> 2. Kyar-bo (Striped Bon) whose priest is the *Kyabri* which possibly dates from around 100 B. C.
> 3. Lam-bo (White or Gyur Bon) whose priest is the *Lambo* which dates from 838 A. D . . .
>
> Some Tamus settled in the northern Bagmati region, having gone through the Kerung or Ku-ti Pass, and became Tamangs (pp. 481–2).

Others crossed over into Mustang. When they moved on to Manang,

> Those remaining in Mustang became the Thakali when other Tibetan groups, and probably some Tamangs, arrived. . . While they inhabited the banks of Mha-ri-syo (Marsyangdi river) in Manang, they adopted a new *Klye* (master) as their

is certainly not now. The anthropologist is actively engaged in the process of the creation and re-interpretation of ethnic identity. This is now a co-operative venture with the peoples themselves, whose lives it affects and who themselves are literate and able to communicate their views to the anthropologist, whether he or she is in Nepal or anywhere in the world.

It is not surprising that the Gurungs are asking fundamental questions about 'Who are we?', about birth, marriage, death, about priests, history, social structure. Resolutions to these problems are as important as are those concerning the very many desperate practical problems facing the Gurungs. In the attempt to resolve them, the anthropologist is suddenly allowed to peer into a newly active volcano. In this, there is an unique opportunity for understanding of the deeper levels of both present and past.

NOTES

My recent research on the Gurungs has been carried out together with Sarah Harrison, hence the use of the first person plural. We are grateful to the Economic and Social Research Council, the Renaissance Trust, and the University of Cambridge for financial support in this work.

[1] C. B. Ghotane's reminiscences on working with Bernand Pignède are published as a preface in Pignède (1993).

[2] The original translation was undertaken by Gill and Alan Macfarlane in 1969 and a copy deposited at Tribhuvan University. The whole was re-translated by Sarah Harrison, with assistance from Penny Lang, in 1990. Professor Dumont and the original publishers very kindly gave us permission to undertake this work, and the Centre d'Etudes de l'Inde et de l'Asie du Sud, Paris, was most helpful in making Pignède's papers available to us.

[3] Dr. Sarah Green did much of the work on the desk-top production of the book; the Pokhara fax was made available through the kindness of Dr. Don Messerschmidt. Judith Pettigrew orchestrated much of the work at the Nepal end.

[4] Further work on this subject has been undertaken by Judith Pettigrew and Yarjung Kromche Tamu (1994).

CHAPTER SIX

The Heavy Loads of Tamang Identity

Ben Campbell

INTRODUCTION

Changes in the political culture of Nepal set in motion by the events of 1990 have enabled the rise of new associations of political alignment, some of which draw on ethnic and religious identifications. Assumptions of correspondence between shared ethnonym, culture, socio-economic condition, and political consciousness, might seem inherently problematic given the geographical spread of a population as large as the Tamang. In this paper I will none the less argue that the people of the Tamang-speaking heartland have carried a particular historical and continuing burden in their relationship to the mercantile economy of Kathmandu, the power structure of unified Nepal, and access to the fruits of national development. The effects of this relationship on the production of identities will be examined in the context of Rasuwa district, north-central Nepal, where social group categories and relations have operated in a distinctly peripheral environment to mainstream Nepali society. But it is a periphery that has been historically constituted in economic and cultural relationships with the state.

The problem could be formulated in terms of asking what interests have been served by the perpetuation of marked social and cultural difference in this hinterland population, from the dominant social models? What are the conditions that reproduce social relations only minimally influenced by notions of caste difference? And what have been the historical processes that by accident or

REGIONAL PERSPECTIVES OF IDENTITY

The 1971 and 1981 censuses recorded a Tamang population of well over 80% in Rasuwa District, the highest for any district in Nepal. There is a noticeable overall social and cultural homogeneity in Rasuwa (Hall, 1982) if one excludes the mixed-caste villages in the south of the district. The construction of a road in the 1980s from Trisuli Bazaar has, however, led to a growth in the non-Tamang population (Tamangs were only 65% in the 1991 census), centred on the administrative, commercial, and military enclave in the district capital of Dhunche, the effects of which I discuss later. Learning the dialect of Tengu village, roughly in the middle of the district, I could detect accent and vocabulary variation with other Tamang villages, but not to the point of incomprehension. These differences are talked about, and often made fun of, according to

FIGURE 16   *Circle dance during the Gosainkund pilgrimage. Women look on in the exchange of verses with men (Ben Campbell)*

a schema of social geography, which contains a value hierarchy linking adaptive economic patterns, cultural practice, and social estimation.

In these estimations a major divide is provided by the course of the Trisuli river. In Nepali the river is known as the Bhote Kosi north of the confluence (near Dhunche) with the tributary flowing from the sacred lake of Gosainkund. In Tamang it is known as the Kyirong Gendi. To its west people are *Nuppa* ('West People') to its east *Shyarpa* ('East People'). I stayed on the *Shyarpa* side of the valley from where the *Nuppa* are regarded as more traditional Tamangs. The *Nuppama* (the *-ma* suffix creates a plural) generally dress more traditionally using more home-woven items, and whereas women on the eastern side of the valley (*Shyarpa-shya-ma*) like to wear bazaar-bought towels on their heads, the *Nuppashyama* mostly wear beautifully embroidered felt hats.

FIGURE 17   *At Gosainkund the singing traditions from Rasuwa mingle with those of Helambu. Here the dignitaries of Dhunche take centre stage to announce the arrival of their party (Ben Campbell)*

From Tengu with its roughly 45 households only one woman had married *mur* (down), though this does not include emigrants to Kathmandu. No Tengu women had married across the valley to the west, though some *Nuppashya* had married in, laterally as it were. As noted by Clarke (1980b) in Helambu, there is an impression of women moving uphill. Women generally explained this to me in economic terms. The higher up the valley you go the more forest there is, the easier it is to collect fodder, and livestock are more important in the agro-pastoral mix. People, men and women, tend to speak with some pleasure of animal herding, particularly of cattle rather than the more time-consuming buffaloes, moving between pastures, having milk to drink and making butter, as compared to the hard grind of working crops. Livestock has a stronger symbolic power than land in valuations of relative wealth. Several women had resisted the attempts of their parents to arrange marriages with cross-cousins in lower villages, perceiving such moves as entailing economic hardship.

The association of 'up' and the north with a better material and cultural life cannot be discussed without mention of the myths of origin. The oral texts chanted by the *bombo* (shamans) and *lhaben* (hereditary sacrificial specialists) refer to migration down from *Wi Samye* in Tibet.[2] *bSamyas* was the site of the first monastery that was built in Tibet after the introduction of Buddhism by Padmasambhava (*Guru Rimpoche*). What is important in the texts, however, is not the foundation of the monastery, which they do not mention, but that a socio-political order originated up there from which some of the contemporary clans are descended. There are many local oral variants of the original clans. In Tengu this order is said to have consisted of "*Ghale-raja, Shyangba-mantri, Tokra-kaji*" (Np. *rājā*: 'kings', *mantri*: 'ministers', *kāji*: 'officers'). All members of Ghale clans have a royal suffix to their first names: '-gyelbo' (Tb. 'king') for men, '-gyalmo' (Tb. 'queen') for women. *Shyangba* could be derived from the Tibetan *zhang,* a term referring to the maternal uncle ministers of Tibetan kings (Uebach, 1981; Richardson, 1977). I have not so far traced a Tibetan etymology for the Tokra but Vinding does mention a medieval King Thokarchan ("the king with the white turban")[3] in the region of the Thak Khola

(1988: 174–7). Toffin (1976) also mentions an 'ur'-socio-political order in the Ankhu Valley in which the Ghale were royalty and the Tokra ministers. However, in Dhunche I was told of four original clans: Tidung-*pandit* (priests), Gyaldang-*shipai* (soldiers), Bongtso Ghale-*raja/ponpo* (kings/leaders), and Tokra-*kaji* (officers). Another clan, the Loptsen, claim to be the original lamas in the area.

Claims to a history of royal status by Ghale clans are locally justified by linking particular clans with ruined forts, *dzong*, in the valley. Stories of old conflicts between clans are remembered, such as the fighting between Bongtso Ghale and Gyaldang Ghale in Dhunche, where the two clans each had their own *dzong*. The most numerous Ghale clan in Tengu is Bongtso Ghale. On a high ridge, known as 'Bongtso la' are the remains of one of these *dzong*, sitting in a commanding position overlooking the main valley and that of the Chilime, an important tributary to the west. The ancestor of the Bongtso Ghale is said to have flown to this point from Tibet, and later on to Tangdor in the upper reaches of the Palangu Khola to the east of the Trisuli, from where the Bongtso Ghale arrived in Tengu. A Bongtso Ghale *rājā* is said to have entered into ritual friendship (*mīt*) with a visiting Newar king. In the ensuing feast the Bongtso Ghale *rājā* asked what was the meat he was eating and was told it was buffalo, which he would have previously never eaten. None of the Ghale eat beef and to this day only the Bongtso Ghale eat buffalo meat. Several clans thus have particular dietary taboos that mark them off as unique rather than implying a hierarchy of purity.[4]

It is interesting that the Bongtso Ghale remember the relationship between their ancestor and the Newar king as one of *miterī* rather than subjugation or vassalage. The relationship contains sufficient ambiguity as to imply a notional equality between partners, the ritual itself bears certain resemblances with a wedding, and yet it is frequently contracted between people of vastly different objective status and power (Okada, 1957; Messerschmidt, 1982b). Prior to the capture of Nuwakot by Prithvi Narayan Shah in 1744 (Stiller, 1973: 111) the area of the upper Trisuli valley must have been a region of petty, *dzong*-centered chiefdoms alternately drawn

The bazaar has had a centripetal effect on commercial activity, drawing in shopkeepers from outlying villages, and, combined with National Park controls, has eliminated much of the traditional barter between communities of complementary ecological zones. Though the common greeting given to lowlanders arriving on foot in the village is still "what have you brought?", the overall importance of such encounters has diminished, and, with it, the economic basis for interactions between different ethnic groups being founded on mutually advantageous exchange. These encounters have ceded to mediation by the bazaar economy and the institutions of the state as structures of national integration, displacing the locus of significant social and commercial exchange away from villages. The sale of village produced commodities is furthermore subject to the arbitrary periodicity of official regulatory enforcement. This was particularly the case with home-distilled alcohol, fuelwood, timber, and the butchering of female buffaloes.[10] Many of the villagers' traditional economic survival strategies have been criminalized or rendered unprofitable on a small scale by licensing requirements. New evolving survival strategies depend on familiarity with the dominant cultural practice of officialdom and patronage cultivation.

Dhunche is the central focus of the local experience of 'development'. The bazaar is something of a cultural melting pot and has the feel of a frontier town. Madheshi snake-charmers enthrall local people, bureaucrats take Tamang mistresses, soldiers frequent liquor dens, and the male youth dresses in the style of 'Nepali punks'. At the same time structural disparities of opportunity are evident between locals and outsiders.[11] The most lucrative enterprises are controlled by outsiders (the few Tamang exceptions tend to be migrant returnees from India). Tourist hotels tend to he owned by people of high castes or locally married Thakalis. Dhunche promises opportunity, but villagers' investments in small enterprises, mostly liquor shops, are risky and frequently fail. Land values there have rocketed beyond the means of all but a few local people. Tamangs encounter derogatory attitudes from high-castes in service provision such as health and agricultural extension.[12] And casual prostitution can lead on to young women being sucked into the Bombay sex industry – the latest form of commoditizing Tamang labour power.

TAMANGS IN REVIEW

If this outline holds for the local, contemporary operation of identities among Tamang-speakers of Rasuwa, what of the situation elsewhere? There has been a noticeable shift in the literature on Tamangs from a tribal essentialist concept to a more subtle appreciation of the ways in which ethnic labels are constructed by dynamic processes of self-definition in relation to other groups, and also by interventions of the state in these processes. As one of the numerically largest ethnic minorities recognized in census takings in Nepal we might expect considerable variation within this grouping in the way in which the label is applied. Graham Clarke's work was an important step in the direction of understanding Nepalese ethnic labels as they are reworked in their different, local contexts. The contrast of Tamang and Lama in Helambu was presented as opposed categories in a symbolic hierarchy, correlating with contrasts of wealth and morality, rather than as empirically isolable groups, such that "one group's Tamang is another group's Lama" (Clarke, 1980b: 25). I did not find 'Tamang' being opposed to 'Lama' in this way in Rasuwa, where 'Tamang' and 'Ghale' is the locally salient opposition, though it is not as similarly permeable as in the contrast Clarke discusses in Helambu.[13] The explanation for this could be sought in the different histories of settlement and land tenure: religious endowments of *guṭhī* land controlled by Lama communities is important in Helambu, and virtually absent in Rasuwa.

At the extreme end of what might be called ethnonymic artificiality in the application of the Tamang label is the case referred to by Levine of a seemingly arbitrary manipulation of categories by the state. Speaking of Humla in the west she says,

> Tibetan speakers long were considered Bhotiya. Some decades ago they were instructed by government representatives that their *jāt* (caste and ethnic label) had become Tamang. The reason given was that the government needed to circumvent Tibetan claims to Nepalese populations and territories, and that the change in *jāt* was to their advantage, Tamang being of higher caste status (Levine, 1987: 79–80).

Similarly, Tom Cox notes that

> Langtang Tibetans, in their routines of self-presentation,
> often do not even admit to being Tibetan, but instead claim
> to be *Tamang* ... By identifying themselves as *Tamangs*
> Langtang Tibetans reinforce their self-presentation as well-
> integrated citizens of Nepal, and avoid being disparaged as
> 'squatters from Tibet' ... Within the context of their own
> community Langtang Tibetans do not refer to themselves
> as *Tamang* (Cox, 1989: 16–17).

Clearly the decree issued in 1932 that first recognized
'Tamang' as a legitimate *jāt* designation not only served the purpose
of self-identification as separate from Bhotiya,[14] but also enabled
the state to extend the term's use for its own ends of national
integration in administering geographically and culturally marginal
peoples.

Levine's position that the Tamang label was created "to
facilitate interactions with the state" was argued against Höfer's
notion that "the ancestors of the present Tamang had minimal or
latent identity, based on common cultural and linguistic criteria and
on the awareness of a common, mostly mythically substantiated
origin" (Höfer, 1979: 148). Macdonald follows Levine's standpoint
claiming that

> Tamang identity as it can be said to exist is a Nepalese
> administrative invention and a concept formulated by non-
> Nepalese researchers to facilitate written communications
> between themselves. There does not seem to be much
> evidence to show that isolated Tamang villagers are
> conscious of belonging to a pan-Tamang social identity
> (Macdonald, 1989: 176).

While I would not dispute that a shared status of being Tamang *per
se* holds little importance in encounters between strangers, discovery
of clan affiliations can provide a more significant basis for mutual
interaction. When two strangers know their respective clans it is
then possible to initiate a relationship in terms of kinship or affinity.[15]

In contrast to the way in which Levine and Macdonald reject the idea that people who have acquired the label of Tamang display any features in common, Holmberg has developed an analysis of the ethno-construction of Tamang grounded on research in a particular locality, but claiming some generality as to its applicability to many if not all Tamang. The central and ironic twist in his argument is that though much ethnography in the early phase of research in Nepal, was overly obsessed with the notion of "autonomous 'tribal' groups", and that in Nepal "a social order has emerged that is irreducible to separate Indic, Tibetan, or tribal perspectives" (Holmberg, 1989: 15), at the same time he considers that the historical and social conditions behind the emergence of the Tamang reinforced some quasi-tribal features:

> Tamang culture ... was as much created as undermined in the genesis of contemporary Nepal ... An insular or 'tribal' character of Tamang culture emerged in response to the evolvement of sociopolities in the greater Himalayas where local sectors of Tamang turned in upon themselves in a process of involution (*ibid.*: 12).

The essential feature of this tribal character for Holmberg is the predominant equality of 'restricted exchange' between exogamous clans, rather than the asymmetrical relations of endogamous castes. However, the involuted effect of restricted exchange produces an appearance, filtered by the perceptual frame of Hindu legal and interactive ideology, of the Tamang as an endogamously separate caste.

Holmberg describes any notion of pan-Tamang identity as "a recent phenomenon", but he does suggest some objective features, *as perceived by the Hindu Gorkha rulers*, common to the Murmi people, later to become Tamang. "They were incorporated into the state as a subjugated population; they were marked off from other groups in Nepal as the consumers of beef and particularly carrion beef; and they were associated with lamas and Buddhism" (*ibid.*: 23). This amounts to a view of the "emergent Tamang as outside the fold of the nascent state order." In the caste Legal Codes the

"Bhote-Murmi-Tamang" occupied the lowest rung of the *matwālī* alcohol-drinking groups and unlike the other Tibeto-Burmans were 'enslavable'.

I would argue that Holmberg's analysis does not give due prominence to the place occupied by Tamang communities in the marked regionality of Nepali economy and society. From his account we get an image of the way Tamangs have been excluded from effective participation in the dominant Hindu society, kept at a distance but maintained in service as a source of labour. He tells us of the forms of land tenure under which Tamangs were obliged to perform corvée labour for portering, herding, postal services, paper making, gunpowder production, timber cutting, and so on. The densest concentrations of Tamangs is in the hinterland surrounding the Kathmandu Valley. The importance that this population has had as a source of labour and products from the hills for the economy of Kathmandu and its trading base should not be underestimated.[16] Hamilton wrote at the beginning of the nineteenth century that "in the rude and more mountainous parts of Nepal Proper, the chief population consisted of these Murmis ... They never seem to have had any share in the government, nor to have been addicted to arms, but always followed the profession of agriculture, or carried loads for the Newars, being a people uncommonly robust" (1986 [1819]: 52–53).

The full significance of Kathmandu's dependence on the labour supply of its immediate periphery can be indirectly appreciated by a telling silence in historical accounts of the relationship between the state of Nepal and its southern colonial neighbour. I have thus far searched in vain the formal treaties signed by the rulers of Nepal and British India for any reference to the fact that recruitment for Gurkha troops was effectively prohibited from the districts contiguous with Kathmandu. To my knowledge Anup Pahari (1991) is the first to have addressed this issue in print.[17] He claims that "Nepali rulers and the British collaborated formally and informally to close non-military employment to the so-called 'martial races'" (*ibid.*: 8), and that "Nepali rulers preferred to retain their 'monopoly' over Tamangs, who lived close to the Kathmandu valley. The Tamangs were used as semi-captive labourers for everything from portering to soldiering, mining and construction. Their bondage to the state and Kathmandu elite was often formalised through ... 'rakam'" (*ibid*.: 9). Tamangs living in the main recruiting areas of the British and Indian armies were in fact enlisted, but many changed their names in order to do so. Those that claimed to be Gurung in Gorkha District came to be known as 'Bahra Saley [Year Twelve] Gurung', changing their name in the year 2012 V.S. (= 1955) (Tamang, 1992: 25).

Parshuram Tamang (1992) has pointed out that among the groups listed by Vansittart (1915) as not to be recruited was that of 'Pipa'.[18] He says "it was the term for 'porter', which was the occupation reserved by the Ranas for Tamangs. The Pipas were used to carry loads, pitch tents, and provide other menial physical labour for the military, but were excluded from the military hierarchy." They were administered from the 'Pipa Goswara' at the gate of the Singha Darbar Secretariat in Kathmandu.

The Tamang-populated area to the north of Kathmandu was the site of the two most important routes into Tibet, via the trade-entrepots of Kuti and Kyirong. Until the British opened up the way to Lhasa through Sikkim at the beginning of the twentieth century most of the trade between India and Tibet passed through here (Stiller, 1973: 28). The wars fought with Tibet in the eighteenth and nineteenth centuries were also primarily conducted through these routes with the Nepalis attempting to annex both Kyirong and Kuti during each conflict (Uprety, 1980). This area was thus of crucial economic and strategic importance to Kathmandu, which must explain its importance as a preserve to be left alone by British recruitment. This is not to deny the state's exaction of compulsory labour elsewhere in Nepal,[19] but the greater volume of trade that passed through the area in which Tamangs carried loads under obligation to the state or for wages should be remembered. The majority of Tamang communities were therefore isolated from the social, cultural, and economic effects of large-scale male out-migration: they lacked experience of the world beyond Nepal's immediate borders, and the flow of mercenary cash into the hills. The differential access of Nepal's hill peoples to the opportunities for escape from poverty and oppression at home has from a trip telling me he thought people in Tengu live like grubs in the soil after seeing other places. They themselves remark on the ethnic division of labour in the trekking industry, with the Sherpas of Solu-Khumbu in particular doing very well out of the role of *sardār* guides, and keeping for themselves all the best items of bakshish gifted by the foreigners. This division of labour may represent a change in the historical alignment of certain groups such as the Sherpa, but the overall structure is one that only has a role for Tamangs as human beasts of burden. The details may have changed but the Tamangs are still carrying loads to make profits for the Kathmandu elite.[21]

CONCLUSION

I have attempted to show in this paper how it may be possible to view a combination of economic, political, and social factors as having conspired in the arrested development of the Tamangs in the Kathmandu hinterland. I would suggest that an historical relationship with the centre characterized by neglect, distrust, repressive tolerance, and exploitation has been perpetuated by the following conditions. The insufficiency of the Tamang communities' ecologically marginal subsistence base has forced them into exchange relations with more powerful neighbours. The importance of human porterage to the commercial activity of Kathmandu and a history of coercive induction to state labour services have linked perceptions of cultural difference to a division of labour. The effective exclusion of the Tamang heartland from Gurkha recruitment preserved the state of underdevelopment in Kathmandu's close periphery. And the tenacity of Tamang society to cultural practices (cross-cousin marriage, Buddhism, relatively non-hierarchical gender relations, etc.) inconsistent with the dominant Nepali cultural doxa accentuates a cultural divide that produces incongruity in the constitution of social identities and gives rise to cross-cultural "creative misunderstandings" (Höfer, 1986).

The articulation of subsistence, as the dominant mode for reproduction of labour power, with the periodicity of portering labour demands of transhimalayan trade, state corvée labour, and more recently the trekking industry, has prevented a fuller development of class in this relation. Yet, a definite consciousness of it is evident in the idiom and connotations of 'load-carrying people', while of course not all porters are Tamangs. The Tamang case does not quite test the limits of the validity of Blaikie's analysis from west-central Nepal that "a characteristic set of relations of production and conditions of work which are at the root of class relations do not emerge from portering alone" (1979: 90). There would seem to be some irony in the fact that engaging in paid portering is an indigenous marker of socio-economic differentiation. It is virtually a form of class consciousness without meeting textbook criteria of being a class in itself. Extra-community relations of socio-economic hierarchy are kept at a distance, and the conditions of a rural proletariat not fully realized, by the maintenance of local identities, bound up in the subsistence economy and the symbolic and material logic of bilateral exchange as opposed to caste and class asymmetry.[22]

If being porters does not systematically encapsulate identity, what of a sense of greater-Tamang solidarity? In Rasuwa at least this was not politically manifest in the elections of 1991, when material inducements for votes overrode any such possibility. Was it only coincidence that the pro-Panchayat parties achieved their only successes in this region of north-central Nepal? The relative isolation of this area from 'modernizing' political consciousness is perhaps connected with its history of underdevelopment as a cheap labour preserve. One of the educated Nepali office workers in Dhunche expressed to me his frustration with the local lack of awareness of national political issues, saying that in Rasuwa human life (i.e. votes) could be bought for the price of a chicken. The amount of money offered to villagers by representatives of the successful party were indeed in the region of 100 to 150 rupees. The votes of whole villages were rumoured to have been bought for 20,000 rupees. Few villagers expressed much sense that the multi-party elections were different in kind from those held under the Panchayat regime. Elections in general were perceived as 'world turned upside-down' occasions when the poor, briefly, could expect the path to go in single-file through wooded sections, and with the flock keepers out of sight, men would descend from above the path and rush on down into the undergrowth below bearing their prize in their arms.

6 *Yangna Yamhu makye, yangna Kerong makye. Parki sala kenna, tomtom rere chungsum.* This is the ritual language derived from Kyirong Tibetan, and the translation into colloquial Tamang was offered me by a village shaman.

7 To what extent this regard for the culture of higher communities constitutes a reverse pull to that of 'Hinduization' is an interesting question. Höfer (1986) writes of parallel frames of reference between Tamang and Hindu ritual practice in Dhading, even giving rise to 'creative misunderstanding', but he rules out a push towards religious assimilation. His identification of Dasain as a key Hindu ritual reworked through Tamang myths of origination as well as political subjugation is intriguing. In Tengu it would be impossible to categorize the Dasain festival as unambiguously Hindu, since lamas perform a crucial role in leading the funeral dance for the sacrificed buffalo (*mai mane*). Differences in death rites specifically were what I was told distinguish people of Buddha Dharma, with cremations on ridges rather than by water. Hindus are seen as giving inadequate attention to the dead, which is why their country (*Jyarti lungba*) is full of ghosts.

8 Lakshmiprasad Devkota, the great Nepali poet (1909–1959), wrote of his reflections on encountering a Tamang family in their mountain *goth* during a pilgrimage to Gosainkund, "In such a place, people live a shifting, wandering existence; they travel in search of sunshine and warm air. For them the world is stingy, nature is tightfisted. If forced, the earth yields maize and nettles. Whyever did people come to such a place? What pleasure, what happiness did they seek? Was it just to eat thorns, just to stand like a few frost-ravaged leaves and rattle in the wind, to demonstrate their alienation?" (From an unpublished translation by Michael Hutt of *Pahari Jivan*).

9 The son of the old *mukhiyā* of Tengu claimed his father was the first man in Rasuwa to learn to read and write in Nepali. I only heard of one Rasuwa Tamang to have got a BA, and he was helped by Japanese sponsors.

10 Michaels (above, p. 92) refers to the ambiguous status of female buffaloes even in the Muluki Ain's code on animal slaughter. It is one instance of "a striking uncertainty of the law, . . . [but] such inconsistencies . . . did not hinder the achievement of the law's real objective."

It seemed to me ironic that after the 1990 'revolution' even stricter Hindu laws concerning both female buffalo meat and alcohol were enforced in Dhunche. These laws were resented as a nuisance, but quite simply circumvented by butchering female buffaloes, and distilling, away from the authorities' gaze.

[11] This observation was confirmed by a Newar school teacher who had known Dhunche for twelve years and commented on the fact that the major beneficiaries of the growth of the bazaar were outsiders.

[12] Bista (1991: 141–2) writes of the attitudes of Nepali civil servants implementing development programmes: "The plight of ethnic villagers in remote places is hard to identify with, they are invariably of low status (which decreases the amount of consideration due to them), and the actual physical nature of their environment is largely unknown ... [M]any of the people who go to agricultural colleges have absolutely no interest in agriculture. Instead, they are hierarchic high caste people for whom agricultural labour, and work of any kind, is unthinkable ... What they learn is never applied."

[13] 'Lama' did seem to be in occasional use in Rasuwa as a last name for correspondence. Parbatiyas would also use it as a respectful term of address. I was eventually given the nickname Ur-Lama ('Yellow Lama'), derived from the fact that Westerners, if not called *deshi,* or *Amrikan,* are referred to as *kra-ur* ('hair/head yellow').

[14] See Lall (1969). and Höfer (1979: 147–149). It should be noted that in Newari Tamangs and Tibetans are both refered to as *sē.*

[15] Conversely, Tamang women often keep their clan identities a secret on occasions such as pilgrimage, so that the possibilities for erotic liaison remain at their initiative. Unwelcome suitors, challenged to reveal their clan identities first, can then be repelled by declaration of inappropriate kinship.

[16] Fürer-Haimendorf's famous thesis (1975), positing a correlation between Tibetan Buddhism and adventurous trading dispositions, ends up looking plausible only by cutting off from view all but the high altitude-dwelling, pack-animal-owning traders. It seems ironic that in the account of his first visit to Nepal he remarks that his luggage was being carried "by the Tamangs from villages in the vicinity of the Nepal valley. In the absence of roads suitable for wheeled traffic beyond the immediate vicinity of the capital, porters were then the only means of transport, and in Kathmandu there was an efficient agent who provided any desired number of reliable men at a few days notice. Most of these professional porters were members of the Tamang

tribe" (1990: 133–4). Further on he wrote "among the Tamangs, Buddhism is an active force" (*ibid.*: 141).

[17] Previously, it had only been mentioned in passing. For example, Gibbs wrote: "Until recently the only Tamangs known to the Gurkha Brigade were those enlisted from eastern Nepal and Darjeeling for the 7th. and 10th. Gurkhas" (1947: 25), and described West no.1 District, which included Rasuwa, as "*closed by the Nepal Government against recruiting for the Gurkha Brigade*" (*ibid.*: 21, my emphasis). He also noted that many Tamangs had enlisted under the names of 'Gurung' and 'Ghale' (*ibid.*: 23, 26). Höfer writes of Dhading District, which was also part of West no.1, "the first Tamangs were recruited to the then British-Indian Army during World War II. They all enlisted as Gurungs ... because the army did not accept Tamangs at that time" (1978: 180).

[18] *Pipā*: "Labourer, hired labourer;-tent-pitcher (of whom several are attached to each battalion in the Nepalese Army)" (Turner, 1931: 381).

[19] Nicky Grist's work confirms the general historical importance of labour/transportation tax in the operation of trade across Central Asian states (Grist, n.d.).

[20] Upadhyay presents data on ethnic distribution among porters in Ramechap and Sindhuli, noting that "the majority of Tamangs work as porters" (1990: 51). Lewis's (1984: 143) survey of the economy of Asan Tol market in the centre of Kathmandu specifies the role of Tamangs as porters. Steinmann presents a different formulation of the relationship between portering and Tamang culture. For her the porters are the most 'de-ethnicized' of the community (1987: 24), and she points to the rural economic crisis since the 1970s as the cause of increasing numbers having to take to portering, rather than arguing as I have that portering has been the traditional articulation of grain-deficit Tamangs with the national economy. This could well be a factor of the socio-economic conditions in different fieldwork sites. My experience of speaking Tamang with numerous rickshaw, tempo, and taxi drivers in Kathmandu is that a very large proportion have come from Kabhre Palanchok the district of Steinmann's research).

[21] Fricke *et al.* (1990) discuss contemporary labour patterns of a Tamang community on the northern rim of Kathmandu Valley, but while highlighting the post-1960s increased monetization of the economy, they stress that "there has never been a time in living memory when people from these villages were not combining outside labour with family farm activities" (*ibid.*: 288).

[22] In my PhD thesis I discuss village-level exchanges and compare specifically different forms of labour reciprocity across a range of communities in Nepal (Campbell, 1993). Equality of gender in labour exchange emerges as a feature which sets communities like Tengu apart from mixed-caste agricultural relations.

[23] One piece of anti-communist propaganda in circulation, though, was that if the Communists came to power people over sixty years old would not be allowed to do any work.

PART THREE

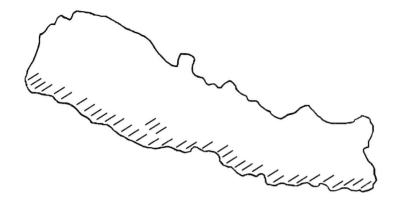

PART THREE

The Tarai

At the southern border of Nepal is a long strip of flat land, geographically indistinguishable from the land over the frontier in India. In the eighteenth century most of it was thick forest and infested with malaria, so that travellers and merchants could only pass through safely in the winter months. Only in certain areas was the forest cleared and settled agriculture practised, as around Janakpur. Here the language and the culture of the settlers was indistinguishable from those on the other side of the border with India. Even in the early days, there were sufficient cleared areas for the Tarai, with its fertile soil and flat land, to be a major source of revenue for the elite and for the state.

Gradual expansion of the cultivated area continued and cultivators were attracted into the region from India. As in the hills, the inhabitants were divided into many different castes and ethnic groups, but, in contrast to the hill region, the Nepalese state made little effort to regulate the Tarai caste system and the relative ritual status of many of these groups has remained in dispute. The

239

demographic situation was further complicated with the eradication of malaria in the 1950s and 1960s, which brought mass migration to the Tarai and elsewhere, and the clearance of much of the remaining forest. In 1984–5 the Tarai was providing 56.5% of Nepal's GDP (H. Gurung, 1989a:109).

As described in chapter 7, the Tarai people, here Maithils, are caught between Nepal and India. Politically Nepalis, culturally and linguistically, and even economically, they have more in common with their neighbours over the border in India than with their compatriots in the hills. Thus the Maithils were and are bound to be alienated by the symbolic construction of Nepali nationhood, since it focuses so strongly on opposing the hills to the plains, Nepaliness to Indianness. The feelings that Gaige (1975) described, of being second-class citizens in their own country, are clearly continuing in the 1990s.

Such settled pockets as Janakpur apart, the Tarai (especially in the west) was originally thinly inhabited by various tribal peoples practising swidden or non-intensive agriculture. The largest and most dispersed such group, or collection of groups, was called Tharu. The changing relations of the Tharus of Dang with immigrant Parbatiyas from the hills are described in chapter 8.

CHAPTER SEVEN

Defining Maithil Identity: Who is in Charge?

Claire Burkert

INTRODUCTION

When I first came to Janakpur in 1988, the signboard posted by the Nagar Palika (town hall) on public ground near the police offices and the government rest house was brightly painted. It showed the national bird, the national flower, national dress, and so on. As we passed the symbols one day in a rickshaw, a Janakpur friend commented that he'd never seen the national bird or the national flower, and the national dress was too hot for him. The sign is so faded now that one hardly can decipher its meaning, and after a few more monsoons it will merely be a board with nothing on it, unless there is a change in local priorities and someone is found who can repaint the bird, the flower, and the national dress of Nepal. The local advocates for Maithil culture, though divided on certain issues, are united in their belief that it is not the time for them to restore signboards with the national symbols of Nepal, but rather that all people in Nepal should know what beautiful Gold Mohar trees bloom in Janakpur, and what the religious monuments of the city are, and how sweet is the sound of the Maithili language.

The culture of Maithil people extends from Nepal's eastern Tarai into Bihar in India, and the region has unofficially retained the name of Mithila. During the age of the Videhan kings, Mithila was a kingdom and Janakpur its capital. King Janak, Sita's father, was the King of Mithila. Hindu scholars have combed ancient texts for allusions to Mithila and to Janakpur and have found references

241

in various texts, including the *Upanishads*. The degree of Janakpur's importance as part of a succession of kingdoms until the time of the unification of Nepal is under conjecture. While Richard Burghart's work has done much to provide a solid basis for our knowledge of Janakpur, a good deal of the scholarship on Janakpur and Mithila is backed by religious faith and poetic feeling. Shivendra Lal Karna writes in a publication issued for the occasion of the Fifth International Conference on the *Ramayana* held in Janakpur in November 1989:

> Nurtured in the soft and sweet lap of the Himalayas, Janakpur's contribution to the enhancement of the glory of free Nepal is undeniable. Although it is difficult to present accurately and correctly the historical and geographical relations of ancient Janakpur in the absence of archeological basis, yet according to the scriptures, it is evident that Janakpur, the capital of Mithila, which bestowed upon Sri Janaki 'motherliness': had provided spiritual and intellectual leadership to the whole world in the Upanishad Age: owing to passage of Time, this world-famous part, which remained in oblivion for a long time has again reemerged and revived (Karna, 1989: 23–24; spelling and punctuation as in the original).

This quote evinces the same sentiment which prevailed in Janakpur just after the advent of democracy in 1990: according to popular feeling (similar to the title of Burghart's article, 'The Disappearance and Reappearance of Janakpur', 1978) Janakpur would emerge to prove its greatness as a religious and cultural centre, and its Maithil people would find a role in the governing of Nepal.

Kathmandu was twice under the rule of kings from Mithila, and during this time both the Newari language and Newar culture came under Maithil influence (Jha, 1993: 2). In 1097, Nanyadeva, whose capital was Simraungarh, dethroned the two princes who ruled Kathmandu, Lalitpur, and Bhaktapur. The last king of Nanyadeva's dynasty, Harisimhadeva, fled to the hills after Mithila was attacked by a Muslim conqueror in 1326. Sthiti Malla married Harisimhadeva's grand-daughter and later Malla kings in the Kathmandu Valley claimed direct descent from a dynasty founded by Harisimhadeva (Slusser, 1982: 57, 66).

During the Malla period, the Malla kings invited Maithil priests to Kathmandu and Maithil families settled in the heart of the city near Hanuman Dhoka and Asan. Maithili was the language of the court and dramas and poems were composed in Maithili. On some level (varying according to class and caste) memories of past privilege or eminence linger in Maithil culture. The educated have heard that the Maithili language affected Newari, while the less educated have heard about the kingdom of Mithila. In the new democracy, Maithil people have not just a hope that their status in the political life of Nepal may be raised; perhaps more than any other Tarai people they have the conviction that their cultural eminence can be regained, and their access to power reclaimed.

JANAKPUR AS THE CAPITAL OF MAITHILI SPEAKING PEOPLE IN NEPAL

Janakpur is unlike other cities of the eastern and middle Tarai: renowned for its temples and ponds, it attracts visitors from India and from around Nepal in a way that Birganj, Butwal, and Biratnagar do not. As a prelude to further discussion of Maithil people's cultural identity, a few observations may be made on some of Janakpur's landmarks. From the point of view of the educated, politically aware, and high-caste male of Janakpur, the landmarks have either risen from the culture of its Maithil people, or like the signboard, are symbols of national unity and serve to remind Janakpur people just who is in power.

Janaki Mandir, the city's famous temple, draws visitors from India and all across Nepal (Figure 19). It was built in 1911 by a donor from central India, and in all of Nepal there is nothing like this large white Moghul style temple which contains an idol of Janaki (Sita). In Janakpur, Sita's name comes up in conversation as if she and her husband Ram were alive today (even Mynah birds sold on the streets say 'Sita Ram'. People love Sita and they love her temple. The temple itself gives Janakpur a heart. Within the temple

FIGURE 19   *The Janaki Mandir, Janakpur, built in Moghul style by an Indian donor (Claire Burkert)*

or on its grounds, pilgrims eat and sleep, festival processions converge, students give speeches, political parties hold rallies, Mithila art exhibitions and cultural programs are presented. While nearby is an open space for large events, the grounds of the Janaki Mandir host many of the activities of Janakpur.

During the Panchayat period, the government of Nepal erected the Bibah Mandap on a site adjacent to the temple (Figure 20). The Bibah Mandap commemorates Sita and Ram's marriage, although the actual site is in another location nearby Janakpur. With its narrow pedestrian entrance gate (preventing processions, banners, and elephants), its entrance fee, and formal walkway lined with lights and trees (and no mess of discarded leaf plates from pilgrims' feasts, or leaflets from the rallies of every political party), the Mandap is the opposite of the Janaki Mandir. While its neighbour throbs with the beat of drums, the Mandap has the silence of a museum.

The Mandap was funded by taxes levied on purchases of land or materials such as cement and bricks, and these taxes were

FIGURE 20   *The Bibah Mandap, Janakpur, built in 'Nepalese' style by the government during the Panchayat period (Claire Burkert)*

gathered in Janakpur and surrounding Tarai districts. The government provided the design which was modelled after the pagoda style temple of the hills. (In Mithila, a mandap is usually a small raised platform with bamboo columns and a thatch roof.) However, despite its marble pillars and glassed-in idols in fancy dress, it retains an institutional coolness and contrasts severely with its gracefully ornate neighbour. Since the advent of democracy, the true story of how the Mandap was constructed has been embellished. One young village Congress leader, for instance, tells of how the government posted the army with guns when the Mandap was being built so that there would be no interference. Even so, he claims, lives were lost by those unable to tolerate the government's imposition. One of Janakpur's Sadbhavana Party leaders has termed the Mandir an example of the "bland [sic] nationalism" of the Panchayat period. By those who are most aware of issues of cultural identity, the Mandap is perceived as an act of humiliation: Maithil culture must fit into hill culture forms.

Every Hindu will stop to worship at the Janaki Mandir, but few local people care enough to pay the entrance fee for the Mandap. Even during Bibah Panchami (the large festival celebrating Sita's marriage), the procession of idols of Ram and Sita begins at the Mandir, bypasses the Mandap, and terminates at the true site of the marriage. In general, the activity around the Mandir is so vibrant that the Mandap can easily be ignored.

If the comparison of these two buildings reveals a prevailing view of government suppression or of calculated insensitivity towards Maithili culture, other 'proof' is to be found in Janakpur's statues. King Mahendra in the form of a statue had intruded on the grounds of Janaki Mandir facing the temple, but during the democratic movement in 1990 he was attacked and toppled. It is now widely agreed that its place should be taken by the statue of a Maithil Brahman boy from a village near the Indian border. When King Mahendra visited Janakpur in January 1962, Durganand Jha threw a bomb at King Mahendra's car and was accordingly hung. Prior to the movement, sympathy for this boy was shown somewhat quietly (for example, sorrow was expressed for his wife who was widowed as a teenager). Today Durganand Jha is hailed as one of the greatest martyrs of Janakpur. Legend has it that the King himself told the boy that he would spare his life for an apology, to which Durganand Jha boldly replied that the King was the one who should apologize for all the lives that had been lost in the quest for democracy. It is believed that the statue should be erected in exactly the same spot as the one occupied by King Mahendra, but in 1993 concern about disapproval from the government still prevented supporters of the idea from carrying out the plan (the mayor admits he, too, has reservations). Durganand Jha was a Congress Party member, however, and because of party advocacy it is believed likely that the statue will eventually be built.

One of Janakpur's statues which survived 1990 but continues to provoke resentment is the statue in Bhanu Chowk of the hill poet Bhanubhakta, who first translated the *Ramayana* into Nepali (see Figure 21). To the intelligentsia of Janakpur, the erection of the poet's statue was proof of the government's intentions to deny Maithil people expression of their own superior culture; the statue should have been of the fourteenth-century Maithili 'Adikavi' (first poet) Vidyapati, whose lines such as "the language of one's own country is the sweetest" are regularly quoted or sung. It was recently decided to create a Vidyapati Chowk and to erect a statue of the poet. According to a statement in the press, the decision had been made at an 'all-party meeting'. In fact, not all parties signed

FIGURE 21   *The memorial to the Nepali 'Adikavi', or 'first poet', Bhanubhakta Acharya, in Janakpur, which irritates partisans of Maithili (Claire Burkert)*

the minutes, and there was some dispute as to who should be the chairman of the statue committee. Yet eventually a consensus was reached, and this unifying symbol of the culture began to be constructed at one of the city's most important intersections. (But now, in 1996, because of another dispute over land owned at the chowk, completion seems to be delayed indefinitely.)

The landmarks of Janakpur express the culture in its classical religious and literary form and now, too, its democratic spirit. (Just after the advent of the current democracy, one other chowk was created in honor of the martyrs.) The monuments of Janakpur in turn shape the view the Maithils have of themselves. There is yet to be a statue of a Chamar woman performer of a favourite local dance, of a fisherman catching the fish Janakpur is renowned for, or of a Maithil woman artist. But it is certain there will never be another pagoda building, or statue of a hill poet or politician.

Paul Brass has written about the importance of "symbol pools" out of which a culture forms a distinct identity. "Nationalism, then, is the striving to achieve multi-symbol congruence among a group of people defined initially in terms of a single criterion" (Brass, 1974: 410). In his analysis of the Maithil political movement and the absence of regional consciousness in Bihar he notes that "the regional elite has failed to extend the cultural symbols of Mithila and Maithili to the non-Brahman castes of the region and build a common Maithil identity" (*ibid*.: 60). As the "symbol pool" of Janakpur is now being assembled, the first step has been to weed out the symbols of the power of the Kathmandu Valley and to establish symbols that empower the culture of Janakpur. Whether this symbolic representation of culture will be accepted and adopted by the lower castes, or expanded to include symbols with which all the castes can identify, remains to be seen.

The 'Master Plan for the Development of the Religious Sites of Janakpur', which was created in the new democracy, recognized the importance of preserving Janakpur's religious heritage, but to date most investment in preservation or development of religious sites has come from India or from local sources. It is believed that if Janakpur were a city in the hills, or had Ram and Sita been married in Bhaktapur, interest from the government of Nepal would be greater. The lack of preservation and development in Janakpur does not stem from a paucity of interest in its religious subject matter, but rather from a fundamental distrust of its people, who are viewed either as Indians or as strongly influenced by Indian politics.

After the time of the Malla rule, Maithil people lost favour with the government. When Jaya Prakash Malla was attacked by Prithvi Narayan Shah he had a force called the 'Tirhutia army' (Tirhutia is synonymous with Maithil). When Jaya Prakash was defeated, Prithvi Narayan Shah suspended the Tirhutia army, and to this day recruitment of Madheshis in the army has been very low. One Maithili speaker from a village outside Janakpur changed his name from Thakur to Thakuri, but after his recruitment, when it was found that he was a Madheshi rather than a hill Thakuri, his service was terminated (Jha, 1993: 68).

During the early Shah period a rich and powerful Maithil named Subba Kulanand Jha sided with the lunatic King, Rana Bahadur Shah – an act which cost him his large trust and his land. (The 'Jha Guthi', however, still survives.) Under the Ranas, the influence of Maithil people gradually declined and after 1951 the government remained generally unsympathetic. A year after the parliamentary government was banned, Durganand Jha threw his bomb. The act of the bomb was never forgotten; it is believed that the subsequent lack of interest in developing Janakpur and Dhanusha district was a protracted punishment.

It is still the belief of local people that the government suspects them of anti-national sentiment (rather than recognizing that earlier acts of protest during the Panchayat period had been for the cause of democracy) and is therefore retarding their development. And, as Paul Brass points out with regard to Maithils in Bihar, the Janakpur Maithils fail to perceive that one reason their development lags behind is that they have been incapable of organizing to press for change (Brass, 1974: 114–15). The supposed lack of interest in developing Janakpur explains why there is no investment in industry or large-scale development projects. In fact, the government of Nepal has little money to invest in any of its municipalities. Even so, the mayor of Janakpur laments that the municipality of Birganj receives "a hundred times" the budget of Janakpur, and that most cities have a budget many times as large. The city, he claims, is thirty years behind because any plans for development were suspended during the Panchayat period. He cites B. P. Koirala's plan for a Dalkebar-Kathmandu highway which was halted by the Panchayat government. Current support for development of Janakpur and Dhanusha District is unlikely to increase since, despite the number of Tarai MPs in government, only a few people from the Tarai have positions in ministries.

Even so, the mayor is hopeful; there are signs of change. For the first time in twenty years, the mayor of Janakpur is a native Maithili speaker. Janakpur's one major industry, the Janakpur Cigarette Factory (part government-owned), never had a Maithili speaker as its General Manager until recently. And fifteen out of sixteen ward representatives are Maithili speakers: this, too, has never been the case before.

In a comparison of Newar and Maithil language movement, David Gellner (1986: 144), citing Brass (1974), has pointed out two reasons why Maithils have "failed to carve out a political unit" for themselves: (1) "Maithils lack a religious identity different from that of their neighbours", and (2) "the Maithili-speaking area, and the people living there, lack sharp boundaries." However, Janakpur provides this people without a boundary with a city centre which has the capacity to develop. One occasionally sees news articles about plans to build an international airport, a major hospital, or a university. Currently there is a local plan called The Greater Janakpur Project which intends to make a ring road out of the traditional 93 kilometre Parikrama route and to develop facilities for pilgrims. As yet, most of Janakpur's residents are native Maithili speakers, and a city centre in Nepal may become all the more important if the governing leaders of Bihar continue to be anti-Maithil. While it is said that 'pure' Maithil culture is found in the villages around Madhubani in Bihar (according to Brahmans, the language among upper castes is unadulterated, art flourishes, and the low castes remember their place), Janakpur overshadows Madhubani in size, religious activity, and historical importance.

Since the Indian serial of the *Ramayana* has become perhaps the most popular TV programme in all Nepal, Janakpur's legendary importance may now be even greater than it ever has been. Maithil people have some claim on Ram and Sita, hence the creation of huge festivals drawing pilgrims from all over Mithila to commemorate Sita's marriage (Bibah Panchami) and Ram's birthday (Ram Nawami). The legend of Ram (the dutiful son, the virtuous leader) and Sita (the devoted wife) informs the daily life of people of Mithila. These two figures are regarded almost as ancestors, and provide Maithil people with a religious identity which is their own.

Furthermore, the perpetuation of the name 'Mithila' shows that a legendary boundary can serve as a substitute for a political one in helping to retain cultural identity in a modern nation-state. People speak of the foods of Mithila, the customs of Mithila, the language or the art of Mithila. In recent history there have been efforts to recreate an independent Mithila. Dr. L. N. Jha was not a Congress Party member, and despite suffering repeated torture during the Panchayat period, and his final disappearance after imprisonment in Kathmandu, he will not be immortalized in statue form. Nevertheless, he is remembered for having raised his voice against the treatment of Janakpur by the government, and for his call for a free 'Mithila State'. Jagannath Mishra, previous Chief Minister in Bihar, has also urged that there be a separate Mithila state within India. It may be that without being an actual state, kept alive as it is in festivals, cultural programs, literature, and now TV, the legendary boundaries of ancient Mithila will still serve to unify Maithil people.

WHAT IS A MAITHIL?

Being Maithil is more than speaking Maithili, or chewing *pān* and quoting Vidyapati.

Maithil people claim to look different. Legend has it that the goddess Parvati broke into pieces and her eyes fell on Mithila, hence people have almond-shaped eyes. But far more important, there are prescribed acts of politeness and complicated rituals (particularly as regards marriage). People will not elaborate on how Maithil culture also means a rigid caste system or the confinement of women in purdah, although such features are notably Maithil. Politeness to guests seems to be a unifying characteristic, and in this it is implied that the culture has grace and generosity. Even people of lower caste will exemplify the culture this way: when you enter the house, you are given water to wash your feet and your hands. You are given a mat or cloth on which to sit. Then, without asking, you are presented with food. "This is the traditional hospitality of Mithila." Often the guest will be reminded that he is receiving the special foods of Mithila: beaten rice (*ciurā*) and yoghurt (*dahi*), batter-fried vegetables (*taruwā*), fish, and an assortment of sweets (such as *ṭhakuwā* and *khajur*).

The romanticized view of the hospitality of Mithila (which, it is agreed, is changing with the times) underscores the deep sense of being treated with disrespect when a Maithil person goes to Kathmandu. People will say that the hospitality of Maithil is far greater than that of hill people who often won't offer even a cup of tea. "When the sun sets, the people of Kathmandu get drunk" (*sūrya bhayo asta, Kathmandu bhayo masta*), whereas people of Mithila maintain politeness and serve the guest like a god. Never mind such dignity, when they go to Kathmandu they are abused for wearing dhotis, and people call them derogatory names.

In fact, the Maithil people receive no more abuse than other Tarai people, and it cannot be said whether a man on his visit to Kathmandu is more aware of being Madheshi or Maithil. But in his reaction to the disrespect he encounters in Kathmandu, he is certainly Maithil. Maithili speakers, it will be repeated again and again, are superior people – superior to Awadhi speakers, superior to Rajputs ("ask them and they will agree") – and this superiority comes from being born of such an ancient cultured civilization. I once heard an educated man comment that the marriage of the current Kayastha mayor of Janakpur to a Newar is not so very strange as the value placed on ritual in both cultures is similar. (I have also heard it said by an unlearned man that Newars are the lowest caste. For example, they perform worship of the gods with eggs while Maithils worship with *laḍḍu* [a sweet, and therefore a vegetarian and pure offering, unlike eggs].) It is the belief of many Maithil people that the Newars received culture from Mithila (as when Brahman priests came to the court of the Malla kings). Furthermore, the present King's own great-grandmother came from a village outside Janakpur. It is astounding to the people of Janakpur that nobody in Kathmandu sees the connection.

The most evident sign of being Maithil, however, is the language. Although many people mix Maithili with Hindi and there are dialects of Maithili, most people would say they are Maithili because they speak Maithili. It is the language, therefore, with its rich literary heritage, that is most often cited as evidence of a distinct Maithil identity.

Maithil activists are anxious to see the language recognized in the constitution. One Maithil intellectual listed the inadequacies of government policy regarding Maithili as follows:

1. Although it usually focuses on the upliftment of Nepali language and culture, the Royal Nepal Academy recently commissioned two Janakpur scholars to compile a Maithili-Nepali dictionary. While the gesture is appreciated, it also rouses ire not only because the payment was paltry (8,000 rupees) but because the agenda for the development of Maithili language is continually being set by non-Maithili speakers. Whether it be a dictionary, a collection of folklore, or scriptures, Maithili speakers should determine the priority for projects in Maithili.

2. Those who receive an M.A. in Maithili are given no points for this on public service exams. However, those who receive an M.A. in Nepali receive 15 points.

3. At the Rajbiraj campus one can earn a B.A. in Maithili and at Janakpur an M.A.; however, there is no possibility of receiving a job either in government service or in primary education. As of 1993, the Janakpur department is only being kept active by the contrived enrollment of two unenthusiastic students. The current situation will cause further study of Maithili to die out. While the Constitution gives each community the right to use the mother tongue as a medium of instruction in primary

schools, the government has yet to provide assistance for instruction in the mother tongue. In general, textbooks for primary and adult literacy instruction contain references to things Tarai people are not familiar with, and illustrations which never represent Tarai people. In February 1993, a Seminar on the Tarai Community and National Integration in Nepal was held in Janakpur. Dr. Hari Bansh Jha proposed that Hindi become the medium of instruction and the unifying language of the Tarai, a notion which fails to generate much enthusiasm among the Maithili speakers of Janakpur.

4. Radio and TV should offer more programs in Maithili to spread awareness of the culture as a whole. (In 1993 Radio Nepal did begin broadcasting news bulletins in Maithili once a day.)
5. When given the chance to present Nepali culture to the outside world, the government should include the art, music, dance, and literature of the Maithils.

In Janakpur, there are several publications in Maithili, and after 1990 the 'Maithili Development Council', comprised of a group of youths under twenty years of age, was established to encourage poetry, stories and dramas through the organization of competitions. However, as discussed below, the issue of language is not a burning one among non-intellectuals, and where it does arise, it tends to divide Maithils between high caste and low.

MADHESHI OR MAITHIL: SADBHAVANA PARTY VS. CONGRESS

One man of the Kayastha caste says, "First I am Maithil, then Madheshi, and thirdly Nepali." Not everyone lists his identities in this order: it may be that as regards residence, people are Nepali, for political reasons they have taken allegiance with the Madheshi, and culturally they are first Maithil.

Much has been written about the Madheshi identity problem (Gaige, 1975; Dahal, 1992), but I would argue that from the Maithil point of view, it is more of a hill people's problem. The wearing of khadi cloth or the dhoti may be the first signal that a man is Madheshi, and to hill people that means more Indian than Nepali. To Maithils this assumption is an injustice and they point out how obtaining a citizenship card may take two years for a person from the Tarai, whereas a hill dweller from Ramechap gets his quickly without question.

As regards the difficulties of gaining citizenship, and under-representation in the government and military, Maithil people will become one with all who are Madheshi. Thus when a Maithil Brahman or a Mandal (Farmer-caste man) speaks of "us" (Madheshi) versus "them" (Pahari) he will overlook the deep differences in Maithil culture and believe there is indeed a solid "us". Within the Congress party, this unity was shown through the wearing of white khadi cloth. (Khadi was daily wear during the elections, now jeans and polo shirts are back in fashion, though khadi reappears on Janakpur's streets when there is a political meeting.)

The Sadbhavana party expresses the feelings of Maithil people that the government does not represent the interests of Tarai peoples, but the Congress party has a long history in Janakpur. After the movement of 1990, people of Janakpur believed that democracy, and the subsequent success of the Congress party was as much an outcome of their efforts as it was the efforts of those in the Kathmandu Valley. Congress MPs won in all five constituencies of Janakpur's district, Dhanusha. When Congress won a majority of seats nationally, it was assumed that the Tarai would be duly represented. Moreover, it was assumed that locally elected leaders would further the interests of the Tarai and of Janakpur. Now there is a strong feeling that the Congress Party Central Committee is guilty of a kind of casteism. For example, some of the candidates chosen to contest the elections were selected not on the basis of political acumen but because they were Yadav, the caste with the largest population. Once elected, it is said, these weak politicians became pawns of the party and were more interested in retaining their position in the party than in taking on Tarai concerns and siding with Sadbhavana.

People comment that before the movement, Congress people couldn't afford to chew *pān*, and now they eat the four-rupee, rather than the common two-rupee variety. (In local terms, this observation may be just as disturbing as the fact that the leaders are now seen eating in Janakpur's most expensive restaurant, or driving Toyota Landcruisers.) But while representatives may have neglected the Maithil cause, the original struggle of the Congress party is too fresh in the people's minds to be forgotten, and until Sadbhavana can bring forth leaders people know and trust, it will not gain ground in Janakpur.

Another reason Sadbhavana has not become popular is that the ruling elite are first Maithil and secondly Madheshi. It is somewhat beneath them to join with other Tarai peoples (particularly 'tribals') when what they really desire is to have equal if not superior power in a party which is national. In other words, they don't want to be 'left out of the clubs' which are currently dominated by hill Brahmans and Newars. Ram Saroj Yadav, District Development Committee of Dhanusha President, has quoted B. P. Koirala as saying that in fact Tarai people are the most nationalistic (Jha, 1993: 74) – which in Nepal counts as a compliment. In sum, he says that Tarai people may not like the way Sadbhavana divides the country into two, particularly since that leaves Maithils on the side without power.

Finally, and as important as the above points, Sadbhavana urges recognition of Hindi as a national language, but this is not an issue for those Maithils whose identity is strongly centred on speaking Maithili, a language they view as far superior to Hindi and one which has influenced Newari. Maithili speakers would rather not be clumped with Bhojpuri speakers or Tharu speakers in an all-Tarai party. They are not all-Tarai, they are Maithil with a legendary boundary which separates them from other Tarai communities.

Both Paul Brass and Richard Burghart have noted that one reason for the failure of the Maithili language movement is that there is a division between the Brahmans and Kayasthas who speak a pure Maithili, and the other castes, who mix theirs with Hindi or speak in dialect. The high-caste "chaste Maithili speakers sometimes claim ... that they alone speak Maithili; what the others speak is not rustic Maithili but simply rustic language ... Maithili

is the preserve of those who cultivate their minds, not their fields"
(Burghart, 1996a: 367). As long as high-caste Maithils hold power,
or as long as lower-caste politicians attempt to win favour by
espousing the Maithil cause, Sadbhavana's promotion of Hindi will
have little chance of success. If the lower castes were to increase
their power, depending on how they chose to define their identity,
it could be that lower castes would see more to be gained in the
pro-Hindi movement.

CASTE AND JANAKPUR POLITICS

In questions of residence (i.e. their 'ancestors' land is now
included within the boundaries of Nepal) and political rights, the
Maithili speaking people of Janakpur are united as Nepali. In their
frustration and humiliation regarding the Kathmandu government
they are united as Madheshi. It is when they begin to define
themselves as Maithil that divisions within the culture open up. In
the long term, such divisions are bound to affect political unity.

Burghart points out that there are only a few castes who are
unique to the Maithils, of whom Maithil Brahmans are the most
prominent: others are found equally in other parts of the Tarai and
north India (Burghart, 1996a: 373). Maithil castes are divided
among the four main *varṇa* categories: Brahman, Kshatriya,
Vaishya, and Shudra. In the addition there are the Kayasthas who
did not fit into any of the *varṇa*s, and the Untouchables below the
Shudras. Most Vaishya, Shudra, and Untouchable castes are listed
in Table 7.1.

In the new democracy, caste organizations are increasing. The
Nepal Vaishya Welfare Organization has its central office in Janakpur
where efforts are now being made to connect Vaishya (business caste)
people from Janakpur to Patna and in all Tarai districts. While the
organization is not said to be political, one of its chief aims is to put
pressure on the Brahmans, Kayasthas, and Yadavs whom the
Congress Party continues to put in power. The Vaishyas, among
whom there are engineers, lawyers, doctors, and businessmen –
frequently educated and/or wealthy –, believe they are not trusted

FIGURE 22   *A typical wall painting in the village of Kuwa, near Janakpur (Claire Burkert)*

FIGURE 23   *A traditional aripan design of the Kayastha caste (Claire Burkert)*

developed during the art for income programme initiated in Bihar in 1967. The highly ornate painting which developed in India became known as Madhubani painting or Mithila painting, and artists from Madhubani and nearby villages have travelled all over the world to show their skills in making highly ornate paintings with pen or a stick covered with cloth.

When I began the Janakpur project I decided that rather than imitate exactly the meticulous pen and ink paintings of Madhubani, women could try to put on paper the same bold, bright, often humorous images that appear on the walls of their homes. We used Nepali handmade paper rather than the finer bleached paper used in Madhubani, and substituted brush and poster colour for the stick wound with cloth and the pigments bought in the bazaar because the latter did not work well on paper. In this way the Janakpur Women's Art Project (JWAP) began to promote the women's art as 'Janakpur Art'.

In May of 1990, just after 'the Movement', JWAP held its first exhibition. Julia Chang Bloch, the US Ambassador to Nepal,

FIGURE 24   *A village-style painting produced at the JWDC by Urmila Mandal (Mandal/Farmer caste) (Claire Burkert)*

FIGURE 25   *Detail of a painting of Ram and Sita by Sita Karna (Kayastha caste) (Claire Burkert)*

and Dhanusha District's Mahendra Narayan Nidhi, who later became General Secretary of the Nepali Congress Party, cut the ribbon. The exhibition appeared on TV and in the newspapers, and obviously inspired a pride that was not only local but national.

Trouble began when, in order to receive outside funding, JWAP had to ally itself with the local chapter of an international men's club. (At that time it was still difficult for an NGO to become offical and receive international aid.) The then chairman of the Janakpur chapter agreed to the club becoming the partner of JWAP, although many in his organization were not aware of it. He set himself up as Chairman of the project, with a few other members as Secretary and Treasurer and board members. JWAP's wish to be equally represented was never met.

Soon Project funds were helping to support an NGO newly established by the chairman. This organization purported to promote Maithili culture, which it did at events of the Nepali Congress party (such as the Party's national pre-election convention in Jhapa). When the Prime Minister came to town, the club chairman organized an exhibition of the women's paintings under the auspices of his new NGO. The women were left to wander somewhere in the background while the Chairman gave the Prime Minister a tour of the exhibition.

There came a time when members of JWAP were no longer allowed to see the account books, and JWAP decided to protest. Help was sought from UNDP, UNIFEM, and the Social Services National Coordinating Committee (SSNCC). At a joint meeting of club members, JWAP women, and SSNCC officials, the Chairman read a letter he had just sent to the UNDP, SSNCC, and the Ministry of Finance. In it, he claimed that the organization was destroying culture: for instance, the artists were "presenting not only untraditional things but shocking things." When asked for concrete examples of paintings he found untraditional or shameful, he cited as an example scenes of childbirth and paintings of tigers. The tigers which he alluded to were copies of those found on lower-caste village houses. The birth pictures illustrated the real-life scene in Maithil culture after a child is born, with the Chamar midwife massaging the mother and various items arranged to ward away ghosts.

"Ask the women if their culture is being ruined," the club members were asked, to which an elderly doctor replied, "They don't know their culture. We must teach it to them." Although I did not expect the doctor to come sit on the floor and teach the women how to paint *aripan*, I was shocked. The tables had turned: the culture these men had once claimed to know nothing about was now their property. And I saw that just as the women had presumably lost their culture which now belonged to the men, Mithila art had lost its innocence.

The painting project had called attention to women's skills and proposed to uplift women in a culturally appropriate manner, i.e. offer them empowerment through the practice of what is traditionally theirs. As soon as the male power elite understood that the project's promotion of Maithil art had an aim of empowering women and not the promotion of men, they needed to claim that what was traditionally the women's was not the women's after all. These men claimed, then, that the women lost their tradition and the men recovered it, and now they were the champions of artistic preservation.

Not only did the men want the power and prestige that this women were earning, they felt that their domination, which was always a presumed right, was threatened. For this reason, they demanded the keys to the women's painting workshop and pasted up rules and regulations for them to follow. In the letter to the government, the Chairman added that the project was breaking up families and exploiting women, and thus the men also became the champions of family values, and the defenders of innocent and mistreated women. About me, he wrote in his letter:

> She is reported to have been striving to ruin the Nepalese families with her so called faministic [sic] efforts to bolster up the morale of the gullible women stand against husbands and other respectable members (like in-laws) in the family. The report is a subject to be probed.

Fortunately since the advent of democracy it is easier to establish an NGO, and so the women formed their own NGO, the Janakpur Women's Development Centre (JWDC), and the club soon had no more involvement with them. But the event presaged what might be the future of Maithil art, and something I had never foreseen, art's close relationship to power.

A significant aspect of the conflict was that the members of the club, though many were Vaishyas, were adhering to the Brahman/Kayastha model of what was Mithila art. One way to control the women would be to control the art. By making sure the women only repeated the Brahman/Kayastha traditional images, they could also monitor what the women expressed. Although we had successfully held an exhibition with 'scenes from a woman's life' with the club on the occasion of Women's Day, the men began to think that things were getting out of hand. The desire to promote 'Janakpur Art' which encompassed the designs of all castes and also illustrated traditions in Mithila culture did not receive support – rather, it was used against the JWDC. In the past few years local art contests have continued to award prizes to Jhas and Karnas.

The Yadavs, Tatamas, and Chamars are not aware of such contests nor are they invited to attend. And in the future, if they do, will they imitate the Brahman forms? It is likely that they will, for once they realize that their art is 'unsophisticated' they begin to imitate the Brahman and Kayastha style. However, though the style is more and more Sanskritized, what is expressed is not. There are marriage scenes, scenes of wife-beating, literacy classes, etc.

Local journalists and scholars from time to time bring up the subject of Maithil art and its demise through Western influence and commercialization. As yet there has been no reflection on the fact that new directions in the art may be coming out of the culture itself, and in particular women's culture. As women get outside their homes and begin to learn about the world around them they are naturally going to wish to express what they see. Since most Maithil women are illiterate, it is especially natural that they will express themselves in visual form.

The high profile of Mithila art in Kathmandu, due mainly to the Janakpur Women's Development Centre, has raised general awareness of the unique culture of Maithils. But Mithila art is also becoming associated with the JWDC and the effort to generate income for women. As women painters of all castes step outside to earn income from their paintings, it is only natural that they will expand their subject matter and develop caste and individual differences.

This is not how some of Janakpur men have intended it. They would prefer that the art continue to express the classical, religious, and romantic view of the culture and for some time within Janakpur, it will be Maithil men, not women, who determine what acceptable Mithila art is. Should casteism result in the strengthening of other castes, will other caste leaders of society take an interest in the art – and if so, will it be in its Brahman/Kayastha form or will it be redefined?

The question of whose culture it is comes up in situations of power between men and women in Mithila, and between castes. As yet it has not come up with regard to the commercialization of the art. The Janakpur Women's Development Centre maintains that since it is a women's art, women should have jurisdiction over how it is commercialized and women themselves should reap the majority of the profits (rather than being labourers employed by a middleman). However, since the project proved there was commercial interest in Mithila art, Mithila art also meant money. And that was why not only the men's club was interested, but so were some Shresthas in Kathmandu, a team comprised of a Sherpa papermaker and a local Maithil Brahman boy with a fine arts degree, the son of one of our Muslim artists, an arts school for Dharan earthquake victims in Kathmandu, some Janakpur Congress Party men, and a Magar woman politician of Janakpur. Most recently, in 1995, an exhibition of Mithila art was organized at the Bal Mandir in Kathmandu. The organizing board was largely Newar.

Before the project's success, unlike the language and literature issue, Mithila art was innocent and, perhaps unlike Maithil language and literature, could be appreciated without stirring up trouble. When it is in the hands of politicians, the educated elite, or entrepreneurs, it is 'currency' in actual or political terms.

As the women change, so does the meaning of the art, and so does a tradition which is central to the definition of cultural identity. For the conservative, the only way to 'manage impressions' may be to attempt to impose a Brahman/Kayastha ideal of the art. Casteism, however, may affect the definition of what is Mithila art, and Mithila art redefined to include the art of Chamars, Mandals, Musahars, etc. could, in fact, help to unify the culture more successfully than its language and poetry.

CONCLUSION

Maithil people have a rich political, religious, and artistic heritage. Today the myth of greatness still prevails, perpetuated by Brahmans and Kayasthas who for the most part define the culture and its values. The growth of casteism may affect the forms Maithil culture takes. Should the image of Maithil culture undergo some revision, the path to achieving political goals may change. For example, the issue of recognition of the Maithili language may be less important than all-Tarai issues, or the advancement of lower castes. Meanwhile, certain traditions of the culture, such as Maithil art, have been politicized. Although Maithil women have always produced their art without influence from men, this politicization could affect the subject matter of the art they produce for income. In any event, because Maithil women remain excluded from political life, it will be a long time before women artists can benefit from their art's connection to issues of cultural identity and power.

ACKNOWLEDGEMENTS

I would like to thank Dr. Rajendra Prasad Rimal, Ganga Prasad Jha, and Brikesh Chandra Lal for the information they supplied me for this chapter. I thank Charles Ramble for his encouragement. I am especially appreciative of David Gellner's assistance and guidance during both writing and editing processes.

CHAPTER EIGHT

Losing Ground, Gaining Ground: Land and Change in a Tharu Community in Dang, West Nepal

Christian McDonaugh

INTRODUCTION

Difficulties over access to land, rather than wider questions of cultural and ethnic identity, have been a central concern for Tharu communities in Dang particularly over the last few decades. Issues surrounding land, therefore, have been one of the key elements in shaping Tharu communities' wider outlook and in underpinning what sense of common concerns they have had. The aim of this paper is to review changes over access to land, mainly in one village community particularly during the period 1980 to 1993, but also against the wider background of changes experienced by Tharu communities throughout Dang over this century.

It is true that since 1990 Nepal has been in a state of considerable political ferment and one of the central issues on the political landscape is the increasing prominence of ethnic political groupings making political demands or providing the basis for actual political parties. How to assess such emergent ethnicities is a major concern of commentators and is generating a growing literature of various kinds, including this book itself. Thus far, however, there is little in the way of a common pan-Tharu ethnic identity or unity, though there are attempts to forge such an identity between the various different groups of 'Tharu' spread throughout the Nepalese Tarai.

A national organization, Tharu Kalyankarini Sabha (Tharu Welfare Association) was set up in 1949. Through the publication of a magazine *Tharu Sanskriti*, and by holding conventions bringing

275

together Tharus from all over Nepal, this organization has sought to promote a common ethnic consciousness at the same time as making demands for the support and development of Tharu communities. Guneratne has described this organization as the attempt by an elite to forge a common identity and unity between the cultural and linguistically diverse endogamous groups subsumed under the Tharu ethnonym (n.d.: 1). Referring to it as Tharu Kalyan Samiti as it is known locally in Chitwan, Guneratne explains that this organization is very much elite led and dominated but nevertheless it

> can claim to represent a significant sector of Nepalese society, even though not all Tharus have heard of the Tharu Kalyan Samiti and of those who have, not all support it. Despite this qualification however the Tharu Kalyan Samiti has brought together in a common arena of symbolic action a diversity of groups from every corner of the Terai and successfully asserted a claim to common community (Guneratne, n.d.: 8–9).

In my experience support for this organization among Tharu villagers in the western Tarai is very limited. This is partly because it is seen as an association of richer and elite members of Tharu communities, particularly drawn from the eastern Tarai. This has also been reported for Tharu communities in Kailali district (Oder-gaard, forthcoming). One of its main areas of demands has been for better educational opportunities for the Tharu, but as Guneratne points out "only the elite itself is in a position to benefit from the fruits of such activities" (n.d.: 3). Its relative lack of a grass-roots following in the west at least is probably also because it appears to have done little to address other issues of real concern to most Tharu, such as their problems over access to land. To the extent that it has been successful in promoting a pan-Tharu sense of 'common community', this has mainly been among sections of the Tharu elite.

As I have described elsewhere (McDonaugh, 1989: 200), in Dang in the early 1970s, a radical group of Dangaura Tharu set up an organization calling itself 'The association for the improvement of Tharu language and literature in the west of Nepal'. This group initially addressed itself primarily to the Dangaura Tharu and published books of songs in that language. It seems to have had mixed aims, including reform of cultural practices, such as drinking, along higher caste lines. It also aimed to promote Tharu unity in the face of adversity, calling on Tharu peasants to stand together in the struggle for their rights against exploitative landlords. Some of this was contained in their magazine *Gotchali*. Only one issue of this magazine was published and soon afterwards it was banned by the then government, an act which is a good indication of its radical political tone. Some members of the editorial committee, who were also founders of the association were also jailed and the group was thus prevented from continuing to operate. In the early 1980s one of the original association's members published three further books of songs in the Dangaura Tharu language, but the editorial introductions to these were careful not to make any references, for example to the Tharus' economic situation, which could have been taken as politically inflammatory (Chaudhari and Chaudhari, 1981/82; Chaudhari, 1982/83a, 1982/83b; McDonaugh, 1989: 200–203). Although the original association through the *Gotchali* magazine had a significant impact in Dang at the time, government pressure effectively prevented any further overt organization and expression of a more militant Tharu identity by this association.

More recently, since the 1990 revolution, there has been the emergence and extremely rapid growth of BASE (Backwards Society Education), an NGO set up by young Tharus.[1] The creation and development of BASE has apparently been driven to a significant extent by the energy and ideas of its director, Dilli Bahadur Chaudhari, a young Tharu of humble origins from the west of Dang.[2] Dilli Bahadur's work has recently received international recognition when he was awarded the Reebok International Human Rights Award in December 1994. BASE grew out of earlier attempts in the late 1980s by Dilli Bahadur Chaudhari and other young Tharus to start up local development associations in the west of Dang and like earlier movements also experienced considerable opposition from government and powerful local Paharis. Originally BASE was focused on education and consciousness raising among the Tharu community and started a programme of non-formal education including literacy classes for adults and especially women. The idea behind this was that ignorance and lack of education have been at the root of the problems Tharu have suffered in recent decades. Through education the Tharu will become more aware of their rights and better able to assert these in dealings with landlords and other external agencies including government offices. The organization has seen a phenomenal growth, now being the largest local NGO in Nepal, and it has diversified its programmes into additional areas such as health education and income-generating initiatives. It is active throughout the western Tarai, but apparently almost exclusively among Dangaura Tharu communities, though officially, at any rate, it has had to move beyond operating explicitly as an ethnically oriented organization.

BASE does not align itself with any political party and in this sense is non-political, but its activities are obviously of considerable local political significance, particularly its support for the disadvantaged Tharu tenant farmers and landless households. Moreover, it has begun to organize annual Tharu cultural conventions with a view to revitalizing Tharu culture and this has brought it directly into the arena of cultural politics as well. At this stage it is not clear what its wider political impacts have been or will be, but to my mind its success in the sphere of grass roots education in the more open political atmosphere since 1990 must be linked to a general impression one now has of Dangaura Tharu communities as more positive, vocal, confident, and outward looking than they ever were before. I am not in a position to assess the impact of its education programmes, but the rapid spread and uptake of this programme strongly suggests that it has touched on areas of widespread concern to the Tharu. Nevertheless, BASE itself has apparently recognized that education on its own will not be enough radically to improve the Tharu situation. Consequently it has also begun to run other programmes including significantly some relating to *kamaiyā*s or landless labourers/bonded labourers, land distribution, legal support, and agricultural development (Odergaard, forthcoming). Apparently education and consciousness raising, though very important, need to be accompanied by efforts towards more structural and developmental changes.

BASE is a new organization and one that is rapidly evolving. It has patently acquired a major following and membership among the Dangaura Tharu, but at this stage we do not have the detailed information to assess its true impact at a grass roots level. Research is required if we are to understand if and how BASE may have affected and indeed even shaped notions of cultural or ethnic identity among the wider Dangaura Tharu population.

Thus far no ethnically based political party has emerged among Tharu communities. In the west Tharu allegiance is given either to Congress or the UML. Overall it seems that the Dangaura Tharu tend to follow the UML, but in Dang itself there is also some support for Congress. The Sadbhavana Party, which has its power base in the eastern Tarai, has made no impact among western Tharu communities as far as I can tell.

The question of the emergence or not of a Dangaura or even of a wider Tharu ethnicity is an important issue but it is also a difficult and frustrating topic to discuss principally because we lack detailed information to generalize confidently about what is happening at grass roots level in Tharu communities. In relation to BASE and even the earlier organizations we can get some impressions of what is happening but for the most part we are restricted to looking at the level of leaders and elites. It is tempting to extrapolate from this to make generalizations about the Dangaura Tharu as a whole, but such generalizations would run the severe risk of lacking substance and validity. This may be a particular danger when we are dealing with such vague, slippery, and rapidly changing notions as identity and ethnicity. The rather narrow focus of the rest of this paper reflects in part a reaction against such a temptation to make broad but potentially vacuous generalizations. It may well be that the findings I will present about some of the changes in land ownership and land use in one village cannot easily be generalized to the Tharu community as a whole, but at the same time they may have something to contribute to filling in the picture, albeit a small part of it, of how social and economic change is taking place on the ground.

LOSING GROUND

The general picture of the Tharu situation in Dang over the last few decades at least is that they have been losing ground. They have lost their hold on positions of local administrative and political power and over this period they have also lost ownership of land in some cases and experienced deteriorating conditions of access to land they cultivate as tenants. The groups who have made gains at Tharu expense are the Hindu high castes originating from the hills to the north, and collectively referred to by the Tharu as Pahari (*Pahāḍi*, i.e. the Nepali-speaking Parbatiyas or Bahun-Chetris as they are known in the hills). Misra in his study of the political economy of Urahari village in Dang, summarizes this overall situation while bringing out the centrality of the Pahari-Tharu relationship in structuring recent Tharu social and economic experience:

> The everyday life of the Tharus thus emanates from their relation with the Pahadi zamindars [landowners] ... [the] Tharu-zamindar production relation appears to have become more and more exploitative, despite periodic lulls, through the last one hundred years. A large proportion of Tharu families have had an extremely uneasy livelihood during the last three or four generations (Misra, 1984: 3).

The progressive extension of the apparatus of the Nepalese state was accompanied by a steady erosion of local Tharu influence. From the late nineteenth century on, the central government sought to undermine the position of the powerful Tharu Chaudharis, who were responsible for the administration of revenues and other duties for the various *pargannā* into which the valley was divided (Krauskopff, 1989: 49). Towards the end of the nineteenth century the position of *jimidār* was introduced into the valley. The *jimidār* was the person appointed by the Government to be responsible for the collection of taxes at one or more villages or *maujā* which thereby progressively replaced the much larger *pargannā* as the key unit of local administration. At the same time the Government appointed hill people as *jimidār* so that when the system was abolished in 1951 virtually the only remaining Tharu *jimidār* were concentrated in the Deukhuri valley to the south which had experienced much less Pahari immigration (McDougal, 1968: 77, 88). The position of Chaudhari itself was abolished in 1933 (Krauskopff, 1989: 49).

Alongside the increasing presence of Pahari in the administration came their encroachment into Tharu-held land. Over the last century, by one means or another, more and more of the land has come under Pahari ownership. Whereas in the 1912 revenue settlement most of the landlords were Tharus, by the late 1960s McDougal's survey found that the great majority of landlords were Pahari (1968: 86–7). In Dang by this date some 80% of the Tharu were tenants and the great majority of these tenants had little or no land of their own. Around 90% of the land cultivated by Tharu tenants belonged to Paharis.

The rise in Pahari control over land was accompanied by an increasing rate of immigration of hill people into the valley. This process accelerated rapidly after malaria eradication in the early 1960s and has continued up to the present. The Land Reform measures in 1964 in the short term had unfortunate consequences for the Tharu. The reforms appear to have sparked a phase of land sales by the larger and often longer established of the Pahari landowners. In general, however, the Tharu were not able to buy. Instead land was bought by immigrant Pahari households.

Over this century, accompanying the massive influx of Paharis and the increasing pressure on land, the tenancy conditions for the Tharu have also worsened dramatically. The earlier system of tenancy called *potet* was progressively replaced by *batāyā*. Under the *potet* system, the tenant cultivated some land taking the whole crop, but approximately for every 5, 6, or 7 *bighā* of land the tenant had to provide labour to cultivate 1 *bighā* of the landlord's land. For the Tharu this system was preferable to *batāyā* under which the tenant has to pay a share of the crop on all the land he cultivates to the landlord. The early decades of this century saw a steady movement away from *potet* towards *batāyā* so that the previous system had gone by the time of Land Reform. Initially under *batāyā* the shares were *pānchkur*, *caukur*, or *tinkur* with the tenant providing one fifth, one fourth, or one third respectively to the landlord. Such customary shares of the crop should have been protected by the Land Reform measures, but landlord pressure resulted in an inexorable shift to *adhiyā* ('halves', i.e. a half share going to the landlord) or in a few cases to *tinkur* by the mid to late 1960s (McDougal, 1968: 87–89; Krauskopff, 1989: 54, 55; Misra, 1984: 6–8).

Tharu emigration from Dang to the Tarai districts further west, and Bardia and Kailali in particular, had been going on at a low level throughout this century. As a result of the Pahari influx and deteriorating land situation, however, Tharu emigration from Dang increased dramatically in the 1960s, reaching its highest levels between the late 1960s and early 1970s (Rajaure, 1978: 28; Macdonald, 1975a: 268; Krauskopff, 1989: 55; Misra, 1984: 8). Emigration to the west continued throughout the 1970s but has trailed off since the early 1980s. This movement of Tharu households out of Dang was a very pronounced feature of the social landscape in the 1970s as is evidenced by the refrain from one of the songs published in *Gotchali: "e morā gotcāli jin karo cārā"* meaning "oh, my friends, do not leave (Dang)". During my first period of field research between 1979–1981, in the months following the rice harvest, it was still not unusual to catch sight of Tharu families moving west along the trails carrying their belongings with them. In some cases whole village communities migrated, leaving their original village site to households of incoming Paharis who replaced the original Tharu inhabitants over the space of a few years.

These trends, then, formed the broad background to the situation when I began research in the village of Sukhrwar in 1979. The village population was predominantly Tharu with 35 Tharu households and approximately 355 Tharu individuals. There were 12 Pahari households with a total population of around 70, but 4 of these households also had residences in other parts of Dang so there was continual fluctuation and movement of population. The Tharu owned approximately 23% of the village land. On the western edge of the village lands a small religious educational foundation, known locally as the *vidyālaya*, held about 12% of the land. The remaining 65% of land was held by 15 Pahari families. There were 5 landless Tharu households whose members worked as *kamāyā* or agricultural labourers paid on an annual basis. The ownership of land by Tharu households was as shown in Table 8.1. In addition approximately 20 of the 30 farming Tharu households also owned relatively small amounts of dry *bārī* land in the Deukhuri valley to the south of Dang, where most of them also had small secondary dwellings. In short, in Sukhrwar, apart from one owner-cultivator household the Tharu households were owner-cum-tenant farmers with the majority owning very little and in some cases no land themselves.

The Tharu households were, therefore, directly dependent to a very great extent on the Pahari landowners for access to the land. The main social and economic division within the village as a whole was thus very clear cut with the Pahari as landlords on one side and the Tharu as tenants on the other. The notable social distance between these two groups was, of course, also due to caste-hierarchical distinctions as well as linguistic and cultural differences. Tharu-Pahari interaction took place in a number of contexts, but overall there was a marked lack of interaction. Paharis, for example, very rarely if ever attended the *khel* or village council of Tharu household heads which organized all the ritual and many of the other administrative aspects of everyday village life. Relations between tenants and landlords were generally uneasy and character-ized by restraint and formality on the part of the Tharu. Easier

TABLE 8.1 THARU LANDOWNERSHIP IN SUKHRWAR (1980)

Area of Land	Number of households	Percentage of total village land
9–10 *bighā* [a]	1	5
3–4 *bighā*	3	5
2–3 *bighā*	3	4
1–2 *bighā*	6	5
0–1 *bighā*	22	4
	35	23%

[a]   One *bighā* is approximately 0.67 hectares.

relations were maintained with smaller Pahari landlords and with Pahari families from neighbouring villages in a few instances. It would not be oversimplifying too much to say that for the Pahari in general, the Tharu were considered lower, backward, uneducated, and primitive: connotations all implied by the term *jaṅgalī*, which I heard used of the Tharu on some occasions. For some of the longer established landlords, however, their attitudes also contained a strand of paternalism. As it was explained to me, in times of hardship due to illness or food shortage for instance, it was the duty of a landlord to look after his tenants. Equally the other side of this view was that the landlord could expect the tenant to carry out a range of duties beyond simply cultivating the land. This traditional model of landlord-tenant relations was, however, rapidly breaking down under the impact of the sorts of economic and social changes described above. It is not clear to what extent, if any, the Tharu for their part had ever been happy to accept this view of their relations with their landlords.

Tharu tenant-Pahari landlord relations were not only charac-terized by social distance and hierarchy, there was also considerable disagreement and tension over the rights of the respective parties. Unlike many other villages in Dang, the issue for the Tharu was not of actually having lost ownership of land through indebtedness or as a result of other sharp practice on the part of the Pahari immigrants.[3] Originally the village land had been given as *birtā* to a Brahman family, and over generations lands had been split up between family members and sold off to others, some to Tharus but most to other Paharis. Two descendants of the original Brahman owner still owned about 25% of the village land and were two of the three largest landowners in the village. The disputes and tensions between the Tharu tenants and the Pahari landlords focused on three issues: shares of the crops, obtaining *mohī* or legally secure tenancy rights, and to a lesser extent rendering *begārī* or free labour to the landlords.

The Tharu were resentful of the fact that they had been forced to accept declining shares of the crop on the landlords' lands. This area of dispute was largely over by the end of the 1970s, but was alive in Tharu memory. Some time in the early 1960s the landlords had pushed for half shares or third shares with the tenant providing all of the inputs of seeds and fertilizer in the latter case. The Tharu had tried to maintain the previous arrangements of fifths or quarter shares for the landlord and this had resulted in a village-wide dispute during which all the crops were left on the communal village threshing ground. The case had gone as far as the courts in Kathmandu, but whatever the legal outcome, which I was never able fully to ascertain, the end result was that the Tharu had been forced to accept *adhiyā*, or *tinkur* in some cases. During this dispute considerable pressure via the police and by physical assault and intimidation had been brought to bear on the Tharu households and attempts had been made, latterly with limited success, to split up the solidarity of the Tharu community. Incidents from this past were recounted to me on a number of occasions, particularly at the time of minor disputes during my time in the village. The issue had not entirely disappeared since there was still disagreement about which crops had to be shared. For instance, did the landlord have a right to the share of winter wheat or only to the main rice crop planted on the *khet* land? Or again did the landlord have a right to shares of all the dry land (*bārī*) crops of mustard, maize, pulses, and barley, or only to some of these crops?

Tensions over obtaining legally recognized tenancy rights were more acute and were still in the process of resolution while I was in the village. Given its intrinsically controversial nature, this was not an aspect of village life that I was able to explore in great detail, but the general picture was clear. It was not in the landlords' interests to agree to their tenants getting *mohī*. Since the mid-1960s, therefore, most of the landlords had been slow to agree to this new arrangement and had in some cases placed numerous obstacles in the tenants' path. Such obstacles included various forms of harassment and intimidation as well as the more standard ploy of seeking by various means to have the legal and administrative process interminably delayed. By the late 1970s many of the Tharu tenants had managed to secure *mohī* but while I was in the village several farmers were still having to make regular visits to the district capital, Ghorahi, doing what they called *tārikh bokne*, literally 'carrying the date', while waiting for a hearing for their tenancy application. In support of their cases it was also necessary to have the actual sharing out of the crop and delivery to the landlord's house recorded and witnessed officially by local elected members of the panchayat. It was apparent, however, that the tide was running in the tenants' favour and *mohī* rights were being steadily gained by the Tharu.

Traditionally Tharu tenant households had to perform *begārī* by providing unpaid labour for landlords, *jimidār*, and other higher authorities. This system of forced labour had been officially abolished in 1951, though local practice only gradually followed the law. Over the 1960s and into the 1970s landlords had continued to demand *begārī* from their tenants but to an ever decreasing extent as their leverage over the tenants was undermined by tenants' acquisition of *mohī*. The rendering of forced labour on a relatively large scale and in a structured manner gave way therefore to a continuation of the practice on a customary and *ad hoc* basis with landlords asking tenants to do some porterage, and other small odd jobs and sometimes to provide mostly female labour for domestic chores. This kind of demand was resented by the majority of tenants, though some were still continuing to provide such labour from time to time. The increasing refusal by the Tharu to perform such duties and even in some cases their demand to be paid for such work was a further cause of antagonism between these two groups. Although the provision of free labour was not by this time a matter of great economic significance, symbolically it was important in that it reflected and embodied the changing nature of the relationships between landlord and tenant. The refusal to do this unpaid work constituted and reflected a shift in the balance of power, albeit a minor one, between Tharu tenant and Pahari landlord. Symbolically its significance was that it expressed a rejection by the Tharu of their position of subordination to and dependence on the Pahari.

During my initial fieldwork, then, there was a relatively clear-cut social division between the Tharu and the Pahari. For the reasons outlined above the Tharu in general felt themselves to be under pressure from the incoming Pahari. At the same time, however, the Tharu community in this village were consciously and with some degree of success asserting their rights, to *mohī* for instance, and thus resisting any further encroachment on their livelihood. The solidarity of the Tharu community in this struggle was clearly evidenced shortly after I arrived in the village. A dispute erupted with a non-resident landlord on a visit to the village in the course of which he was forced to run through the village while being showered with lumps of dung by some of the Tharu. I was only able to glimpse some of this event from a distance. The Tharu pradhan panch, also from this village, was with me at the time and he quietly advised me not to go into the village to observe events. He himself, of course, did not want to go anyway since had he done so he would have had to become involved immediately. The upshot was that a day later the police came and took some young Tharu men away for questioning, though they were later released. The Tharu were conscious that the situation might deteriorate and a short but intense meeting of many of the Tharu men was held in which it was unanimously resolved that come what may the Tharu would stand together and that even if things got very bad no households were to contemplate leaving the village and migrating to the west.

The Tharu-Pahari division took on political aspects in the run up to the national referendum which the king had called on the future of Panchayat Democracy in 1980–81. The Tharu were unanimously in favour of the multi-party (*bahudal*) side. Pahari allegiances were probably more split, but many of the landlords favoured the Panchayat system, partly because the multi-party camp drew support from the Tharu and tenants and poorer households from all social groups. Tharu support for the opposition in this village was obviously well known to the authorities since some months before the election several Tharu men from the village were put in jail. These men included the Tharu pradhan panch who had resigned his position in order to campaign for the multi-party side. At the same time a small police post was set up in the village. By now it had become apparent to me that I had inadvertently chosen a highly 'political' village as my research base. The jailing of the Tharu men as well as the police presence served to emphasize the Tharu sense of oppression in their continuing struggle with the landlords who for the Tharu were seen in a loose way as aligned with the government administration at local and national levels. The referendum victory for the Panchayat side was perceived as a severe blow by the Tharu.

In a longer term perspective, although the referendum marked a low point for the Tharu, there were signs that the deterioration in their situation was being halted and that in some respects they were even gaining ground. It was true that Tharu shares of the crop had declined but many of the tenant households had won *mohī* rights or were in the process of doing so. The formal imposition of *begārī* had gone and in its residual forms also it was disappearing. The solidarity of the Tharu village community had been maintained over the years through various challenges and disputes, and even if the referendum was lost, this too had provided the Tharu with a powerful experience of solidarity in the face of external pressures. To my mind the solidarity of the Tharu community had been crucial and had provided the essential framework for the degree of success that their quiet but persistent assertion of their rights had achieved.

The basis of such solidarity is complex and is related to various aspects of their social and cultural organization within and beyond the village. Certainly of considerable importance here are aspects of Tharu village social and ritual organization centered around the institution of headman and village council. It is beyond the scope of this paper to explore this issue further, but certain particular features of this village are relevant, since such solidarity is not necessarily so strong a characteristic of all Tharu villages. The fact that the Tharu of this village stood their ground cannot be simply explained, but it may be partly related to the fact that the village has a strong identity and relatively high standing in the local area related to its association with a clan (*gotyār*) of household priests (*gharguruwā*) who take their clan name, Sukhwariyā Guruwā, from the name of the village. Such priests exercise considerable influence in Tharu society and households of this clan comprise the largest clan grouping in the village and include the household of the village headman. Another factor may be that several households already owned some land in the village, and many more own land, albeit in relatively small amounts, in the neighbouring Deukhuri valley. This was something that they would not have been easily

FIGURE 26   *The Maghi Dewani meeting of Tharu household heads of*
Sukhrwar in the village headman's courtyard (1980). This
meeting marks the beginning of the administrative year (which
falls on Magh Sankranti). The village recordskeeper (baidhār)
notes down matters such as fines for missing days of village
communal labour, which families will be building new houses in
the coming year, and so on (C. McDonaugh)

prepared to give up. Equally, if not more important, was the
fact that by the 1970s landownership in the village was distributed
between some 15 Pahari households which meant that the Tharu
did not have to contend with a smaller group of closely related
Pahari households, often descended from one or two much larger
landowners, who between them owned the majority of the land. It
is true, nevertheless, that the two Pahari households descended from
the original village landlord's family, who between them still owned
some 25% of the land, represented the vestiges of such a
landowning group. In some other villages in Dang, where land
ownership was concentrated in fewer households and sometimes in
the hands of closely related households, Tharu tenants would have
found it much more difficult to oppose the landlords' interests.

GAINING GROUND

There were a number of important changes in the patterns of land ownership, tenancy, and land use between 1981 and 1993, which was the last time I was able to visit the village. Village population increased significantly, with the Tharu population growing to around 625 and the Pahari population to approximately 110. The number of individual households also increased, the Tharu to 56 and the Pahari to around 22, though a few of the Pahari households as before have other houses elsewhere in Dang. The increase in numbers of households was due in the case of the Pahari mainly to immigration into the village, though there had also been splitting of earlier established households. The Tharu increase was very largely due to splitting of previous joint households, since there were only three immigrant Tharu households, and one of these, quite a wealthy family, had another house in a neighbouring village.

Land ownership changes began to unfold in the 1980s when several of the main Pahari landlords sold most of their lands. I do not know the reasons for these land sales, but there is probably some truth in the local rumour that for some Pahari one reason was that they found the Tharu in this village too combative and assertive. Over the following years there were a number of transactions in land, for which I do not have the details, but the overall trends and the resulting situation can be broadly summarized as I found it in 1993. Tharu ownership of village land was as shown in Table 8.2. This represented a significant increase in land owned by the Tharu. In the bottom category 0–1 *bighā*, the number of households as a proportion of all Tharu households had decreased from approximately 63% in 1980 to 36% in 1993, while for categories 1–2 *bighā* and 2–3 *bighā* there had been an increase with the proportion of households doubling from 17% to 36% and from 8% to 16% respectively.

Tharu ownership of village land had increased overall from around 23% to about 40%, while Pahari ownership had decreased from around 65% to 46% of which some 6% was owned by non-resident Pahari households. There were now also 6 non-resident

TABLE 8.2 THARU LANDOWNERSHIP IN SUKHRWAR (1993)

Area of Land	Number of households	Percentage of total village land
6–7 bighā	1	3
4–5 bighā	1	2
3–4 bighā	5	9
2–3 bighā	9	10
1–2 bighā	20	13
0–1 bighā	20	3
	56	40%

Tharu households which owned only small amounts of land. The *vidyālaya* ownership of land was still at about 12% of village land as before.

Overall for the Pahari there has been a decrease in the number of larger landowners and a significant increase in the number of smaller landowners and of owner cultivators. The situation is actually quite complex, but an indication of the changing ownership profile of village land can be gained from the records kept of the numbers of households having to make grain payments to the Tharu chairman of the local canal irrigation system, proportional to the amounts of land they owned. These records have become more exact and now are careful to include all households which had taken unregistered (*ailānī*) village land into cultivation and were making use of irrigation water on this new land. Whereas the canal record for 1980 gave around 31 households as making grain payments, in 1993 there were about 90 households assessed, though it is true that some of these were only paying very small or nominal amounts: 11 Tharu households had to pay less than one *mānā* (approximately half a litre) of grain each.

The broad trends which emerge from this data are that there has been increasing diversification in the land ownership pattern, and in particular that more Tharu households now owned land. It seems that increased Tharu ownership had resulted from outright purchase of land in a few cases, but more frequently it has come about because a number of Tharu *mohī* tenants had over time agreed to give up their tenancy rights in lieu of one quarter of the *mohī* land. It seems that by the early 1980s all those Tharu households which were in a position to hold *mohī* tenancy rights had acquired these rights. However, by 1993, Tharu *mohī* tenants were in a minority in the village. From forming a large majority, by 1993 some 29 out of 45 Tharu tenant households no longer had protected tenancies but worked land on a casual year-to-year basis. There were a further 11 households which still held *mohī* land. The remaining 5 tenant households either cultivated *vidyālaya* land on a contract basis, or worked the land of a Brahman owner who had disappeared in India and whose estate was therefore frozen for the time being, so that the land could not be sold or alienated in some other manner.

This shift away from *mohī* tenancy meant that most of these Tharu households now owned some, or more, land than before, but at the same time they cultivated other lands wherever they could get them on a casual *adhiyā* basis from year to year. Given the

FIGURE 27   *Kul Bahadur Chaudhari broadcasting germinated rice seeds into the paddy fields. This was still the predominant method of sowing in 1980 when this picture was taken (C. McDonaugh)*

prominence of disputes over *mohī* in the period before and during my first research visit, this was indeed a remarkable change. One reason was that the Tharu were keen to seize the opportunity to become owners of land, even if in only relatively small amounts. Such ownership apparently brought with it a sense of independence, but also some degree of status. It did not necessarily bring greater day-to-day economic security, since such households now had to compete to some extent to get hold of land on a casual basis. However, in view of the rapidly rising monetary value of land, ownership meant that households now had an appreciating capital asset.

The other, and probably more important, reason for this shift has to do with the changes in cultivation practices which took place throughout the 1980s. The village as a whole has gone through a sort of 'green revolution'. Whereas before the predominant method of rice planting was by broadcasting the germinated seed directly

FIGURE 28   *A group of Tharu men and women transplanting rice seedlings into paddy fields. This form of cultivation is much more labour intensive but also gives much higher yields. It was beginning in 1980 and has subsequently become the standard method of rice cultivation (C. McDonaugh)*

into the fields, now everyone has switched to transplanting paddy seedlings. In addition the variety of paddy seed used has changed with nearly all of the older local varieties giving way to new seeds. In 1993 Bindeswari was the name given to the main form of rice cultivated. At the same time there has been an increasing use of fertilizer which is being used universally for paddy and also to a varying extent for other crops, and winter wheat in particular. The cost of inputs has gone up, but the yields for paddy for example have increased by between 3 and 6 times. This very considerable increase in crop yields, then, means that a farmer is able to get enough, and in most cases grow a surplus, from smaller amounts of land. Many Tharu houses now have large temporary grain storage silos (*bakhāri*) in their spacious hall areas where previously they had been relatively rare.

There are a number of changes in Tharu social and economic circumstances related to these shifts in access to and use of land. In some cases the causal links between changes to do with land and those in other areas of social life seem quite direct, but in other cases change is also related to concurrent developments affecting for example, the general political atmosphere since 1990 or the greatly increased uptake of school education or the changing nature of the communal village organizational structures.[4] There is no space here to examine all these other areas of change, but it is necessary simply to make it clear that land distribution and cultivation changes cannot ultimately be taken in isolation and cannot be seen as the only basis and background to some of the developments I shall touch on below.

The period 1980–1993 has seen an increase in the prosperity of the Tharu community. The rise in ownership of land and in the standard of living, however, has not been shared equally by all households. There has been, to a limited extent, increasing differentiation in wealth. Previously the Tharu headman's household had been significantly richer than all the others. This household has now split into 5 separate houses, producing a levelling down in landownership. A larger proportion of households, however, are wealthier than before. This is indicated by the facts that the percentage of households owning land in the 2–4 *bighā* range has increased from 17% in 1980 to 25% in 1993 and that the percentage of households owning land in the 1–2 *bighā* range has increased from 17% to 35% over this period. One other of the original households of 1980 has remained a large joint establishment and has managed to build up a land holding of slightly over 6 *bighā*, making it one of the largest Tharu landowning households in the village. Two of the three households which had settled in the village during the 1980s, however, are among the wealthiest when their landholdings in other villages are taken into account. One owns about 4 *bighā* in the village of which it rents out about 1.5 *bighā*, but it owns slightly more than one *bighā* elsewhere. The other is a satellite household, forming part of a large joint unit of some 40 people. It owns just under 4 *bighā* in the village, but it also owns some 10.5 *bighā* in neighbouring villages, of which it rents out about 2 *bighā* as *adhiyā*.

FIGURE 29   *The Tharu communal threshing ground of Sukhrwar village (1980). Each household makes its own haystack. Pahari households thresh in their own courtyards. When Tharu sharecroppers have threshed their grain, landlords (usually Pahari) come to the threshing ground to claim their share (C. McDonaugh)*

It also owns a further 1.75 *bighā* in Deukhuri. By comparison the two Pahari households with the largest amounts of land own approximately 10 and 8 *bighā* respectively. The advent of Tharu landlords is a completely new development in this village, and when I was gathering this data the wry comment was made to me that things had indeed changed now that Tharus were taking on the role of landlord alongside the Pahari.

In broad terms the social and economic division between the Tharu and the Pahari has changed. The economic divide between the Pahari and the Tharu is still apparent, but the larger number of smaller landowners among the Pahari combined with the increase in Tharu ownership means that between some households the gap is smaller and there is now some degree of overlap in the middle ranges. The division appears less clear cut. There is less of an atmosphere of opposition and antagonism. There is more and easier social interaction, especially between some of the Chetri and Tharu households. In some cases now the men of such households have begun to eat and drink beer in each other's houses. The fact that the majority of Tharu tenants have given up *mohī*, and rent lands on a casual *adhiyā* basis seems to have made for more flexible and easier landlord-tenant relations. The previous more rigid and hierarchical landlord-tenant relationships have gone. There are, however, accompanying changes in this relationship which have brought with them new but different problems. There is an element of competition between tenants to obtain land and to this end tenants have begun to engage in what some ironically referred to as a 'new *begārī*' in that in some cases in order to secure land tenants are prepared to do various small favours for their landlords such as repairing a roof or cultivating some vegetable plots for the landlord's household. In contrast to the past, however, such 'new *begārī*' is negotiable rather than structurally built in to the landlord-tenant relationship.

The attenuation of the Tharu-Pahari opposition seems to have been accompanied by a greater sense of confidence and of a positive outlook on the part of the Tharu. Inequalities in the overall distribution and control of land between the Pahari and the Tharu is still an issue, but it has lost something of its force and urgency. Tharu identity is no longer so clearly defined in opposition to the

Pahari around the question of land and at the same time there are signs that the structures of Tharu communal organization and the communal solidarity they underpinned are both becoming weaker. The political changes since 1990 have contributed significantly to the greater sense of confidence and of openness among the Tharu community. It is somewhat ironic, however, that just at the time that the Tharu have become able openly to pursue their interests in the arena of politics, the issues around land, which provided them with much of their common ground and which had been the focus for their opposition to the Pahari, have begun to lose some of their force and salience. The distribution of and access to land is still an important concern, but the Tharu agenda appears to have extended to include other matters, such as access to good educational opportunities, availability and cost of agricultural and other development resources such as fertilizers, seed, credit, and irrigation, as well as the provision of infrastructural inputs ranging from wells to local roads.

The social and economic situation in which the Tharu find themselves is one of gradually increasing diversity and complexity. It is possible that in this situation we will see the development of an ethnically based Tharu political movement, emerging from the experience of the relative success of an organization such as BASE. Certainly there are some Tharu who are keen to establish themselves as equal to the Pahari higher castes, and perhaps to achieve this without sacrificing their cultural distinctiveness. This has been one of the motives behind the very considerable increase in school attendance and in educational achievement among the Tharu in this village. Equally, however, the 1980s and early 1990s have seen a process of Nepalization, with the Nepali language, metropolitan patterns of dress, and popular media-based culture all gaining ground at the expense of Tharu traditions. On the basis of this village, however, there is little evidence at the moment that there is a developing Tharu ethnicity. The possibility for the emergence of any such political ethnic grouping will probably depend in the future on whether the Tharu find that they are being excluded from access to state resources, particularly through government offices at district level. Up to 1993, however, the Tharu community in this village have aligned themselves politically with the UML, and politics at local, district, and national levels is seen very much in terms of an opposition between the UML and Congress parties, rather than in terms of allegiance to any ethnically based party.

NOTES

I am grateful to the ESRC, the British Academy, and the Research Committee of the School of Social Sciences, Oxford Brookes University, for financial support for fieldwork in 1979–81, 1986, and 1993 respectively.

[1] For my description of BASE I have relied heavily on Odergaard's excellent account (Odergaard, forthcoming).

[2] Originally a revenue collector's title, 'Chaudhari' is now used as a surname by all the Tharu of Dang.

[3] For reference to such land loss due to Pahari sharp practice in Dang, see Misra (1984: 7); and for a good comparative example for a Tharu community in Kapilavastu District, see Gaige (1975: 75).

[4] See McDonaugh (forthcoming) for an account of changes in village communal organization.

PART FOUR

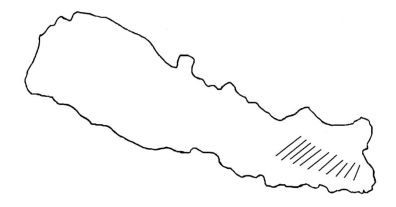

East Nepal

The eastern hills of Nepal are dominated by two
large ethnic groups, the Rai and the Limbu, though there are other
smaller groups, such as the Sunuwar and Jirel (as well as the
Sherpas, a 'Tibetanid' group dealt with in part 5). The Rai are an
agglomeration of a very large number of smaller groups. The
Yakha, described in chapter 10, are in fact somewhere in between
the Rai and Limbu.

In the eighteenth century large tracts of the eastern hills, as
in the whole of the middle hills of Nepal, were forested. There was
land to spare and, as described in chapter 9, Parbatiya immigrants
were welcomed; or at any rate, there was little active hostility to
them. When Prithvi Narayan Shah conquered this part of his new
kingdom, he confirmed large tracts of land in a particular, communally held tribal form of tenure, called *kipaṭ*. Despite this, as described in detail by Lionel Caplan (1970), Parbatiya settlers were able to
gain access to land and become locally dominant.

The process whereby these groups have adopted the dominant Parbatiya practices and ideas, almost without being aware of having done so, is described in chapter 9, which was originally written at the beginning of the 1970s. This forms an interesting contrast to the more flexible view of Yakha identity outlined in chapter 10 and the emergence of an assertive urban-based, culturally revivalist notion of Rai identity described in chapter 11.

CHAPTER NINE

Hinduization:
The Experience of
the Thulung Rai

N. J. Allen

INTRODUCTION

One approach to the question of Rai cultural identity would be to situate it along a tribe-caste continuum. One could set up polar ideal types – the isolated tribe at one end, the caste within a more or less Hindu state at the other – and discuss the multiple dimensions involved in the passage from the one condition to the other, the variety of pathways linking the end-points, the criteria for assessing passage along them, the modalities of causation, and so on (cf. Urhahn, 1987; Caplan, 1990; Gellner, 1991). But this would be to look at the matter from the outside, and my purpose here is rather to look at it from the inside, to undertake an exercise in empathy. What does it feel like to undergo Hinduization, to move along the tribe-caste continuum, to 'enter the caste system'? How does a Thulung who is caught up in the process experience it or conceive of it? Hinduization has so many different aspects than I cannot aspire to any completeness. For instance, I do not enter the debate on Hinduism as a subcontinent-wide phenomenon (cf. Stietencron, 1989), or even attempt to characterize the Nepalese variety of the religion.

ANALYTICAL VOCABULARY

In posing the question one immediately encounters a paradox. Unsatisfactory though they may be, we, the outsiders, have at our disposal the terms tribe, caste, Hindu and non-Hindu, with which to discuss the topic, but equivalent vocabulary is virtually absent from the languages of the people concerned. This needs qualification.

Firstly, I am not saying that it is impossible to express the ideas at all, but that to do so would need periphrases and explanations, and could not draw on one-word equivalents. Secondly, I am not talking of the educated élite, who would often know the English terms, but of the ordinary hill people. Thirdly, the point concerns Nepal, not India, which presents a different situation. In India, outsiders, i.e. the British administration, set aside areas specially intended for tribes, and thus deliberately kept them spatially and conceptually distinct from castes. The distinction became embodied in the legislation on 'Scheduled Tribes and Castes', and has hence entered everyday politics and become very widely known.[1]

The reality of the paradox can be illustrated by the following sentence from Fürer-Haimendorf (1966b: 17): "The Magars seem to be close to the point where a tribal group may enter Hindu society as a caste of recognised status." How could one possibly translate this statement into Nepali (let alone Thulung) in such a way as to make it intelligible to an ordinary native speaker? One problem lies in the word Hindu, which is not to be found in Turner's *Nepali Dictionary* (except as part of Hindustan and Hindustani). I did once hear it used by someone who had been in India when I asked him why most Thulung wear *ṭupī*s or scalp-locks on their closely cropped or shaven heads: it was, he said, to show that they were Hindus and not Muslims. Nevertheless the word is not part of everyday hill vocabulary. Secondly, there exists only the single word *jāt* to cover both tribe and caste. Indeed, as is well known, *jāt* covers not only these two meanings but also *varṇa*, groups smaller than the caste, and species. For instance, Chetris in the Thulung area when asked their *jāt* usually give their exogamous clan name – Basnyet, Khadka, Thapa, etc. – rather than saying they are Chetris. A Damai who had been in contact with egalitarian ideas in Darjeeling once commented to me that restrictions on Untouchables were illogical because all men can interbreed – humans are not really of different *jāt*s like cows and buffaloes.

The lexical ambiguity of *jāt* as between tribe and caste is significant for our purposes because it helps to render the transition from the one to the other virtually imperceptible, indeed meaningless, to those involved in it.[2] The point is well illustrated by the contrast between the attitudes of the Indian and Nepalese states. Whereas the Raj legislators distinguished sharply between tribe and caste, the Nepalese Muluki Ain (of which I was unaware in 1972) took an approach that is far more characteristic of Hindu thinking. They simply treated the tribes as if they were castes, and hierarchized them along with everyone else (cf. Sharma, 1977; Höfer, 1979).

THE THULUNG

In the present context, I need not elaborate on the linguistic and self-perceived distinctness of the Thulung among the other Rai peoples, nor on the wider issue of the classification of the Kiranti people in general (discussed in chapters 10 and 11 below). The Thulung live scattered across the hillsides in some eight or ten contiguous 'administrative villages', south of the Sherpas and Khaling Rai, and more or less due south of Mount Everest. I guess that there are around 8000 Thulung who have remained in their traditional homeland (there has been considerable emigration).

To conceptualize their changing experience of the Hindu world, one can divide their history into four periods. The evidence concerning the first two is obviously scanty.

1. At one time, like most Tibeto-Burman-speaking hill people, the Thulung must have been shifting cultivators in whose economy hunting played a considerable part.
2. The establishment of the first sedentary village at Mukli was followed by secondary foundation of other sedentary villages. Towards the end of this period we can probably envisage the existence of Thulung 'petty rajas'. The historicity of these figures might be doubted, but they appear not only in myths but also in traditions about the orginal four clans (Allen, 1978b: 8–9).

Moreover, villagers claimed that the 'palace' of the raja was formerly located at a site not far from the oldest part of Mukli.[3]

3. The Gorkha conquest around 1770 led to a system of indirect rule through local clan headmen (*tālukdār*s), who acted as tax-collectors.

4. The period since 1950 has seen the introduction of widespread primary education and of more or less democratic political institutions, as well as the spread of weekly markets and a great increase in the circulation of money.

Globally, the most important single trend throughout this history must have been the demographic/ecological one (cf. now Caplan, 1990; Gaenszle, 1991a: 50). The Rai believe that they were once the sole occupants not only of all the territory they now inhabit, but also of the whole hill tract stretching right up to the high mountains on the Tibetan border. We have no reason to doubt their belief, since the long-established Hindu peoples now in the area are undoubtedly immigrants from the south and west, and the Sherpas apparently only began to migrate southwards over the high passes in the sixteenth century. The Thulung have no tradition of displacing or absorbing previous populations in the area, and I suppose that in periods 1 and 2 the whole area, apart from small clearings, was covered with thick forest, the human population density being extremely low. Nowadays some 15 *jāt* (counting the Chetris as a single *jāt*) are represented on the closely terraced hillsides around Mukli, and apart from a few small and deliberately preserved coppices here and there, the forest has been pushed back to the high ridges. It was one of the sadder experiences of fieldwork to hear the blows of axes echoing round the hills on the edge of the forest in April, when every household cuts down a fair-sized tree to maintain its supply of firewood during the rains.

The definitive destruction of the jungle seems to me central to the experience of becoming a Hindu. This can be argued in several ways. Firstly, from an external point of view, I doubt if shifting agriculturalists (not to mention hunters and gatherers) ever constitute a Hindu caste in the ordinary sense, and this mode of subsistence is absolutely dependent on the availability of large tracts of jungle (cf. Nag, 1968). To destroy an area of jungle and settle down more or less permanently as an intensive farmer is not a sufficient condition for becoming a Hindu, but it is surely a necessary one.

Secondly, and more importantly for our purposes, the connection between living in the jungle and being what we should call 'non-Hindu' is often made explicit in Nepali and other Indic languages (cf. Gellner, 1986: 114–5). For instance a group living in Almora and regarded as particularly backward used to be known as either the Raji or the Banmanu (literally 'forest man'), and its language was reported in the Linguistic Survey of India as Janggali (*ban* and *jangal* here being treated as synonymous). A Brahman with whom I was discussing the demographic distribution of his caste in the Thulung area once referred disparagingly to Dewsa village (the neighbour of Mukli to the north-east) as "pure *ban*". There is not appreciably more forest there than anywhere else. What he meant

FIGURE 30   *A primary school celebrates the King's birthday: a pupil pays his respects to the royal portrait. The programme included sports, recitations, and prize-giving. The school is a significant force in promulgating a Nepalese, and by implication, a Hindu identity (N. J. Allen, 12/6/1970)*

was that no Brahmans were resident in the village, hence that the village was a backwoods, 'non-Hindu' sort of place (but he may have been exaggerating – some households in Dewsa do call in Brahmans from other villages to perform rites). In the same way I have heard some of the most actively Hinduizing Thulung (the Sadhus – of whom more later) make use of the term *jaṅgalī* in referring to the tribal customs they have abandoned. To sum up, the expression *jaṅgalī jāt* is the nearest equivalent an ordinary Nepali has at his disposal to render our term 'tribe' with all its connotations of non-Hindu and non-literate.

Another line of argument would call on myth, in which the jungle stands for the state of nature out of which mankind has emerged. Thus in the Thulung myth of creation, Miyegma, the primal mother, gives birth (after obstetric difficulties) to a whole series of beings: the list starts with two separate species of wild thorny creeper, then jumps to the tiger, the bear, the monkey, and, last of all, Mini the man, who is born naked with a bow in his hand. Eventually the tiger kills the mother, and the bear and monkey, sent to bury the corpse, eat it instead. Mini sends them away into the jungle, and takes to growing crops (text and translation in Allen 1976b, summary in 1980: 2).

This narrative is actually known to rather few of the older Thulung, and the knowledge is probably dying out. One obvious explanation is that the ceremonies at which it was recited are now seldom or never performed. But there is more to it than that. More than once I was in the company of young Thulung when an old man told a traditional myth, and when afterwards I asked the young men for the gist of the story, they were unable to give it. Nepalis enjoy telling stories, and many young people could retail versions of Puranic stories; but they seemed to reject their own myths. They would not have gone so far as to say "Now we are no longer a jungly people these stories from the forest are nothing to do with us"; but at an unconscious level some such feeling was perhaps the reason why the stories failed to catch the imagination of the younger Thulung and stick in their memory, whereas, to an anthropologist of similar age but different attitude, they seemed so vivid and memorable. In some sense then, I think the Thulung are aware of their past history as a process of alienation from the jungle.

OTHER COMMUNITIES

Apart from taking to sedentary agriculture, what are the other preconditions for qualifying as a caste? The essential one is surely contact, and reasonably sustained contact, with other castes. One cannot be a caste without being part of a caste 'system'.

Thulung contact with other castes has indeed come to be direct and frequent. The latter have immigrated into the Thulung area in considerable numbers, and many have been established there for at the very least four generations (an influx which has naturally contributed to the conversion of forest into terraced farmland). What has been the Thulung attitude to this aspect of the Hinduizing process? More precisely, what did they make of these outsiders

FIGURE 31   *Dimajit Rai beside the grave of his wife, buried the previous day (Hindus, of course, normally cremate). As here, the head of the grave usually points downhill. The technical terms (e.g. the* yachari, *which encircles the tops of the slender split-bamboo* serbungsəng) *were unknown to my younger informants (N. J. Allen, 23/1/1970)*

when they first came into contact with them, and what do they make of them all now?

I cannot say when exactly the immigration began or in what order the various *jāt*s made their appearance. The Thulung can give little information on the subject and I did not enquire from other *jāt*s. However, my impression is that the earlier immigrants were not forced on the Thulung as a result of the Gorkha conquest, but were welcomed by them – very likely before the conquest. In particular several informants agreed in stating that Brahmans were actually invited by the Thulung to settle at a place just half an hour south of Mukli; the place is still called Bahunli, although the Bahuns or Brahmans have moved to lower ground and have been replaced by Chetris at that particular place. The invitation was issued because the Brahmans knew about *din-bār*, i.e. the auspicious and inauspicious days for doing things. The Rais were illiterate, and appear to have lacked calendrical lore; at least none has survived. The Brahmans were known as specialist astrologers, and presumably enjoyed the prestige which generally attaches to literacy. I presume (this is speculation) that anyone claiming to be a raja who knew of them and could attract them, would want such people to advise him on his undertakings.

But the Brahmans can hardly have immigrated before the Untouchables, being dependent on them for services which would seem to be essential to their way of life as Brahmans. It is difficult to imagine a Brahman immigration not preceded or accompanied by an immigration of Kamis to make the iron ploughshares that Brahmans need in order to grow rice, of Damais whom they need to make their clothes, and perhaps of Sarkis to remove their dead cattle.

If the Thulung welcomed the Brahmans for the skills they had to offer, presumably they welcomed other castes including the Untouchables for the same reason. Certainly the names the Thulung gave them referred to their useful functions: the Kamis were called *sel kokpa*, literally 'iron-hammerers', the Damais *phirpa* 'sewers', the Sarkis *koksiuriu phirpa*, apparently 'leather sewers'. The Newars may well have been among the earliest immigrants; Hodgson (India Office Library mss, vol. 22, fol. 106) gives the Thulung for Newar as *ye chakpa* 'cloth dyer', and even now they have not entirely lost this function in the areas remote from bazaars. Moreover, the Thulung have no recollection of ever having made pottery for themselves, and in the ritual name for pot (its *depcinang*, cf. Allen, 1978a), *kumalip timalip*, the first syllables refer to the Kumhale, a caste of Newar potters who live some six hours south-west of Mukli at a place having good clay deposits. Some of the other immigrants too could offer skills and services such as may well have assured them a welcome. The Majhi are ferrymen (originally the rivers are said to have been crossed by using the overhanging branches of large trees growing on the banks); the Sonars are makers of gold and silver ornaments (they are thought of as a variety of Kami); the Kamer Jogi can perform Sanskritic prophylactic rituals. More doubtfully perhaps, the Gharti could have been useful as personal servants, the Magar as miners, the Gurung as suppliers of wool.

It is probably significant that, apart from some fighting with the Sherpas, the only clear record I have of opposition to the immigrants concerns the Chetris, who have no caste-linked speciality except (in principle) fighting. The story was that at the period when the Dudh Kosi was still crossed on tree branches, the Thulung used to make raids across to Jubu village and slaughter Chetri infants. Even now one may hear the *baji thari* included in a list of evils and afflictions to be warded off by some Thulung ritual; it is true that the word *baji* may be applied to Brahmans as well as Chetris, but in the context it probably applies to the latter. It is not surprising that the Chetris should have been unpopular. During Period 3 their caste relationship to the Rana rulers of the country gave them political advantages in dealing with the administration, as peasants they were very likely more industrious and efficient than the Rai, and their wearing of the sacred thread and abstention from alcohol gave them a confidence in their ritual superiority which may have been galling.

In assessing the Thulung attitude to immigrant *jāt*s, we must constantly bear in mind the ecology. In making their economic transition away from shifting agriculture plus hunting towards sedentary agriculture, the Thulung came to have less and less need of vast tracts of virgin jungle, which many of them now envisage chiefly as the home of potentially harmful wild beasts (one is told that even today a prowling tiger occasionally makes off at night with a goat). Lacking the concept of a population explosion, the Thulung simply had no reason to deny petitioners, even those without special skills to offer as inducements. In period 3, under the *kipaṭ* system of land tenure, clan land could be leased to non-Thulung subject to the permission of the *tālukdār* or clan headman. When I asked how it came about that so much land had been granted to outsiders in this way, I was told: "They came to us with gifts of *rakśī* (liquor) and said *bābā* [a term of respect], and we were simple and let them have it."[4]

To summarize the last section: A tribe only becomes a caste when it comes into close contact with other castes. This can happen either when the tribe or some of its members emigrate (one thinks of the Thakali: cf. Fürer-Haimendorf, 1966b; Manzardo and Sharma, 1975), or else – as with the Thulung – when castes immigrate into tribal territory.[5] Looked at from the outside, the immigration must have been a matter of demographic pressure, of castes moving away from the south and west, where rice-growing farmland was scarce, into Thulung territory where it was plentiful. From a Thulung point of view it seems, for the most part, to have been a matter of welcoming outsiders with some particular and useful expertise; and when outsiders had nothing particular to offer it seems to have been a matter of being good-humoured and easily won over with a few drinks and in some cases apparently a token annual gift.

In any case, it would *certainly* not have occurred to them that in admitting the outsiders they were changing their religion so as to become Hindus. To an analyst, it is obvious that immediately a tribe comes to have dealings with touchable and untouchable castes (and there has been a settlement of Damais within four minutes' walk of the reported site of the Mukli raja's palace for at the very least five generations), then the tribals must make a choice: either they associate with the Untouchables so as to become untouchable thems elves, with all that is thereby entailed for their dealings with other outsiders, or they do not. To remain neutral, to try and stand outside the system is simply impossible; any compromise would make one untouchable. Thus the immigration of even small numbers of Brahmans and Untouchables puts a tribe in a position where it cannot help acknowledging one of the fundamental beliefs of Hinduism: that some *jāt*s are purer than others, and that one's behaviour must reflect the differences. Presumably, it has never been very difficult for any group to accept the idea that they are born superior to another group, even if it has as corollary some inferiority to a third party.

I now move on to the synchronic angle, to the present-day classification of other *jāt*s, looking at the local 'caste system' first through Western eyes, then through those of a Thulung. Using the tribe-caste dichotomy, the four clean *jāt*s (Brahman, Chetri, Sanyasi, and Jogi) and the four Untouchable *jāt*s (Sonar, Kami, Sarki, and Damai) are immediately recognizable as forming a bloc of Indo-Nepalese or Hindu castes. None of them speak any language apart from Nepali, and so far as we know they never did. The remaining *jāt*s would then be distributed between, on the one hand, the more or less Hinduized tribes, viz. Rai, Limbu, Gurung, Magar, Sunuwar, and probably Majhi, and on the other the Buddhist peoples, the Tamang and the Sherpa, with the Newar probably fitting somewhat awkwardly into either the Hindu or the Hinduized group. All of these have, or like the Majhi and the local Gurung, once had, languages of their own.

The Thulung, as we have seen, do not operate the opposition 'Hindu caste versus non-Hindu tribe'. For them the fundamental divide is between the *jāt*s from whom one may accept water (or rice cooked in water), and those from whom one may not. Together with the latter prohibition goes a ban on eating in close proximity, on the passage of Untouchables into the clean castes' houses, and on sexual contact. The term Untouchable is so deeply entrenched in the literature that it is difficult to avoid, but non-sexual bodily contact is unselfconscious and not uncommon. In fact, the usual local term for Untouchables is 'the small castes' (*sāno jāt*), though their position may be more fully specified by noting that rice or water cannot be received from them (*bhāt mildaina, pāni caldaina*). Of course there are degrees of bigness and smallness within clean castes and Untouchables, but the fundamental fact remains that a Thulung can and does invite indoors any clean *jāt*, Sherpa, Brahman, Magar, even anthropologists, but *never* the Untouchables.[6]

After distinguishing the Untouchables, what other groupings would a Thulung make? Chetris and Brahmans tend to be grouped together as teetotal in contrast to the *matwālī* (alcohol-drinking) *jāt*s. Rais and Limbus share a fellow feeling as Kiranti and admit free intermarriage, but informants disagreed on whether Sunuwar were included among Kiranti, as the linguist would expect them to be. The Sanyasi, Jogi, and (curiously enough, but definitely) the Majhi, are recognized by the Thulung as their ritual superiors because they refuse from the Rai certain food which the Rai would take from them (informants never referred to the Ain). I cannot say whether Thulung would recognize Gurung, Magar, and Newar as ritually superior.

An interesting problem concerns the Buddhist peoples, i.e. (here) the Tamang and Sherpas. Just as there is no ordinary word exactly corresponding to Hindu, so there is no exact equivalent for Buddhist; the expression *bauddha dharma* for Buddhism appears in the school textbooks of the last decade, but is not common parlance. The nearest Nepali equivalent for Buddhist is 'Bhote', but the connotations of the two words are quite different. In the context of Nepal (if we ignore the Newars), Buddhism connotes geographical and cultural closeness to Tibet, monasteries, a religion looking back to a historical founder and having a distinct scriptural tradition, and a social system ignoring caste and having for many outside observers an attractively egalitarian atmosphere. 'Bhotiya/Bhote' connotes distinctly only the first of these, the relationship to Tibet and the north; it has the additional connotation, not present in the English, of disreputable habits such as eating meat which, even if it is not actually beef, is unpleasantly close to it (cf. Michaels, this volume). The Thulung have little familiarity with Sherpa monasteries, which have only been established for some fifty years (Fürer-Haimendorf, 1964a: 130; Ortner, 1989); previously the Buddhist ritual specialists of the Sherpas were not celibates resident in an institution, but merely officiants attached to shrines, such as still exist among the Tamang around Mukli. Shrines with attached officiants are familiar among many *jāt*s in the area, both among the Thulung themselves and among long-established Hindus, and there is nothing characteristically

FIGURE 32   *Announcing* (sela goak-) *the Sakhle Tosi, one in the annual series of village-based agricultural fertility rites* (tosi =Np. bhūme). *The priest* (dewa dhāmī) *dances to the drumming. His fringe and satchel are decorated with porcupine quills. The gourd periodically ejects spurts of local beer* (unconscious phallic symbolism?) (N. J. Allen, 18/6/1970)

match on that basis, but increasingly to perform other minor or major *pūjā*s or rites to obtain supernatural favours. Only quite recently, I think, have they been called on by certain individuals (probably ones of higher standing, but I did not study this) to replace tribal priests in the performance of a certain style of wedding (cf. Allen, 1987). I made several enquiries as to when such employment of Brahmans had begun – in the informant's generation, in that of his father, or how many generations ago – and found it very hard to get definite answers. People had simply forgotten, or never known. This aspect of the Hinduization process, like so many others, had been a matter less of memorable initiatives than of almost imperceptible absorption over the generations.

But how would the superior ritual purity of a Brahman have presented itself to a Thulung when he first met it? It must, I suppose, have appeared simply as a fact of life. Not only was it the logical counterpart of the existence of Untouchables, and admitted by everyone else who had dealings with Brahmans, but the actual behaviour of the Brahman must have seemed to constitute proof of his claim to purity. If you invited him to your house and offered him your finest hospitality, pork and alcohol, he would refuse it as being impure. Thulung has no native word for purity, and to challenge the Brahman's claim a Thulung would have had to undertake a foreign-language exercise in semantic anthropology. As we saw with regard to Untouchables, if as a tribal you have dealings with Hindu castes, it is not an option to *decide* whether to adopt the values of the caste system. They are embodied in the discourse and behaviour inseparable from the interaction.

In the context of Hindu ritualists I need at least to mention the Sadhus. The Sadhus of Mukli and Kangel are not mendicants, as the term tends to imply in India; they are respectable Thulung householders, male or female. After they have had families, individuals who are attracted to the idea may join a particular religious order (whose headquarters are near Kalimpong), and by means of initiation and other ritual practices, and by abstaining from meat, alcohol, and interdining with non-Sadhus, strive towards a state of purity, conceptualized in the Hindu sense. They consider themselves purer than Brahmans, whose rice they would refuse. Like Brahmans,

FIGURE 33   *Hinduization in action. A Brahman blows a conch during what he referred to as a Rudri Puja (a Thulung informant called it a Satya Narayan Puja). The flower-covered structure on the Brahman's left represents Shiva, that on his right, Vishnu. My landlord, a fairly conservative Thulung who paid for this small-scale ritual to be held on his veranda, rang a bell during the conch-blowing (N. J. Allen, 15/11/1970)*

they may be invited by other Thulung to their houses to perform *pūjā*s in Sanskrit or Nepali for the benefit of the household. There have been one or two Sadhus in the area for at least half a century, but their numbers have been growing rapidly during Period 4, and I estimate that in Mukli they are now a much stronger Sanskritizing influence than the Brahmans are.

Many Thulung are puzzled as to the relative spiritual authority of Brahman and Sadhu. On being asked what priests one ought to call on, they usually replied with some tolerant phrase like *āphnu man anusār*, i.e. (to paraphrase) "a person has to decide according to his own inner feelings". A certain number of Thulung, without formally becoming Sadhus, have imitated them in such matters as the wearing of sandalwood *ṭīkā*s on ordinary days and the giving up of meat, but one does not hear any suggestion that all

Thulung ought to do likewise. The behaviour appears to express sincere individual leanings towards religious purity.

CULTURE

The Sadhus have been associated with a very tentative and unsuccessful Thulung effort towards political unity, in that the eldest son of the leading local Sadhu became an important politician in the area. The significance of this must not be exaggerated. Some Sadhus I spoke to remarked on the 'darkness' and jungly quality of Rai life, but they did not regard it as their responsibility to change the situation; nor did they look forward to the day when their own numbers would be very much greater than they are now, or when, relative to other castes, the Rai as a whole would hold a higher position in the eyes of the twice-born. Over the centuries the Thulung have absorbed a vast amount from Hindu culture, but they very seldom conceive of this as a matter that has involved or will involve deliberate collective action, let alone competitive action relative to other castes. I only once heard of the possibility of forming a caste *sabhā* or assembly to improve the customs of the caste, and this was certainly a very recent notion. The only subject that the informant could suggest that the council might discuss was the desirability of Thulung women continuing to wear their old-fashioned three-inch diameter gold earrings. Much of the literature on Hinduization or Sanskritization (and the two processes differ essentially only in whether the group concerned is envisaged as starting off as a tribe or as a caste) supposes that the innovations are motivated by an attempt to raise ritual status relative to other comparable groups. But for the Thulung one can usually suggest other motivations that are at least as important, or more so.

If the Thulung conceive of their tribal past in terms of the jungle, can anything be said of their general conception of the world of caste and Hinduism, which must represent their future? The better educated sometimes use the Sanskrit loan-word *sabhyatā*, for which the dictionaries give translations such as "civilization" (Meerendonk), "politeness, good manners" (Turner), "discipline, gentleness, good behaviour, well-being, generosity, aristocracy" (Sharma – I translate). The ordinary peasant usually says of a custom borrowed from Hindu culture either that it is *ājkal ko calan* "the fashion nowadays", or that it is a *rāmro calan, rāmro* being an everyday commendatory word, connoting "good, nice, decent, beautiful". The maker of such judgments naturally has no reason to discriminate between technological, ritual, and other innovations. When the Thulung took to ploughing and gave up hoeing each field by hand, or when they took to replacing their one-storey wooden shacks by two-storey or multi-storey stone houses, their motives need no gloss; we can see as well as they did that the innovations represent improvements. When they took to inviting Damais to play music at weddings during the Removal of the Bride, they probably said it was *rāmro ko lāgi* "to make a decent ceremony" of it, and it does just that. The whole system of greetings to different categories of relatives is in its present form a borrowing; one has no reason to doubt that this formal etiquette of gradations of bowing was more 'polite', more 'cultured' than whatever preceded it.

Another borrowing is the post-harvest Dasain-Tihar complex, the major holiday period in the whole annual calendar of the Thulung (and I suspect of all Rai). But if, as we have claimed, every *jāt* is supposed to have its own customs, which are right for it, why should the Thulung have taken over this whole elaborate alien complex? In this area perhaps, one might hope at last to find evidence that the Thulung, feeling themselves excluded from Hindu society, took over Hindu customs in order to make themselves more socially acceptable. Such an explanation would be unnecessary. As Thulung culture has become more and more intensively agricultural, the monsoon period has become an extremely busy one, in which people are too hard-worked to enjoy themselves. Dasain and Tihar are tremendous fun. The weather's good, there's plenty to eat – what better time to paint the house, buy new clothes, make garlands of flowers, put up swings, call on relatives, cook special delicacies, drink, gamble, and thank the gods? Who would not borrow such an enjoyable complex? There can be little question here of prestige-seeking by imitation of the higher castes, for the complex is no less the heritage of the Untouchables than it is of the Brahmans or Chetris.[7]

CONCLUSION

An interesting paper by Höfer (1986) poses in programmatic fashion four questions about the Tamang that he studied. What in their religion is of Hindu origin, and how are Hindu and non-Hindu elements related? Through what channels were Hindu influences received, and why were they accepted? Höfer's approach is very different from that taken here, which underlines the richness of the theme. His notion of Hinduization is more rigorously focused on religion than mine, and the first three questions, though discussed in some of my other papers (e.g. ritual specialists in 1976b, weddings in 1987), have not been central here. His fourth question is the most directly relevant, but while I would not deny that the acceptance of Hindu elements is related to "identity management" (*ibid*.: 16), the thrust of my argument has been elsewhere. It seems to me that the Thulung have been experiencing and reacting to a massive historical process in a manner so fragmented and piecemeal that its systematic nature has not been apparent to them and can hardly be forced into a single formula by the analyst. Nevertheless, if we hope to understand the politics of culture in Nepal, there is no escaping the task of analysing the integration of the 'ex-tribals' within a Hindu state.

NOTES

This is a revised version of a seminar paper given in the School of Oriental and African Studies in May 1972, a year after my return from fieldwork. Although I have retained the ethnographic present from the original, the Thulung in question are those of *one generation ago*. Virtually all my informants were male.

[1] Before the British Raj, the generalized distinction was probably as difficult to make for an Indian as it is nowadays for an ordinary hill peasant in Nepal. Sanskrit has available terms such as *mleccha* ('foreigner', 'barbarian') and *kirāta* or *niṣāda* (which seem to connote greater ethnic specificity), but there is no term which quite coincides with 'tribal'. No doubt the same was true of other Indian languages until administrative needs led to the coining of the quasi-Sanskrit *ādivāsī* ('primal inhabitant, aborigine').

2 Cf. E. Gellner (1962) on the social function and historical importance of the ambiguities and incoherences in collective representations in all societies.

3 Probably the same period saw the flourishing of the regional *bhume* cult extending beyond the Thulung into Khaling terrritory (Allen, 1981: 169–74). Cf. Holmberg (1989: 132n.) for a comparable phenomenon.

4 Incidentally, on the basis of the types of argument mentioned in Allen (1987: 26), *raksī* seems to be something the Thulung only learned of from outsiders: previously liquor would have been fermented but not distilled.

5 Naturally the Thulung too have encountered Hindu influences when they move outside their home territory, e.g. when serving in the Gurkhas or when seeking work. However, I suppose the most significant contacts have been within the locality.

6 One sometimes finds in the literature suggestions that Untouchables are ex-tribals, or similar to tribals. Whatever may be their ultimate origins centuries or millennia ago, they nowadays clearly belong within the Hindu world, for instance as regards their language and rituals. Their rituals are of course not performed by Brahmans, but by men of their own caste who can read the Nepali books in which they are detailed.

7 I have left this paragraph essentially as it stood in 1972, even though it surely oversimplifies by omitting any reference to the state as having encouraged, perhaps even imposed, the festival. Cf. Pfaff-Czarnecka (1989: 155; 1993a; and chapter 13 below), and more generally, Toffin (1993: chapter 4).

CHAPTER TEN

Identity Management and Cultural Change: The Yakha of East Nepal

Andrew Russell

INTRODUCTION

In 1976 Allen wrote with regard to Nepal that "in thinking about the hill peoples the attitude one tribe/one culture is a positive hindrance" (1976a: 501), a point reiterated elsewhere (Allen, 1981: 168) and taken up by other writers (e.g. Fisher, 1978: 50; Holmberg, 1989: 12–3). What Allen intended by his comment was to alert us to the danger of overlooking the possibility that features could be shared by different groups, or of ignoring questions of the "Y-a-t-il un civilisation Himalayenne?" ['is there a Himalayan civilisation?'] variety (Macdonald, 1981: 38). Allen, Macdonald, and others are interested in cultural forms which predate the arrival of Hindu culture to the middle hills of Nepal. Yet if we are looking for evidence of cultural homogenization, it is models of Hinduization or Sanskritization (Srinivas, 1962), which see tribal groups losing their traditional values and beliefs in the wake of overbearing Hindu influence, that offer more potent explanations for relatively recent convergences in Himalayan civilization. However, studies of the interactions of tribal and Hindu groups (e.g. Caplan, 1970; Jones, 1976; Manzardo, 1982; Messerschmidt, 1982a; Allen, 1987 and this volume) have shown this process to be more complex and less unidirectional than the 'Sanskritization' model might imply.

A reverse danger of the 'one tribe/one culture' approach is that it can contribute to the representation of a particular ethnic group as an overly unified, coherent whole, to the "exaggeration of differences" which Boon suggests is a mark not only of ethnographic writing but

325

and northern Dhankuta districts, although in none of the panchayats in the region do they constitute the largest group. Analysis of
the 1981 census and investigations during our fieldwork, however,
revealed ward 5 of Tamaphok panchayat to have a population over
95% Yakha (n = 415), the rest of the population in this ward being
made up of untouchable Kami and Damai families. Pockets of
Yakha are located elsewhere in Tamaphok panchayat. While there
is some evidence of clustering of households, the dispersed
settlement patterns and mobility characteristic of much of the
eastern hills means that Berreman's model of geographical isolation
is unlikely to have been a major factor in explaining the differences
within the group labelled 'Yakha', or between it and other groups,
at least at the micro-level.

I hope to demonstrate that the Yakha are not pawns in
the externally-derived manufacture of a single ethnicity but rather
can be seen as active participants in the negotiation, manipulation,
and indeed subversion or 'Yakhafication' of multiple ethnic realities,
both in their activities within the group and in their dealings with
the world around. Like the Mewahang Rai (Gaenszle, this volume),
it is possible for an individual (or indeed the group) to assume
multiple identities depending on context. I shall look at this both
historically (by re-examining the concept of Hinduization) and as a
contemporary process (by looking at the enactment of Hindu rituals
and Yakha participation in the current political environment).

THE MANAGEMENT OF YAKHA IDENTITY

The Yakha are in many ways an anomaly for the broad-based
ethnographic 'maps' of Nepal presented by some authors (e.g.
Hagen, 1961: 61; Dobremez, 1976: 108; Gaborieau, 1978: 302),
since not only are they numerically too small to be represented on
such maps, but also there are internally and externally felt
ambiguities concerning their ethnic identity (i.e. what it means to
be Yakha). On the one hand, the Yakha sometimes present
themselves (and are assumed to be) one of the Rai tribes. On the

other, they see themselves as culturally and linguistically closer to the Limbu than the Rai, but distinct from both larger groups.

Various reasons, demographic and economic, can be postulated for this rather peculiar state of affairs. The Yakha present a demographic and spatial picture far more akin to other Rai groups than to the more populous Limbu, who numbered 129,234 in the 1981 census (His Majesty's Government, 1984) and are widely distributed across the districts of the Mechi Zone as well as various places in Sankhuwasabha, Terhathum, and Dhankuta districts. The Limbu are a relatively unified group, possessing only four distinct dialects (Weidert and Subba, 1985; van Driem, 1987). The Rai, by contrast, form a disparate collection of small tribal groups with marked social, cultural, and linguistic variation (McDougal, 1979). In wishing to maintain their cultural distinctiveness the Yakha cannot afford to be lumped, in the eyes of outsiders, amongst the numerically dominant Limbu.

We can also speculate on the advantages to Yakha men of presenting themselves as Rai in dealings with Gurkha recruitment officers.[1] Gurkha officers in their turn seem to have been happy to accept the Yakha as Rai. Morris (1933: 85), for example, writes that "the Eastern tribes are known collectively as Kiranti. Included in this group are the Limbus, or Yakthumbas, and the Rais, known also as Khambus or Yakkas... There appears now to be no difference between Khambus and Yakkas; and whatever their former status may have been the latter now definitely form part of the Rai tribe." To be singled out as Yakha was not necessarily useful. According to Northey and Morris, "though the characters of Rais do not differ much where their *thars* [clans] are concerned; the Yakkas and men of the Lohoron thar are generally considered less tractable than the rest" (1927: 239). On the other hand, it is possible that the Limbu, although respected for their supposed martial characteristics, may have had a reputation at the national level for recalcitrance following the 'Limbu uprising' of 1950–1 (when Limbus in certain parts of east Nepal rose up against Brahman domination).[2]

This split allegiance between Rai and Limbu may be indicative of a more general tendency of the Yakha to select strategically from a range of ethnic labels in different social settings. At one end of the scale are terms such as 'Nepali' or 'Kiranti'. 'Kiranti' is a term encompassing the neighbouring Limbu and Rai groups. 'Kirata' are mentioned in the *Mahabharata*, and there is no reason to doubt the long-term existence of a group or groups identifying with this name from the earliest times.[3] The term 'Nepali', by contrast, is of relatively recent origin (Burghart, 1984) and we heard it used on several occasions by Yakha schoolchildren wishing to indicate some sort of identification with the nation-state. 'Kiranti' similarly expresses a relationship to the nation-state, but in this case a degree of opposition to it. We only heard this used by Rai intellectuals living in Kathmandu.

The title 'Yakha' holds little weight in national terms, and is generally only to be heard in the local inter-ethnic social environment. Even then, when asked "what is your *jāt?*" [caste/type], terms like *jimi* or *dewān* are more likely to be used in reply. The term *jimi*, derived from *jimindār* ['landowner'] after the *kipaṭ* landrights traditionally held by the Kiranti, is shared with other Rai groups (Bista, 1967: 32; McDougal, 1979: 28; Dahal, 1985; Hardman, 1989). It is the label often used by Yakha children attending Sri Chamunde Secondary School in the village. The term *dewān* is, by contrast, more distinctively Yakha (Bista, 1967: 32) but is in something of a decline. We only heard it used by older Yakha men during our time in Tamaphok. The word *dewān* derives from Persian, via Hindi, and means 'magistrate' (Turner, 1931: 318). It is said to have been granted to the Yakha by the Gorkha kings (like the word Rai). Both *jimi* and *dewān* thus indicate a historical status nationally which the term Yakha itself lacks.

Identity, though, is also expressed in the household environment, and here clan names such as Linkha, Challa, and Koyonga are more appropriate. These are the smallest units which Yakha generally recognize, although below this certain clans can be divided into subclans such as the Pãc Bhāi ('five brothers') or Iknap Linkha. These subdivisions, like the clans themselves, are important in defining potential marriage partners as well as one's funeral and other ritual obligations. As Hardman observes for the Lohorung Rai (1989), there is a tendency for Yakha clans to be associated with particular locations and for these locations to be associated with linguistic distinctiveness. There is no recognized hierarchical ranking of clans (as is arguably the case with other ethnic groups in Nepal: cf. Macfarlane, pp. 185, 193 above), but there is pride in one's clan and the myths and legends specific to it.

At the individual level, personal first names, 'flower names' (more affectionate names given by parents to their children and used in preference to their more formal first name), nicknames, and kinship terms all help to distinguish people within the local environment. Finally come the *sammetling* or spiritual clan names, an identity relevant for dealings with the spirit world.

These different identity labels, some internally generated, some externally derived, provide a socio-cultural repertoire easing their bearers' passage through a variety of worlds including home, the village, the nation-state, the world beyond, and the spirit world. As these spatial and social transitions occur, similarities and differences both with other groups and within the group itself are expressed and negotiated. Certainly it is hard to identify a distinctive 'culture' to go with the Yakha 'tribe'. There is, as suggested above, both variation within the group labelled Yakha and similarities between the Yakha and other groups.

There are also different levels of cultural focusing which take place. Intra-group variation at one level (e.g. when comparing a Yakha Gurkha soldier who has retired to the Tarai with a *dhāmī* [traditional healer] in the village) can be seen as intra-group sharing at another (e.g. when the *dhāmī* in question is summoned to the Tarai to perform a healing ritual for the Gurkha soldier). Similarly, as I shall go on to demonstrate, inter-group similarities (such as the observance of the Hindu festival of Dasain) can also be seen as inter-group difference (such as in the particulars of the rituals performed).

YAKHA CULTURE: IN SEARCH OF A CORE

When one asks what the 'core' of Yakha culture might be the answer most Yakha give refers to their language and traditional religion. However, neither of these are the unambiguous markers of identity they might at first appear. Tamaphok Yakha speak a language known colloquially as Das Majhiya, (named after the ten *majhiyā*, or headmen, who were once supposed to have ruled the area). Yet in Marek Katahare panchayat, in neighbouring Dhankuta district, there is a population claiming to be Yakha but speaking a totally different language, which Tamaphok Yakha speakers called 'Chathare'. Tamaphok Yakha seem uncertain as to the cultural status of these Chathare speakers, whom they generally called 'Mareki' (after their panchayat name). One informant, a student from Marek, claimed to be Yakha (although he called himself 'Subba', an autonym used by many Limbu), and furthermore believed he spoke the true Yakha language, the Das Majhiya language of Tamaphok being a dialectal variant, a viewpoint with which the Yakha of Tamaphok overwhelmingly disagree.

The ambiguities of language as a marker of Yakha identity do not derive solely from the fact that there are people claiming to be Yakha who speak Tibeto-Burman languages incomprehensible to the Yakha of Tamaphok. In Tamaphok, it is true, the use of Yakha is sometimes a public face or expression of Yakha identity. However, in neighbouring panchayats it is also common to find people claiming a Yakha identity who do not speak their own language. For example in Madi Mulkharka, a panchayat across the valley from Tamaphok where clusters of Yakha are to be found, older Yakha tend to speak their own language. However, it is unusual to find Yakha children there speaking anything apart from Nepali. Even in Tamaphok, supposedly a heartland of Yakha culture and identity, everyone speaks Nepali with some degree of fluency, and, as might be expected, Nepali is making great inroads into the Yakha language, particularly in certain subject areas.[4]

The situation is not seen by the Yakha themselves as the slow suffocation of their language by Nepali, however. There remain significant differences in the pronunciation and use of words between 'standard' Nepali and 'Yakha' Nepali.[5] More importantly, in Yakha eyes, even when using Nepali vocabulary it is always in the context of 'speaking Yakha'. Although people are generally well able to distinguish Nepali loanwords from 'pure' Yakha words, as long as the words in question appear in the context of Yakha speech, they are generally seen as part of Yakha and not some Nepali intrusion.

Because of this, the Yakha do not have much sense of their language as 'dying'. Their ethnolinguistics takes a very pragmatic view of language as a medium of communication which, if it no longer performs this function, is perhaps better dispensed with. Thus people are not unduly perturbed about the changes occurring in the Yakha language, nor the uncertain future it faces. They also do not consider that there might be certain concepts and ideas that it is possible to express only in Yakha, and are confident that a direct translation of every individual sentence or phrase is possible from Yakha into Nepali. Similarly the idea that the phonemes of Yakha might be different and could not be adequately recorded in Devanagari script seems incredible to most Yakha.[6]

Thus the relationship between Yakha and Nepali is more complex than might at first appear. On the one hand, Nepali can be seen as dramatically increasing its influence over the Yakha language. On the other, Yakha is incorporating Nepali into its structures and forms. This occurs at different rates in different places. Even in communities closely linked through ties of kinship and marriage, there is variety in the inflections of Yakha and the loanwords used. This variation contributes to the intra-group differences associated with locale, which can be partly attributed to Berreman's 'cultural drift' hypothesis mentioned in the introduction.

The willingness to accommodate change and not see it as a jarring intrusion reflects what might be considered a central aspect of Yakha culture. The 'core' can change but, with a finesse which is itself part of the culture, the 'core' is consequently maintained in the face of outside influences. The various elements constituting this 'core' provide the sources for the contrasting, conforming, and contested nature of Yakha identity.

A similar state of affairs pertains to Yakha traditional religion. The word representing the oral tradition on which Yakha indigenous religious practice is based is *muntum*. "If they themselves were asked what it was that made them a distinct social group, the more traditional among them would probably reply that it was possession of their own *Diumla"*, wrote Allen (1978a: 237) of the equivalent word in Thulung Rai. Comparison of the literature on other Kiranti groups suggests that this is a shared concept.[7] According to Gaenszle, "the concept semantically implies a certain unity, both in a spatial as well as in a temporal sense. On the one hand, it emphasises the common root of the oral traditions of the various Kiranti groups in East Nepal, and on the other hand, it depicts the tradition as a divine knowledge which has been handed down in a basically unchanged way by a long line of ancestors since times immemorial" (1993: 117). Thus Yakha traditional religion is only partly "a set of ritual practices which are totally idiosyncratic and represent a guarded series of rituals" as Manzardo writes of the Thakali (1982: 52). Participation in certain rituals, it is true, is restricted to the Yakha in general or to members of particular clans or households. On the other hand, many of the rituals contain elements common to other groups.

In Gaenszle's view, the incorporation of the traditions of one Kiranti group into those of another is the result of "a process of identification based on the assumption of an essential identity" (*op.cit*: 117). This can be seen in the Yakha case with the easy identification of Hindu gods with certain of the panoply of Yakha spirits. The Yakha O'aa'mi, for example, is also called Basudev, father of the god Krishna. The Yakha *muntum*, like the Yakha language, appears extraordinarily open to change and the incorporation of outside elements (just like the Mewahang Rai *muddum*: Gaenszle, *op.cit*.). This leads to a marked degree of cultural variation within the Yakha *muntum*, both within a single account and between practitioners. Within a single account, the variety is reflected in the languages used to relate it, a complex mixture of Yakha, Limbu, Rai, Nepali, and *'dhāmī* language' (presumably similar to the 'ritual language' of the Thulung Rai described by Allen, 1978a).

For Gaenszle, there is a danger of other written traditions "twisting the meaning of indigenous institutions in a way unnoticed by the people, thus slowly alienating them from their past" (1993: 123). This is, as he himself observes, an 'etic' model, not fully shared by the people studied. We found that, although people equate elements of the Hindu and indigenous traditions, they are not necessarily unaware of essential differences between them. This is the case between Kiranti traditions as much as between Kiranti and Indo-Nepalese. In the eyes of most Yakha religious practitioners, for example, the Yakha and Limbu versions of the *muntum* are essentially the same, and different from those of the Rai. Even then certain spirits in the Yakha panoply, such as *Dungdungi*, are said to be 'Limbu'.

Thus those elements we might try to identify as a Yakha cultural 'core' are in principle fluid, malleable, and open to outside influences. I should emphasise when I say this that I am talking at the level of the group and not at the level of the individual. While Yakha women may marry into Limbu households and their children are born Limbu, it would be very difficult indeed to find other examples of a Yakha joining another ethnic group within his or her lifetime.[8] It seems that the basis for Yakha culture (if indeed such a homogeneous entity can be said to exist) has always been an openness to outside influences. This should not be seen in negative terms so much as a reflection of Yakha abilities to manipulate, negotiate, and subvert the cultural heritage to make new, renewed, and contested 'Yakha' forms. The next section looks at how this manipulation and subversion can be seen through the idiom of 'Hinduization'.

HINDUIZATION RECONSIDERED

The ethnic diversity of the eastern hills today derives in part from the Gorkha king Prithvi Narayan Shah's 'conquest' of east Nepal, which began in 1773. In the ensuing years, the Shah kings and later the Ranas encouraged the settlement of land by non-Kiranti wherever possible. This settlement occurred through a number of channels: the government made arrangements for the reclamation of wasteland by non-Kiranti settlers (Regmi, 1978a: 537) but, more frequently, the Kiranti seem to have made land grants themselves. Settlement of the east by non-Kiranti was advantageous to the government not only because of the increased revenue such settlement promised but, more importantly, because of the government's need to establish hegemony over the eastern area. For the Kiranti, settlers provided both labour and a following for the landlords, as well as a monetary pittance for the transaction (Caplan, 1970).

These non-Kiranti settlers, although by no means a homogeneous group, brought the Nepali language and Hindu culture with them to the middle hills of east Nepal. Amongst the 'caste Hindus' were Brahmans and Chetris, and the 'untouchables' such as the Kami (blacksmiths), Damai (tailors), and Sarki (cobblers). There were also Newars, not all of whom were Hindu or spoke Nepali as their mother tongue. Tribal groups such as the Gurung, Magar, and Tamang (the latter mainly Buddhist) also migrated eastwards before and after the conquest.[9] While a degree of spatial distinctiveness and hence 'cultural isolation' has persisted (Berreman, 1960), such a model cannot explain the adoption of Nepali language, Hindu religion, and new agricultural techniques (amongst other things) by the Yakha. It would be difficult to underestimate the importance of these changes to the lives of the Yakha today, although their significance as regards Yakha identity could easily be overestimated or, at least, misunderstood. Perhaps, as Barth (1969) suggests, more contact in such situations has meant more differentiation, culturally speaking, from others.

One major change associated with the influx was the change from shifting agriculture to intensified production in which rice cultivation plays a central part (as Sagant (1976) describes for the Limbu). Hodgson, one of the few nineteenth-century European men of letters to describe the landscape of the eastern hills, wrote:

> The general style of cultivation is that appropriate to the uplands, not the more skilful and profitable sort practised in the level tracts; and though the villages of the Kirántis be fixed, yet their cultivation is not so, each proprietor within his own ample limits shifting his cultivation perpetually, according as any one spot gets exhausted. (Hodgson, 1858: 400)

He added that the plough was rarely used, and the main crops to be seen by a traveller were maize, buckwheat, millet, legumes, dry rice, and cotton. From the stories we heard, it would appear that the diet of the people at that time was supplemented by hunting and gathering in forests rich in game, plants, and honey. Today, however, shifting cultivation has been abandoned for as long as anyone can remember. As Sagant (*op. cit.*) observes for the Limbu, rice cultivation has transformed the agricultural landscape, with variations in agricultural techniques being largely the result of altitude rather than culture (cf. Schroeder, 1985).

The changes associated with Hinduization are more complex and less one-sided than those of agricultural transformation, and are in many ways similar to those of the Thulung Rai (Allen, 1987 and this volume). The Yakha ostensibly demonstrate many of the trappings of Hinduism such as the caste system and the observance of certain festivals. In this selective absorption, the elements in question are now as much part of Yakha identity as the 'core cultural' elements of language and religion discussed above. The cultural trappings of Hinduism are similarly fluid and malleable, open to negotiation as to their meaning and manipulation as to their effect. Far from a one-way process of acculturation, there is a 'Yakhafication' of Hinduism (at least in the eyes of the Yakha themselves) as well as a 'Hinduization' of the Yakha.

The caste system undoubtedly adds a potent, perhaps more hierarchical dimension to Yakha identity. The Muluki Ain (Legal Code) promulgated in 1854 outlined commensal and marriage rules which were to apply across Nepal. The Muluki Ain can be seen as an attempt to codify the place of people speaking Tibeto-Burman languages in Nepalese society, and to integrate the people as a whole under the banner of a Hindu nation with a caste ideology. Because of their size the Yakha, unsurprisingly, do not appear in the work, but would have been classed with the Limbu Kiranti amongst the 'enslavable alcohol drinkers', in an intermediate position below the Gurung and Magar ('non-enslavable alcohol drinkers') but above the *pāni nacalne* ('water unacceptable') and untouchable castes (Höfer, 1979: 141).

Despite their relatively lowly position within it, the Yakha appear largely to have accepted their position in the caste system and to have adopted its norms in their dealings with members of other groups. In Tamaphok, one finds ample evidence of caste rules dictating not just what one can eat or drink, but from whom one can take food, to whom one can give it and expect it to be accepted, and into whose house one can enter. According to the rules, Yakha should not accept water from the Kami ('blacksmith'), Damai ('tailor'), or other *pāni nacalne* castes. Nor are Brahmans and Chetris supposed to accept cooked food from a Yakha (although they can accept water, we were often emphatically told).

Much has been made of the contrast between the caste hierarchy of the Indo-Nepalese and the egalitarianism of Tibeto-Burman groups such as the Tamang (Holmberg, 1989), the Sherpa (Fürer-Haimendorf, 1975), and the Gurung (Doherty, 1975). While the Yakha show no evidence of internal clan hierarchies, in their dealings with other groups they appear to have adopted the principles of the caste system wholeheartedly. Caste-like attitudes are associated with relations not only with Brahmans and Untouchables, but also with Tibeto-Burman groups closer to the Yakha in the hierarchy of the Muluki Ain. For example, one informant told us how the Rai groups were once regarded by the Yakha as lowly and not to be married with. However, there are now many examples of Yakha men who have brought Rai women into the community as marriage partners. The Gurungs are supposed to be higher than the Yakha: they are not supposed to eat pigs or buffalo (although some Gurung living in Tamaphok panchayat keep pigs which they sell to the Yakha), and until quite recently, it was said, they would not have eaten at all in a Yakha household (although again they would have taken water from the Yakha). Only the Limbu, the mythical brothers of the Yakha, appear not to have been classified by the latter in caste terms.

Thus caste, while important, is not a hard and fast set of rules, but something which is in a state of constant negotiation and debate. While some visiting Brahmans asked for (and were given) utensils, firewood, and uncooked rice and dal to prepare their own, unpolluted meal, on the other hand Brahman, Chetri, and Gurung guests frequently visited our Yakha family's house and were enticed into the kitchen to break caste norms by eating and drinking Yakha food. Even in Yakha-Untouchable relations we saw plenty of evidence of *de facto* rule violations through *de jure* rules being overlooked or even deliberately transgressed. *Mīt/mitinī* (Y:*nibak/nimak*), formal relations of ritual brotherhood/sisterhood as have been described for other groups by Okada (1957), Prindle (1975), and Messerschmidt (1982b), amongst others, are another way in which caste rules are somewhat subverted, even across the 'untouchability' barrier.

What is interesting is that, despite their small numbers and (it might be argued) consequent vulnerability to change from the outside world, the Yakha of Tamaphok seem to have been less influenced by certain aspects of Hinduism than their supposedly more powerful and independent 'brothers' the Limbu (about whose Sanskritization, Jones (1976) and Caplan (1970) provide differing accounts). Yakha in Tamaphok, for example, never consult Brahman astrologers for a horoscope (or name) for their child, and never bother with a rice-eating ceremony when the child reaches six months of age (cf. Jones, *op.cit*: 70). Those life-cycle rituals which are performed, such as weddings and funerals, are predominantly 'non-Hindu' affairs. There are elements of Hinduization at weddings, such as the involvement of low-caste Damai as tailors and musicians, and at least in the lip-service which is generally paid to the concept of 'arranged marriage' (cf. Jones, *op.cit*.; Allen, 1987). In other respects, such as their adoption of the caste system and some Hindu festivals (to be described), the Yakha are at least superficially 'Hindu'. However, the Hindu order is being manipulated and subverted even in these avowedly 'Hindu' domains.

Just as with language and traditional religion, while there is a tendency to incorporate new cultural elements into the Yakha's own, the absorption of Hindu practices and values has been selective and does not necessarily mean old forms have been completely done away with. There are limits to the borrowing which has occurred, and it could be argued that elements that 'fit' the pre-existing and shifting matrices of Yakha culture are more likely to have succeeded. It is surely significant that, of the range of possible

Hindu festivals (cāḍ) during the year, the Yakha in Tamaphok observe five: Dasain, Tihar, Saun Sankranti, Magh Sankranti, and Chait Dasain. Festivals such as Nag Panchami, Tij, and Saraswati Puja are largely ignored. "We don't bother with Saraswati because we don't have a tradition of learning" was the general Yakha line. Thus while the Brahman teachers at the Sri Chamunde Secondary School, Tamaphok, assembled by the small, idol-less temple beyond the school playing field for this pūjā, Yakha (even Yakha teachers) were conspicuous by their absence. I thought it symbolic that in the porch of the village headman's house, there was a picture of Saraswati in a frame which had been almost entirely covered over by a black-and-white photo of his daughter when young. We did not see pictures of Saraswati in any other Yakha houses. Ganesh, whose worship might offend the household god, is another Hindu god conspicuous by his absence from Yakha porches. When we asked about him, we were told he was a 'Chetri god'. In the case of the Dasain festival to be described below, it is surely noteworthy that Durga, the killer of demons, forms such a prominent focus of ritual activity.

'Cultural drift' (Berreman, 1960) could again be invoked to explain some, but not all, of the differences between Yakha and non-Yakha practices. The culture and traditions of the incoming caste Hindus is unlikely to have remained static any more than the culture and traditions of the Yakha. Allen, writing about the Hinduization of marriage rituals amongst the Thulung Rai, suggests that, "if there is one thing we can be sure of in the absence of historical records, it is that the Khās [sic] (as they are sometimes still called), when they first immigrated into the Thulung area, brought with them a culture very different from the Hinduism of their descendants, the Chetris of today" (1987: 33). Thus in some cases it is quite possible that the incomers' own tradition has changed while the borrowed Hindu traditions of the Yakha have stayed the same. However, an equally plausible reason for the divergence is that, where cultural borrowing has taken place, in the process of transition the cultural elements have been changed subtly, either knowingly or unconsciously, by the Yakha themselves as they have became part of the loosely bounded field we could label

Yakha culture. Whatever the reason, the performance of even ostensibly Hinduized rituals, such as the festivals of Dasain and Tihar, can be viewed as part of the Yakha expression of distinctiveness as much as commonality. I shall go on to demonstrate this by looking specifically at the Yakha observance of Dasain, which should be compared with the more 'mainstream' observance of the festival described by Pfaff-Czarnecka (chapter 13 and 1993a).

In terms of public ritual there are four main days to the Dasain festival in Tamaphok. The first distinctive feature is the killing of a buffalo on the first day (*phulpātī*). This is done through groups called *baijo*. *Baijo* are formed primarily on the basis of kinship but are open to those of other lineages, clans and ethnic groups, if the organizer is in agreement. On *phulpāti* day itself, as well as home-produced victuals, there is a great exchange of meat (mixed with *iskus* [christophine] or pumpkin) and full pots of *tuṅgbā* (millet beer sucked through a straw) between houses.

The events of *phulpāti* are quite specific to the Yakha and are celebrated by the release of gunpowder charges (*baḍhai*), which make a voluble expression of ethnic difference. On the second day (*mahāṣṭamī*), by contrast, the chief explosions come from nearby Brahman/Chetri communities, since this is the day when these high-caste groups hold their main animal sacrifice (*mār kāṭne*). For the Yakha of Tamaphok, however, the day after *phulpāti* is something of a lull, during which time people continue to exchange meat and drink with their neighbours and carry on with the spring cleaning they still have to do. The Yakha *mār kāṭne* rituals take place on the following day (*mahā-navamī*).

Again the generalities of the *mār kāṭne* sacrifice are the same as other groups, although Brahmans and Chetris reportedly organize theirs on a household-by-household basis while the Yakha rituals are performed in the courtyards of local headmen (*majhiyā*). First the Yakha slay model animals made out of fruits or vegetables and pieces of straw. After this a young animal, either a buffalo, goat, or pig, is brought out. It is vital that the beast be dispatched with a single blow through the neck and a young chick is kept on the sidelines to be sacrificed at the last minute if anything goes wrong. Once the beast is beheaded, a group of men run forward and drag

FIGURE 34   *Model animals prepared for 'sacrifice' during Dasain, Tamaphok (Tamara Kohn, 28/9/1990)*

the carcass around the sacrificial area (*rekhī*) to encircle it with blood after which carcass and head are discarded. The Brahmans and Chetris, by contrast, are said to carry the head of the sacrificial animal in from outside and place it in the far left hand corner of their kitchens (looking from the main entrance). While highlighted as a Yakha custom in Tamaphok, the action of dragging the carcass round the sacrificial area has been observed elsewhere in Nepal (Whelpton, personal communication).

An extra ritual to protect the house during the coming year is performed by taking a small boy and placing his hands and feet in the sacrificial blood, after which he is carried to the front entrance of the house where hand and foot prints are made, left hand and foot to the right of the door, right hand and foot to the left. "Everything for Durga is back to front", we were told.

Kami and Damai families, interestingly, are said to have rituals more similar to those of the Yakha: at least, they are held on the same day, after the Yakha have completed theirs (and the Damai musicians who, as at weddings, are involved in making music for the Yakha are consequently able to attend to their own affairs). Somewhat like the Yakha, too, several households join together in a group to perform the ceremony. According to a Kami woman I was able to visit discreetly during my first village Dasain, their customs during the period are the same except for the fact they do not drink millet beer.

The final day (*vijaya-daśamī*) is marked by *ṭīkā lagāune*, when the male household head gives a *ṭīkā* blessing to all friends and relatives who come to visit. This seems to be more akin to Brahman and Chetri practices than are the rituals of the preceding days, although the Yakha characterize the Brahmans as marking the occasion with the recitation of religious texts. The Yakha *ṭīkā* is normally a broad band of white rice and yogurt (*dahi*) applied across the forehead. Chetris are said to apply pink-coloured *ṭīkā* and we heard Yakha walking around with pink *ṭīkā* being jokingly referred to as having followed the Chetri custom. The eldest unmarried daughter is supposed to receive *ṭīkā* first, followed by whoever is around, in a vague order through daughters-in-law (including brothers' daughters-in-law) and their children, nieces, and male relatives. However, much seems to depend on when people turn up to receive their *ṭīkā*, a rather different story to the highly symbolic order of *ṭīkā* dispensing which Bennett (1983) observed in Brahman/Chetri households.

Thus the changes which have and have not occurred as a result of the growing influence of Hindu practices and doctrines in the lives of the Yakha make the situation more complex than the model of Hinduization, which sees Yakha traditions inexorably moving towards those of their caste Hindu neighbours, might suggest. While not denying the influence of Hinduism, it is wrong to view it as either a mere superficial encrustation on top of a pristine base of Yakha tradition, or as a totally dominant new world view. Rather, the Hindu tradition has become part of a cultural repertoire which is, arguably, uniquely Yakha in its manifestation. The Yakha themselves would argue that the rituals they perform show they are 'Hindu'. For the Brahmans and Chetris to whom we spoke, they are seen as distorted versions of true (*pakkā*) Hinduism. In this way the Yakha both conform to the Hinduization model and, in some ways, subvert it.[10]

POLITICIZATION AND YAKHA IDENTITIES

We could leave things there: Yakha culture as a polythetic and selectively absorbent sponge, with Hindu beliefs and values, far from obliterating it, providing new social and ritual forms for the expression of Yakha distinctiveness and identity. However, during fieldwork we also observed the changes which took place as a result of the success of the 'pro-democracy' movement and demise of the Panchayat system at the village level. The transformation this represented in political terms was immense. Under the Panchayat system, party politics were illegal and the village leader (pradhan panch), while elected, was first and foremost a representative of the

FIGURE 35   *A village Panchayat meeting in progress (Andrew Russell* 16/11/ 1989)

King. With the triumph of the pro-democracy movement in April 1990 pradhan panchas were stripped of their posts and there was promise of party-based 'democracy'. The explosion of open meetings, organizations, and tea-shop debates in the ensuing months invigorated the range of new ideas, beliefs, and values being brought into the midst of the Yakha of Tamaphok. This fresh flow was sifted through in ways akin to those I have tried to demonstrate in 'traditional' patterns of Yakha cultural change. In the process, as before, Yakha identity was sharpened while at the same time changed and renegotiated.

Many Communist Party rallies and 'cultural meetings' took place in the school playground after the demise of the Panchayat system. Often speakers came from the Tarai towns or elsewhere in the hills, and were touring around the area. As I argued above, the Yakha are not isolated and unused to outsiders: there has long been movement of people from the outside world through the village, and Yakha themselves regularly leave Tamaphok to attend bazaars, or to migrate further afield in search of work. But what was unusual

FIGURE 36   *A Communist Party rally in Tamaphok (Tamara Kohn, 29/5/ 1990).*

was the way in which these new visitors articulated and analysed social problems in a public forum.

However, it is difficult not to feel that the Communists' message was losing its full effect because of a lack of understanding about the cultural background of the Yakha. For a start, the Nepali words that speakers used were often Sanskritic in their derivation. This, despite the general fluency of the Yakha in Nepali, only served to emphasize their differences from the speakers and made understanding difficult. When speakers argued for the need to respect all languages and religion "such as those of you Rais", they did not seem aware of Yakha distinctiveness from this larger group. Visiting speakers argued for the right to love marriages over arranged marriages, despite the Yakha already having a tradition of love marriages. Other customs which were highlighted as odious, such as expecting a woman to massage the feet of her mother-in-law and husband's elder sisters, giving a daughter-in-law different food to the rest of the family, or expecting them to remain silent in group situations, similarly did not apply to the Yakha. The speeches, by offering comparative models in this way, probably helped to cement a stronger, more positive feeling of Yakha identity distinct from the problems the speakers were addressing.

Many Yakha supported or had sympathy for the Communist cause (as was the case across large swathes of east Nepal), but as the debate developed, some people became less impressed with aspects of the Communist line. The main criticism levelled against Communism by many Yakha, apart from the question of why someone who had perhaps become impoverished playing gambling games like *juwa* should be supported by the hard work of others, was the restrictions on travel abroad which countries like China were believed to place on their citizens. "How would people go outside [i.e. abroad] to work?" our village sister opined one day. It seemed as if she saw Communism as threatening what she had come to realise was a fundamental part of Yakha identity.

Thus as political debate developed in 1990, issues were discussed which challenged people's basic values and priorities. Polarization of political allegiances, sometimes even within single households, led to kinship and other types of social ties becoming strained and reformulated. For example, the ex-ward 5 *adhyaksa* (ward chairman) had an eldest son who, as a model capitalist, used money saved from his father's service in the Indian army to start a sweet-making factory in Kathmandu. The *adhyaksa* was incensed, however, when his younger son became a leading light in the Communist Party at the school.

We also noticed acute changes in the personality of one of our informants. He sang us a song one day which he had composed for a big political meeting at the beginning of August 1990, a poignant reflection on the hardships of life in Tamaphok. The constant articulation of all the problems his community faced seemed to be affecting his mental state, and his once open and cheerful demeanour changed to one of subdued introspection. He stopped working for us, saying he was "too busy". In terms of the political struggle, despite our sympathy for the cause, it seemed we were becoming classed with the capitalist enemy.

Thus as the political changes played themselves out in Tamaphok, social relations sometimes became strained. Yakha identity became more complex and perhaps solidified as new allegiances were established and people related the new doctrines to their own lives and cultural values. New dimensions of knowledge about and from the world outside also had to be added to the cultural repertoire.

Many of the political debates since the pro-democracy movement have tended to emphasize ethnic rights and empowerment. The initiation of news bulletins in Hindi and Newari on the radio has also aroused interest and ethnic sensibilities. People jokingly asked how long it would be before news bulletins in Yakha appeared. Two of our Yakha teacher friends independently asked to borrow our copy of van Driem (1987) because of the Limbu orthographies it contained. They were interested in the possibility of writing Yakha, and in using something other than the Devanagari script to do so, as well as teaching such a script in the school.

On the other hand, none of the Tamaphok Yakha to whom we spoke appeared interested in becoming involved in a political movement based on ethnic affiliation, although this was an option which was being pursued by factions in some of the larger ethnic groups (such as the Limbus' 'Limbuwan Liberation Front' (*Nepal Press Digest*, 1990: 220) and the 'Magurali' (a loose confederation of Magar, Gurung, Rai, and Limbu groups which has become prominent since our fieldwork). Just like their apparent reluctance to become subsumed into a larger Limbu cultural identity, and ambivalence regarding their relationship to the Rai, so too it seems the Yakha remain cautious about becoming part of broader political movements based on ethnic lines.[11]

CONCLUSION

In this paper I have queried the notion of Yakha culture as something either unified or unique. Diverse cultural practices within the Yakha and similarities between the Yakha and other groups lend support to the arguments of Allen, Fisher, Holmberg, and others (outlined in the introduction) concerning the inadequacy of a 'one tribe/one culture' view. I have also argued for the assimilation and, if you like, 'Yakhafication' of cultural forms as an intrinsic part of whatever it is we might call Yakha culture, with implications for our perceptions of Hinduization and other processes of 'accultura- tion'. There is certainly no evidence, despite their relatively small numbers, that the Yakha are falling into a cultural 'melting pot' as their integration with the nation-state increases. Rather the negotiation of 'what it means to be Yakha' is assuming new forms.

Manzardo (1982) uses Goffman's concept of 'impression management' in his study of Thakali hotel owners on the trail from Jomsom to Pokhara in west central Nepal to explain the apparent fluidity of Thakali religion and other cultural forms. There were echoes of this process amongst the Yakha, but rather than the conscious subterfuge implied by the term 'impression management' (or "cultural chameleonism": Manzardo 1982: 57) I would argue that, for the Yakha, 'identity management' would be a more appropriate term. Identity in this formula is the complex product of cultural change, both conscious and unconscious, internally and externally derived, negotiated, manipulated, and (potentially) subverted. If we accept, as I think we have to, that Yakha culture is at its core open to change, and that Yakha identity is only one of a range of identities which people take from as they think appropriate in different social situations, then it is perhaps our ideas about Nepalese culture and identity which are changing rather than the nature of the identities themselves.

NOTES

The research on which this paper is based was funded by a U.K. Economic and Social Research Council 'CASS' award studentship and was carried out together with Tamara Kohn. I am grateful to the contributors to the 'Politics, Identity, and Cultural Change' workshop, in particular David Gellner, Joanna Pfaff-Czarnecka, John Whelpton, and Nick Allen, for their comments on my original paper. I am also grateful to members of the Department of Anthropology at the University of Durham, including Tamara Kohn, Susanna Rostas, Bob Simpson, Sandra Bell, and Michael Carrithers, for their comments on a subsequent draft.

[1] Recruitment to foreign armies has been and continues to be a major source of employment for young Yakha males, and is only one of a range of migration patterns open to the Yakha (Russell, 1992). The Yakha propensity to migration adds weight to criticisms of geographical isolation as an explanation of ethnic diversity.

[2] See, for example, the account by Upreti (1975).

[3] For an analysis of the history and current status of the Kirata, see Subba (in press).

[4] E.g. the vocabulary associated with wet-rice cultivation, which consists almost entirely of Nepali loanwords and has apparently always done so; cf. Allen on the Thulung Rai (1978a).

[5] This is well demonstrated in the case of place names, some of which have Yakha equivalents (e.g. *Tumok* for Tamaphok and *Waling* for Madi Mulkharka) and some of which have what could be called 'Yakha Nepali' equivalents. For example, a part of Tamaphok known as *Mājhagaū* in Yakha is *Bīcgaū* in Nepali (both translating as 'middle village'). Yet '*Mājhagaū*' could as well be Nepali as Yakha, since the Yakha *ten* ('village') is absent and *mājh* and *bīc* are both Nepali words with virtually synonymous meanings. Despite this people were adamant

that if they were speaking Yakha they would say *Mājhagaũ* rather than *Bīcgaũ*. The kinship term *phupū*, which for caste Hindus means simply 'father's sister' for the Yakha also means 'mother's brother'. This is another example of a Nepali word being used in a distinctive way by the Yakha of Tamaphok.

[6] For an interesting discussion of the problems inherent in using the Devanagari script for such a purpose, see Yadav (1992).

[7] For example, the words *muddum* in Mehawang Rai, *mundhum* in Limbu, *mukdum* in Sunuwar, *dum-la* in Chamling (Gaenszle, 1993), as well as the Thulung Rai *diumla* (Allen, 1978a).

[8] In this, the Yakha evidence contrasts with Levine's experience of the Nyinba Tibetans (1988), and Crandon-Malamud's experience of ethnicity in highland Bolivia (1991), but is supported by Adhikary (1993) who considers that the prospect of a Magar shifting to another equivalent group identity within a single lifetime is 'culturally unthinkable'.

[9] According to Hamilton, the Magar came as government soldiers (1819: 160).

[10] Jones makes the point that "high-caste Hindus frequently make use of Limbu shamans in the diagnosis of disease or simple acts of divination" (1976: 70). We saw ample evidence of this occurring in our observation of Yakha relations with other groups in Tamaphok, giving further support to the notion that, in some respects, 'Yakhafication', not just of Hindu rituals but of caste Hindus themselves, has taken place at the same time as the 'Hinduization' of the Yakha.

[11] Particularly as members of a small ethnic group, I suspect many Yakha would agree with O'Neill (1994) when he writes that "communalism may strike the western reader as an admirable thing, but in South Asia the word carries darker associations. The murderous civil war between 'Buddhist' Sinhalese and 'Hindu' Tamils in Sri Lanka is perhaps only the most visible example of ethnic conflict in a subcontinent wrought by similar upheavals."

CHAPTER ELEVEN

Changing Concepts of Ethnic Identity Among the Mewahang Rai

Martin Gaenszle

INTRODUCTION

In recent years more and more ethnic organizations have been established in Nepal with the aim to represent the interests of the various ethnic groups within the national context and to preserve their cultural heritage. For example the Tamang have the Nepal Tamang Ghedung (founded in 1956), the Tharu have the Tharu Kalyan Karini Sabha ('Tharu Welfare Society', since 1949), the Thakali have the Thakali Sewa Samiti (since 1982), the Newar have the Nepal Bhasha Manka Khalah (since 1979), the Limbu have the Kirat Yakthung Chumlung, and the Rai have, since 1988, the organization called Kirat Rai Yayokkha.[1] Since the restoration of multi-party democracy and the promulgation of the new constitution in 1990 such organizations have come out more openly and gained new political importance. Twenty of them have joined to form the Nepal Janajati Mahasangh ('Nepal Federation of Nationalities'), which was founded in July 1990. What had been non-issues during the Panchayat days (multi-ethnic society, secular state, privileging backward groups) have since become a matter of much public debate. Though some have informal links with political parties which represent ethnic issues (e.g. Rastriya Janamukti Party, Mongol National Organization), these organizations usually are not aligned with specific parties.[2] It is true that they are becoming now more active in the political arena, but generally their aim is above all to maintain and strengthen a cultural identity based on ethnicity.

351

This general development raises questions about the character of such relatively new and emergent forms of identity. Gellner (1986) describes the "modern" kind of Newar identity, which is mainly confined to the young and educated, as more assertive and strongly focused on the common language and a unique culture, whereas the "ancient" traditional kind is "much weaker and largely implicit" (1986: 137). McDonaugh (1989) confirms the importance of a distinct language for the formation of a new identity in the case of the Tharu, but stresses the traditional significance of the mythology which links all the Tharu through 'common origin' – though the situation is not unambiguous (1989: 202).

It seems that for the modern kind of ethnic identity, to which I will restrict the term 'ethnicity',[3] cultural attributes are especially important as distinctive markers, which are often instrumentalized for political and economical interests in a national context. In the traditional outlook, however, where ethnic affiliation is less clear-cut but nevertheless shapes identities, culture is more than that: it is in fundamental ways constitutive of social reality and thus the perception of groups and their boundaries. In this perspective myths, for example, are not only culture traits which, at best, 'reflect' a pre-existing social structure, rather they are part of the process which generates the relevant distinctions. If these propositions can be confirmed, they have important consequences for the concept of ethnic identity outlined by Fredrik Barth in 1969 (I will return to this point in the conclusion).

In general terms, I understand ethnic identity to be the cognitive and emotional attachment to a particular ethnic unit (in contradistinction to another such unit) as the result of the continuous attempt ('identity management')[4] of individuals or groups to harmonize concrete experienced reality, such as encounters with other persons and new situations, with an ethnic self-image inherited from the past.[5] Accordingly ethnic identity in the premodern sense can be seen as deriving from concepts and self-images which are firmly rooted in an encompassing cultural tradition and thus remain relatively stable. Ethnicity, on the other hand, would then be the kind of ethnic identity which is formed under the conditions of modernity, i.e. in the context of an emerging nation-state. Here tradition is no longer something unquestioned and taken for granted, but something which is consciously valued and used for strategic purposes in dealing with an enlarged social world.[6]

In the following outline of the situation among the Mewahang Rai I will also deal with the difference between a more traditional sense of ethnic identity and its modern version. How can this difference be described? And how does the role of culture change in the course of this historical transformation?

First I will sketch the socio-historical setting of the Mewahang Rai and their various ethnic categories. Then I will show the importance of the oral tradition of the *muddum* (M.)[7] for the construction of a self-image. Finally I will discuss the historical changes which affect and transform this traditional world-view.

GROUPS AND CATEGORIES

The Mewahang Rai are one of the numerous (more than fifteen) subtribes which make up the problematic ethnic unit called Rai, and as such they belong to the autochthonous stratum of Eastern Nepalese inhabitants known as Kiranti. They are settled for the most in eight major villages on the western bank of the Arun River, ranging from the Chirkhuwa Khola in the south to the Apsuwa Khola in the north (for ethnographic details on this and the following issues see Gaenszle, 1991a). Their more or less distinct language can be classified as belonging to the East-Himalayish Section of the Bodic Division of Sino-Tibetan (Shafer, 1955), or, according to a more recent classification, to the North-Eastern sub-group ("Meohang-Saam") of Central Kiranti (Hansson, 1991: 111).

But what kind of group are the Mewahang? Ethnographers have often naively assumed that where there is a name, there must be a clearly defined group: ethnonyms are taken as evidence for the existence of a distinct ethnic group. But ethnonyms have often complex histories: they may originally have been vague and inclusive and only later came to refer to specific social groups (e.g. the general term Tb. *shar-pa* 'easterner' which became the ethnonym Sherpa), and/or there may have been a prior discrepancy between self-designation and outside-designation, which was erased in the course of time (e.g. the term 'Gurung' replacing the indigenous term 'Tamu').

Though the term 'Mewahang Rai' can be regarded as an ethnic name which is used by the people, it does not refer to a clear-cut unit with a unique and distinct common culture. Especially in the fringe areas of the Mewahang territory, there are numerous ambiguities which make it impossible to draw impermeable boundaries: the same clan names are sometimes found among two different Rai groups, or incongruities exist in the terms which people ascribe to themselves and those which others ascribe to them. The cultural practices of the Mewahang differ from village to village, and at the same time they have such a lot in common with those of neighbouring Rai groups that it is difficult to speak of a homogeneous Mewahang culture. Even the language can be subdivided into two or three subgroups.

What meaning does the use of the ethnonym 'Mewahang' have under these circumstances? Or, in other words, to what extent does there exist an ethnic identity among the Mewahang? It should first of all be emphasized that language usage varies in a fundamental way on this point. On the one hand, the category refers to the subtribe, which is primarily associated with the roughly delimitable settlement area under its control; on the other hand, the members of this subtribe themselves also include – as the myths show – all the autochthonous Rai of the Arun Valley (i.e. Lohorung, Bantawa, Yamphu, etc.) under this label, thus giving it a more general, inclusive meaning.

For the Mewahang themselves, the question of how to determine the boundaries of the subtribe does not represent a problem; it has no significance for practical matters. Rather, in everyday interaction various categories are used: they constitute levels associated with a particular identity both above and below the level of the subtribe (in the narrow sense of the term) and are at least as relevant as that of 'Mewahang'.

On the highest level there is the category of 'Kiranti' (*Kirãti*) which usually includes the Rai, Limbu, and Yakha (cf. Bista, 1967: 32, Russell, chapter 10), and also the Sunuwar, Jirel, as well as some

Tarai groups such as Dhimal and Rajbanshi. This is a highly evocative and emotionally charged concept, as it is associated with former political autonomy and the status of royalty. It is widely believed that the Kiranti groups of east Nepal are direct descendants of the ancient *Kirāta* (Skt.), the dynasty which according to the chronicles ruled the Kathmandu Valley before the Licchavis. Though there are good reasons to regard these *Kirāta* and the present day Kiranti as having a common (however distant) ethnic background,[8] it is highly doubtful whether one can accept the popular view that the Rai, Limbu etc. are descendants of people who fled from conquering kings (see also below, section 3).[9] Rather, there is evidence that the term '*Kiranti*' was first used in the political centre, Kathmandu, as a general designation for the hill tribes of the eastern region called *Kirāt* (cf. Burghart, 1984: 107) and only later developed into an ethnonym used by the people themselves (cf. Gaenszle, 1991a: 4–13). Nevertheless, the concept of a roughly corresponding unit is implicit in the mythology. According to a well-known myth (see below) there were Four Original Brothers: Khambuhang, Mewahang, Limbuhang, and Meche Koche (this latter expression referring to the Tarai groups). Though the term 'Kiranti' is usually not used in this context, the myth can be taken as evidence for an ancient Kiranti solidarity. The mythic fraternal unity is strengthened by the specific historical experience of being subjugated for the past two centuries, and so this most comprehensive kind of traditional ethnic identity is of special political significance. Today the term is often used in a very wide sense, including all 'Mongol' groups, such as Gurung, Magar, Tamang, and even Tibetans.

The unit which one most readily would regard as an ethnic group is that called *Rāi*. This is the ethnonym which is generally used for purposes of self-designation in multi-ethnic contexts, and, as the ethnic organizations show, this is a unit which is emphasized in the present political arena (though this is not unproblematic as we will see). It is well known, however, that the use of the term *rāi* as an ethnonym is of quite recent historical origin: the word, which is etymologically linked with Sanskrit *rājan* 'king', was first used as a title granted to the local headman by the Shah kings in order to acknowledge their semi-autonomous status. As land documents from the research area show, still in the early 1960s it was a privilege of the headman and authorized tax functionaries to have *Rāi* as their surname, whereas the ordinary settlers on ancestral territory were called *Jimi* (see below). In fact this kind of usage is preserved in nicknames even today. Though it is difficult to reconstruct the timing and social dynamic of the process (cf. Gaenszle, 1991a: 70, 108), it is clear that in the course of time the title of a small elite became the term used by outsiders and by the people themselves as the name of an ethnic group. As there is no indigenous term for this group, one has to assume that ethnic identity on this level is an outcome of this somewhat contingent development.[10]

In a more local context, the term *Jimi* is still widely used among the Mewahang for self-designation (it is similarly used by other subtribes: cf. Russell, p.330 above). This word (*jimi* < *jimidār* 'landowner') points to their status as the original owners of communal *kipaṭ* lands,[11] and it is generally used in conceptual opposition to the word 'Khambu', which refers to the Rai subtribes from the Dudh Kosi basin. Many of the latter, mainly Kulunge, but also some Chamling, Thulung, and Khaling, have been migrating into the Arun Valley since about seven or eight generations ago. Under the *kipaṭ* system they were dependent on the landholding Mewahang and had the politically inferior status of *dhākre* (lit. 'one who carries a basket'). Another distinction which marks the Mewahang off from other Rai groups is the former's taboo on goat meat, even though there are some other Rai groups which have this restriction (e.g. the Namlunge and Sotange, see McDougal, 1979: 19). Moreover, there is the widely spread but highly inconsistent distinction between *Lhāsā gotra* and *Kāśi gotra* groups, which cuts across all these previous distinctions. The underlying idea is that a part of the ancestral groups migrated through Tibetan country before settling on their present territory (Gaenszle, 1991a: 126f.); this apparently is a later modification of the migration myths.

Turning now to the level below the subtribe, there is a 'group' defined on the basis of descent from the first settler (i.e. persons sharing a common ritual name, M. *same*) which ideally occupies a specific ancestral territory (M. *ca:ri*). This is the largest precisely determinable and socially more or less coherent unit, even if its significance in territorial and kinship terms has undergone great change in the course of history (Gaenszle, 1991a: 129–47). The sense of identity with one's own locality continues to be very strong, and it is made even stronger by the current trend towards village endogamy, so that in encounters with strangers the question of a person's place of origin may be as important as that of his subtribe (usually called *thar*). The *ca:ri* localities often differ, too, according to objective criteria: the ritual cycle, its symbolism, and the myths vary, and even the language exhibits dialect-based differences.

Traditional ethnic identity is relational and situational: it is constituted on a number of levels, and it would be an error to fix on one of them as the 'true' one. The crucial point appears to me to be that on none of the levels can the groups be talked of in an essentializing, 'corporative' sense. In none of the cases is it possible to determine with complete precision where the 'boundaries' of a group run. No one is able to say who is to be regarded as a Kiranti: do the Tharu, for example, belong to the group, as some opine, or not? The same problem exists for the determination of the category 'Rai'. Here again there are several borderline cases, such as the Yakha, the Sunuwar, and the Jirel, not to mention the fact that most Mewahang are scarcely familiar with these peripheral groups. And even on the level of the *ca:ri* groups there are numerous ambiguities as migration movements have complicated the situation.

From all of this it becomes clear that ethnic identity does not necessarily refer to an objective, well-defined ethnic group; it exists primarily as a concept – in other words, on the level of ideas. So if we want to understand how the Mewahang traditionally see themselves, and how they view their place in the order of things, we have to look at their mythology, because this is the idiom in which they discuss the matter.

MYTH, HISTORY, AND IDENTITY

In the totality of Mewahang myths which belong to their oral tradition of ancestral knowledge, known as *muddum*,[12] we find a conceptual framework which relates and situates the ethnic categories within a history of origins. The mythology is structured like a huge genealogical tree (though not all links are remembered), and because it recounts the origin of all beings in terms of descent and the continuous process of branching-off, the levels of group division are reflected in the mythic model.

I shall now roughly summarize the major myths which are of importance in this respect (for a detailed discussion of the mythology see Gaenszle, 1991a: part 3).

After the first divine ancestors created the variety of species and the First Man, Tumna, the next prominent descendant is the culture hero Khakculukpa who established Kiranti traditions. It was he who introduced hunting and agriculture, he built the first house and he married by capturing a wife, later on holding a great domestic feast which resembles both a house inauguration and a wedding. His descendants are the Four Brothers, Khambuhang, Mewahang, Limbuhang, and Meche Koche (in order of seniority). These four, who originally lived close to the Place of Origin, known as *khowalung* (down in the Tarai), eventually walked northward towards the hills, but the youngest brother got lost and stayed behind in the plains.[13] The eldest brother arrived first at the Saptakosi River and after crossing it with the help of a small blood sacrifice he tricked the second brother, Mewahang, into sacrificing his sister. When the latter found out about the wickedness of his elder brother he cursed him, but Khambuhang likewise cursed his younger brother Mewahang. The three brothers eventually split up, dividing their share of inheritance, *aṃśa*, and each followed a different valley upwards: Khambuhang went up the Dudh Kosi, Mewahang followed the Arun River, and Limbuhang settled in the Tamur Valley.

The next series of myths then recounts the migration of the Mewahang forefathers, who continued walking up along the eastern bank to the upper Arun Valley, intermarried with the Bhotiya but later returned south and finally settled on the western bank – on their present territory. Here, according to a widespread myth, Mewahang and Khambuhang met again. They decided to divide up the land, but again the elder brother tricked his younger brother and ended up with the greater share. This story, which seems to be a more recent variation on an older theme,[14] is often grudgingly recounted as a reason for the demographic fact that the Khambuhang, who generally occupy the higher altitude lands, today tend to outnumber the Mewahang on the latter's ancestral territory.

Once the ancestors have arrived in their specific settlement areas, which are identified by their familiar place and river names, we come to the level of locality myths. These tell about the 'first settler' ancestors who found the proper place to stay and to establish villages. Sometimes the founding ancestor was not the very first to occupy the land, but in all cases he was the first *legitimate* settler: always the spirit of the territory (*ca:ri*) signaled in one way or another (e.g. through dreams, or through the behaviour of a pig) who was to be the proper one to stay, and thus others could be chased away without scruple. But still these 'first settlers', powerful *hang* (M. 'king') who are often regarded as brothers, did not live peacefully each in his respective territory: numerous myths describe the quarrels between them, wars with bow and arrow, which typically lead to the eventual forging of marriage alliances. The descendants of the first settlers then split up and become the founders of the various clans: usually the clan names are said to be those of their founders. In this way the myths lead directly into the remembered genealogy of the living.

It becomes clear, then, that the mythology as a whole can be seen as a history of creation and migration. The various groups are the result of fraternal division: they result from a common ancestor and are thus not different in substance (i.e. Rai and Limbu and Meche Koche are all Kiranti brothers and their differences are only the result of historical developments). In the course of fraternal division different *ca:ri* territories have been occupied, and thus the continuous segmentary division coincides with a continuous localization of smaller group units (development of local dialects, local ritual traditions etc.). It is interesting that a more recent version of the mythology also includes the branching off of other *jāt*s, the Chetris, Tibetans, as well as Russians, English, etc. (Gaenszle, 1991a: 267). They are all part of the genealogical tree and history of creation, but happened to branch off at an earlier stage.

Because of this spatio-genealogical structure, the mythology is able to serve as a kind of charter for identity:[15]

- the culture hero is the founder not only of Mewahang but – implicitly – of Kiranti culture in general;
- the four brothers' migration accounts for the internal divisions of the Kiranti: there is no base for a unit called Rai, but instead there is one for the rift between Jimi and Khambu;
- the village founders are the focus of *ca:ri/same* group identity;
- and their offspring are credited with the creation of the present-day localized clans.

As in any segmentary structure these groups are not conceived as substances with an identity in themselves; rather they exist only in relation to each other. One group is opposed to another at one level, but both are a unit opposed to another unit on another (higher) level of the spatialized genealogy. In thus forming a cognitive paradigm for moving back and forth between the various levels, the mythic model of a genetic hierarchy allows groupings of different sizes to be identified in an unambiguous manner.

The merging of spatial and temporal images in the mythic account of origins appears to be a typical feature of the Rai *muddum*. The question 'Who are we?' is almost synonymous with the question 'Where do we come from?', because the past is seen essentially as a history of migration (also cf. Macfarlane, chapter 5 above). It is this latter question which is often passionately discussed by elders and which typically leads to the telling of myths. Thus, to use a term coined by Rosaldo, one could speak here of the "spatialization of time" (Rosaldo, 1980: 55). Identity is derived from this linking of experiences in the present with the events and localities of origin and migration in the past. On certain occasions the Mewahang enact parts of this mythology, thus temporarily 'returning' to the ancestral times and places.[16]

So it can hardly be said that the Mewahang are a 'people without history', as 'tribes' have often been held to be. It may be surprising that a people who are among the oldest inhabitants of Nepal seems to remember more of the past than many 'late-comers'.[17] But considering their background of shifting cultivation and the importance of mythic land claims, especially in a time when there were no land documents, the concern with ancestral migration and settlement makes good sense. And particularly today, after the communal *kipaṭ* system has been abolished, there are strong reasons to keep up the memory of a time when the Rai were the 'owners' and rulers of *Kirāt*.

INTEGRATION AND TRANSFORMATION

With this particular kind of historic consciousness enshrined in their oral tradition, how have the Mewahang dealt with change? Or, more specifically: How has the traditional ethnic self-image as it has been outlined above been transformed in the modern context? As I want to focus on the more recent changes, I will not attempt to reconstruct the complex history of this transformation. But for a rough sketch one may distinguish the following processes: the translation, juxtaposition, and homogenization of culture.

Though there are good reasons to assume that during the time of the Sen kings of Makwanpur the Mewahang had already come into contact with Hindu culture, the major impact occurred with the formation of the Gorkha empire. With an increasing number of Hindu caste immigrants settling in the eastern hills, the Rai were confronted more and more with a rich tradition that had established itself in the region. However, rather than rejecting this tradition as something 'alien', the Rai have integrated parts of it into their own tradition by translating them into their own familiar idiom. Thus, for example, village goddesses, like Jalpa Devi or Sat Kanya Devi, began to 'appear' in Mewahang settlements in natural formations like trees and rocks, and were worshipped and addressed in a similar manner as the local spirits of the soil (*ca:ri*). Likewise many other Hindu deities, like Shiva/Mahadeo or Sansari Mai, became part of the ritual, especially the shamanic, tradition. Various rituals, festivals and myths were simply juxtaposed to the existing

FIGURE 37   *Praying to Durga represented by a number of swords in the courtyard of the village headman (Dasain festival,* navamī *day, 1985, Sankhuwa Valley) (Martin Gaenszle)*

cultural forms.[18] In general these modifications remained quite superficial as they did not really change much of the indigenous tradition of the *muddum*. Rather the introduction of new symbols and the reinterpretation of old symbols in terms of the new ones can be seen as the result of identity management in a changing environment: it is an attempt to link up with the symbolism prevalent in the wider region (cf. Gaenszle, 1993).

But the interaction with the Hindu tradition increasingly had also political implications. During the administrative consolidation of the emergent nation-state, the dominant political model was that of Hindu caste society protected by the king. This was, in principle, accepted by the local elites, who through the title of *rāi*, were given local powers on the condition of loyalty to the king in Kathmandu. Having thus become like "the king's younger brothers", the local headmen, by representing the royal function on the village level, became a significant force in the process of Hinduization.[19] For example, the festival of Dasain, with its blood sacrifice for the

FIGURE 38   *The headman, as the local representative of royal sovereignty,*
distributes ṭikā to his subjects during Dasain (as Figure 37)
(Martin Gaenszle)

warrior goddess Durga, is hosted by the headmen who, like the king
in Nepal, distribute *ṭikā* to the 'subjects' – a ritual celebrated still
today. In engaging in such symbolic practices, the Rai did not
subscribe to all aspects of Hindu ideology (e.g. food symbolism, the
role of Brahmans); but they acknowledged the general framework of the Shah kings' sovereignty, which they emulated on a
smaller scale (cf. Gaenszle, n.d.). Only very recently, caused by the

democratic changes, have some of the young and educated started to question the political significance of this festival.

There are also indicators of oppositional voices in the oral tradition. For example, in one mythic episode, which is clearly a later addition, the Mewahang ancestor, when migrating towards the hills from the place of origin, eventually "lost his way" and ended up in the Kathmandu Valley. There his descendants became kings of Nepal, the so-called *kirātsore rājā*. But after some time they were attacked by a foreign power, and losing in battle they were finally chased away. So they returned to the Arun Valley where they began to settle on the different territories (Gaenszle, 1991a: 300). This obviously alludes to the ancient *Kirāta* dynasty with which the Rai today like to identify. The myth gives expression to the feeling that the Rai at one time were the rulers of the country, but eventually were overpowered by a superior force. In a similar way, the Rai today, when coming to the Kathmandu Valley, worship certain deities as Kiranti kings who were subdued but may rise again in the future.[20]

Generally, even when asserting their 'tribal' identity, the Rai cannot avoid using idioms derived from the 'high religions' which they have encountered. For example, at some stage, at least a part of the Rai elite was no longer satisfied with having 'only' an oral history, so that some started to write genealogical chronicles which they conceived as *vaṃśāvalī* (Skt.), thus assimilating the genre which was common among the Hindu (but also Tibetan) kings. Recently, more and more such attempts to 'scripturalize' the *muddum* have come into print (e.g. the *Mewahāṅ Kirātīko vaṃśāvalī* by Madan Dāś Rāi, 1989/90), though, ironically, they are often meant as a means of revitalization, in a move against Hindu dominance. Obviously such a reinterpretation of tradition precipitates its transformation. The written *vaṃśāvalī* emphasize the genealogical aspects to the detriment of the spatial ones. This, significantly, coincides with the loss of traditional land rights.

Since the abolishment of former privileges and the *de facto* integration into the mainstream of the Nepalese nation-state, the Mewahang increasingly identify themselves with that distinct ethnic group or 'nationality' (*janajāti*) which they regard as being a more or less homogeneous constituent of Nepal's multi-ethnic society: the group with the ethnonym 'Rai' is seen, according to a common metaphor, as one among many flowers in the colourful garden of the kingdom.[21] As already indicated, particularly since the restoration of multi-party democracy – and especially in the urban centres – this trend of ethnic awareness has found open expression in the widespread establishment of ethnic organizations which are meant to preserve the cultural heritage and safeguard the interests of the group.

In the case of the Mewahang Rai this process is only in the beginning. In the villages pamphlets appear and issues such as the former autonomy of the Kirantis and the subsequent dominance of the "Khas" or "Chetri *rājā*" are discussed (mainly, but not exclusively, by the adult male part of the population). Especially during the parliamentary elections 1991, when the Rastriya Janamukti Party (National People's Liberation Front) was comparatively popular in this area,[22] these discussions had also strong political overtones. But generally the bases of the relevant ethnic organizations are in the urban areas, such as Dharan, where a high number of Mewahang pensioners from the Gurkha army have settled, and of course the Kathmandu Valley.

As mentioned above, at present the major Rai organization is Yayokkha, which is based in the capital but has supporters in Dharan, Bhojpur, Darjeeling, and elsewhere. In the first issue of its 'mouthpiece' (*mukhpatra*) *Yayok* the purposes of this organization are given as the following:

1. Establishing unity (*ektā*) among all Kirant Rai (*Kirāt Rāī*);
2. Facilitating research, protection, and promotion of the language, script, religion, art, culture, and history of the Rai;
3. Raising awareness within the Rai ethnic group (*rāī jātimā cetanāko abhivṛddhi garne*);
4. Developing all Rai languages in a coordinated manner by studying and teaching them at schools and universities;
5. Helping to build a great national culture by furthering the cooperation with other ethnic groups and ethnic organizations (Gangārāj Rāī, 1992/93).

Typically what is stressed here is not only the common interest and solidarity of the ethnic group, but also its non-separatist, 'national' character: one does not want to be reproached with communalism. This was written, of course, in Nepali, the only written medium in which all literate Rais can communicate.

Significantly, for the Rai the formation of ethnicity is not without complications. For one thing, there is the problem of the proper name of the ethnic group represented. As they are aware of the historic contingency of the term 'Rai', it is avoided, but in the absence of an equivalent indigenous name compromise solutions are the only way out. So Yayokkha, for its part, opts for the term 'Kirant Rai'. But this binomial remains somewhat ambiguous, because it is not clear how inclusively the term 'Kirant' should be understood (if both words were synonymous one would be redundant). Others suggest using the term 'Khambu' (e.g. Noval Kiśor Rāī, 1992/93), but here the problem is whether the term covers all the Rai, because, as we have seen above, local usage restricts it to those Rai groups from the Dudh Kosi area.[23]

Another problem is the strong internal diversity of the Rai. The proverbial multiplicity of Rai languages (*jati Rāi uti kurā*: 'There are as many (Rai) languages as there are Rai') is certainly a serious impediment for Rai ethnicity. In a recent conference organized by Yayokkha this has led some participants to the suggestion to make one Rai language – namely Bantawa – the standard language (and in fact, Bantawa was the language selected for newscasts in Rai in 1994). This, of course, has met with a lot of resistance, not only from non-Bantawa. Obviously, as long as Yayokkha claims to be representing all Rai it is not possible to privilege one Rai language without losing credibility. Already the Kulunge have formed a separate organization (called *Mā Kuluṅ Ridumchā*).

While linguistic diversity is usually accepted as a fact, there is a general tendency to emphasize cultural unity. This not infrequently leads to the somewhat simplifying view that all Rai have basically the same traditions, with differences being restricted to the level of language. An interesting illustration of the problem is the annual festival called Sakkhewa which is one of the major events organised by Yayokkha. As a handout explains, "'SAKKHEWA' is one of the main cultural festivals of the Kirant people of Nepal, which has, indeed, a long history that goes as far back as the Kirant civilization ... SAKKHEWA is known with various names viz: 'SAKLE', 'SAKELA' and 'TOSHI'." The celebration, held in recent years on the full moon day of the month of Baisakh on the open space in front of the zoo in Jawalakhel, consists mainly of a dance which is led by a priest wearing a turban (called *sili makpa*) and is accompanied by drums and cymbals. Numerous groups of both men and women dance in circling lines, in distinct styles varying according to the locality of the dancers. The whole performance is a poignant metaphor of 'unity in diversity', and, significantly, it has recently acquired political overtones, as when such a dance was organized on Tundikhel (May 8, 1993) with a Rai minister in the lead role of *sili makpa*. The point, however, is that this dance is not a pan-Rai tradition. I do not know about its exact background among the Bantawa, from whom it seems to derive, but among the Mewahang this dance does not exist. There are indications that the festival is linked to the territorial soil cult (called *sakhewa* (M.) among the Mewahang, and *tos* among the Kulunge[24]), but this is an entirely different context (see Gaenszle, n.d.). So the tradition, which unites the urban Rai in Kathmandu, is largely 'invented' (cf. Hobsbawm and Ranger, 1983): it is a new tradition created from local ones, and it contributes to the homogenization of 'Rai culture'.

CONCLUSION

To sum up, we have seen that the Mewahang have a variety of ethnic concepts which may be used in different social situations. Traditionally these concepts derive their meaning from the mythology, which describes a history of common origins, continuous descent, and subsequent group differentiation in the course of migration.

The attempt has thus been made to reconstruct the conceptual base of a traditional, more or less implicit ethnic identity. This has here been characterized as relational, non-essential, and contextual.

In interactions with Hindu castes or ethnic groups like Gurung, Sherpa, etc. a Mewahang will identify himself as a Rai or Kiranti, while in local contexts he is likely to be Jimi, or Mewahang, or – for example – Yaphule (from the village of Yaphu), depending on each specific social situation, which may thus be interpreted – as well as manipulated – by evoking the relevant myths. None of these identities is singled out as the 'true' and emotionally dominant one, and as all the groups ultimately have the same origin they are all equally important as a focus of affiliation. Just as the difference between two Mewahang villages is accounted for by the split of two brothers, so too the difference between Mewahang and, say, Limbu, is seen as the result of earlier fraternal division – only it happened at a more distant time, on a higher level of the genealogy. So what makes the groups different is not a distinct inherent essence, but rather their specific historical experience of migration and land occupation. That even 'foreign' groups are included in the cosmic genealogy may be seen as an inclusivist ethnocentrism, but one that underlines the basic unity of all mankind.

In distinction to this traditional kind of ethnic identity, the modern form of ethnicity is characterized by a shift in focus. Now, in the context of an emergent nation-state with its model of a multi-ethnic society, the Mewahang are 'forced' to identify with an ethnic group, or 'nationality', which is on an equal footing with other such groups. Therefore the unit of Rai – which is not so vague as the encompassing unit of Kiranti, and wider than the numerous and often small linguistic groups – is picked out and essentialized: in the common idiom, the Rai are, like the Gurung, Sherpa, Limbu etc. a distinct 'flower' in the garden of Nepal. In this new context the older mythic model tends to be forgotten and is often replaced by a new one which regards all Tibeto-Burman *janajāti*s as Kiranti, drawing the crucial line between them, the *ādivāsī* (indigenous people), and the 'Aryan', Hindu caste immigrants. Thus the specific territorial links which are so important in the mythology are transformed into political claims on a national level: being under-privileged despite being the original inhabitants of Nepal, they assert their demand for special treatment in the access to education, employment, and other such resources (cf. Despres, 1975).

Returning to the last of our initial questions: How, then, has the role of culture changed in the transformation of ethnic identity? In the more traditional context the values and categories which are embedded in the mythology of the *muddum* are important as constituents of the Mewahang's experienced world ('Lebenswelt').[25] As we have seen, social reality is interpreted in terms of the myths, just as the latter are seen in the light of ordinary experience, and this dialectical process affects action even as it may modify ideas.[26] The Mewahang Rai of the Arun Valley, for the most, still today see themselves as descendants of Khakculukpa, the culture hero, and, for example, the episode of the four brothers who divided their territory is still important for the perception of social divisions. Thus culture is here intrinsically part of the construction of a world- and self-image, or ethnic identity.

In the modern phenomenon of ethnicity, on the other hand, there is a tendency to instrumentalize culture and use it primarily as a distinctive marker, separating a bounded 'we' group from others. Through the process of cultural homogenization, moreover, local traditions are reinterpreted and stripped of their specific social context, thus leading to the 'folklorization' of tradition, i.e. its reduction to a mainly aesthetic enterprise. Though it may still affect the 'Lebenswelt', culture loses its pervasive, unquestioned founding qualities. It is often reduced to nothing more than an occasional reminder of one's 'true' identity.[27]

These observations should make one cautious about generalizations concerning the role of culture in the formation of ethnic identity. When Fredrik Barth in his influential contribution (1969) shifted the focus away from ethnic groups as clear-cut culture-bearing units to the processes of ethnic ascription and boundary maintenance it was an important step towards a proper understanding of the constitution of ethnic identity. But his downplaying of the "cultural stuff" (1969: 15) as mere signals or, at best, basic value orientations raised doubts whether this approach, though particularly appropriate for modern ethnicity as described above, does not unnecessarily reduce culture to a mere epiphenomenon. In fact, in a more recent article, Barth calls for an updating of our views of the structure of social action: "Such revision will primarily need to attend to the *cultural* construction of reality: that human social behaviour is intended and interpreted in terms of particular cultural understandings and is not transparent, objective, and uncontested" (Barth, 1992: 21, my emphasis). But in order to thus understand the formation of ethnic identities and ethnicity, one has to be aware that the role of culture itself may be subject to change.

NOTES

I am grateful to Joanna Pfaff-Czarnecka and David Gellner for their comments on earlier versions of the paper, and to Philip Pierce for revising my English.

[1] The dates in brackets are given in Fisher (1993: 12), except for the date on the Tharu organization which I have from Chris McDonaugh.

[2] During the Nepal Janajati Mahasangh's first conference in Kathmandu July 11–14, 1992, leaders not only from these but also from other major parties were invited to speak.

[3] Of course the underlying term 'ethnos' is the same, but the nominalized form ('ethnicity') appears to be more appropriate to express the essentializing qualities of modern ethnic self-definitions. The adjective 'ethnic' in contrast may be associated with groupings of varying scope.

[4] Cf. Höfer (1986: 48 f.) as well as Russell (p.348 above) as examples for the use of this term in other Nepalese contexts.

[5] The close link between ethnic identity formation and history has poignantly been expressed in the double question 'How did the past lead to the present?' and 'How does the present create the past' (Chapman, McDonald, and Tonkin, 1989: 1).

[6] The traditional sense of ethnic identity can be seen as a form of what Geertz, drawing on ideas developed by E. Shils, has called primordial attachment (Geertz, 1973: 259 ff.). On the opposite pole of this are the civil sentiments of the modern citizen. Ethnicity, then, would be somewhere in between these two poles, as primordial ties continue to be important while civil consciousness forms in a modern political set-up.

[7] If not otherwise marked, expressions in italics are transliterated from the Nepali language according to the system of Turner (1980). Mewahang expressions are marked by 'M.' (phonological details and

the conventions for transcription are given in Gaenszle, 1991a: 357), Sanskrit words by 'Skt.', and Tibetan words by 'Tb.'

[8] Licchavi inscriptions in the Kathmandu Valley have been shown to contain a high degree of non-Sanskrit vocabulary which seems to derive from the *Kirāta* (Vajracharya, 1969) and may also be regarded as belonging to a "proto-Newari" language (Slusser, 1982: 10fn.). As Newari may be classed together with Kiranti as "East Himalayish" (van Driem, personal communication), linguistic evidence points to a common heritage.

[9] A scholarly reference on this issue is Wright (1990 [1877]: 112) though the passage is not clear about expulsion from the Kathmandu Valley.

[10] As Höfer (1979: 142) writes: "Perhaps it is due to this new name that the various groups, now called Rai, became aware of their ethnic identity."

[11] The *kipaṭ* system is a form of land tenure under which control over the land is exercised by a community that cannot alienate its ownership rights (Regmi, 1978a: 534 ff.). Among the Mewahang the system was closely linked with traditional notions of ancestral territory, M. *ca:ri* (Gaenszle, 1991a: 138 f.).

[12] Like the cognate terms *muntum* (Yakha, cf. Russell, this volume), *mundhum* (Limbu), *ridum* (Kulung), *dum* (Chamling), *ḍiumla* (Thulung, cf. Allen, 1976b: 256 ff.), the word stands for the tribal way of life and has strong emotional overtones as it epitomizes a distinct cultural heritage which is not found among the Hindu castes or the Bhotiya groups.

[13] An obviously related story, told from the perspective of the left-behind brother, was reported by B.P. Upreti from the Dhimal in the Tarai: they regard themselves as the descendants of a younger brother who got lost, whereas his elder brother, the forefather of the Limbu, eventually reached the hills (Bista, 1967: 142).

[14] Similar myths about quarrels over land are documented for the Thulung Rai (Allen, 1976b: 151 ff.) and the Chamling Rai (Ebert, personal communication).

[15] As I have outlined above, I regard identity as resulting from an adaptive and dialectical process. Thus, unlike in Malinowski's theory, the charter itself may be subject to some degree of change.

[16] For example during the *Ma:mangme* (M.) ritual the priest 'travels' down the Arun Valley to the place of origin, *khowalung*, in order to guide away a harming spirit (see Gaenszle, 1995).

[17] Significantly the Brahmans and Chetris, who are recent immigrants, do not usually remember the route of their ancestors' migration. Among many Tibeto-Burman ethnic groups in Nepal, however, such a memory is an important part of their tradition.

[18] E.g. rituals like the *pāsni* (first-rice feeding), and festivals like Tihar or Nag Panchami are commonly celebrated, though they have no functional equivalent in Rai tradition. Similarly certain Hindu myths, like those deriving from the *Ramayana*, are known but remain clearly distinct from the mythology of the *muddum*.

[19] I do not think that this close identification with Hindu values necessarily gave the local elites any material advantages. The reason behind it may just as well have been the attempt to redefine one's identity in terms of a new and more 'universal' symbolism.

[20] For example the Sleeping Vishnu at Budhanilakantha is worshipped as a deified Kiranti king. The same is true for the statue of Virupaksha at Aryaghat at the Pashupatinath temple. Of this figure, which has a mongoloid face, only the upper half is visible. I was told by some Rai friends that it slowly emerges from the ground, and when it has fully reappeared, Kiranti rule will be established again!

[21] This often used metaphor goes back to Prithvi Narayan Shah's *Dibya Upadesh* (cf. Stiller, 1989: 44). There, however, it was meant as a negative image: "If my brother soldiers and the courtiers are not given to pleasure, my sword can strike in all directions. But if they are pleasure-seekers, this will not be my little painfully acquired kingdom but a garden of every sort of people."

[22] In constituency Sankhuwa Sabha No. 1 this party came third behind Congress and the Communist Party (UML).

[23] Nineteenth-century publications yield no clear evidence on former usage. Campbell, for example refers to the "Kambung rai" as one of the Rai "families" (1840: 599), whereas Hodgson regards "Khombo" as an original self-designation, synonymous with "Kiranti" (1880: 398).

[24] For details on the *tos* rites of the Kulunge see McDougal (1979: 38 f.).

[25] I regard the term 'Lebenswelt', coined by Husserl and developed by Schütz and others, as a useful concept to stress the unthematic or implicit character of this outlook.

[26] As I have tried to show elsewhere (Gaenszle, 1993), the traditional concepts have also in the past been subject to change as encounters and interaction with various groups have led to a modification and reinterpretation of cultural characteristics.

[27] This may be seen as as an extreme case of "long term change of culture" (cf. Ohnuki-Tierney, 1990).

PART FIVE

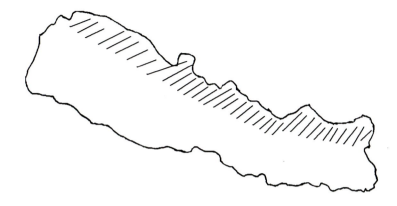

The Northern Fringe

Ecologically, Nepal is made up of three horizontal bands; the northernmost band, the zone of the high Himalayas and the valleys between and beyond them, is the most sparsely inhabited part of the country. In terms of area it may be nearly one third of Nepal's total territory. On the most restrictive definition, the population of these areas, known as 'Bhotiya' to other Nepalis, comprises just 0.1% of Nepal's total population; a very loose (though controversial) definition of 'Bhotiya' that included Tamangs, Gurungs, Thakalis, and Sherpas, would give a total near to 9%. As described in chapter 12, the Bhotiyas proper live in a series of enclaves strung out along the Himalayas, and, despite their common religion and related Tibetan dialects, they do not see themselves as belonging to a single ethnic group.

Despite this lack of political solidarity, they all equally have a high profile in romantic Western writing as Tibetans and Buddhists, and latterly – at least as far as the Sherpas are concerned – as 'stalwart' guides of mountaineering and trekking expeditions. Furthermore, as Tibetan Buddhists, they all have potential links to

377

Tibetan refugee settlements in India and to the wider global Tibetan diaspora. If, in spite of this, they show no inclination to see themselves as one group, part of the explanation for this must lie in the fact that the Nepalese state has strongly discouraged them from identifying themselves as Tibetans for obvious strategic reasons, just as it has discouraged the inhabitants of the Tarai from identifying with Hindi or India.

CHAPTER TWELVE

Tibetan Pride of Place: Or, Why Nepal's Bhotiyas are not an Ethnic Group

Charles Ramble

INTRODUCTION

The few years that have elapsed since the extinction of the Partyless Panchayat System have seen an intensified insistence on cultural distinctiveness on the part of a number of communities, a trend denounced by one commentator as "nascent ethnic egotism" (Bhandari, n.d.). The political orientation of these manifestations covers a considerable spectrum, ranging from exclusively cultural concerns at one end to the rhetoric of secessionism at the other. The appropriation of ethnicity for political ends is certainly nothing new in Nepal. As we shall see presently, the phenomenon has been observed, at various periods in the present century, among the Newars, Limbus, Rais, Tamangs, Magars, Gurungs, Tharus, and Maithils, to cite the most conspicuous examples.

Equally conspicuous is the absence from this list of the Bhotiyas, the indigenous Tibetan-speaking people of Nepal. There is, at present, no organization in Nepal claiming to represent the Bhotiyas as a single ethnic group. Nor indeed, I believe, is there any sentiment among the people in question that they constitute a distinguishable ethnic category. This is all the more surprising given that Lamaist civilization is so different from the dominant culture of the Nepalese state. Moreover, the latter has never made a secret of its contempt for the Bhotiyas, and its policies with regard to the high valleys have often been blatantly negligent. Why, then, have the Tibetan-speakers of northern Nepal never mobilized the fact of their common religion, language, and culture as the basis for an ethnic forum, much less used such a forum to articulate their discontent against the state? The following pages will attempt to answer this question.

It has often been observed that the national identity of Tibet was thickly suffused with the awareness of being Buddhist. From at least the thirteenth century on, religion was the distinctive idiom in which Tibet presented itself in its dealings with other nations. This is apparent in official statements, such as the following extract from a letter sent by the National Assembly to Chiang Kai-shek in 1946:

> Tibet remains the special fountainhead of the precious teachings of Buddha. China and all those who share this sacred tradition and who value it more than life itself should endeavour to promote and expand it ... There are many great nations on this earth who have achieved unprecedented wealth and might, but there is only one nation which is dedicated to the well-being of humanity in the world and that is the religious land of Tibet which cherishes a joint spiritual and temporal system (cited in Goldstein, 1989: 541–42).

Tibet was accustomed to formulating its position with regard to its neighbours in terms of the relationship between priest and patron (*mchod-yon*).[1] As the basis of a foreign policy the notion had worked well enough with the Mongols in the thirteenth century, and it continued to be effective down to the end of the Manchu Dynasty in the early twentieth. The fragility of this position first became apparent in dealings with the Chinese Nationalists, who were not, however, in a position to assail Tibet's *de facto* independence. The Communists, who succeeded them, could and did take full advantage of Tibetan weakness on this point.

Buddhism continues to be the main vector of nationalist, anti-Chinese sentiment, both in Tibet and among the diaspora community. One cannot help feeling, among younger Tibetans who have been educated abroad, that their adherence to Buddhism is motivated at least in part out of solidarity with the nationalist ideology. An admission of religious doubt implies an imperfect patriotism, and agnosticism is a political luxury a Tibetan patriot cannot afford.

However, there is evidence, particularly in the People's Republic of China, of the emergence of an apparently secular framework for the expression of Tibetan identity. The as appertaining to the indigenous culture: namely Bon – or rather 'Bon' – and the epic of Gesar. Unlike Buddhism, which is a foreign import, made in India, Bon is believed to come from Zhang-zhung, which was annexed to Tibet in the seventh century. The word Bon itself may be cognate with Bod, meaning Tibet (Stein, 1972: 31). Bon, as it is used here, has little to do with the Lamaist religion (or, as some prefer, sect) of that name, but seems to designate the entirety of folk belief and ritual. It is, in effect, a residual term to denote whatever is left when everything that is demonstrably Buddhist has been subtracted.

The official approval accorded to studies of Tibetan folklore is indicated by the number of publications in this field that have appeared in the PRC.[2] The approval that the field enjoys apparently stems from a feeling that a Tibetan identity constructed around folklore is potentially less conducive to 'splittist' tendencies than Buddhist faith and scholarship. Folklore studies also contain the potential for demonstrating that the Tibetans badly need the protection of the mother nation in facing the modern world:

> One reason for the shamanic belief of the nomads [of western Tibet] is the way in which people think. From their facial expressions and the excited way in which they talk about the stories of the sacred mountains and how seriously they believe the tales to be the truth, we can judge that they have the kind of psychology that takes illusion for reality. The sacrifices offered to the mountains also express the naivety and humour in the nation's characteristics (Ma Lihua, 1993: 197).

The Gesar epic, the quintessentially Tibetan tale of a Buddhist warrior-king that is still sung, and is continuing to grow, in all areas of Tibetan culture, has also benefitted from state approval, apparently on the grounds that it is fundamentally anti-Buddhist. The point is inevitably emphasized by certain scholars:

> Even though the epic of Gesar has been covered with the dust of history and of certain religious factors, especially of Buddhism ... a deeper study of Gesar and its origins has enabled us to unearth traces of Bon from its contents and forms of chanting .... The time of Gesar was the period (the Tubo [i.e. Yarlung] Dynasty) when Bon was at its highest peak (Yang En-hong, 1993: 440).

In a recent analysis of Tibetan nationalism, George Dreyfus suggests that an additional factor in the official encouragement of Gesar studies is the implied regionalism of the epic. Ling, the homeland of Gesar, is in Eastern Tibet, and the prevailing hostility between Eastern and Central Tibet (not to mention subdivisions within the latter) is something that the Chinese have exploited in the past (especially in 1950–51) to their considerable advantage. A myth that undermines the pan-Tibetan unity provided by Buddhism is clearly a major asset in the perpetuation of this policy (Dreyfus, 1994).

The quantity of published Gesar literature, cassettes, and posters that one sees in Tibet – particularly in the east – is a strong indication of official support for the promulgation of the epic. Samten Karmay adds the significant observation that, among the assorted Gesariana he has seen in Tibet in the past decade "the most glamorous printed poster was not of King Gesar but of his elder half brother, Gyatsha Zhalkar, whose mother is supposed to be Chinese" (Karmay, in press). But the mythic Ling of the Gesar epic is no more regarded by the majority of Tibetans as being in eastern Tibet than the New Jerusalem is understood by Christians to be in Israel. Under the circumstances, as Dreyfus (*op. cit.*) points out, Ling has come to be identified with the Tibetan nation as a whole.

Yang's assertion, cited above, that "the time of Gesar was the period (the Tubo Dynasty) when Bon was at its highest peak" is a further interesting example of myth-making. The first literary references to Gesar apparently date from no earlier than the sixteenth century, some six hundred years after the collapse of the dynasty, but the person of Gesar and his martial career have been conflated with those of the kings, principally Songtsen Gampo and Trisong Detsen, who built the Tibetan empire.

It is not difficult to see why such a conflation should be in the interest of both the official and nationalist positions. From the point of view of the former, the association with Gesar would tend to colour the 'kings of religion' (chos-rgyal) as pagan warlords with healthy Chinese connections and little time for Buddhism. For the great majority of Tibetans, however, it is impossible to dissociate Songtsen Gampo (d. 650) the empire-builder from the archetype of the promulgator of Buddhism. A. W. Macdonald has suggested that, whatever the historical religious proclivities of Songtsen Gampo, tradition associates him with the paradigm of Ashoka, in which territorial expansion and Buddhist diffusion were concomitant, if not synonymous, activities (Macdonald, 1987). Furthermore, however ambivalent a figure Gesar may be from the Buddhist point of view (cf. Dreyfus, 1994: 211), the Bonpos regard him as unequivocally hostile.[3]

Buddhism may have been the single most important unifying force in Tibet, but the theocratic framework that conveyed and claimed to represent it had no such universal support. The mythic complex of Songtsen Gampo and Gesar is in fact an evocation of the heroic age of Buddhism in Tibet: a golden epoch before the doctrine became tainted by its association with political intrigue and social injustice, and, above all, was still innocent of emasculating an invincible warrior tradition.

The sense of a common religion was radically opposed to the very strong divisive tendencies of regionalism. A particularly vivid illustration of the disjunction between religious and political interests in Tibet is provided by the Chinese invasion of the country in 1950. When the PLA arrived in Kham they were actively supported against Lhasa by sections of the laity as well as a number of major religious institutions:

> For Khamba villagers, it was difficult to see how great
> lamas and scholars such as these could support the Chinese

Communists if the Communists were really going to
destroy religion as the Tibetan government claimed ... The
motivations of the lamas and learned monks are difficult to
assess. Political expediency, belief in the Communists'
promised policy toward minorities, disenchantment with
the traditional system in Tibet, and enmity to Taktra [the
regent] and the Lhasa government all play a part. It is
reasonable to assume that none of these religious figures
ever dreamed that the Communists would totally destroy
the monastic system as they actually did during the years
following the Tibetan uprising in 1959 (Goldstein, 1989:
686–87).

In short, religion and locality were of greater importance to the
Khambas, and probably to Tibetans in general, than the integrity
of the state.

It would be possible to stretch the point and argue that
religious unity was actually *detrimental* to national sentiment. The
conventional representation of Tibet in Buddhist literature has
nothing in it of national pride: while India, the 'White Expanse'
(rGya-dkar), is the 'exalted' (*'phags-pa*) home of Buddhism, Tibet is
a barbarous (*mtha'-khob*), benighted (*mun-pa*) wilderness inhabited
by savage humans ignorant of Buddhism and ferocious demons
hostile to it (cf. Dreyfus, 1994). There is probably considerable truth
in the remark, made by the radical monk Gendun Choephel
(1905–51), that Buddhism was responsible for destroying the
Tibetan national identity (Stoddard, in press).

As Dreyfus points out, the figure of Songtsen Gampo, the
seventh-century unifier of Tibet, as a symbol of national unity has
become inseparable from the notion of the all-embracing Buddhist
faith. Not only is Songtsen Gampo regarded as the first 'religious
king' (*chos-rgyal*) of Tibet, but he is acknowledged as an incarnation
of Avalokiteshvara, and hence a precursor of the Dalai Lamas. And
yet there is evidence to suggest that Songtsen Gampo was once the
focus of a very different myth of Tibetan national unity. The earliest
Tibetan works revere the king as an incarnation of the mountains
of heaven, the ruler of an empire that gloried in its military power.
The patriotic rhetoric is strikingly different from the self-effacing

tone of later Buddhist works. A panegyric to the first ancestor of
the Yarlung dynasty runs as follows:

> Since his adoption of the earth as his land,
> 'O-lde spu-rgyal, the god-king with magical power
> ... has become the great king of Tibet.
> When he came from the sky-gods
> as the king of men, to the centre of the high
> snow-mountains, to the source of the mighty rivers,
> in this high country, this pure land,
> he founded a lasting empire
> (A.D. Macdonald, 1975: 341, in French).

Another passage, in praise of King Tride Tsugtsen (Khri lDe-gtsug-
brtsan) (704–755) extols the land of Tibet in similar terms:

> From the country of the gods,
> from the blue sky with seven stages,
> a son of the gods, a master of men
> came to Tibet,
> which has no parallel, no equal
> among all the lands of men,
> because it is a high country, a pure land
> (*ibid.*: 343–44).

Samten Karmay, who cites another early Tibetan hymn that
praises the country ("Tibet is high and its land is pure"), emphasizes
the incompatibility between Buddhist tenets and national pride:
"Nationalism requires will, self-assertion, self-identification and
self-determination and these notions have no place and receive no
respect in Buddhist education as we know it" (Karmay, in press). If
the Yarlung kings were symbols of national unity, it was not
originally by virtue of their services to Buddhism but because of
their association with the cult of mountains. Describing a ceremony
for a local mountain divinity in Amdo, Karmay suggests that
"participation in such a ritual ... implies being totally integrated
into the community, thereby inheriting social and political
obligations, moral and individual responsibility, and affirming

communal and national solidarity in the face of external aggression" (*ibid.*).

Cults of mountain gods are widespread through Tibet, but the following that they command varies from place to place. The sense of nationhood that prevailed during the period of the empire may perhaps be understood as a nation-wide extension of a local mountain cult: the king himself was a *cha* (Tb. *phywa*), a descendant of the mountains of heaven, and his clan divinity (*sku-bla*) was the mountain Yarlha Shampo in central Tibet (A. Macdonald, 1975: 346, 350, and *passim*). "Buddhism exerted no influence at all on the policy of the government of Tibet and had no place in the theory of power worked out for the Spu-rgyal dynasty" (*ibid.*: 349). On the contrary,

> The stability of the dynasty and the power of all the kings descended from 'O-lde spurgyal therefore derives from their identity with this god, their observance of religious practices – the cult of the *sku-bla* – and their application of the system of government that he brought to earth (*ibid.*: 342).

Karmay points out that "this is one of the reasons why the Tibetan national flag has an image of a snow mountain ..." (Karmay, in press).

This more archaic dimension to the Gesar-Songtsen Gampo myth may have considerable relevance for understanding the ethnic identity of Nepal's indigenous Tibetans, and we shall return to it presently.

THE HIMALAYAN REGION

The Tibetan-speaking peoples of the Himalaya are in a comparable position to their neighbours in the PRC, to the extent that they regard their ethnic distinctiveness as being menaced by more vigorous cultures pressing on their boundaries. The genuineness of this threat is not the subject of discussion here; the point is that it is felt to be real, and certain strategies have been devised in order to meet it. Before exploring the situation in Nepal, it is worth considering some of the manifestations of Tibetan ethnicity in neighbouring Himalayan areas.

Bhutan has recently been the focus of a certain amount of international attention because of the bitter conflict between its two main ethnic groups, the Tibetan-speaking Drukpas in the north and the Nepali-speaking Lhotshampas in the south. Bhutan is unique insofar as it is the only country in the world where the politically ascendant community comprises adherents of Lamaist Buddhism and speaks a Tibetan language. 'Drukpa', literally 'Bhutanese' gives a rather deceptive impression of unity: the name encompasses a number of Tibetan-speaking people apart from the politically dominant Ngalung, and helps to mask the considerable tensions between them.

In the early 1980s the growing Lhotshampa population came increasingly to be seen as a potential threat to the essentially Tibetan character of the country. The fate of Sikkim, which lost such limited independence as it had in 1975 precisely because of its large Nepali population, was as sharp a warning as any could wish for. The Bhutanese government consequently took steps to homogenize the country along 'Drukpa' lines, in an effort to offset the consolidation of Nepali ethnicity in the south. Nepali was removed from the school curriculum in 1985, the *gho* (for men) and *kira* (for women) became obligatory wear, and Dzongkha, the *lingua franca* of Western Bhutan, became the national language. The policy of integration, known as Driglam Namzhag, was not racist insofar as it sought to incorporate people of Nepalese provenance into the national melting pot, even offering pecuniary incentives for mixed marriages. The code received a cool reception among the Lhotshampas, who objected to the abuses which its enforcement often involved, as well as the threat it represented to Nepali ethnicity; and, not least, to its disastrous consequences for the Lhotshampa political agenda. The resistance that the policy encountered, and the sharp Drukpa response to this resistance, culminated in the exodus of some 88,000 Lhotshampas to seek shelter in the crowded refugee camps of eastern Nepal.[4]

The Tibetan-speaking people of Sikkim do not have the Bhutanese option of preserving their culture by encouraging the perceived threat to go away. The kingdom was independent until its annexation by India in 1975. A century ago, the population of Sikkim consisted almost entirely of Tibetan-speakers, Lepchas, and some long-established Limbus. From about 1875 onward there came the first waves of Nepalese immigrants, largely with British encouragement, and by 1890 these already outnumbered the indigenous people. By 1980, the proportion of the latter had been reduced to less than a quarter of the overall population. British land reforms, and later, the end of the Sikkimese monarchy, effectively put an end to the privileged position occupied by the twelve dominant Tibetan-speaking clans.

In a recent study of ethnic categories in Sikkim, Anna Balikci describes the strategies that have been adopted by the Sikkimese Bhutias[5] to confront the perceived threat to their identity. In broad terms, the procedure involves a weakening of ethnic partitions within the Tibetan-speaking population and the fortification of other, more distant boundaries that circumscribe a larger group. The group in question is more comprehensive than the composition of the "Bhutia" category that the government officially recognizes as a scheduled tribe. For example, the fact that the Tibetan language is itself less important a criterion than Buddhism permits the inclusion of groups such as Tamangs, Lepchas, and the Limbu Tsong (Balikci, n.d.).[6]

A number of devices are used to fortify the links between the groups that comprise the 'Himalayan Buddhists'. The history of the Sikkim, as it is taught to the children of this community, stresses the political harmony that prevailed when the land was administered equally by representatives of the Bhutias, the Lepchas, and the Limbus under the reign of the divine Chogyal. The decline of the nation is presented as being the result of a corrupt system of government introduced by the British and shored up by Nepalese labour. But the figure of the quintessentially Sikkimese Chogyal has limited significance for Himalayan Buddhists such as the Tamangs and more recent immigrants from Tibet. The icon that has been adopted as a symbol of unity among the Himalayan Buddhists is

Guru Rimpoche, who is not only universally revered by Nyingmapa Buddhists but also has a special connection with Sikkim. According to local tradition Guru Rimpoche visited the land on his way to Tibet and 'opened' it as a sacred sanctuary (*sbas-yul*). Finally, efforts are being made to strengthen the Buddhist tradition in Pemayangtse, a monastery that has important political associations deriving from its customary recruitment of monks only from the twelve ruling clans. The process is particularly interesting since it involves the resurrection of obsolete rituals and the invention of others that are justified on the grounds of their supposed antiquity.

In Bhutan, the significance of the state's role in defining cultural correctness was keenly noted by its critics. A pamphlet published by Lhotshampa opponents of the Bhutanese government condemns the official protection extended to Drukpa culture. If the latter is so fragile that it cannot survive in the presence of Nepali culture, then it is "not worth preserving" (cited in Dixit, 1992: 11). The Drukpas themselves use the image of the 'endangered species' to describe their own culture, but evidently neither they nor the Sikkimese Buddhists subscribe to the opinion that the resilience of cultures is best tested by abandonment to the forces of natural selection. It frequently happens that a culture under pressure produces a coterie that takes upon itself the responsibility of defending the threatened heritage. The custodians, having good reason to believe that the sustaining traditions will inevitably vanish in their natural habitat, adopt the measure of nurturing them in a safe, artificial environment. The traditions themselves are necessarily adapted to the new medium, and although, as Gellner observes, the product is exhibited as low, popular culture, it is in reality a high culture that may be only partially reconstituted from folk traditions (E. Gellner, 1983: 57).

The studied preservation of folk culture as an assertion of ethnicity is perhaps even more clearly apparent in Ladakh than it is in Sikkim and Bhutan. The institution primarily responsible for sustaining Ladakh's folk heritage is the Leh Cultural Academy, founded in 1969. Ladakhi scholars publish volumes of folksongs, folktales, and local history, and are periodically awarded honours for their services by the Academy. A radio station that opened in Leh in 1971 broadcasts plays, songs, and other aspects of official culture to the Ladakhis, and 1982 saw the inauguration of *Sheeraza*, a Ladakhi language quarterly. The Chinese crackdown on Tibet in 1959 ended the tradition of Ladakhi monks receiving higher education in Tibetan monasteries, but the continuity of religious training was assured by the establishment of a school of Buddhist philosophy in Leh in 1962.[7]

Not unexpectedly, there is a political dimension to this cultural assertiveness. Ladakh's agitation in 1985 for greater independence from Srinagar, the Muslim-controlled capital of Jammu and Kashmir, was led by the Ladakh Buddhist Association. At the time of writing, discussions are in progress concerning the possible designation of Ladakh as a Hill Council, a status that would entitle the region to considerable autonomy in planning and funding development projects (Malyon, 1993).

In spite of the differences in their particular circumstances, the four examples summarized above – Tibet, Bhutan, Sikkim, and Ladakh – contain certain similarities that may be formulated in terms of a single process. Each case presents a number of groups speaking a range of Tibetan or Tibeto-Burman languages (Ladakh, for example, is linguistically more homogeneous than Sikkim). Whether or not the groups in question are politically dominant (as in the case of Bhutan), they consider their ethnic identity to be threatened by the adjacent culture, be it Nepali, Muslim, or Han. In each case the putative threat has caused the groups to submerge the cultural distinctions within them and to present themselves as a single ethnic group. The consolidated identity is based on the emphasis, invention, or imposition of certain common denominators that circumscribe the composite group and mark it off from others.

NEPAL

On the face of things, the indigenous Tibetan speakers of Nepal are in the same position as the four groups discussed above. They comprise a Tibetan-speaking Lamaist group embedded in a wider society (the state itself) that is distinguished by a markedly different Hindu culture. However, far from compiling a manifesto of distinctive ethnicity to present to the rest of the kingdom, the population does not even have a common name. It is for this reason that, in speaking of them as a collectivity, we are obliged either to use language as a metonym for ethnicity ('Tibetan speakers') or adopt the Nepali term 'Bhotiya', which, as we shall see, is unsatisfactory for reasons even beyond its pejorative overtones. Since we must have recourse to names applied by outsiders, perhaps the most useful term is Höfer's "Tibetanid" which designates "groups being Lamaists or followers of the Bonpo religion and speaking a dialect closely related to High Tibetan" (1979: 43). The main disadvantage of the name is a certain awkwardness owing to its having acquired little currency in ethnographic literature.[8] Since we are concerned here with Nepal's Tibetanid people, it is worth reviewing briefly the Nepalese usage of the term Bhotiya, the approximate equivalent in the Nepali language.

Literally, a Bhotiya ('Bhote') is someone from Bhot. 'Bhot' in turn derives from the Tibetan word 'Bod', meaning Tibet, via the late Sanskrit 'Bhotaḥ' (Turner, 1931). In Nepal, 'Bhot' was tradi-tionally used not only of the Tibetan state but also of ethnically Tibetan areas that the Gorkha conquest had brought within the boundaries of the new kingdom. It is still used as a suffix to certain toponyms, as in Mustangbhot, Manangbhot, Charkabhot (Tsharka in Dolpo), and so forth.

As a number of authors have pointed out, an important feature of Nepal's caste system that distinguishes it from its Indian counterpart is the central location it accords to ethnic groups; Indian tribes, by contrast, have a marginal position. In the Muluki Ain of 1854, Nepal's ethnic groups are clustered mainly in the second and third of three 'pure' categories, below the wearers of the sacred thread and above the impure and untouchable castes. The Bhotiya fall in the third pure category, the enslavable alcohol-drinkers (*māsinya matwālī*) (Höfer, 1979:45).

The application of the term 'Bhotiya' is not limited to the Tibetanid people, but encompasses 'Tibetanoid' groups, primarily the Tamang and Thakali. Höfer adds the observation that "to my knowledge, some high caste speakers label even the Guruṅ as

Bhoṭe" (*ibid*.: 147 fn. 58). Not only is 'Bhotiya' decidedly vague as an ethnic category, it was also apparently used as a non-ethnic designation of legal status. Höfer cites a passage in the Muluki Ain to the effect that members of the 'non-enslavable alcohol-drinkers' (*namāsinya matwālī*) could be degraded to "enslavable Bhoṭyā" as a punishment for incest. Thus in addition to its specifically ethnic application "Bhoṭyā" was also "a sort of reservoir for degraded persons of various ethnic origin" (*ibid*.: 147).

The ethnographic literature on Nepal contains numerous examples of groups who have tried, with varying degrees of intensity and success, to distance themselves from the sobriquet of Bhotiya. The Thakalis have long claimed Thakuri origins (Fürer-Haimendorf, 1966a); a Nepali tract written in 1955 has it that the Gurungs were Rajputs who had lost their sacred thread (Höfer, 1979: 173). Tibetan documents relating to the origins of the rulers of Baragaon (southern Mustang) boast their descent from the Yarlung kings, whereas their present-day oral account shifts the point of departure to Jumla, thereby justifying their present name of Bista. The commoners of the same area, who used to put to 'Bhotiya/Bhote' after their given names on legal documents up to the second half of this century, are now officially known as Gurungs.

The change in nomenclature cannot be understood simply in terms of Sanskritization. Levine (1987), who cites numerous other instances of identity change among the Tibetanid groups, emphasizes that ostensibly 'Hinduized' communities may revert to being Tibetan in response to exigencies of kinship and economy. Even in the case of permanent identity changes, the goal is not necessarily the achievement of a superior caste designation. A reasonably well-documented instance of ethnogenesis in Nepal is provided by the case of the Tamangs, whose relations with the political and economic centres of Nepal are discussed in this volume. Although the name Tamang was certainly used by certain groups – notably in the Thak Khola – in quite early times,[9] it was only in 1932 that the name received recognition as the official designation of a number of groups who until then had been known as Murmi (or Murmibhotiya) and regarded as a variety of Bhotiya (Macdonald,

1983: 129). The legislation may have entitled the emergent Tamang no longer to use the name Bhotiya, but it seems not to have raised their legal status in any way. As Höfer remarks "it is striking that, according to the context the Tamang cease to be called Bhote but continue to be regarded as belonging to the Bhote" (1979: 147).

Höfer attributes the proto-Tamangs' insistence on a nominal distinction from the Bhotiya to their contact with Parbatiya castes, for whom the term Bhotiya even now evokes stock images of beef-eating, alcohol-drinking, and doubtful standards of personal purity. The adoption of the name Tamang is apparently not motivated by a desire to be raised into a superior caste group but rather represents an effort to be regarded as unequivocally Nepalese (cf. Holmberg, 1989: 30). A Bhotiya is someone from Bhot, and Bhot not only denotes the Tibetanid areas of Nepal, but also the polity of Tibet. Relations between Nepal and Tibet were often far from amicable, and indeed at the time of the promulgation of the Muluki Ain in 1854 the two countries were about to embark on a bloody two-year war.

The middle ranks of the Legal Code are made up principally of ethnic groups. This observation implies the syllogism that, in order for a collectivity to have a secure legal status in the Code there are considerable advantages in being recognized as a Nepalese ethnic group. An interesting case in point is the creation of the Chantel of Dhaulagiri. This group emerged only in the present century from an assortment of freed slaves, Bhotiyas, criminals who had been reduced in caste, products of incestuous liaisons and suchlike, who banded together to work the copper mines of Dhaulagiri in the nineteenth century. They have a shamanic tradition that owes much to that of the neighbouring Magars, and a corporate origin myth that has their ancestors stumbling upon some copper mines during the course of a deer-hunt. While the name of the group implies Thakuri antecedents (Chantel is the name of a Rajput clan), it is clear that the overriding priority is not acknowledgement by others of their high-caste status but an official recognition of their identity as a distinct ethnic group (de Sales, 1993; n.d.). In the context of Nepal, the Bhotiyas are not so much a distinguishable ethnic group as a sort of matrix from which ethnic groups crystallize, or whose members assume, for periods of varying duration, the names of Nepalese peoples.

A prerequisite of ethnic identity is consensus. Members of a collectivity must agree, whether voluntarily or under duress, that they are constituents of a given ethnic group, and should preferably have this distinctiveness recognized by others. There is little to suggest that the Tibetanid groups of Nepal conceive of themselves as a single group in any circumstances. There are approximately fifteen enclaves of Tibetan-speakers extending across the northern region of Nepal, from Limi in the west to Walung in the east (cf. Jest, 1975: 33–34). A summary description of what constitutes an 'enclave' in this case would include the following points: enclaves are geographically separated from one another by natural barriers, such as high mountains; they are largely endogamous units; each enclave speaks a different dialect of Tibetan which is not necessarily comprehensible to neighbouring enclaves. A number of other, less important features might be added, such as distinctions of dress, hair-style, architecture, and so forth.

The linguistic variations between these groups should not be underestimated. The variants of Tibetan that are spoken here are usually referred to by writers as dialects, but the differences between some of them are greater than those between certain European languages. The Scandinavian 'languages', for example, are mutually comprehensible; most of these Tibetan 'dialects' are not. The dialects of Khumbu and Lo are probably not much less different than, say, Italian and Spanish or Hindi and Nepali. Sherpas who visit Dolpo, Mustang, or Nubri, as they frequently do in the company of trekkers and mountaineers, communicate with the people of these areas in Nepali or, in the event that both parties have received some classical education, in the dialect of central Tibet.

It is also noticeable that the various groups tend to emphasize the differences between them, and, as commonly happens in cases where distinctions between communities are marked, the boundaries are often expressed in the idiom of purity. Thus people of areas X and points westwards are all abominable because they practise cross-cousin marriage; the inhabitants of Y drink the warm blood of slaughtered animals; if you wish to commit adultery with a woman of Z you have to go to her house (or tent) already naked or you'll never be rid of the fleas and lice afterwards; and so forth.

An important consequence of the geographical distribution of the enclaves is that they have very little indeed to do with one another. It is no exaggeration that Tibetans travel a great deal. But in Nepal, in the nature of their commercial enterprises they travel north or south, and only very rarely east or west. Broadly speaking, each group occupies the same niche on a given trade route between Tibet and the Nepalese middle hills, and there is little that can be profitably exchanged along a latitudinal axis. Villagers of Dolpo may visit Lo as wage labourers, and the Baragaonles used to cross the Thorang pass to help with Manang's harvest, but there is no reason to travel further than that. True, good horses may be purchased quite inexpensively in Tsum and Nubri, but the difficulties of the intervening trails means that they have to be brought back to Mustang via Tibet. People of Mustang and Manang do indeed collaborate in international trade, but their operations are coordinated in Kathmandu. The only people who seem to have spent much time on lateral journeys were religious figures whose biographies reveal them to have been inexhaustible travellers to monasteries and other places of sacred interest. The significance of this will become apparent presently. The insularity that distinguishes the Tibetanid enclaves will be examined in greater detail below, but some attention should be given first to the relationship between these areas and the Nepalese state.

As Martin Gaenszle points out in his contribution above (pp. 365–7), the ethnic organizations that have emerged in Nepal are motivated less by explicitly political considerations than by the desire to fortify a cultural identity. Whatever the degree of politicization these organizations exhibit, it is clear that they have coalesced in distinction to the dominant Parbatiya culture, with which they have rubbed shoulders for generations. Whether the opposition is articulated in terms of territorial dispossession by Bahun-Chetri settlers, as in the case of the Tharus, Rais, and Limbus, or concerns more general cultural oppression, which is where the stress seems to be laid by the Tamang, Magar, and Newar representatives, the point is that the groups in question have lived close enough to the Parbatiyas and the culture they represent to feel stifled or otherwise disadvantaged by them.

The Tibetanid groups have never lived close to orthodox Parbatiya culture, and the representatives of the state with whom they traditionally had dealings were not Bahun-Chetris. Nepalese policy for administering the Bhotiya areas minimized contact between the two cultures. In the majority of these areas the collection of taxes was the responsibility of local officials who either retained a measure of the power they had held prior to the unification, or were raised to these positions by the Kathmandu government. A few examples may serve to illustrate the point.

The King of Mustang, who had offered no resistance to the Gorkha army that passed through on its way to subjugate the sovereign kingdom of Jumla, retained his rule over the principality and administered it on behalf of the Nepalese state. In 1790, not long after the subjugation of Jumla, King Rana Bahadur Shah wrote to the King of Mustang, Wangyal Dorje:

> We hereby confirm your rule over the territories occupied by you from the time of your forefathers, adding thereto the territories situated north-east of Bandarphat, along with Bharbung-Khola, Tarap-Khola, Langu-Khola and Chharkagaun, which had been encroached upon and occupied by Jumla. We also confirm the customary payments which you have been collecting in Thak, Thini, Barhagaun, Manang, Nar, Nisyang and other areas. Jumla, when it occupied your country, used to forcibly collect the Chhyakpol tax from those who visited it for trade. We hereby grant you (authority to collect) this tax ... Be faithful to us, and comply with our orders. Rule over and enjoy your territories situated [within] the (prescribed) boundaries from generation to generation (Regmi, 1970: 99).

The nobles of Baragaon were later entrusted with the collection of taxes in Dolpo, and held this responsibility well into the present century. Latterly, legal authority over much of Mustang district was in the hands of the Thakali subbas, who had secured the right to collect taxes on the salt trade, and eclipsed the authority of the King of Mustang within his own realm (cf. Bista, 1971:57). Khumbu, Walung, and the Shingsa area of the upper Arun were ruled by local potentates known as *gowa*s (Tb. *'go-ba*) (Steinmann, 1988; 1992). Officials such as these were frequently zealous, not to say oppressive, in their collection of taxes and the imposition of their authority, and it sometimes happened that the state was obliged to intervene directly to curb their excesses. The principal reason for such intervention was probably to prevent the rulers concerned from developing sufficient confidence to secede from the kingdom; but to the eyes of the oppressed villagers concerned the state appeared as a kind of saviour (cf. Ortner, 1989: 99; Regmi, 1984: 33–42).

As was the case with other outlying areas, such as east Nepal (Kirat), Shah and Rana policy consisted in ensuring the loyalty of provincial elites by permitting them a reasonable degree of authority and only gradually assuming more direct control. Walung did not become part of Nepal until the Nepal-Tibet war of 1854–56. The time of Nubri and Kutang's incorporation into the state is also a matter of uncertainty. It was still apparently under Tibetan rule in 1810. "In practice, however, the area is so remote and inaccessible that for all intents and purposes its people always seem to have managed their own affairs independent of governments" (Aris, 1975: 62).

There are, in short, a number of critical impediments to the coalescence of a unified ethnic identity that the Nepalese Tibetanids might oppose to the Brahmanical culture of the state. There are considerable linguistic, as well as cultural, differences between the enclaves; for reasons of geography and economy there is effectively no direct communication between them; and the national culture is too remote to provide the stimulus for the reactive creation of an ethnic organization.

It may be mentioned that there are at least two organizations that have been created to represent Tibetanid groups. One is the Sherpa Sewa Kendra, and the other, created only in 1992, is the Lode Tshodun Baragaon Samiti, which represents the interests of the northern (Lode Tshodun) and southern (Baragaon) Tibetan-speaking areas of Mustang. Neither of these organizations is particularly concerned with fortifying the cultural identity of the people they represent; they are mutual-aid associations, comparable to the *kyiduk* (Tb. *skyid-sdug*) networks operating among the diaspora Tibetans, and they are intended to serve members of the respective communities who are resident in Kathmandu. The main point, however, is that neither of these groups can be construed as representing Nepal's Tibetan-speakers as a whole: their concerns are emphatically local.[10] Furthermore, whereas the organizations created by other ethnic groups tend to be left-wing in their political orientation, the Sherpa and Baragaon associations are, insofar as they are political at all, supporters of the government.

How, then, are we to understand the identity of Nepal's Tibetanid enclaves? It was suggested above that the single most important component of national identity in Tibet was, and still is, Buddhism, but that the unity provided by the sense of a common religion was opposed by a close attachment to a limited territory that found expression in cults of local gods. I believe that it is in terms of the cult of gods of place that the identity of Nepal's Tibetanid enclaves in modern times is best understood. The people of these regions are certainly Buddhist (or Bonpo) at least in name, but the influence of these religions has generally not been strong enough that it could shift people's primary allegiance away from an identity determined by locality to one based on more abstract religious ideals. In Tibet proper, and among the diaspora Tibetans, the most conspicuous boundary of collective identity is marked by the terms *nangba* (Tb. *nang-pa*), 'insider', and *chiba* (Tb. *phyi-pa*), 'outsider'. These are primarily religious designations, such that the first is often extended to members of any Buddhist country. In Mustang the similar terms *nangmi* (Tb. *nang-mi*) and *chimi* (*phyi-mi*) are frequently heard, but here they denote respectively someone who is a member of one's own *community* and someone who is not.

Place may have a very direct bearing on an individual's identity in an objective sense. The people of Baragaon are stratified into a number of ranked castes that enjoy certain privileges in function of their status. Caste is said to be patrilineally transmitted, and this is how the system seems to work on the surface of things. But in practice, heredity is always overridden by residence. For example, if a man of caste A marries uxorilocally into a village inhabited by people of caste B, the children he fathers in the village will belong to caste B (Ramble, 1984).

Some of the most important rituals performed in Nepal's northern borderlands concern the reaffirmation of community solidarity within a given territory. A ceremony that was performed annually in Kagbeni, in southern Mustang, involved the sacrifice of a yak to the territorial god (*pho-lha*). The carcass of the yak was divided so that every household received a portion of the meat. If a household was omitted from this distribution it was considered to have been temporarily suspended from membership of the village, and was exempted from civic duties. The actual sacrifice was performed by a priest, called the *aya*, from the nearby settlement of Marpha, but the organization of the ritual and the reconsecration of the shrine were the responsibility of the headmen (*rgan-pa*). As in a number of other villages in Mustang, the sacrificial component of the rite was brought to an end by the Shangpa Rimpoche about the middle of this century.[11] However, the annual sacrifice of a sheep to territorial divinities is still performed by at least four other villages north of Kagbeni. Diemberger has described a similar cult among the Khumbo of eastern Nepal, where the deity concerned is also seen as a focal point for the identity of the enclave (1993: 67–68).

The close association between mountain gods and local headmen has been emphasized by Philippe Sagant, who provides examples of sacrificial cults from Manang in Nepal, and from the Chumbi Valley, north of the Sikkimese border (Sagant, n.d.). As for Sikkim itself, in spite of the current efforts to organize a non-Nepali sector of the population defined in terms of Buddhism, the only real unity, as Balikci maintains, is found in the cult of Mt. Kanchenjunga (Balikci, n.d.).

I have suggested elsewhere that headmanship in the borderlands utilizes certain important symbols derived from notions of Tibetan royalty (Ramble, 1992–3). But kingship may provide the unity of an enclave in a more literal sense. The annual horse-racing festival of Baragaon unites representatives of the enclave's constituent castes in a dance around a spear representing the clan god of the local rulers, who are a branch of the royal family of Lo (Ramble, 1987). The seat of this god, A-bse mdung-dmar, who is revered primarily as the *sku-bla* of the Mustang kings, is a snow-capped mountain north-west of the city of Lo. There is little doubt that cults of place continue to play a central role in other Tibetan-speaking enclaves, but detailed ethnographic descriptions are lacking. Snellgrove, writing about the significance of territorial gods in Dolpo, states that

> Every village and monastery has its own local god ... They are conceived of as living in lordly style in palaces inside the mountains. They appear dressed in fine white clothes with turbans of coloured silk and jewelry of all kinds, sometimes riding on horseback with a large horse-borne following (Snellgrove, 1967: 15).

Recent research-by Guntram Hazod and Christian Schicklgruber reveals the importance of the relationship between dominant lineages and territorial divinities in Dolpo (Hazod, n.d.; Schicklgruber, n.d.).

Following the escalation of the conflict between Muslims and Buddhists in Ladakh in 1988, there appeared an article by the Ladakhi Muslim journalist Siddiq Wahid that placed the blame for the conflict squarely on the shoulders of Western writers. From the first missionaries, through colonial agents and down to modern scholars, ran the argument, the prevailing image of Ladakh has been culturally Tibetan. The conception of the area "was such that the idea of a Ladakhi Muslim was inadmissible in the Western conception of Tibetan civilization." The past two or three decades have seen the appearance of quantities of Western publications that reinforce this 'Tibetan' image of Ladakh, and in consequence of the 'bookfeeding' of the new generation with this literature,

> the Ladakhis learn about themselves from the English-literate specialist. Thus the Ladakhis learn to perceive themselves as 'unique' ... In point of fact, of course, Ladakh's culture is no more unique than any other: but

rapidly, this sense of uniqueness translates into the Ladakhi's fascination with his own quaintness. There are many aspects to this 'quaintness', but what concerns us is the one which permits the society to be perceived as exclusively Buddhist, no matter what the empirical evidence. What we are witnessing in the riots in Ladakh today is the assimilation of this aberrant perspective by its very victim ... (Wahid, 1989: 25).

In short, Ladakhi Buddhists are victims of intellectual colonialism perpetrated by Francke, Snellgrove, and others of that ilk. (One presumes that celebrated native promulgators of Ladakhi culture such as J. Gergan, S. S. Gergan, Thupstan Palden, Tashi Rabgias, and N. T. Shakspo are to be seen as imperialist lackeys or victims themselves.) The rhetoric is reminiscent of the Communists' announcements to the Tibetan government in 1950 that the PLA would soon arrive to liberate the country from its imperial oppressors, in spite of anxious Tibetan assurances that since there were no imperialists around they did not need to be liberated (cf. Goldstein, 1989: 765).

Wahid's article was criticized by a (Nepalese) writer who pointed to "the tendency among the Indian intelligentsia to blame the West for anything and everything that turns out to be bad", and dismissed Wahid as "just another scholar with a deep-rooted prejudice against the West" (Shrestha, 1989: 1). It is true that both the tone and content of Wahid's assessment suggest a certain partiality. But the possibility of Western influence in the 'Tibetanization' of Ladakh should not be dismissed out of hand. In a more temperate assessment of Bhutanese nationalism, Kanak Mani Dixit suggests that the consolidation of quasi-Tibetan Drukpa culture against the Nepali Lhotshampas is in some measure a response to Western (specifically, aid-donor countries') perception of the kingdom:

When learned *sahibs* keep reminding you of your uniqueness, sooner or later you begin to believe it ... In contrast [with Tibet and Nepal], Bhutan's postcard image has remained constant ... This incredible little country is ruled by a monarch who is modern, speaks chaste English, and yet is fervently in favour of maintaining cultural traditions. ... He is out to save Bhutanese culture, forests and a way of life. It is difficult not to support such a man and his programmes ... International acclaim has helped fuel Drukpa rejection of the Lhotshampas for their potential to ruin this idyll. The Druk Yul political chieftains took to heart the image that travel writers helped create in their coffee-table books. They decided to recreate the country in the image held by the West – culturally pure and ecologically pristine (Dixit, 1992: 15).

In this light, the origins of a few of Nepal's ethnic and cultural movements may be examined briefly.

One of the first Newar cultural organizations, the Institute of Nepalese Literature, was established in Calcutta in 1926. That the Institute should have been created outside Nepal is explained by the hostility of the Rana government to Newar nationalism. The creator of the movement, Dharma Aditya Dharmacharyya, was influenced primarily by Anagarika Dharmapala, a founder of the Maha Bodhi Society and the father of 'Protestant Buddhism' (D. N. Gellner, 1986: 129). The single most important figure in the formulation of Limbu (and, to some extent, Rai) ethnic identity, and the promulgation of the so-called 'Kiranti script', was Imansingh Chemjong, the Darjeeling-educated son of a Christian minister. As for the Magars, K.R. Adhikary refers to a pamphlet, issued by the Magar Langhalee Pariwar Association, that traces the origins of the organization. According to this document,

> The Langhalee was the product of the awareness of Magar ex-servicemen who returned to Nepal after losing many of their fellow villagers in World War II only to find their own Magar-villagers devasted with a sense of loss and low-esteem. They found that many of the Magar youths would timidly identify themselves as Magars if they had to, otherwise they would not like to reveal their Magar identity. This shocked the ex-servicemen and they collectively decided that they should do something to give

a boost to Magar self-esteem, and to uplift the Magar society in general (Adhikary, n.d.).

The Tamu Pye Lhu Sangh, which is concerned with the promotion of Gurung culture, was also established (in 1990) by ex-servicemen.

The aim of citing these examples is not to suggest that the groups in question are all victims of intellectual colonialism. The point I wish to make is that traditionalism is a very different matter from 'being traditional'; the former involves the selection of features of a culture that are regarded by the selectors as being especially traditional and emblematic of that culture, and presenting them in such a way that they will be easily recognizable to others. The selection requires that the person or group in question have a degree of detachment from the culture that makes it possible to decide what is, or can be made, distinctive about it with respect to other cultures. Traditionalism is, in a sense, the end of tradition. A great deal has been written about the matter since Weber first developed the distinction between the primordial condition and instrumental trends in society, but the opposition had already been succinctly expressed by Abu Hamid Al-Ghazali in the eleventh century:

> For anyone who has abandoned the traditional faith there is no hope of return, because the survival of tradition depends on our being unaware that we are upholding it.[12]

THE FUTURE OF BHOTIYA IDENTITY IN NEPAL

The Tibetanid enclaves of Nepal have for the most part been closed to tourism and, with a few exceptions, the foreigners who have visited them have stayed only briefly. There are two notable exceptions. Baragaon, in southern Mustang, which was opened to tourism in 1976, and Solu Khumbu, where the Sherpas have been hosting foreign mountaineers since a good deal earlier. It is true that these are the only two Tibetanid areas that have created representative bodies in Kathmandu. However, we should perhaps not make too much of this fact since, as stated earlier, these organizations are neither particularly political nor cultural in their orientation. External influences are certainly playing an important part in moulding the cultural identity of the borderlands, but the process is a complex one that deserves closer examination.

As we have seen, the identity of Nepal's Tibetanid groups is based very largely on their association with a limited territory. The relatively weak Buddhist tradition has only partly shifted villagers' focus from cults of place gods to the overarching concerns of high religion. This, combined with a lack of communication between the enclaves and the distance of Nepalese national culture that has been experienced at close quarters by other ethnic groups, has prevented the formation of a shared identity.

On the basis of observed trends, predictions concerning the future of the Tibetanid areas postulate three possible directions of evolution. First, the areas may become Westernized; secondly, they may become more 'Nepalified' and third, they may restore and consolidate their Tibetan Buddhist tradition. The three trends are regarded as mutually incompatible, and are variously celebrated or lamented according to the persuasion of the commentator.

An explanation that has acquired a certain vogue in the interpretation of cultural change among Nepalese highlanders is the notion of impression management. The idea is that members of a given group will present themselves as, say, orthodox Hindus or devout Tibetan Buddhists in order to gain acceptance and, ultimately, material profit, within the appropriate milieu. All the time, however, these chameleon traders retain a 'real' cultural identity which is kept hidden from observers. This identity is focused on some centripetal activity, such as the performance of certain tribal rituals that periodically take place in the people's heartland.

In fact, the validity of this assessment diminishes diachronically. It holds good only up to a point: namely, the duration of the generation that acquired its wealth and prestige through the judicious management of its public image. For members of the succeeding generation, who have been educated abroad and have barely lived in their ancestral territory, these rituals are less likely to be accepted as the core of an ethnic identity than regarded as an atavistic curiosity, worth filming. Apart from certain exceptions we shall come to presently, there is little indication that, if the Tibetanid groups have a secret identity, they have any interest in passing it on to their offspring. This is especially evident in the case of groups that have entered, or are entering, the mainstream of modern Nepal. Many of them give their children Nepali names, and speak to them in Nepali, and will sometimes claim, with undisguised pride, that these children can no longer speak their native language. When in Kathmandu they celebrate festivals such as Tihar and Dasain: more accurately, they do not celebrate them as religious occasions so much as mark them as national holidays with a certain amount of domestic festivity, mainly for the children.

Especially when they are in Kathmandu, members of groups such as the Baragaonles project themselves as modern, Westernized Nepalis. But no one in Nepal is merely Nepali. Everyone has a more specific designation pertaining to a recognized caste or ethnic group, and the Tibetanids have little inclination to present themselves as Bhotiyas who speak rude dialects and follow cults of obscure gods in remote places.

Traditionally, prosperity in the Tibetan areas has tended to be translated into patronage for Buddhist institutions. The heyday of religious art and architecture in Lo was the fifteenth century, when the region flourished under the rule of Agon Zangpo (A-mgon bzang-po) and Trashigon (bKra-shis-mgon) (Jackson, 1985: ix). The rise of monastic Buddhism among the Sherpas was a function of wealth generated by new avenues of trade in India at the turn of the century (Ortner, 1989). The Manangis, too, have dedicated a significant portion of their wealth to the construction of monasteries and the sponsorship of religious education. Paradoxically, Westernization among the Tibetanid people brings them closer to high Tibetan culture. In this environment they see themselves, and are seen, as members of the rustic periphery of a sophisticated society with fine manners and an elegant language. Their reaction is best understood as a Tibetan version of Sanskritization, in which the aspirants shed the stigmata of their provincialism and are gradually Tibetanized.

The process of Tibetanization receives substantial impetus from foreign sources. As members of the Tibetan religious community in exile are fond of observing, the new 'conversion field' (*'dul-zhing*) of Buddhism is the international sector, and considerable material support for Tibetan Buddhist institutions derives from patrons in countries such as Malaysia, Taiwan, and Japan, as well as Europe and North America. Patronage is not limited to the exile community but is increasingly extending to indigenous Tibetanid groups in the Himalaya. In the mid-1980s, for example, when the population of monks in Tengboche, in Khumbu, was reaching a critically low level,

> Substantial contributions from foreigners and increased receipts from tourist lodges owned by the monastery ... resulted in improved living facilities, which made the monastic life feasible for more monks than it had been when each monk had to be self-supporting (Fisher, 1990: 149).

Many foreigners tend to regard Nepal as a kind of Tibet manqué, where Buddhist culture is suppressed by interfering Hindu southerners. Bhutan, as we have seen, is perceived in a similar light. Dixit refers to a recent guide book on the country which

> has a single sentence on the Lhotshampas ... The rest of the book is on the Ngalung lifestyle and institutions, their Dzongs (forts), the western valleys, close-ups of monks and dashos, and whirling dancers. There is not one picture of a Lhotshampa, even in background (Dixit, 1992: 13–15).

Foreigners who visit the Tibetanid areas of Nepal frequently carry with them an image of Tibet, acquired from books or from encounters with Tibetan religious insititutions in India or overseas, that they project onto the Nepalese landscape: Muktinath, Mustang, and Dolpo are vestiges of a vanished Tibet. The peculiarities of local religion and culture have no place in the image, and consequently remain invisible.

One might have thought that the Nepalese government would be nervous about the Tibetanization of its northern borderland. This is, in fact, one of the more convincing reasons offered for the exclusion of foreigners from these areas. However, the regions where Tibetanization is occurring are of unimpeachable loyalty, and the process is congruent with Nepalese national interests. Manang, which for a long time benefitted from unrescinded tax concessions on international trade, was understandably a staunch supporter of the Panchayat regime (cf. Regmi Research Series vol. 15: 67–68). The Sherpas, too, whose prosperity derives in part from the cultivation of an image of independent-spirited Tibetan Buddhist highlanders, have established a healthy symbiotic relationship with the national government. The reopening of Tengboche monastery following its restoration after the 1989 conflagration was celebrated as an event of national importance, attended by the Prime Minister and other dignitaries. Furthermore, certain facets of Sherpa culture have been adopted by Nepal as respectably international images of the country. For example the Tibetan dress of Sherpa women has ceased to be "an object of scorn, from the Hindu point of view", and become

> high fashion – worn in the fashionable restaurants, hotels, and discotheques of Kathmandu, and on board Royal Nepal Airlines Corporation aircraft on international and domestic flights by women who would not have dreamed of wearing anything but a sari a few years before (Fisher, 1990: 140).

On the basis of responses to questionaires, Fisher draws the interesting conclusion that schoolchildren in Khumbu are more keenly aware than monks of equivalent age in Kathmandu that they are citizens of Nepal, and have correspondingly greater respect for national institutions (*ibid.*: 92–93).

It is a significant fact that the only forum in which representatives of the Tibetanid regions ever congregate is the Lama Sanskriti Bhraman, known in Tibetan as the Lama Tshokpa (Bla-ma tshogs-pa) or 'Lamas' Association'. This organization consists of fifty or sixty influential lamas from the borderland communities, organized in a number of groups under regional chairmen. Periodically the entire group gathers in Kathmandu to attend

FIGURE 39   *Lamas participating in the Lama Sanskriti Bhraman being*
lectured in Kwa Baha, Lalitpur, on how the Newars helped to
bring Buddhism to Tibet (David N. Gellner, August 1986).

conventions hosted by the government. The members hear speeches
assuring them of government commitment to the economic
development of the borderlands and support for Buddhist traditions,
and they are taken by bus to visit appropriate places, such as
Lumbini. The present chairman of the organization is the abbot of
Tengboche.

The organization cannot be accused of being merely a vehicle
for the dissemination of unsubstantiated government propaganda
in the borderlands. It earns support among the religious community
by complementing economic development programmes (construction of water mills, river training, electrification, and so on)
with cultural undertakings such as the restoration of monasteries.
As the border regions are progressively brought into contact with
the central government in the form of the official machinery that
accom panies tourism, development projects, and education, there
is no reason why monastic Buddhism should not benefit as a

consequence. Tibetanization, in its modern 'international' form, seems to suit the Tibetanid people very well: the image of the cultivated modern Tibetan is a great advance on that of the rural Bhotiya. Foreigners are keen to subsidize Tibetanization, and the government of Nepal has the politics of the situation well under control.[13]

In short, contrary to the common misconception, Nepalification, Tibetanization, and Westernization are entirely compatible processes. As always, it is the small god who is the loser.

CONCLUSION

The Nepalese category known as Bhotiya is not identical with, although it subsumes, the group we have been referring to as Tibetanid. As an ethnic term, Bhotiya has traditionally included various 'Tibetanoid' populations, and it has also been used as a non-ethnic legal designation. From among the Bhotiya there have emerged a number of populations claiming the status of distinctive ethnic groups, the most notable among them being the Tamang. The 'emergence' in question may have amounted to little more than the official recognition of a name, but, as Höfer remarks, the importance of an ethnonym should not be underestimated as an agent in the consolidation of group identity (1979: 149). Equally important is the fact that an ethnonym makes possible the fabrication of a group identity by an elite that decides what cultural features that name should evoke, and what its common political aspirations should be.[14]

There is a suggestion that conditions are appearing which might favour the development of a common ethnic identity among the Tibetanid groups themselves. Contact among the areas is increasing through the agency of government institutions and the spread of monastic Buddhism. Traditionally, identity was based on association with a given geographical area and articulated through territorial cults that were intimately linked to systems of local political organization. While this situation remains visible in much of the northern borderlands, the conditions for such ecocentrism have gradually been dismantled. The political relevance of local leaders was dramatically reduced by the implementation of a system of local representatives under the Panchayat Regime. The influence of Buddhist missionaries at various periods in the present century has further contributed to a weakening of territorial cults, especially in cases where their performance has been appropriated by the monastic community from the traditional specialists. For example, the Loyak ceremony of Kagbeni, described above, is now performed by Sakyapa monks who substitute a dough effigy of a yak for the real thing. The famous Mani Rimdu of the Sherpas is fundamentally a mountain cult that has been absorbed into a liturgical ritual, and the priestly traditions that sustained the worship of place gods such as Khumbi Yul-lha are being displaced by "the general twentieth-century movement in Khumbu toward a more orthodox, monastic, transcendental form of Buddhism" (Fisher, 1990: 159).

Nevertheless, it does not follow from this that the Tibetanid people of Nepal will gradually be forged into a single ethnic group. The spread of monastic Buddhism and the dissolution of the traditional criteria of regional identity are being opposed by mutant forms of regionalism. Territorial gods have a limited relevance outside their territory and away from the political framework that housed their cults, but other markers of distinctiveness can always be found if required. The Sherpas provide an interesting illustration of the way in which an enclave has espoused the respectability of monastic Buddhism at the expense of local cults and specialists, and yet has found ways to retain an advantageous insularity.

> Part of the reason for this tenacious cultural identity is the mutual admiration of Westerners and Sherpas ... Sherpas are so massively reinforced at every point for being Sherpas that they have every reason not only to 'stay' Sherpa but even to flaunt their Sherpahood. One might say that tourists pay Sherpas in part for being Sherpa, or at least for performing the role that accords with the popular image of Sherpas (Fisher 1990: 136–7).

It is surely significant in this regard that Tibetanids have only entered the Janajati Mahasangh (the Nepal Federation of Nationalities or NEFEN) as Sherpas, people of Hyolmo, etc., that is, precisely as 'ethnic groups' based on particular enclaves.

Since Nepal is still in the preliminary stages of an accelerating tendency to long-term or permanent migration to Kathmandu from the high mountains, it is still too early to offer a descriptive typology of the ways in which the Tibetanid enclaves retain their distinctiveness in a setting peopled by members of other enclaves, not to mention a wide range of other ethnic groups and castes. Nevertheless, it is certain that, if an enclave perceives any advantage in retaining a separate cultural identity it will find markers that are sufficiently conspicuous to be visible in a complex new environment.

NOTES

Research for this article was carried out in the course of a project funded by the Deutsche Forschungsgemeinschaft.

[1] The history of this and related terms, and the various applications of the concept, are discussed in Ruegg (1991).

[2] Buddhism, by contrast, is considered inappropriate as a subject for scholarly research. A recent survey of Masters degrees in Tibetan studies submitted in China between 1978 and 1989 shows that, of seventy-one theses submitted, more than half were concerned with classical textual studies. Two subjects were conspicuously absent, Buddhist studies, "a subject for which in China monasteries are considered the proper place" and social anthropology, "which is not taught the way it is outside China" (Wehrli, 1993: 427).

[3] For example, in the *gZi-brjid*, one of the main compilations of Bonpo mythology, Gesar is the commander of one of the three armies (the other two being led by Kong-rje dkar-po and Khyab-pa lag-ring) that unsuccessfully oppose the Bonpo hero, sTon-pa gShen-rab, during his Kongpo campaign (cf. Ramble, in press a).

[4] For a more detailed examination of the events leading up to the departure of the Lhotshampas, see Hutt, pp. 133–9 above.

[5] 'Bhutia', an Anglicized variant of 'Bhotiya', is the name conventionally used to designate the indigenous Tibetan-speaking people of Sikkim.

[6] I am indebted to Ms. Balikci for permitting me to read and refer to this unpublished work.

7 For a summary of Ladakhi cultural institutions, see Thupstan Palden (1990).

8 Goldstein had already coined the term 'Tibetanoid' for the group (1975: 68), but Höfer reserves this name for groups such as the Gurungs, Tamangs, and Thakalis (1979: 43 fn. 2).

9 For example, the *Gung-thang gdung-rabs* of Rig-'dzin Tshe-dbang nor-bu, written in the seventeenth century, refers to a group called the Tamang (Ta-mang) in the upper Kali Gandaki, and probably corresponding to the Thakalis. The name appears in the compound 'Ta mang se mon'. While Jackson (1978) takes this term to be a single ethnonym, there are grounds for supposing that it actually denotes three groups, the Tamang, the Se, and the Mon (Ramble, in press b). It is worth noting that Gurung origin myths replace the usual self-referent 'Tamu' (a name undoubtedly related to 'Tamang') with 'Se' (Strickland, 1982: 1–2), while variants of the term 'Se' are also sometimes applied to the Tamang. The significance of this sharing of ethnonyms is discussed in Ramble (in press b).

10 As it happens, a serious rift in the Lode Tshodun Baragaon Samiti has already developed, with the two regional components pursuing their respective interests at the expense of any pretence at unity.

11 Concerning this lama, see Snellgrove (1981: index, but especially 40–41).

12 The passage has been glossed from a French version cited as the epigraph to Stoddard's *Le Mendiant de l'Amdo* (1986): "Il n'y a aucun espoir, pour qui l'a délaissée, de retourner à la foi de la tradition, puisque la condition essentielle du maintien de la tradition est d'ignorer qu'on la détient." Dr. Stoddard informs me that she has been unable to trace the original source.

13 Interestingly, as members of this association have privately remarked, the favour of the government has cooled since the abolition of the Partyless Panchayat system in 1990. The chairman until that time, the 'Drukpa Lama', Tshechu Rimpoche, was entitled to an armed police escort. The present chairman, the Tengboche Lama, is not. Alterations to the way in which the association is included in its administrative framework also suggest a diminished official interest in maintaining the goodwill of the Bhotiya areas. The Lamas' Association is a function of the Monastery Management and Development Committee (Gumba Vyavastha tatha Vikas Samiti). As an integral part of the Remote Areas Development Committee (Durgam Chetra Vikas Samiti) within the Ministry of Local Development, the MMDC was not required to

compete for its annual allocation of funds. After 1990, however, it was detached from the RACD, and must now fight with representatives of other ethnic groups for a share of the funds allotted to Nepal's twenty-two officially remote districts. Although the overall budget of the DCVS rose from approximately forty to nearly sixty million rupees between 1992–93 and 1993–94, the MMDC's share of this fund has decreased since 1990. The subsidy for the periodical meetings of the Lamas' Association is also less generous than in the past. Whereas the figure was previously adequate to subsidize an event lasting up to twenty days, the duration of the conference now has shrunk to ten or eleven days.

[14] Not that there is always a consensus within the group about forms of cultural correctness. Among the Gurungs, for example, there is a lively debate about whether healing ceremonies and other rites performed by Gurung priests should, as purists insist, include animal sacrifice, or whether, as those who have been influenced by Buddhism maintain, all rites should be sacrifice-free. Concerning recent efforts to achieve a revised standard version of Gurung culture and history, see Macfarlane (chapter 5 above).

PART SIX

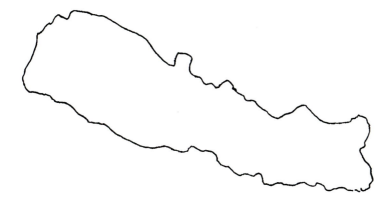

PART SIX

Conclusions

Is the outburst of ethnic revivalism since 1990 a natural and healthy phenomenon? Is it essentially superficial, a movement of intellectuals that is far removed from the concerns of ordinary people and will have little effect on them? Or is it dangerous and irresponsible, threatening the gains in political and economic development of preceding decades, as well as undermining national integration? Has a new pluralist and multi-cultural model of national integration emerged since 1990, and if so, how far should it go in legitimating and encouraging diversity? Is national integration a meaningful goal for ordinary Nepalis? Are Bahuns being scapegoated or are they at the root of the problems Nepal faces in the years ahead?

These are some of the questions any general diagnosis of Nepal's political and cultural future must face. Chapter 13 gives a detailed analysis of the evolution of Nepali ideas of national integration and the challenges they have faced and sketches the international context which influences Nepalese intellectuals in various far-reaching ways. Chapters 14 and 15 were independently composed by two differently situated, but equally highly respected Nepali scholars: they represent two of the possible Nepali responses to foreign analyses of the politics of contemporary Nepalese culture.

CHAPTER THIRTEEN

Vestiges and Visions: Cultural Change in the Process of Nation-Building in Nepal

Joanna Pfaff-Czarnecka

INTRODUCTION

The growing scholarly interest, as reflected in this volume, in processes of cultural change in contemporary Nepal mirrors the increasing concern among many Nepalis publicly to redefine their national identity and to establish how it relates to the cultures and traditions of ethnic minorities.[1] Recent events in cultural politics are closely interwoven with the political transformation that was marked, among other things, by the promulgation of a new constitution in November 1990. The new Nepalese Constitution does not merely shift sovereignty from the King to the people, re-introducing a multi-party parliamentary democracy. It declares the kingdom to be multi-ethnic and multi-lingual, which is a drastic departure from the governmental measures aimed at the homogenization of Nepalese society during the preceding decades.

The Nepalese citizens have presently taken upon themselves the fascinating task of rethinking the characteristics of their national society and accordingly of redefining their mutual rights and duties. However, such endeavours are also risky. As Prof. Prayag Raj Sharma recently warned: "Today, whether they fully realise it or not, those who would rule Nepal are weighted down by the responsibility of managing multi-ethnic, multi-linguistic and multi-tribal divisions" (1992: 7). Nor should it be assumed that the task of accommodating Nepal's varied cultures was easy in the preceding political epochs. Since the 'unification' of Nepal in 1769, its successive rulers and governments sought to cope with the unusual heterogeneity of the subjected peoples' cultural and political traditions while striving to rule and to forge Nepal's image according to shifting internal and external requirements.

This article seeks to explore the major efforts to accommodate Nepal's varied cultures in the course of three subsequent political epochs and to examine the related processes of cultural change. While discussing the first two (the Shah and Rana rule between 1769 and 1951 and the Panchayat 'democracy' between 1962 and 1990), it is especially intriguing to compare the different ways in which the state attempted to unify Nepalese society. In their efforts to centralize and to expand their polity, the Shah and Rana rulers created a Hindu state, combining diversity with hierarchical organization. In contrast, the Panchayat rulers sought to promote modernizing imperatives, among other things by advocating homogenization. In the third part of the article I turn to contemporary cultural politics in Nepal which are basically characterized by two interrelated processes. As exemplified in several articles in this volume, various members of minority groups seek to break away from former accommodative practices and to react to the cultural change induced by these measures. This involves internal reform processes as well as public action. Consequently, the very fact that ethnicity issues enter the public arena is an important indicator of the substantial changes in Nepalese society that need to be explored.

Cultural change, whether consisting in assimilation to a new, dominant culture or revitalization of one's own old one, or in a combination of both, relates to social dynamics at four different levels (see Brass, 1985). First, within the ethnic groups themselves struggles occur over their material and symbolic resources. This does not only involve defining the group's boundaries and its rules for inclusion and exclusion; struggles may occur over defining a proper public image of a given culture as well as over establishing who is in charge of defining and promoting a specific image of an ethnic minority group.[2] The second level pertains to the inter-ethnic competition for rights, privileges, and resources, where, among other things, culture can become a 'political currency'. Thirdly, struggles occur "between the state and the groups that dominate it, on the one hand, and the populations that inhabit its territory" (Brass, 1985: 1) when attempts to participate in the state's resources and the decision-making process are counterbalanced by the state that seeks to maintain and to extend its control. Finally, ethnic representations are increasingly being geared to promote images not only in the national context but also to 'fit' into valid international models ... or publicly to resist them.

I shall turn to the emerging Nepalese public sphere where visions, grievances, and conflicts at all four social levels are being carried to the open and where they are negotiated while discussing the contemporary processes of cultural politics. Let me first concentrate on the state's shifting attitudes towards its ethnically diverse subjects since 1769.

Despite Nepal's relative remoteness from centres where the modern ideas of nation-state and nationalism were formed, the country's politics and ideological patterns have been increasingly influenced by the related Western notions, as analysed by Burghart (1984). With its distinct cultural traditions and specific geo-political situation Nepal provides an interesting example of the process of forging a nation. As in other parts of the world, Nepal's notions of national identity, as promoted by successive rulers/governments have differed in the course of history. Obviously, nations are historical products. Over time, historical conditions change and so do the cultural contexts within which social constructions are based. As Giesen (1991: 12) argues, different kinds of national identity have been propagated by successive leaders,[3] who attempted to orient themselves, among other things, to shifting cultural traditions. For the Nepalese case I propose to distinguish three different models of national integration.

A. THE 'EMPIRE MODEL': The first model relates to what is usually known as the period of Shah and Rana rule. The beginning of this period is marked by the forceful 'unification' of Nepal, when about 60 former political units were combined to form one polity under the sword of the Shah rulers, themselves forced by the Ranas to give up their *de facto* power in 1846. Until the overthrow of the Rana autocracy in 1951, the Gorkha Kingdom was undergoing a continuous process of unification and consolidation.

These changing structural conditions called for an adequate symbolic expression. The overall conditions during this period lie in specific exigencies of hierarchically ordered monarchies with an agrarian base where autocratic rule does not presuppose popular consent (in contrast to the notion of the people's sovereignty in democratic systems). As indicated by Ernest Gellner, in agrarian societies "the state is interested in extracting taxes, maintaining the peace, and not much else, and has no interest in promoting lateral communication between its subject communities" (1983: 10). Even when they attempt to define an ideological national framework, the ruling groups are simultaneously interested in displaying differences: "Among the higher strata of agro-literate society it is clearly advantageous to stress, sharpen and accentuate the diacritical, differential, and monopolizable traits of the privileged groups" (*ibid.*: 11). Hence, the first model resembles the pluralism of the Byzantine Empire, with a high degree of structural differentiation against the background of a unifying socio-political framework with differing social functions attributed to hierarchically differentiated strata (Eisenstadt, 1991). After the 'unification', the Nepalese rulers created a representative public domain (a term introduced by Habermas, 1962: 60f.) where they sought to display their status, power, and grandeur *in front of their subjects*.[4] Rather than enforcing Hinduization, they linked specific cultural elements to political power and created a ritual framework, a hierarchically differentiated Hindu Kingdom, within which aspirants to powerful positions could orient themselves (Pfaff-Czarnecka, 1989).

B. THE NATIONALISTIC MODEL: The second model refers to the period between 1962 and 1990 when the Panchayat system of a "guided democracy" was established. With the Nepalese Kings of this period holding *de facto* power over the executive, judicial, and legislative bodies, as well as the army, Nepalese politics was characterized by a high degree of power concentration. Among the major imperatives as expressed by the rulers was the creation of a societal framework suitable for ensuring economic development. In this endeavour, national unity was presented as an indispensible means for effecting societal communication and new value orientations geared towards progress. In this quest, ideas of the

German Romantic period, especially the idea that the nation is, among other things, a project to be made complete through conscious cultural measures, are combined with imperatives of modernization theory, such as the search for progressive cultural attitudes (e.g. Huntington, 1967). Cultural production is no longer merely a process of being nationally self-aware, but a means of creating, describing, and asserting the identity of a given society (Giesen, 1991: 12). The Panchayat era is characterized by the rulers' claims to national homogeneity under the aegis of the cultural traits of those in power, i.e. of high-caste Parbatiya Hindus. Especially towards the end of the Panchayat era, many members of minority groups reacted strongly to what they saw as enforced assimilation.

C. THE 'PATCHWORK OF MINORITIES' MODEL: The third model pertains to the very recent democratization process characterized by the institutional enforcement of numerous civic rights, and especially by vesting sovereignty in the people rather than in the King. The 1990 Movement, carried through by various social forces, has given an enormous impetus to minority demands: minorities may now operate freely in the public sphere. The question of national identity and the process of its redefinition is an intrinsic element (and cannot be avoided) in the quest for participation in policy-making and in the distribution of national welfare resources. Besides relating to the institutions of the state, cultural processes relate also to actions through associations which are free of state tutelage (Taylor, 1990: 98) as well as to international cultural flows (e.g. new development imperatives that stress elements of minority groups' community ethos as a development resource). With increasing social complexity, minorities, more often than not confined to social peripheries, threaten the national unity envisaged and enforced by central measures. The more minority groups come into being (ethnic, regional, linguistic minorities constituting just some of the emerging patchwork of minorities – see Lyotard, 1977), the more complicated the task of central administration becomes. The major idea in 'thinking' the nation is no longer a common culture but rather mutual recognition and the recognition of difference.

The following discussion of processes of nation-building and ethnicity formation is organized 'around' four *leitmotifs* or major areas of investigation.

1. Processes of nation-building and of ethnicity formation are to be examined within the shifting international framework. Besides market forces and political strategies, international cultural flows affect national cultural politics. Legitimatory endeavours of those in power may be addressed to international patrons or allies, such as the British rulers during the Rana period; international aid institutions, including the World Bank (with their shifting policies and underlying value orientations); the Indian Congress, social-democratic parties and liberal associations in the West, and various Communist Parties in India and China for the past decades.

2. Legitimacy patterns that relate values to power relations change considerably. In the first place, they pertain to the changing legal-political systems with their specific patterns of dominance; furthermore they vary according to the specific requirements of different patterns of production (agrarian vs. industrial societies). Forms of publicity change with new technological tools and according to the exigencies of capital formation. The public character of legitimizing measures depends upon the source of sovereignty; in civic societies, forms of publicity correspond to discursive modes that condition the formation of political opinion, legitimacy of protest, and participation. Additionally, in the context of 'developmental' value orientations have implications for the extent to which states are allowed to act as preceptors towards societies.

3. Ethnic tensions in the processes of nation-building also relate to the ways through which centres and peripheries are linked to each other and/or how centrally governed societies increasingly establish poly- (or hetero-) centric structures (e.g. by-passing the state in attempting to solve societal problems). In the Nepalese context, centre-periphery links relate to processes of minority formation in manifold ways, especially to the ways in which the centre dominates peripheries (force, legal provisions, cultural dominance); how the dominance of the centre over peripheries is

legitimized; how peripheries can withdraw from the grip of the centre and/or how they can counteract central measures.

4. Nation-building and minority formation depend to a large degree upon individual action of national and local elites who act, among other things, as cultural brokers. As indicated by Brass (1976), minority formation and minority competition especially affect those groups that either contain threatened traditional elites or groups that benefit by modernization and industrialization sufficiently to produce an educated intelligentsia or an entrepreneurial class in a position to compete for prestige and economic advantage.

NATIONAL IDENTITY AND ETHNIC PROCESSES DURING THE SHAH (1768–1846) AND THE RANA ERAS (1846–1951)

But if anyone is alert, this will be a true Hindustan of the four jats, greater and lesser, with the thirty-six classes. Do not leave your ancient religion. Don't forsake the salt of the king (Prithvi Narayan Shah, *Dibya Upadesh*, 1968: 44).

The integration model, as established under the Shahs and later under the Ranas, differs from the 'bourgeois' models of nation-building emerging during the same period in the Western world in one fundamental respect: under the Shahs and the Ranas sovereignty remained *de jure* with the King, and *de facto* with powerful individuals and factions able to manipulate and/or represent the monarch. From the point of view of the rulers, the plurality of Nepalese society was conceived of within a uniform sociopolitical framework: diverse castes and ethnic categories were incorporated into a holistic framework of a 'national caste hierarchy' (Höfer, 1979). The diversity has been translated into inequality: positions were increasingly ascribed to different ranks that corresponded with caste/ethnic divisions (Pfaff-Czarnecka, 1989: 37–109). Rather than seeking to establish a national unity through a vision of a culturally homogeneous population, the rulers sought to define a national identity which allowed for cultural variation but which had Hinduism as its major pillar. They then sought to present themselves as being at the focus of the political and of the ritual order (Burghart, 1984). The two major elements in this process of identity formation were the premodern form of patriotism expressed via loyalty to the King (being true to the salt of the King) as well as the prominence of the Hindu religion. The subjects, as opposed to 'citizens', were not asked to participate in processes of national identity formation. The principle of *cuius regio eius religio* was realized not so much through proselytizing measures (on the limitations of such measures see Michaels, chapter 2)[5] as by declaring Nepal to be the last pure Hindu kingdom – notwithstanding the differing religious and cultural orientations of the subjects. By establishing themselves at the apex of the Hindu hierarchy, the rulers could accentuate their superiority over their political clients and opponents and ally themselves, for instance through marriages, with high-status families outside the kingdom. As members of ethnic groups were increasingly relegated to the societal periphery and denied a voice, the high-caste Hindu rulers could promote their own vision of the Gorkha kingdom.

By consolidating their political and economic power, the dominant Hindu elites in the centre were creating a specific idelogical framework which linked prestige to high-caste Hindu status. In the course of the nineteenth century, the Hindu rulers in Nepal enforced various changes upon the Nepalese population by increasingly ascribing duties and privileges (see below) according to rank, and by promoting the transfer of land rights to those of high caste. The desire to improve one's status within the Hindu hierarchy resulted from local elites' endeavours to attain a higher social position. Hence, processes of Hinduization among the minority groups of Nepal are in the first place to be attributed to central elites' efforts to concentrate their dominion in peripheries on the one hand, and to legitimatory measures of local powerholders on the other. Within the framework of the emerging Hindu polity, ethnic populations, notably ethnic elites, responded with the adoption of specific cultural symbols of those in power.

It is of course dangerous to treat almost 200 years of Nepalese history, that is the Shah and the Rana era, as a single historical period. Several processes initiated by the Shah Kings were only completed (or just continued) under the Ranas, as for example the extension of the centre's effective political control over remote areas, the centralization of the taxation system, and the rationalization of the land-tenure and taxation systems. Unlike the Shahs, the Ranas always maintained friendship with the British rulers of India, even if this was sometimes precarious. It was under British influence that the Prime Ministers were exposed to Western ideas and institutions. The promulgation of the first Nepalese Legal Code (Muluki Ain) in 1854 was at least partly inspired by the Western emphasis on codification, even though in terms of content the code was largely based upon the major Hindu/Indian texts and upon existing Nepalese practice.[6] In general however, the main features of the social process – in terms of absolute rule, ascribed status, forms of central dominance over the periphery, and legitimacy patterns – did not change significantly during the entire period.

In the middle of the eighteenth century, the principality of Gorkha had begun a military expansion which resulted in uniting some 60 political units within the present Nepalese borders. This expansion came to an end in 1816 with the defeat by the British East India Company, whose victories in north India coincided with the 'unification' of the Gorkhali state. The Gorkhas lost the territory they had conquered in Sikkim, Kumaon, and Garhwal and, subsequently, the British presence on Nepal's western, southern, and eastern borders (with Tibet to the north) seriously affected Nepalese politics. The British presence meant that expansionism was not a practical option for Nepal. With the boundaries fixed, the Gorkha elites did not have any other choice but to expand their economic resource base within the realm, with the large standing army (which was not reduced after the defeat of 1816) playing an important role in the subsequent process of administrative consolidation.

The 'unification' and the subsequent factional struggles among the political elites (that is, high-caste landowning families, partly with marital ties to the royal family) reinforced legitimatory endeavours.[7] The Shah kings of Gorkha were by no means considered superior to other princely houses whom they had defeated and the same was the case with their political clients. When the Ranas came to power, they also were forced to elevate their own status, since initially they belonged to a minor Chetri (Kshatriya) family. In this process, the assistance of the Brahmans was indispensable, as a consequence of which Brahman interests could never be ignored.

Of course, political changes were not confined to the centre. With the on-going consolidation of the administrative system (including the stationing of military units throughout the country) local elites in remoter parts of Nepal were increasingly drawn into the centralizing process. The centralization of Nepal was seriously hampered by the difficulties of the terrain with, for example, transport and communication from the capital to the far western regions of Nepal taking 40 days in relays for letters carried by runners. Still, despite such barriers, the nineteenth century was characterized by widespread migration in the course of which Hindus moved into tribal areas. Their movements were at least partly due to the centralization process: on the one hand escaping the increasingly tight grip of the central elites, and on the other, seeking to acquire land by clearing forests in areas inhabited by different ethnic groups. Local ethnic societies apparently welcomed the migrants, assuming that their presence was only temporary. Some of the groups appear to have hoped that whatever tax duties there were, the new settlers would help to share the burden. Another reason was to acquire the settlers' skills. Apparently the 'ethnic' hosts did not anticipate that the Hindu settlers had allies among the central elites. This was the case however: as a result, the state was able gradually to turn lowly-taxed tribal lands into state lands, or clear new lands, the revenue from which enriched the state treasury.

While the centralization of the Nepalese state was causing people to migrate (Pfaff-Czarnecka, 1991),[8] the settlement of Hindus in tribal areas was certainly an important factor facilitating centralization. Economically, more land could be put under state taxation; politically, the high-caste Hindus were gradually attaining dominance over the tribal populations and even partly over the tribal leaders, or at least threatening their dominance – an aspect which most probably was to the central elites' liking since *divide-et-impera* tactics appear not to have been alien to them.

To some extent, cultural change was rooted in the political struggles among local elites. In the case of ethnic communities, these local leaders were members of founding lineages, with specific political and partly ritual prerogatives, and in the case of Hindus they were high-caste people with large landholdings. Both Hindu and ethnic elites had networks linking them beyond the local context. In view of the central rulers' status as high-caste Hindus, some ethnic local elites striving to be their clients appear to have seen an advantage in publicly displaying some elements of the Hindu culture valued by those rulers.[9] This strategy was all the more necessary as their major political rivals were Hindus. However, there is another process to be considered, which, although it did not always take place, did occur in the case of some Rai groups described by English (1982) and by Gaenszle (1986), the Limbus described by Sagant (1976) and by Jones (1976), and the Thakalis described by Manzardo (1978). During the time of political and administrative consolidation in Nepal, several ethnic groups appear to have undergone a process of social differentiation with some local families, usually ranking high within clan hierarchies, emerging as more affluent and more powerful than the rest of their societies. In the course of this process, displaying elements of Hindu culture in order to create a social distance from 'those below' seems to have been a successful measure. Ethnic elites' endeavours to elevate their status or to split into hierarchically ordered groups have frequently been reported.[10] These processes were also encouraged by occupational changes occasioned by the adoption of new agricultural practices (see Allen, p.305ff.). By turning to irrigated agriculture on terraced lands, former pastoralists and swidden cultivators had to learn from the high-caste Hindus (adopting – among other things – the hierarchized exchanges with low-caste specialists, indispensable in the process of agricultural production).[11] Displaying, and possibly adopting, elements of Hindu culture can be further explained by the wish to acquire the control of supernatural forces which their rituals appeared to give those who were more successful. Finally, as Gaenszle suggests (above, p.362), they may have wished to redefine their identity in terms of a new and more 'universal' symbolism.

The Nepalese rulers reinforced such ongoing struggles by strengthening the links between duties and privileges and hierarchical rank. In the first place, there is some evidence that in the course of the consolidation period members of some ethnic groups lost their prerogatives. While, for instance, in Gorkha before 'unification' there were Magars among the six ruling houses (Riccardi, 1977) and Magars and Gurungs were found among the ruling elite until the opening years of the nineteenth century, elite membership was afterwards reserved for the twice-born Parbatiyas with those members who were actually of ethnic minority descent having to conceal their origins. Furthermore, while all ethnic groups could be enslaved in the first half of the nineteenth century (Hamilton, 1819: 234; Höfer, 1979: 124), this could not (or could no longer) be done to the high-caste Hindus. It was only in the course of the nineteenth century (second half) that first the Magars and Gurungs and then the other minority ethnic groups were freed from liability to the penalty of enslavement. Some documents exist which suggest that only those ethnic groups which were free from enslavement could, for instance, enroll into the well-paying British Gurkhas. Similarly in the first half of the nineteenth century high-caste people, starting with Brahmans, gradually became exempt from unpaid labour, such as military service in the national army (see RRS, 18: 143; RRS, 5: 140; Regmi, 1972: 104).

Against this complex background of various changes instigated by the emergence and consolidation of the Nepalese state, I hope to have indicated some reasons why ethnic minorities oriented themselves towards Hinduism or to symbols displayed by the Hindus.[12] Interestingly, there is also some evidence that in the course of the nineteenth century, high-caste Hindu groups themselves abandoned some of the local customs which were contrary to north Indian Hindu rules[13] (e.g. cross-cousin marriages among Jaisi Brahmans).[14] In the year 1761 Prithvi Narayan Shah forbade the Jaisi Brahmans to conduct Vedic rituals (RRS, 2: 278ff.).

FIGURE 40   *Bajhang, far west Nepal, 1990: The high-caste, twice-born*
dhāmī *of Bhate Khola, one of the two main* dhāmīs *connected to
the Bajhangi princely family. In Bajhang* dhāmīs *are both oracles
and mediums believed to be possessed by the major local god, Lango.
Many* dhāmīs *were killed by the Shahs after 1769, even though
Bajhang was a semi-autonomous principality; this example of the
state's interference in customary practice is still today an important
part of local lore* (Joanna Pfaff-Czarnecka)

M.C. Regmi has documented the ban on high-caste Hindus performing levirate marriages (which are nowadays shunned).[15]

As members of minority groups struggled for political positions, lost land to new settlers, were impressed by rituals of the powerful and the skillful, turned to new forms of livelihood, or simply came into contact with other peoples, various cultural processes were coming into being. The extensive ethnographic literature provides numerous instances of minority groups displaying or adopting elements of Hindu practice.[16] For example: worshipping Hindu deities[17] and performing sacrifices;[18] associating local gods with those from the Hindu pantheon; including Hindu elements alongside local ones; sponsoring Hindu rituals such as the Satya Narayan Puja, which is often performed in the Nepalese hills as a purification rite, for instance before a *bartaman* ritual; pilgrimages to Hindu holy places; including Hindu gods among lineage deities (for the Chepang, see Jest, 1966); accepting the Hindu hierarchy (that is deferential behaviour towards those accepted as higher);[19] adding Hindu elements to original myths (including Hindu holy places);[20] reforming the tribal hierarchy with some clans striving to emerge as ritually higher than others; adopting rites of passage performed by Brahman priests; employing low-caste specialists on a *bali* basis (this being also dictated by economic changes, e.g. with blacksmiths being indispensable for agriculturalists); reorganizing hierarchical relations within the family; adapting marriage prescriptions according to local Hindu norms.

THE PANCHAYAT ERA

The state-enforced homogeneity is the practice of nationalist ideology. In Boyd C. Schafer's (1955: 121) witty comment, "patriots had to be made. Nature was credited with much by the eighteenth century, but it could not be trusted to develop men unassisted." Nationalism was a programme of social engineering, and the national state was to be its factory. National state [sic] was cast from the start in the role of a collective gardener, set about the task of cultivating sentiments and skills otherwise unlikely to grow. In his addresses of 1806 Fichte wrote "If you want to influence him at all, you must do more than merely talk to him; you must fashion him, and fashion him, and fashion him in such a way that he simply cannot will otherwise than you wish him to will" (Bauman, 1990: 154).

To put it crudely, by dividing their subjects into castes, the pre-1951 rulers united large sections of the Nepalese population under the aegis of a Hindu ritual framework, thus allowing for diversity. After the overthrow of the Ranas in 1951, the Shah monarchs, now again in full power, by striving to establish a peculiar political form, the so-called Panchayat democracy, instigated divisive tendencies among the Nepalese precisely by proclaiming their unity as one nation sharing a common culture.[21] Beyond the process of establishing national identity in a changing geopolitical environment, the requirements of modernization, as understood worldwide during the 1960s and '70s, called for national unity, among other things in the sense of sharing one culture.[22] Thus, the Panchayat government adopted an assimilation policy,[23] insisting upon creating a homogeneous 'development' society.[24]

After 1951, when King Tribhuvan emerged as a 'hero of the revolution', the Nepalese political outlook changed considerably. With the Nepalese king dominating the legislative, judicial, and executive bodies as well as the army, Nepal entered a very specific democratization process. Its main elements – as gradually became clear – were the following: equality of all citizens under the constitution (though the caste system was not explicitly abolished: see Höfer, 1979: 203f.); the political process was constituted through popular elections (partly indirect); a uniform administrative system was established throughout the country (abolishing of the *rājya*, autonomous principalities within the realm); Nepalese borders were opened to outside influences (especially to foreign aid); and, last but not least, a new idea of the Nepalese nation was forged, with the former subjects now turned into citizens. Cultural unity was perceived as a means of value integration

FIGURE 41   *Schoolchildren sing the national anthem in celebration of King Mahendra's birthday (Belkot, Nuwakot district, 1979) (Joanna Pfaff-Czarnecka)*

and a means of communication that was indispensable within the development process. Any claim to ethnic identity was reduced to political subversion. Nepal's delicate geopolitical position may explain some of the fears.[25]

With the monarch and the majority of top officials being high-caste Hindus, the emerging distinctive national characteristics (Nepali language, Nepalese dress, Hinduism as the state religion) were those of the dominant groups. In official rhetoric the Nepalese nation was now presented as made up of equal citizens sharing a common culture, that is, 'sharing' cultural elements of the reigning Parbatiya Hindus (Burghart, 1984). Hence, equality was proclaimed but apparently it could only be achieved by suppressing differences. In striving to promote cultural unity as a means of political control, the government now had forceful tools at its disposal: road and air transport; telecommunications; mass media, especially the radio; and an education system and an administrative system in which only the Nepali language could be employed.

FIGURE 42   *A schoolboy worshipping the national flag and pictures of the King and Queen (Belkot, Nuwakot district, 1979) (Joanna Pfaff-Czarnecka)*

During the Panchayat period, the cultural language of the dominant Hindu groups emerged as the *language of modernization*. Since the high-caste elites were able to establish themselves as brokers between international allies/donors and Nepalese society, they could claim that 'their' cultural symbols and means of expression were a successful means of progress in the national context. This rhetoric of modernization encapsulated the dualism thesis, namely the idea that peripheral societies are divided into two sectors: a dynamic 'modern' sector which seeks and achieves integration within the global (economic) system; and a second 'traditional' and stagnating sector, devoid of links to the developed world. In striving to establish development ideals, the elite has promoted an image of villagers as backward (Pigg, 1992); traditional forms lived by non-Hindus are viewed as opposed to progress. Hence, imposing Nepalization has been understood, among other things, as a process of civilizing a backward population. The majority of the ethnic population remained confined to the social periphery defined in these terms.

With the King at the apex of the 'national' hierarchy, any attempt at decentralization of the administrative and the political system was doomed to fail.[26] The capital Kathmandu and its surroundings were increasingly becoming the economic centre of Nepal with developing industries (tourism, carpet manufacture, construction), infrastructure, real estate markets, and above all labour markets. The centralizing tendencies were decisively reinforced by booming international aid.

Though heavy taxation was considerably reduced at the outset of the Panchayat era, the state clearly had 'something' to take from its citizens, not just from the prosperous Tarai but also from other areas. The most striking measure was the nationalization of the bulk of the Nepalese forests with some ethnic minority areas and communally held natural resources being turned into national parks – a drastic means to prevent people from continuing previous forms of livelihood and organization. On the other hand, with substantial foreign funds pouring into Nepal (rendering the central elites stronger), those in charge of public expenditure also had 'something to give', basically in the form of various development project, promising improvement in production and consumption levels.

Despite the egalitarian rhetoric, cleavages persisted: the caste system was never really abolished, and caste/ethnic distinctions were reinforced by the fact that ethnic groups largely lacked networks giving access to high positions, and displayed cultural modes differing strongly from those prevailing among the elites in the centre. Economic disparities persisted; with Kathmandu and the surrounding areas developing economically at a much quicker pace than most of the other areas of Nepal, regional disparities became more apparent, and the majority of ethnic groups – along with numerous Parbatiyas, however – were living in the stagnating peripheries. The first indications of tensions were regionalist sentiments in the Tarai. In the 1960s, Tarai activists claimed that state expenditure in the Tarai was far below the amount of taxes and revenues flowing from this region to the state treasury (Gaige, 1975).

Within the particular political context of the Panchayat era, only the state, dominated by the high-caste Hindus, had the opportunity publicly to develop its definition of the national culture. With civic rights such as freedom to organize and freedom of expression seriously restricted, the members of Nepalese ethnic groups were prevented from displaying any diverging visions in public. In addition to public displays of national symbols and modernizing ideologies, the state had various means at its disposal to undermine pre-existing 'parochial' identities, authority struc- tures, and 'traditional' ways of life. In the course of its centralizing efforts, the state was increasingly able to interfere in the private domains and to submit its citizens to bureaucratic regulation (e.g. by unifying the land-holding system, and by surveying and registering the land). The state began to control and to normalize its citizens' ways of living, and to shape experience "by categories which may cut across those in which one wants to live one's life" (Taylor, 1990: 99). Some measures meant disempowerment of communal self-management and local or corporative mechanisms of self-perpetuation; it meant "sapping the social foundations of communal and corporative traditions and forms of life" (Bauman, 1990: 157). Though promoted all over the country, assimilation was primarily an invitation extended to those individual members of stigmatized groups who were able to respond to it. By enabling individual members of local communities to embark on a new mode of life, the right of those communities to set proper standards of behaviour was challenged.[27] Inherent in this was the idea that one form of life (and hence one cultural form) which promised deliverance from 'underdevelopment' was superior to all others. The 'undeveloped' sector, persisting in its very 'otherness', was by definition inferior. Discrimination against the 'inferior' sector within the existing power structure could be publicly attributed to its own flaws, in short, to its backwardness and enslavement to tradition. However, the government's firm stand on cultural matters was to be increasingly challenged by various social forces during the last decade of the Panchayat period.

With new governmental measures and the persisting forms of dominance within local societies, cultural change continued, partly reinforcing tendencies to adopt aspects of Hinduism, but mostly leading people into a variety of new orientations. Several factors promoted cultural change during the Panchayat era. The most striking feature about this process is its multidirectionality: despite the central rulers' efforts to homogenize Nepalese society, several opposing tendencies were current during this period. Foreign influences promoted new consumption patterns among the upper and middle classes, and the general impact of market forces called for new cultural forms and value orientations that were only partly compatible, or even opposed, to governmental strategies. We cannot ignore the force of modernization apart from Hinduization or Nepalization. When analysing the cultural changes which took place in the last decades it is sometimes difficult to discern why and how particular changes came about. For instance, the new tendency among high-caste Parbatiyas in central Nepal to ask for substantial dowries could be an indicator of their increasing orthodoxy. However, as in north India, it is questionable whether the increasing dowry-demands are due to religious change. Another example shows that such ambiguities probably already existed before the Panchayat era. The Thakalis took several measures in order to raise their collective status such as: producing new genealogies; removing stigmatizing practices such as drinking beer and marriages by capture, which formerly rendered them 'wild and uncivilized', and employing Brahman priests. The special feature here is that the Thakalis claimed that Hindu rituals were cheaper to perform. The same point is made by those Newars who prefer Theravada modernism to the highly ritualized forms of their traditional Vajrayana Buddhism (Gellner, 1992: 327). Thus their acceptance of some Hindu cultural forms was not so much explained by religious conversion, but at least partly by economic considerations.

The spread of Parbatiya Hindu culture, which was a government objective, was indeed an important trend during the Panchayat era. While the state saw itself as a guardian of the Hindu religion (Sanskrit schools, donations to temples, cow protection, elaborate Hindu state rituals), at the same time secular features such as the Nepali language were increasingly promoted (Gaborieau, 1982). Elements of this 'Nepali' culture, propagated via schools, school textbooks, and the mass media, have reached most people in Nepal (women to a lesser degree). The most exposed people were (male) aspirants for governmental employment and local politicians, and above all those who were successful. Especially within the government, public conformity in such aspects of the culture as language, dress, and hierarchy-conscious behaviour was one of the proofs of loyalty.

Not all members of ethnic groups, however, were confined to the peripheries. Members of several ethnic groups emerged as private entrepreneurs and increasingly established themselves in Kathmandu during the Panchayat period (Zivetz, 1992). Most of them were former Gurkha soldiers (Gurungs, Magars, Rai, Limbus), descendants from former tax collecting families ('Subbas') in remote border areas (Thakalis, Sherpas, Manangis), and members of the few ethnic families involved with the government or at officer level in the Nepalese army. Additionally, members of several ethnic groups who were able to establish durable contacts with foreign donors and foreign entrepreneurs have expanded into new economic sectors. Tibetan refugees have started the booming carpet industry, 'Bhotes', especially the Sherpas, run major tourist enterprises, and Thakalis, Gurungs, and Manangis, along with Parbatiyas and Newars, are very successful in all sorts of import-export business. Among the main resources at the ethnic entrepreneurs' disposal have been capital, Indian and Western partners, as well as (mainly high-caste) patrons within the political and administrative elites. By and large, business people have not so far organized themselves into pressure groups trying collectively to influence state policies, even though civic formations based upon economic interests have developed. Rather, individuals have sought access to powerful patrons as a risk-minimizing strategy in view of inconsistent economic policies and loopholes in the law. While entrepreneurs from various ethnic groups provide employment to members of their communities and in this way tend to enforce cultural norms and social ties within their groups, they are not likely to adopt the role of ethnic mobilizers.

Entrepreneurs have, of course, to manage the cultural system within which they operate (knowing Nepali, understanding rules and regulations, communication ability with government officials). However, this does not necessarily imply assimilation: the framework within which they operate goes beyond a single cultural context (in addition to the government, they have to deal with foreign business partners on the one hand and their 'own' communities, for instance as a reservoir of labour power, on the other). Entrepreneurs do not have to adapt culturally to their powerful patrons among the central elites because there are other, more forceful, means of establishing loyalty and durable relationships, such as bribes and holding out the prospect of future exchanges and mutual gain. Hence, entrepreneurs have to display a variety of progressive characteristics such as work ethos, dynamism management, and technological skills that exceed the context of what is considered 'the' national culture. Their characteristics are necessarily tied to foreign norms and values that may be unrelated to any political ideology. On the other hand, the majority of Nepalese entrepreneurs of ethnic origin maintain manifold ties with other members of their communities. Many of them have emerged as 'reformers', inducing friends and relatives to cut the costs of rituals, refrain from alcohol, abandon habits considered dubious within a 'modern' context (e.g. marriage by capture), or to turn to 'high' religions such as Buddhism (see Ramble, pp. 405–7 above).

The expanding labour market has equally induced members of different groups to reorient themselves culturally. Entrepreneurs tend to employ people from their own communities. In this field readjustments to new authority and subordination requirements, or cooperative forms, are necessary and can be expressed in different idioms. More often than not, 'old' community values are moulded according to new, market, exigencies, and additionally new strategies are adopted in order to avoid conflicts among members of the same group, especially when business hierarchies cut across solidarity patterns based upon egalitarian ideals (Zivetz, 1992: 125ff.). Within the emerging labour market, members of various communities come into frequent contact with one another, be it in cooperation (e.g. in the Chambers of Commerce), or in competition. Within this context, relationships are established not only between members of ethnic groups and high-caste entrepreneurs and/or officials, or between members of ethnic groups and foreign partners and investors, but also among various ethnic groups. Already during the last years of the Panchayat era the more entrepreneurial ethnic groups have become patrons of employees from other ethnic groups (especially porters for tourists, and workers in the carpet weaving industries). Even though little is known about any related conflicts as yet, there is some reason to expect ethnic tensions in future.

The homogenizing efforts of the high-caste Hindu elites have been increasingly opposed throughout Nepal for a variety of reasons. It is precisely in systems claiming to be egalitarian that those dominant groups presenting themselves as guarantors of equality, but actually promoting inequality at the expense of others, are increasingly taken to task. Since the mid-1970s the state has been losing its legitimacy. The state claimed for itself a focal role in the development process and proved a failure. After the modernizing euphoria of the early Panchayat days started to subside, large sections of Nepalese society came to realize that they could hardly get ahead through the government. The highly centralized state apparatus dominated by high-caste officials and politicians has proved unsuccessful in instigating economic growth and/or extending welfare measures beyond the capital and a few other economic centres (some parts of the Tarai, major tourist areas). Oppositional voices attributed the inefficiency of the state apparatus and internal corruption, on the one hand to the destabilizing effects of donor policies (Pandey, 1989), but also to the manipulative strategies and fatalist orientations of high-caste Hindus (Bista, 1991). It was claimed that educated members of ethnic groups were not able to find employment within the central organs due to their lack of personal networks. Within the political and administrative bodies, ethnic 'elites' were not able to compete with high-caste Hindus.

Ethnic activists have increasingly claimed that Nepalese society has undergone a process of differentiation, with the bulk of the ethnic population confined to peripheries – be it in the sense of not having access to welfare, or in the sense of lacking a political voice. In this process, old grievances were coming into the open such as resentment over the abolition of the *kipaṭ* system (communally held land) among several Kiranti groups (see Gaenszle, chapter 10). The century-long migration of Hindu population into ethnic areas has been increasingly branded as 'internal colonization'. Towards the end of the Panchayat era, some ethnic activists started to adopt the internationally current label 'indigenous people' (see Pradhan, 1994), initially just hinting at specific minority rights. Political symbols that have been propagated by the state as well as – increasingly – symbols that have been attached to the crown have acquired a new dimension: in the process of the opposition political mobilization, they were increasingly understood and openly labelled as symbols of oppression. One such symbol was the annual Durga Puja or Dasain, a major state power ritual (Pfaff-Czarnecka, 1993a). Any homogenizing effort linking the idea of national unity with high-caste Hindu cultural elements was increasingly resented among ethnic activists. At the same time, however, individual members of the ethnic groups have continued to adopt and display high-caste manners and symbols as a means of social mobility.

Towards the end of the Panchayat era, members of ethnic/ regional/language communities were increasingly carrying their specific demands and objectives into the open. When they protested against the government and its cultural measures, ethnic mobilizers were also responding to other factors such as economic change and, above all, the changing international context. Among these foreign influences were: the world-wide evolution of ethnicity as a new form of political formation;[28] the changing global development discourse, stressing such elements as people's participation, 'community involvement', solidarity, and cooperation patterns at the local level; the development of ties between ethnic elites, on the one hand, and foreign business partners, foreign scholars, foreign members of global organizations, and foreign admirers of Asian religions, on the other; the growing interest in 'native' culture reinforced by national and international research institutions, and, finally, the arrival in the public forum in Nepal of the growing critical debate over epistemological and ethical issues raised by the Western representation of 'the Other'. These factors gained a tremendous momentum over the course of the 1990 Movement. Powerful cultural cleavages were only brought into the public domain with the crucial political change which came about after the bloody unrest in the spring of 1990.

THE 'PATCHWORK OF MINORITIES' AFTER 1990

> How to tend this garden? – Prithvi Narayan bequeathed a 'garden' of 'four caste division and thirty-six tribes'. Why not pull down the hedges and let a hundred wildflowers bloom? (P.R. Sharma, 1992)

The democratic movement of 1990 was successful in inducing crucial political changes, especially by stripping the King of his dominant role and re-establishing a multiparty system. The mobilization which occurred all over the country raised extremely high hopes and expectations, with many people saying aloud that henceforth all expectations and demands were legitimate and ought to be met quickly! In view of the country's economic backwardness and the institutional constraints obstructing the democratization process, tensions are in fact likely to get only more severe.

It would not be correct to analyse recent ethnic tensions simply as one of the outcomes of the 1990 Movement and nothing more. Activists from ethnic groups formed part of the Movement, which comes closest to a 'bourgeois revolution', either as party members[29] or as members of ethnic/regional organizations. It was a combined effort of wide sections of the population – ethnic groups along with the Parbatiyas – to overthrow the existing Partyless Panchayat system, to proclaim a new constitution vesting the sovereignty in the people, and to create a new social order, about the nature of which manifold visions exist. One clear-cut tendency can however be discerned: in the aftermath of the 1990 'revolution', ethnic tensions have gained momentum.

Aside from political parties being formed and re-formed, various new ethnic organizations have emerged and several of those previously existing underground have entered the public domain (Fisher, 1993; pp. 20–1, 59–62, 67–8 above). However, although the ethnic groups together form the majority of the population, they are scattered, with no single one of them exceeding 12%. Thus opposition on an ethnic basis has been difficult to orchestrate (Fisher, 1993), though there are examples of ethnic organizations uniting, for instance into the Nepal Janajati Mahasangh (the Nepal Federation of Nationalities). After 1990, the fierce public debate as to whether the Constitution should continue to describe Nepal as a Hindu state or declare it a secular one was an important rallying point for many organizations. Suddenly a variety of groupings including ethnic organizations, Buddhist activists, the Muslims, the Christians, and some Communist fractions were united against forces which, backed by various Indian Hindu associations, demanded that Nepal remain a Hindu state.[30]

The debate over this crucial cultural issue reinforced sentiments and resentment on both sides. Pro-Hindu state forces won, with ethnic demands being disappointed.[31] The process of mobilization on ethnic grounds continues, however, with various organizations either representing single ethnic groups or their conglomerations. Though there are large disparities in their demands – some opting for a quota system after the Indian model, some forcefully objecting to this – several political aims are being often repeated: a higher representation of ethnic members in political and administrative bodies; a higher degree of decentralization with a greater scope for self-government (a wish shared by many

Parbatiyas); abolition of Nepali's status as the only national language; and correction of the national statistics which present the Nepalese population as approximately 85% Hindus, with most of the rest classified as Buddhists and Muslims.

The prolonged debates concerning the contents of the new Constitution (promulgated in November 1990) have been a clear indicator of the continuing relevance of cultural considerations and negotiations in the process of nation-building. The international scene, notably Eastern Europe which is observed in Nepal with attention, has seemed to demonstrate that the complex relationship of 'nation' and 'state' has not lost its pertinence. The very fact that old states were falling apart and new ones were emerging at the same time called the concept into question, and, on the other hand, reinforced its validity.

Until the end of the Panchayat era, the rulers and/or the government had focused on the task of defining the essential characteristics of the 'nation', but in the present context, 'people' insist on participating in this process. Ethnicity, so far understood as opposing the national idea, is being propagated by some ethnic activists as one intrinsic aspect of Nepalese society, calling for a redefinition of what should be considered national culture. The idea of Nepal as a nation-state is not contested. There seems to exist a wide consensus that defining a national identity and a basis for national unity is an important task. On the other hand, ethnic activists challenge the necessity for a homogenized Nepalese society on high-caste Hindu lines. It is widely accepted in Nepal that *some* common cultural denominator is necessary in order to allow for communication, given – among other things – new requirements for production and exchange. But in the view of many, the necessity for a common means of communication does not preclude the coexistence of differing customs, languages, worldviews, and ways of life – at least in theory.

Since 1990 various ethnic activists have insisted on taking part in the project of forging a new notion of Nepal's national culture. However, nation-building processes in emerging democracies such as Nepal, besides establishing the cultural characteristics of a 'nation', consist basically of processes of building a civil society.[32] Such processes are essentially independent of the states containing them and depend upon the establishment of civil rights. In this wider sense, citizens (and no longer subjects) strive to have a say in defining civil rights and duties, to take part in calling institutions and procedures into existence, to establish legal and public channels for popular protest, and to demand accountability of popular representatives.[33]

Within the present political process in Nepal, minority formation on ethnic, linguistic, and regional bases seems to face a contradiction. On the one hand, the emergence of minority demands in public is concomitant with, and an indicator of, the Nepalese democratization process. On the other hand, specific minority demands, and especially the ways that these are expressed, appear to threaten the democratization process. In the view of many, pursuing collective goals such as quota systems or 'positive discrimination' is contrary to establishing institutions enabling the process of social integration at the national level. Whether the future political process will involve accepting the either/or dichotomy (individual vs. collective integration) is questionable. It remains to be seen whether (and if so, how) particular demands pertaining to collective identities in Nepal will be incorporated within a broader integration process based upon defining and protecting individual rights and duties. For a better understanding of the present institutional set up, let us now turn, once again, to the relationship between Nepalese citizens and the state.

Towards the end of the Panchayat era, the rulers had to acknowledge that the state could not retain the desired control over society either in the cultural sphere or in political and economic domains. Despite the state's struggle to promote a centrally controlled economy based upon five-year plans, there emerged an ever growing number of private entrepreneurs. Nepal's 'mixed' economy has been shifting towards a market economy, promoted among other things by the state elites who have been collaborating with various partners – ethnic economic elites numerous among them. The privatization of state enterprises in recent years has also been encouraged by the structural adjustment measures forced on Nepal by foreign organizations. None the less, several factors still make for a strong grip by the state and state elites over the national economy: by means of patronage, state elites, if not the state itself, have been able to retain a considerable control over market forces; government economic policies have been geared towards state elites, and quite a few state enterprises have been developed. At the same time powerful economic actors have developed outside state institutions and have been striving to influence government policies. In the aftermath of the 1990 Movement, numerous organizations pursuing various economic interests (e.g. chambers of commerce, trade unions, and particular organizations such as 'Women Entrepreneur Association of Nepal') have been reorganizing themselves or have been called into being. However, their role in affecting state policies (corporatism), and as an integrative social force through market mechanisms, cannot yet be evaluated. A new section of the private market continued to open up in the last several years, in the form of Non-Governmental Organizations, sponsored to a substantial extent by international agencies. The weight of this new sector is probably best indicated by the fact that numerous individuals have been abandoning low-paid governmental positions and engaging in this private market. In addition, an increasing number of government employees engage on a part-time basis with NGOs or entertain close personal ties with them (this is discussed further below).

While until the end of the Panchayat era the state decided for its subjects which religion to choose (cf. p.520 below) and how to organize themselves,[34] the new Constitution provides for extensive civic rights such as freedom of speech, freedom to organize, freedom of religion, and the right to information. Despite some remaining restrictions on groups deemed separatist, the new Constitution's provision for establishing political parties, and for public displays of religions other than Hinduism, has allowed ethnic organizations and activists to emerge from their confinement. On paper at least, the Constitution of 1990 allows Nepalis the opportunity to abandon their subject status and emerge as citizens (cf. Ellingson, 1991).

During the Panchayat era, elections under universal franchise were held at local level and, after 1980, at national level also, and

formation in contemporary Nepal. Before proceeding further some remarks on the notion 'public sphere' are necessary.

ON THE PUBLIC CHARACTER OF ETHNICITY FORMATION IN CONTEMPORARY NEPAL

The 'public sphere' refers to the arena where individuals act in a way that is visible/transparent to potential observers. As such, it is on the one hand a domain where aims or grievances can be exposed to the public, and on the other hand it is, or rather should be, an arena where any civic action can be subjected to public scrutiny. The public sphere refers to a general audience that can be addressed. Hence, individuals who enter the public arena approach a section of the national civil society with its existing patterns of intercourse (including the specific political culture), institutions, and procedures. However, social barriers prevent individuals from addressing the public and/or from being part of the audience.

Public spheres emerge as a constitutive element of demo-cratization processes (whereas a representative public pertains to autocratic systems: see the discussion of the 'Empire Model' above). Civic participation consists, among other things, in the freedom of the individual to form his/her opinion and to carry it into public discussions. The process of opinion formation presupposes access to information as well as participation in ongoing debates about the conditions of society and the state.

The mode of the debates, and of reasoning, pertains, among other things, to public culture, not only understood as a means of collectively thinking about aspects of modern life, but also as a type of cultural phenomenon and as a zone of cultural debate where different "types, forms and domains of culture are encountering, interrogating and contesting each other" (Appadurai, 1988: 6). Debates on the character of national culture form part of public culture; as such, "public culture is a contested terrain, for national culture is itself a contested mode, embattled, on the one hand, by transnational cultural messages and forces (which sometimes threaten the nation-state), and, on the other hand, by indigenous critics from the various sectors that continuously threaten the cultural hegemony of the nation-state" (*ibid.*).

Coming back to the specific situation in Nepal the public processes pertaining to ethnicity bring up several questions which I shall try to answer in the remaining part of this article: where are ethnicity debates carried out? Who are the major actors in the debates? What are the contents of ethnicity debates? What are the objectives of the ethnicity mobilizers? Who are the addressees of ethnic messages? Following on from this, questions need be raised about the relationship between public displays of ethnicity and collective experiences of marginalization and expropriation; about the reasons for entering the public sphere; about the cultural processes which come into being, once ethnic activists have entered the zone of public culture, and finally about the differences between ethnic representatives and those being represented by them.

Without doubt, success in taking active part in the drafting process of the Constitution, as well as the general success of the Movement, have shaped the national political culture: displaying dissent or even civil disobedience,[39] and stressing distinction rather than compliance, are marks of status for many activists.[40] At present, besides demonstrating in the street, there many ways to push particular demands, be it through conventions, meetings, assemblies; through communications in various mass media, notably in the press (*Chahara, Vishleshan, Janamukti* – these periodicals have been listed by Burghart *et al.*, 1991); forming 'interest groups' (e.g. for the restoration of the Tengboche monastery); forming 'reform organizations' (see Zivetz, 1992; Ramble, chapter 12); or estab-lishing Non-Governmental Organizations. Some activists have been striving to correct their community's image in scientific publications, or generally within scientific discourse (see Macfarlane, pp. 191–2 above; Onta, 1992).

Who are the ethnic activists I have so often referred to? During the last decade or so, it has often been repeated that ethnic mobilizers are to be found in the first place among (young) men constituting a 'frustrated middle class'. It is difficult to make generalizations, but the existing data indicate that many important minority leaders do not fall into such a category. However, ethnicity is not to be confounded with ethnic conflicts. Should ethnic conflicts escalate in Nepal in the future, it is possible that new, more radical activists could emerge, who would have less to lose. Presently among the promoters of 'cultural politics' are many prominent politicians and parliamentarians, intellectuals employed in key positions, entrepreneurs (see below), highly regarded priests and religious teachers, and even government officials. Those coming closest to the category 'frustrated middle class' may be local teachers and local politicians who might have aspired for higher positions, but it is not possible to treat all of them under one simplifying label. We still know little about the scope of ethnic mobilization as displayed in public life in the capital in comparison with related processes occuring in the 'homelands' of various ethnic, regional, or linguistic groups, though some indications can be found in this volume.

Resentment against statistical distortions (especially since those who embrace neither Hinduism nor Buddhism are not represented) is an important indicator of the present direction of the changing cultural orientations. Since 1990, the democratization process has been accompanied by a sort of 'back to the roots' movement, with some sections of the ethnic population publicly displaying the distinctive aspects of their own culture and maintaining that they will try to remove some of the Hindu influences on it. The 'back to the roots' movement in Nepal is at present strongly reinforced by changing attitudes among many development organizations which publicize their work with slogans such as 'small is beautiful', 'people's participation', and 'community involvement'. Numerous project documents present 'indigenous' ethnic institutions as the proper bodies to carry out development efforts. The renowned Nepalese social anthropologist Dor Bahadur Bista has recently argued that the strength of ethnic solidarity and ethnic cooperative spirit is the most powerful tool for social progress. He claims in his widely discussed and controversial book, *Fatalism and Development*, that the Brahmanic values dominating Nepalese society are to be blamed for the overall fatalistic attitude of the bulk of the Nepalese population and for development failures. Himself a Chetri, he criticizes the Brahmanic attitudes widespread among Hindus. He particularly attacks hierarchical thinking, which values ascribed status above achievement, and results in people striving primarily to please their superiors, whether ritual superiors, those in power, parents, or superiors within professional hierarchies. Ethnicity, which is implicitly associated with egalitarian ideals, has entered the discourse of the international aid experts as a value and as a resource.

In the context of the Nepalese democratization process, the emerging public sphere becomes an arena for (a) discussing cultural issues; (b) influencing government policy, as regards, for example, the shaping of the national outlook or the share of state benefits going to minorities; (c) designing and carrying out action independent of the state (e.g. 'self-help programmes'). Processes within the three fields reinforce one another; drawing clear-cut boundaries between the indicated areas is not possible. This relating of cultural issues over control of the state and to the pursuit of specific goals within the public sphere shows that minorities' efforts to stress certain cultural features may have an instrumental value. In ethnicity debates, a majority of scholars adopt the instrumentalist stand, claiming that ethnic leaders tend to take advantage of existing cultural divisions and similarities in order to promote collective action to obtain access to political, social, and material resources.[41] However, while acknowledging that emotions can be made use of in this way, we cannot ignore primordial factors: people simply do feel an attachment to their territory, language, customs, or to other members of their community and this sense of attachment is characterized by intense feelings of solidarity and obligation. More often than not, people's endeavours to display their culture become instrumental but this does not mean that all forms of public manifestations pertaining to one's culture are necessarily, or primarily, directed toward attaining any 'material' ends. Therefore, before considering the ways in which attachment to a culture is displayed for tactical purposes, let us consider first the 'primordial' reasons for the interest in one's own culture which is seen in Nepal today.

Many ethnic activists currently claim that their cultures have been subject to Brahman oppression for centuries. In particular, Brahmans are accused of having faked ethnic groups' *vaṃśāvalī* (see, e.g., Macfarlane, p.185, pp. 202–3 above) – a valid claim, though one which ignores the fact that Brahmans were asked by ethnic elites to do so (Höfer, 1979: 135–150; 171–6 mentions several instructive examples). As discussed above, during the Shah and Rana periods, the rulers created an ideological framework based upon Hindu rules and customs. Some rules and mores were forced upon their subjects. More importantly, however, the ideological framework created by the Hindu rulers has served ethnic elites' objectives. Their leading role in adopting, or at least displaying, certain Hindu traits has rarely been discussed so far. Although the high-caste Hindus' role in the Hinduization process is crucial, the ethnic elites' contribution to the process should not be underestimated.

During the Panchayat period, minorities' cultures were certainly neglected, if not suppressed; if ethnic culture was present in the public arena at all, it was folklorized, as for instance in the case of Tamang songs performed by Brahmans on Radio Nepal. However, even though the majority of the poor ethnic population continues to carry the "heavy loads of its identities" (Campbell, chapter 6), an increasing number of people now dare to assert publicly that their cultures are not inferior, but different. Stressing minority cultural traits should be seen, among other things, as a reaction to former governments' stand on cultural matters. Such reactions consist in displaying a sense of pride in a particular ethnic group's contribution to the national culture. "If Nepal is a nation, it requires additional national motifs," claims Saubhagya Shah; Gopal Singh Nepali suggests that "celebrating the memory of Yelambar, an ancient Kirat king would be a good start in tracing authentic Nepali roots" (Shah, 1993: 9). After several centuries of Hindu symbols and values overtly or covertly determining the culture of public life, the new-found legitimacy of displaying defiance reflects a substantial change in the political climate. Public challenges contesting the validity of the established Hindu hierarchy have already started to inform political action.

People's new self-concious interest in their own cultures is additionally reinforced by scholarly awareness.[42] Western universities[43] increasingly tend to expect foreign students to conduct research among their own societies. During the last decade, Nepalese researchers have engaged in 'subaltern studies', striving to uncover how, among other things, images of their societies have been misrepresented in Western discourses.[44] Former 'research objects' read books written on themselves by 'strangers' many feel that it is time to take command of the process of shaping their public images. This tendency is reinforced by the spread of a new notion of culture, understood as pertaining to people's identity. Linguists, anthropologists, archeologists, and historians are put to work in order to uncover the past. A search for origins goes on in the capital as well as in various ethnic 'homelands' (see Gaenszle and Russell, this volume). After decades of homogenizing measures, it is now cultural diversity that orients cultural discourse. Differences are being stressed by insisting upon distinct language, distinct origins, distinct religious orientations, and distinct chronicles (compare chapters 5, 10, and 11 above).[45] In this process, the uniformity of cultural endeavours is striking. Distinctions are being worked out by constantly referring to language (often seeking to invent a new script), to a highly valued origin (*vaṃśāvalī*), and to 'authentic' religious forms – as if there were no question that identity should be defined, and as if there were only one valid way of doing it. The search for identity is apparently informed by the dominant cultural patterns of the moment.

A third factor leading to an increased interest in cultural matters can be located among the entrepreneurial group. Here, primordial and instrumental considerations mingle most visibly. On the one hand, the religious ethos of several entrepreneurial communities, notably that of the Tibetan Buddhists, induces successful individuals to serve their societies by donating to religious institutions, by helping the poor, by supporting relatives and friends, and by contributing in various ways to the well-being of their local ethnic communities. On the other hand, promoting social reforms by cutting costs of rituals or by banning excessive alcohol drinking and establishing rotating credit associations aims clearly and consciously at promoting a community's chances in the economic sphere (Ramble, chapter 12; see also von der Heide, 1988). These related strategies not only pertain to establishing and enlarging entrepreneurial networks, but also to particular groups promoting images such as being 'modern' or 'progress-oriented', which may impinge upon individual success (Ramble, chapter 12).

As noted above, actions relating primarily to defining cultural 'content' can eventually evolve into mobilization, especially if control of state resources and state policies is at stake. When access to governmental and political positions is perceived to be restricted to particular cultural groups with access to the right networks, ethnic conflicts can swell (Wimmer, 1994). Especially where the cultural dominance of a core group is no longer considered legitimate, public assertion of ethnic distinctiveness may be the answer: stressing the numerical strength of a group; insisting upon the importance of the impact of one's own culture upon the national culture (implying that members of one's group should be better represented in crucial bodies); opposing privileged treatment for some sections of society; insisting upon cultural traits, unacknowledged so far, as new devices in social development; insisting upon special rights to specific territories and demanding recognition of wrongs perpetrated in the past. Interestingly, as Rajendra Pradhan (1994) suggests, those who struggle for legal recognition of particular rights usually have to accept a lower status. Those who seek protection have to comply with the government's patronizing language calling people 'backward', 'ignorant', 'incapable of taking care of themselves', and 'needing protection'.[46]

When ethnic organizations and activists use cultural characteristics in struggles over state resources and state policies, 'culture' becomes all the more a tactical device within the heterogeneous field of the public life. This field contains various interest groups aiming to influence governmental measures, private organizations trying to uplift needy members of their communities, more-or-less profit-oriented Non-Governmental Organizations as well as organizations with 'cultural' objectives, such as promotion of local art, or 'religious' goals, such as support to temples or monasteries.

The latter organizations link the Nepalese public with foreign organizations and individuals towards whom cultural manifestations are also oriented. 'Cultural' and 'religious' projects have been discussed by Ramble and Burkert in this volume, the first in connection with the Western support for the Tengboche monastery, the second with the American Ambassador's presence at the opening ceremony of the Maithil paintings by The Janakpur Women's Development Centre. In this latter case, it is also apparent, and holds for a variety of projects, that attracting Western donors is crucial for the project's future, as is attracting Western buyers.

Where prestigious or wealthy foreigners are present, however, ambitious individuals often strive to establish themselves as go-betweens. Burkert's description of how influential men try to represent women, the actual bearers of the project, is most illuminating: while women are confined to the backstage, men act in the public as custodians of the culture. In order to legitimize their own role, they say "They don't know their culture. We must teach it to them," they prevent the women artists from introducing a dynamic element into their art which would enable them to represent the changing conditions of their life. Burkert is right to remark (above, p.272) that "before the project's success, unlike the language and literature issue, Mithila art was innocent and ... could be appreciated without stirring up trouble. When it is in hands of politicians, the educated elite, or entrepreneurs it is 'currency' in actual or political terms."

Ramble's article indicates yet another development that links the form of displayed images to the question of to whom such displays are directed. Western Buddhists, eager to support Tibetan monasteries, are interested in versions of purified Buddhism. More unorthodox, folk elements tend to be considered as interesting, but deviating from the expected text. Foreign expectations cannot hold as the unique explanation for the scope of purifying processes among the urban-based Buddhist elites, but their importance cannot be underestimated, for, as Ramble (above, p.406), suggests:

> Foreigners who visit the Tibetanid areas of Nepal frequently carry with them an image of Tibet, acquired from books or from encounters with Tibetan religious institutions in India or overseas, that they project onto the

Nepalese landscape: Muktinath, Mustang, and Dolpo are vestiges of a vanished Tibet. The peculiarities of local religion and culture have no place in the image, and consequently remain invisible.

Non-Governmental Organizations, including the various ethnic associations mentioned in this volume, institutions providing 'development' expertise and, nowadays above all, associations pursuing environmental goals form the major arena for intercultural meetings, and consequently for cultural readjustments. The democratization process, so thoroughly interwoven with minority movements, coincides with new international socio-cultural trends brought into Nepal through foreign funding agencies that (a) strive to by-pass the state (according to the demands of the structural adjustment imperatives, and due to reluctance to cooperate with cumbersome bureaucracies); (b) follow new ideologies, partly contrary to those promoted during the 1960s and 1970s, by pointing out the development potential of traditional forms of communal life; and (c) are under pressure to legitimate their action by showing that they have immediate 'access' to the people and that people themselves participate in the projects. Thus, the booming arena of Nepalese NGOs operates between foreign 'partners' who provide the funding and who themselves are under pressure to act according to 'democratic' procedures, and the Nepalese 'people' represented by the NGOs themselves, on the other side. The latter have to present themselves publicly as embodying certain cultural traits ('communal spirit', 'diligence'), and have to display an intimate relationship, or 'solidarity', with the rural 'partners'. Little is known, however, about how firm a base such urban intermediaries have at the local level. Where, as is the case in the field of the NGOs, the majority of actors consist of generalists, it is especially important to display temporarily valid cultural traits and value orientations that combine local 'peculiarities' with global exigencies. The ability to represent members of local societies and to manage a currently internationally dominant cultural code determines the success of individual NGOs and their foreign partners/sponsors.

In view of the extreme complexity of ongoing cultural processes in Nepal, with the extent of assimilation to the dominant culture varying among the different local societies, with the differing degree of politicization of the various issues, and with some forms of opposition just about to start, it is presently very difficult to reach any firm conclusions. But we can ask: Is it possible to undo the cultural changes which have occurred over the last two centuries as some ethnic leaders appear to claim? Obviously not. Martin Gaenszle, who has studied one of the more remote ethnic communities that was rather marginally exposed to external influences, stresses that among this group, religious adaptations were extremely superficial (1991a). He attributes such superficial adaptations to the wish to demonstrate that the local religious system conforms to Hindu tradition, but "underneath" nothing has changed in the cultural content. I believe that he is right in his interpretation of this process amongst one of the less Hinduized groups. On the other hand, I have tried to show that Hinduization was occurring in manifold ways among the bulk of ethnic populations which were more exposed. Among these groups, public conformity with some Hindu practices as a political tactic was just one of the processes leading to Hinduization. Therefore, with a variety of cultural processes reinforcing each other, aspects of high-caste Hindu culture have penetrated the cultural systems of minority groups far beyond the surface. Thus any attempt to root out 'Hindu influence' is bound to be highly contentious and divisive for the group concerned. Furthermore, any attempt to follow indigenous cultural practices in a public display of opposition to another, thus far dominant culture, almost inevitably tends to be expressed in terms *derived from* the dominant culture.

CONCLUSION

At this early stage of Nepalese democratization it is doubtless risky to attempt any general statements about the future political forms: to assess how Nepalese people, the new sovereign, will think about and define the essential characteristics of their national culture, and how they will link up their national belonging to other forms of solidarity. Growing interest in one's own culture, the search for origins, new cultural projects, public discussions of culture, cultural comparison, and cultural competition are partly a reaction to earlier neglect, partly tactical manoevres, and partly a new type of hobby among the intelligentsia.

While struggling for rights and resources some members of minorities have taken recourse to 'cultural' arguments; some members of the majority, notably the supporters of Hindu organizations, seek to preserve the status quo in a countermovement. It is not possible to discern one single tendency for cultural change, or one major factor underlying the unfolding processes. Some major tendencies can be outlined, as follows.

First, minority manifestations as an intrinsic element of the emerging public sphere are powerful indicators of new social forces forming themselves in Nepal: outside state institutions, striving for social integration through self-organization and/or striving to determine the national outlook and state policies. The way minority organizations and their individual exponents are active indicates the nature, direction, and discontinuities of the broader process. Since the 1990 Movement, the previously neglected, marginalized, or even suppressed groups and organizations have been able to act within a new legal framework. At least in theory, all Nepalese citizens are invited to participate in the development process: as clients to welfare, through party politics, and also as concerned citizens with access to the public sphere.

On the other hand, however, it has become obvious that in the overall democratization process (provided of course that this is the direction in which Nepalese polity is now heading), minority formation has been closely connected to the politics of representation. If we envisage the public sphere as being an arena where any civic action can be subjected to public scrutiny, one is immediately confronted with the question as to the actual share of the ethnic population involved in 'cultural politics'. One may ask whether the majority of members of the Nepalese minorities know that they are being represented by their leaders on public occasions, and whether they agree with the way in which they are represented as well as with the objectives particularly stressed by their self-appointed spokesmen. Is it legitimate, we may ask, for any member of a particular community to speak on behalf of his/her own society when – contrary to party politics – minority representatives can claim to have a mandate to represent their fellow members but cannot substantiate their claims? Obviously, there is an increasing gap between the publicly invoked images of community life and everyday communal life.

The ideal of community refers to a model of association patterned on family and kinship relations, on an affective language of love and loyalty, on assumptions of authenticity, homogeneity, and continuity, of inclusion and exclusion, identity and otherness. The modern notion of community, as evoked in some civic society discourses and displayed through various forms of public event, offers images of solidarity and reciprocity that are grounded in a collective experience of marginalization and expropriation. The language of community provides a powerful matrix of identification and thus may function as a mobilizing force for transformative politics. There is a difference, however, between the fashionable rhetoric "as a trope of impossible authenticity, reinventing the promise of community through synthetic and syncretistic images" (Hansen, 1993: 207), and the complex exigences of communal life. In particular, the current rhetoric denies difference and differentiation within communal borders, and fails to accept multiply determined sexual-social identities and identifications.

Minority representations are a pertinent factor in the present political process in Nepal. As such, they indicate the scope of an emerging pluralism corresponding to the enhanced access of citizens to ongoing debates. However, pluralism does not preclude inequality, especially where the decision-making process is concerned. In the present field of popular representation, new forms of differentiation are likely to emerge and old inequalities may well be reinforced.

Second, the emerging public sphere is a contested ground. Institutionalized rules governing the ways in which "potential issues are kept out of the political process" (Lukes, 1974: 21) and "control over political agenda" (*ibid.*: 25) are being produced and reproduced. It is a heterogeneous field, with shifting barriers preventing access, and a changing distribution of power. In the process of minority

formation in Nepal, the public sphere is simultaneously moulded by
the international aid scene, international 'capital', international
audiences (tourists, religious disciples), members of the ruling
groups and their clients (as a counter-movement), as well as various
spokesmen for minorities promoting sectional visions. In pursuing
these interests, current values which guide action are being
negotiated. In the present context, a particularized notion of
ethnicity emerges as a political resource since it serves various
interests such as: the new 'development discourse'; the new entrepreneurial culture; the Western 'dream' of authenticity presently
invoked in the aid scene; the power-holders' image as politically
progressive; the minority leaders' newly acquired role of
intermediaries as a new type of political resource.

It could be claimed, thirdly, that the entry of the minorities
into the public arena results in a 'tragic' instrumentalization of
primordial feelings, reinforcing internal cleavages, and politiciz-
ing every single aspect of culture.[47] Whether it is really so is
for the 'represented' minorities to judge. Certainly, in the complex
and contested public sphere, a variety of cultural manifestations
confront each other. Ethnic activists display their progressive
attitudes (as entrepreneurs, as promoters of self-help actions
for their own groups, as concerned citizens) but at the same
time show they remain tradition-conscious. Apparently, being
modern does not require the abandonment of traditional cultural-
religious forms.[48] Forms of solidarity and reciprocity are subject
to negotiation in a field where political legitimacy, economic
growth, and the international development discourse provide
major patterns of orientation. The Nepalese public sphere contains
a broad spectrum of cultural repertoires, some of them conflicting.
None the less, it provides an opportunity to express one's
arguments, to discuss, negotiate, and possibly shape public action
accordingly.

Fourth, the more homogeneous and harmonious the images of
minorities, the easier it is for their public spokesmen to claim a focal
role as representatives for entire collectivities. However, all available
data suggest that especially in the present context, all Nepalese
'communities' are divided in manifold ways: into castes (the Newars,

the Maithils), into religious communities (the Newars), into more or less prosperous, urban- or village-based, progressive or traditional sections (several groups seen as entrepreneurial such as Thakalis, Sherpas), and of course by gender. When differences of opinion break into the open, among the major arguments which come up is the question of who is in charge of defining the culture of a particular social entity, especially if the culture once defined can be used as a sort of currency, be it in international (labour) markets, be it in the contest for social prestige (see, e.g., Burkert, pp. 269–73 above). Being in charge of representing one's own 'community' means attaining the role of a cultural 'broker' – and hence of instrumental value.

The simultaneity and the interrelatedness of assimilation to a new, dominant culture and revitalization of one's own old one results in a paradox: the search for distinction and uniqueness somehow creates a unifying factor in the national perspective, as if those seeking to distinguish themselves are striving to establish a common denominator at the same time. Whenever cultural forms are being made official or public, specificities or 'inconsistencies' fall prey to the difficult process of cultural translation. Traditionalism tends to simplify tradition for the same reason, as well as because those who choose traditional elements to be displayed subject their cultures to careful scrutiny. If shamanism – fascinating for foreign tourists but embarassing to many among the Nepalese intelligentsia – is to be considered an intrinsic part of the tradition, shamanism without blood sacrifice may appear as a compromise solution in the process of adopting a progressive outlook.

Several of the articles in this book reveal that within minority groups, discussions about valid versions of their cultures abound. Diverse sections of ethnic groups, guided by estranged elites, differ in their visions of 'cultural correctness'.[49] While cultural purists opt for retaining practices disapproved of by others, reformers advocate modifications in ritual practice. Such cultural disputes may provide new fuel to old factionalisms, or contribute to erecting barriers where there was formerly affinity. One can be sure that a variety of current and future disputes will affect the Nepalese minorities' perception of their cultural vestiges … and visions.

NOTES

I am grateful to Martin Gaenszle, David Gellner, Axel Michaels, Charles Ramble, Andrew Russell, Sarah Strauss, John Whelpton, and Andreas Wimmer for their comments on early drafts of this article as well as to Nick Allen, Graham Clarke, and Gregory Sharkey for their comments on my paper presented during our seminar 'Politics, Identity, and Cultural Change in the Himalayan Region, upon which this article is based.

1 Strictly speaking all Nepalese population groups are minorities, even though the high-caste Parbatiya Hindus are usually referred to as a dominant group (see Whelpton, p.57 above).

2 I concur with Said (1993: 260) and with Anderson (1983: 67ff.) in their view that the widespread global movements to achieve solidarities are often based on an essentially imagined basis.

3 Eisenstadt (1991: 21) speaks in this context of "Trägergruppen", a group of "bearers" constituted by the cultural intelligentsia, as well as of political "entrepreneurs".

4 For a discussion of the processes by which subjects turn into citizens, see especially Bendix (1980; 1991).

5 Among some further enforcing measures are a decree by King Girvana Yuddha (1802) to "all Gurung, Ghale and Tamang" to employ Brahman priests (Höfer, 1979: 174) and a decree of 1836 to Magars not to accept cooked rice from lower castes (RRS, 17: 191).

6 See Höfer (1979). On earlier codification attempts in Nepal, see Whelpton (1992: 216–220).

7 While stressing here the instrumental aspect of promoting Hinduism, however, we must not forget that some of the Nepalese rulers were devout Hindus.

8 Numerous migrants from Nepalese ethnic minorities who settled down in Darjeeling and Kumaon have significantly contributed to forging elements of 'Nepali culture'. On this, rather paradoxical, process, see Hutt (chapter 2, above).

9 I do not suggest that publicly displaying certain Hindu traits meant abandoning previously practised cultural forms, nor do I equate 'displaying' with 'accepting'.

10 For Gurungs, see Höfer (1979: 145); for the Koch, see Höfer (1979: 174); for the Sunuwar, see Fournier (1974). In 1985 K.P. Malla commented:

Not long ago, the Khas-Magars who came to political power after the Kot massacre of 1846 laid a claim to Kṣatriya descent. The Brahmins invented pedigree and genealogy connecting Jang Bahadur Kūwar's ancestors with the Ranas of Udaypur, and Jang's family succeeded in marrying into the Thakuri ruling family. Since then, all the tribals have been making social claims to Ksatriya descent. The Gurungs in the 1920s made similar claims but did not succeed; the Thakalis continue to make such claims, particularly the affluent ones ... [T]he Limbus make the same claims ... [T]he Rais have recently made similar claims (Malla, 1985: 78).

[11] On tribes turning into peasants, see Caplan (1990).

[12] We cannot assume that adopting religious elements of an alien group immediately relates to the religious system. Religious elements of a dominant group can also be incorporated by a subordinated group as power or status symbols.

[13] Höfer (1979: 166) comments: "Here we are obviously faced with a turning away from a hitherto practised form of marriage which is now regarded as structurally opposing 'Brahmanical standards'."

[14] Cross-cousin marriages still occur among the high-caste Hindus in far west Nepal (see Krause, 1980).

[15] See RRS (3:1); Höfer (1979: 171f.); RRS (16: 82–3); RRS (17: 188). Regmi also, published the following astonishing document from 1836: "From King Rajendra, to people of the four castes and thirty-six sub-castes throughout the kingdom. It appears that sexual intercourse with the married wife [the document uses the term *vivāhitā:* see Höfer (1979: 171): JPC] of one's own elder brother is a great sin. What has been done in the past has been done. Since this is a Jungly country, it is necessary to make arrangements relating to caste matters. Henceforth, no person, except among the Kiratas, Limbus, Lapaches and Jumlis for the time being, shall knowingly commit sexual intercourse with the married wife of his own elder brother" (RRS, 3:1 – translation by M.C. Regmi). Whelpton suggests that this document was probably issued at this time in an attempt to embarass a relative of Bhimsen Thapa's family who had taken his brother's widow as a concubine (1992: 50).

[16] All the ethnographic evidence presented here was collected after 1951. It is safe to assume, however, that adoptions, or mere displays, of Hindu elements were occurring long before the middle of the

commodity markets, since the economy is presently only now in the process of establishing itself independently of the state. Hence, the term 'civil society' used here is more extensive than, for instance, Habermas's (1990) restricted notion of *Zivilgesellschaft* as non-state, non-economic associations on a voluntary basis. But it follows Habermas and other authors in their conception that such free associations can only emerge within the institutional framework of a democracy. For minorities to pursue their claims, they must address themselves to a broader civic framework: courageous citizens, sophisticated constitutions, and functioning institutions (Kleger, 1992). How then can minorities pursue their objectives if crucial social institutions are lacking?

[34] People were asked to join so-called 'class organizations', viz. of women, of peasants, of workers, of ex-soldiers, and of youth.

[35] Little has been written about political elections in Nepal at the local (village and district) level. The existing data suggest that ethnicity has been only one factor in support base formation, the others being: patterns of patronage and subordination; factionalism within local groups; party politics (though forbidden before 1990); and the strength of local leaders.

[36] POLSAN (1992: 63) comments: "Ethnically the composition of Parliament reinforces the notion that Nepalese politics is dominated by three principal groups: the Brahmins (39.1%), Chetris (18.8%) and Newars (9.4%). Compared to our data on party members, while the figures for the Brahmins and Chetris are quite similar, we find a drop by more than half in terms of representation of Newars in Parliament. Both the NC and CPN-UML appear to be heavily influenced by these three groups. The remaining one-third of MPs are dispersed between 14 ethnic communities, with the representation of Rais and Limbus being somewhat higher in the CPN-UML than in the ruling party ... [T]he positions of the Newars, Hill tribes and Terai groups has changed very little in the embryonic stage of the new system, despite the importance given to ethnic Terai communities in particular by the NSP."

[37] "Religion-wise, the parliamentarians were found to be predominantly Hindus ... Interestingly enough, despite their communist ideology, only about one-third of the CPN-UML MPs claim to be secular; while among MPs of the Nepali Congress none identified themselves with the concept" (POLSAN, 1992: 64).

[38] See Wimmer (1994) for a theoretical discussion on related phenomena in other parts of the world.

[39] Civic disobedience emerges as an important element of the national political culture. Being ostracized by those in power marks political dedication as, for instance, indicated by POLSAN (1992: 65):

> If a yardstick for measuring political dedication and sacrifice can be developed by examining whether politicians had been imprisoned, then the parliamentarians would rank quite high. As opposed to the 40% of party members who said they had been detained ... 84% of the MPs claim to have been arrested at one time or the other during their political career.

[40] K.P. Malla points to the (so far) peaceful character of public displays of 'ethnic' sentiments, but warns of the potential for future escalation:

> The aggrieved sentiments of the terai, the janajatis, the Matawalis of the Hills, and the Newars of the Valley may be fake political gimmicks, but the two millennia of Brahmin domination in the social and cultural life of Nepal's recorded history is not. So far these sentiments have been expressed in psychological metaphors, newspaper columns, or Sadbhavana public meetings, and rarely if ever in organised political activities of any damaging value. But if these sentiments, as expressed by Ganesh Man Singh, Gajendra Narayan Singh, Gopal Gurung, Sitaram Tamang, Suresh Ale, M.S. Thapa and Padma Ratna Tuladhar are translated into organised political movements, then into military action, Nepal will never remain the same. We will all be commiting national *harakiri*, unwittingly converting Nepal into a Sri Lanka of the north (Malla, 1992: 23).

[41] For a discussion of this concept, see for instance McKay (1982).

[42] Among Nepalese scholars opinions on contemporary ethnic formations differ significantly. See, for instance, the very disparate points of view displayed by K.B. Bhattachan (1995) and D.R. Dahal (1995).

[43] Nanterre in Paris, Cambridge University, University of Pennsylvania, among others.

[44] See for instance recent articles in *Himal*: e.g. Onta (1992) and Tamang (1992).

[45] Activities aimed at promoting vernacular languages certainly cannot fall merely under the 'instrumentalist' rubric. Nepali remains the major national language; a good command of Nepali is a *sine qua non* for social mobility, and at the upper reaches English is required as well. Of course, under specific conditions promoting an 'ethnic' language can prove instrumental as well.

[46] "In any case, many poor Nepalis, whatever their origin, do need 'special facilities' One might then ask why then indigenous people should be singled out for special treatment, particularly if indigenousness encompasses 80 percent of the population as Gopal Gurung claims? And why do the leaders of these groups insist on being classified as indigenous when the term is derogatory? We need to be careful in implementing positive discrimination and learn from mistakes made elsewhere. For example, in India, hundreds of castes and tribes struggle to be classified as 'backward' even though it is a derogatory term, so that they become eligible for positive discrimination from the state, although it is usually the more wealthy and powerful of the marginalized groups that benefit from positive discrimination" (Pradhan, 1994: 45).

[47] For a valuable critique of this kind of approach, see van der Veer (1994).

[48] Cf. Parming and Cheung (1980), Tiryakian (1992).

[49] For stimulating discussions on related phenomena in other countries, see Anderson (1983) and Smith (1984).

CHAPTER FOURTEEN

Nation-Building, Multi-Ethnicity, and the Hindu State

Prayag Raj Sharma

INTRODUCTION

I have been asked to write an epilogue for the present volume in my capacity as a Nepali person writing from Nepal on the overall theme of the book. The focus of the book is on nation-building and ethnicity. The contributions deal, very broadly, with the following four areas: (1) state formation and nation-building efforts since Nepal's unification in 1768–9; (2) the upsurge in ethnicity and ethnic identity among the various linguistic and regional minorities; (3) some broad trends of socio-cultural change; (4) the implications of Hinduization in a multi-ethnic state, which, according to its Constitution, is still the world's only Hindu kingdom.

Most contributors writing for the volume are well-known anthropologists, who have many years experience of working in Nepal in their respective areas. As anthropologists their perspectives are naturally drawn from village-based single-community studies. But the volume also has contributions from others, including a historian, a specialist of language and literature, and an Indologist, who use a broader time-scale and geographical area in their discussion. On the whole this seems to provide a good combination of perspectives and research methods. The introduction by David Gellner tries to pull together the diverse chapters and brings out in sharper relief some of the issues, as well as making some theoretical excursions.

The task of making adequate comments on all the papers and of offering an alternative perspective is far from easy. In the first place, all the contributors are scholars of great standing. Then the

471

problem of nation-building itself, overshadowed by the emerging trends of ethnicity of which Nepal had remained blissfully ignorant until little over a decade ago,[1] is difficult to see through clearly. To hazard any guess as to what shape they might take in the coming months and years is an impossibility. In these circumstances what I have done in the few paragraphs below is to react to some of the points raised in the book, agreeing with some, while offering some of my own observations regarding the others.

In a sense the political change of 1990 could be said to have brought with it far broader socio-political ramifications for Nepal than the political change which it witnessed earlier in 1951. It is true that both changes helped to usher in an era of democratic rule and popular government. In 1951 democracy was established after the popular revolt that overthrew the rule of the Rana feudal oligarchy of one hundred and four years. This change also ended forever Nepal's centuries old self-imposed political isolation which had kept the country virtually cut off from all modern developments happening in the rest of the world. The political freedom brought forth by the change of 1951 lasted barely a decade, after which the country reverted once again to the authoritarian regime of an absolute Hindu monarchy under the Panchayat system. This fact notwithstanding, there was, however, no going back for Nepal to its former political isolation. The authoritarian Panchayat policy could not hope to insulate Nepal from exposure to the outside world. The change of 1990 was shaped by the cumulative force of Nepal's continuing contacts and exposure to the rest of the world since 1951. The second phase of democratic experience in the early 1990s was itself the outcome of a democratic resurgence sweeping across Europe at the close of the 1980s. In these decades the world also saw a strong rise in ethnic awareness and identity among peoples across all the continents of the world. All these developments have come to affect and characterize Nepal's post-1990 democracy as well. Most people in Nepal have liked to believe that, despite its cultural diversity, its history has been marked by an ethnic harmony in a multi-ethnic society, free of all kinds of ethnic tension. Its transition to democracy could be expected to produce other kinds of problems, but no serious ethnic stirrings. Have all these hopes been belied by the new developments in ethnic politics?

The end of the era of isolation in the early 1950s brought a stream of people from outside to visit Nepal in the form of tourists, visitors, resident foreigners, aid workers, scholars and researchers. Today Nepal has become one of the most well-researched countries of the world, thanks to the painstaking work of these foreign scholars – anthropologists in particular. Nepalis have learnt about Nepal more through the writings of these foreign researchers than through works written by the Nepalis themselves, and these readings have distilled through into their new consciousness.

The multi-party democratic Constitution has given the people of Nepal a new sense of power, freedom of expression, and a voice of dissent. As people have organized themselves in diverse associations and according to various political ideologies, expectations of a better deal from government have become commonplace. But no one had bargained for the bitterness that it would arouse in ethnic feelings amongst various groups who had lived together amicably in the past. Nepal must find a way to come to terms with this new reality of ethnic politics in coming days.

Thus a look back at Nepal's nation-building process over the last two hundred years or so, such as is attempted in this book, becomes a very pertinent enquiry. Any misplaced perspective on an issue of such crucial importance could have serious consequences. Therefore, what the contributors have to say on these and other related issues is going to be of great relevance.

In the following few paragraphs I too shall be talking mainly about two things: the process of nation-building and the problem of ethnicity and ethnic politics. I am not sure that on an important and controversial subject like this one, only one or two views or perspectives from Nepal can be enough. All the same, since I am asked to join in the debate, I shall do my best to give my observations on the subject below.

THE PROCESS OF NATION-BUILDING

The papers by John Whelpton and Michael Hutt deal directly with the questions of Nepal's nation-building and Nepali nationalism starting well back in the past and coming down to the present, and examining the issues beyond Nepal's borders among the émigré Nepalis in Darjeeling, Bhutan, and Assam. Although there is no paper by the late Richard Burghart appearing in the present collection, his paper on the concept of the nation-state which came out in 1984 has permeated the discourse of the book. The editors quote a passage from this paper in the beginning of the book. Naturally the question to ask would be whether or not Nepal became a nation-state at the time of its unification by Prithvi Narayan Shah of Gorkha (c.1722–1775) in 1768–9. Nepal's political status in the late eighteenth century seems to be closer to Yapp's definition of 'nationism' (cited by Hutt), which characterizes it as a state aspiring to be a nation. This urge was well evident from early on, as the sayings of Prithvi Narayan Shah compiled in his *Dibya Upadesh* bear out. Some people think that Nepal's work of national integration, especially the integration of its diverse ethnic groups, is far from over. On the face of it, it would seem that the status of nation-state still remains elusive for Nepal. Ethnic leaders of the 1990s allege that they have been subject to political oppression, economic exploitation, social subjugation, and cultural annexation by the Hindu state in the present as well as in the past. Although the truth of this cannot be wholly denied, it would be wrong to assume that even authoritarian feudal regimes of the past only ever succeeded in unifying their subjects in a purely political sense. Those who would like to minimize integration are only out to exploit the situation for other ends.

For Burghart (1984) the concept of nation-state has entered and become part of governmental discourse in Nepal. Burghart conceptualizes the state and the functions of the King and his subjects in it at three levels through the use of the terms *muluk* (the king's entire territorial possessions), the *deśa* (the territory over which he exercises his ritual authority), and just *deś* (a smaller sub-division of the early *deśa* inhabited by a culturally distinct group of his tenants, cultivators, and subjects). Although his article has the great merit of understanding the development of the notion of the nation-state in the terms described, his arguments sometimes seem to be over-laboured. The authority of the king over his dominions can be said to be of two sorts. One is derived from divine sanctions. This authority earns him the attributes of a sovereign lord, protector of the kingdom's territory including his subjects, a guardian of the moral order, an upholder and custodian of traditions, and the source of all spiritual and temporal power. In this capacity his territorial authority extended over his entire territorial possessions. This authority was deemed to be one indivisible whole. The other kind of authority resided in the king's power to realize payments of tribute, presents, gifts, revenue, levies, tolls, and taxes from the land and natural resources in his entire domain for the fulfilment of his earlier functions. This latter authority, however, could be alienated or delegated by the king to his vassals, feudal chiefs and rulers, civil and military servitors, priests, religious establishments, or ordinary farmers. His subordinates exercised the same authority as the king over their respective areas as long as they obtained this privilege from him. The areas over which they exercised such authority could be referred to by any number of names.

In the days when political prowess was determined by the strength of the sword, and when sovereign rulers were ever keen on conquering other kings' territories in order to expand their own, political boundaries were always fluid, and the question of a subject's political affiliation was, at best, indeterminate. This was true not only of Nepal but of the mediaeval period practically everywhere. Such a state of affairs describes the politics of Nepal before unification most aptly. Nepal's political boundary after unification became more durably fixed, receiving international recognition from China in 1792 and from the British East India Company after the treaty of Sagauli in 1816. Despite this, the idea of citizenship for the people in the modern sense was slow to evolve. The notion of citizenship in post-unification Nepal was not shared by everyone alike, with the result that an individual subject's political affiliation tended to remain loose. This condition was not any better in British India either.

Burghart is right to say that a person's identities based on family, kinship, home, and land were more important than any political ties. He might be led to forsake his home and his land by economic reasons, which resulted in a constant migration of people from and into Nepal (this latter migration characterized the *ryot*s of the Tarai). There is no need to make this act of migration look more emotionally significant than it is with the use of the term *deś tyāg* ('abandonment of one's country/land'), as Burghart has tried to do. The term *deś tyāg* is more usually seen in works of literary fiction intended to dramatize the individual experience of migration triggered by rural indebtedness. Migration should not be viewed as evidence of weak political affiliation. Political affiliation in the premodern state may not have been as strong, but the idea of a corporate existence or the abstractions of a state with which people identified themselves was not wholly lacking. Of course, the sense of a common belongingness was confined to the aristocracy, the nobles, the ruling elites, courtiers, and the more privileged class of people. The identification of these men with Nepal, or more properly, with Gorkha, was total. The citizenship ideal of the state takes its early form here. This idea of common belongingness was reinforced by a feeling of powerful nationalism, which led these people to fight in its defence and to die for it. Nationalism has been a preserve of the rich and privileged class in all times and places. Even in modern nation-states, nationalism is by and large articulated by members of the more conscious middle class. Consequently the loose affiliation of its subjects to a premodern state does not necessarily contradict its status as a nation-state.

The foundation of Gorkha by Prithvi Narayan Shah was laid upon a feudal matrix. It fitted Max Weber's definition of a patrimonial state, in which the king was the patriarch, a protector and a provider. The king was the patron par excellence, and all others under him were his clients whose position was hierarchically and ascriptively defined. The polity gave the key role to monarchy in which the ruler's words were a command (*hukum*); it followed the dynastic and hereditary principles. Familial networks and loyalty to one's patron were the assured means of career success and personal fortune. The values of such a state derived from Hinduism; from it all the king's divine sanctions flowed. Hinduism provided the king (state) not only with its rational basis, but also all its popular legitimacy.

The enlarged state of Gorkha was created mainly out of the dreams and vision of one person. It is expressed most clearly in Prithvi

Narayan Shah's *Dibya Upadesh* in which he spoke to his heirs, nobles, and military generals. True, such a vision was not a collective one to begin with. It was more like the personal ambition of one man, but he wanted to pass it on and entrust it to a wider group of people in his state. That is what made him say what he did about his military campaigns, share his concern about the integrity of the state with his successors and members of the nobility (*bhāradārī*), and bequeath this responsibility to them.

The overriding concern of Prithvi Narayan Shah for his newly enlarged Gorkha was to keep it one and indivisible. He would not be pressured into dividing it among his brothers as a patrimony, which some kings customarily did both in the Chaubisi states and in the Newar kingdoms of the Kathmandu Valley. The term *ḍhuṅgo* (literally 'stone'), which the Gorkhalis used to designate their state, was a fitting metaphor, conveying the idea of its solid, indivisible, and sovereign political character. Whelpton writes in his paper how the (*bhāradārī*) council enjoyed the right to veto the king if he sought its division. This places the new Gorkhali state altogether on a qualitatively different footing.

Prithvi Narayan Shah was able to rally a broad cross-section of Gorkhali society, including the Brahmans, the Khas, the Gurungs, the Magars, and others to his cause. His army of Gorkhalis comprised men of all these castes and social groups. The term 'Gorkhali' represents the first example of national blending and assimilation. Even the Newars of Gorkha who originally went to settle there from Patan (Lalitpur), assumed the Gorkhali title after their names. For a long time people outside Nepal understood 'Gorkhali', or just 'Gurkhas' as the British popularly called their soldier recruits from Nepal, to refer to a distinct caste or ethnic group from Nepal. Of course this was a mistaken notion. Nevertheless, it indicates an integration of some sort.

Before he died Prithvi Narayan Shah had enlarged his state till it extended from the Marsyangdi river in the west to the borders of Sikkim in the east. His ambitions in the west were held in check by the powerful confederation of principalities just west and north of Gorkha. He was waiting for the right opportunity to strike them. He had his eyes set on Lamjung, Tanahun, and Palpa. He had already won the ruler of Jajarkot to his side to help him in his cause. He had watched the politics of the state of Palpa at first hand during his travel to and from Banaras. All this indicates that he had planned the expansion of Gorkha from very early in his career.

Nepal's unification process can be said to resemble and parallel to some extent Italian and German unification in Europe in the nineteenth century, which it anticipated by a hundred years. As in Europe, the psychological conditions for unification can be said to have been ripe in Nepal also. In all the Baisi and Chaubisi clusters of states, as well as in the string of Sen states starting in Palpa and extending to Makwanpur, Chaudandi, and Bijayapur along the Tarai of Nepal, a large proportion of the population was of the same stock (i.e. Khas-speaking Parbatiyas). Furthermore, in many cases they were also linked together by common familial ties. The groundwork for unification had also been laid by the quick spread of the Khas language (the precursor of the Gorkhali or Nepali language) right across the hills of Nepal. Its speakers had moved to settle down in sizeable numbers everywhere. These people and their language had made a significant dent in the Kathmandu Valley of the seventeenth century. As in the European cases mentioned above, in which the unification was directed against French and Austro-Hungarian imperialism, the motivation for combining all the hill states into a single, powerful entity was not merely personal ambition but the wish to build a sacred Hindu land, distinct from and secure against the non-believing Muglan (Moghul Emperor) and the English 'Phiringis' poised on the coast.

Prithvi Narayan Shah was also the first ruler in what is now Nepal to acknowledge the idea of cultural diversity, although some have rejected this interpretation (see, for example, Gellner's introduction, p.24 above). The words of Prithvi Narayan Shah in the *Dibya Upadesh* have been understood by many in Nepal in this sense. I would like to quote in full the relevant passage:

> ... bhāradār le svakh garenan bhanyā cārai khuṭmā mero tarvār bajnyai cha svakh garyo bhanyā merā sānā dukha le ārjyā ko muluk hoina sabai jāt ko phulbāri ho sabailāi cetanā bhayā yo phulbāri ko choṭā baḍā cārai varṇa chattis

jāt le yo asil hindusthānā ho āphnā kuldharma na choḍnu
khvāmit ko nun ko udhār garnu ... (Saṃskṛta Saṃdeśa 1:
8–9)

... If members of the council of nobility eschew luxury [the
sound of] my sword will ring out on all four sides of [my
kingdom's] boundary markers. If they take to [a life of]
luxury, the country is not earned out of my small pains; it
is a garden of all castes, if they have the sense to realize it.
All [those] of this garden, high and low, belonging to the
four *varṇa*s and thirty-six *jāt* [castes], since it is a pure land
of the Hindus, should not abandon the customary religion
of [their respective] lineages. [They] should redeem the
master's [king's] salt ... (my translation).

A measure of integration of the newly acquired territory was
also achieved through a system of revenue administration and
taxation policy pursued by the revenue-hungry state (Regmi, 1971:
55–74). Such a system was a highly centralized one, like all other
systems of the administration. All military and civil appointments
in the districts and outlying provinces were made by the centre.
There was a good network whereby all revenues collected from
districts and villages were remitted to the state treasury in
Kathmandu. Although some changes in the style of revenue
collecting were made from time to time – for example, revenue
rights were farmed out to individual contractors through a system
of bidding (*ibid.*: 124–41) – there was no change in the requirement
that all revenue be received eventually at the centre.

This brought about a uniform pattern of cultural and
administrative behaviour among diverse groups in different parts of
the country. Local officials aped the manners of the central court as
they were granted a multi-faceted authority over farmers and
tenants in their area. A common culture was engendered through
the ritualized behaviour in which tenants and farmers paid their
respects and brought gifts to the local chiefs (*mukhiyā, jimmawāl,
talukdār, dwāre,* and *amālī*) during the annual Dasain festival. It
helped to forge a strong link connecting the districts with the
political centre (see Pfaff-Czarnecka above). Such a link was also

established through other forms of levies collected directly on behalf of the centre and which the centre would under no circumstances alienate to anyone. Such levies included the *gaddīmubārak* (collected from every household at the time of the king's ascension to the throne), the *cumāwan* and *goddhuwā* (collected at the time of the sacred thread and marriage ceremony of the king's sons and daughters), *sāunyāphāgu* (twice-yearly levies collected from all homesteads), and fines imposed in connection with capital offences (*pañcakhaṭ*) (Regmi, 1971: 63–4). Apart from the above, the social and juridical integration of the country was made through the promulgation of the Legal Code (Muluki Ain) of 1854.

Among other attributes of a democratic country, the 1990 Constitution (Article 4.1) applies to Nepal the epithets "multi-ethnic" and "multi-lingual". The clause referring to multi-ethnicism and multi-lingualism made a smooth, non-problematic entry, requiring no ethnic pressure or political agitation at the time of drafting the Constitution. The idea of cultural diversity has been a part of and is implicit in Nepal's historical legacy.

The notion of cultural diversity has gone deeper into Nepal's collective consciousness than people are willing to credit. As shown above, Prithvi Narayan Shah himself acknowledged this idea in his *Dibya Upadesh*. Of course this idea of cultural diversity fell short of actually embracing cultural pluralism as a positive value. Some commentators have also cast doubt on the meaning of Prithvi Narayan's words. In his introduction David Gellner refers to Prithvi Narayan Shah's "indifference to the question of language" (p.24 above), but this sounds somewhat like blaming Queen Elizabeth I for not allowing women to vote in her time in England.

The Legal Code of 1854 endorsed the idea of the inviolability of 'customary practices' of different *jāti*s (Höfer, 1979: 171–6). There are any number of decrees to be found issued by the rulers of the centre even during the Rana regime in which social and cultural groups were left free to follow their customary traditions and practices under their council of elders (*Regmi Research Series*, Vols. 1, 4, 7, etc.). The *bhāradārī*, or Council of Nobles, gave its adjudication on disputes over infringements of customary practices or of the customary rights of specific castes (*jāt*) or ethnic groups (*jāti*). They would respond to petitions brought by specific members of such groups and would take care to ensure that the customary practices followed by a large majority of the group in question were respected and passed on intact (J.L. Sharma, 1992/93; Höfer, 1979).

The terms to describe a caste (*jāt*) and an ethnic group (*jāti*) in the Nepali language stem from a common root. In early writings the word *jāt* was used as much to refer to a person's ethnic status as to his caste. It might therefore be possible to interpret Prithvi Narayan Shah's use of the expression *cār varṇa chattis jāt* to describe the social universe of his state in a slightly different way than is usually done. In fact *varṇa* could be said to allude to the people of the caste order, while *jāt* referred to the ethnic multiplicity of Nepal.

Carl Degler has described how the underlying principles of inclusion and equality were applied to American Blacks after the Civil War (Degler, 1992). Despite the USA's celebration of the idea of multiculturalism in their society, it was the principle of inclusion which guided their outlook in race relations for a long period. Similarly, in the case of Nepal the Legal Code of 1854 worked more in the spirit of inclusion. One outcome of it was the promulgation of a single national hierarchy. But this hierarchy must be understood as only a loose arrangement, leaving enough room to the various ethnic groups to enjoy their customary traditions freely within it. The social hierarchy should not be understood as an attempt by the state at full cultural annexation.

Against the historical background sketched above, the process of Hinduization in Nepal should not come as too much of a surprise. Hinduization happened neither in the same degree nor in a uniform manner amongst all groups and individuals. Nor did the state proselytize or force people to accept Hinduism, although in some cases tax exemptions were available to ethnic groups as an incentive to conform to some cherished Hindu cultural values (see *Regmi Research Series, passim*). More properly, it was left to the individuals or groups themselves to decide to what extent and in what form to take it or leave it. In general the Hinduization process never cut deeper than the imitation of the Hindu high castes' mannerisms by the others (see Pfaff-Czarnecka, chapter 13). Nor was Nepal's acculturation process one-way traffic. The Hindus

FIGURE 43   *An intercaste feast, celebrating the* bartaman *of two Newar boys, by the shore of the Tadi river, Nuwakot, 1980. The intimate connection of purity, caste, and eating is here displayed. The ground is purified before eating, the cooks are Brahmans, and high-caste men and women purify themselves before eating and wear unstitched clothes. Men of the highest castes are served first. (Girls and uniniated boys are allowed to eat at the same time, but at a distance.) Castes are kept segregated* (Joanna Pfaff-Czarnecka)

themselves have been no less influenced in their many beliefs and practices by the religion of the smaller traditions.

From the preceding discussion certain conclusions inevitably follow. Remove monarchy and there is no state, and minus the state, there is no nationalism. The only form of nationalism the ethnic groups have known about or been familiar with is in the framework of the Nepali state. Even from a distance and across the political divide, Nepal serves as a powerful symbol of cultural and emotional unity to Nepali expatriates living in various diasporas in India (see Hutt, chapter 3).

There is bound to be an element of history behind all concepts of specific nation-states and the formation of identities based on them. Such a historical process cannot ever be ignored or completely set aside from the consideration of nation-building. Respect for such a historical legacy is needed for the health and integrity of a nation-state. The emerging culture of a multi-party polity in a young democracy such as Nepal's is expected increasingly to assimilate new ideas and new values of social justice and human rights in the practice of its national life. Once these have struck root, one might expect that a national identity incorporating them will gradually replace older, more parochial identities.

ETHNICITY AND ETHNIC POLITICS

The ethnic politics of Nepal in the 1990s seems to have elements conforming with both the primordialists' and the instrumentalists' models. In a democratic set-up the ethnic groups of Nepal feel an urge to discover pride in their ethnic identity. At the same time, however, they are also conscious that they can take advantage of the democratic situation and bargain for a good share in the political and economic pie, which fits the instrumentalist model. Such an urge on the part of the various ethnic groups need not be in conflict with the idea of a nation and nationalism. Still, much unnecessary heat and passion gets generated over the many issues relating to ethnic demands (O. Gurung, n.d.; Bhattachan, n.d., 1995). No serious attempt seems to have been made to bridge the gap which lies in the mutual perception of the problem between the ethnic activists, on the one hand, and the government, on the other. If one group pitches its demands too high and uses radical rhetoric, the other appears complacent and mired in a do-little attitude.

Ethnic politics in Nepal first surfaced in the year leading up to the referendum of 1980. Then it disappeared as quickly as it had arisen, because the national referendum confirmed the Panchayat system in power. In the decade of the 1980s ethnic activists concentrated on bringing out cultural magazines devoted to the study of their respective groups. Among these were *Kongpi* (the Kirat group), *Tamu* (Gurung), *Khanglo* (Thakali), and *Tharu Sanskriti*

(Tharu), not to mention the many publications devoted to Newar culture from early on. Since the political changes of 1990 ethnic politics have become a permanent fixture in Nepal's multi-party democracy. Today practically every ethnic group of some note has a cultural forum or association of its own. A larger organization called the Nepal Federation of Nationalities (Nepal Janajati Mahasangh) was established in 1990 to bring all the smaller ethnic forums under a single umbrella. In a pamphlet published in 1993 nineteen such forums are listed as federating units (NCIWIP, 1993). This Federation claims to speak on ethnic matters on behalf of all its federating units. Although it calls itself a non-political organization, the 17-point charter it submitted to the government in 1993 includes unmistakeably political demands. I will return to this below. So far four ethnic political parties based in the hills are known. They are the Limbuwan Mukti Morcha, the Khambuwan Mukti Morcha, the Mongol National Organization, and the Rastriya Janamukti Party (*ibid.*). The first three parties were barred from contesting the general

FIGURE 44   *Brahmans reading the* Devimahatmya *during Dasain* (*Belkot, Nuwakot district, 1986*) (*Joanna Pfaff-Czarnecka*)

elections of 1991. The Election Commission alleged that they were overly communal and parochial in their stated aims. Only the last-named party, the Rastriya Janamukti Party, was allowed to contest elections in 1991 and 1994, and it contested them chiefly on the issue of establishing a quota of representation for the members of various ethnic groups (see Whelpton, p.59 above). Although it fielded 50 and 82 candidates in the 1991 and 1994 elections respectively, it failed to win even a single seat in the National Parliament and it managed to win only around 1% of the total votes in both elections (*ibid.*; see also Election Commission, 1994).

The other facet of Nepal's ethnic/regional politics consists of the Tarai-based Sadbhavana Party which is an all-Madheshi party. In their stated aims and objectives the Sadbhavana party and the hill-based ethnic parties stand a world apart from each other in their perception and assessment of the ethnic problems. While the Janajati Mahasangh is anti-Hindu and anti-Brahman in sentiment, the Sadbhavana Party is anti-Pahari (anti-hill people). It is opposed to the numerical domination of the Tarai by immigrants from the hills (whether 'Hindu' or not); it is against the prejudiced way the hill population regards Madheshis in general, it is unhappy with the distribution of citizenship certificates to Tarai people, and it is critical of discrimination against the recruitment of Tarai people into the Nepalese army. It also demands that Hindi be recognized as a national language of Nepal. This party won a total of six seats in the 1991 elections, but was reduced to only three in the 1994 elections. One obvious conclusion would be that the country's political agenda is still largely determined by the three major national political parties, the Nepali Congress Party, the Communist Party of Nepal-United Marxist-Leninist (CPN-UML), and the Rastriya Prajatantra Party, which are all organized along ideological lines.

In his very useful paper, Charles Ramble has provided a good insight into the ethnicity question as it affects Nepal's different Tibetanid groups living in the Himalayan foothills and in its trans-Himalayan valleys. These groups provide a study in contrast with the Madheshis living in the south. From what he writes there is still no evidence of any strong sense of ethnic solidarity amongst these Tibetanids which might bind them together. There is also no feeling of resentment on their part against the Hindus or the Hindu state, although the Bhotiya population has not been treated with any great esteem by them in the past. Ramble links the rise of ethnicity directly to the economic and political benefits it can bring to the groups concerned. From this one can probably infer that the Tibetanids do not see Hindu predominance or the Hindu state in Nepal as posing any serious obstacle to the practice and propagation of their culture, religion, or economic vocation.

The phenomenon of Newar ethnicity has some puzzling and inexplicable aspects uniquely its own. The more ethnically minded Newars are strongly anti-Hindu and anti-Brahman in their feelings. The Nepal Bhasha Manka Khalah – their cultural forum – is a federating member of the Janajati Mahasangh, and joins issue with it on all questions of ethnic rights against the government and the predominant Hindu majority. Perhaps no other social group of Nepal enjoys the same degree of advantage as the Newars do in terms of their opportunities for participation in the economic and political spheres of national life. Newars can adopt several identities, separately or all at once, depending on their calculation of what will bring them the highest political and economic dividends on a particular occasion. They can present themselves as either caste Hindus, Buddhists, or indigenous people of Nepal. There is no job, no profession, which they have not entered freely from the highest to the lowest ranks. A mere 5% of the total population enjoys a share as high as 35% of government jobs. As Nepal's traditional trader and merchant class their market outposts are spread throughout the length and the breadth of the country. In spite of this, Newar ethnic activists join hands with the Janajati groups claiming to be among those exploited by the Hindu majority. This psychology can only be summed up by the English proverb 'hunting with the hounds and running with the hare'.

The brand of ethnic politics espoused by the Nepal Janajati Mahasangh and others reflects a totally different perception of Nepal's political, economic, social, and cultural processes from that of the Hindu majority.[2] Space does not permit a detailed examination of this here. The first blueprint for ethnic resentment appeared in 1985 in a book by Gopal Gurung (Gurung, 1985). His book was banned by the then Panchayat government for its allegedly communal overtones and for inciting mutual hatred between different cultural groups. The ethnic politics pursued by subsequent ethnic forums in Nepal continue to follow more or less the same line as Gurung's book. Their attack is directed against the Hindu state, Hindu rule in Nepal over the past 200 years, and Brahmans. They question Nepal's political unification, resent Hindu exploitation and domination, and the denial of their legitimate cultural rights. The Hindus are accused of depriving them of their rights to communal land, such as *kipaṭ*. A supposed 20% of Hindus are said to rule an 80% non-Hindu country. The numbers game is an intimate part of ethnic politics.[3] To the ethnic activists, Hindu rule amounts to internal colonization. The Hindus are regarded as refugees fleeing from India and as followers of the religion and culture of India. The recruitment of ethnic groups into the army of the Hindu state and their recruitment as 'Gurkhas' in the British army is taken as proof that they have been made into a subservient class.

Irredentism lends a sharper edge to the ethnic politics of this region. There is no space to deal with it in detail here. The Indian subcontinent has been home to scores of cultures and peoples who have enjoyed freedom of spatial movement in all directions for the greater part of their history. The open border between India and Nepal even today could be said to be part of this lingering relic of the past. Recent political developments in the region, however, have led to many independent sovereign states being created out of a subcontinent that had formerly been a single political unit. The drawing up of strictly regulated borders restricting the free movement of people has, in many instances, divided a single linguistic and cultural group, rendering its members citizens of different countries. Thus ethnic disturbances in the region acquire a transnational character that threatens to engulf a larger area. Ethnic tensions in one country arouse the suspicion that they may be orchestrated by another country, usually its neighbour, for its own political advantage. The Bhutanese refugees in Nepal are the latest example of this, souring the relationships between Nepal, Bhutan, and India. The Indian press accuses Nepal from time to time of harbouring intentions of creating 'greater Nepal' by claiming the areas where Nepalis are resident in India.

During 1990 when the new Constitution was being drafted, ethnic and religious minorities – especially Newar Buddhists (of all hues) – joined forces to oppose the idea of Nepal again being declared a Hindu state. However the Constitution-drafting committee, which was drawn from the Nepali Congress Party, the various factions of the Communist Party making up the United Left Front, and nominees of the Royal Palace, decided otherwise and let Nepal continue as before as a Hindu state. The new Constitution is regarded as a document of national consensus today as never before in the past. The Hindu state seems to have been left untouched more for reasons of historical continuity than to make Nepal resemble, however remotely, a theocratic state (Acharya, 1993). The next battle waged by the Janajati Mahasangh was over the teaching of Sanskrit as a compulsory subject in Nepal's middle and high schools, which they opposed tooth and nail, with eventual success. Sanskrit to them provides a focus for their anti-Brahman stance. In the heat of ethnic passion their leaders even at one time questioned the place of Nepali as the nation's lingua franca.

The above-mentioned 17-point charter submitted by the Janajati Mahasangh exhibits the mix of the realistic and the unrealistic characteristic of their political approach. Some of their concerns relate to the question of strengthening their cultural identity. The Constitution of 1990 has already endorsed this idea by calling Nepal a multi-ethnic, multi-lingual country. Their other demands concern the right to education in the mother tongue. The Nepali Congress set up a separate commission to look into this matter and make recommendations. In 1993 the Commission submitted its recommendations which the government accepted, agreeing to implement them gradually.[4] The new CPN-UML government which came into power after the general elections of 1994 took further steps in this regard. It set aside funds for the preparation of textbooks for mother-tongue teaching. It also announced a number of other programmes to benefit the people of some of the most economically backward ethnic communities in Nepal.[5] These include the provision of income earning opportunities, a cash grant of six hundred rupees per annum to purchase educational materials for ten students from each district, and other schemes of social upliftment.

The democratic government of Nepal is expected to expand its schemes to benefit the economically most backward ethnic communities in the near future. It may also be willing to grant such communities further cultural rights and gradually to increase their level of political representation. Among the most improbable and unrealistic demands put forth by the Janajati Mahasangh, there is particularly one which asks that Nepal be made into a multi-national state (the ethnic activists like to refer to all their federating groups as separate nations). They want political units to be established along ethnic lines with defined boundaries, and to have the right to self-rule, self-determination, and full autonomy. In a similar vein the Janajati Party (NRJP) has produced a map of Nepal cut up into twelve federal provinces, with one province for each of the twelve ethnic/linguistic/regional groups.[6] What is very striking in this is the fact that neither the upper-caste Parbatiya Hindus, nor their less fortunate lower-caste brethren, are given any place whatsoever.

The leaders of ethnic organizations in Nepal have shown a preference for presenting their case in terms of two sets of opposing ideas, cultures, values, or situations, or even, unfortunately, in racial terms. This can be seen in the use of contrasts such as Hindu versus Janajati, indigenous versus non-indigenous, Pahari (i.e. of the hills) versus Madheshi (of the plains), Mongol versus Aryan, or the pointed nose versus the flat nose. There seems to be a constant implication of 'them' versus 'us' (Bhattachan, 1995). These are examples either of political naiveté or of deliberate ethnic brinkmanship. Whether they like it or not, only the state such as we have it today is able to provide all of us with an overarching sense of national identity. Sequestered ethnic groups, either singly or collectively, have nothing similar to parallel it. If they try to invent something artificially so late in the day, they cannot do it without first destroying the idea of the state.

In short, even the feudal and autocratic Hindu state of the past succeeded, in my opinion, in achieving a measure of integration which is not just a figment of the imagination. The Hindus of Nepal have shared a common physical, economic, social, and cultural space with other ethnic groups living there. In fact the Limbus, the Rais, the Gurungs, the Magars, the Tamangs, and, not least, the Newars have lived and worked more like economic competitors in a common framework, although some groups have shown their skills, aptitudes, and preferences for one activity rather than another. As farmers holding land of their own they stood on an equal footing. The Hindus no more look apart from the other people of Nepal than a tree does from its trunk. It is inappropriate therefore to call them colonizers. This mutual living and sharing together is far more intimate than in most other parts of South Asia. As a matter of fact, in the Nepali case, castes and ethnic groups form a continuum rather than a dichotomy.

The domination of Brahmans in the political parties, in the National Parliament, and in government today is a reality which cannot be denied. This is cited as an example of the much publicized term *bāhunbād* ('Brahmanism'), which is the subject of Bista's much publicized critique (Bista, 1991). However, one would like to believe that the present imbalance in caste/ethnic representation will be corrected and that this will be reflected in the internal hierarchies of the political parties and in other organs of government in the years to come. The predominance of Brahmans is only proportionate to the level of interest Brahmans have taken in politics and political activity. It should be recalled here that Brahmans have been in the forefront of all political change and in adopting new and emancipatory political values in recent decades.

In the general socio-economic and political life of post-1990 Nepal, with the increasing emphasis on ethnic politics, the image of the Brahman has suffered the most. In this context the word in most common use in political vocabulary is this same *bāhunbād*. No one, however, knows precisely what this word means. Or rather, it means different things to different people. The Brahmans are held to be the *bête-noirs* who are responsible for perpetrating most of the country's ills, both now and in the past. It is not so much what a Bahun (Brahman) actually does, or what he believes in, it is the Bahun himself who seems to be the object of their hatred. As a result, today Bahuns find themselves caught on the wrong foot by the 'ethnic wave'. Unlike the other ethnic groups, who claim a putative tribal origin and build a new identity based upon it, the Bahuns have no comparable tribal identity to fall back upon. Brahmans are believed to have come from India by the more radical ethnic activists. But the Parbatiya Bahuns have known no other home except Nepal. Bahuns cannot ever hope to revive their patriotism to return to the different Baisi and Chaubisi principalities of old to which they belonged before 1769. Regardless of their former political allegiance they have all accepted the larger Gorkha or Nepal as their new state. The privileged Brahmans forming part of the ruling class have always been in a small minority compared to the general Brahman population of Nepal. The continued predominance of Bahuns in the politics and administration of Nepal today causes a resentment which expresses itself by means of the term *bāhunbād*. But the Brahmans' share in Nepal's politics and administration is not unduly disproportionate to the size of their population, when their education and their interest in politics are taken into account. This picture should alter as the members of other groups come and compete with them in the years to come. The negative image of the Bahun today has much to do with political corruption and bureaucratic inefficiency, which they are associated with more than any other social group.

The Bahun's image may have suffered a decline for yet another reason. Most anthropological studies by foreign scholars have centred on the different ethnic and linguistic minorities of Nepal. In the presentation of their ethnographic studies their main sympathy naturally goes to the group they have studied. It is the anthropologist's accepted method of research to look for differences in every aspect of culture and lifestyle that set their group apart from the rest (N. J. Allen's chapter above is a welcome attempt to correct for this). The stress is on pointing out the dissimilar rather than the similar. Such studies set off the ethnic group in question from the Hindus or the Bahuns who can be found living not far away from them. The points of contrast are sharply delineated. Unlike the ethnic groups who tend to be centred in a single habitat, the Bahuns have managed to spread throughout Nepal's middle hills. Each time an ethnographic study is made the ethnic group will change, but the Bahun, playing his various social roles, everywhere remains the same. This has produced a common stereotype of the Bahun, which potrays him as a greedy priest, a crafty village moneylender, a stealer of other people's land, who shuns rough and dirty work, carries with him an air of haughtiness, and is presumptuous and patronizing. This is an image which sticks to all Bahuns. It is the image which is most often sold to the outside audience. Any good impression which Bahuns may make is submerged beneath all this. The truth is that Bahuns are neither more good nor bad than members of other social groups in Nepal. However their negative image weighs more heavily in people's minds and may hang for long like a millstone around the Brahmans' necks. Brahmans find themselves at the centre of all this ethnic imbroglio in Nepal today. Could this be a prelude to a more serious ethnic conflagration in the future?   January 1996

FIGURE 45   *A Brahman widow from Belkot (1987) wearing a yellow blouse. Older high-caste women are considered to be the 'bearers of tradition' (Joanna Pfaff-Czarnecka)*

NOTES

[1] The unrest among the Limbu population in eastern Nepal in the early 1950s was caused by concern over their *kipaṭ* system of communal land tenure rather than by ethnic assertiveness in the broader sense.

[2] See G. Gurung (1985), O. Gurung (n.d.), and Bhattachan (n.d., 1995).

[3] See Whelpton's paper for tables of percentages of caste/ethnic population and mother-tongue speakers based on the 1991 census; cf. Bhattachan (1995).

[4] See Rastriyabhasa (1994) (Report of the Advisory Commission of Policy towards the National Languages).

[5] See His Majesty's Government (1994).

[6] See Sharma (1994) for their names; Dahal (n.d.) has reproduced a map of these twelve federal provinces.

CHAPTER FIFTEEN

State and Society in Nepal

Harka Gurung

INTRODUCTION

This book is a collection of essays on the changing nature of cultural identity in Nepal with the focus on ethnicity and politics. It is dedicated to the late Richard Burghart whose seminal paper on the formation of Nepal as a nation-state (1984) is quoted by nine of the authors. All the contributors are foreigners who have researched in Nepal for considerable periods of time. The editors have asked me to provide reactions to the papers as a Nepalese. My response below, with some supplementary material, begins with comments on perspectives in Nepalese social research. This is followed by a short note on the formation of the Nepalese state. The third section deals with Hinduization and Nepal's reliance on Indic symbols for national identity. The main section, the fourth, reviews adaptation and resistance by the ethnic groups included as examples in the book. In conclusion, there are sections on the present social composition of Nepal and the political expression of ethnic issues.

PERSPECTIVES

Gellner in his introduction refers to the essays in this collection as being both top-down and bottom-up perspectives. Accordingly, Gellner's introduction itself and the pieces by Whelpton (chapter 1), Michaels (chapter 2), and Pfaff-Czarnecka (chapter 13) belong as overviews to the first category. The bottom-up perspective is represented by eight contributions on particular ethnic/language groups. Those on Nepali-speakers abroad and Tibetan-speakers in Nepal fall in the intermediate category that provide instances of how cultural persistence leads to political alienation.

Interpretation is also influenced by other contrasts in perspective. These would be outside/alien versus inside/native and dominant versus marginal. On the first dichotomy, Burghart (1984) referred to theoretical advantages of adopting a native approach for a better understanding of alien cultures. Although the contributors to this book evince high field intimacy, in so far as they are all foreigners, they provide an outside perspective in generic terms. Within the inside/native perspective itself, there is a distinction between the dominant and marginal approach. Two contributors to this volume are quite explicit on this aspect. Gellner (Introduction, p.3) notes, "Just what it means to live in a Hindu polity varies a great deal depending on who you are", and Whelpton (chapter 1, p.39) adds, "Being Nepali, then, means different things to different Nepalis and we need to be constantly aware of the gap that may exist between official aspirations and the actual feelings of a population divided along ethnic, caste, and class lines."

The formulation of Nepalese history and the interpretation of Nepalese culture has been very much the construct of dominant castes. Thus, Nepalese socio-cultural discussion has remained a monologue with no voices from below. Until recently, the marginal groups or the ethnic minorities had neither the intellectual resource nor the freedom of expression to record or present their viewpoint. It is significant that the first two histories of Nepalese ethnic minorities were produced outside the country. These were *Tamba Kaiten* by Santbir Lama (1959)[1] and *History and Culture of the Kirat People* by Imansingh Chemjong (1966).[2] Burghart (1984: 101), in another context, noted that "it is nonetheless reasonable to assume that just as the anthropologist can get inside an alien culture so the native can get outside his." The extent of political and cultural dominance in Nepal is evident from the irony that the marginals were able to express their nativity only outside their country!

One should also note a certain congruence in the perspectives of outsiders and native marginals. The outsider may be an intruder but has the advantages of objectivity and critical analysis. However, some undertake an exercise in empathy and others are actively engaged in the process of the creation and re-interpretation of ethnic identity. Therefore, the penchant of foreign anthropologists for carrying out ethnographic studies is viewed with some disapproval by the authorities as giving encouragement to communal movements. And Nepalese scholars, mostly from higher castes, tend to criticize foreign scholars for what they see as their divisive habit of romanticizing the culture of minorities. That so much research has been accomplished has been mainly due to Nepal's increasing dependence on outside aid and influence. Meanwhile, the ethnic minorities tend to view the printed exposition of foreign researchers as more authentic. Thus it is that there emerges on the one hand a nexus between the outside and marginal perspectives and on the other a divergence in perception between the natives according to whether they subscribe to dominant or marginal aspect viewpoints.

In addition to perspectives, the medium of communication between the researcher and subject greatly influences the interpretation. Earlier social scientists visiting Nepal relied heavily on Nepali interpreters recruited mostly from educated high castes who would be as alien to the group under study as the foreign researcher. This contributed to lack of understanding and mis-interpretation. Even in rare cases when interpreters were educated members of ethnic minorities, their elite status tended to produce bias or distortion.

More researchers are now equipped with some knowledge of the language of the group they study. Here also, there is a lack of clarity in their interpretation of native terms due to two constraints. Firstly, most tribal languages simply lack conceptual terms or those that did exist have been subsumed by Nepali ones. However, many Nepali colloquial terms have lately been superseded by Sanskritic ones.[3] Secondly, since there is no standard form in pre-literate languages,[4] researchers are tempted to have recourse to Nepali words readily available in dictionaries. Even in the case of diction-aries of minority languages, there is a preponderance of Nepali loan-words. The essays in this book include varieties of such interpretation of native terms and these will be considered in the relevant context.

STATE FORMATION

The land corresponding to present-day Nepal in the Central Himalaya represents an area of interface of two culture worlds: Indic and Bodic. Their contact zone runs north-west to south-west at a tangent to the mountain axis whereby the Caucasoids (Khas) predominate in the Karnali basin and the Mongoloids (Kiranti) eastwards. The rugged relief fostered numerous tribal units, chiefdoms and petty states. How was it that a sizable state emerged to encompass such a diverse land and culture? The case of Nepal was no different from most states that grow round a nucleus and expand by aggrandizement. The extended Nepal was created through conquest, an outcome of territorial unification by force. The House of Gorkha had to contend with three types of political system for supremacy. One was represented by the forty-six lordships of Chaubisi and Baisi with a culture and technology similar to the Gorkhalis' own. Another group was of tribal hegemonies in the Gandaki and Kosi basins. The third type of adversary included Newar and Sen kingdoms that were more developed and endowed with greater resources. The former had been weakened by internecine feud since the division of the kingdom after Yaksha Malla in the mid-fifteenth century. The Sen kingdom of Palpa had the potential to be a larger state but Mukund Sen squandered it by parcelling his realm into four patrimonies.

The Gorkhali could only turn east as they came out of the west. Various factors contributed to the primacy of Gorkha in the ensuing struggle. One was its geographic location as the eastern vanguard of expanding Khas power at the threshold of the dissonant Newar kingdoms. Gorkha represented a transition between the rustic Khas and cultured Newar as their kings had matrimonial ties with the western lordships and a *mīt* (ritual friendship) relationship with the Newar kings. It had also adopted innovations from the

Nepal Valley. Particularly important in this regard were the initiatives of Rama Shah (1606–36) in social and legal systems and the establishment of a commercial Newar community (*caubīs koṭhī*) by courtesy of King Siddhi Narasingha of Lalitpur. In addition, the Gorkhali army had a multi-ethnic character, being composed of Khas-Bahun commanders and tribal followers. This fighting force had been moulded through a long campaign and well-armed with arsenals captured from the expeditionary forces of Murshidabad Muslims (1763) and Kinloch (1767). Thus, during the brief period 1806–1815, Gorkhali rule extended nearly 1,500 km from the Tista to the Sutlej including the Barah Thakurai (Twelve Lordships) of the western Himalaya. This domain was not only overextended but also a challenge to a newly emerging power in the plains. The Anglo-Nepal war (1814–16) confined Nepal by and large to its present geographic limits.

In tracing the evolution of the concept of nation-state in Nepal, Burghart (1984) identifies six analytically separable stages:

1. 1816 – demarcation of an external border;
2. c. 1860 – convergence of realm (core) and possessions' (periphery) boundaries;
3. c. 1860 – interpretation of country (people) as species (castes);
4. c. 1930 – designation of Nepali as the official language;
5. c. 1960 – differentiation between kingship and the state; and
6. c. 1960 – construct of a cultural polity.

The first three episodes have relevance to the question of interpretation of terms referred to in closing the perspective section above. Burghart's formulation of three indigenous spatial notions is based on his rendering of, native terms: *muluk* as possessions, *deśa* as realm, and *deś* as country. He then relates these to types of authority as respective sources of legitimation: proprietary to 'possessions', ritual to 'realm', and ancestral to 'country'. Despite their divergent etymology, *muluk* (Persian) and *deśa* (Sanskrit) are in fact synonymous terms for country, possession, or realm, since vernacular usage lacks conceptual clarity. Similarly, *deśa* and *deś* are mere variations which means country or territory and the subtle distinction Burghart alludes to would better fit *deś* (core) and *prades* (periphery) despite the Nepali marginalization of the related term *madheś* (*madhya-deś* = heartland). Burghart makes a valid distinction between a core of Hinduized proto-Nepal and a periphery of climatic and culture regions both together making up a 'pan-Nepal', but his attempt to ascribe discreteness and precision to the relevant native terms is weak.

Similarly, Whelpton (chapter 1) refers to Mahesh Regmi's rendition of another term, *dhuṅgo* (stone), as the concept of loyalty to the state. Prithvi Narayan's *Dibya Upadesh* has only two references to *dhuṅgo*, both negative. One pertains to the imperial barriers, likening Nepal to a squeezed yam between British India and imperial China and the other is a reference to the three Newar cities as unresponsive, cold stone. Regmi's interpretation diverges from the usual imagery of a country with *māṭo* (soil) or stone eroded into a fertile earth.

Burghart's episode one, demarcation of borders, was a formality when national boundaries were porous. Tibetan territorial claims extended down to Tengu cave in Nuwakot (Campbell, chapter 6) and included Nubri-Kutang in Gorkha (Ramble, chapter 12). In Mugu, people paid *cultho rakam* (women's tax) to Tibet until 1856 (H. Gurung, 1980: 61). There was similar flexibility along the southern border. Burghart (1984: 108) draws the distinction between possession (*muluk*) and country (*deś*) by citing the case of hill people emigrating east rather than turning to the nearby Tarai within Nepal. Such a migration trajectory, however, had both ecological rationale and political acquiescence. The Tarai then was a hostile land for hill migrants due to endemic malaria. And, despite the demarcation of the boundary, there was no restriction on border crossing for livelihood as each state encouraged outside settlers. Thus, while Nepal enticed yeoman farmers from the Company territory to its Tarai, the British welcomed Nepalese migrants in their hill domain.

HERITAGE HINDUSTAN

Nepal territory is mostly cis-Himalayan, i.e. it lies along the southern flank of the mountain range. Hindu cosmology included it within Himavatkhand as the northern extension of Jambudvip-Bharatkhand. Prithvi Narayan, despite his claim "I am king of the Magars" (*Magarāt ko rājā mai hum*), confirmed this Indic alignment by declaring of Nepal "This is the pure land of Hindus" (*yo asil Hindustān ho*). Thus, Hinduization of the conquered people became the *raison d'être* of the Gorkhali state.

The project of Hinduization, however, was not a Gorkhali invention. In reviewing the sweep of Nepalese history, Sylvain Lévi, characterized the country as an 'India in the making'. With reference to the rise of Shaivism that contested Buddhism in Licchavi Nepal, he noted, "Sacerdotal Brahmanism menaced with death by the triumph of heresies, skillfully searched for refuge in popular cults; it adopted them, consecrated them, and took up the struggle with rejuvenated gods and a renewed pantheon" (Lévi, 1905: 38). Hinduization in the hills gained momentum after the Muslim onslaught from the tenth century onwards. With Muslim advance further east, the retreat of Hindus to hill sanctuaries became a regional phenomenon.

The spread of Hinduism as a religious ideology also meant social ordering according to the Hindu framework based on a hierarchical caste system. Eleven chapters in this book refer to Höfer's (1979) exposition of the Muluki Ain (National Legal Code). The Code was promulgated in 1854 to impose Hindu caste rules on various ethnic groups. However, Jang Bahadur was not the first to introduce the caste system in Nepal as the Code was merely the culmination of a long-standing tendency. Inscriptions attest to the beginnings of a caste system during the Licchavi period. A prominent one was that of Jaya Sthiti Malla (1382–95) which categorized Newars into sixty-four castes (Petech, 1958). A similar exercise occurred during the reign of Mahendra Malla (1506–75). This Hindu social code was later introduced in Gorkha by Ram Shah (1603–36). The Sen rulers, whose claim to being Hindupati preceded that of Prithvi Narayan, also subscribed to such a division of society.

The main significance of the Muluki Ain was in its scope, the fact that it encompassed all people under the Gorkhalis' rule. Another important feature was its modification from the classical form which reflected the political dominance of three Parbatiya castes (Bahun, Thakuri, Chetri). Not only were the Tarai Brahmans ranked in a lower position than the Parbatiya Chetri, the hill caste system had provisions for co-option through miscegenation by legitimizing hypergamy (Sharma, 1993). The state had a more active role in the maintenance and even alteration of caste status to accommodate politico-economic power. Thus some high-ranking members of ethnic minorities, particularly Magars, were absorbed into the Chetri caste.[5] On the other hand, the various ethnic/tribal groups were lumped together as *matwālī* (alcohol drinkers) and a their national identities converted into castes. The *matwālī* block of ethnics were further categorized into *māsine* (eliminable) and *na-māsine* (non-eliminable), meaning enslavable or not, depending on the group's political relation to the Hindu regime. The impact of the Muluki Ain was felt most among the non-Hindu groups, mainly Mongoloid, who had been inducted from egalitarian *jāti* (nationality) to hierarchical *jāt* (caste) and associated norms. How some of these ethnic groups reacted to state intervention of this sort is described in various chapters of this volume.

Burghart (1984) examines the intent of Muluki Ain as the interpretation of country (people) in terms of species (*jāt*) as the third episode in the formation of the concept of nation-state in Nepal. This change in the process of nation-building is elaborated by Pfaff-Czarnecka (chapter 13) into three models. They are termed empire model during Shah-Rana rule (1769–1951), nationalistic model of the Panchayat era (1962–90), and patchwork of minorities since the restoration of democracy in 1990. The intent of the empire model was the creation of a Hindu theocracy by subsuming diversity with social stratification to consolidate and centralize power. The ideology of the Panchayat and immediately preceding periods was homogenization according to Parbatiya Hindu culture with some modernizing imperatives. The recognition of a multi-ethnic society since 1990 is a major departure from the past.

Hinduization was accompanied by the colonization of tribal areas. The migration of Hindus from the drier west to the humid east was basically a search for economic space. These were followed by other ethnic groups from the central to the eastern region in concert with the conquest. The tribal economy relied mainly on

FIGURE 46   *A Khas woman of Bhote Khola village, Bajhang (1990), a member of the caste known as 'alcohol-drinking Chetri' (Joanna Pfaff-Czarnecka)*

swidden cultivation and pastoralism. Hindu migrants and their Hinduized cohorts brought new agricultural methods (terracing and irrigation) and artisan skills with Untouchable castes. In a way, these had 'modernizing' influences on primitive economies that met the state's expectations of increased revenue.

State advocacy was the primary vehicle for the spread of Hinduism in Nepal since punishments prescribed in the Muluki Ain were according to caste ranking. Here, one might also highlight the role of Gurkha soldiers in the dissemination of Hinduism and the Nepali language. Of the ten Gurkha regiments in British India, only the 9th Gurkha Rifles was reserved for Chetri and Thakuri, the rest being of Mongoloid tribals. Since the soldiers were subjects of a Hindu king, each Gurkha battalion had a Bahun chaplain who officiated according to Hindu customs. In addition, the recruits, who had their own Tibeto-Burman mother tongues, were instructed in Nepali with Roman script. Therefore, the Gurkhas, who provided role models with enhanced income, were an important agent for the introduction of pan-Nepali values among ethnic communities.

The polity and society of Nepal was indeed devised in the image of a Hindustan. To begin with, the etymology of the place-name Gorkha itself was rationalized as *goraksa* (cow protection), symbolic of the sanctity of the cow for Hindus.[6] The cow played a special role in the process of defining Hindu identity and the extent of centralized power (Michaels, chapter 2). The ban on cow slaughter was probably first enforced in the whole kingdom in 1805. Its subsequent incorporation as a proviso in the Muluki Ain represented consolidation of the regime including the periphery of beef-eating people. According to Michaels: "That is how Nepal could show herself more Catholic than the Pope, more Hindu than India" (p.92 above).

In relation to the divergent boundaries of the realm (religious) and possessions (political), Burghart refers to the Gorkhali king's patronage of shrines outside the country (Banaras and Kedarnath) and he cites the 1866 regulations as reversing the situation by defining the two borders as coextensive (Burghart, 1984: 116). In fact, the Nepalese rulers, whether Rana or Shah, continued to maintain extra-territorial religious links in their search for legitimacy. Jang Bahadur paid homage at Hindu shrines in India *en route* to Europe while Juddha Shamsher made generous grants to Indian temples and was eulogised for upholding the spirit of *hindutva* (Michaels, p.93 above). Recent Shah kings have followed this tradition and during the Panchayat period, the designation of

Nepal as 'the world's only Hindu state' was utilized to cultivate the RSS and VHP in India as sources of support for the regime.

States often adopt symbols and myths to promote a sense of oneness. In the Nepalese case, this has involved appropriation of mostly Indian traditions. The Nepal Samvat of the Newars was introduced in 879 AD and since its associated Bansdhar Sakhwal legend is too plebeian, it remains a mystery as to why the rulers of the time instituted it. However, the Gorkhali rulers adopted the Saka and Vikram era and Chandra Shamsher recognized the latter as the official calendar in 1911. Both are Indian calendars with no linkage to any Nepalese historical experience.

Similarly, the regime has held a strong attachment to the Sanskrit language. It is a spiritual medium that harks back to Vedic India. Sanskrit has been patronized with free education from school to the university level despite a lack of students. It is to be noted that Sanskrit students of Tindhara Pathshala went on strike in support of the nationwide *satyāgraha* in May 1947, demanding that they be taught modern subjects. The past persists in attempts by some parliamentarians to make the language compulsory in schools and it has been recently introduced as a medium for the radio news.

The Panchayat regime devised a set of national symbols. These were the crown, sceptre, royal crest, royal standard, coat-of-arms, cow, national flag, pheasant, rhododendron, and red blob. The first four are associated with dynamic monarchy, while the cow, flag, and red colour are symbolic of Hindu dominance. The designation as a Hindu kingdom even in the new democratic Constitution (1990) and adoption of its sectarian symbols are clear evidences of the long shadow of heritage Hindustan.

COMPLIANCE AND RESISTANCE

The territorial expansion of Nepal was achieved through diplomacy, cunning, and conquest. The Gorkhalis resorted to various measures to deal with the vanquished people. These ranged from induction as followers (Magar, Gurung), accommodation with *kipaṭ* concession (Limbu, Rai), labour exploitation (Tamang), and vengeance (Kirtipur Newars). They were equally ruthless in their treatment of Khas subjects. In the Karnali basin, harsh punishment was known as *gorkhe-lauri* (Gorkhali-stick) while Kumaon-Garhwal experienced much exploitation and enslavement. But the excesses of Gorkhali rule were neither a racial vendetta nor a *jihad* for Hinduization. It was sheer pursuit of regime consolidation and social ordering. Indeed, the contest for power was most intense within the contending Chetri clans as exemplified by the Kot and Bhandarkhal massacres and fatricide within the ruling Rana family.

Political conquest was followed by the imposition of the Hindu social order on the subjects. Hindu influence was more palpable among ethnic elites since where two culture groups impinge, the privileged tend to associate with the powerful. This created cleavages within tribal groups whereby some sections adopted caste tenets and even invented genealogies to claim *kāśī-gotra* (Indic) Aryan ancestry as against *lhāsā-gotra* (Bodic). Thus emerged status schisms within ethnic communities such as Athar Jat/Bara Jat (Tamang), Bara Thar/Das Thar (Sunuwar), Char Jat/Sorah Jat (Gurung), Kutag/Righin (Bhotiya), Pradhan/Apradhan (Tharu), Pukunthali/Kachare (Chepang), and so on (Bista, 1967). The Hindu caste ideology based on the concept of purity did not, however, preclude the process of status enhancement through power as evidenced by the upgrading of the Khas to Chetri status and the Ranas' own attempt to climb the social ladder. In the case of the tribals, Hinduization was a viable route to promotion and recognition. Some of these tendencies of compliance as well as resistance are noted below.

A. CENTRAL HILLS

Newar: Newar ethnic identity is basically associated with language and locale. To these might be added the feeling of resentment at the dominance by the Parbatiya/Gorkhali (Gellner, chapter 4). Since the Muluki Ain placed all Newars below the Parbatiya *tāgādhārī* castes, their attempt at integration was in the form of upward social mobility: Newar Brahmans tended to emulate Parbatiya Bahuns while the Jyapu resorted to Hindu practices to seek Shrestha status. Caste division among Buddhist Newars was predominantly a Hindu borrowing although their exclusion of the Khadgi (butcher caste) has a parallel in the ostracization of the Gara (butchers) in Tibetan society.

Gellner examines Newar nationalism and his evidence points mainly to cultural activism with the emphasis on language. Internal divisions between Hindu Shrestha, Buddhist Newar, and indigenous Jyapu seem to have precluded a common political agenda. Their feeling of anti-Brahmanism, on the other hand, is grounded both on culture and on competition for opportunities.[7] Newar activism during the people's movement including the Jyapu propensity towards communism may be seen as opposition to the *ancien régime*. Newar cultural activism has significance for other ethnic groups since it has a repertoire sophisticated enough to contend with the Parbatiya culture. One area where the Newars have attempted to lead is in the Buddhist cause by bringing together other ethnic groups through the Dharmodaya Sabha.

Gurung: Macfarlane (chapter 5) deals with social and economic changes taking place among the Gurung. In contrast to Pignède's Indianist model of dual marriage within the four clans, he posits a three-fold schema in their clan system. He is unclear about the preferred system in Gurung cross-cousin marriage. However, a Gurung saying (rendered in Nepali) is quite unambiguous:

> *Māmā-ko chorī, rojī-rojī* (A wide choice among maternal uncle's daughters)
> *Phupū-ko chorī, khojī-khojī* (Seek and search father's sister's daughter).

Macfarlane describes significant transformations in the Gurungs' economic life. Once they were pastoral and dry crop farmers, but a long tradition of mercenary service and associated income has turned them to irrigated farming and to urban areas with much change in their tribal culture.

The Gurungs gave up beef-eating and adopted other Hindu customs. Since their Lamaistic attachment made it problematic to assimilate them into the Hindu fold (as in the case of the Tamangs), the alternative for social upgrading was internal cleavage. There were indeed superior and inferior clans among the Gurung and the Ghale chiefs, as among the Tamang (Campbell, chapter 6), were later usurpers from Tibet. The main issue with regard to the status cleavage among Gurungs was in its Brahmanic interpretation subscribed to by some of their elites.[8] The genealogical version attributing *kāśī-gotra* to Gurungs is untenable on the basis of their Mongoloid physiognomy as well as Bodic language. Obviously, the terms 'Char Jat' and 'Sorah Jat' originated not as the literal number of their respective clans but as status symbols derived from Hinduism. The number four is a transposition of the four Hindu *varṇa*s and the 16 of the *Bhāṣā Vaṃśāvalī*'s sixteen minorities of which thirteen are identifiable as marginalized ethnic/caste groups.[9]

The recording of *pyeta-lhuta* (oral tradition) provides some hints on the early migration of the Gurungs but reconstruction of their history will be an arduous task as in most pre-literate societies. The religious debate mentioned by Macfarlane is a search for identity with multiple motives. At the macro level, it is rejection of Hinduism in favour of familiar faiths. At the meso level, it is inclination towards Buddhism with its literary and philosophical appeals. And at the micro level, it is a conflict between tribal tradition and higher religious belief symbolised by the Pa-chyu tradition of blood sacrifice versus the Lama credo of *ahimsā*. This conflict is also symptomatic of the stress urban migrant Gurungs are experiencing, many of them ex-servicemen with leisure, whose spiritual needs remain unfulfilled by tribal rituals alone. They wish to preserve their heritage yet aspire for a reformed version to suit the new life style. The tussle between the Pa-chyu and Lamaist traditions has been a long process of competition for minds only made dramatic in the modern context. Perhaps, the path to resolution is the one already traversed by Taoism and Shinto into the Buddhist embrace.

Tamang: The ethnonym *Tamang* can be interpreted as highlander (*ta* = up, high; *mang/mu* = people) and the people have a larger fraternity. This includes the Gurung (Tamu) and Thakali (Tamhang) with whom they have considerable linguistic and cultural affinity. Tamang *bombo*, Gurung Pa-chyu, and Thakali *dhom* priests follow similar shamanistic traditions, the former two groups recognize the Ghale as a royal clan, and Tamang *ghewa* and Gurung *pye* are parallel mortuary rites.

The Tamang aspiration has been basically to dissociate from the Bhotiyas who are denigrated in Hindu Nepal. The process of upgrading to Tamang status is attested by the 1932 decree that first recognized 'Tamang' as a legitimate *jāt* (Höfer, 1979), the Humla tradition of state imposition of this label (Levine, 1987), and the Mugu version of receiving the designation for services rendered during the Nepal–Tibet war of 1856 (H. Gurung, 1980: 61). However, as Campbell (chapter 6) demonstrates, the Tamang are still burdened with old identities due to the power structure and economic exploitation.

Campbell also refers to aspects of social geography among Tamangs. Esteem of the north or higher (*turpa*) land over the south

FIGURE 47   *Two Brahman women, one a widow, still wearing the golden jewellery given at her wedding but forbidden to wear 'colourful' clothing, the other a maiden with pierced ears ready for the jewellery to be presented at her wedding (Belkot, Nuwakot district, 1980)* (*Joanna Pfaff-Czarnecka*)

or lower (*murpa*) is related to their highland origin and has parallels with other pastoral communities. The east–west (*shyarpa-nuppa*) distinction in culture and economy has more to do with external exposure since the area east of the Bhote-Kosi/Trisuli river was once a trade route and has now a road with its own frontier town, Dhunche. Incidentally, the western area also had some external connection. In contrasting Ghale-Tamang (Rasuwa) with Lama-Tamang (Helambu) hierarchies, Campbell seeks an explanation in the virtual absence of *guṭhī* (grant) land in Rasuwa. Such land grants for a *gompa* in Helambu was first made by a Newar king. But in Rasuwa also, particularly west of Bhote-Kosi, there were a number of villages that were considered the *guṭhī* of the Dharma Raja of Bhutan.[10] Swayambhunath was also included among Bhutanese religious grants and when the stupa fell in 1813, they completed its renovation in 1817.[11]

The Tamangs were incorporated into the state as a subjugated people and the Muluki Ain considered them enslavable.[12] Their Lamaistic faith associated them with Bhotiyas and upward social mobility was limited to local claims as Gurung (west) or Sherpa (east). Their economic exploitation to serve mercantile interests of Kathmandu was compounded by a restriction on army recruitment. They have remained economically marginalized as porters and labourers. Their underdevelopment as a cheap labour reserve was reinforced by factors of religion and culture differing from those in power. And the Tamang hinterland still remains the stronghold of traditional Panchayat politics.[13]

B. EASTERN HILLS

The three ethnic communities of the eastern hills included in this compilation belong to the Kiranti group recorded in early annals of the Nepal valley. It is not known whether these proto-Kirants later evolved into the Jyapu-Newar of the Valley or moved westward as the Magar. According to the tradition of the eastern Kirantis, they entered the hills from the Morang plain (Chemjong, 1967). Their communal *kipaṭ* land tenure system must predate Gorkhali recognition of it, probably going back at least to the time of the Sen confederacy. Similarly, the migration of caste people into their region must pre-date the Gorkhali conquest as the Bhojpur area was taken with the connivance of a Pokharel-Bahun in the service of a local ruler. Be that as it may, the ethnonyms this amorphous group acquired as Dewan, Jimidar, Rai, and Subba (Mughal terms for land functionaries) were later identity labels given by outsiders.

Thulung-Rai: Allen (chapter 9) touches on the tribe-caste continuum with reference to Thulung-Rai cultural identity. Despite the lexical ambiguity of *jāt*, which means both tribe and caste, there is a real difference beteen the two kinds of group and educated speakers of Nepali now recognize the distinction by employing *jāt* for caste and *jāti*, particularly *janajāti*, for ethnic community or nationality. The usual question framed to seek identification is not "What caste are you?" but "What are you in?" The response will be contextual: tribal name to outsider, clan name to tribal fellow, and lineage name to clansman. There is no ambiguity according to the level and type of interaction (see Gaenszle, p.360 above).

Allen associates Hinduization with agricultural colonization as illustrated both by the Hindu propensity for forest clearance and the Thulung-Rai perception of alienation from the jungle as a process of refinement. He also rightly posits that initial immigrant intrusions were welcomed for their occupational expertise. Once in close contact, there was no room for neutrality; the Thulungs had to subscribe to the norms of caste relationships. This was followed by imperceptible absorption of Hindu customs such as the festivals Dasain and Tihar. The Thulung experience of Hinduization was basically exposure to a higher culture and the patronage of the Pranami sect by Mukli sadhus is only one of many different expressions of this.

Mewahang-Rai: The case of the Mewahang-Rai described by Gaenszle (chapter 11) illustrates changing perceptions in identity management. They have multiple levels of ethnic identity with decreasing intensity, from Mewahang territoriality to Rai tribe and then a supra-Kiranti group including the Mech and Koch. The same can also be said of many other ethnic groups. On the other hand, one may contrast such concentric layers with the division of a single ethnic group: Koch as tribal, Rajbanshi as Hindu, and Tajpuriya as Muslim (Chemjong, 1967). The Mewahang may not have a unique culture of their own but they do possess aspects that distinguish them from others. As Gaenszle points out (p.357), ethnic identity, under whatever ethnonym, is relational and exists primarily as a concept.

Gaenszle makes a distinction between traditional and modern kinds of ethnic identities, the former rooted in tradition and the latter formed in today's emerging context. The changing concepts of identity among the Mewahang are visualized as translation, juxtaposition, and homogenization. The first two relate to Hinduization by adopting some Hindu practices, not necessarily all aspects of its ideology. The homogenization Gaenszle refers to, however, is not in terms of pan-Nepal Hinduism but rather to the broader Rai or Kirant culture. This modernist approach in the context of an emerging nation-state also draws sustenance from the mythic fraternal unity of *muddum*. In order to preserve one's cultural heritage, the emphasis is on cultural unity even if the Bantawa *sakkhewa* festival is 'invented' as a pan-Rai institution. These developments have parallels among the Gurung who now turn to their own oral history (*hyule-pye/kyahle-pye*) and have revived *lhosar* as a tribal celebration. The Mewahang also tend to align with other Mongoloids for socio-political space. Eastern Nepal being more exposed to ethnic movements across the border has, thus, become a fertile ground for ethnic activists, spawning organizations such as the Limbuwan Liberation Front, Mongol National Organization, and Rastriya Janamukti Party.

Yakha: The Yakha, a small group at the interstices of Rai and Limbu territory, subscribe to the Kiranti *muntum* tradition and have an ambiguous alliance with their larger neighbours (Russell, chapter 10). Colonization of their area by caste groups brought not only new modes of cultivation (hoe to plough) but also the Hindu religion and Nepali language. The associated changes were complex and are described by Russell as a process of negotiation, manipulation, and subversion (compare with Gaenszle's translation, juxtaposition, and homogenization). Their interaction with other people is based on group identity as blocks of superior Khas-Bahun,[14] equal Rai-Limbu, intermediate Gurung-Magar, and inferior untouchable castes. Russell refers to *nibak/nimak* (ritual brotherhood/sisterhood) as an instance of subversion. However, this institution, equivalent to the Nepali *mīt/mitinī*, should be seen as a device for interethnic relations not unlike the use of *ciurā* (beaten rice) among the Newar for inter-caste dining without the pollution stigma of cooked rice.

The Yakha have been selective in incorporating external cultural elements and these are not mere encrustation on the pristine base. Their religious pantheon includes both local spirits and imported deities while Hindu festivals are celebrated in local idiom. They have also vernacularized the Nepali language to conform to Yakha concepts. Thus, Yakha culture is seen as polythetic with Hindu beliefs providing new social forms to express Yakha identity. Russell observes that there is certainly no evidence that the Yakha, despite their small numbers, are falling into a 'melting pot'. And the new democratic environment has brought more ethnic awareness among the Yakha.

C. BORDERLANDS AND BEYOND

The essays on Bhotiyas of the mountain, Tharus and Maithils of the Tarai, and Nepalese abroad deal with diverse groups on the frontier of Nepal's hill heartland.

Bhotiya: Ramble's account of the Bhotiya (chapter 12) commences by giving the broad regional context of their kind in Tibet, Bhutan, Sikkim, and Ladakh. Nepal itself included a Buddhist kingdom, Mustang, which had marital ties with Ladakh and Lhasa. Also, high Lamas of Bhutan had priest-patron (*mchod-yon*) relations with both Newar and Gorkha kings while Tamur valley *gompa*s used to be under the ministry of Sikkim Lamas. These traditional relations were discarded as Nepal turned increasingly towards Hinduization. The Bhotiya of Nepal are migrants from Tibet and their marginal status has been much influenced by the political relation between the two countries. The treaty following the Nepal–Tibet war of 1854–56 established the former's supremacy not only with imposition of annual tribute but an unusual custom of assigning national status to children of mixed unions whereby males were considered Nepalese and females Tibetan!

The treaty also referred to the priest-client relationship between Tibet and Nepal but Chandra Shamsher was partisan to the British and provided men, mules, and material to the Younghusband mission of 1904 (Fleming, 1961). Such disdain for Lamaistic culture by Nepal would later find expression in neighbouring Buddhist states. If the demise of Sikkim as a sovereign kingdom in April 1975 had its genesis in the antagonism of Hindu migrants from Nepal, recent Lhotshampa opposition to Bhutan's *driglam namzhag* (integration policy) can partly be attributed to such attitudes.

The Bhotiya constitute a cultural group with distinctive linguistic (Tibetan) and religious (Lamaistic-Buddhism) markers. The root word *bhot (Nepali) from bod* (Tibetan) can be translated as 'trans-Himalayan'; hence used as suffix (*bhot*) for territories and as prefix (*bhote*) for rivers with Tibetan connection. In the search for a neutral term in place of the pejorative 'Bhote'/Bhotiya, Ramble prefers Höfer's 'Tibetanid' rather than Goldstein's 'Tibetanoid'. However, the most appropriate one seems to be 'Bodic', coined earlier by Shafer.

The Bhotiya live in enclaves but their isolation is only relative. As great seasonal travellers, they interact regularly at trade and pilgrimage centres and these regular contacts promote cultural homogeneity. The earlier perception of Bhotiya as beggar pilgrims has been much modified by new experiences in metropolitan Kathmandu, now home to affluent Bhotiya of diverse origin. First came Tibetan refugees in 1959 not all of whom were poor; some later became rich through the carpet business. Then, after the Sino-Indian war (1962) closed Darjeeling, Kalimpong, and Gangtok, handicraft entrepeneurs from these areas came to take part in the Kathmandu tourism industry.[15] Other Bhotiya settlers in Kathmandu included the wealthy displaced by the Tibetan trade blockade (Thakali, Walung-Bhotiya), affluent international traders (Manangi), and tourism professionals (Sherpa). Thereafter, the metropolis was exposed to *lhosar* gatherings of various Bhot communities and Tibetan dress became fashionable.

Ramble highlights the cult of local gods, *hyul-lha*, as the primary identity of Bodic enclaves and its increasing constriction by Buddhism as a Tibetan version of Sanskritization. He refers to the spread of Buddhism with substantial foreign impetus, including tourism that projects *bhot* areas as vestiges of a vanished Tibet. The Lama programme cited by Ramble was also externally induced, under the aegis of the Remote Areas Development Committee (established in 1968 with foreign aid), to counter communist influence from Tibet. This Desh Darshan Karyakram was basically an orientation programme to solicit lama support for development activities. In the process, Buddhism was tolerated, *gompa*s were repaired, lama trumpets joined Bhaktapur minstrels in Panchayat processions, and the Mao badge was countered with the Mahendra badge along with the spiritual badge of the Dalai Lama. Modernization has freed the Bhotiyas of the shackles of the Muluki Ain and in the process they are adapting to a cosmopolitan environment in the image of their own identity.

Tharu: McDonaugh (chapter 8) finds little in the way of a common pan-Tharu unity and instead focuses on the dynamics of access to land among the Tharu of Dang. However, he refers to the Tharu Kalyankarini Sabha at the national level and also local activist groups engaged in ethnic demands. The different experiences in Dang of the early radical group censored by the government and a later NGO expanding into new activities are indicative of the changed political climate.

The past of the Dangaura-Tharu was one of economic exploitation and political domination by hill people. With Pahari administration came encroachment on Tharu land, first as landlords and then as migrants following malaria eradication in early 1960s. The land reform (1964) measures also had negative consequences for the Tharu and their struggle against *begārī* (unpaid labour) and their demand for *mohī* (tenant) right was long contested and sustained only by ethnic solidarity.

The recent change in land ownership pattern recorded by McDonaugh is indeed remarkable for such an exploited people. During the period 1980–1993, Tharu households increased by 60% as against a Pahari increase of 83.3%, the latter mainly through migration. On the other hand, Tharu land ownership increased from 20% to 38% while that of the Pahari declined from 68% to 46%. Along with a considerable increase in land owned by Tharu households, there were also improvements in cultivation practices with increased productivity. These changes minimized hierarchical landlord-tenant relationships between the Pahari and the Tharu and the atmosphere of antagonism was replaced by one of competition. Earlier Tharu activism despite its literary/cultural garb emphasized Pahari exploitation. The current Tharu agenda includes homogenization of their own culture as well as access to state resources.

Maithili-speakers: Sindhuli-Garhi lies about 30 kilometres due north of Janakpur. On the steep trail below the fortress, where Captain Kinloch's 2,400 men floundered in 1767, there is a massive gateway that once served as a checkpoint for travellers (H. Gurung, 1980: 301). In effect, it marked the Tarai land southwards as a political and cultural frontier. On the other hand, the Tarai people described by Burkert (chapter 7) take pride in their heritage of the Videha kingdom as well as the Maithili language that later embellished the court of Newar kings. So they resent the imposition of 'bland nationalism' of the hill variety. This includes unfamiliar national symbols, statues of Bhanubhakta[16] and King Mahendra instead of Vidyapati and martyr Durganand Jha, and Bibah Mandap in contrast to Janaki Mandir. That the pagoda style of Bibah Mandap is considered more obtrusive than the seventeenth century Mughal architecture of Janaki Mandir, a gift of the Tikamgarh (Bundelkhand) queen in 1910, has to do with the former's hill association.

Maithil identity is based on a language with a rich literary heritage. Other aspects such as politeness and grace cited by Burkert are secondary to their Hindu orthodoxy of a rigid caste system and servile status of women. On the latter aspect, her account of how 'Mithila art lost its innocence' in the politics generated by the Janakpur Women's Art Project is an eloquent exposition. The Maithils share grievances with other Madheshis (Tarai) people at the domination by the Pahari (hill) group. These pertain to discrimination in citizenship, under-representation in government service, exclusion from the military, and insensitivity towards Tarai culture. At the same time, they hold to a Maithili identity with a legendary boundary which separates them from other Tarai communities. Indeed, the last two general elections show a decline in the appeal of the Nepal Sadbhavana Party. In the five constituencies of Dhanusha district, the Sadbhavana share of the total vote fell from 4.9% in 1991 to only 2.6% in 1994.

Given the Maithil cultural axis extending from Madhubani to Janakpur, one would assume pervasive influence of Bihari politics ridden with caste factions. Burkert cites such activism among Vaishyas, Kayasthas, and Yadavs, and also the significant impact of Laloo Prasad Yadav.[17] The evidence of recent elections, however, does not suggest that casteism is the key factor in the politics of Dhanusha district. Of the district's total population, 88.9% are of Tarai origin, of which the largest proportion (20.9%) is Yadav. People of hill origin constitute less than 10% of the district's population. But both in 1991 and 1994 elections, two Bahuns were elected. In 1994, the second highest vote went to Thakuri candidates (18.3%) who number only 532 in the district population. Kayasthas are 1.1% in population but one Kayastha seat was passed on from father (1991) to son (1994). The two Yadavs elected in 1991 lost to a Brahman and a Suri in 1994. Although votes garnered by hill-caste candidates declined from 42% in 1991 to 37% in 1994, the voting pattern did not obviously follow caste divisions. This may be attributed to the influence of major political parties. The shift in party vote in Dhanusha between the 1991 and 1994 elections indicates a decline in the clout of parties closer to India. The Congress Party vote declined by 13.6% with the loss of two seats out of five. The Sadbhavana vote declined drastically, by 43.8%, and none of its candidates secured 5% of the total vote. The leftist UML gained 47.8% in its share of the vote and won two seats out of five. The most dramatic gain, 156%, was made by the traditionalist Rastriya Prajatantra Party whose candidates, all of hill caste, secured a fifth of the total vote.

Nepalese Abroad: Hutt (chapter 3) surveys internal and external factors in the development of 'Nepali/Gorkhali' identity in India. Among internal or positive factors are included their ethnicity, language, and culture. Ethnicity as such is a very weak basis for Nepalese identity. First, the group includes many ethnic communities, and second, Bhotiyas and Lepchas also sometimes tend to align with the broader Nepali-speaking group.[18] As in the case of 'ethnic Nepalese', there is no Nepali *jāti* (Nepalese race) but a collectivity that includes many ethnic groups who speak Nepali and originally came from Nepal. The majority of the Nepalese emigrants are Mongoloids with Tibeto-Burman languages from adjacent Kiranti territory in Nepal. Though most were economic migrants to escape exploitation, many were political exiles from Gorkhali persecution as evidenced in Limbu manuscripts. Their culture is basically Pahari or Parbatiya of the eastern variant with Nepali language as the distinguishing marker. Although political stirrings among Nepali-speakers in India pre-date the founding of the Nepali Sahitya Sammelan in 1924, initiatives for recognition of their language were an important factor in identity mobilization.

The external factors contributing to assertive identification referred to by Hutt are economic exploitation and Indian attitudes. Despite being longtime settlers, most Nepali-speakers continue to live under economic hardship. The negative Indian attitude towards the Nepalese may be traced to the role Nepal and the Gurkhas played as a lackey to the British, be it during the 1857 Mutiny or later during the independence struggle. Hutt refers to the Indian ban on the wearing of the *khukri* as being unenforceable. Perhaps it was relaxed following the 1948 memorandum of Padma Shamsher, which endorsed the All-India Gorkha League's case that the *khukri* was a Hindu ritual weapon.[19] The above intervention of Padma Shamsher on behalf of All-India Gorkha League added ambivalence to the status of Nepali-speakers abroad. Such wider interpretation of being Nepalese gave the image of a waiting homeland to the emigrés. Refugees from Bhutan in Jhapa camps are only the most recent arrivals of a series. When Burma introduced its Nationalization Act in 1964, many Nepalese emigrants, despite being given the option of citizenship on becoming Buddhist, returned to Nepal and were rehabilitated. Thereafter came refugees from Assam, Manipur, Meghalaya, and Mizoram.

The nationality and citizenship status of Nepali-speakers in India is complicated by the legacy of the 1950 Treaty of Peace and Friendship that provides for national treatment for each other's citizens along with free movement across the border (H. Gurung, 1992: 41). The demand for abrogation of this clause was raised not by the Nepal government but by the Gorkhaland National Liberation Front (GNLF) in 1986. The demand for an autonomous Gorkhaland has been dropped (or rather postponed) with the creation of the Darjeeling Gorkha Hill Council in July 1988. Yet it has come a long way since early demands made by an informal hill group (1907), Hillmen's Association (1917), and All-Indian Gorkha League (1943).

Hutt provides a judicious account of the Nepali-speaking population in Sikkim and Bhutan. One might be tempted to regard the Nepalization of Sikkim as now in the past and the resolution of the Lhotsampa-Drukpa conflict in Bhutan as an issue for the future.[20] Yet the two experiences converge in terms of people's identities and state formation. Bhutanese concern needs to be appreciated in the light of the Sikkim experience and Darjeeling conflict led by Nepali-speaking activists. At the same time, socio-political processes operating in the two Indian territories provide some future indicators for Nepal itself. In culture, these Nepali-speakers, free from the strictures of the Muluki Ain, have created a multi-ethnic society with a modern outlook. In politics, caste elitism has been superseded by a democratic spirit, in which leadership of the state is passed on from a Chetri to a Limbu and then a Rai, while the Hill Council leadership is contested between a Tamang and a Limbu.

PERSISTENCE OF THE PERIPHERY[21]

The preceding section describes the processes of adaptation and resistance in sampled population groups. One might now turn to the content of the country's social composition. These relate to religion, language, and ethnicity which form the principal bases of political expression. The evidence of relative magnitude is drawn from census data with due regard for the subjectivity of the respondents' declarations as well as the propensity for official manipulation.

A. RELIGION

Nepal's long promotion of Hinduism as the state religion is reiterated by the new democratic Constitution (1990). Naturally, a high proportion of the total population claims adherence to Hinduism although such claims may not conform to their actual religious beliefs. The process was further facilitated by the definition prescribed in the census schedule. The guideline to enumerators for the 1952/54 census (Statistics Dept., 1957, Appendix, p.36) stated:

1. Assign as Hindu the worshippers of the five deities (Ganesh, Shiva, Vishnu, Sun, Devi) such as Bahun, Chetri, Magar, Gharti, Gurung, Sarki, Damai, etc.

Thus, ascription to the state religion had a broad basis both as to deities worshipped as well as ethnicity. The census of 1952/54, the first to provide data on religion, classified 88.9% of the population as Hindus, 8.6% as Buddhists, and 2.5% as Muslims. In the 1991 census, Hindus were 86.5%, Buddhists 7.8%, Muslims 3.5%, and 'others' 2.7%. The preponderance of Hindus in both censuses is obvious. The percentage increase of believers was highest for 'others', followed by Muslims and the lowest for Buddhists. The large increase in the 'others' category was due to a new category ('Kiranti'), to conversion (Christian), and to migration (Jain, Sikh, Muslim).[22] During 1981–91, the percentage increase of the Hindu population was lower (19.0) than for the total population (23.1). The decennial increase of the Hindu population during the Panchayat period was 25.1% for 1961–71, 30.2% for 1971–8, and 19.0% for 1981-91. Thus the proportion of Hindus in the total population declined from 89.5% in 1981 to 86.5% in 1991. This partly reflects the recent tendency of ethnic minorities to assert a separate religious identity, rejecting the Hindu ascriptions of the past.

B. LANGUAGE

The population census 1952/54, the earliest source of statistics on language in Nepal as a whole, recorded 54 mother tongues. This list contained many Tarai languages devised to downplay the magnitude of the main groups. However, regrouping of regional dialects yields much larger totals for Awadhi, Bhojpuri, and Maithili than those actually reported.[23] The number of Nepali speakers, despite official preference, fell short of a majority and came to 48.7% of the total population. Most significant has been the change in the rate of growth from census to census of the numbers speaking Nepali. The intercensal growth rate rose progressively from 19.5% for 1952/54–1961 to 26.4% for 1961–1971 and 44.7% for the period 1971–1981, but there was an increase of only 6.1% for 1981–1991. And the proportion of Nepali-speakers in the total population declined from 58.4% in 1981 to 50.3% in 1991.

The 1952/54 census reported 19 Tibeto-Burman languages but excluded small groups such as Bramu, Chantel, Dura, Lepcha, and Raute. The 1991 census also did not include these and in addition excluded Hayu, Khambu, Meche, Pahari, and Sunuwar, all included in 1952/54. The omission of Sunuwar is surprising as it had 17,299 speakers in 1952/54 and there was an ethnic Sunuwar population of 40,943 in 1991. The various mother tongues spoken in Nepal can be classified as 14 Indo-Aryan, 20 Tibeto-Burman, and one each of the Munda and Dravidian families. The proportion of the population speaking an Indo-Aryan language has increased from 77.5% in 1952/54 to 80% in 1991, while the figure for Tibeto-Burman speakers has declined from 21.9% to 17% during the same period. The number of Nepali speakers more than doubled from 4 million to 9.3 million during 1952/54–1991.

The adoption of the Nepali language is quite pronounced among hill ethnic groups who originally spoke Tibeto-Burman languages and especially so at migration destinations outside their native area. Ethnicity and language data available for 19 ethnic groups provide information on this change. While the speakers of seven Indo-Aryan languages[24] spoken by caste groups increased by 126.9% during 1952/54–1991, only four of the ethnic languages (Danuwar, Dhimal, Rajbansi, Tharu), all of them lowlands tongues, exceeded such increase. Of the hill ethnic languages, the increase in speakers ranged from 40.6% for Thami to 86.1% for Rai-Kiranti.

Those in the intermediate range were Gurung (40.5%), Magar (57.4%), Limbu (74.6%), Newar (80.1%), and Tamang (82.6%). The number of Kumhale speakers declined by 59.7%.

The comparison of the 1991 census data on ethnicity and language indicate the level of mother tongue retention by ethnic groups. In this regard, again the Kumhal show the least level of retention: 1,413 speakers against a population of 76,635. It is also low among the Majhi with only a fifth of the population retaining their language. Among the hill ethnic groups, only one third of Magars and half of Gurungs and Thakalis retain theirs. The percentage of language retention among other hill ethnic minorities are: Chepang – 68.5, Newar – 66.1, Thami – 75.4, Rai-Kiranti – 83.6, Limbu – 85.5, Jirel – 86.5, and Tamang – 88.8. Language retention is fairly high among the 'Bhote'-Sherpa (90%), Raji (90.4%), and Dhimal (89.5%). Rajbanshi appears as an exception with the number of speakers (85,558) actually exceeding the number of ethnic Rajbanshis (82,177), perhaps due to the inclusion of Koch (tribal) and Tajpuriya (Muslim) speakers of the language.

C. ETHNICITY

The 1991 census provides for the first time detailed data on ethnic/caste composition of Nepal. Table 15.1 provides the distribution of ethnic/caste population by geographic regions.

In terms of native area, the mountain people include three ethnic groups with no castes. The low number of Bhotiyas ('Bhote') may be ascribed to their tendency to use other ethnonyms. The mountain group constitutes only 0.7% of the total population. The hill group has 11 ethnic groups and 9 castes. The hill castes constitute 40.3% of the total population, of which 29% are Bahun-Chetri. Another block of 8.7% is made up of artisan castes (Kami, Damai, and Sarki). The hill ethnic minorities make up a quarter of the total population, among whom the Magar, Newar, and Tamang account for sizable proportions. The hill group of ethnic communities and castes together account for 67.2% of the total population.

The people of the inner Tarai are represented by seven small ethnic groups. They represent only 1.1% of the total population.

TABLE 15.1 ETHNIC/CASTE COMPOSITION OF NEPAL, 1991

Geographic Region	No. of Groups	Population	Percent
Mountain			
Group	3	138,293	0.7
Caste	–		
Ethnic	3	136,552	0.7
Others		1,741	0.0
Hill Group	20	12,420,157	67.2
Caste	9	7,457,170	40.3
Ethnic	11	4,776,993	25.8
Others		185,994	1.0
Inner Tarai Group	7	206,068	1.1
Caste	–	–	–
Ethnic	7	206,068	1.1
Tarai Group	25	5,718,770	30.9
Caste	20	2,939,175	15.9
Ethnic	5	1,452,652	7.9
Others		1,326,943	7.1
Unstated/ foreigners	–	7,809	0.0
Total	55	18,491,097	100.0

Source: Salter & Gurung (1996: 3).

The Tarai group includes 20 castes, 5 ethnic communities and 'others' (including Marwari, Muslim, Sikh, and Bengali as religious or language groups). Their share in total population is 30.9%. Of this 16.1% are castes, 7.9% ethnic communities and 7.1% 'others'. The Tharu and the Yadav constitute the largest individual groups in the Tarai.

Of the 18.5 million total population of Nepal, 56.2% belong to the caste group. These include 9 hill castes of 7.5 million and 20 Tarai castes of 2.9 million. The proportion of the population belonging to the ethnic communities is 35.5%. This includes 4.8 million members of 11 hill groups and 1.7 million from 12 Tarai

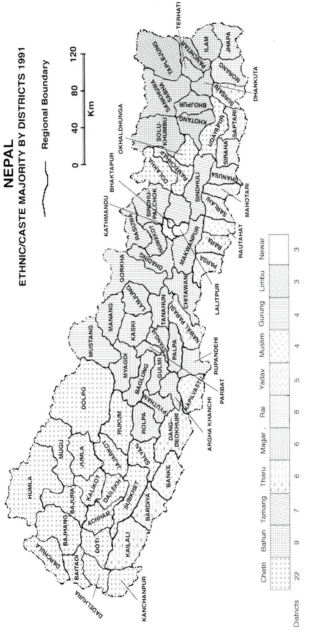

FIGURE 48   *Map of Nepal showing largest caste/ethnic group in each district.*

or Inner Tarai ones. The remaining 8.3% or 1.5 million in the 'other' category are mostly from the Tarai.

There has been a considerable dispersal of people from their native area with two main migration trajectories. The west-to-east population movement is exemplified by the distribution of hill castes. Of the 7.5 million belonging to hill castes, only 18.2% is reported in western hills, their native area. They constitute 51.1% of the central hill and 40.9% of the eastern hill population. The north-to-south migration is obvious from the large number of hill and mountain people in the lowlands. Nearly a third, 3.9 million out of 12.5 million, of those of highland origin now reside in the lowlands. In contrast, people of lowland origin are a mere 2.2% of the hill and 0.9% of the mountain population.

The map (Figure 48) shows the most numerous ethnic/caste population in each administrative district as reported in the 1991 census. For the 60 ethnic/caste groups listed in the census, only 11 form the largest segment of the population in one or more districts. These include seven ethnic groups (Tamang, Tharu, Magar, Rai, Gurung, Limbu, Newar), three castes (Chetri, Bahun, Yadav), and one religious group (Muslims).

POLITICAL EXPRESSIONS

Many assign ethnic activism in Nepal to the aftermath of the 1990 people's movement, the assumption being that the subjugated people had previously accepted the inevitability of their fate. But resistance based on the politicization of ethnicity did take place in Nepal only to be consigned to local lore.[25] Moreover, due to the despotic regime, cultural or political opposition became exile exercises. One early episode of Newar activism was initiated through a linguistic institute in Calcutta (1926). The hanging of the four martyrs (three were Newars) in 1941 was preceded by the expulsion of Buddhist activists in 1937. They were allowed to return in 1947 after the intervention of Ven. Narada Mahathera of Sri Lanka. The political turmoil of 1950-51 also included a Limbu revolt while the Muktisena insurgents mobilised by the Congress were mostly ex-servicemen from ethnic minorities.

Some ethnic organizations were established during the 1950–60 decade of political freedom. For example, the Backward Classes Organization (Pichadieka-Barga Sangathan), created in 1956, included the Gurung Kalyan Sangha, Tharu Kalyankarini Sabha, Kirant League, and Dalit (Depressed) Sangha. Those that developed political overtones were duly contained by the Panchayat regime (1960–1990) with recognition given only to the five official Class Organizations (*bargīya saṅgaṭhan*). Actually, the referendum announcement of 1979 marked the watershed for open expression of ethnic demands. This was encouraged by the regime's attempt to seek the support of minority groups (Bhotiya Buddhists, Muslims) for the Partyless Panchayat and also by inclusion of members of ethnic groups and artisan castes in the Constitution Recommendation Committee. Although the third amendment of the Constitution (1980) made no major departure on social issues, ethnic expressions were tolerated. One early instance was the Newar *bhintunā* (new year) processions in urban areas (Gellner, 1986: 122–3). Then followed 'Magurali' (Magar-Gurung-Rai-Limbu) as an informal coalition of hill ethnic minorities. The post-referendum period saw the emergence of various ethnic organizations, some with their own mouthpieces. Examples of these publications are: *Tharu-Sanskriti* (Tharu), *Tamun* (Gurung), *Khanglo* (Thakali), *Paru-hang* (Kiranti), *Kongpi* (Kiranti), *Kairan* (ethnic minorities in general), and *Chahara* (ethnic minorities in general). Two of the organizations had a federal character. The Nepal Sarvajatiya Manch (Nepal All-Peoples' Platform) formed in 1982 later evolved into the Janajati Mahasangh (Federation of Nationalities). Another was the Utpidit Jatiya Utthan Manch (Depressed People's Upliftment Platform) set up in 1987 to unite low-caste people.

The 1990 Constitution declares Nepal a multi-ethnic and multi-lingual state despite the hang-over of also calling it a 'Hindu kingdom'. The new freedom whereby subjects have become citizens has unleashed political pressures. In so far as their cultural aspirations remain unmet, the ethnic demands have potential for politicization. As a platform for the common cause, the Janajati

Mahasangh includes twenty-two entities mostly from Mongoloid and originally non-Hindu ethnic groups.[26] Most of these groups were represented at the national convention of Nepalese Indigenous People in April 1994. The meeting defined the characteristics of indigenous people as: (1) non-Hindu, animist believers; (2) possessing territory and language; (3) deprived of tribal resources; (4) devoid of policy-making role; and (5) egalitarian, opposed to caste (see chapter 1, pp.21–2 above). In effect, they equate 'indigenous' with 'ethnic minority'. The meeting dwelt on religious, cultural, educational, economic, and political problems. The 14-point resolution included a demand for Nepal to be made a secular state and opposed Sanskrit as a compulsory language in school (Vishwa Adivasi, 1994: 18–19).

Whelpton (chapter 1) and Pfaff-Czarnecka (chapter 13) deal with substantive aspects of the ethnic debate. These range from cultural to economic and constitutional demands. In the field of culture, the claim is for ethnic, linguistic, and religious equality. The ethnic organizations oppose the caste system, Nepali language supremacy, and Hindu hegemony. In the economic arena, the pressure is for a fair share of state resources and against the Khas-Bahun-Newar monopoly in government employment. In politics, the call is for proportional representation and regional autonomy.

One might enquire briefly into the government initiatives taken since the restoration of democracy. In 1992, the government appointed a committee to formulate programmes for a national cultural policy. The committee devised a range of modest recommendations including formation of a national coordination agency (Rastriya Sanskritik Samiti, 1992). These remain to be implemented and the leftist Nepal Majdur Kisan Party (NWPP) has recently called for a strong bill on cultural protection.

In April 1994, a commission on minority languages made a 58-point recommendation on their development and use in teaching, and on the formation of a council of minority languages (Rastriyabhasa, 1994). Of these, the suggestion for radio broadcasting was followed in mid-August 1994. The news bulletin includes all languages (now 12) whose speakers exceed 1% of the total population as well as in English and Hindi.

On the economic front, recent budget speeches make reference to the socio-economic upliftment of depressed classes. However, there is divergence in the identification of these people by the Communist and Coalition governments. The former listed 16 groups of which 11 are castes and 10 from the Tarai. The latter listed 12 groups of which 8 are castes and 8 from the Tarai.

The demand for more employment opportunities for members of ethnic minorities remains problematic simply because of their low literacy. The country has an average literacy of 39.3%. It exceeds 60% among the Kayastha, Tarai Brahman, hill Bahun, and Newar. Among the 96,977 with a first degree or higher qualification recorded in the 1991 census, 34.1% were Bahun, 23.7% Newar, and 12.4% Chetri (CBS, 1993: Vol.1, Part VII,

FIGURE 49   *Seasonal migrants (mostly Khas) resting during their journey from the far western districts of Nepal to the Indian districts of Kumaon and Garhwal. These men seek work in India less for money than in order to "eat outside", so that those left behind can survive on the food left in the store (Bajhang, 1989) (Walter Pfaff)*

Table 26). Such an imbalance calls for drastic affirmative action in the field of educational opportunities.

Measures for better political representation also face some constraints. The main one is the skewed nature of political participation by ethnicity/caste. In the 1994 general election, the three major parties – Nepali Congress, NCP-UML, and Rastriya Prajatantra party (NDP) – fielded 604 candidates. Of these, 70.7% were caste people and 27.7% from the ethnic communities. The caste group included 35.6% Bahun and 15.4% Chetri while the ethnic groups were led by the Newar (7.3%). Among those elected were 41.5% Bahun, 15.1% Chetri, 13.2% Tarai castes, 12.2% hill ethnic minorities, and 6.3% each of Newar and Tharu. Therefore, some mechanisms seem necessary to ensure better political representation of the minority groups.

The Rastriya Janamukti and Sadbhavana parties have made the case for federalism based on ethnic/linguistic division. This seems to be fraught with problems of area demarcation and the sustainability of Nepal itself. While large-scale inter-regional migration of people has eroded discrete culture areas, a federal structure could encourage centrifugal forces. Since most of the present administrative districts are too small to be economically viable, some reorganization seems justified. Such a re-grouping, however, should be for decentralization purposes that would ultimately lead to the devolution of power.

Hutt (chapter 3) raises the issue of nationalism and nationism as defined by Yapp (1979). The latter ('the desire of a state to have a nation of its own') is exemplified by Nepal's past attempt at homogenization. The former ('the desire of a nation to have a state of its own') is expressed by the activism of Nepali-speakers for Gorkhaland in India and those of the Sadbhavana Party in Nepal. The call for Tarai autonomy was first raised in the late 1950s and fuelled by the 1983 migration report (H. Gurung, 1992). Their grievance is based on the particularistic historic identity devised by the state which Whelpton (chapter 1) elucidates. Basically, the political identity of Nepal evolved through accretion round a kernel of Parbatiya high-caste conquistadors. The people of the Tarai and mountain frontier lands remain the least integrated due to this emphasis on a national identity based on the hill castes.

Political expressions, ethnic or otherwise, become especially salient during periods of power transition. This is what Nepal is experiencing presently under a democratic environment. However, Gellner (Introduction, p.6) seems nearer the truth when he argues that ethnic harmony may previously have been exaggerated. There were ethnic conflicts in the past of which recent apparitions include the Hindu furore over Padma Ratna Tuladhar's comments on beef eating and the Hindu–Muslim clashes in Nepalganj in October 1995. Ethnic demands so far have been mostly of the secondary type, i.e. civil ethnicity, seeking to compete for resources within the system. The trend of the last two general elections also indicates people's preference for mainstream politics. However, there is still the possibility of more aggressive expressions, even violence and irredentism, if legitimate demands for social justice and political equality are not entertained by those entrenched in power. What Nepal now needs to devise is a polycentric nationalism that fosters feelings of belongingness and promotes national integration.

NOTES

I am grateful to John Whelpton for providing information and helpful comments on the first draft.

[1] See Macdonald (1983b).

[2] Lama and Chemjong were both born in Darjeeling and the latter's book, date-lined 'Phidim', was actually published in Darjeeling.

[3] Nepali dictionaries show retrogression from that of Turner (1931) with increasing constriction by Sanskrit. Turner's etymology perhaps derives its vitality from the colloquial language of the ethnic-minority Gurkhas who were his source.

[4] For example, compare *muddum* (Mewahang-Rai), *mundhum* (Limbu), and *muntum* (Yakha).

[5] J.M. Gurung (1985/86) cites the case of descendants of commander Angad Ghale ('Ghale' is a Gurung and Tamang clan) living as Khawas (a Chetri clan) in Lalitpur.

[6] Most scholars connect it with Gorakhnath of the Kanphata sect while Gyawali (1963: 211) interprets it as a derivation from *garkhā* (revenue division) or *kharka* (pasture). *Garkhā* is still a prevalent term in the western hills between the Mahakali and Seti rivers.

[7] Competition between Sharmas and Shresthas is particularly keen in the bureaucracy.

[8] The debate on the relative status of 'Char Jat' and 'Sorah Jat' Gurungs provides an interesting example of state intervention in caste matters. The first documentary evidence is a *tāmra-patra* (copper-plate) of 1828 which proclaimed that all Gurungs were of equal status. This was followed by a *lāl mohar* (red seal) of 1867 that re-affirmed the decision of the 1828 copperplate. Then in 1921 came a *bhāradārī* court decision that ordered a fine of Rs.20 on Sikarnath Subedi and banned his book *Thargotra-Pravarāvalī* (Benares, 1911) that referred to Sorah Jat as inferior Gurungs. All the relevant documents are reproduced in Kishor (1958/59) and those of the 1867 red seal and the court decision as appendices in J.L. Sharma (1992/93).

[9] Of those listed in the *Bhāṣā Vaṃśāvalī*, Khapang, Palahari, and Panchari are unclear.

[10] *Vide* notes of Jean Smith on biographies of Bhutanese Lamas since the seventeenth century concerning their missions to Nepal based on the traditional patron–priest relationship between the King of Nepal and the Lama of Bhutan.

[11] Sakya (1978), Document no. 114.

[12] During our Gosainkund trek in 1973, Pasang Goparma related the Chhekampar incident as told by historian Baburam Acharya. This was in Bhimsen Thapa's time when the Tamang village was visited by a Gorkhali force and males were incarcerated to yield 200 females to serve the Kathmandu nobility.

[13] Of the seven Tamang majority districts, five sent six Rastriya Prajatantra Party representatives to the Parliament in the 1994 election.

[14] The term 'Khas' was and is still used by non-Parbatiya groups in Nepal to refer to the Parbatiyas exclusive of the Brahmans and the Untouchable castes. This usage links together the remaining non-*tāgādhārī* Khas with the dominant Chetris, who are for the most part descendants of Khas who were allowed to assume the sacred thread. The Bahun (Brahmans) are viewed as ethnically separate because of their own claim to have originally migrated into the hills from Kanauj region of Uttar Pradesh.

[15] A recent parallel is the influx of Kashmiri Muslims into tourist-related activities in Kathmandu and Pokhara after the intensification of hostilities in the Kashmir Valley since 1989.

[16] His statues in Darjeeling and Kalimpong were desecrated in 1991 by GNLF activists campaigning for the replacement of the name 'Nepali' by 'Gorkhali' (see fig. 5, p.110 above).

[17] Yadav's campaign in Bihar for 'Backwards' (Dalits) has also affected Uttar Pradesh politics with violent reactions by high castes in Uttarakhand.

[18] *Nebula* (i.e. *Ne* = Nepali, *bu* = Bhutan, *lā* = Lapche) was coined in 1935 to indicate this confluence (see Hutt, p.129 above).

[19] This reference to religious symbolism might have influenced the decision as one may note that the 1947 tripartite agreement on recruitment includes a clause forbidding the use of Gurkhas against Hindu states.

[20] Bhutan's 'one nation, one people' policy is ironically the echo of Nepal's 'one nation, one dress, one language' slogan of Panchayat days.

[21] This section is based on Salter and Gurung (1996).

[22] The 1961 census was the first to report the number of Jains (831) and Christians (458) in Nepal. The 1991 census recorded 7,561 Jains and 31,280 Christians, which shows their considerable increase in three decades.

[23]
Mother tongue	Reported	Inclusive of dialects
Awadhi	27	69,473
Bhojpuri	16,335	275,335
Maithili	300,768	1,485,726

[24] Awadhi, Bengali, Bhojpuri, Hindi, Maithili, Marwari, and Nepali.

[25] Some of these episodes include the Limbu expulsion in 1770 for resisting the Gorkhali attack, the Murmi/Tamang revolt (1793) after the Chinese retreat from Nuwakot, and the rebellions of Lakhan Thapa-Magar (1870) and Sukdev and Supati Gurung (1877) in Gorkha.

[26] These include Chepang, Chantel, Danuwar, Dhimal, Dura, Gurung, Jhangar, Jirel, Jyapu, Kirat, Magar, Majhi, Meche, Newar, Rai, Rajbanshi, Sherpa, Sunuwar, Tamang, Thakali, Thami, and Tharu.

Glossary

NOTE: Where the anglicized spelling of a word is identical to the exact transcription except for the absence of diacritics, that word has been entered in the glossary in Roman type with diacritics added. Where the spelling differs, the transcription is given as a parenthesis in italics. Except as otherwise indicated, words are Sanskrit and/or Nepali. The abbreviations used for other languages are: D. (Dzongkha); Gur. (Gurung); Mai. (Maithili); M. (Mewahang Rai); Nw. (Newari); P. (Persian); Tam. (Tamang); Tb. (Tibetan).

adhirājya: kingdom

adhiyā: share-cropping system under which the landlord normally received 50% of the main crop

Ādikavi: 'First Poet' (title given to the first major poet in a particular language, e.g. Bhanubhakta (19th century) for Nepali and Vidyapati (14th century) for Maithili

adhyakṣa: Chairman, ward representative, leader

ādivāsī: a Sanskritic neologism coined to mean aboriginal, indigenous inhabitant(s)

ahiṃsā: non-violence, in particular the avoidance of animal sacrifice

Ahir: see Yadav

Ain (*āī'n*) (P.): law, statute; *see* Muluki Ain

Akhil Bhāratiya Nepālī Bhāshā Samiti: All-India Nepali Language Committee

533

ambal: province, territory

ambālī: official in charge of an *ambal*

aṃśa: part, share of inheritance

āphno mānche: 'one's own person' (someone in your kin group or personally linked to you in some other way who may be relied upon for assistance)

aripan (Mai.): floor designs made with rice paste by Maithil women

Arthashastra (*Arthaśāstra*): treatise on statecraft traditionally attributed to Kautilya

arjī: affidavit, petition

Ārya Samāj: 19th-century Indian reform movement to revive 'Vedic' Hinduism

asal hindustān: 'real/pure land of Hindus': what Prithvi Narayan Shah hoped for Nepal

Aṭhāra Jāt/Bāra Jāt: Eighteen 'Clans'/Twelve 'Clans' (referring to supposedly superior and inferior Tamang clans)

Awadhī: a language spoken in the western Tarai

bahudal: multi-party

Bāhun: Parbatiya Brahman

bāhunbād: 'Brahmanism': pejorative term for Brahman nepotism and for policies perpetuating the allegedly dominant position of Brahmans in the Establishment

Baiśākh: first month of the Nepali calendar (mid-April to mid-May)

Bāisī: twenty-two statelets in the Karnali basin before unification

Bajracharya (*Vajrācārya*): among Newars the Buddhist priestly caste, known colloquially as Gubhaju; cf. Shakya

bālī: share of the crop owed to a caste specialist, especially to a Tailor (Damai) or Blacksmith (Kami) in return for year-round services

Baniyā: plains caste (Merchant); also found among the Newar Uray

Bansdhar Sakhwal: legendary Kathmandu merchant who established the Nepal Samvat (Era) in 879 AD

Bantāwā: a Rai sub-group

Bāra Thar/Das Thar: Twelve Clans/Ten Clans (referring to supposedly superior and inferior Sunuwar clans)

bargīya saṅgaṭhan: 'class organizations': government-sponsored corporate groups under the Panchayat system representing youth, peasants, workers, women, and ex-soldiers

bārī: unirrigated land, garden

bartaman (from Skt. *vratabandha*): 'tying the loincloth': the life-cycle ritual by which a boy becomes a full member of his caste with all the ritual obligations that implies (for high Hindu castes this involves also taking the sacred thread)

BASE: Backwards Society Education, a Tharu-run NGO

batāyā: share-cropping

begārī: a form of unpaid labour

Banaras: Hindu sacred city on the Ganges in Uttar Pradesh

bhāradār: 'bearer of the burden'; term for a person, who, whether or not currently in state employment, was one of the kings's counsellers

bhariyā: porter

Bhāṭ: hill and Tarai caste (Genealogists, Minstrels)

bhintunā: 'Good Wishes' in Newari; now used in Nepali for procession/demonstration, on the New Year's Day according to the Nepal Era, in favour of adopting the Era as the official era of Nepal

Bhojpurī: a language spoken in the central Tarai

Bhoṭiyā('Bhoṭe'): (often derogatory) label for peoples of Tibetan or related language and culture

Bhutia (Indian English): as above, but used especially when referring to Sikkim

Bibah Mandap (*Vivāha Maṇḍapa*): Wedding Pavilion, a shrine to Ram and Sita in Janakpur

Bibah Panchami (*Vivāha Pañcamī*): festival celebrating the marriage of Ram and Sita

bighā: unit of land-measurement used in the Tarai (=1.6 acres)

bikās: development

Bikram Samvat (B.S.): *see* Vikram Samvat

bīrtā: land granted on a tax-free basis

BJP: Bharatiya Janata Party: Indian political party opposed to India's secular Constitution; often labelled as Hindu fundamentalists

Bodic: relating to Tibet or Tibetan language or culture

bombo: (Tam.) shamanic healer

Brahman (*brāhmaṇa*): caste (or, more strictly, varṇa) associated with priesthood

buddha dharma/bauddha dharma: Buddhism

Chait Dasain (*Caitra Dasaī*): a minor festival celebrated during the month of Chait (mid-March to mid-April); also known as 'small Dasain'

cākarī: seeking the favour of a person of higher status by frequent visits, flattery etc.

Chamar (*Camār*): plains caste (Leatherworkers)

Chantel (*Cantel*): ethnic group in western hills; of diverse origins including Thakalis, Ghartis, and miners

Char Jat/Sorah Jat (*cār jāt/sorāh jāt*): 'Four Clans' 'Sixteen Clans' (referring to supposedly superior and inferior Gurung clans)

Chathare: Rai dialect

caubīsī: twenty-four pre-unification statelets of the Gandaki basin

Chepang (*Cepāṅ*): an ethnic group living in a section of the Mahabharat range south-west of Kathmandu; one of Hodgson's "broken tribes"

Chetri (from Sanskrit *kṣatriya*): dominant Parbatiya caste, formerly known as Khas

Chitrakar (*Citrakār*): Newar caste (Painters)

Chitragupta (*Citragupta*): the scribe of Yama, the lord of the dead

chowk (*cok*): courtyard, quadrangle

ciurā: beaten rice

class organization: see *bargiya sangathan*

Congress: Nepali Congress Party, founded in 1947; it formed the first democratically elected government in 1959 under B.P. Koirala; his brother, G.P. Koirala, was Prime Minister from 1991–4; it returned to power in September 1995 as senior partner of a coalition with the RPP and Sadbhavana Parties with Sher Bahadur Deuba as Prime Minister

CPN-UML: Communist Party of Nepal (United Marxist-Leninist), often known as UML for short; the most important of the communist factions, formed by the merger of the CPN (Marxist-Leninist) and CPN (Marxist) in 1991; it formed a minority government under Man Mohan Adhikari for nine months in 1994–5 but was ousted by a vote of no-confidence after the Supreme Court disallowed its attempt to hold mid-term elections

culṭho rakam: 'plaited-hair levy' (tax on women)

cumāwan: levy collected at time of king's son's sacred thread ceremony

dahi: curd

Dalit Sangha (*Dalit Saṃgha*): Association of the Oppressed, i.e. of ex-Untouchables

Damāī: ex-untouchable Parbatiya caste (Tailors)

Danuwār: small ethnic group found in low hills and Tarai of east Nepal

Darai: small group similar to Danuwar found in central inner Tarai

Darjeeling: town and district in West Bengal with a largely ethnic Nepali population

Daś Majhiyā: a Rai dialect

Dasain (*Dasaĩ*) (Skt.: **Durgā Pujā**) ten-day festival, the biggest of the year and a national holiday which all families attempt to celebrate together; religiously it celebrates the triumph of the goddess Durga over evil demons, and it also marks the beginning of harvesting

deś/deśa: country

ḍhakre: 'basket-carrier'; normally used figuratively for the unemployed

dhāmī: traditional healer, (in some regions) diviner

Dhānuk(h): ethnic group in the Maithil area

dharma: religion; duty; even 'essential nature'

dharmādhikārī: '*dharma* supervisor': title given to the Brahman guru responsible for enforcement of caste regulations in Nepal

Dharmaśāstra: generic term for compilations of Hindu law, the most famous being ascribed to the legendary sage, Manu

Dharmodaya Sabhā: a Buddhist association

Dhimāl: small ethnic group in the far eastern Tarai speaking a language of the Tibeto-Burman family

Dhobī: caste of Washermen (found among, Newars and in the plains)

dhotī: traditional male garment in the Tarai and India, wrapped around the upper legs (see illustration on page 48)

dhotīwālā: *dhoti*-wearer (derogatory term for plainsmen)

ḍhuṅgo: lit. stone, an early term also used for country, kingdom, state

Dibya Upadesh (*Divya Upadeśa*): ('Divine Counsel') collection of reminiscences and policy guidelines dictated by Prithvi Narayan Shah shortly before his death

Driglam Namzhag (D.) (=Tb. sgrigs-lam snam-bzhag): traditional code of dress and behaviour imposed by the Bhutanese government as part of its homogenization policy

Drukpa (D.) (=Tb. 'brug pa): dominant group in Bhutan

Durgā: mother Goddess and chief object of worship at the Dasain festival

Durgam Chetra Vikās Samiti: Remote Areas Development Committee

Duṣadh: plains caste (variously described as Swineherds, Basket-Markers, and Thieves)

dwāre: a type of revenue collector and local administrator

Dyaḥlā (Np. Poḍe, Nw. Pwaḥ): Newar Sweeper and Fisherman caste

dzong (Tb.): fort

Ekadashi (*Ekādaśī*): eleventh day (of the bright or dark half of the lunar month), sacred to Vishnu, on which animals should not be killed or eaten

Firaṅgī: foreigner, European (derived from 'Frank')

gaddīmubārak: levy collected on king's accession

Garhwāl: district of the Indian Himalaya west of Nepal

Ganesh (Gaṇeśa): Hindu elephant-headed god, son of Shiva, worshipped for auspicious beginnings

garkhā: (revenue) subdivision in the western hills

Ghale: clan claiming royal descent and now found in both Tamang and Gurung communities

gharguruwā (Tharu): household priests

Ghartī: Parbatiya caste (descendants of freed slaves)

ghewa (Tam.): funeral rites (cf. Tb. *dge-ba*, lit. 'virtue' i.e. the merit gained by the ritual on behalf of the dead person); in Np. as *ghewā*

gho (D.): traditional Bhutanese dress (male) (cf. Tb. *gos*, garment)

Gīrvāṇa Yuddha: King of Nepal (reigned 1799–1816)

GNLF: Gorkhaland National Liberation Front; founded in 1980, it staged a violent agitation in 1986–88 for a separate Nepali-speaking state within India and based on Darjeeling; in 1988 it accepted the compromise of a Gorkha Hill Council within the state of West Bengal

goddhuwā: levy for marriage of king's daughter

Gorakhnāth: Hindu saint who gave his name to the town of Gorkha

Gorkhā: hill town approximately 50 miles west of Kathmandu that is the origin of the Shah dynasty; also used as a synonym of Gorkhali (the spelling 'Gurkha' is used in British military contexts)

Gorkhā Bhāshā Prakāshinī Samiti: Gorkha Language Publication Committee

Gorkha Parishad (*Gorkha Pariṣad*): 'Gorkha Council': common designation of the Nepal Rastrabadi Gorkha Parishad (Nepal Nationalist Gorkha Council), a 'Rana revivalist' group originally founded in 1951 as the Bir Gorkha Dal ('Brave Gorkha Party'); won 19 out of 109 seats in the 1959 election and formed the official opposition but later merged with Congress

Gorkhālī: 1. a person from or a subject of Gorkha; hence an ethnonym for persons of Nepali hill origin, used especially for Parbatiyas; 2. the language of the Parbatiyas, otherwise known as Nepali

gompa (Tb. *dgon-pa*): Tibetan Buddhist shrine or monastery; in Np. as *gumbā*

gorkhe-laurī: 'Gorkhali stick' (= harsh punishment)

goṭh: shepherd's hut

gotra: descent group

Gurung (*Guruṅ*): ethnic group found in the midwestern hills who call themselves Tamu

Gurung Kalyāṇ Sangha: Gurung Welfare Association founded in 1954

guṭhī: 1. religious fund or association; 2. a form of tax-free land tenure for holdings dedicated to religious purposes

hang (M.): king

Harisimhadeva: Maithil ruler who in 1326 fled to the hills after defeat by the Muslims; was claimed as the founder of their dynasty by the later Malla kings

Hāyū: small ethnic group originally living along the lower course of the River Kosi in the eastern hills

Hindutva: modern neologism coined to translate 'Hinduism', lit. 'Hinduness'

hukum: order, command

Hurkya: Parbatiya untouchable caste of Musicians and Dancers

Hyolmo: region to the north-east of Kathmandu known in Nepali as Helambu

Indo-Nepalese: synonym of Parbatiya (q.v.)

Jaisī: lower status Parbatiya Brahmans, the offspring of Brahman men and Brahman widows

jan āndolan: People's Movement (used of the protest campaign of 1990 that ended the Panchayat system)

janajāti: 'ethnic community' (a newly popular term for originally non-Hindu or 'tribal' ethnic groups)

Janajāti Mahāsangh: see Nepal Janajati Mahasangh

jaṅgal: forest, jungle, uncultivated area

jaṅgalī: (adj.) of the jungle, wild, uncivilized

Jaṅg Bahādur Rāṇā: Prime Minister (1846–77), founder of the Rana regime

jāt: 'species', hence: descent group, clan, caste, ethnic group

jāti: Sanskrit term from which *jāt* derives, now often employed by educated Nepalis to mean 'ethnic group'

jātiyatā: Sanskrit neologism to translate 'ethnicity'

Jaya Prakāsh Malla: last Newar king of Kathmandu (reigned 1735–68)

jimi/jimi(n)dār: landholder, landlord

jimmawāl: headman, revenue collector, usually for irrigated land

Jirel: Tibeto-Burman-speaking ethnic group group found mainly in Ramechap district (eastern hills)

Juddha Shamsher: Prime Minister from 1932 to 1945

Jyāpu: see Maharjan

Jyarti (Tam.): Tamang term for high-caste Nepali-speakers

kājī: senior grade in the old administrative hierarchy

kamāyā: bonded labourer

Kāmī: ex-untouchable Parbatiya caste (Blacksmiths)

Kanphaṭā Yogī: 'Split-Eared Yogi': member of an ascetic sect supposedly founded by Goraknath

Kasāī: see Khadgi

Kāyastha: plains caste (Scribes); also found among the Newars

Khaḍgī: low Newar caste (Butchers, Milk-Sellers), known in Nepali as Kasāī, and in colloquial Newari as Nāy

khadi (*khādī*): homespun cloth, a symbol of the Gandhian belief in home production and self-reliance, consequently now associated with Indian politicians

Khakchulukpa (*Khakculukpa*) (M.): legendary ancestor of the Kiranti

Kham: area of eastern Tibet

Khamba: inhabitant of Kham, a person originally from Kham, east Tibet

Khambuhang (M.): mythical ancestor of the Rai peoples in the Dudh Kosi basin

Khambuwān Mukti Morchā: Khambuwan Liberation Front, an ethnic political movement based in east Nepal

Khas/Khasa: old name for the ethnic group/caste now known as Chetri and sometimes used for the Parbatiyas as a whole; today the term is generally restricted to the *matwālī* Chetris of far west Nepal

khas kurā: 'the language of the Khas': old name for Nepali

Khasān: area originally inhabited by the Khas in west Nepal

khet: (irrigated) field where rice can be grown

Khlibri (Gur.): Gurung priest (alternative form: *ghyabre*)

khuk(u)ri: curved Nepali knife

kipaṭ: system of communal tenure for Limbus and other ethnic groups; it was eroded in practice throughout the 19th and 20th century and finally abolished in 1968

kira (**D.**): traditional Bhutanese garment (female)

Kiranti (Kirāi): name of a people who supposedly ruled the Kathmandu Valley in prehistoric times; generic term for Limbus, Rais, and kindred peoples, and for their languages

Kirāt Rāī Yayokkhā: an association of Rai peoples

Kirāt Yākthung Chumlung: an association of Limbu peoples

Kirāta: classical (Sanskrit) term for Kiranti

Kshatriya (*kṣatriya*): second of the four varnas (see also 'Chetri'); rulers, warriors

Kulung: a Rai sub-group

Kumāl/Kumhāle: ethnic group in the Tarai and hills traditionally working as potters; also used of Newar Potter caste found also in the hills

Kumhār: plains caste (Potters)

Kunwar (*Kũwar*): *thar* (surname) of Jang Bahadur's family

Kusalyā/Kusle (Nw. Kāpālī): ex-Untouchable Newar caste of marr-Jogiied Shaivite ascetics who act as death specialists

Khushawaha (*Khuśawāhā*): Kshatriya-status plains caste

***kyiduk* (Tb. *skyid-sdug*)**: mutual aid society

lāhure: someone who serves in a foreign army

lālmohor: (lit. 'red seal'); royal decree

lama (Tb. *bla-ma*): 'teacher': monk or priest in Tibetan Buddhism; in Np. as *lāmā*

Lama: a clan name among the Gurungs; used as an ethnonym by some Tamangs and Bhotiyas

Lamaism: Tibetan Buddhism

Lamas' Association: government-funded organization of lamas from remote areas (Np. *Lāmā Saṃskṛti Bhramaṇ*, Tb. *Bla-ma tshogs-pa*)

Lepcha (*Lāpche*): ethnic group formerly dominant in Sikkim

Lakshmi Puja (*Lakṣmī Pūjā*): festival of the Goddess of Wealth, forming part of Tihar (q.v)

lhaben (Tb. *lha-bon*): sacrificial priests, usually hereditary

lhosar (Tb. *lo-gsar*): Tibetan New Year celebration, also observed by Gurungs and others

Lhotshampa (D.): people of Nepali origin inhabiting southern Bhutan

Licchavī: dynasty ruling Kathmandu Valley c. 2nd. to 8th. century AD, claiming descent from the Licchavis who ruled Vaishali (in Uttar Pradesh) in the Buddha's time

Limbu: ethnic group inhabiting the far eastern hills of Nepal

Limbuhang: mythical ancestor of the Limbus

Limbuwān Mukti Morchā: Limbuwan Liberation Front

Lohorung: a Rai sub-group

Madhesh (*madés*): the (Gangetic) plain, the lowlands; India

Madheshi (*madhésī*): inhabitant of the Tarai or north India

Magar: ethnic group inhabiting the western hills of Nepal

Magar Langhalee Parivār Association: an ethnic Magar organization

Magh Sankranti (*Māgha Saṃkrānti*): festival marking the start of the month of Magh (mid-January)

Magrat (*Magarāt*): territory occupied by the Magars

Maha Ashtami (*Mahā Aṣṭamī*): eighth day of Dasain festival

Mahābhārata: one of the two great epics of Hinduism

Maha Nawami (*Mahā Navamī*): ninth day of Dasain festival

Mahādev(a): 'the great god': title of Shiva (q.v.)

Maharjan: Newar caste (Farmers) known colloquially as Jyapu

Maithil: inhabitant of Mithila (q.v.)

Maithilī 1.'of Mithila' (adjective); 2. the language of Mithila

Mājhī: ethnic group of Tarai and hills traditionally working as ferrymen

majhiyā: headman

Ma Kulung Ridumcha (*Mā Kuluṅ Ridumchā*): Kulung Rai Association

Maṇḍal: plains caste (Farmer)

Maṇḍale: the name for pro-Panchayat activists in 1990 (from Rastriya Swatantra Vidyarthi Mandal)

māne: prayer wheel; Tibetan style prayer wall with carved stones bearing the mantra *oṃ maṇe padme huṃ*

Mārwārī: ethnic group/caste originally from Rajasthan, now famous traders all over the subcontinent

Masāl: Maoist communist faction

māsine: enslaveable (lit. 'eliminable'), an important category in the 1854 Muluki Ain

matwālī: alcohol-consuming

maujā: village, sub-division of a district in the central hills

Meche Koche (*Mece Koce*): mythical ancestors of the Kiranti peoples of the Tarai

Mewahang: a Rai sub-group

mīt/mitinī: ritual friend (masc. and fem. forms)

miterī: ritual friendship

Mithilā: region of the Tarai and North Bihar

mleccha: barbarian, non-Hindu

mohī: status of legally recognized tenant

Mongol National Organization: political grouping established in 1989 and advocating special assistance for Mongoloid groups

muddum (**M.**): Kiranti scriptures, relating to origins

Muglān(a): obsolete term for India ('land of the Moghuls')

mukhiyā: headman, revenue collector for unirrigated land

muluk (adj. *mulukī*): country, territory

Mulukī Ain: national Legal Code

Murmī: earlier term for 'Tamang'

Musahār(i): plains caste (Labourers)

Nag Panchami (*nāga pañcamī*): festival of the serpent gods

Nagarpālikā: municipality (pre-1990: Nagar panchayat)

Nagarkoṭe: a sub-category of hill Newars

Nānyadeva: king of Mithila (c. 1097–1145)

NC: Nepali Congress Party

NDP: see Rastriya Prajatantra Party

NEFEN: see Nepal Janajati Mahasangh

Nepāl Bhāshā Mankā Khalaḥ: an umbrella organization of numerous locally based Newar cultural groups

Nepālī Bhāshā Prakāshinī Samiti: Nepali Language Publication Committee, formerly Gorkha Bhasha Prakashini Samiti

Nepālī Sāhitya Sammelan: Nepal Literature Conference

Nepāl Janajāti Mahāsangh: Nepal Federation of Nationalities (NEFEN), a confederal grouping of ethnic organizations

Nepāl Majdoor Kisān Party: Nepal Workers' and Peasants' Party (NWPP), a leftist party based in Bhaktapur

Nepāl Rāṣṭriya Janajāti Party: Nepal National Ethnic Communities Party

Nepāl Rāṣṭriya Swatantra Bidyārthi Maṇḍal: Nepal National Independent Students' Grouping (pre-1990 pro-Panchayat student union)

Nepāl Samvat: the Nepal Era which began in Oct-Nov 879

Nepāl Sarvajātiye Manch: Nepal Pan-Ethnic Platform, founded in 1982; forerunner of the Nepal Janajati Mahasangh

Nepāl Tāmāng Ghedung (Sangh): Nepal Tamang Council

Newā Guthi: a Newar cultural nationalist organization

Newār: ethnic group based in the Kathmandu Valley

NGO: Non-Governmental Organization: refers to numerous charitable or aid-related bodies; there are reportedly over 17,000 in Nepal

NPD: Nepal Press Digest, produced by Regmi Research Ltd (Pvt.), Lazimpat

N.S.: see Nepal Samvat

NSP: Nepal Sadbhavana ('Goodwill') Party, a Tarai-based regionalist party, part of the coalition government formed in 1995

NWPP: see Nepal Majdoor Kisan Party

Nyingmapa (Tb. rNying-ma-pa): the oldest 'sect' of Tibetan Buddhism; the form of Tibetan Buddhism most widespread in Nepal

Pa-chyu: traditional (non-lamaistic) Gurung priest

Padma Shamsher (Padma Śamśer): Prime Minister of Nepal from 1945 to 1948

Pahari (*pahāḍī*): hillman

Pahari/Pahi (*pahari*): a peripheral Newar caste

Panchayat (*pañcāyat*): system of government in Nepal (1962–1990) under which political parties were banned

panchayat: town or village council operating under the Panchayat system

pañcagavya: 'five products of the cow': milk, curd, clarified butter, urine, and dung

pañcakhat: fines levied for capital offences

pānī nacalne: 'water unacceptable' (label for impure groups usually known as 'Untouchable' from whom 'clean' castes could not accept water)

Parbatiyā: member of one of the hill castes that has always been Nepali-speaking: a Bahun, Thakuri, Chetri, or one of their associated service castes

pargannā: revenue division in the Tarai

Pashupatinath (Paśupatināth): 'Lord of Creatures': form under which Shiva is worshipped at the temple of that name in Kathmandu, the foremost temple of Nepal and protector of the kingdom

patiyā: ritual purification of an offender

People's Movement: see *jan āndolan*

Phulpātī: the seventh day of the Dasain festival

PLA: People's Liberation Army, the army of the PRC

Poḍe: Nepali for 'Dyaḥlā' (q.v.)

pönpo (D.) (Tb. *dpon-po*): lord, ruler

potet/pote: tenancy system under which the tenant works for the landlord in lieu of rent

pradhan panch (*pradhān pāc*): head of a panchayat (q.v.)

Prajā Parishad: 'People's Council' (Nepal's first political party, formed to oppose the Ranas in 1935)

prajātantra: democracy

Pratinidhi Sabhā: House of Representatives (Lower House of the Nepalese Parliament)

PRC: People's Republic of China

Prithvi Narayan Shah (Pṛthvī Nārāyaṇa Śāh): ruler of Gorkha who created the kingdom of Nepal by his conquest of the Kathmandu Valley in 1768/69

pūjā: worship

Purāṇa: narrative text accepted as Hindu scriptures

purdah (*pardā*): the practice of enclosing women

pwe/pye lava (Gur.): Gurung funeral ritual

pye (Gur.): funeral rites (cf. Tb. *dpe*, example, epic)

pyeta-lhuta: (Gur.) oral tradition

Rāī: ethnic group based in the eastern hills

Rājbanshi (*Rājvaṃśī*): ethnic group based in the eastern Tarai, also known as Kuch (Kooch)

(Rāj)bhāt: hill and plains caste

Rājopādhyāyā: Newar Brahman caste

Rājput: plains caste (lit. 'kings' sons'); see also Thakuri

rājyābhiṣeka: royal consecration, coronation

rājya: kingdom; principality

rakam: wealth, tax; specifically corvée labour

rakṣī: liquor distilled distilled from millet or rice

Ram Nawami (*Rām Navamī*): annual festival of the god Ram

Rāmāyana: one of the two great epics of Hinduism telling the story of Ram and Sita

Rānā: family name adopted by Maharaja Jang Bahadur to claim descent from the Ranas of Mewar in Rajasthan

Rana Bahādur Shāh: king of Nepal from 1777 to 1799, and *de facto* head of administration for his son 1804–06

Rañjitkār: Newar caste (Dyers) known colloquially as Chipā

rāstra: nation

Rāstriya Janamukti Morchā: National People's Liberation Front (later known as Rastriya Janamukti Party), a hill-based movement in favour of reservations for ethnic minorities

Rāstriya Janamukti Party: see preceding entry

Rāstriya Pañchāyat: national assembly under the Panchayat system

Rāstriya Prajātantra Party (RPP): the National Democratic Party, formed by leading ex-Panchayat politicians; known in Nepal by the acronym *rā-pra-pā*; joined Congress-led coalition government formed in Sept. 1995

Rāstriya Sabhā: National Assembly (Upper house of Nepalese Parliament)

Rāstriya Swayam Sewak (RSS): National Volunteers (a right-wing Hindu association in India)

rāstrabhāsā: 'language of the nation' (i.e. Nepali)

rāstriyabhāsā: 'national language' (i.e. any other language spoken as mother tongue in Nepal)

Rasuwā: Tamang-majority border district north of Kathmandu

Rig Veda (Rg Veda): oldest Hindu scriptures

Rin-po-che (Tb. *rin-po-che*): 'precious one': title of reincarnate lamas in Tibetan Buddhism

RSS: Rastriya Swayamsevak Sangh, a militant Indian Hindu organization linked to the VHP *ryot*: peasant

Saun Sankranti (*Śrāvaṇa Saṅkrānti*): mid-summer festival

sabhā: assembly, council

Sadbhāvanā Party: see NSP

sādhu: ascetic

Sagauli: village in Bihar where the 1815 treaty ending the Anglo-Nepal War was signed; older spelling is 'Sugauli'

sakhewa: Mewahang earth cult

Sakkhewa: pan-Rai festival now held in Kathmandu

sambat (*saṃvat*): year, era

sampradāya: community

sampradāyiktā: communalism

Sanyasi (*sannyāsī*): ascetic; caste of married former ascetics, assimilated to Parbatiyas

Sanskrit: sacred language of the Hindu (also Mahayana Buddhist) scriptures; associated with Brahmans because of their priestly status; Nepali, Maithili, and other languages of the Tarai derive from Sanskrit

Sanskritic: 1. derived from the Sanskrit language; 2. associated with Brahmanical Hinduism

Saraswati Puja (*Sarasvatī Pūjā*): annual festival of Saraswati, goddess of learning

sardār: chief (grade in the traditional administrative hierarchy; also head porter)

sarkār: government, ruler

Sārkī: ex-untouchable Parbatiya caste (Cobblers)

Satya Narayan Puja (*satyanārāyaṇa pūjā*): fast in honour of the god Narayan (Vishnu)

satyāgraha: 'struggle for truth': civil disobedience

sāunyā-phāgu: household levy collected in August

Shakya (Śākya): Newar caste: their socio-religious identity is that of married monks; with the Bajracharyas they are the leaders of Newar Buddhism

Sherpa (Tb. *shar-pa*): lit.'easterner': used as an ethnonym by the people of Solu-Khumbu and some others

Sherpā Sevā Kendra: Sherpa Service Centre

Shiva (Śiva): one of the two principal Hindu gods (the other being Vishnu)

Shivaratri (Śivarātrī): 'The Night of Shiva', festival usually falling in February

Shrestha (Śreṣṭha): high Newar caste, mostly Hindu

Shudra (Śūdra): lowest of the four *varṇa*s

sino, sinu: meat of a cow that has died naturally; animal carcass

Songtsen Gampo: first king of unified Tibet

Sorāh Jāt: see Char Jat

Sotang(e): a Rai sub-group

Sunār/Sonār: plains caste (Goldsmiths); also found among the Parbatiyas

Sunuwār/Sunwār: small ethnic group in the eastern hills, similar to and living nearby the Jirel

tāgādhārī: 'wearing the sacred thread' (label for the high, 'twice-born' castes)

tālukdār: local headman, revenue collector

Tamang (Tāmāṅ): ethnic group living around the Kathmandu Valley

Tamhang: Thakalis' name for themselves

Tamoli: plains caste (Betel Sellers)

Tamu: Gurung name for themselves

Tamu Di: a Gurung cultural association

Tamu Pye Lhu Sangha: Gurung cultural association

Tarāi: lowlands separating the Himalayan foothills from the border with India

Thakālī: small but commercially very successful group originally from the Thak Khola (river); linguistically closely related to the Gurungs and Tamangs

Thakālī Sewā Samiti: Thakali Service Committee

Ṭhakurī: high Parbatiya caste from which rulers usually come; concentrated particularly in far west Nepal and in the Kathmandu Valley

Thāmī: small ethnic group close to the Tamang

thar: clan, persons bearing the same surname

Thāru: tribal ethnic group found in the Tarai

Thāru Kalyāṇkāriṇī Sabhā: Tharu Welfare Association (founded 1949)

Theravāda: the form of Buddhism practised in Sri Lanka and South-East Asia, now a strong reformist current among the Newars and a few others in Nepal

Thulung (Thuluṅ): a Rai sub-group

Tibetanid: a technical term for people following Lamaist Buddhism or Bonpo religions and speaking a dialect closely related to High Tibetan

Tibetanoid: a technical term for those of Lamaist or Bonpo religion speaking a Tibeto-Burman language not a form of Tibetan, e.g. Tamangs, some Gurungs

Tihār: autumn 'Festival of Lights' (known as Diwali in India)

Tīj: women's festival (late August or early September)

ṭīkā: mark placed on the forehead as part of religious worship

Tirhut (adj. Tirhutia): Mithila

ṭopī: cap, particularly the style typically worn in the hills

Tulādhar: Newar trading caste from Kathmandu

tungba (*tumba*): alcoholic drink made by pouring hot water on fermented millet

ṭupī: scalp-lock: lock of hair at the top of the head left when the head is shaved to mark the state of a householder in Hinduism

ULF: United Left Front: broad front of leftist forces joining the Congress Party in the *jan āndolan* of 1990

UML: see CPN-UML

Urāy: high (Buddhist) Newar caste made up of several sub-groups, including the Tuladhar (q.v.)

Utpīdit Jātiya Utthān Manch: Platform for the Upliftment of Oppressed Groups

Vaishya (Vaiśya): third of the four *varṇa*s

Vajrayāna: 'The Diamond Way' (Tantric Buddhism), part of both Lamaism and Newar Buddhism

vaṃśāvalī: genealogy; written historical chronicle

varṇa: the four 'estates' or 'orders' into which Hindu society is traditionally divided: Brahmans (priests), Kshatriyas (rulers, warriors), Vaishyas (herders, tradesmen, agriculturalists), and Shudras (servants)

vartaman: see *bartaman*

VHP: see Vishwa Hindu Parishad

Vijaya Dashami (*vijayā daśamī*): 'The Victorious Tenth' (last day of Dasain, commemorating Durga's slaying of the demon Mahisur)

Vikram Samvat: Vikram Era (currently in official use in Nepal, reckoning from 57 B.C.); V.S. for short

vintunā (**Nw.**): see *bhintunā*

Vishnu (Viṣṇu): one of Hinduism's principal gods

Vishwa Hindu Parishad (Viśva Hindu Pariṣad): World Hindu Federation or Council (an India-based organization for the defence of Hinduism)

V.S.: see Vikram Samvat

Yādav: large plains caste (Farmers, Herders)

Yakha: small ethnic group in the eastern hills

yogin: yogi, Hindu holy man

Yolmo: see Hyolmo

References

1. Literature in Nepali and other South Asian Languages

Acharya, N. 1993. 'Yo Samvidhān Nepālī Mathingal ko Upaj ho' [This Constitution is the Product of Nepali Genius]. Interview, *Saṃsadiya Gatividhi* [Parliamentary Affairs Bulletin] 3(8): 7–9, 12.

Adhikari, R. 1975. *Nepālī Nibandh Yātrā* [The Evolution of the Nepali Essay]. Darjeeling: Nepali Sahitya Sanchayika.

Bhattachan, K. n.d. Nepālkā Ādivāsīharu: Avadhāraṇā ra Pahicān' [Nepal's Indigenous People: Definition and Identity]. Unpublished paper presented at a seminar organized by CNAS on the World Indigenous People's Year, 1993.

Chaudhari, M. 1982/83a (2039 V.S.). *Guru Babak Jalmauti* [The creation of the Guru Baba]. Dang: the author.

Chaudhari, M. 1982/83b (2039 V.S.). *Jhumrā Gīt* [Jhumra Songs]. Dang: the author.

Chaudhari, M. and S. Chaudhari 1981/82 (2038 V.S.). *Barkimār* [The Great Battle]. Dang: the author.

Dahal, D.R. n.d. 'Nepālkā "Ādivāsī" haru: Sāmājik samracanā ra ārthik sthiti ra yas bāre uthekā kehī praśnaharū' [Nepal's 'Indigenous' People: Their Social Organization, Economic Condition, and some Issues Raised in this Respect]. Unpublished paper presented at a seminar organized by CNAS on the World Indigenous People's Year, 1993.

Devkota, G.B. 1967/68 (2024 V.S.). *Nepālko Chāpākhānā ra Patra-Patrikāko Itihās* [The History of Printing and of the Press in Nepal]. Kathmandu: Keshav Prasad Lamsal.

Dhakal, G.P. 1992. *Jan-Āndolan: 2046* [The People's Movement: 1990]. Lalitpur: Bhupendra Purusha Dhakal.

555

Election Commission 1994. *Pratinidhisabhā Nirvācan 2051: Nirvācan Pariṇām Vivaraṇ* [Election of Members to the House of Representatives 1994: Report on Results]. Kathmandu: Election Commission.

Gautam, R. 1989/90 (2046 V.S.). *Nepālko Prajātāntrik Āndolanmā Nepāl Prajā Pariṣadko Bhūmikā* [The Role of the Praja Parishad in the Democratic Movement in Nepal]. Kathmandu: the author.

Gurung, G. 1985. *Nepālī Rājanītimā Adekhā Saccai* [Hidden Truths of Nepali Politics]. Kathmandu: the author.

Gurung, H. *et al.* 1992. *Nepālmā Āntarik Tathā Antarāṣṭriya Basāi-Sarāi: Mūl Prativedan* [International and National Migration in Nepal: Main Report]. Submitted to National Commission on Population, August 1983. Kathmandu: HURID International.

Gurung, J. 1985/86 (2042 V.S.). *Nepālko Ekīkaraṇmā Guruṅgharūko Bhūmikā* [The Role of the Gurungs in Nepal's Unification]. Pokhara: Bauddha Arghon Sadan.

Gyawali, S.B. 1962/63 (2019 V.S.). *Nepāl Upatyakāko Madhyakālīn Itihās* [Medieval History of the Kathmandu Valley]. Kathmandu: Royal Nepal Academy.

Kishor, Y.B. 1958/59 (2015 V.S.). *Guruṅgko Vaṃśāvalī* [Chronicle of the Gurungs]. Syangja-Nuwakot.

Lama, N. 1992. 'Janajāti Samasyā Bāre' [On the Problem of the Ethnic Communities] *Sāptāhik Bimarśa* 17/17/92.

Lama, S.B. 1959. *Tambā Kaiten* [Tamang Lore]. Darjeeling.

Malla, K. 1968/69. 'Hali' [The Ploughman]. In B. Aryal (ed.) *Sājhā Kathā*. Kathmandu: Sajha Prakashan.

Malla, K.P. and D. Vajrācārya (eds.) 1985. *Gopālarājavaṃśāvalī*. Stuttgart: Franz Steiner.

Mishra, T. 1985. *Maithilī Lok-Sāhityakā Adhyayan* [A Study of Maithili Folk Literature]. Patna: Janaki Prakashan.

Naraharinath, Y. 1965/66 (2022 V.S.). 'Rāmaśāhako Samayamā Gorkhāle Gareko Kehī Pragati' [Some Progress Made by Gorkha in the Time of Rama Shah]. In Y. Naraharinath (ed.) *Itihāsa Prakāśamā Sandhipatrasaṃgraha* [Collection of Treaties and Letters in Illumination of History]. Dang: Adhyatmik Sammelan, Pt. 1: 684–688.

Naraharinath, Y. and B. Parajuli (eds.) 1953. 'Divyopadeśa' [Divine Counsel] *Saṃskṛta Sandeśa* 1(8): 25–8; (9): 21–5.

Nepal Communist Party (United Marxist-Leninist) 1994. *Cunāv Ghoṣaṇā-Patra* [Election Manifesto]. Kathmandu.

Nepali Congress 1994. *Cunāv Ghoṣaṇā Patra* [Election Manifesto]. Kathmandu.

Nepali, N. 1963/64 (2020 V.S.). *Śrī Pā̃c Raṇa Bahādur Śāh* [His Majesty Rana Bahadur Shah]. Kathmandu: Shrimati Meri Rajbhandari.

Pant, D.R. 1965/66 (2022 V.S.). 'Lāhormā Nepālī Bīrharū' [Nepali Heroes at Lahore] *Purṇimā* 5: 63–70.

Pant, D.R. 1969/70 (2026 V.S.). 'Svāmīmahārāja Raṇabahādura Śāhako V.S. 1862 ko Bandobasta' [Renouncer King Rana Bahadur Shah's Measures in 1805/6] *Purṇimā* 24: 238–67.

Paudel, N. (ed.) 1963/64 (2020 V.S.). *Bhāṣāvaṃśāvalī* (Part 1). Kathmandu: Rastriya Pustakalaya.

Pokhrel, B.K. (ed.) 1986/87 (2043 V.S.). *Pā̃c Say Varṣa* [Five Hundred Years]. Lalitpur: Sajha Prakashan.

Pradhan, K. 1982. *Pahilo Pahar* [First Watch]. Darjeeling: Shyam Prakashan.

Rai, G.R. 1992/93 (2049 V.S.). 'The Kirāt Rāī Yāyokkhako Choṭo Cināro' [A Short Introduction to Kirat Rai Yayokkha] *Yāyok* 1: 1–4.

Rai, M.D. 1989/90 (2046 V.S.). *Mewahāṅg Kirātko Vaṃśāvalī* [Genealogy of the Mewahang Kirantis]. Yamdang: Mewahang Prakashan.

Rai, N.K. 1992/93 (2049 V.S.). 'Rāī (Khambu) Bhāṣāharūko Vikās Garne Jamarko Gardā' [Attempting the Development of the Rai (Khambu) Languages] *Yayok* 1: 5–11.

Raj, P.A. 1992. 'Nepālmā Bhāṣā ra Jāt-Jāti Tathyāṅka' [Language and Caste/Ethnic Group Statistics in Nepal] *Sāptāhik Bimarśa* 28/8/92.

Rastriya Prajatantra Party 1994. *Cunāvi Ghoṣaṇāpatra* [Election Manifesto]. Kathmandu.

Rastriyabhasa Niti Sujhav Ayog 1994 (2050 V.S.). *Rāṣṭriyabhāṣā Nīti Sujhāv Āyogko Prativedan* [Report of the Advisory Commission on Policy Towards the National Languages]. Kathmandu.

Rastriya Sanskritik Samiti 1992 (2049 V.S.). *Rāṣṭriya Sāṃskṛtik Nīti tathā Kāryakram Tarjumā Samiti dwārā Prastut Prativedan* [Report Submitted by the Committee on National Cultural Policy and Programme Preparation]. Kathmandu.

Royal Nepal Academy 1983. *Nepālī Bṛhat Śabdakoś* [Comprehensive Dictionary of Nepali]. Kathmandu.

Sakya, H.R. 1978 (1098 N.S.). *Śrī Svayambhū Mahācaitya* [The Great Stupa of Swayambhu]. Kathmandu: Swayambhu Vikas Mandal.

Sharma, H.P. 1965/66 (2022 V.S.). *Gorakṣa-Śāha-Vaṃśa: Aitihāsikam Mahākavyam* [The Gorkha Shah Lineage: An Historical Epic Poem] (Goraksagranthamala, 92). Benaras and Pyuthan.

Sharma, J.L. 1992/93 (2049 V.S.). *Hāmro Samāj: Ek Adhyayan* [Our Society: A Study]. Kathmandu: Sajha Prakashan. (2nd ed.)

Subedi, S. 1992. 'Bāhunbād: Ṣaḍyantrakā Nayā Nayā Rūp' [Brahmanism: A Brand New Form of Conspiracy] *Janamanch* 27/2/92.

Tamang, P. 1991a. 'Saṃsadiya Ām Nirvācan 2048 ra Janajāti' [Parliamentary General Election of 1991 and the Ethnic Communities] *Jhilko* 16: 27–33.

Tamang, P., S.A. Magar, and A. Kanduwa 1993. *Kāryaśālā-Goṣṭhī: Nepālmā Bhāṣik Samasyā ra Nirākaraṇkā Upāyaharū* [Workshop: Language Problems in Nepal and Methods of Solving them]. Kathmandu: Nepal Janajati Mahasangh.

Vajracarya, D. and T.B. Shrestha 1980/81 (2037 V.S.). *Śāhakālako Abhilekha* [Inscriptions of the Shah Period]. Kathmandu: Tribhuvan University.

Vishwa Adivasi Antar-Rastriya Dasak tadartha Rastriya Samiti 1994. *Nepālkā Ādivāsīharū: Sva-Pahicān ra Punaḥsthāpanātira* [Indigenous People of Nepal: Towards Identity and Rehabilitation]. Kathmandu.

2. References in European Languages

Acharya, M. 1980. *The Women of Sirsia* (The Status of Women in Nepal Report Vol. 2, Part 1). Kathmandu: CEDA, Tribhuvan University.

Adhikary, K.R. 1993. 'The Participation of the Magars in Nepalese Development'. PhD thesis, University of Austin, Texas.

Adhikary, K.R. n.d. 'The Quest for Unity among the Magars of Nepal'. Paper for panel "Ethnicity and Nation State in South and Southeast Asia", American Anthropological Association annual meeting, Chicago, November 20–24, 1991.

AHURA Bhutan 1993. *Bhutan: A Shangrila Without Human Rights*. Damak: Association of Human Rights Activists (AHURA).

All India Nepali Bhasa Samiti 1979. *Case for Constitutional Recognition of Nepali*. Darjeeling.

Allen, N.J. 1976a. 'Approaches to Illness in the Nepalese Hills'. In J.B. Loudon (ed.) *Social Anthropology and Medicine* (ASA Monograph 13). London: Academic Press.

Allen, N.J. 1976b. 'Studies in the Myths and Oral Traditions of the Thulung Rai of East Nepal'. Unpublished DPhil thesis, University of Oxford.

Allen, N.J. 1978a. 'Sewala Puja Bintila Puja: Notes on Thulung Ritual Language' *Kailash* 6(4): 237–56.

Allen, N.J. 1978b. 'Fourfold Classifications of Society in the Himalayas'. In J.F. Fisher (ed.) *Himalayan Anthropology: The Indo-Tibetan Interface.* The Hague and Paris: Mouton.

Allen, N.J. 1980. 'Tibet and the Thulung Rai: Towards a Comparative Mythology of the Bodic Speakers'. In M. Aris and Aung San Suu Kyi (eds.) *Tibetan Studies in Honour of Hugh Richardson.* Warminster: Aris and Phillips.

Allen, N.J. 1981. 'The Thulung Myth of the *bhume* Sites and Some Indo-Tibetan Comparisons'. In C. von Fürer-Haimendorf (ed.) *Asian Highland Societies: An Anthropological Perspective.* New Delhi: Sterling.

Allen, N.J. 1987. 'Thulung Weddings: The Hinduisation of a Ritual Cycle in East Nepal' *L'Ethnographie* 83: 15–33.

Alsdorf, L. 1962. *Beiträge zur Geschichte von Vegetarismus und Rinderverehrung in Indien.* Wiesbaden: Harrassowitz.

Amnesty International 1992. *Bhutan Human Rights Violations Against the Nepali-Speaking Population in the South.* London.

Amnesty International 1994. *Bhutan: Forcible Exile.* London.

Anderson, B. 1991 (1983). *Imagined Communities: Reflections on the Origin and Spread of Nationalism.* London and New York: Verso.

Appadurai, A. 1988. 'Why Public Culture?' *Public Culture* 1(1): 5–9.

Aris, M.V. 1975. 'Report on the University of California Expedition to Kutang and Nubri in Northern Nepal in Autumn 1973' *Contributions to Nepalese Studies* 2(2): 45–87.

Armstrong, J. 1982. *Nations before Nationalism.* Chapel Hill: Carolina Press.

Baird, Robert D. 1991. *Essays in the History of Religions.* New York: Peter Lang.

Balikci, A. n.d. 'Inter-Ethnic Relations and Ritual in West Sikkim'. Unpublished research report.

Banks, M. 1995. *Ethnicity: Anthropological Constructions.* London: Routledge.

Baral, I. 1964. 'The Life and Writings of Prithvi Narayan Shaha'. Unpublished PhD thesis, London University.

Baral, L.R. 1989. 'Political Culture and Political Process in Nepal'. In K.P. Malla (ed.) *Nepal: Perspectives on Continuity and Change.* Kathmandu: CNAS, Tribhuvan University.

Baral, L.R. 1993. *Nepal: Problems of Governance.* Delhi: Konark.

Barnett, S. 1976. 'Approaches to Change in Caste Ideology in South India'. In B. Stein (ed.) *Essays on South India.* Delhi: Vikas.

Barré, V., L. Berger, L. Feveile, and G. Toffin 1981. *Panauti: Une ville au Népal*. Paris: Berger-Levrault.

Barth, F. 1969. 'Introduction'. In F. Barth (ed.) *Ethnic Groups and Boundaries*. Boston: Little, Brown.

Barth, F. 1992. 'Towards Greater Naturalism in Conceptualizing Societies'. In A. Kuper (ed.) *Conceptualizing Societies*. London: Routledge.

Bauman, Z. 1990. 'Modernity and Ambivalence'. In M. Featherstone (ed.) *Global Culture: Nationalism, Globalization and Modernity*. London: Sage.

Bendix, R. 1980 (1978). *Könige oder Volk: Machtausübung und Herrschaftsmandat* Vol. 1. Frankfurt: Suhrkamp.

Bendix, R. 1991. 'Strukturgeschichtliche Voraussetzungen der nationalen und kulturellen Identität in der Neuzeit'. In B. Giesen (ed.) *Nationale und kulturelle Identität: Studien zur Entwicklung des kollektiven Bewusstseins in der Neuzeit*. Frankfurt: Suhrkamp.

Bennett, L. 1983. *Dangerous Wives and Sacred Sisters: Social and Symbolic Roles of High-Caste Women in Nepal*. New York: Columbia University Press.

Berreman, G.D. 1960. 'Cultural Variability and Drift in the Himalayan Hills' *American Anthropologist* 62: 774–94.

Berreman, G.D. 1972. *Hindus of the Himalayas*. Berkeley: University of California Press.

Beyer, S.V. 1992. *The Classical Tibetan language*. Albany: State University of New York Press.

Bhandari, D.P. n.d. Welcome speech delivered to international seminar 'The Anthropology of Nepal: Peoples, Problems and Processes', Kathmandu, September 7–14, 1992.

Bhattachan, K.B. 1995. 'Ethnopolitics and Ethnodevelopment: An Emerging Paradigm in Nepal'. In D. Kumar (ed.) *State Leadership and Politics in Nepal*. Kathmandu: CNAS, Tribhuvan University.

Bhattachan, K.B. and K.N. Pyakhurel n.d. 'Ethnoregional Perspectives on National Integration in Nepal'. Paper presented at seminar on Ethnicity and National Development, Kathmandu, December 21–22nd, 1995.

Bista, D.B. 1971. 'Political Innovators of the Upper Kali Gandaki' *Man* 6(1): 62–80.

Bista, D.B. 1987 (1967). *People of Nepal*. Kathmandu: Ratna Pustak Bhandar.

Bista, D.B. 1991. *Fatalism and Development: Nepal's Struggle for Modernization*. Calcutta: Orient Longman.

Bista, D.B. 1995. 'Khas of Chaudabisa' *Himal* 8(3): 45–8.

Blaikie, P. 1979. 'Porters'. In D. Seddon, P. Blaikie, and J. Cameron (eds.) *Peasants and Workers in Nepal*. Warminster: Aris and philips.

Blaikie, P., J. Cameron, and D. Seddon 1980. *Nepal in Crisis: Growth and Stagnation at the Periphery*. Delhi: Oxford University Press.

Bonk, T. 1990. *Dawn of Democracy: People's Power in Nepal*. Kathmandu: Forum for Protection of Human Rights (FOPHUR).

Boon, J.A. 1982. *Other Tribes, Other Scribes: Symbolic Anthropology in the Comparative Study of Cultures, Histories, Religions, and Texts*. New York: Cambridge University Press.

Borre, O., S.R. Panday, and C.K. Tiwari 1994. *Nepalese Political Behaviour*. New Delhi: Sterling.

Brass, P.R. 1974. *Language, Religion and Politics in North India*. Cambridge: Cambridge University Press.

Brass, P.R. 1976. 'Ethnicity and Nationality Formation' *Ethnicity* 3(3): 225–41.

Brass, P.R. 1985. 'Ethnic Groups and the State'. In P.R. Brass (ed.) *Ethnic Groups and the State*. London and Sydney: Croom Helm.

Brass, P.R. 1991. *Ethnicity and Nationalism: Theory and Comparison*. Delhi: Sage.

Brass, P.R. 1994. *The Politics of India since Independence* (2nd edition). Cambridge: Cambridge University Press.

Breuilly, J. 1993. *Nationalism and the State* (2nd ed.). Manchester: Manchester University Press.

Brinkhaus, H. 1993. 'The Textual History of the Different Versions of the Swayambhupurana'. In G. Toffin (ed.) *Nepal, Past and Present*. Paris: CNRS.

Brown, T.L. 1996. *The Challenge to Democracy in Nepal: A Political History*. London: Routledge.

Burghart, R. 1978. 'The Disappearance and Reappearance of Janakpur' *Kailash* 6(4): 257–84.

Burghart, R. 1984. 'The Formation of the Concept of Nation-State in Nepal' *Journal of Asian Studies* 44(1): 101–25. Republished in Burghart (1996b).

Burghart, R. 1996a. 'A Quarrel in the Language Family: Agency and Representations of Speech in Mithila'. In Burghart (1996b).

Burghart, R. 1996b. *The Conditions of Listening: Essays on Religion, History and Politics in South Asia*, C.J. Fuller and J. Spencer (eds.). Delhi: Oxford University Press.

Burghart, R., M. Gaenszle, J. Whelpton, and S. Wolf 1991. 'Private Newspapers, Political Parties and Public Life in Nepal' *European Bulletin of Himalayan Research* 1: 3–15.

Campbell, A. 1840. 'Note on the Limboos, and Other Hill Tribes Hitherto Undescribed' *Journal of the Asiatic Society of Bengal* 9: 595–615.

Campbell, B. 1993. 'The Dynamics of Cooperation: Households and Economy in a Tamang Community of Nepal'. Unpublished PhD thesis, University of East Anglia.

Caplan, L. 1970. *Land and Social Change in East Nepal: A Study of Hindu-Tribal Relations*. London: Routledge and Kegan Paul.

Caplan, L. 1990. '"Tribes" in the Ethnography of Nepal: Some Comments on a Debate' *Contributions to Nepalese Studies* 17(2): 129–45.

Census of India 1981. *Series 1 India, Series 19 Sikkim, Series 23 West Bengal*. ('Households and Household Populations by Language Spoken Mainly in the Household'.)

Census of West Bengal 1961. *District Census Handbook Darjeeling*, Table C-V Mother Tongue. Calcutta, 1967.

Central Bureau of Statistics 1993. *Nepal Census of Population*. Kathmandu.

Central Bureau of Statistics 1994. *Statistical Pocket Book Nepal*. Kathmandu.

Central Bureau of Statistics 1994a. *Population of Nepal by Districts and Village Development Committees/Municipalities (Population Census 1991)*. Kathmandu.

Chapman, M., M. McDonald, and E. Tonkin 1989. 'Introduction: History and Social Anthropology'. In E. Tonkin, M. McDonald, and M. Chapman (eds.) *History and Ethnicity* (ASA 27). London: Routledge.

Chaudhuri, K. 1991. 'A Himalayan Bogey' *Frontline*, 3-16/8/91: 33–5.

Chaudhuri, T.K. 1982. *Demographic Trends in Assam 1921–71*. Delhi: B.R. Publishing Corporation.

Chemjong, I.S. 1966. *History and Culture of the Kirat People*. Phidim/Darjeeling: Tumeng Hang and Chandraw Hang.

Clark, T.W. 1969. 'Nepali and Pahari'. In T.A. Sebeok (ed.) *Current Trends in Linguistics:* Vol. 5, *Linguistics in South Asia*. The Hague and Paris: Mouton.

Clarke, G.E. 1977. 'Who Were the Dards? A Review of the Ethnographic Literature of the North-Western Himalaya' *Kailash* 5(4): 323–56.

Clarke, G.E. 1980a. 'Lama and Tamang in Yolmo'. In M. Aris and Aung San Suu Kyi (eds.) *Tibetan Studies in Honour of Hugh Richardson*. Warminster: Aris and Phillips.

Clarke, G.E. 1980b. 'The Temple and Kinship among a Buddhist People of the Himalaya'. Unpublished DPhil thesis, University of Oxford.

Clarke, G.E. 1996. 'Blood, Territory, and the History of National Identity in Himalayan States'. In. S. Tonreson and H. Antlov (eds.) *Asian Forms of Nation*. Copenhagen: NIAS/Curzon Press.

Clarke, G.E. and T. Manandhar 1988. 'A Malla Copper-Plate from Sindhu Palchok' *Journal of the Nepal Research Centre* 8: 105–39.

CNAS 1987. *CNAS Current Issue Series no. 4: Seminar on Nepali Emigrants in India*. Kathmandu: Centre of Nepal and Asian Studies, Tribhuvan University.

Cohen, A. 1969. *Custom and Politics in Urban Africa*. London: Routledge and Kegan Paul.

Cohen, A. 1974. 'Introduction: The Lesson of Ethnicity'. In A. Cohen (ed.) *Urban Ethnicity* (ASA 12). London: Tavistock.

Collins English Dictionary 1979. London: Collins Publishers.

Constitution 1992. *The Constitution of the Kingdom of Nepal 2047 (1990)*. Kathmandu: Law Books Management Board.

Cox, T. 1989. 'Langtang Tibetans and Hindu Norms as Political Language: A Critical Perspective on Sanskritization Theory' *Contributions to Nepalese Studies* 16(1): 11–20.

Crandhon-Malamud, L. 1991. *From the Fat of Our Souls: Social Change, Political Process and Medical Pluralism in Bolivia*. Berkeley: University of California Press.

Cüppers, C. (forthcoming). 'A Ban on Animal Slaughter at Buddhist Shrines in Nepal'. In P. Sagant and S. Karmay (eds.) *Festschrift for A.W. Macdonald*. Paris.

Dahal, D.R. 1979. 'Tribalism as an Incongruous Concept in Modern Nepal'. In M. Gaborieau and A. Thorner (eds.) *Asie du Sud: Traditions et Changements*. Paris: CNRS.

Dahal, D.R. 1985. *An Ethnographic Study of Social Change Among the Athpahariya Rai of Dhankuta*. Kathmandu: CNAS, Tribhuvan University.

Dahal, D.R. 1992. 'Grasping the Tarai Identity' *Himal* 5(3): 17–8.

Dahal, D.R. 1995. 'Ethnic Cauldron, Demography and Minority Politics: The Case of Nepal'. In D. Kumar (ed.) *State Leadership and Politics in Nepal*. Kathmandu: CNAS, Tribhuvan University.

Das, B.S. 1983. *The Sikkim Saga*. New Delhi: Vikas Publishers.

Datta-Ray, S.K. 1992. 'Juggling with the Himalayan Balkans' *International Herald Tribune* 13/10/92.

Degler, C.N. 1992. 'A Challenge for Multiculturalism' *Dialogue* 98: 36–40. Washington: US Information Agency. Reprinted from *New Perspectives Quarterly*.

Des Chene, M.K. 1991. 'Relics of Empire: A Cultural History of the Gurkhas 1815–1987'. Unpublished PhD thesis, Stanford University.

Desideri, Father Ippolito 1932. *An Account of the Kingdom of Tibet*. London.

Despres, L.A. (ed.) 1975. *Ethnicity and Resource Competition in Plural Societies*. The Hague and Paris: Mouton Publishers.

Diemberger, H. 1993. 'Gangla Tsechu, Beyul Khenbalung: Pilgrimage to Hidden Valleys, Sacred Mountains and Springs of Life Water in Southern Tibet and Eastern Nepal'. In C. Ramble and M. Brauen (eds.) *Anthropology of Tibet and the Himalayas*. Zürich: Ethnological Museum.

Dixit, K.M. 1988. 'Highlanders on the Move' *Himal* 1(1): 3–5.

Dixit, K.M. 1992. 'The Dragon Bites its Tail' *Himal* 5(4): 7–9.

Dixit, K.M. 1993. 'Looking for Greater Nepal' *Himal* 6(2): 15–9.

Dhanagare, D.N. 1983. *Peasant Movements in India 1920–1950*. Delhi: Oxford University Press.

Dobremez, J.F. 1976. *Le Népal: Ecologie et Biogéographie*. Paris: CNRS.

Doherty, V.S. 1975. 'Kinship and Economic Choice: Modern Adaptations in West Central Nepal'. Unpublished PhD thesis, University of Wisconsin, Madison.

Dreyfus, G. 1994. 'Proto-Nationalism in Tibet'. In P. Kvaerne (ed.) *Tibetan Studies: Proceedings of the VIth Meeting of the International Association of Tibetan Studies, Fagernes, 1992*. Oslo: Institute for Comparative Research in Human Culture.

van Driem, G. 1987. *A Grammar of Limbu*. Berlin: Mouton de Gruyter.

Dumont, L. 1980 (1966). *Homo Hierarchicus: The Caste System and its Implications*. Chicago: University of Chicago Press.

Durkacz, V.E. 1983. *The Decline of the Celtic Languages: A Study of Linguistic and Cultural Conflict in Scotland, Wales and Ireland from the Reformation to the 20th Century*. Edinburgh: Donald.

Eichinger Ferro-Luzzi, G. 1987. *The Self-Milking Cow and the Bleeding Lingam*. Wiesbaden: Harrassowitz.

Eisenstadt, S. 1991. 'Die Konstruktion nationaler Identitäten in vergleichender Perspektive'. In B. Giesen (ed.) *Nationale und kulturelle Identität. Studien zur Entwicklung des kollektiven Bewusstseins in der Neuzeit*. Frankfurt: Suhrkamp.

Eller, J.D. and R.M. Coughlan 1993. 'The Poverty of Primordialism: The Demystification of Ethnic Attachments' *Ethnic and Racial Studies* 16: 183–202.

Ellingson, T. 1991. 'The Nepal Constitution of 1990: Preliminary Considerations' *Himalayan Research Bulletin* 11(1–3): 1–68.

English, R. 1982. *Gorkhali and Kiranti: Political Economy in the Eastern Hills of Nepal.* New Haven: Human Relations Area Files, Yale University.

English, R. 1985. 'Himalayan State Formation and the Impact of British Rule in the Nineteenth Century' *Mountain Research and Development* 5(1): 61–78.

Epstein, A.L. 1978. *Ethos and Identity: Three Studies in Ethnicity.* London: Tavistock.

Eracle, Jean n.d. *Kamadhenu: La Vache qui satisfait tous les désires.* Genève: Musée d'Ethnographie.

Eriksen, T.H. 1993. *Ethnicity and Nationalism: Anthropological Perspectives.* London: Pluto.

Fezas, J. 1990 (V.S. 2047). 'The Nepalese Juridicial Tradition and its Sources: A List of the *ain* Books Kept in the National Archives' *Abhilekha* 8(8): 121–134.

Finance Ministry (Nepal) 1995. Budget Statements, July (Communist Government) and October (Coalition Government). Kathmandu.

Fisher, J.F. 1978. 'Homo Hierarchicus Nepalensis: A Cultural Subspecies'. In J.F. Fisher (ed.) *Himalayan Anthropology: The Indo-Tibetan Interface.* The Hague and Paris: Mouton.

Fisher, J.F. 1990. *Sherpas: Reflections on Change in Himalayan Nepal.* New Delhi: Oxford University Press.

Fisher, W.F. 1993. 'Nationalism and the Janajati: Diversity in Ethnic Identity Strengthens Nepali Nationalism' *Himal* 6(2): 11–4.

Fleming, P. 1961. *Bayonets to Lhasa.* London: Rupert Hart Davis.

Fournier, A. 1974. 'The Role of the Priest in the Sunuwar Society' *Kailash* 2(3): 153–166.

Fricke, T. 1994 (1984). *Himalayan Households: Tamang Demography and Domestic Processes.* New York: Columbia University Press.

Fricke, T., A. Thornton, and D.R. Dahal 1990. 'Family Organization and the Wage Labour Transition in a Tamang Community of Nepal' *Human Ecology* 18(3): 283–313.

von Fürer-Haimendorf, C. 1964a. *The Sherpas of Nepal.* London: Murray.

von Fürer-Haimendorf, C. 1964b (1975). *Himalayan Traders.* London: Murray.

von Fürer-Haimendorf, C. 1966a. 'Caste Concepts and Status Distinctions in Buddhist Communities of Western Nepal'. In C. von Fürer-Haimendorf (ed.) *Caste and Kin in Nepal, India and Ceylon.* London, Bombay: Asia Publishing House.

von Fürer-Haimendorf, C. 1966b. 'Unity and Diversity in the Chetri Caste of Nepal'. In C. von Fürer-Haimendorf (ed.) *Caste and Kin in Nepal, India and Ceylon.* Bombay: Asia Publishing House.

von Fürer-Haimendorf, C. 1990. *Life among Indian Tribes: The Autobiography of an Anthropologist.* Oxford: Oxford University Press.

Gaborieau, M. 1978. *Le Népal et ses Populations.* Brussels: Editions Complexes.

Gaborieau, M. 1982. 'Les rapports de classe dans l'idéologie officielle du Népal' *Purusartha* 6: 251–90.

Gaenszle, M. 1986. 'Hinduisation among the Mewahang Rai'. ms.

Gaenszle, M. 1991a. *Verwandtschaft und Mythologie bei den Mewahang Rai in Ostnepal: Eine ethnographische Studie zum Problem der 'ethnischen Identität'.* Stuttgart: Steiner.

Gaenszle, M. 1991b. 'Blut im Tausch für Demokratie: Der Kampf um eine neue Verfassung in Nepal 1990' *Internationales Asienforum* 22(3–4): 233–58.

Gaenszle, M. 1992. 'The Topicality of History: An Interview with Mahesh Chandra Regmi' *European Bulletin of Himalayan Research* 4: 40–6.

Gaenszle, M. 1993. 'Interactions of an Oral Tradition: Changes in the *muddum* of the Mewahang Rai of East Nepal'. In G. Toffin (ed.) *Nepal, Past and Present.* Paris: CNRS.

Gaenszle, M. 1995. 'Journey to the Origin: A Root Metaphor in a Mewahang Rai Healing Ritual'. In M. Allen (ed.) *The Anthropology of Nepal: Peoples, Problems and Processes.* Kathmandu: Mandala Book Point.

Gaenszle, M. n.d. 'Political Aspects of the Territorial Cult among the Mewahang Rai'. ms.

Gaenszle, M. and R. Burghart 1991. ' "Martyrs for Democracy": A Review of Recent Kathmandu Publications' *European Bulletin of Himalayan Research* 2: 5–15.

Gaige, F. 1975. *Regionalism and National Unity in Nepal.* Berkeley: University of California Press.

Gaige, F. and J. Scholz 1991. 'The 1991 Parliamentary Elections in Nepal: Political Freedom and Stability' *Asian Survey* 31: 1040–60.

Geertz, C. 1967. 'The Integrative Revolution: Primordial Sentiments and Civil Politics in the New States'. In C.E. Welch (ed.) *Political Modernization: A Reader in Comparative Political Change.* Belmont,

California: Wadsworth Publishing Company. Reissued as chapter 10 of Geertz (1973).

Geertz, C. 1973. *The Interpretation of Cultures*. New York: Basic Books.

Gellner, D.N. 1986. 'Language, Caste, Religion and Territory: Newar Identity Ancient and Modern' *European Journal of Sociology* 27: 102–48.

Gellner, D.N. 1991. 'Hinduism, Tribalism and the Position of Women: The Problem of Newar Identity' *Man* (N.S.) 26: 105–25.

Gellner, D.N. 1992. *Monk, Householder, and Tantric Priest: Newar Buddhism and its Hierarchy of Ritual*. Cambridge: Cambridge University Press.

Gellner, D.N. 1993. 'From Sacred Centres to Communist Strongholds? Reflections on the Cities of the Kathmandu Valley, Nepal'. In Z. Uherek (ed.) *Urban Anthropology and the Supranational and Regional Networks of the Town*. Prague: Institute of Ethnology.

Gellner, D.N. 1995. 'Sakyas and Vajracaryas: From Holy Order to Quasi–Ethnic Group'. In D.N. Gellner and D. Quigley (1995).

Gellner, D.N. and D. Quigley (eds.) 1995. *Contested Hierarchies: A Collaborative Ethnography of Caste among the Newars of the Kathmandu Valley, Nepal*. Oxford: Clarendon Press.

Gellner, E. 1973 (1962). 'Concepts and Society'. In E. Gellner (ed.) *Cause and Meaning in the Social Sciences*. London: Routledge. (Reissued 1986 as *The Concept of Kinship and Other Essays*, Oxford: Blackwell.)

Gellner, E. 1983. *Nations and Nationalism*. Oxford: Blackwell.

Gibbs, H. 1947. *The Gurkha Soldier*. Calcutta: Thaker, Spink, and Co.

Giesen, B. 1991. 'Einleitung'. In B. Giesen (ed.) *Nationale und kulturelle Identität: Studien zur Entwicklung des kollektiven Bewusstseins in der Neuzeit*. Frankfurt: Suhrkamp.

Glagow, M. 1992. 'Die-Nicht-Regierungsorganisationen in der internationalen Entwicklungszusammenarbeit'. In D. Nohlen and F. Nuscheler (eds.) *Handbuch der Dritten Welt: Grundprobleme, Theorien, Strategien*. Bonn: J.H.W. Dietz Nachf.

Glover, W.W., J.R. Glover, and D.B. Gurung 1977. *Gurung-Nepali-English Dictionary*. Canberra: Australian National University Press.

Goldstein, M.C. 1975. 'Preliminary Notes on Marriage and Kinship among the Sherpa of Helambu' *Contributions to Nepalese Studies* 2(1): 55–69.

Goldstein, M.C. 1993 (1989). *A History of Modern Tibet, 1913–1951: The Demise of the Lamaist State*. New Delhi: Munshiram Manoharlal.

Grist, N. n.d. 'The Use of Obligatory Labour for Porterage in Pre-Independence Ladakh'. ms.

Guneratne, A. n.d. 'The Role of Elites in the Creation of Ethnic Identities: The Tharus of Nepal'. Paper presented at AAA, San Francisco, December 1992.

Gurung, D.B. 1960. 'Political Problems of Bhutan' *United Asia* 12/4/60.

Gurung, H. 1980. *Vignettes of Nepal*. Kathmandu: Sajha Prakashan.

Gurung, H. 1989a. *Regional Patterns of Migration in Nepal* (Papers of the East-West Population Institute, no. 113). Honolulu: East-West Population Institute.

Gurung, H. 1989b. *Nature and Culture: Random Reflections*. Kathmandu: Mrs. Saroj Gurung.

Gurung, H. 1992. 'Representating an Ethnic Mosaic' *Himal* 5(3): 19–21.

Gurung, H. 1994. *Nepal: Main Ethnic/Caste Groups by Districts, Based on Population Census 1991*. Kathmandu: the author.

Gurung, O. n.d. 'Formation of a Nation-State and Creation of National Identity'. Unpublished paper presented at the Ethnic Forum of Tribhuvan University Students, 1992.

Habermas, J. 1962. *Strukturwandel der Öffentlichkeit*. Neuwied: Luchterhand. English translation 1989 as *The Structural Transformation of the Public Sphere: An Enquiry into a Category of Bourgeois Society*. Cambridge: Polity.

Habermas, J. 1990. 'Vorwort zur Neuauflage 1990'. In J. Habermas *Strukturwandel der Öffentlichkeit*. Frankfurt: Suhrkamp.

Hachhethu, K. 1990. 'Mass Movement 1990' *Contributions to Nepalese Studies* 17(2): 177–201.

Hagen, T. 1960. *Nepal: Königreich am Himalaya*. Bern: Kümmerly & Frey. (*Nepal: the Kingdom of the Himalayas*, 1961 same publisher.)

Hall, A. 1982. 'Religion in Tamang Society: A Buddhist Community in Northern Nepal'. Unpublished PhD thesis, SOAS, University of London.

Hamilton, F.B. 1986 (1819). *An Account of the Kingdom of Nepal*. New Delhi: Asian Educational Services.

Hansen, M. 1993. 'Unstable Mixtures, Dilated Spheres: Negt and Kluge's *The Public Sphere and Experience*, Twenty Years Later' *Public Culture* 5(2) 179–212.

Hansson, G. 1991. *The Rai of Eastern Nepal: Ethnic and Linguistic Groupings* (Findings of the Linguistic Survey of Nepal). Ed. W. Winter. Kirtipur: Linguistic Survey of Nepal and Centre for Nepal and Asian Studies.

Hardgrave, R.L. and S.A. Kochanek 1993. *India: Government and Politics in a Developing Nation*. Fort Worth: Harcourt Brace Jovanovich.

Hardman, C. 1989. 'Conformity and Self-Expression: A Study of the Lohorung Rai of East Nepal'. Unpublished PhD thesis, SOAS, University of London.

Hasrat, B.J. (ed.) 1970. *History of Nepal as Told by its Own and Contemporary Chroniclers.* Hoshiarpur: V.V. Research Institute Press.

Haugen, E. 1966. 'Dialect, Language, Nation' *American Anthropologist* 68: 922–34.

Hazod, G. n.d. 'The yul lha gsol of mTsho yul: On the Mythology of the Mountain and the Lake in the Context of the "Land God Ritual" of Phoksumdo (Northwestern Nepal)'. ms.

von der Heide, S. 1988. *The Thakalis of North Western Nepal.* Kathmandu: Ratna Pustak Bhandar.

Herring, R.J. 1983. *Land to the Tiller: The Political Economy of Agrarian Reform.* New Haven: Yale University Press.

HIMAL, 1993. Vol. 5, no. 3 (Special issue on Ethnicity).

His Majesty's Government 1984. *Population Census 1981.* Kathmandu: Central Bureau of Statistics.

His Majesty's Government 1994. *(Supplementary) Budget Speech for the Fiscal Year 1994–5.* Kathmandu: Ministry of Finance.

Hitchcock, J.T. 1966. *The Magars of Banyan Hill.* New York: Holt, Rinehart, Winston.

Hitchcock, J.T. 1979. 'An Additional Perspective on the Nepali Caste System'. In J.T. Fisher (ed.) *Himalayan Anthropology.* The Hague and Paris: Mouton.

Hobsbawm, E.J. 1990. *Nations and Nationalism since 1780: Programme, Myth, Reality.* Cambridge: Cambridge University Press.

Hobsbawm, E.J. and T. Ranger (eds.) 1983. *The Invention of Tradition.* Cambridge: Cambridge University Press.

Hodgson, B.H. 1858. 'On the Kiranti Tribe of the Central Himalaya' *Journal of the Asiatic Society of Bengal* 27(5): 446–56. Reprinted in Hodgson (1880).

Hodgson, B.H. 1880 (1858). *Miscellaneous Essays Relating to Indian Subjects.* Vol. 1. London: Trübner.

Höfer, A. 1978. 'A New Rural Elite in Central Nepal'. In J. Fisher (ed.) *Himalayan Anthropology: The Indo-Tibetan Interface.* The Hague and Paris: Mouton.

Höfer, A. 1979. *The Caste Hierarchy and the State in Nepal: A Study of the Muluki Ain of 1854.* Innsbruck: Universitätsverlag Wagner.

Höfer, A. 1981. *Tamang Ritual Texts: Preliminary Studies in the Folk-Religion of an Ethnic Minority in Nepal.* Wiesbaden: Franz Steiner.

Höfer, A. 1986. 'Wieso hinduisieren sich die Tamang?'. In B. Kölver and S. Lienhard (eds.) *Formen kulturellen Wandels und andere Beiträge zur Erforschung des Himālaya*. Sankt Augustin: VGH Wissenschaftsverlag.

Holmberg, D. 1989. *Order in Paradox: Myth, Ritual, and Exchange among Nepal's Tamang*. Ithaca and London: Cornell University Press.

Hughes, M. 1995. Letter published in *Spotlight* 29/12/95.

Humphrey, C. 1985. 'Barter and Economic Integration' *Man* (N.S.) **20**: 48–72.

Huntington, S.P. 1967. 'Political Development and Political Decay'. In C.E. Welch (ed.) *Political Modernization: A Reader in Comparative Poltical Change*. Belmont, California: Wadsworth Publishing Company.

Huntington, S.P. 1968. *Political Order in Changing Societies*. New Haven and London: Yale University Press.

Husain, A. 1970. *British India's Relations with the Kingdom of Nepal, 1847–57*. London: George Allen and Unwin.

Hutt, M.J. 1988. *Nepali: A National Language and its Literature*. New Delhi: Sterling.

Hutt, M. 1991a. *Himalayan Voices: An Introduction to Modern Nepali Literature*. Berkeley: University of California Press.

Hutt, M. 1991b. 'Drafting the Nepal Constitution, 1990' *Asian Survey* **31**: 1020–39.

Hutt, M. 1993. 'Bhutan: Refugees from Shangri-la' *Index of Censorship* **22**, 4/4/93.

Hutt, M. (ed.) 1994a. *Bhutan: Perspectives on Conflict and Dissent*. Gartmore: Kiscadale Publications.

Hutt, M. (ed.) 1994b. *Nepal in the Nineties: Versions of the Past, Visions of the Future*. Delhi: Oxford University Press.

Hutt, M. and G. Sharkey 1995. '"Nepalese in Origin but Bhutanese First": A Conversation with Bhim Subba and Om Dhungel' *European Bulletin of Himalayan Research* 9: 32–42.

Indigenous 1994. *Indigenous Peoples of Nepal Towards Self-Identification and Re-establishment* (Proceedings of the National Consultation on Indigenous Peoples of Nepal). Kathmandu: National Ad Hoc Committee for International Decade for the World's Indigenous Peoples, Nepal.

Jackson, D. 1978. 'Notes on the History of Se-rib and Nearby Places in the Upper Kali Gandaki' *Kailash* 6(3): 195–228.

Jackson, D. 1985. *The Mollas of Mustang.* Dharamsala: Library of Tibetan Works and Archives.

Jest, C. 1966. 'Les Chepang: Ethnie Népalaise de langue Tibéto-Birmane' *Objects et Mondes* 6(2): 169–84.

Jest, C. 1975. *Dolpo: Communautés de Langue Tibétaine du Népal.* Paris: Editions du CNRS.

Jha, H.B. 1993. *The Tarai Community and National Integration in Nepal.* Kathmandu: Centre for Economic and Technical Studies.

Jones, R.L. 1976. 'Sanskritization in Eastern Nepal' *Ethnology* 15: 63–75.

Joshi, B.L. and L. Rose 1966. *Democratic Innovations in Nepal: A Case Study of Political Acculturation.* Berkeley: University of California Press.

Josse, M.R. 1992. 'Recognition of Nepali in India' *The Independent* (Kathmandu) 11/11/92.

Kansakar, V.B.S. 1989. 'Population of Nepal'. In K.P. Malla (ed.) *Nepal: Perspectives on Continuity and Change.* Kathmandu: CNAS, Tribhuvan University.

Karmay, S.G. in press. 'The Question of National Identity in Tibet'. Paper delivered at international conference "Forty years on: Tibet 1950–1990", School of Oriental and African Studies, University of London, April 5–6, 1990.

Karna, S.L. 1989. *A Glance on the Parikrama of Janakpur.* Janakpur (Issued for the Fifth International Conference on the Ramayana).

Khare, R.S. 1970. *The Changing Brahmans: Associations and Elites among the Kanya-Kubjas of North India.* Chicago: the University of Chicago Press.

Kirkpatrick, W. 1811. *An Account of the Kingdom of Nepaul.* London: W. Miller.

Kleger, H. 1992. 'Die Rückkehr der Bürgergesellschaft' *Widerspruch* 23: 49–62.

Knall, B. 1993. 'Economic Development, Participation, and Decentralization in Nepal' *European Bulletin of Himalayan Research* 5: 26–29.

Kölver, B. 1986. 'Der Staat und die Anderen: Formen institutioneller Auseinandersetzung'. In B. Kölver (ed.) *Formen kulturellen Wandels und andere Beiträge zur Erforschung des Himālaya.* St. Augustin: VGH Wissenschaftsverlag.

Kondos, V. 1994. '*Jana-Sakti* (People's Power) and the 1990 Revolution in Nepal: Some Theoretical Considerations'. In M. Allen (ed.) *Anthropology of Nepal: Peoples, Problems and Processes.* Kathmandu: Mandala Book Point.

Krämer, K.-H. 1991. *Nepal: Der lange Weg zur Demokratie.* Unkel/Bad Honnef: Horlemann.

Krause, B. 1980. 'Kinship, Hierarchy and Equality in North Western Nepal' *Contributions to Indian Studies* (N.S.) 14(2): 169–94.

Krauskopff, G. 1989. *Maître et Possédés: Les rites et l'ordre social chez les Tharu (Népal).* Paris: CNRS.

Kumar, D. (ed.) 1995. *State, Leadership and Politics in Nepal.* Kathmandu: CNAS, Tribhuvan University.

Lal, M. 1967. 'Cow Cult in India'. In A.B. Shah (ed.) *Cow-Slaughter: Horns of a Dilemma.* Bombay: Lalvani Publishing House.

Lall, K. 1969. 'The Tamangs' *Nepal Review* 3: 39–41.

Lecomte-Tilouine, M. 1993. *Les dieux du pouvoir: Les Magar et le hindouisme au Népal central.* Paris: CNRS.

Lensch, J.H. 1985. 'Probleme und Entwicklungsmöglichkeiten der Rinderund Büffelhaltung in Indien unter besonderer Berücksichtigung der "Heiligen Kühe": Eine interdisziplinare Betrachtung'. Unpublished PhD thesis, Universität Göttingen.

Lévi, S. 1905–1908. *Le Népal: Etude historique d'un royaume hindou.* 3 vols. Paris: Ernest Leroux.

Levine, N.E. 1987. 'Caste, State and Ethnic Boundaries in Nepal' *Journal of Asian Studies* 46(1): 71–88.

Levine, N.E. 1988. *The Dynamics of Polyandry: Kinship, Domesticity, and Population on the Tibetan Border.* Chicago: University of Chicago Press.

Levy, R. 1990. *Mesocosm: Hinduism and the Organization of a Traditional City in Nepal.* Berkeley: University of California Press.

Lewis, T.T. 1984. 'The Tuladhars of Kathmandu: A Study of Buddhist Tradition in a Newar Merchant Community'. Unpublished PhD thesis, Columbia University.

Lewis, T.T. and D.R. Sakya 1988. 'Contributions to the Study of the Newar Diaspora' *Contributions to Nepalese Studies* 15(1): 25–65.

Ling, T. 1985. 'Max Weber and the Relation of Religious to Social Change: Some Considerations from Sikkim and Nepal'. In A.E. Buss (ed.) *Max Weber in Asian Studies.* Leiden: E.J. Brill.

Lodrick, D.O. 1981. *Sacred Cows, Sacred Places: Origins and Survivals of Animal Homes in India.* Berkeley and London: California University Press.

Lukes, S. 1974. *Power: A Radical View.* London: Macmillan.

Lyotard, J.-F. 1977. *Das Patchwork der Minderheiten.* Berlin: Merve.

McCrum, R. *et al.*, 1986. *The Story of English.* London: Faber and Faber.

Macdonald, A.D. 1971. 'Une lecture des Pelliot tibétain 1286, 1287, 1038, 1047 et 1290: Essai sur la formation et l'emploi des mythes politiques dans la religion royale de Sroṅ-bcan sgam-po'. In A.D. Macdonald (ed.) *Etudes tibétaines dédiées à la mémoire de M. Lalou*. Paris: A. Maisonneuve.

Macdonald, A.W. 1981. 'Recherches Ethnologiques: Bhutan, Sikkim, Ladakh et Népal 1975–79' *La Recherche en Sciences Humaines, Humanité 1979–80*. Paris: CNRS.

Macdonald, A.W. 1983a (1975). 'Two Festivals among the Tharu, 1. Holi'. In A.W. Macdonald (ed.) *Essays on the Ethnology of Nepal and South Asia*, Vol. 1. Kathmandu: Ratna Pustak Bhandar.

Macdonald, A.W. 1983b (1975). 'The Tamang as Seen by One of Themselves'. In A.W. Macdonald (ed.) *Essays on the Ethnology of Nepal and South Asia,* Vol. 1. Kathmandu: Ratna Pustak Bhandar.

Macdonald, A.W. 1983c (1975). 'The Hierarchy of the Lower Jat'. In A.W. Macdonald (ed.) *Essays on the Ethnology of Nepal and South Asia,* Vol. 1. Kathmandu: Ratna Pustak Bhandar.

Macdonald, A.W. 1987. 'Religion in Tibet at the time of *Srong-btsan sgam-po*'. In A.W. Macdonald (ed.) *Essays on the Ethnology of Nepal and South Asia,* Vol. 2. Kathmandu: Ratna Pustak Bhandar.

Macdonald, A.W. 1989. 'Note on the Language, Literature and Cultural Identity of the Tamang' *Kailash* 15(3–4): 165–190.

Macdonald, A.W. and A. Vergati Stahl 1979. *Newar Art: Nepalese Art during the Malla Period*. New Delhi: Vikas Publishing House.

McDonaugh, C. 1984. 'Die Tharu in Nepal'. In M. Brauen (ed.) *Nepal: Leben und Überleben*. Zürich: Völkerkunde Museum.

McDonaugh, C. 1989. 'The Mythology of the Tharu: Aspects of Cultural Identity in Dang, West Nepal' *Kailash* 15(3–4): 191–205.

McDonaugh, C. in press. 'Aspects of Social and Cultural Change in a Tharu Village Community in Dang, West Nepal, 1980–1993'. In H. Skar and G.M. Gurung (eds.) *Nepal: Tharu and Tarai Neighbours*.

McDougal, C. 1968. *Village and Household Economy in Far-Western Nepal*. Kathmandu: Tribhuvan University.

McDougal, C. 1979. *The Kulunge Rai: A Study in Kinship and Marriage Exchange*. Kathmandu: Ratna Pustak Bhandar.

Macfarlane, A. 1979. *Resources and Population: A Study of the Gurungs of Nepal*. Cambridge: Cambridge University Press.

Macfarlane, A. and I.B. Gurung 1990. *A Guide to the Gurungs*. Kathmandu: Ratna Pustak Bhandar.

McKay, J. 1982. 'An Exploratory Synthesis of Primordial and Mobilizationist Approaches to Ethnic Phenomena' *Ethnic and Racial Studies* 5(4): 395–420.

Ma Lihua 1993. 'Shamanic Belief among Nomads in Northern Tibet'. In C. Ramble and M. Brauen (eds.) *Anthropology of Tibet and the Himalaya*. Zürich: Ethnological Museum of the University of Zürich.

Malla, K.P. 1979. *The Road to Nowhere*. Kathmandu: Sajha.

Malla, K.P. 1981. 'Linguistic Archeology of the Kathmandu Valley: Preliminary Report' *Kailash* 8(1–2): 5–23.

Malla, K.P. 1985. 'Epigraphy and Society in Ancient Nepal: A Critique of Regmi, 1983' *Contributions to Nepalese Studies* 13(1): 57–94.

Malla, K.P. 1989. 'Language and Society in Nepal'. In K.P. Malla (ed.) *Nepal: Perspectives on Continuity and Change*. Kathmandu: CNAS, Tribhuvan University.

Malla, K.P. 1992. 'Bahunvada's Myth and Reality' *Himal* 5(3): 22–4.

Malyon, T. 1993. 'Ladakh at Crossroads' *Himal* 6(5): 15.

Manzardo, A.E. 1978. *To be Kings of the North: Community, Adaptation and Impression Management in the Thakali of Western Nepal*. New Haven: Human Relations Area Files, Yale University.

Manzardo, A.E. 1982. 'Impression Management and Economic Growth: The Case of the Thakali of Dhaulagiri Zone' *Kailash* 9(1): 45–60.

Manzardo, A.E. and K.P. Sharma 1975. 'Cost-Cutting, Caste and Community: A Look at Thakali Social Reform in Pokhara' *Contributions to Nepalese Studies* 2(2): 25–44.

Manzardo, A.E. *et al.*, 1976. 'The Byanshi: An Ethnographic Note on a Trading Group in Far Western Nepal' *Contributions to Nepalese Studies* 6(2): 84–118.

Mayer, A.L. 1990. 'Die Gründungslegende Khotans'. In J.P. Laut and K. Röhrborn (eds.) *Buddhistische Erzählliteratur und Hagiographie in türkischer Überlieferung*. Wiesbaden: Harrassowitz.

Messerschmidt, D.A. 1976. *The Gurungs of Nepal: Conflict and Change in a Village Society*. Warminster: Aris and Phillips.

Messerschmidt, D.A. 1982a. 'The Thakali of Nepal: Continuity and Socio-Cultural Change' *Ethnohistory* 29(4): 265–80.

Messerschmidt, D.A. 1982b. 'Miteri in Nepal: Fictive Kin Ties that Bind' *Kailash* 9(1): 5–43.

Michaels, A. 1992. 'Recht auf Leben und Selbstötung in Indien'. In B. Mensen (ed.) *Recht auf Leben, Recht auf Töten: Ein Kulturvergleich*. St. Augustin: Steyler Verlag.

Michaels, A. 1993. 'Widow Burning in Nepal'. In G. Toffin (ed.) *Nepal, Past and Present*. Paris: CNRS.

Michaels, A. 1994. *Die Reisen der Götter: Der nepalische Paśupatinātha-Tempel und sein rituelles Umfeld*. Bonn: VGH Wissenschaftsverlag.

Michaels, A. (forthcoming). 'Kuhschützer und Kuhesser: Gesetzliche Verbote zur Rindertötung in Nepal'. In A. Wezler (ed.) *Ahiṃsā*.

Michailovsky, B. and M. Mazaudon 1973. 'Notes on the Hayu Language' *Kailash* 1(2): 135–52.

Mikesell, S.L. 1993. 'The Paradoxical Support of Nepal's Left for Comrade Gonzalo' *Himal* 6(2): 31–3.

Mines, M. 1975. 'Islamisation and Muslim Ethnicity in South India' *Man* (N.S.) 10: 404–19. Reprinted in I. Ahmad (ed.) 1983 *Religion and Ritual among Muslims in India*. Delhi: Manohar.

Misra, C. 1984. 'Political Economy of Population Distribution: A Case Study of a Dang Village' *Contributions to Nepalese Studies* 11(3): 1–20.

Mojumdar, K. 1973. *Anglo-Nepalese Relations in the 19th Century*. Calcutta: K.L. Mukhopadhyay.

Morris, C.J. 1985 (1933). *The Gurkhas: An Ethnology*. Delhi: B.R. Publishing Corporation. (Originally published as *Handbook for the Indian Army: Gurkhas, Delhi*.)

Müller-Böker, U. 1988. 'Spatial Organisation of a Caste Society: The Example of the Newar of the Kathmandu Valley, Nepal' *Mountain Research and Development* 8: 23–31.

Mumford, S.R. 1989. *Himalayan Dialogue: Tibetan Lamas and Gurung Shamans*. Madison: University of Wisconsin Press.

Munshi, S. and T.K. Chakrabarti 1979. 'National Languages Policy and the Case for Nepali' *Economic and Political Weekly* 14/4/79: 701–9.

Murty, T.S. 1983. *Assam: The Difficult Years*. New Delhi: Himalayan Books.

Nag, M. 1968. 'The Concept of Tribe in the Contemporary Socio-Political Context of India'. In J. Helm (ed.) *Essays on the Problem of Tribe*. Seattle and London: American Ethnological Society.

Nakane, C. 1966. 'A Plural Society in Sikkim: A Study of Interrelations of Lepchas, Bhotias and Nepalis'. In C. von Fürer-Haimendorf (ed.) *Caste and Kin in Nepal, India and Ceylon*. Bombay: Asia Publishing House.

NCIWIP 1993. 'Country Paper on Indigenous People of Nepal'. National Committee for the International Year of the World's Indigenous Peoples.

Needham, R. 1975. 'Polythetic Classification: Convergence and Consequences' *Man* (N.S.) 10: 349–69.

Nepal National Education Planning Commission 1956. *Education in Nepal*. Kathmandu: College of Education.

Nepal Press Digest 1990. 'Autonomy Demanded for Limbuwan' *Nepal Press Digest* 3(22): 220.

Nepali, G.S. 1965. *The Newars*. Bombay: United Asia Publications.

Nickson, R.A. 1992. 'Democratisation and the Growth of Communism in Nepal: A Peruvian Scenario in the Making?' *Journal of Commonwealth and Comparative Politics* 30(3): 358–86.

Northey, W.B. and C.J. Morris 1987 (1927). *The Gurkhas: Their Manners, Customs and Country*. New Delhi: Cosmo Publications.

NPD = Nepal Press Digest, Regmi Research (Pvt.) Ltd, Lazimpat, Kathmandu.

Odergaard, S. in press. 'BASE and the Role of NGOs in the Process of Local and Regional Change'. In H. Skar and G.M. Gurung (eds.) *Nepal: Tharu and Tarai Neighbours*.

Ohnuki-Tierney, E. 1990. 'Introduction: The Historicization of Anthropology'. In E. Ohnuki-Tierney (ed.) *Culture Through Time: Anthropological Approaches*. Stanford: Stanford University Press.

Okada, F.E. 1957. 'Ritual Brotherhood: A Cohesive Factor in Nepalese Society' *Southwestern Journal of Anthropology* 13: 212–22.

O'Neill, T. 1994. 'Peoples and Polity: Ethnography, Ethnicity and Identity in Nepal' *Contributions to Nepalese Studies* 21(1): 45–72.

Onta, P. 1992. 'Anthropology Still Finding its Feet: Anthropology in Nepal Struggles for a Unique Identity' *Himal* 5(5): 31–3.

Onta, P. 1993. 'Whatever Happened to the Golden Age?' *Himal* 6(4): 29–31.

Oppitz, M. (forthcoming). 'The Bull, the Ox, the Cow and the Yak: Meat Division in the Himalaya'. In P. Sagant and S. Karmay (eds.) *Festschrift for A.W. Macdonald*. Paris.

Ortner, S.B. 1978. *Sherpas Through their Rituals*. Cambridge: Cambridge University Press.

Ortner, S.B. 1992 (1989). *High Religion: A Cultural and Political History of Sherpa Buddhism*. Princeton: Princeton University Press.

Overmyer, D.L. *et al.*, 1995. 'Chinese Religions: The State of the Field: Part II, Living Religious Traditions' *Journal of Asian Studies* 54(2): 314–95.

Pahari, A. 1991. 'Ties that Bind: Gurkhas in History' *Himal* 4(3): 6–12.

Panday, D.R. 1989. 'Administrative Development in a Semi-Dependency: The Experience of Nepal' *Public Administration and Development* 9: 315–329.

Pandey, G. 1990. *The Construction of Communalism in Colonial North India*. Delhi: Oxford University Press.

Pandey, G. 1993. 'Which of Us are Hindus?'. In G. Pandey (ed.) *Hindus and Others*. Delhi: Viking.

Parel, A. 1969. 'The Political Symbolism of the Cow in India' *Journal of Commonwealth Political Studies* 7: 179–203.

Parming, T. and M.-Y. Cheung, 1980. 'Modernization and Ethnicity'. In J. Dofny and A. Akiwowo (eds.) *National and Ethnic Movements* (Sage Studies in International Sociology 19, ISA). London: Sage.

Peel, J.D.Y. 1989. 'The Cultural Work of Yoruba Ethnogenesis'. In E. Tonkin, M. McDonald, and M. Chapman (eds.) *History and Ethnicity* (ASA 27). London: Routledge.

Petech, L. 1958. *Medieval History of Nepal (c.750–1480)*. Rome: ISMEO.

Petersen, E. 1985. 'Zur Dynastischen Mythologie der Śāhas: Darstellung anhand Hariprasād Śarmās "Gorakṣaśāhavaṃśa"'. Unpublished MA thesis, University of Kiel.

Pettigrew, J. and Y.K. Tamu (Gurung) 1994. 'Tamu Shamanistic Possession (*khhlye khhaba*): Some Preliminary Ethnographic Observations'. In M. Allen (ed.) *Anthropology of Nepal: People, Problems and Processes*. Kathmandu: Mandala Book Point.

Pfaff-Czarnecka, J. 1989. *Macht und rituelle Reinheit: Hinduistisches Kastenwesen und ethnische Beziehungen im Entwicklungsprozess Nepals*. Grüsch: Rüegger.

Pfaff-Czarnecka, J. 1991. 'State and Community: Changing Relations of Production after the "Unification" of Nepal'. In H.J.M. Claessen and P. van der Velde (eds.) *Early State Economics*. New Brunswick, London: Transaction Publishers.

Pfaff-Czarnecka, J. 1993a. 'The Nepalese Durgā Pūjā Festival or Displaying Military Supremacy on Ritual Occasions'. In C. Ramble and M. Brauen (eds.) *Anthropology of Tibet and the Himalaya*. Zürich: Ethnological Museum.

Pfaff-Czarnecka, J. 1993b. 'Migration under Marginality Conditions: The Case of Bajhang'. In O. Schwank *et al.* (eds.) *Rural-Urban Interlinkages: A Challenge for Development Cooperation*. Zürich: Infras.

Pfaff-Czarnecka, J. 1995. *Debating the State of the Nation: Ethnicity and Nation-Building in Nepal* (ICES Discussion Paper). Colombo: International Centre for Ethnic Studies.

Pigg, S. 1992. 'Inventing Social Categories through Space: Social Representations and Development in Nepal' *Comparative Studies in Society and History* 34(3): 491–513.

Pignède, B. 1962. 'Clan Organization and Hierarchy among the Gurungs' *Contributions to Indian Sociology* 6: 102–19.

Pignède, B. 1966. *Les Gurungs: Une Population Himalayenne du Népal*. Paris and The Hague: Mouton.

Pignède, B. 1993. *The Gurungs: A Himalayan Population of Nepal*, tr. and ed. S. Harrison and A. Macfarlane. Kathmandu: Ratna Pustak Bhandar.

Pinn, F. 1986. *The Road to Destiny: Darjeeling Letters 1839*. Calcutta: Oxford University Press.

POLSAN, 1992. *Political Parties and the Parliamentary Process in Nepal: A Study of the Transitional Phase*. Kathmandu: POLSAN.

Poudyal, A.R. 1992. 'Nepal: Ethnicity in Democracy'. In L.R. Baral (ed.) *South Asia: Democracy and the Road Ahead*. Kathmandu: POLSAN.

Pradhan, K. 1991. *The Gorkha Conquests: The Process and Consequences of the Unification of Nepal with Special Reference to Eastern Nepal*. Calcutta: Oxford University Press.

Pradhan, R. 1994. 'A Native by any Other Name' *Himal* 7(1): 41–5.

Pradhan, S.K. (ed.) 1992. *Bhutan: An Iron Path to Democracy*. Kathmandu: INHURED.

Prindle, P.H. 1975. 'Fictive Kinship (*mit*) in East Nepal' *Anthropos* **70**: 877–82.

Pyakuryal, K. 1982. *Ethnicity and Rural Development: A Sociological Study of Four Tharu Villages in Chitwan, Nepal*. New Haven: Human Relations Area Files, Yale University.

Quigley, D. 1987. 'Ethnicity without Nationalism: The Newars of Nepal' *European Journal of Sociology* **28**: 152–70.

Quigley, D. 1993. *The Interpretation of Caste*. Oxford: Clarendon Press.

Raeper, M. and M. Hoftun 1992. *Spring Awakening: An Account of the 1990 Revolution in Nepal*. Delhi: Viking.

Ragsdale, T. 1989. *Once a Hermit Kingdom: Ethnicity, Education and National Integration in Nepal*. New Delhi: Manohar.

Rajaure, D. 1978. 'An Anthropological Study of the Tharus of Dang-Deokuri'. MA thesis, Tribhuvan University, Kathmandu.

Ramble, C. 1984. 'The Lamas of Lubra: Tibetan Bonpo Householder Priests in Western Nepal'. Unpublished DPhil thesis, University of Oxford.

Ramble, C. 1987. 'The Muktinath Yartung: A Tibetan Harvest Festival in its Social and Historical Context' *L'Ethnographie* **83**(100–101): 221–5.

Ramble, C. 1992–93. 'A Ritual of Political Unity in an Old Nepalese Kingdom'. *Ancient Nepal* 130–133: 49–58.

Ramble, C. 1993. 'Whither, Indeed, the Tsampa Eaters' *Himal* 6(5): 21–5.

Ramble, C. in press, a. 'The Creation of the Bon Mountain of Kongpo'. In A.W. Macdonald (ed.) *Mandalas and Landscapes*. New Delhi: D.K. Printworld.

Ramble, C. in press, b. '*Se*: Notes on the Distribution of an Archaic Ethnonym in Tibet and Nepal'. In P. Sagant and S. Karmay (eds.) *Festschrift for A.W. Macdonald*. Paris.

Rauber, H. 1980/81. 'The Humli-Khyampas of Far Western Nepal' *Ethnos* 52(1–2): 200–28.

Rao, P.R. 1978. *Sikkim: The Story of its Integration with India*. Delhi: Cosmo Publications.

Regmi, D.R. 1966. *Medieval Nepal,* Part II. Calcutta: Mukhopadhyay.

Regmi, M.C. 1970. 'Mustang Raja, 1790' *Regmi Research Series* 2(4): 99.

Regmi, M.C. 1971. *A Study in Nepali Economic History*. Delhi: Manjusri.

Regmi, M.C. 1976. *Landownership in Nepal*. Berkeley: University of California Press.

Regmi, M.C. 1978a. *Land Tenure and Taxation in Nepal* (Bibliotheca Himalayica Series 1, 26). Kathmandu: Ratna Pustak Bhandar.

Regmi, M.C. 1978b. 'Preliminary Notes on the Nature of the Gorkhali State and Administration' *Regmi Research Series* 10(11): 141–7.

Regmi, M.C. 1984. *The State and Economic Surplus*. Varanasi: Nath Publishing House.

Regmi, M.C. 1969–1989. *Regmi Research Series,* Vols. 1–20. Kathmandu: Regmi Research Institute (Pvt) Ltd.

Regmi, R.R. 1996. "Ethnic Violence Unlikely to Erupt in Nepal" *Spotlight* 12/1/96: 20–1.

Reinhard, J. 1974. 'The Raute' *Kailash* 2(4): 233–72.

RGB (Royal Government of Bhutan) 1989. *Proceedings and Resolutions Adopted in the 68th Session of the National Assembly of Bhutan*. Thimphu, October.

RGB (Royal Government of Bhutan) 1992a. Department of Education, Royal Government of Bhutan. *Eighth Quarterly Policy Guidelines and Instructions*. Thimphu.

RGB (Royal Government of Bhutan) 1992b. Department of Information, Royal Government of Bhutan. *Anti-National Activities in Southern Bhutan: An Update on the Terrorist Movement*. Thimphu.

Riccardi, T. 1977. 'The Royal Edicts of King Rama Shah of Gorkha' *Kailash* 5(1): 29–66.

Richardson, H. 1977. 'Ministers of the Tibetan Kingdom' *Tibet Journal* 2(1): 10–27.

Rogers, J.D. 1994. 'Post-Orientalism and the Interpretation of Premodern and Modern Political Identities: The Case of Sri Lanka' *Journal of Asian Studies* 53: 10–23.

Rosaldo, R. 1980. *Ilongot Headhunting 1883–1974: A Study in Society and History*. Stanford: Stanford University Press.

Rose, L.E. 1971. *Nepal: Strategy for Survival*. Berkeley: University of California Press.

Rose, L.E. 1977. *The Politics of Bhutan*. Ithaca: Cornell University Press.

Rose, L.E. n.d. 'The Nepali Ethnic Community in the Northeast of the Subcontinent'. Paper delivered to a conference at the International Centre for Ethnic Studies, Kandy, Sri Lanka, 20–22 August 1993.

Rosser, C. 1966. 'Social Mobility in the Newar Caste System'. In C. von Fürer-Haimendorf (ed.) *Caste and Kin in Nepal, India and Ceylon*. Bombay: Asia Publishing House.

Ruegg, D. Seyfort 1991. '*mChod yon, yon mchod* and *mchod gnas/yon gnas*: On the Historiography and Semantics of a Tibetan Religio-Social and Religio-Political Concept'. In E. Steinkellner (ed.) *Tibetan History and Language: Studies Dedicated to Uray Géza on his Seventieth Birthday*. Wien: Arbeitskreis für Tibetische und Buddhistische Studien, Universität Wien.

Russell, A.J. 1992. 'The Hills are Alive with the Sense of Movement: Migration and Identity amongst the Yakha of East Nepal' *Himalayan Research Bulletin* 12(1–2): 35–43.

Rustomji, N. 1987. *Sikkim: A Himalayan Tragedy*. Ahmedabad: Allied Publishers.

SAARC Jurists 1992. *The Bhutan Tragedy: When will It End? First Report of the SAARC Jurists' Mission on Bhutan*. Kathmandu and New York.

Sagant, P. 1976. *Le Paysan Limbu: Sa maison et ses champs*. Paris and The Hague: Mouton.

Sagant, P. n.d. 'Les tambours de Nyi-shang (Népal)'. ms.

Sahlins, M. 1993. 'Goodbye to Tristes Tropes: Ethnography in the Context of Modern World History' *Journal of Modern History* 65: 1–25; reissued in R. Borofsky (ed.) 1994. *Assessing Cultural Anthropology*. New York: Mcgraw-Hill.

Said, E. 1993. *Culture and Imperialism*. London: Vintage.

de Sales, A. 1993. 'When the Miners Came to Light: The Chantel of Dhaulagiri'. In G. Toffin (ed.) *Nepal, Past and Present*. Paris: CNRS.

de Sales, A. n.d. 'The Chantel Claim for Identity: From Integration to Separation'. Paper delivered at international seminar "The

Anthropology of Nepal: People, Problems and Processes", 7–14 September 1992, Kathmandu.

Salter, J and H. Gurung 1996. *Faces of Nepal*. Kathmandu: HIMAL Books.

Schafer. B.C. 1955. *Nationalism: Myth and Reality*. London: Gollancz.

Scharfe, H. 1968. *Untersuchungen zur Staatsrechtslehre des Kautalya*. Wiesbaden: Harrassowitz.

Schicklgruber, C. n.d. 'Holy Mountains, Mighty Men: *yul lha* and Politics in Dolpo'. ms.

Schrader, H. 1988. *Trading Patterns in the Nepal Himalayas*. Saarbrücken: Verlag Breitenbach.

Schroeder, R.F. 1985. 'Himalayan Subsistence Systems: Indigenous Agriculture in Rural Nepal' *Mountain Research and Development* 5(1): 31–44.

Seddon, D. 1987. *Nepal: A State of Poverty*. Delhi: Vikas.

Seeland, K. 1993. 'Sanskritisation and Environmental Perception among Tibeto-Burman Speaking Groups'. In C. Ramble and M. Brauen (eds.) *Anthropology of Tibet and the Himalaya*. Zürich: Ethnological Museum.

Shafer, R. 1955. 'Classification of the Sino-Tibetan Languages' *Word* 9(1): 94–111.

Shah, S. 1993. 'Throes of a Fledgling Nation' *Himal* 6(2): 7–10.

Shaha, R. 1982. *Essays in the Practice of Government in Nepal*. Delhi: Manohar.

Shaha, R. 1990. *Modern Nepal: A Political History 1769–1955*. 2 vols. Delhi: Manohar.

Shakya, S. 1991. 'Sikkim Surges, Darjeeling Trails' *Himal* 4(3): 32–3.

Sharma, P.R. 1977. 'Caste, Social Mobility and Sanskritization: A Study of Nepal's Old Legal Code' *Kailash* 5(4): 277–99.

Sharma, P.R. 1978. 'Nepal: Hindu-Tribal Interface' *Contributions to Nepalese Studies* 6(1):1–14.

Sharma, P.R. 1986. 'Ethnicity and National Integration in Nepal: A Statement of the Problem' *Contributions to Nepalese Studies* 13(2): 129–136.

Sharma, P.R. 1989a. 'Values in the Doldrums: Does the West Meet the East in Nepal?' *European Journal of Sociology* 30: 3–21.

Sharma, P.R. 1989b. 'Nepali Culture and Society: Reflections on Some Historical Currents'. In K.P. Malla (ed.) *Nepal: Perspectives on Continuity and Change*. Kathmandu: CNAS, Tribhuvan University.

Sharma, P.R. 1992. 'How to Tend this Garden' *Himal* 5(3): 7–9.

Sharma, P.R. 1993. 'Caste Societies in the State of Nepal: A Historical Perspective'. In C. Ramble and M. Brauen (eds.) *Anthropology of Tibet and the Himalaya*. Zürich: Ethnological Museum.

Sharma, P.R. 1994. 'Bahuns in the Nepali State' *Himal* 7(2): 41–5.

Shaw, B.C. 1992. 'Bhutan in 1991: "Refugees" and "ngolops"' *Asian Survey* 32(2): 184–8.

Shaw, B.C. 1993. 'Aspects of Nation-Building and the Southern Problem in Bhutan'. In M. Hutt (ed.) *Bhutan: Perspectives on Conflict and Dissent*. Gartmore: Kiscadale Publications.

Shrestha, B.G. and B. van den Hoek 1995. 'Education in the Mother Tongue: The Case of Nepalbhāṣā (Newari)' *Contributions to Nepalese Studies* 22(1): 73–86.

Shrestha, N.B. 1989. 'Against the West' *Himal* 2(5): 1.

Simoons, F.J. 1973. 'The Sacred Cow and the Constitution of India' *Ecology of Food and Nutrition* 2: 281–96.

Sinha, A.C. 1975. *Politics of Sikkim*. Faridabad: Thomson Press.

Sinha, A.C. 1991. *Bhutan: Ethnic Identity and National Dilemma*. New Delhi: Reliance Publishing House.

Slusser, M.S. 1982. *Nepal Mandala: A Cultural Study of the Kathmandu Valley,* vol. 1. Princeton: Princeton University Press.

Smith, A.D. 1971. *Theories of Nationalism*. London: Harper and Row.

Smith, A.D. 1984 (1981). *The Ethnic Revival*. Cambridge: Cambridge University Press.

Smith, A.D. 1986. *The Ethnic Origins of Nations*. Oxford: Blackwell.

Smith, G. 1967. 'Summaries of Several Bhutanese Sources on the Relations between Nepal and Bhutan'. ms.

Snellgrove, D. 1989 (1981). *Himalayan Pilgrimage*. Boston and Shaftesbury: Shambhala.

Snellgrove, D. 1992 (1967). *Four Lamas of Dolpo*. Kathmandu: Himalayan Book Sellers.

So, D.W.C. 1987. 'Searching for a Bilingual Exit'. In R. Lord and H.N.L. Cheng (eds.) *Language Education in Hong Kong*. Hong Kong: Chinese University Press.

Sonntag, S.K. 1995. 'Ethnolinguistic Identity and Language Policy in Nepal' *Nationalism and Ethnic Politics* 1: 108–20.

Sontheimer, G.D. and H. Kulke (eds.) 1991. *Hinduism Reconsidered*. Delhi: Manohar.

Southall, A. 1970. 'The Illusion of Tribe' *Journal of Asian and African Studies* (Leiden) 5: 28–50.

Srinivas, M.N. 1962 (1955). 'Sanskritization and Westernization'. In M.N. Srinivas (ed.) *Caste in Modern India and Other Essays*. Bombay: Asia Publishing House.

Statistics Department (Nepal) 1957. *Census of Population, 1952/54* (Appendix Volume). Kathmandu.

Stein, R. 1972. *Tibetan Civilization*. London: Faber and Faber.

Steinmann, B. 1987. *Les Tamang du Népal: Usages et religion, religion de l'usage*. Paris: Editions Recherches sur les Civilisations.

Steinmann, B. 1988. *Les Marches Tibétaines du Nepal*. Paris: Editions l'Harmattan.

Steinmann, B. 1992. 'The Political and Diplomatic Role of a Tibetan Village Chieftain ("go-ba") on the Nepalese Frontier'. In E. Steinkellner (ed.) *Tibetan History and Language: Studies Dedicated to Uray Géza on his Seventieth Birthday*. Wien: Arbeitskreis für Tibetische und Buddhistische Studien, Universität Wien.

von Stietencron, H. 1989 'Hinduism: On the Proper Use of a Deceptive Term'. In G.D. Sontheimer and H. Kulke (eds.) *Hinduism Reconsidered*. Delhi: Manohar.

Stiller, L. 1973. *The Rise of the House of Gorkha*. Kathmandu: Ratna Pustak Bhandar; Delhi: Manjusri Publishing House.

Stiller, L. 1989 (1968). *Prithwinarayan Shah in the Light of the Dibya Upadesh*. Kathmandu: Himalayan Book Centre.

Stoddard, H. 1986. *Le Mendiant de l'Amdo*. Paris: Société d'Ethnographie.

Stoddard, H. n.d. 'Literature and National Identity: Does the One Reveal the Other?' Paper delivered at international conference "Forty years on: Tibet 1950–1990", School of Oriental and African Studies, University of London, April 5–6, 1990.

Stone, L. 1988. *Illness Beliefs and Feeding the Dead in Hindu Nepal*. Lewinston/Quinston: Edwin Mellen Press.

Strawn, C. 1993. 'Falling Off the Mountain'. ms.

Strickland, S. 1982. 'Beliefs, Practices and Legends: A Study in the Narrative Poetry of the Gurungs of Nepal'. Unpublished PhD thesis, Cambridge University.

Subba, T.B. 1992. *Ethnicity, State and Development: A Case Study of the Gorkhaland Movement in Darjeeling*. Delhi: Har-Anand Publications and Vikas Publishers.

Subba, T.B. in press. *Kirata Culture and Nationalism in the Eastern Himalayas*. Hyderabad: Orient Longman.

Tamang, P. 1991a. See Nepali references.

Tamang, P. 1991b. 'Address of Welcome at a Ceremony Organised by the Nepal Janajati Mahasangh in Honour of Ethnic Community Members of Parliament' (July).

Tamang, P. 1991c. 'Open Letter to Prime Minister G.P. Koirala on Behalf of the Various Religions, Languages, Nationalities Action Committee' (August).

Tamang, P. 1992. 'Tamangs under the Shadow' *Himal* 5(3): 25–7.

Taylor, C. 1990. 'Modes of Civil Society' *Public Culture* 3(1): 95–118.

Taylor, D. and M. Yapp (eds.) 1979. *Political Identity in South Asia*. London: SOAS, London University.

Thinley, J.Y. 1994. 'Bhutan: A Kingdom Besieged'. In M. Hutt (ed.) *Bhutan: Perspectives on Conflict and Dissent*. Gartmore: Kiscadale Publications.

Thompson, D.L. and D. Ronen (eds.) 1986. *Ethnicity, Politics and Development*. Boulder: Lynne Rienner Publishers.

Thronson, D. 1993. *Cultural Cleansing: A Distinct National Identity and the Refugees from Southern Bhutan*. Kathmandu: INHURED.

Thupstan, P., 1990. 'The Language and Literature of Ladakh'. In N.K. Rustomji and C. Ramble (eds.) *Himalayan Environment and Culture*. New Delhi: Sterling.

Timsina, S.R. 1992. *Nepali Community in India*. Delhi: Manak Publishers.

Tiryakian, E.A. 1992. 'Dialectics of Modernity: Reenchantment and Dedifferentiation as Counterprocesses'. In H. Haferkamp and N.J. Smelser (eds.) *Social Change and Modernity*. Berkeley: University of California Press.

Toffin, G. 1974. 'Les Populations de la Haute Vallée de l'Ankhu Khola' *Objects et Mondes* 14(4): 325–36.

Toffin, G. 1976. 'The Peoples of the Upper Ankhu Khola Valley' *Contributions to Nepalese Studies* 3(1): 34–46.

Toffin, G. 1981. 'L' Organisation Sociale des Pahari ou Pahi, Population du Centre Népal' *L'Homme* 21: 39–68.

Toffin, G. 1993. *Le palais et le temple: la fonction royale dans la Vallée du Népal*. Paris: CNRS.

Turner, R.L. 1980 (1931). *A Comparative and Etymological Dictionary of the Nepali Language*. New Delhi: Allied Publishers.

Uebach, H. 1981. 'Notes on the Tibetan Kinship Term *dbon*'. In M. Aris and Aung San Suu Kyi (eds.) *Tibetan Studies in Honour of Hugh Richardson*. Warminster: Aris and Phillips.

Unbescheid, G. 1980. *Kānphatā: Untersuchungen zu Kult, Mythologie und Geschichte śivaitischer Tantriker in Nepal*. Wiesbaden: Franz Steiner.

UNESCO 1953. *The Use of Vernacular Languages in Education*. Paris.

UNHCR (United Nations High Commissioner for Refugees) 1995. *Situation Report on Bhutanese Refugees and Asylum Seekers in Nepal Covering the Period 1 July – 30 September 1995*. Kathmandu.

United People's Front 1991. *Election Manifesto*. Kathmandu.

Upadhyay, K.D. 1990. 'A Socio-Economic Profile of the Porters in the Central Mid-Hills of Nepal'. In S. Mikesell (ed.) *Occasional Papers in Sociology and Anthropology*. Kathmandu: Central Department of Sociology and Anthropology, Tribhuvan University.

Upreti, B.P. 1975. 'Analysis of Change in Limbu-Brahmin Interrelationships in Limbuwan, Nepal'. Unpublished PhD thesis, University of Wisconsin, Madison.

Uprety, P.R. 1980. *Nepal-Tibet Relations 1850–1930*. Kathmandu: Naga Pura.

Uprety, P.R. 1992. *Political Awakening in Nepal: The Search for a New Identity*. Delhi: Commonwealth Publishers.

Urhahn, M. 1987. 'For a Sociology of India: "Tribe" and "Caste" Reconsidered'. In C. Effenberg (ed.) *Developments in Asia: Economic, Political and Cultural Aspects*. Stuttgart: Steiner.

Vajracharya, D. 1969. 'Kirat Influence in Licchavi History' *Regmi Research Series* 1(1): 7–9.

Vansittart, E. 1915. *Gurkhas*. Calcutta: Superintendent Government Printing.

van der Veer, P. 1994. *Religious Nationalism: Hindus and Muslims in India*. Berkeley: University of California Press.

Vinding, M. 1988. 'A History of Thak Khola Valley, Nepal' *Kailash* 14(3–4): 167–211.

Wahid, S. 1989. 'Riots in Ladakh and the Genesis of a Tragedy. *Himal* 2(4): 24–5.

Weber, M. 1968. *Economy and Society*. 3 vols. New York: Bedminster Press.

Webster, P. 1981. 'To Plough or not to Plough? A Newar Dilemma: Taboo and Technology in the Kathmandu Valley, Nepal' *Pacific Viewpoint* 22(2): 99–135.

Wehrli, E. 1993. 'Tibet Research in China by Tibetans and Chinese After 1949'. In C. Ramble and M. Brauen (eds.) *Anthropology of Tibet and the Himalaya*. Zürich: Ethnological Museum of the University of Zürich.

Weidert, A. and B. Subba 1985. *Concise Limbu Grammar and Dictionary*. Amsterdam: Lobster Publications.

Weiner, M. 1968. 'Political Integration and Political Development'. In H.G. Kebschull (ed.) *Politics in Transitional Societies: The Challenge of Change in Asia, Africa and Latin America*. New York: Appleton-Century-Crofts.

Wezler, A. 1985. 'Dharma und Deśadharma'. In H. Kulke and D. Rothermund (eds.) *Regionale Traditionen in Südasien*. Wiesbaden: Franz Steiner.

Whelpton, J. 1983. *Jang Bahadur in Europe*. Kathmandu: Sahayogi Press.

Whelpton, J. 1987. 'The Ancestors of Jang Bahadur Rana: History, Propaganda and Legend' *Contributions to Nepalese Studies* 14(3): 161–91.

Whelpton, J. 1991. *Kings, Soldiers and Priests: Nepalese Politics and the Rise of Jang Bahadur Rana, 1830–1857*. Delhi: Manohar.

Whelpton, J. 1993a. 'The May 1991 Elections'. In M. Hutt (ed.) *Nepal in the Nineties*. Delhi: Oxford University Press.

Whelpton, J. 1993b. 'Being Nepali: The Construction of a National Identity in South Asia'. Paper Presented to the 34th International Congress of Asian and North African Studies, Hong Kong, 22–28 August 1993 (to be published in *Modern Asian Studies*).

Whelpton, J. 1995. 'Nepalese Political Parties: Developments since the 1991 Elections' *European Bulletin of Himalayan Research* 8: 17–41.

Wimmer, A. 1994. 'Der Kampf um den Staat: Zur vergleichenden Analyse inter-ethnischer Konflikte'. In H.P. Müller (ed.) *Ethnische Dynamik in der Aussereuropäischen Welt* (Zürich Arbeitspapere zur Ethnologie 4). Zürich: Argonaut-Verlag.

Witzel, M. 1987. 'The Coronation Rituals of Nepal: With Special Reference to the Coronation of King Birendra'. In N. Gutschow and A. Michaels (eds.) *Heritage of the Kathmandu Valley*. Sankt Augustin: VGH Wissenschaftsverlag.

Wright, D. 1990 (1877). *History of Nepal*. New Delhi: AES Reprint.

Yadav, R. 1992. 'The Use of Mother Tongue in Primary Education: The Nepalese Context' *Contributions to Nepalese Studies* 19(2): 177–90.

Yang En-hong, 1993. 'The Forms of Chanting Gesar and the Bon Religion in Tibet'. In C. Ramble and M. Brauen (eds.) *Anthropology of Tibet and the Himalaya*. Zürich: Ethnological Museum.

Yapp, M. 1979. 'Language, Religion and Political Identity: A General Framework'. In D. Taylor and M. Yapp (eds.) *Political Identity in South Asia*. London: SOAS, London University.

Zivetz, L. 1992. *Private Enterprise and the State in Modern Nepal*. Madras: Oxford University Press.

Author Index

Subject Index

591

myths, of origin
  Bahun 41, 51 n.14;
  Chantel 393;
  Chetri 60;
  Gurung 43, 199–200, 412 n.9;
  Mewahang 358–61;
  proposed for Nepal 73, 454;
  Newar 14, 156, 162;
  Rai 356–7;
  Tamang 216, 222;
  Thakuri 41, 73;
  Tharu 352;
  Thulung 308;
  Tibetanid 392;
  Yakha 331

Nagaland 105, 200
Nagarkote 207
Nag Panchami 340, 372 n.18
Nakarmi 162, 170
Namgyal, Palden Thondup 132
Namlunge Rai 356
Nanyadeva 242
Nar 202, 396
Narada, Mahathera 525
Narbhupal Shah 214
nationalism 39–48, 70
  Brass on 16, 65, 248;
  common-sense view of 11;
  condemned 245;
  cultural 11–12, 164, 177, 182, 364, 395, 402, 507;
  and ethnicity 10–11, 48ff.;
  Indian 46, 121, 157;
  as modern 7–8, 24–5, 44–5, 157, cf. 40;
  and monarchy 46–7, 482, cf. 73;
  pro-word in Nepal 10, 256, 482;

as social engineering 432–3, cf. 248;
  supposedly incompatible with Buddhism 385;
  Tibetan 381–6;
  v. nationism 101, 474, 529
national parks 436; see also Langtang
National Assembly, of Bhutan 134, 144 n.35
National Assembly, of Nepal 26, 50, 61–2, 159, 176–7, 448, 485
National Assembly, of Sikkim 131–3
NC, see Congress
NDP 64, 485, 517, 529, 531 n.12
NEFEN 20–2, 27–8, 51, 178, 180, 351, 411, 444, 484–6, 488–9, 526–7
Nehru, Jawaharlal 134
Nepal
  'Greater Nepal' accusation 37, 129, 139, 488;
  purer than India 92–3;
  substitute for Tibet 406, 515
Nepal Bhasha Manka Khalah 180, 351, 486
Nepalganj 530
Nepali
  adopted by non-Parbatiyas 36, 43, 297, 405;
  basis of diaspora identity 116, 518;
  basis of national unity 478;
  in Bhutan 108–9, 115–16, 134;
  brought to east Nepal 336;
  development as national language 45, 35, 63, 113–14;